The Media Book

Edited by
Chris Newbold
Oliver Boyd-Barrett
Hilde Van den Bulck

A member of the Hodder Headline Group
LONDON

Co-published in the United States of America by
Oxford University Press Inc., New York

First published in Great Britain in 2002 by
Arnold, a member of the Hodder Headline Group,
338 Euston Road, London NW1 3BH

http://www.arnoldpublishers.com

Co-published in the United States of America by
Oxford University Press Inc.,
198 Madison Avenue, New York, NY10016

The advice and information in this book are believed to be true and accurate
at the date of going to press, but neither the author[s] nor the publisher can
accept any legal responsibility or liability for any errors or omissions.

British Library Cataloguing in Publication Data
A catalogue record for this book is available from the British Library

Library of Congress Cataloging-in-Publication Data
A catalog record for this book is available from the Library of Congress

ISBN 0 340 74047 7 (hb)
ISBN 0 340 74048 5 (pb)

1 2 3 4 5 6 7 8 9 10

Production Editor: Jasmine Brown
Production Controller: Bryan Eccleshall
Cover Design: Terry Griffiths

Typeset in 9.25/14pt News Gothic by J&L Composition Ltd,
Filey, North Yorkshire
Printed and bound in Malta by Gutenberg Press Ltd.

What do you think about this book? Or any other Arnold title?
Please send your comments to feedback.arnold@hodder.co.uk

The Media Book

06

'3

Contents

List of Contributors

Chris Newbold is Lecturer and BSc Course Tutor at the Centre for Mass Communication Research, University of Leicester. He has taught film, media studies and television production at all levels of education. His research interests are film as mass communication, video production in education, and research methods in the study of film. He has written and edited three books: *Approaches to Media* (1995) (with Oliver Boyd-Barrett) London: Arnold; *Media: Communication and Production* (1996) (Newbold *et al.*) Harlow: Longman; and *Mass Communication Research Methods* (1998) (Hansen *et al.*) London: Macmillan. His new book, *Cinema, Film and Mass Communication*, is due to be published by Arnold in 2002.

Oliver Boyd-Barrett is Associate Dean, College of the Extended University at California State Polytechnic University, Pomona. He previously pioneered distance learning courses in communications, at the Open University and at Leicester University (both in the UK). He has written and edited many books and articles on international communications and educational communications, including *The Globalization of News* (with Terhi Rantanen) Sage; *Media in Global Context* (with Annabelle Sreberny Mohammadi *et al.*) Arnold; *Approaches to Media* (with Chris Newbold) Edward Arnold; *Education in Democratic Spain* (with Pamela O'Malley) Routledge; and *The International News Agencies* (Constable). He has worked as communications consultant for the Government of Dubai, NATO, the UK's Royal Commission on the Press, the UK's Parliamentary Technology Committee, USIA and UNESCO.

Hilde Van den Bulck is a Lecturer at the University of Antwerp (UIA) in Belgium. She wrote a PhD on 'Public Service Broadcasting as a Project of Modernity' and has published widely on audiovisual media culture and identity.

Daniël Biltereyst is an associate professor at the University of Ghent (Belgium), where he teaches film, television and cultural media studies. Most of his work is at the crossroads of cultural media studies and international communication issues, on which he has published widely.

Alina Bernstein has a PhD from the Centre for Mass Communication Research, University of Leicester. She lectures on various aspects of television studies at the Film and Television Department, Tel Aviv University, Israel. Her principal interest is the media coverage of sport, an area in which she has published several articles. She is currently co-editing a 'media and sport' special issue of *Culture, Sport, Society*, which will also be published as a book in 2002 (by Frank Cass).

Rachel Eyre has an MA from the Centre for Mass Communication Research, University of Leicester, she has taught widely on the media, advertising, journalism and health. She has researched and published on women journalists, local news and women politicians in the media. She is now a part-time Lecturer, a freelance researcher and writer on the media, and full-time mother to Larissa and Danielle.

Roland van Gompel is a research assistant at the Department of Communication, KU Leuven, Belgium. He is currently preparing a PhD on historical developments in election press coverage. He teaches on institutions and structures of print media, a field in which he has several publications.

John Lough has an MA in Mass Communication from the Centre for Mass Communication Research, University of Leicester. He has taught media theory to degree level at the University of Lincolnshire and Humberside, the University of Winnipeg, Canada, and is presently Head of Media Theory at West Kent College in Kent, England. His research interests include post-modernity, and contemporary popular television and film.

Michel Walrave is a Lecturer at KU Leuven, Belgium and at URL Barcelona. He teaches about marketing communications, e-marketing and privacy issues.

Gillian Youngs is a Lecturer at the Centre for Mass Communication Research, Leicester University. She has a PhD From Nottingham Trent University, and is a former journalist and communications consultant. She has taught and conducted research in Asia, Africa and Europe. She has written widely on subjects including the Internet, culture and technology, gender and spatiality, and global political economy. Her publications include: *International Relations in a Global Age: A Conceptual Challenge* (1999) Polity Press; and *Political Economy, Power and the Body: Global Perspectives* (2000) Macmillan. She is co-editor of *International Feminist Journal of Politics* launched in 1999.

Acknowledgements

The editors and publisher would like to thank the following for permission to use copyright material in this book: McQuail and Sage for Table 19.1 'Two models of media power', from McQuail, D. (1994) *Mass Communication Theory: An Introduction*. London: Sage, p. 70; Siebert *et al.* and University of Illinois Press for Table 20.1 'Four theories of the press', from *Four Theories of the Press*, Siebert *et al.* (1956) Urbana: University of Illinois Press, p. 7; Suine and Hulten, and Sage for Table 20.2 'Old and new media structures' from Siune and Hulten (1998) 'Does Public Broadcasting have a future', in McQuail and Siune (eds) *Media Policy: Convergence, Concentration and Commerce*, London: Sage, p. 36; Pictorial Press Limited for Figures 29.1, 29.2, 29.3 and 30.1; *Country Life* for the front page from 28 March 1903 (Figure 33.1); Wright's for the advert for the Wright's Coal Tar Soap advert from *Country Life* March 1903 (Figure 33.2); Cadbury Schweppes for the Cadbury's Cocoa advert from *Country* Life March 1903 (Figure 33.3); R&A Main Ltd for the Main Gas Cookers advert from *The Daily Mail* 13 May 1937 (Figure 33.4); Playtex for the Wonderbra advert from *Cosmopolitan* November 2000 (Figure 34.1). Warner Bros for the still from *Unforgiven*; Twentieth Century Fox Film Corporation for the still from *The Gunfighter*.

We would also like to express our thanks to Rakesh Kaushal for his work on the piece of research into media studies courses that helped to set this book on the path it eventually took, and Jackie Gardner for her help in obtaining examples of American advertisements. Thanks to Bernd Reggers, Alexande Dhoest and James Okemwa for their useful comments and constructive criticism.

Introduction

The Media Book was conceived and designed as a guide to the complex worlds of the media and media studies. It is structured with the student in mind, to focus on the subjects and issues that are central to knowledge of the media, how they work, the kinds of influence they exert, and the many debates they both inspire and provoke. *The Media Book* aims to provide students with a thorough briefing in the core areas of their chosen field, as well as introducing them to some of its emerging themes. Its purpose therefore is to provide a basic single-source support for students studying the media at undergraduate level. Our ambition is for *The Media Book* to act as a guide to the exciting and dynamic world of the media and media studies.

WHAT IS THIS BOOK ABOUT?

This book is ostensibly about the media and the study of the media. The media in our societies are seen to be all-pervasive (but not necessarily persuasive). The audience are seen as either willing participants who are hailed by media producers and their products, through the allure of pleasure, information and communication, or as detached and possibly critical observers. We the audience, experience media in almost all phases and aspects of our lives. From this point of view, the book is accessible in that it deals with a phenomenon about which most of us have accumulated a very considerable corpus of knowledge and direct experience. Prevailing social values may seem, paradoxically, to undermine the value or usefulness of such knowledge and experience. This sometimes leaves us with feelings of guilt about our media use, or with sentiments of disapproval about other people's media use; or even with a sense of virtue if, like diets, we consume less media overall, or we are careful to select what we do consume according to 'wholesome' criteria of personal and social health.

To convince yourself of the centrality of the media to our lives, we recommend that you make a media diary – i.e. that you write down, for one day (or, better, one week), where, when and under what circumstances you experienced or consumed media in general (what programme, why, with whom, with what result, etc.). Consider how you are defining media. Are you including or excluding certain uses of the computer, for example, or of the telephone, or of paper and pen, and why? Make a note of any particular feeling or observation you have about particular media encounters. We think you will be surprised to find how many times a day/week you consumed, interacted with or used the media, the variety of and the diversity of your media experiences, and by the extent to which your use and consumption of media invokes not just intellectual response, but profound cultural, personal, ethical and other reactions. *The Media Book* will be a guide to this complex and all-pervasive world and will help you, the student, make sense of that world, and of your own experiences and feelings about it.

One consequence of the ubiquity of the media is that everybody has an opinion on them and their workings. For instance, most people will have an opinion on the impact on society of violence in the media. These opinions are often based on a gut feeling, some moral or ethical value system or prejudice, or on some rare examples that people have witnessed or heard about. There is nothing wrong with having opinions. What we want to achieve for our students, though, is that they develop a more rounded and informed opinion that is based on knowledge, evaluation and research. To this extent our aim is to provide facts and theories, research and findings that should help you, first, to understand matters better, second to learn new and important facts regarding structures and processes, and, third, to be able to offer a qualified and more informed opinion about all these facts, structures and processes. We expect that, after you have worked your way through this book, you will also feel more confident in critiquing the design and execution of research, and the value of particular theories. This is what we want you to do with this book; these are the outcomes that we want you to take away from it.

Another consequence of the pervasiveness and indeed the centrality of media, of media-generated images in society, of media-mediated representations of the world, is that the study of the media has prospered and flourished all over the world. More and more educators and students have come to realize the importance of providing society with people who have a grounded understanding of the workings of the media in all its different aspects. This kind of expertise, of critical awareness, is ever more important in a society whose political, economic, educational, cultural and social structures and processes are ever more intertwined with the works of the communications media. The nurture of such critical skills, expertise and awareness is a further goal of this book, which is structured with student use in mind, around the sorts of subjects that are central to an understanding of the media, how they work, their influence and the many debates that surround them.

One further consequence of this pervasiveness of the media, and important for this book, is that media studies comprise a *field* rather than a *discipline*. As the media are present in so many different guises, it seems very hard to pinpoint what exactly comprises media studies. Its roots are in English literature, sociology, psychology, the study of economics, history and, of course, journalism. It goes under many names: media studies, mass communication, cultural studies, communication studies. It has many sub-areas, such as film studies, technology, international relations, politics, advertising and marketing, as well as the practical subjects such as video production, radio production, printing and journalism. So, in order to come up with one volume suited for all these different students studying all these many and various aspects of separate media and multi-media, we had to ask a great many questions of ourselves, about our subject area – and about you, our students. To help with your use of this book, we will now explore some of these questions; we hope that this introduction, and indeed the book itself, will go some way towards answering them.

WHAT SHOULD BE IN A BOOK ON MEDIA AND MEDIA STUDIES?

Given the extensiveness and diversity of the field, it was important to decide what's hot and what's not, what should be in the book and what falls out of the scope of this academic effort. Our choices were determined, not only by our years of experience teaching in the field, but also by a small piece of research carried out in 1998. This was an analysis of the content of media courses taught in Britain, Europe and America, which enabled us to identify a number of core areas that appeared in all media courses, as well as some areas that were becoming increasingly popular and relevant to the study of the media. We have written a book that incorporates the major features of media studies as the subject is actually taught worldwide. *The Media Book*, then, provides students with an array of the most important areas of teaching and research in contemporary media studies; it contains as extensive and comprehensive a range of material as is possible and necessary in order to support your study of the media at undergraduate level.

Of course, there are a lot of other good books on media studies; we do not pretend to provide the ultimate answer to all your questions. We do feel, though, that our book is distinctive in its commitment to a review of the media from a variety of different theoretical and pragmatic perspectives, interests and starting points. To students it may sometimes seem that media studies is 'all over the place', a bit of everything but not really connected. We thought it was important to show the student reader that even though the field is wide and varied, there are lots of commonalities and underlying links between the many different aspects that make up media studies. Bringing together and integrating the different areas into one book, will help the student to see the wood for the trees. Throughout the book it will become clear how the seemingly different areas interconnect; for example, how trends in media technology are related to changes in the media industries, or how post-modern trends in identity are reverberating in advertising as well as in television genres or the wider field of cultural representations. Books that focus on only one area of media studies do not, and cannot, track such cross-influences. *The Media Book* aims to help students to see the *Gestalt*, the overall picture, in the composing features.

WHAT ARE THE PEDAGOGICAL PRINCIPLES OF THE BOOK? HOW DO WE EXPECT STUDENTS TO USE IT AND LEARN FROM IT?

This book was written in order to provide much-needed clarification and direction in the debate as to what is the core of our field, what are the important debates and organizing theories, and what empirical findings can improve our knowledge of the field. We have written it to provide a comprehensive guide for students.

The book very consciously pays attention to theory. Theories reduce complexity by mapping an explanatory framework onto seemingly random phenomena. But, at the same time, theories can also heighten complexity as they show that phenomena are not as plain and simple as is generally assumed. Theories are, in the words of Förnas (1995: 7), instruments to look with, glasses to look through, and maps to look at. They help to grasp complex phenomena intellectually. Theories can help us, first, to deconstruct the area of interest into its main parts, and then to reconstruct and interpret its mutual relationships and relevant context. As media and communication studies is a field, not a discipline, we have tried to work by Halloran's (1995: 33–42) adagio of a 'critical eclecticism'. Thus, you will find theoretical considerations from a variety of disciplines such as sociology, social psychology, political economy, English, and cultural studies.

At the same time the book pays considerable attention to actual research. One of the main steps a media student needs to take is not just to read about media but also to go out and try to understand the media – their operations, representations and influences – for themselves. This requires analysis. The book therefore provides the tools to study the media as well as numerous examples of research undertaken in the diverse area of media studies. Most students on undergraduate courses are required to complete some form of dissertation or long study. The research methods section in this book will prove invaluable in helping you construct an original and informed piece of work, while the other sections provide a wealth of findings within which to contextualize your own research.

Finally, through all the different sections dealing with different aspects of media, we have tried to map multi-dimensionally, holistically. Phenomena do not exist on their own, in isolation, but must rather be studied in relation to the context and environment in which they appear and function. For instance, to understand why western Europe at one point witnessed the proliferation of commercial television stations leading to the current multi-channel environment, we need to look (among other things) at the changing political-economic climate, the lobbying of advertisers, entrepreneurs and other special interests, the (attitude to) new technologies and how they inflect prevailing cultural norms and values, and the changing needs of the media recipients. In a way this is what being a media student is all about: learning to see the bigger picture behind the manifold isolated media facts we are confronted with from day to day.

All these aims can only be achieved if the material is easily accessible, both intellectually and practically. To this end, the book is divided into eight sections and is designed to be as user-friendly as possible, with distinctive chapters and sub-sections, box-outs to provide further information, asides and summaries, an extensive index and a glossary for further explanation of selected key terms (glossary entries appear in bold in the text). Additionally, each section ends with a summary, a conclusion, suggestions for further reading, a list of useful websites and a list of references.

WHY DO WE THINK WE CAN MAKE A DIFFERENCE? WHY IS OUR BOOK SPECIAL?

A further distinguishing intent of this book is to look beyond the narrow national boundaries that have so often in the past typified policy debates, research and thinking about media operations. Without being too general, we have aimed to provide material that is of interest to students across the globe, paying attention to media and research from all parts of the world. The integration of so many different countries and cultures into a global economy whose commonalities and differences are increasingly structured by a global capitalist rationale, makes it ever more important that students should learn to see 'the bigger picture'. To achieve this we have selected contributors, not only from a variety of fields, but also from a variety of backgrounds. The authors are all committed teachers and scholars. Together we represent an extensive range of experience, at all levels and across all boundaries of media teaching and research. Between us, we have taught students from almost every country across the globe and many of us have taught in several countries. This has better enabled us to understand our reading public, which is comprised of the largest constituency of media scholars in the world: undergraduates. Our students go out into the world to a vast range of occupations; we hope that their knowledge of the media and media studies gained from this book will help them, not only in their working lives, but also in their everyday interaction with the media itself.

References

Förnas, J. (1995) *Cultural Theory and Late Modernity*. London: Sage
Halloran, J.D. (1995) The context of mass communication research. In Boyd-Barrett, O. and Newbold, C. *Approaches to Media*. London: Arnold

Theory in Media Research

Oliver Boyd-Barrett

Introduction

In the first chapters of this section my purpose is to demonstrate the importance and inevitability of **theory** in media research. The process of explaining any phenomenon is shot through with theory, whether it is explicit or implicit, sound or weak. I first of all provide some examples of the uses of theory in media research. In my second chapter I consider the extent to which theory is different from ideology, and I look at the relationship between theory and descriptive data. I then assess the principal benefits and risks of theory-building.

In the third chapter, I go back a step to show how the range of different theories about media communications are contoured by understandings about what constitutes the 'field' of media study. One helpful starting point for defining the field of study is a set of key concepts that was developed by the British Film Institute (BFI).

From this mainly descriptive exercise of identifying a broadly consensual acceptance of what the field of study comprises, I proceed in Chapter 4 to trace some of the many influential approaches to research about media. Approaches are sometimes distinguished according to whether their primary purpose is to contribute to the success or effectiveness of communications media (administrative) or to explain how communications relate to their broader social contexts – within the compass of a concern for the general social or public good (critical). In Chapter 5, I ask whether this distinction is valid or useful. In Chapter 6 I discuss four major different phases in media research, identifying each phase chronologically over a 60- to 70-year history of media research, and consider how each approach

appears to relate to broader social and political changes. These approaches may be identified in terms of a combination of the kinds of questions they ask, the views of the world they
express, and the range and balance of methodologies they employ to arrive at answers to
their questions. In the seventh and final chapter I concentrate in greater depth on what I
consider to be the three most powerful theoretical influences on media research, namely the
'effects' tradition, **cultural studies** and **political economy**.

CHAPTER 1

On the Uses of Theory: an Example

I will start with what I call a 'middle-level' set of theories, an example that I believe illustrates
the inevitability and usefulness of theory in addressing issues that have a practical significance for everyday life. I have also adopted a 'new media' example, in a bid to emphasize
the challenge to media research, at the time of writing (2000), of encompassing all forms
of technologically mediated communication within the compass of the field. In a conference
paper that he delivered at the Chinese University of Hong Kong, Charles Steinfield (2000)
considered the significance of electronic commerce for business. He identified three
reasoned predictions ('theories') that were then common. The first claimed that electronic
commerce would bring about 'disintermediation' in the value chain (that is, it would allow
producers of goods and services to bypass various intermediary firms to reach their end
customers). The second said that it would encourage 'frictionless commerce' by reducing
transaction and switching costs that formerly made it more difficult to find and conduct business with new trading partners, so that alliances between trading partners would become a
good deal more volatile. The third prediction was that it would lead to the 'death of distance'
by making it as easy to do business with distant firms and customers as with local ones.

Steinfield set out to critique this 'everyday wisdom' (one that was also supported by
selected economic theories). First, he argued that electronic commerce can actually
increase rather than reduce the role of intermediaries. This may occur where the **Internet**
reduces intermediaries' own transaction costs. For example, a firm that decides to sell
directly to end consumers incurs additional management and communications costs. The
Internet may strengthen the case for outsourcing such services to intermediaries. As transaction costs get smaller due to electronic services, there may be a growth of highly
specialized intermediaries. Intermediaries provide many additional functions that are attractive to businesses; in other words, they have value beyond the fact that they simply match
what would otherwise be internal services. These include functions that are difficult for producers to replicate. For buyers, intermediaries select and evaluate the products available on
the market, assess buyer needs and suggest products that meet them, absorb some of the
risk, and distribute the product to the buyer by maintaining an inventory or delivery capability.
For sellers, they help disseminate product information, influence the purchase of products,

provide marketing information about buyer tastes and demands, and absorb risks such as faulty payments. Because they typically carry the products of several producers, they can aggregate transactions and benefit from economies of scope that are not available to a single producer attempting to sell directly to consumers.

Does electronic commerce also promote 'frictionless markets', where buyers switch effortlessly to another supplier of a good or service without incurring prohibitive costs? It is sometimes argued that because the Internet provides a standards-based technology for electronic commerce, it reduces the need for firms to invest narrowly in doing business with a specific trading partner. The Internet can open formerly closed trading relationships, lower the costs to firms of switching suppliers, and generally reduce friction in the market. But, in practice, argued Steinfield, there is contrary evidence suggesting that network-based trans-actions actually promote longer-term, more tightly coupled linkages between businesses that have a continuing need for a given product and its suppliers. For example, pre-existing social relations between buyers and sellers may lead firms to develop the capability for elec-tronic transactions with trusted and established suppliers. Internet use in business is asso-ciated with higher investment in equipment and software for the purpose of trading with specific suppliers.

The prediction that the Internet makes distance irrelevant claims that companies no longer need to establish a physical presence in any geographical location for the purpose of doing business there. Steinfield argued that this is too limited a view of the types of costs consumers encounter in the market-place. A significant inhibitor for electronic commerce is the lack of trust that consumers have in Internet merchants; a physical presence in a locality helps to nurture trust. Also, consumers who need immediate gratification may be reluctant to rely on electronic commerce vendors who ship goods by courier. Steinfield preferred arguments that gave greater weight to the advantages of 'hybrid' electronic commerce. Hybrid models offer the advantages of both virtual and physical presence to meet the needs of buyers, where 'physical presence' is defined to include any assets that enable potential buyers to interact in person with a firm's personnel or on a firm's premises. The benefits are ones of:

- cost reduction (e.g. reduction of local inventory for infrequently purchased goods, while still offering them on delayed Internet basis)
- trust building through local presence
- value adding (e.g. encouraging Internet orders that complement the goods and services offered in physical outlets)
- market extension/reach, where the Internet is used to extend the physical market rather than replace it.

What does this example tell us about theory? First of all, it reflects the fact that new theory often develops as a form of reaction to existing theory, with the objective of confirming exist-ing predictions or explanations, or refining them, or rejecting them in favour of some alter-native predictions or explanations. In his paper, Steinfield showed that there are some sound economic reasons, and empirical evidence, to support the 'common wisdom' about the impact of e-commerce on aspects of business practice, but also that there are sound reasons and some empirical evidence that undermines it, certainly enough to demonstrate that the 'common wisdom' is unlikely to be universally correct. His paper also showed how the act of interrogating existing theories and of proposing alternative ones, contributes to an understanding of the complexity of the subject or process that the theories purport to explain. The example is a healthy reminder that a great deal of theory-building occurs at what is sometimes described as a 'middle-range' level of analysis. That is to say, theory does not have to be about matters that relate in especially profound ways to the human condition, nor does it have to address social life as a whole, in order to count as worthwhile.

CHAPTER 2

Theory and Ideology

The challenge of developing explanations for why things are as they are, of establishing evidence for such explanations by means of methodologies that command the respect (rarely universal, of course) of professional scientists and other intelligent people, is a serious and worthwhile endeavour. One criterion for winning the respect of others is to demonstrate that a proposed theory has not been constructed simply to satisfy some special interest. In other words, that findings have not been 'fixed' simply to suit the beliefs, expectations or hopes of some sponsor or benefactor. None the less, the worlds of theory and ideology do easily inter-penetrate. Let us consider an example.

Writing this section in 2000, it seems clear to me that I am living in an era of unparalleled activity in media industries. Media scholars such as Hamelink (1994) or Schiller (1999) identify at least six main forces at work that explain at least the recent evolution of the communications industries. The first is digitization (the transfer of communications from analogue to digital technologies). Digitization contributes, second, to convergence. This has to do with the merging of what were previously discrete media delivery systems: for example, film can now be delivered through projection at a cinema, terrestrial or satellite television, video cassette, compact disc, broadband telephony. Third, digitization and convergence contribute to intensification of industrial concentration, which in turn has been assisted, fourth, by the privatization and deregulation of what were once publicly owned or state-owned media enterprises or private enterprises subject to regulatory controls that required them to operate in the public interest. The result is, fifth, intensification of commercialization, or the heightening of profit over public service as the key fact that helps account for communications activity. Finally, all these processes contribute to globalization, which is the extension of media markets, industries and products worldwide.

On closer inspection, however, this list of major forces turns out to be somewhat problematic and partial. These trends can each be documented, but do they really capture all the important elements? For instance, there is reference to increasing 'concentration', but is there not also increasing competition (for example, competition between the quondam state-owned telecommunications industries or private monopolies and new competition riding on the back of technological innovations such as the mobile phone or wireless Internet)? There is staggering competition between the terrestrial television networks in the United States and the spread of cable television; and cable television is increasingly under threat from the changing fortunes of satellite television; while the television medium as a whole is challenged by the growth of the Internet, since more people are spending more time working or playing on computers. The world of the Internet embraces hundreds of new content and service suppliers.

In many countries of the world, the decline of state broadcasting monopolies has been succeeded by a much more diverse range of private, semi-public as well as public television enterprises, using digital and analogue terrestrial, satellite, cable and video modes of delivery. The one-time fixed-line telecommunications companies, whose markets and profits in 1999–2000 have been ravaged by new competition, are moving into delivery and content for cable, satellite and wireless technologies, and into both wired and non-wired fast-speed access to the Internet. Looking around the world, there is clearly much more competition in the telecommunications business than there was even a decade ago, both between and within fixed-line and mobile markets.

Many of these developments have come about not simply because of changes in technology, but because of changes in regulation. We are not dealing here with a system of capitalism that has spiralled out of control of state intervention. Major expansion in cable in the United States came about in 1977 when the Federal Communications Commission (FCC) changed the regulatory structure to make it possible for cable companies to import an unlimited number of signals for local distribution. Technology is, in some cases, a strictly secondary consideration. The Telecommunications Act 1996, made it possible for telecommunications providers to acquire cable companies and hence to control content. In so doing it merely reversed previously established 'common carrier' principles that had favoured separation of control over content from delivery of content, and had been an arrangement of convenience that had suited the telephony, telegraph and wireless industries of an earlier era (Winseck, 1995).

The year 2000 witnessed two developments that at least give pause to assertions about trends towards increasing concentration and deregulation, respectively. One was the decision by the United States Supreme Court auguring the possible dissolution or fragmentation of the Microsoft empire (though the company may yet be reprieved under the Bush administration). Another was the decision of the board of AT+T (not for the first time in its history) voluntarily to split itself into a number of separate companies. Other giant telecommunications companies were considering similar strategies of divestiture and asset sales (amid speculation that even AT+T might be subject to takeover). Rather than an ineluctable trend, are we witnessing a continuous cycle of competition and concentration that predates digital technology, and is related to processes of technological innovation in general?

Deregulation reconfigures market opportunities, domestically and internationally, and invites competition. To reduce the uncertainty effects of competition, established players typically seek alliances or mergers with others. To protect domestic markets against foreign invasion they often seek alliances or mergers with foreign players. What was principally a struggle for domestic supremacy that sometimes involved foreign acquisitions, becomes a struggle for global supremacy that leverages domestic market strength. Globalization is evident in the marketing success of powerful multi-national communications corporations who manufacture the equipment, own the stations, produce and distribute media product; yet despite the highly visible activities of multi-media conglomerates, based mainly in the United States, western Europe and Japan, there is contrary evidence of continuing media regulation and practice serving, in effect, to support and maintain distinctive patterns of local control, production and genre, in many different countries (Curran and Park, 2000).

The initial list of major forces thus begins to look potentially selective. Industrial concentration at the turn of the century has been prevalent and highly visible in media reporting. Recent instances, at the time of writing, include giant mergers or buy-outs between AT+T and MediaOne, Viacom and CBS, AOL and Time Warner, Vivendi and Seagram, Bertelsmann and Barnes & Noble. But focusing on these and building on them to yield theories that have explanatory power for the field as a whole inevitably privileges the importance of certain aspects of the structure and process of communications over others in ways that are ultimately difficult to justify. The 'political economy' approach to media, which typically celebrates diversity in media and condemns forces that limit access to and representation of different interests or voices, attributes a special and negative importance to the concentration of capital.

It is sometimes difficult to disentangle a value-based belief system (one that, in this instance, celebrates diversity) from efforts of theory-building on the basis of available evidence, and both run the danger of ignoring or minimizing contrary evidence. What appears as 'contrary' evidence may be accounted for within the theory of 'dominant trends'. For example, the appearance of greater competition might be explained as a temporary phase of a longer-term trend. New communications regulation might be represented simply as the death of a 'public service' regulatory system in favour of a system that exists solely to regulate between industrial competitors. Diversity of channels (from systems of one to four to systems that offer from 50 to a 100 or more) may be disparaged on the grounds that ownership of channels and of channel content remains highly concentrated and that the range of available genres is limited. The continuing, and in some cases increasing, strength of national systems of media regulation and production merely obscures, it might be said, the internationalization of finance, the hybridization of content, the influence of multinational advertising revenue . . . and so on. All these may or may not be good arguments that can be supported by evidence. But there is always a danger of committing to a theory beyond its useful life. This may happen because the 'theory' has converted to a 'belief system' or ideology. Or it may happen because the sheer possibility of developing more and more sophisticated and dialectical explanations as to why apparently 'contradictory' evidence is in fact 'supporting' evidence, discourages the search for fresh theoretical frameworks.

A 'purely theoretical' approach would certainly demonstrate strong commitment to the classical scientific project of continuous testing of a proposition. This involves the search for evidence that might discredit the prevailing theory. Such a search is motivated by the principle that only through continuous challenge can theories be replaced or strengthened (stronger theories are those that explain a greater number and variety of instances than the weaker theories they displace). This kind of open-minded commitment does indeed help to distinguish the deliberateness, discipline and the tentativeness of theory-building from the taken-for-granted, fixed and 'self-evident' assertions of an ideology. Even the 'purely theoretical' approach is problematic, because researchers choose to apply scientific methodology to certain problems and issues, and not others, and in such processes of choice there are often sources of non-random bias (for example, available financial sponsors favour certain areas of enquiry over others). Given methodologies may rest on debatable presuppositions (e.g. that quantitatively demonstrable propositions are superior).

In my example it looks as though ideology influenced the process of theory-building. Ideology is less self-reflective than theory, less systematic, has greater fixity, is more directly associated with affective dimensions of life and more easily accounted for by individual life circumstances. In reference to media, I do believe that issues of ownership and finance are important. I am attracted by the 'political economy' approach to the study of media, which is one that places things structural above things cultural. I am sometimes inclined therefore to rank structural phenomena high on my list of research foci that are likely to yield theories with comprehensive explanatory power. The theory here, at its simplest, is that media owner-ship and finance (capital, advertising, etc.) greatly influence the ways in which the world is represented through the media. For the theory to be a good theory, it will need to account for the interconnections between ownership, structure and content, drawing on a variety of different kinds of evidence from different sources. Yet, I accept that theories that privilege structure are often only able to establish rather tenuous or superficial links to content and reception. Understanding how the potential for meaning is inscribed within media texts and how media consumers interact with texts to realize meaning requires the help of many more lines of inquiry than those favoured by the school of 'political economy'. Later chapters of this section exemplify this.

Good research requires attention to theories. It is virtually impossible to collect 'mere facts' in research, as though mere facts could be free of theory. Suppose a researcher focuses attention on the circulation figures of selected national newspapers over time; he, presumably, would do this because someone has paid him to do it, and he obliges, or simply because, explicitly or implicitly, he considers that circulation figures are indicators of something significant. He may know that changes in circulation figures can have a dramatic effect on advertising rates, and perhaps on the value of news media stock on the stock exchange. Such effects may be demonstrated by reference to actual advertising or stock rates, and by discussions with circulation and advertising managers, advertising agencies and brokers, among others, that explore their reasons for decisions about rates and investments. He may also believe that high circulation figures are a measure of news-papers' influence in society. The supposition of social influence needs to be carefully artic-ulated if it is to be dealt with systematically. Social impact cannot be gauged from circulation figures alone, for these merely indicate the likely scale of potential exposure to given news items and other items of content. Upon thinking about what might constitute 'influence', the weakness of circulation figures as a measure becomes clearer. One news-paper that is read by only a small number of powerful people could be as, or more, influ-ential than one that is read by a large number of relatively powerless people. Influence can operate at the institutional level (for example, the influence of the press on the election strategies of political parties) or at the individual level (the influence of the press on voter intentions). It may be expressed in terms of changes in reader cognition, in value or attitude, or in behaviour. The ambition to demonstrate that a given change in cognition, attitude or behaviour has occurred in response to a media stimulus, as shall be seen, is fraught with methodological challenges.

What are the merits of theory-building? First, it is motivated by the desire to understand and explain the world. A strong theory explains much and often; a weak theory is beset by exceptions to the rule and limitations on the range of phenomena to which it refers. Because the social world is generally one of continuous change, the tentative nature of theory-building is suited to the challenge of explaining things, and helps to sustain an open mind as to the adequacy and durability of particular theories. Second, theory-building is both a challenge to the intellect and a framework that helps advance the intellect. A good theory posits certain relationships between different parts of the social world, and between the social and physical worlds, and provides a rich treasure of questions to be investigated. Third, the questions that are provoked by a good theory suggest the range of data and therefore the kinds of approaches and measurements that are most relevant. Fourth, a strong theory enables us to make reasoned predictions about the future. If in the course of observation predictions are not realized in accordance with the theory, then at least there is evidence that will contribute to a refinement or replacement of the theory.

Are there dangers in theory-building? The principal danger is that a theory becomes a cage, and the researcher becomes so intent on proving or disproving the theory that he does not take account of alternative perspectives or phenomena, that are relevant to his search, but that lie outside the cage. A similar danger is that a theory becomes a marker of identity, even of self-concept, and takes on some of the characteristics of an ideology, defensively expropriating or ignoring contradictions without adequately adjusting to these or allowing itself to be transformed by them.

What is the relationship of theory to descriptive data? Good theory generally comes from detailed knowledge of the object of investigation even in advance of quantitative methods. In addition to extensive reading of existing publications, knowledge is acquired through close association with the field of research, and with the subjects of investigation. It is acquired from people who have worked within the field, and from time spent by the researcher as participant or ethnographic observer. The resulting evidence or data will not be free of bias. Bias may result from the position of the researcher within the field or organization, or from the dynamics of the relationship that the researcher is able to sustain with those within the situation that is being studied. Participants and observers have their own hunches as to the kind of evidence that is most relevant to the purpose and object of study. Such hunches may reflect preconceived or ill-founded ideas, but researchers do need hunches to help them achieve progress within the constraints of time and expense. If attentive, they will be on the alert to cues that point in new directions, to things that they had at first excluded as being of likely relevance, or to things of which they may have been entirely unaware. Prejudice is structured into the way in which a situation or organization is commonly regarded or looks at itself, through existing statistics, reports and conversation. Yet such evidence is generally and inevitably an important primary source of information. The point is that 'raw data', while it may be the outcome of initial field investigations designed to develop a descriptive basis upon which to generate theory, is itself framed by implicit theories, by the values and ideologies of both the observers and of those who are observed. This does not make the descriptive phase of research any the less important. In general, familiarity with and comprehensive knowledge of the object of study is an important asset in research, provided that the researcher can maintain a sense of curiosity and can sustain a relationship with the field of study that does not compromise his or her commitment to discovery and revelation.

What makes for good theory?
- Good theory illuminates the world by explaining the world.
- Good theory claims strong relevance to human concerns.
- The intellectual processes of good theory are transparent.
- The intellectual processes of good theory are both creative and systematic.
- Good theory takes account of, and evaluates the usefulness of, preceding theories.
- Good theory takes account of all the relevant data.
- Good theory is testable and verifiable by methodologies that are appropriate to its subject matter.
- Good theory generates good (meaningful, relevant, precise) questions, propositions or hypotheses.
- Good theory is open to contest.
- Good theory is tentative.
- Good theory holds ideology at as much distance as it can achieve.
- Good theory is succeeded by even better theory.

CHAPTER 3

Demarcating the Field

The dialectic between description and theory begins even in the process of determining what the field of study includes. The authors of this volume are contributors to the study of media within society. Not all such researchers have a sense of shared intellectual history. However, various attempts have been made (e.g. *Journal of Communication*, 1983, 1993; McQuail, 2000; Boyd-Barrett and Newbold, 1995) to construct such a history. These demonstrate that whatever else it is, the field is multi-disciplinary, and that consensus as to what it includes, and what are the significant milestones of its history, is fragile and elusive. This elusiveness is evident in the 'what' of study, as much as in the 'how'. In its earlier years and for much of its subsequent history, we can say that the study of media in society has tended to focus on the more popular media. There has been a tendency, for example, to disassociate the term 'media' from the ancient medium of the book and its associated activities of publishing, printing and reading. This omission therefore tended to marginalize the study of literature and of educational publishing within the field of media study. The early field favoured newspapers, comics, film, radio and television over theatre, opera and ballet. There may have been an implicit assumption that the absence of a 'mass' audience was equivalent to the impossibility of a mass 'influence'. Large audience media were preferred, as were issues that seemed to be problematic for society. Even within the general category of 'popular' media there was a curious selectivity of focus. Newspapers were looked upon primarily as purveyors of formal news, principally of the doings of government, yet the fact that they were also sources of entertainment, gossip, scandal, sport and classified advertisements barely registered. News agencies attracted little interest until the 1970s. Some technologies, such as the telephone and telecommunications were for several decades overlooked (Pool, 1983), as though only the province of tedious technical and regulatory issues. Even at the turn of the twenty-first century, telephony and computing were relatively new arrivals to the established field of media study.

Equally, consensus was absent in the determination of what were the proper questions to ask about media. In the early days, the principal concern was the 'effects' of the media on the morality of the masses, or on the effectiveness, for good or ill, of media as tools of political and commercial persuasion. Over time, however, a much broader range of questions has been formulated, addressing the history and structure of media industries, issues of media regulation, production practices, the production and structure of media texts, the relationships of media with other social institutions and with the overall transformations of society itself. The issue of what we should incorporate within the domain of media study has implications for the generation of theory because it helps alert us to the range of possible factors that are likely to impact on the particular object of investigation in any specific study.

Alvarado and Boyd-Barrett (1992), in a reader on media education, organized the field of media study into three major traditions: the interpretative, the social science and the practice. This division broadly recognized the differences between a tradition that drew on the analysis of literature and film and that focused mainly on the structure of the **text**, and a second tradition that used empirical methodologies for the analysis, primarily, of production and audiences. The tradition of practice is the 'how to' approach to working *in* the media, which – at least in the United Kingdom – had been largely separate from studies *of* the media.

One useful framework for the descriptive demarcation of the boundaries of communications research emerged from the BFI in the early 1990s, a summary of which appeared in a chapter of the aforementioned Alvarado and Boyd-Barrett reader (see Bazalgette, 1992a). Within this framework, its authors argue, it is possible to locate all the questions and issues that typically concern people about the media. The framework consists of six 'key aspects' (see the accompanying box) each representing a cluster of concepts. The boundaries between the clusters are not intended to be watertight:

If you look at one aspect of a building and then another, you may be able to see the same feature of the building each time, although it will not look the same. Each aspect will also reveal things that could not be seen from anywhere else, and if you really want to get a sense of the whole building, you need to look at several different aspects. (Bazalgette, 1992a: 201)

Key aspects

Signpost question	Key aspect
Who is communicating and why?	Media Agencies
What type of text is it?	Media Categories
How has it been produced?	Media Technologies
How do we know what it means?	Media Languages
Who receives it, and what sense do they make of it?	Media Audiences
How does it present its subject to us?	Media Representations

Source: adapted from Bazalgette, 1992b

AGENCY

This aspect is concerned with the people, whether singly or in teams, working within or outside institutions, who produce media texts. ('Media texts' is a term I use generically to incorporate oral, print, still and moving image, and computer-generated communications.) Producers of such texts typically undergo a lengthy and sometimes rigorous process of learning and training, whether formal or informal, and acquire 'professional' knowledge. Training and professional knowledge help them function effectively in production teams and to develop texts that suit the genre and other requirements of the media for which they work, and that are considered likely to be popular with their intended audience(s).

The 'multi-authored' character that is typical of mass communication texts entails an array of distinct specialist roles and knowledge. These include technical (relating to design, choice and manipulation of technical equipment), directive (relating to the management and organization of creative human talent), administrative (relating to the management of non-human financial and material resources), and creative or 'performative' (writing, editing, reporting, drawing, filming, photographing, drawing, acting, dancing, 'hosting', composing, playing, singing, etc.).

Agents are typically concerned that media products should be 'effective', according to some set of criteria, or that they should make a profit, or that they should contribute to the overall health and viability of the institutions within which, or for which, they work. By extension, therefore, questions of agency also include issues of distribution and scheduling, media ownership and control, financing, industrial concentration, and the relationship of media organizations to political, legal, regulatory and similar environmental influences upon media operations. Such factors can often be situated at a range of different levels from local, through national, to international or global.

CATEGORY

Media texts are generally recognized by their consumers or interpreters as belonging to one or more different categories of text. The concept of 'genre' is sometimes employed to denote a textual category. Film and television studies routinely make use of genre categorizations such as horror, western, musical, news, situation comedy, quiz show, chat show, sport, and so on. Genre categories can be useful for all media, including newspapers (hard news, foreign news, editorial, 'op ed.' articles, women's features, fashion, motoring, etc.), magazines (women's interest, soft porn, hobbies, health), books (romance, biography, murder mystery, science fiction), music (country and western, hard rock, rap), radio (call-in programmes, record requests), Internet (portal pages, search tools, e-commerce).

Some genres, as the lists in the previous paragraph indicate, are applicable across different media. The success of new media may depend on how easily they can assimilate previously established genres. Early film, for example, borrowed heavily from the traditions of music hall, theatre, the popular novel and comic books, even as it transformed these genres in a variety of ways, not least through the visual language, editing and other production techniques unique to film. Not all media products can easily be identified in terms of genre. Some programmes or products represent more than one genre (e.g. hybrid forms such as the drama-documentary or comedy western). There can be significant similarities between programmes of supposedly different genres. Identification of a media text by genre may vary between different people, depending on such factors as their relative experience of media texts, their interests and expectations, and cultural factors that influence how media are used, discussed and thought about. In some media, genre categories are less established than in others: in the early twenty-first century, the Internet would be a good example. Genres develop over time, so that associations that are commonly evoked by genre labels are likely to evolve. The more exposure an audience has to a particular genre, the more sophisticated it will become in its appreciation of the possible variations around a generic theme, and the more tolerant it is likely to be of innovation, play, involution and intermixture of generic characteristics.

The aspect of 'category', then, draws our attention to the expectations we bring to different kinds of text and how they can be used. In the United Kingdom, for example, viewers would expect a television news bulletin to be introduced and 'held together' by a presenter or anchor-person speaking directly to camera, using Standard English and received pronunciation, characteristic of the English upper and middle classes, especially of the south of England. The presenter will introduce each of the different news items and each of the different segments within a news item. These will include introductions to on-location reporters who, in turn, will typically address the presenter in order to contextualize any on-location film for which they will provide voice commentary. Such features enable most UK viewers to recognize, almost instantly, whenever they switch on to a news programme, that

they are watching 'the news'. Similarly, newspaper readers soon acquire an intimate knowledge of the lay-out conventions of their preferred newspapers, knowing where to look for
such categories of news as sport, financial or foreign. They also acquire a general knowledge of newspaper conventions that apply to most newspapers or groups of newspapers.
These include such things as the significance of story position and size of typeface, and
differences in the ways in which the audience is addressed – as demonstrated by uses of
lexicon and syntax, structures of narrative or exposition, etc. – between news stories,
feature articles and editorials.

Although there may be idiosyncrasies in the ways in which individuals categorize
media, categories also have a cultural and sociological reality in that they form the basis,
for example, of explicit production, promotional and scheduling practices, even of training programmes and career structures. Many journalists spend substantial periods of
their entire careers identified as specialist sports journalists, say, or crime correspondents, while television producers may specialize in news, current affairs, consumer,
sports or drama programme-making. The sociological reality of media categories has
implications for 'reading' practices. Viewers or readers who have relatively little experience of the conventions of a certain category of text may have more difficulty than others in understanding or 'making sense' of it. They may not position themselves in relation
to a text in a way that affords them the use or pleasure that its producers had hoped to
achieve. That is to say, they may bring inappropriate expectations to the text, they may
not understand the significance of some of its conventions, and so on.

T E C H N O L O G Y

The technologies of any given system of media production and delivery may seem just
another way of categorizing media. Communications technology has to do with the tools and
materials that are used for the inscription and delivery of meanings. Identification of technology as a key aspect of the study of mass communications has the heuristic value of
focusing attention on the extent to which media communications reflect technological
choice. Choice operates at an infra-structural level (e.g. design of telephone systems for
point-to-point rather than for mass communication, replacement of valve radio by the tran-
sistor) and at the level of individual programmes or messages (choice of camera or sound
system, depth of field, wide-angle lens, position of microphone). Technologies, in other
words, are human constructions, the outcome of human motivations, processes and institutions. Technology helps determine the range of non-verbal signs or communication conventions that are possible, and therefore the potential complexity of meanings that different
media can generate. Technology affects the relative costs and necessary skills of particular
forms of media expression. Technologies define significant differences between media (for
example, audio cassette as opposed to computer disk), while also undermining those
differences (as in the convergence between television, cable, computing, CD-ROM and
telecommunications for the delivery of moving images). Technologies are important not just
for the production of meaning, but also for the manner of its reception: the technology of

delivery is part of the complex of sensation and meaning that is the outcome of the inter-action between media content and consumer.

LANGUAGE

The media constitute important contexts for the use, experience and decoding of spoken and written, or printed, languages. There is an immense range of issues that touch upon choice of languages and language styles in the media, to do with different language 'regis-ters' or 'patterns of discourse' that are associated with different media, genres, audiences and purposes. What may be called the 'socio-linguistics' of media, a flourishing subdiscipline of linguistics, addresses such issues as the political implications of language choice for media in multi-lingual societies and the extent to which media language is restricted to standardized and official language categories. It also has to do with relative degrees of formality and informality of language use, variation in language use according to genre, to the relationships between participants within media programmes, and to producer percep-tions of their audience. There is considerable interest in the particularities of the language structure of media texts, and in the diversity of ways in which visual design and printed language interact. There has also been study of the uses of 'oral' mode in printed media (to create the illusion of informality and equality between producer and consumer) and of 'literary' mode in audio-visual media (with the purpose of capturing some of the authority of printed text).

Increasingly, the study of media texts is influenced by post-modernist approaches. These stress the interrelationships between given texts, and their implicit and explicit borrowings from, and representation of, existing 'discourses' in society. Such discourses often com-prise clusters of ideas and associations that are shared by members of a social, ethnic, occupational, gender or social class grouping (sometimes referred to as 'interpretative communities'). The repertoire of discourses available to particular groups, whether through media or non-media sources, is influenced by wider structural features of society that influence the distribution of resources and skills that people need in order to generate and appropriate meanings. Consider debates about the 'digital divide' in relation to the spread of computing and of opportunities to use computers between national, social, ethic, age and gender groups. In post-modernism, texts do not have single authors; if a production team is identified as responsible for, say, a given film, it need not actually constitute the 'author' for that film (see Bell, 1991, for extended discussion of this in relation to news media). Rather, a film – like most texts – is multi-layered, containing echoes of all manner of previous texts and of the broader social discourses on which those texts have drawn.

A newspaper article about a political conference is not merely authored by the journalist whose byline heads the article, but is the product of many other contributors. These include: the editorial team; the photographer whose work appears alongside the story; the news-paper itself, its news values and policies; news agency dispatches and archive cuttings from which the journalist has borrowed indirectly or explicitly quoted; quotes from sources that the journalist has interviewed; statements distributed by party spokespersons; public relations handouts. All these source texts will have been prepared for other, perhaps rather different, audiences in different contexts. The newspaper article therefore not only contains echoes of other texts, but it also contains echoes of the audiences for which those texts were prepared. These texts may be framed by the journalist in order to relate closely to the contents of his main lead (which we can imagine may have to do with major policy issues of the day – nationalization as opposed to privatization, perhaps – and debated in preparation for a party manifesto). They may draw on ideas or concepts that reflect philosophies, ways of seeing the world and value systems that have been in circulation for decades, if not for centuries. These are part of a cultural data bank or storage system of concepts, values, ideas, turns of phrase, into which individual writers dip for inspiration, sometimes quite unconsciously.

The media do not generate meaning only through spoken and written language. Just as language has 'paralinguistic' features – including tone, inflection, posture, and gesture, that constitute related but distinctive semiotic (sign) systems – so too the media represent complexes of interdependent semiotic systems of visual, aural, even tactile (as in touch-screen interaction for some computing) communication. Some of these, like the 'languages' of bodily proximity, architecture, dress, and food preparation, are found in the everyday world. Others are peculiar to the media – like the conventions governing the use of different styles and sizes of type, page lay-out, the relationships between visual and verbal communication on the printed page, camera positions and movements, juxtapositions of shots, continuity editing, framing, lighting and montage.

AUDIENCE

Studies of audiences were at one time mainly concerned with the 'effects' of media on audience beliefs, attitudes and behaviour. They asked how such effects were differentially distributed according to the social positioning of audience members, especially in terms of their social class, education and occupation. Audience studies are now as likely to be concerned with the ways in which members of audiences use the media in their day-to-day lives, how different cultures appropriate media content, and with the range of different meanings, interpretations and pleasures that audience members take from the media. Naturally, they are also interested in how media use varies according to age, culture, gender, social class and other influences that shape 'personal' identity. Many audience studies are still informed by conventional, institutional (and advertiser) interest in such issues as the popularity of particular programmes or the 'effectiveness' of political or other campaigns. Psychologists, criminologists and others continue to be concerned about such matters as the implications of exposure of children and adults to programmes containing scenes of violence; educationalists are concerned with the potential of the media for education; social anthropologists, who are foremost among those staking out new questions in audience research, are interested in the ways in which people use, experience, relate to, live around and take meaning from the media, and how these factors are contextualized by particular cultures, communities, family structures and ideologies.

A key feature of many contemporary audience studies is their rejection of the view that the 'meaning' of a text can be accessed merely through detailed analysis of the text itself. They favour an alternative view that audiences make meaning, and that to understand the meanings of media texts it is therefore necessary to study, observe and talk to audience members. Critics of this approach worry that an unqualified focus on individual difference may simply reflect a liberal theory of the world that is premised on the supremacy of individual choice as a sufficient explanation for variations in behaviour. The 'rich data' of ethnographic social anthropology offers a route to understanding individual difference through an analysis of cultures and subcultures. This is an approach that usefully augments more quantitative methods of conventional sociology and psychology.

Just as the influence of post-modernism has expanded the concept of authorship, so too it has developed a broader conceptualization of the concept of audience. The term can apply to those who participate, as audiences, in media programmes (the immediate or 'real' audience, as in the case of programmes with studio audiences). Producers may have in mind particular audiences when they produce a programme (e.g. influential peers or news sources), as well as 'imagined audiences' that incorporate ideas about the 'average' viewer or reader (the 'Kansas City Milkman' of Associated Press folklore). Some audiences are directly addressed in a programme (e.g. a programme for people with disabilities), while others are merely 'listeners-in' (non-student viewers of Open University educational broadcasts in the UK, for example). As shown above, a text can contain 'echoes' of previous audiences, audiences for those older components of the text that have been transposed from earlier texts. (Bell, 1991)

REPRESENTATION

With representation we move back to the texts for an understanding not of their codes and conventions, nor of the languages they manipulate to construct their meanings, but of their content, and in particular of how they portray, reflect, filter and negotiate the 'real' world. I put the term real in quotation marks, because all methods of understanding the world, not just the methods of media, are subject to processes of selection; and also because much of the supposedly 'real' world, and of our ways of knowing that world, is influenced by the media and by widespread assumptions about the power of media.

Concerns about how the media represent the world are often expressed through use of terms such as ideology or bias. Today, it is commonly appreciated that the media do not simply mirror reality – even where that is their stated aim. Every form of representation involves selection, exclusion and inclusion. Selection is inherent from the stage of initial perception through to decisions about what aspects of a programme to focus on and from whose point of view. Selection in production extends to decisions about the kinds of evidence that will be used, the style of expression, and all processes of selection in media are driven by an awareness of constraints of time, resources, money and imagination. In this respect the media are merely dramatic examples of the ways in which our own everyday non-mediated representations of 'reality' are subject to similar processes of selection and interpretation. In no way does this reduce the importance of studying how the media represent the world, whether it be political events in news bulletins, the 'news-geography' of news agency wires or gender relations in soap operas.

We can form judgements about such representations in the light of a range of different source of evidence. These include other media texts, and alternative or non-media sources of information, perspective and evaluation. Often, we will be left at the end of the day merely with a *judgement* – perhaps a more reasoned, convincing judgement than that which informed the original media representation, but none the less a judgement – rather than a 'true' picture of 'how it *really* is'. Suppose I conduct a study of prime-time television drama. Imagine I find that of all occupations represented in such productions, those relating to law enforcement and crime account for 30 per cent. Then suppose I compare this finding with various government and other surveys and I find that these alternative sources of evidence show that the actual distribution of such professions among the employed population is 3 per cent. I would probably make a convincing case that the second percentage is more trustworthy than the former (although I would have to acknowledge problems with the data, perhaps relating to definition or methodology). If you accepted my case, we would then discuss the 'meaning' of this finding. What does it signify? Is it a matter for concern? Are children exposed to a suitable range of role models? Are grave-diggers discriminated against? Should we take comfort if the study of television drama shows, for example, that many lawyers in these productions are female, and therefore (we might hope) helping to modify gender stereotypes? Should we worry that too many of the television criminals come from 'minority' groups and are therefore (we might fear) negatively stereotyping such groups? And so on. You will note that such discussions very quickly begin to make reference to our assumptions, explicit or implicit, about media 'effects' on audiences.

It is not intended that the key aspects should be thought of as water-tight compartments. In media research the key aspects commonly interlink. Studies of media agency, for example, are often motivated by an interest in the implications of agency for representation: how far does the ownership and control of a given news medium influence the way in which news issues are covered? If a newspaper belongs to a larger corporation with business invest-ments in satellite television, which would like to extend into terrestrial television, does this influence the newspaper's coverage of issues related to the regulation of media cross-ownership? If a news agency's revenues in a given country derive mainly from the sale of news services to leading financial institutions, does this influence the kind of news the agency covers about that country or that it feeds to it?

To demonstrate the existence of any such influence we would need to show not only that news coverage in either case was favourable to deregulation or was dominated, say, by economic news. We would also need to show that these patterns were the direct result of corporate policy, or that observation of the practices of other media lead us inexorably to the conclusion that news coverage in the case of the subject newspaper or news agency would have been different in a different market context or under different ownership.

The key aspects could be reduced to a smaller number: e.g. 'category' could be fused with 'language', or with 'technology'. The framework is essentially descriptive: it helps define significant phenomena that are encountered in media study, significant questions typically asked about the media, or topics that are frequently discussed. The framework proposes, in a way that most researchers are likely to find reasonably unproblematic, how these foci or questions can sensibly be arranged or clustered. It does not in itself offer any explanation for why things are as they are. It proposes no theories. It is very much media-focused, which is what we might expect. But an intriguing outcome of such a framework is its applicability to a broader range of phenomena than 'just' the media.

I proposed the concept of 'text' as a generic term for all media products, such as book chapters, speeches, film extracts, newspaper stories, but we could apply the term more widely to any form of social expression: the festival of Easter, a school mathematics class, a suburban garden. All of these we could regard as texts in which forms of expression or communication show evidence of rule-governed regularity. The governing rules have mainly to do with the context and purpose(s) of the text, and with the relations that pertain between the parties to the communication or expression event. Also important are 'mode' (the tools and vehicles that are used in order to communicate or express) and the arrangement, the syntax, of the different elements of the 'content' or 'message'. To all forms of communication or expression we can apply the key aspects of agency, category, technology, language, audience and representation. In other words, at least some of the basic conceptual tools that are encountered in the study of mass communications are of much broader applicability. A focus on the media in the BFI's treatment of the key aspects, finally, could divert our attention from the media as situated in society and culture, acted upon and constituted by society and culture just as much as they feed into, influence, serve and transform society and culture.

FROM DESCRIPTION TO THEORY

The distinction between theory and ideology, as I have indicated, is never absolute, but is rather a question of degree of systematicity, reflexivity and openness, and a question of purpose. Any time something is described and explained, processes of selection, exclusion and inclusion entailed, these processes entail theories, even if the theories are only implicit. The following example is of a movement from descriptive data to theory, a theory that is informed, to some extent, by ideology.

Suppose we observe, on listening to recordings of a sample of conversations about media, that people commonly indicate a belief or presumption that some media enjoy high social status and that others do not, that some media sit towards the top of a scale of seriousness, status, prestige, credibility, affiliation with high culture, intellect, commitment to rational discourse, etc., and appeal particularly to a privileged and highly educated minority, while there are other media that sit towards the middle or bottom of that scale. We can hypothesize that the existence of such a scale is acknowledged even by people whose preferences are for the media that lie towards the bottom of the scale and who are inclined, in the presence of interviewers, to mock their own reading preferences. (A similar pattern has been documented among speakers of non-standard language varieties who attribute high status to corresponding standard varieties, and describe their own speech habits as 'incorrect' even as they exhibit strong attachment – referred to in socio-linguistics as 'covert prestige' – to their preferred non-standard variety (Holmes, 1992).)

Why might one generate such a hypothesis? What underlying theory would inform it? A plausible answer relates to a perception of the mass media as brokers of power in societies in which power is unevenly distributed. In this perspective, powerful interests control main-stream media. Some media exist mainly to serve the powerful; others exist to serve, or at least to make money from satisfying, the curiosity of the relatively powerless, through enter-tainment, diversion and sensation. These media offer their popular service in a way that does not threaten their own stake in the existing structure of society; they give their audi-ences 'what they want' provided that this also helps to secure or even reinforce audience consent or compliance with the existing social structure. Despite their concern to maximize audiences through 'popular' programming, popular media none the less maintain the symbolic world on which public order depends, continuing to invest status and authority in symbols of power – for example, in their representations of the parliamentary process, insti-tutions of business and finance, the army and police. Audiences are co-opted into maintain-ing respect for, or compliance with, these institutions. Even if they themselves do not attend to media or programmes that deal with such things in detail, they will tend to recognize that such media or such programmes are prestigious because they deal with matters that are close to the centres of social power.

Such is the theory, for what it is worth, and it is offered merely as an example of a move-ment from description to theory in media study. It may not be a particularly good, challeng-ing or original theory, and it has some holes. It does not really explain why audiences should allow themselves to be duped, and it seems to assume that audiences simply 'read off' media communications in the way that was intended by authors or producers. More funda-mentally, it seems to assume that media communications are indeed 'intended', in any simple sense of the word. It has not accounted for potentially contradictory evidence (for example, in the UK this would include instances of negative coverage of the monarchy by the popular press). To pursue this theory any further a lot more thought is required as to the appropriate evidence that might support or refute the theory and to how one might set about collecting such evidence. Perhaps the weaknesses of the theory would have been avoided had more thought been given to audience ideology. What ideology that might be in this case is not clear. It could plausibly have to do with a presumption of the high saliency of power as something that it is important and worthwhile to examine, something that a morality of social justice requires should be understood so that, through improved knowledge, greater social justice can be attained.

Theories exist at any of a number of levels, from the micro – for example, theories that seek to explain the cognitive processes through which readers are able to make sense of texts (see van Dijk, 1998) – to the macro – for example, theories that seek to explain the relationship between media and the nature of civilization (see Innis, 1950; McLuhan, 1964). Lying behind an explicit theory is often another, implicit, theory. Many of the early theories of 'media effects', for example, seem to have subscribed to an underlying 'transmissional' model of communication. That is to say, they discussed media effects using such central concepts as 'the flow of messages' as moving uni-directionally from 'senders', through 'messengers' to 'receivers', accompanied by 'noise', and 'redundancy'. 'Correct' decoding of the message, in this model, may be subject to interference from noise in the system (rather like the static in radio communication). Perhaps the decoding apparatus has not been tuned to decipher the particular code in which the message is encoded. The speaker may be using a language the receiver does not understand. One problem with this kind of conceptualiza- tion is that it tends to treat meaning as something that is inscribed within the physical property of the text itself. An alternative model of communication regards meaning as the product of the interaction between reader and the system of signs that makes up a text, or as a process of mutual engagement by two or more people in a shared construction of meaning that has no end point. In this model, meaning can never be definitively packaged and delivered to others. This is because newcomers to the interaction will not have partici- pated in the initial process of joint construction. They will enter with their own personal histories and preoccupations; and all parties, whether or not they are new to the exchange, will continuously generate new associations, new thoughts and new meanings the longer they participate in the process of communication.

C H A P T E R   4

Different Theories in the History of Mass Communication Research

The study of mass communications has attracted scholars from many academic disci- plines, including psychology, sociology, economics, politics, history, social anthropology, literature, linguistics, professional studies, mathematics and engineering. Different scholars look at different things, ask themselves different sorts of question. Research into media texts (often drawing on the intellectual heritage and the study of literary criticism) looks very different from research into media industries (often informed by a mixture of political studies, economics and sociology). A research focus on media contribution to 'social reproduction' (i.e. the maintenance over time of specific configurations of the distribution of capital in society) draws on a challenging vocabulary of Marxist political economy (Murdock, 1982; Bennett, 1982). It is very different from the focus of educationalists or psychologists when they research the potential of media for teaching, learning and cognitive development.

APPROACHES TO MEDIA

Boyd-Barrett and Newbold (1995) identified nine different major approaches to the study of mass communications. The term 'approach' was adopted on the grounds that the defining features of different bodies of media research are typically a mixture of four different com- ponents. These are: selective focus as to topic (e.g. news, women in the media, representations of violence); sometimes unexplored ideological presumptions as to the very nature of the topic selected, or why it is important; theories about media in society; and preferences for specific methodologies in finding answers to the questions that have been raised. Any major approach or theory, in common with the construction of any 'text', is a selective process that reflects particular views of the overall field, its boundaries and judgements about the most significant previous contributions. Many media academics nurture a strong sense of the history of their own intellectual discipline and, as the first section of that 1995 volume demonstrated, there have been significant controversies about the ways in which the field has been and should be defined. The cluster of approaches identified were not all of the same kind: some were specifically linked to particular theories, others to particular areas or topics of study. In particular, it should be noted that the classification is not a priori, based on first principles, but reflects areas and movements that have seemed to their proponents and others as distinctive in certain ways, even if the original justification for such distinctiveness may have eroded over time.

Approaches to media (Boyd-Barrett and Newbold, 1995)
- Mass society, functionalism, pluralism
- Media effects
- Political economy
- The public sphere
- Media occupations and professionals
- Cultural hegemony
- Feminism
- Moving image
- New audience research

Mass Society, Functionalism, Pluralism

This cluster of theories and approaches focuses on how the media contribute to the overall social system. It incorporates two radically different views of society. In one view (the **mass society** thesis) modern society (identified at the time principally with North America and western Europe) has been shaped by industrialization and urbanization. Principles of industrial rationalism are applied to the production of cultural goods, including the media, and the shaping of public tastes for such goods result, in this view, in a process of cultural standardization. An alternative view sees the media as reflective of the many different social groups, cultures and interests of a democratic and heterogeneous society, and consequently as a force for social cohesion and stability.

Media Effects

Throughout the history of media research, a prevailing concern has been with whether the media have an influence upon knowledge, beliefs and behaviour. This focus on the individual or group, and its presumption of a one-way 'transmission' of messages that have corresponding impacts on those exposed to them, is in sharp contrast with a great deal of the rest of the research literature.

Political Economy

Mosco (1995) has defined political economy as the 'study of the social relations, particularly the power relations, that influence the production, distribution, and consumption of resources, including communication resources'. As applied to the communications media, political economy studies tend to focus on how the work of media institutions relates to the other major institutions of society – particularly the political, financial and industrial – and how these influences account for media industrial and professional practices.

The Public Sphere

The concept of **public sphere** was coined by Jurgen Habermas in 1962. McKenna (1995) defines it, at its simplest, as a 'forum of public communication: a forum in which individual citizens can come together as a public and confer freely about matters of general interest'. Studies within this approach attempt to identify the role of the media in fostering or in imped-ing the development, operation and survival of such public communication, as well as to explore the conditions that help account for why some manifestations of public sphere appear effective and others not. If the media are controlled by large corporations, for example, and run mainly for their benefit, can the media also function to serve the common good by providing a forum for the exercise of open discussion? Or is such opportunity always tainted and limited by media goals of revenue maximization? Or by the heavy intervention in public communication of media professionals whom nobody has elected and few have chosen?

Media Occupations and Professionals

This descriptive title is self-evident in its area of concern, but invites a variety of different theoretical perspectives. Some studies start from an interest in the analysis of media production and performance, roles and role-relationships – for example, among sources, colleagues, management (see Tunstall, 1971). Others focus on the ways in which media practice is conditioned by institutional economic interests. Still others concentrate on how media workers absorb and recreate prevailing ideas and representations that contribute to the maintenance of a cultural hegemony. Cultural hegemony occurs through the privileging, in the semiotic universe of signs, of ideas and images that reflect the perspectives, inter-ests and ideologies of the ruling class or the ruling alliance of major centres of social power. Such studies also identify areas for authorial freedom, independence or discretion. These are sometimes explained as the spaces created when there are conflicts or dissonance between different sectors of the ruling class, or that are tolerated as commercial efforts to meet audience tastes for novelty, challenge and authenticity.

Cultural Hegemony

Hegemony is defined by During (1995) as the totality of relations of domination that are not visible as such, relying for effectiveness not on coercion but on the voluntary consent of the dominated. The analysis of cultural hegemony is actually but one phase of an intellectual movement that is known as cultural studies. The term hegemony is equally common in political economy; in cultural studies, however, it has a particular inflection – namely, the ideological function of mainstream media texts. Cultural studies is a meeting point in media research, between traditions of study that have grown out of literary analysis and film studies, and traditions of study that have come from the social sciences (principally politics, economics, sociology, anthropology and psychology). Loosely, it may be said that the literary tradition in cultural studies has tended to focus attention on how texts are constructed to make them capable of rendering meaning. The social science tradition has focused more on the significance of texts within specific cultural contexts and the ways in which culture influences the strategies that consumers, audiences or readers employ in order to make meaning of texts.

The cultural hegemony variant of cultural studies was primarily concerned with 'how media contribute to popular consciousness the language, symbolic and cultural codes in which media frame the world' (Newbold, 1995), and in so doing how they reproduce the social relations in which their own power is invested. The media are seen to work principally as conservative forces that reinforce inequalities of power in society. The focus here is on the 'ideological work' of media. For Althusser (1971), individuals are the constructs of ideology, defined as a set of discourses and images that constitute the most widespread knowledge and values – 'common sense'. Ideology turns what is in fact political, partial and open to change into something *seemingly* 'natural', universal and eternal. It achieves this transformation partly by obscuring real connections and replacing them with a picture of social relations that overemphasizes individual freedom and autonomy. This encourages individuals to make sense of the world by flattering their sense of importance and autonomy within it (During, 1995: 187). Ideologies are realized in part through what Bourdieu (1986) has called the 'imaginaries' of the different fields humans typically occupy (family, work, peer groups, etc.), each of which contains particular promises and images of satisfaction and success. But individuals are never, or need never be, completely positioned or determined by the system of fields.

Cultural studies is sometimes seen in opposition to 'structuralist' approaches. That is to say, in cultural studies a great deal of power and influence is attributed to meanings, signs, ideas and language as among primary determinants of the human world. Structuralists, on the other hand, regard manifestations of culture as epiphenomena, merely incidental outcomes of the working of economic determinants through institutions and power relations. By extension of this idea, the term structuralism is applied to any explanatory approach that tends to explain the outer appearances of things by reference to deeper and usually invisible forces. An example would be Freud's explanation of human behaviour in terms of primary impulses such as sex. None the less there is evidence of structural thinking in the analysis of texts. Examples would include the focus on binary oppositions in semiology, an approach which considers that texts achieve meaning by their play of explicit or implicit oppositions. Structural thinking also appears in the analysis of consumers' use of texts when there are references to social class and gender as determinants of the meanings that individuals generate.

In a process of transition from the study of cultural hegemony to a more general interest in cultural studies, there has appeared a dichotomy in the understanding of the relationship of reading to meaning. Cultural hegemony regards the meanings of texts as relatively fixed, while in cultural studies researchers are more inclined to see texts as polysemic – that is to say, open to an infinity of meanings or at least to a limited range of different readings. This transition parallels a change in media studies away from transmissional approaches to communication (in which communication study is essentially the study of how a fixed message gets from source, sent through a channel to a receiver). In more recent years, there has been a tendency to understand communication as something that is negotiated and in which there are no fixed messages, only a series of encounters between texts that have usually been multi-authored (and for whose authors the meanings may also be ambiguous), and readers, who 'read off' meanings from texts, in ways that are influenced by factors that range from cultural membership, immediate task or concern, to general experience and competence in decoding certain kinds of text.

Feminism

The application of feminist theories and concerns to media study applies across the range of other traditions and approaches. It is most evident in cultural studies (which explores the relative importance of sex and gender in relation to social class and patriarchy, and studies gender representations in media texts). It is also evident in 'new audience research', which applies ethnographic methods, involving long-term observation of a community, to study of the ways in which women take meaning from texts and of how their reading practices have been influenced by gender and role. Through these enquiries, feminism has helped to energize and radicalize audience research.

Moving Image

The only approach to media study that is identified by reference to media category, study of the moving image, is intended to refer to the analysis of film, television and video products. It reflects the strength of an independent field of study and practice that for a long time focused solely on film, maintaining a parallel existence with media study. It is largely through film studies that concepts such as genre and narrative were developed for application to media content. Outside the study of literature, it was mainly in film studies that media scholars allowed themselves the luxury of detailed scrutiny of media content, while other approaches to media dealt with content rather summarily, often reducing it to nominal categories. Moving Image scholars came mainly from literature and similar humanistic backgrounds, and they generally felt more comfortable with literary techniques of textual analysis than with the social science techniques of audience analysis. Developing from auteur theory, which regarded the director as the most significant film artist, study of the moving image progressed to theories of genre (as ritual, as ideology, as aesthetic), and narrative (defined by Newbold, 1995, as the 'devices and strategies, the conventions and sequencing of events with characterization, which constitutes a story'). On the way, it introduced, among other things, such considerations as inter-textuality (references in media products to previous products) and the influence of audience expectations and pleasure upon how audiences 'read' film, and on how film is made.

New Audience Research

This is defined largely by its rejection of the role attributed to the audience in traditional media effects studies. These had positioned the audience either as passive receivers in a 'transmissional' model of communication, or as marginally more active receivers whose media preferences were identified mainly by reference to broad categories of content and gratification, and broad categories of membership of social and cultural groupings. New audience research, drawing on ethnographic methodology, regards the processes whereby both authors and readers make sense of texts – their encodings and decodings – to be complex, culturally derived competencies, and that extend to the factors that bring individuals to texts in the first place. The process of 'reading' is influenced by many different factors; these include the structure of the text itself, the social context within which the text is read, the cultural affinities of readers, and the ways in which cultural factors influence their reading competencies, predispositions, opportunities, likes and dislikes.

CHAPTER 5

Administrative and Critical Traditions

Before going on to discuss the above 1995 categorization by Boyd-Barrett and Newbold, I want to look at an important dichotomy in the field between what has been called 'administrative' and 'critical' research (cf. Lazarsfeld, 1941). **Administrative research** was described by Halloran (1995) as a characteristic of most mass communications research in the USA up to the early 1960s. As in the case of other branches of social science, mass communications research had developed, says Halloran:

> essentially as a response to the requirements of modern, industrial, urban society for empirical, quantitative, policy-related information about its operation [that was] geared to improving the effectiveness and profitability of the media, often regarded simply as objects of study, or as neutral tools in achieving stated aims and objectives, usually of a commercial nature. (Halloran, 1995: 64)

Halloran's criticism of such research was less about its focus or its motivation, than about its methods. Too often these were media- rather than society-centred, neglected theory, used crude conceptualizations, were superficial in their analysis of content, and neglected the ways in which the media are linked with other institutions, including political and economic institutions.

> There were few, if any questions about power, organization and control; there was little reference to structural considerations, and rarely were attempts made to study the social meaning of the media in historical or sociological contexts . . . tending to concentrate on one aspect of the process [effects and reactions], to the neglect of the factors that influenced what was produced. (1995: 64)

Research focused on answers that were seen to be useful in the short term. It measured that which lent itself to quantitative measurement rather than that which was important. It focused on the individual, and limited the scope of media influence to imitation, attitude and opinion change.

In contrast to the administrative tradition, Halloran counterposes a tradition of 'critical, problem and policy-oriented' research. This tradition addresses itself to major issues of public concern. It questions the values and claims of the system, by applying independent criteria of effectiveness, suggesting alternatives with regard to both means and ends, and exploring the possibility of new forms and structures. Critical research does not ignore problems that are central to the media, but it tries never to accept without challenge the ways in which problems are defined as problems by media practitioners or politicians. It deals with communication as a social process. It studies media institutions in social context, and does not take the existing system as sacrosanct. It recognizes that research itself is not carried out in a social or political vacuum, but is influenced by a range of factors.

With this in mind, therefore, let us return to the Boyd-Barrett and Newbold (1995) classification that was outlined in the previous section. Overall, the classification is more heavily weighted towards the critical than the administrative tradition, with the important exception of the media effects school, which is home to much of the research in such topic areas as advertising or campaign effects. This critical weighting is only to be expected in a book about theory, in as much as administrative research is not typically oriented to the refinement of theory.

Notwithstanding Halloran's observation that critical research does not ignore problems that are central to media, the weighting in favour of the critical suggests a potential problem with the 1995 classification, and possibly a problem with the field. Halloran has defined his terms to indicate that 'administrative' is not so much a matter of focus, but also of the quality of thinking, analysis and research, particularly with reference to whether the social context is adequately taken into account, as this will affect the way in which questions are asked and answered. The problem with this formulation is that we are in danger of being left simply with a dichotomy between 'good' and 'bad' analysis, and that in itself is too broad to be useful. For much of its history, critical media research has had little time for media-related problems as these have been defined by governments, by the industry and even by many consumer groups that have tried to take action on issues to do with children, violence or media access. In part this is an academic reaction to the failure of much 'administrative' research to take due account of critical research and of the full social, cultural, economic and political contexts in which the media operate and in which people receive or consume them. It also has to do with different agendas of concern between sociologists and 'administrators', and with a corresponding tendency for sociology to deprecate the value of detail in such matters as policy and ethical issues on the grounds of their irrelevance to the grander sociological project of explaining rather than judging society.

The study of media goes a long way beyond sociology (unless we want to argue that sociology encompasses every discipline). Many who work in the study of media, even if they recognize that media operate in a social context, do not share the grander sociological project, but are concerned to achieve certain limited goals for the operation of media systems. I want to argue that their concerns should be as central to the field of media research as the concerns of those who have come to media research through sociology. I also believe that in relation to many of the research questions posed by sociologists, immersion in the details of media policy and organization is increasingly necessary for the demonstration of professional competence, in terms of appropriate knowledge and credibility, in dialogue with the industry and with society at large. This is precisely the area in which social concerns are generally most prevalent and most clearly articulated through government reports, policy discussion papers and enquiries.

Following on from this view, I would argue in favour of including within the 1995 classification a section that could be described as 'media policy', an area in which there is growing interest in teaching and research. Although they could conceivably be subsumed within the notions of 'public sphere' or 'media occupations' or 'political economy', issues of media policy and media regulation are very substantial topics, and the literature comprises many weighty government-sponsored policy and regulatory papers, as well as reports and legislation. I agree that immersion in policy-related research should not be at the expense of a regard for the holistic social context and a 'meta-awareness' of the factors that drive policy-oriented research. I do not believe it is necessary or practical that all industry research should adopt a sociological framework in order to be effective, or even to be useful to sociology. At the same time, 'administrative research' may be the source of much of the data that is available for reworking and re-interpretation by critical researchers.

I will conclude this assessment of the 1995 classification with reference to two other issues. The moving image category did acknowledge in a practical way that film studies has been to some extent a separate tradition in media research. As a discipline it has been informed by the tools and concepts of literary and film analysis, and this background has also contributed fresh and original insights for the analysis of all texts. The moving image tradition has had to come to terms with the specific vocabulary of film, the rich variety of visual and non-linguistic means by which meaning is created and which, until recently at least, have been unique to the media of film and television. None the less, it can be argued that all media represent unique combinations of semiotic systems, some of which owe their genesis to the range of possibilities for sign creation that a particular technology allows. Therefore moving image media are no different in principle to print, say, or to hypertext computer communication. Furthermore, many of the applications of film analysis, relating to such issues as auteur theory, narrative and genre construction, are equally applicable to other media. Rather than thinking of moving image as one of the main categories of a classificatory system, it may be better in future to work with categories that refer in a general way to textual structure and construction.

The 1995 classification did not include a separate category for international communication. This was in part because the book in which it was discussed was one of a series, and a second volume dealt with media in global context. Study of international communication, it might be argued, is not in itself different from the study of media in general. The questions that are asked about media in international or global contexts are much the same as those that are asked of media in national contexts. In both, the main questions have to do with issues of production, content and reception, drawing on a similar range of theories for elucidation.

In practice, the study of international communication has constituted a distinctive thread of investigation in media research for the past 50 years. By the 1990s the term 'international' had become problematic because it implied that political relations between nation-states were the most appropriate focus for a study of media in their full global context. Such a focus would seem to underestimate the importance, for example, of diasporic media (e.g. the Indian cinema's appeal for Indians living throughout the world), or of media that serve ethnic or religious communities. In its place, therefore, the concept of media in a global context is now often preferred. The principal approaches to media in a global context have to do with the following factors.

- Media regulation (e.g. the allocation of radio or broadband spectrum) of transnational or multinational media activity.
- Relations of dominance-dependency that arise from the unequal exercise of power between local, national and transnational media (captured most succinctly by the term 'media imperialism').
- Media in relation to national or economic development. While development may be thought of as an intra-national issue, developmental studies tend to have broader regional or global dimensions. This is in part because development scholars have often investigated groups of countries, as indicated in the phrase 'developing economies', and in part because development scholars have typically been based in western institutions while studying the developing world.

CHAPTER 6

Theory Circles and Spirals

Theoretical models of society, media power and communications process, with indications of prevailing focus, tone and method, 1930s–1990s

Society	Power	Communications	Tone	Characteristic method
		Mass Society, 1930s–1950s		
		(focus on society)		
mass	high	one-way	negative	deductive reasoning
		Pluralism, 1940s–1960s		
		(focus on individual)		
plural	moderate	intervened	positive	empirical
		Cultural Studies 1 (cultural hegemony), 1960s–1970s		
		(focus on society)		
class relations	high	ideological	negative	literary criticism
		Political Economy 1 (neo-Marxist), 1960s–1970s		
		(focus on society)		
class relations	high	ideological	negative	institutional analysis
		Political Economy 2 (public sphere), 1980s–1990s		
		(focus on individual, institution and sector)		
State/capital/ public	moderate	negotiable	positive	policy studies
		Cultural Studies 2 (new audience research), 1980s–1990s		
		(focus on individual, group and culture)		
plural	low	interpretative	positive	ethnographic

PHASE I: 'MASS SOCIETY, MASS MEDIA'

McQuail (2000), Curran *et al.* (1982), and Boyd-Barrett and Newbold (1995) detect certain cycles in the development of media theory. There has been a tendency for one prevailing approach or theory to be supplanted by another, and then for the new dominant theory to be replaced by something that is similar, in certain ways, to a theory that had appeared earlier in the cycle. It has been rare for a theory or approach to completely disappear – rather, the repository of theoretical directions grows richer, or at least more populated, even though at any time one particular theory or approach may be more fashionable than others. In the decades that led up to the Second World War – a period during which scholars and intellectuals began to give more attention to the new 'mass' media (in particular, the press, cinema, and radio broadcasting) – we can say that the prevailing mood was one of patrician angst over the allegedly pernicious effects of the mass media on society. Society itself was conceptualized largely as a nation-state in the process of 'massification'. This came about, it was argued, as the product of the combined forces of industrialization and urbanization, and among the key features of such a society were widespread alienation, a sense of loss of community, and the disappearance of mediating institutions such as trades unions, churches and voluntary associations, which had held society together in pre-industrial times (Kornhauser, 1968). The media's role in this 'mass' society was to offer diversion for the masses, to distract them from political action, to provide a surrogate sense of community, and to manipulate mass consciousness in the interests of the ruling classes.

There were at least three significant versions of this way of thinking about the media. One was a moral or religious anxiety that exposure to the popular media encouraged licentiousness and other immoral behaviour. A different concern, from the intellectual right (best represented by F.R. Leavis (1952; also see Leavis and Thompson, 1948), was that the mass media threatened to undermine the civilizing influence of great literature and high culture that was thought to have played a significant role in helping people make sense of and adjust to social change. A concern among the intellectual left (e.g. Adorno and Horkheimer, 1979) was that the mass media represented the interests of the powerful, and debased the critical and sensory faculties of those who consumed them. Both the intellectual left and right agreed that popular culture was the product of the industrialization of culture. All versions attributed considerable power to the media, and this presumption was reinforced by perceptions of the use of media by governments to influence other countries, notably in wartime but also in the service of imperialism and trade relations. In brief, this first major phase of media research was characterized by a mass society model of society, by a focus on the impact of media on the moral robustness of the community as a whole. It viewed the media as very powerful, and its model of the relationship between media and readers or consumers was a transmissional one, sometimes described as the 'hypodermic needle' model of media effect. Its tone was overwhelmingly negative in its appraisal of the role of at least the popular media. Prevailing methodology was deductive reasoning on the basis of evaluative premises of the nature of human beings and of their potential.

PHASE 2: PLURALISM AND REINFORCEMENT

From some time preceding the Second World War, and in particular during and after it, there developed a more empirical approach to questions of media and their effects. This approach was largely spearheaded by psychologists and social psychologists working for the US armed services to investigate the potential of wartime propaganda to bring about alterations in knowledge, attitude and behaviour of readers, listeners or viewers. This approach was also fostered by politicians and advertisers intrigued by the possibility of predicting the relative impacts of different kinds of media message. Among the leading names of this period those of Katz and Lazarsfeld (1955), among others, stand out. During this period there emerged a number of important findings that have never been effectively challenged. These were that media power is dependent on many 'intervening' factors, not least of these having to do with the educational and other characteristics of audience members, their inter-personal networks and their perceptions of the authority of different media. Reviewing this tradition, Klapper (1960) concluded that the most important outcome of exposure to media was one of reinforcement, not change of existing attitudes and opinions. Reinforcement occurs because audiences are not masses, but are made up of individuals who are located in cultural, social class, community, family and occupational groups. Their choice of media, their perception of what they choose to look at, listen or read, and the things they remember, are significantly filtered by the values and norms of the cultures and groups to which they belong. Even when they are subject to media influence, the influence is likely to be indirect, working in a 'two-step' flow sequence of interpersonal channels. Reinforcement was the combined result of: selective exposure (people choose what they want to read, and they read what they are already comfortable with); selective attention (they attend to that which best fits with their perceptions and expectations); and selective retention (they best remember facts and opinions that fit with their existing views of the world).

This second major phase of media research was characterized by a more 'pluralistic' view of society (i.e. a society in which there are many different centres of power, and in which there are checks and balances, or countervailing forces, that maintain a certain degree of equity between the different centres). The model was supported by the emergence of richer sociological evidence of the diversity of cultures and communities (strongly associated with differences in social class) and the survival even in cities of established, traditional working-class communities. In the work of Hoggart (1957) and Williams (1958; 1961), for example, we find evidence that people have sustained distinctive cultures in the face of industrialization and urbanization, and that they can appropriate mass culture products within the framework of their own cultures. In many ways this model of media analysis is reassuringly empirical, sophisticated, subtle. Yet at the same time it is less critical. In sociology this was the period of the rediscovery of one of the founding fathers of sociology, Max Weber (1965), who had argued that economics was secondary to culture and belief as an explanation for social structure. The leading contemporary sociologist was Talcott Parsons (1949), for whom society was an integrated and self-sustaining system. In the approach to media, the prevailing focus was on the impact of media on individuals, in particular on individual knowledge, belief and behaviour, particularly to do with matters related to politics and consumption. The power of media was seen as limited and conditional, a power that was 'mediated' by an ever-extending range of factors. Greater subtlety of appreciation of media operation in the developed countries of the world, however, had not yet translated to the developing world, where the media were celebrated as the harbingers, through the one-way transmission of new knowledge and attitudes, of modernization and democratization. In general, the relationship of media to their consumers was now seen as more 'negotiable' than before and mediated by many factors. The overall tone or attitude towards media and the relationship between media and society was a good deal more positive than in the first phase.

PHASES 3 AND 4: CULTURAL STUDIES AND POLITICAL ECONOMY

The third and fourth major phases run roughly in parallel. These are the political economy and cultural studies phases or traditions, and they emerge into mainstream intellectual thought from the 1960s. They are both linked to the rediscovery of a more humanistic inter-pretation of Marx (1992) that followed translation of the early Marx in the Grundrisse. It may be said that both phases went through 'Marxist' and 'post-Marxist' periods.

The Influence of Neo-Marxism

Even though cultural studies rejected the reductionism that is inherent in the classical Marxist notion of a cultural superstructure that is determined by an economic base, its title to the Marxist tradition rested on its focus on culture as an expression of the unequal rela-tions between social classes. Its early contribution to the field of media study was its explo-ration of ideology in the maintenance of class relations. The emergence of neo-Marxism during this period may be linked to a variety of factors. Among these was the coming to power in the newly independent ex-colonial countries of leaders who were well versed in Marxist thought. This was also the coming of age for the post-war baby-boomers. In response to their needs, the developed world saw a huge expansion of university systems to incorporate the growing demand from middle- and working-class students. These new-comers to what had previously been enclaves for the offspring of aristocratic elites, were less born to rule than co-opted as functionaries to help make the existing social order work on behalf of the rulers. Alongside all this was the radicalizing influence of the Vietnam War, particularly in the United States where young men were drafted in an elusive cause of con-taining the alleged 'domino effect' of communist expansion. Alternative ways of imagining social order fired new left-wing aspirations and were to be observed in various embryonic, still to be evaluated, socialist experiments in countries such as Chile, China, Cuba, North Vietnam and the then Yugoslavia. Older certainties about patriotism, just war, the desirability of capitalism, the work ethic and economic growth, came under critical attack. In sociology, the structural **functionalism** of Talcott Parsons (1949) and the role analysis of Robert Merton (1958), whose overriding missions had been to explain social stability, gave way to the critical dissection of the power elite by C. Wright Mills (1956), and the radical economics of Paul Baran and Paul Sweezy (1968). These described an economy that was comprised not of multiple entrepreneurs competing in a free and open market, but of monopoly capi-talists who were able to determine both the prices they paid to suppliers and those they charged to customers, and for whom aggression on international markets was the inevitable outcome of domestic market saturation. This line was aptly developed in relation to the media by Herbet Schiller (1969), one of the first scholars to examine in detail the inter-linkages between leading media institutions, the defence industries and the political elite.

The central question was no longer 'How do social systems function to maintain equilibrium?, it was the problematic of 'How do societies in which resources and rewards are so unevenly distributed continue to survive at all without revolution?' The answers were to be found less in the exercise of overt power than in Weberian analysis of the different forms of authority. Part of this analysis requires consideration of the role of the production of ideas, information and cultural representations, and how these reflect the interests of the ruling class (as in Marx) or of the prevailing coalition of dominant interests (as in Gramsci, 1971). The authority of ruling classes in modern society is defined in terms of how successfully they secure the willing consent of the ruled to the conditions of their own oppression (Marcuse, 1964).

The work of a school of British scholars, principally Raymond Williams (1960), Richard Hoggart (1957) and Stuart Hall (1980), demonstrated how mass or popular culture was not something to be 'blamed' on the illiterate or uneducated tastes of working people; it was rather the product of the application to cultural expression of industrial practices. These were concerned with maximizing economy of scale, and hence profit, by reaching the largest number of people with identical product. At the same time, these scholars celebrated the continuing, if diminished, vitality of working-class culture. They could even find reflections of that culture in certain mass media products, and they began to explore in a more positive way some of the nuances and traditions of popular culture itself. They showed how popular culture could sometimes function to subvert the authority of 'high culture' and act as a form of opposition to the values and ideas of the ruling classes.

A Western Focus

Both the political economy and cultural studies traditions in media research therefore started out predominantly as critiques of existing media systems within the western world, and of capitalist societies generally. Their critical purview strangely failed to incorporate the authoritarian press systems of the communist or the developing worlds. While these were not generally defended, they were largely ignored. This omission can be explained by a variety of factors, mostly to do with the dynamics of left-wing thought in the 1960s and 1970s. In the first place, not very much was known in detail about non-western systems. Such systems did not generate their own media research and access to them was difficult for journalists and scholars alike. The real diversity of the Soviet Union and of China was redis-covered by the West only after the fall of the Berlin Wall in 1990. In the 1960s and 1970s there was little opposition to the prevailing western view of communist media systems as deplorably subservient to their respective governments or dominant political parties. Out-side of the traditional communist parties of the West, there was little sympathy with Russian and Chinese communism, although for a brief period of time the thinking of Mao was thought to offer some promise. These communist states were often regarded as 'state capital' systems that had been betrayed internally by nationalist ambitions and the greed of party elites. The real promise was seen to lie elsewhere, as in Cuba, and in the revolutionary move-ments of South America and Asia.

As for the developing world, media scholars shared the general left-wing and liberal ambivalence about the early post-colonial history of countries that were struggling, with little resource, to establish national systems and national identities. Authoritarian press systems could be explained away sympathetically as a necessary evil in the transition to modern, integrated nation-states, or as another unfortunate legacy of imperialism. The real left-wing venom was directed at targets closer to home: at press systems that, according to the rhetoric of orthodox canons of journalism, were meant to function as fourth estates, representing the public interest *vis-à-vis* state bureaucracy, or as independent critical watchdogs of the holders of power. In reality, their news agendas appeared just as much swayed by dependence on advertisers for revenue. Advertisers dictated the media's mode of address to consumers, as did the business and political interests of media moguls or corporate owners, and webs of complicity between major news sources and news reporters. Many media businesses operated internationally. International and notably Anglo-American exports of media product, in particular Hollywood film and advertising, along with western innovations in communications technology, notably satellites and computers, helped to extend western media-society models around the world. The left-wing critique of western media systems was at the same time an international critique.

The Political Economy Model Summarized

Political economy focused on the relations between media and other economic and political interests. It examined regulatory systems that governed such factors as ownership, cross-media ownership, competition and monopoly, public service broadcasting, controls over quantity and content of advertising. It looked at the internal workings of media systems, at different groups of media professionals, and at relations between news workers and news sources. Its principal overriding interest was in the consequences of these various dimensions of media operation for the general public good and for the health of democracy. Whereas the previous **pluralist** phase of media theory concluded that the influence of media was strictly limited, that its most important effect was a kind of non-effect – namely reinforcement – both political economy and cultural studies started from the premise that reinforcement was not neutral. Reinforcement was the inevitable and contrived outcome of a system whose very purpose was to maintain order and to prevent change in societies that were riven by manifest inequalities, and whose media were increasingly driven by the need to 'deliver' audiences to advertisers (Smythe, 1977). Media content, according to this argument, functioned to provide an environment of information and entertainment that was positively conducive to the sale of goods and services. Promotion of goods and services, in addition, was predicated on the assumption of individual and family aspirations, largely illusory, for identities that would set them higher in the social hierarchy. In its vision of alternative modes of social arrangement, political economy did not reach far beyond the politics of social class. It looked for ways of creating voices for the working classes in mainstream media and of lowering barriers to market entry so as to make it more likely that new media, representing a wider diversity of the population, could be established.

The first, or neo-Marxist, episode of political economy, therefore, may be summarized as an approach whose model of society was defined by social class relations, in which order was achieved through the 'manufacture of consent' by means of institutions such as education, religion and the media. Its focus on media was on the totality of relations between media and other social and political institutions in society as a whole. It regarded the media as very powerful contributors to social integration. Its view of the relationship between media and individual readers or consumers reverted to a transmissional model – some political economists adopted Marxist ideas of 'false consciousness' to describe how the media persuaded people to adopt values and positions that were at variance with their 'real interests'. Its overall tone was pessimistic. Befitting an approach whose focus was on institutions and institutional relations, the range of methodologies in political economy was much broader than the psychologistic and positivist-empirical models that had dominated the effects studies of the 'pluralist' phase. They incorporated social history, company research, participant observer, interview and survey.

Political economy has remained vigorous in media study to the present day. For a period during the 1980s it was displaced in visibility by a second or post-Marxist episode of cultural studies (as we shall see below). A re-invigorated and transformed political economy (in its second episode) has been inspired by major shifts in the international communications industries, to which reference has been made at the beginning of this chapter, having to do with such phenomena as digitization, deregulation, convergence, concentration and competition, commercialization, proliferation of media product, and globalization. One particularly notable outcome of these trends for media research in general is the increasing pressure on scholars to widen the scope of their field to take into account telecommunications and computing as well as the traditional content-led media industries such as publishing, broadcasting and cinema. In this second phase, it is much less common to encounter works that are rooted in classical Marxist vocabulary, as in the works of Garnham (1979), for instance, during the 1970s. In particular, the singularity of focus on class relations has disappeared. This can be ascribed to a variety of influences. Principal among these has been the contribution of feminism to an appreciation of the importance of gender relations. There has also been growing interest in and concern about ethnic relations, and the place of minority ethnic groups in society. Some, but not all, scholars argue that gender and ethnic divisions are in part nurtured under capitalism in order to weaken the proponents of class struggle, or as a safety valve for times of insufficient labour. Others, however, see in gender and ethnic relations independent sources of social division, rooted in value systems that predate capitalism, such as patriarchy and racism. A growing volume of literature has championed the causes of other minority groups. All these concerns help to focus attention on issues of representation in the media, and how issues of media organization and economics help to account for characteristics of representation of women, ethnic groups and minorities; but we can also say that a second episode of political economy has opened up to more practical strategies of change.

From Political Economy to Public Sphere (Phase 5)

Continuing attention to media in international and global contexts looks not just at the role of media in the formation of relations between countries, but at their role in the integration of nearly all countries and peoples of the world into a global economy. This is seen as driven by huge concentrations of capital, associated with large multi-national corporations, most of them still associated with the United States and OECD countries. Another factor that helps to explain the shift from the first to the second phase of political economy has to do with transformations of global politics. The demise of communism in the Soviet Union, and in central and eastern Europe, the emergence of the Russian Federation, and the transformation of Chinese communism from a class-based and centralist philosophy to something more pragmatic, nationalistic and market-driven, have required a less Manichean understanding of the world, one that is sensitive to every form of diversity. Such trends have affected parts of the developing world that also once subscribed to authoritarian systems, some with socialist or communistic philosophies, many of them now discredited. These changes have facilitated greater democratization. Around the world, political transitions after the cold war from communism to post-communism, from apartheid to post-apartheid, from dictatorship to democracy, have necessitated vigorous, practical debates about the role of media.

To these debates the Habermas (1989) concept of 'public sphere' has had much to offer. The concept does not carry the baggage of Marxist vocabulary. It has therefore been an aid to politicians, media managers and scholars in debate across a broad political spectrum. It extended a lifeline to scholars who had found themselves imprisoned in theories and vocabularies whose perceived legitimacy had been undermined. It offered a legitimate way to address fundamental concerns about the relationship between commercial, political and public interests and the communications media. There are limitations to Habermas's original historical model for the generation of a media-supported public sphere, but his concept highlighted the value and importance of forums of debate that are independent of church, state and capital. For Habermas, citizens should have equal access to media. The quality of argument in the public sphere should be judged solely in terms of rationality or (since we can no longer assume 'rationality' by itself is a neutral foundation for social judgement, for it privileges an epistemology that is closely associated with science elites and with patriarchy) in terms of their relevance to notions of public interest. In as much as political economy is characterized by a sense of moral commitment, as Mosco argues (1995), the concept of public sphere has provided a broadly acceptable framework for the expression of moral concern in the sphere of media studies. Technological transformations have also had an impact. The proliferation of media content, however commercialized it may be in the mainstream, is undermining the intensity of concern about older bottlenecks in the flow of ideas imposed by notions of scarcity.

Content and Reception: Achilles Heels of Political Economy

Focusing on media institutions, political economy's weakest links have been in the areas of content and audience reception. Analysis of media institutions, their links with other social, political and cultural institutions, goes a long way to identifying their interests as business institutions and/or as strategic components within larger corporate portfolios. Such analysis suggests, more often than it actually proves, a direct link between the business and other corporate interests of the media, media content and the influence of such content. The political economy tradition has not had a good purchase on content analysis, other than fairly crude categorizations. These were based on older quantitative methodologies that were barely able to encompass such subtleties as narrative structure, generic convention, and characterization, and which proceeded on the assumption that quantitative repetition was equivalent to semiotic and/or affective significance. It is quickly evident to even a casual observer that there is a great deal of variety even within mainstream media product, to an extent that does not conform with what institutional analysis would lead one to expect. Explanations for such discrepancy are various, and there is empirical evidence to support most of them. These include the exercise of independent influence of media workers, protected by a culture of professionalism. A need is sometimes imputed for media to secure audience credence by dealing with a broader universe of representations than would be permitted by a narrow definition of self-interest, or by allowing the appearance of some controversy and discordance. It may be argued that real-world divisions of interest and viewpoint between the main centres of power create spaces for content that is ideologically challenging. It is also possible that the suffusion of signs and messages contributes to a form of consumer apathy that is less and less propelled to action upon learning of injustices, scandals and outrages. Apart from explanations for the variety of media content, research also has to take account of the actual meanings that receivers make of the media products they consume. This is a further challenge for political economy, which is not commonly associated with methodologies that are appropriate or effective for audience investigation.

Cultural Studies and Social Anthropology (Phase 6)

It is with respect to these two areas of weakness that cultural studies best complements political economy. Cultural studies is a blend of two different traditions. On the one hand there is a tradition of literary and cinematic analysis. This brings to the study of content a variety of intellectual and conceptual tools, semiotics included, that in general does better justice to the subtlety of actual texts and their construction than the crude categorizations of content that were for a long time common in positivistic social science. For this tradition within cultural studies the central question is 'How are texts constructed so that they have the power to mean?' The challenge of this question also draws upon the fields of linguistics and socio-linguistics, disciplines that were not well established in media studies even in the 1990s. Language studies had primarily focused on interpersonal communication; only relatively recently did this discipline come to terms with the extent to which human communication is technologically mediated. Language studies have only recently given sustained attention to the incorporation of non-linguistic features in media texts, to move beyond the more obvious audio-visual grammars of moving film, to the communicative potential of media forms such as typeface, pitch and intonation, and the visual rhythms established in the play between texts and illustration (see Kress, 1995; Kress and Leeuwen, 1996). Contemporary socio-linguistics, with its focus on the dynamics of interaction between context, purpose, relationship and content in any speech event, has a great deal to contribute to establishing the holistic semiotic significance of media texts (see van Dijk, 1985; 1998).

On the other hand, there is also within cultural studies a socio-anthropological or ethno-graphic influence. This is to be expected in a tradition that has as its primary purpose the exploration of human culture, a tradition that relates uneasily with cruder a priori cate-gorizations of society offered by positivistic sociology. This is a tradition that looks in depth at human relationships in their full social contexts, and that searches for its own categories emerging from the 'thick' data of sustained participant observation. Applied to media, this tradition has provided a far more subtle appreciation of the ways in which media tech-nologies are used in everyday life and the multiple ways in which audiences as cultural members take meaning from texts.

The Cultural Studies Model Summarized

In an early, neo-Marxist, episode cultural studies focused principally on issues of represen-tation in texts in order to demonstrate the links between textual construction and cultural **hegemony**. It did this through the application of methods of literary analysis, with particu-lar reference to genre, narrative and characterization, and their relationships to mythologies and folklore, as well as to psychoanalytic categories. In this period it might be said that cultural studies adopted a view of society in which the meanings embedded in textual con-struction reflected the struggle between the social classes but were essentially supportive of the dominant culture. Although its focus was on the text, therefore, its purpose was the illumination of the relationship between text and society and the understanding of society through the text. In this approach the media are seen as powerful, operating through ideol-ogy, working to construct perceptions of the world that do not challenge its basic social structures of inequality, and that lead readers either to believe that the way things are is the way that they must inevitably be, or to perceive the world in a way that does not reflect the way in which things actually are. Surprisingly, this model of relationship between text and reader was still essentially transmissional, there was little room here for deviant 'readings'. The methodologies were primarily tools of textual analysis. The overall tone of the analysis was pessimistic.

In a later, post-Marxist, episode cultural studies has devoted more attention to contribu-tions from the social anthropological tradition. Sometimes referred to as the 'new audience research', this approach demonstrates and celebrates the diversity of ways in which media technologies are put to use in different family, social and cultural contexts, and also the diversity of meanings that people draw from the media they consume. The process of meaning-making has been shown as surprisingly subtle, with people quite capable of con-forming with prevalent social disapproval or deprecation of certain categories of text, on the one hand, while continuing to take pleasure from those same texts on the other. Curran (1980) has argued that this exploration of the negotiation of meaning in the encounter between textual products and actual readers was simply a re-articulation of Klapper's (1960) **reinforcement effect**, the combined result of processes of selective exposure, attention and retention. However, there is an important difference. In this second episode of cultural studies, the approach to the understanding of meaning is social-anthropological, not psycho-logical. It is more concerned with the ambient contexts of culture, tradition, group and family, and with what Radway (1984) has called 'interpretative' communities, whose shared values influence how people use texts, how they take meaning from them, and through what rituals of interaction, perception and conversation. This approach demonstrates the different interpretative skills that are prized by different cultures. In its analysis of the social ways in which audiences often make meaning from texts (Moss, 1995) it finally shatters the problematic of the language of media 'effects'. People are unlikely to be influenced in a once-and-for-all way by a single media text. All human beings are engaged in multiple projects of meaning-making from the moment of birth; it is from within the vortex of these projects, which are interminable and whose every phase is lived in a more or less tentative and hypothetical mode, that media products are selected, perceived and interpreted. Those interpretations themselves are sustained in hypothetical mode and have the status merely of fleeting contributors to the larger lifetime context of meaning-making. Furthermore the interpretative process is not only, or even mainly, conducted on the cognitive, racio-centric plane, but also on the affective plane, linked with the pursuit of holistic mind-body sensation, emotion and pleasure.

The second episode of cultural studies encompasses, but is not reduced to, movements of post-structuralism or post-modernism. These concepts refer to new epistemologies that shy away from older structuralist traditions that were characteristic of analytical systems such as those of Marx or Freud and that reduce the epidermal complexity of phenomena to the rule-governed operation of a small number of irreducible explanatory concepts. Post-modernism recognizes no 'surface' that is of greater or lesser significance than imputed essence. It resists the impulse to dichotomization of phenomena (e.g. masculine/feminine, colonial/post-colonial, dominance/dependence), on the grounds that the characteristics of one extreme of a social dichotomy are as they are because of the way in which the *other* extreme is. In some senses, therefore, one pole or extreme incorporates, subsumes or transforms the 'other' that it supposedly is not. On the other hand, where structuralism posits unities, such as the 'self', or the 'text', the post-modern sees fragmentation. The 'self' fragments into different identities that are called into play by different contexts of culture, purpose and relationship. 'Texts' reveal themselves to be multiples of different voices, with echoes of the different audiences that those voices once addressed, each voice following different rules of lexical choice, grammatical structure and semantic inflection. Even a single speaker will reflect fragments of different discourses, traceable to a variety of debates, philosophies and experiences, some of them very ancient. No wonder, then, that in the post-modernist perspective texts should be polysemic, available for the making of many different meanings by different readers. Readers do not make sense of texts as isolated individuals. Rather, they do so socially, in relation to previous texts they have experienced, in relation to the language, concepts and semantics they have absorbed as members of families, groups and cultures from childhood, through previous relationships they have lived, and through conversation. At the same time, texts are cultural and historically situated; in particular they embody, in their production, format, address and availability to audiences, relations of power. Post-modernism holds out no hope of stability, fixity or certainty: it catches fleeting moments of phenomena that are in perpetual movement and transition.

Towards an Integrative Model

In the 1990s and into the new millennium it is becoming more common for studies to integrate political economy and cultural studies traditions. This is in part attributable to the internal dynamics and processes of synergy observable in any intellectual project, where the strengths of initially different traditions are bridged and fused. It may also in part be attributable to changes in the external world, again suggestive of the importance of examining the evolution of theory in relation to both the immediate context of intellectual discourse and also to its broader social, cultural and political context. Part of this context has to do with the insistence and magnitude of the turbulence of communications industries and their global spread. This has undermined any temptation to complacent acceptance of the polysemic openness of texts, if such exists, as exonerating media industries of accountability for their exploitation of global communications space (Boyd-Barrett, 1998; 1999). While cultural studies in its post-modern mode has introduced us to the subtleties and variegation of communications phenomena, processes of globalization simultaneously generate variety at the local level as they produce homogeneity in globalized spheres of social life, especially those related to production and employment, consumer goods and related behaviour. These processes then cry out for explanation and meaning. Competing theories variously press upon us competing causes for this dialectic of heterogeneity/homogeneity. These include global capitalism (an economistic explanation: e.g. capitalists need to produce a variety of goods to attract and fascinate consumers, but too much variety interferes with economies of scale), and westernization (a culturalist explanation: e.g. white Anglo-American traditions think their ideas are the best and militantly export them).

CHAPTER 7

The 'Big Three': Further Observations

In broad-brush terms, the current complexity of the field can be accommodated within three of the most significant movements of media study: effects studies, political economy and cultural studies. The trajectory of media effects studies and its transformations has culminated in the second phase of cultural studies, namely in a radically new way of conceptualizing the relationship of texts to readers. I shall look first at the movement from 'effects' to the study of texts and readers within the cultural studies tradition, while recognizing that a complete fusion or integration of the different approaches, agendas and disciplines has not been achieved. I shall also look further at political economy.

FROM EFFECTS TO CULTURE

Do media have the power to change people? Well, yes, of course. What could be simpler? I hear on the radio as I drive to work along the 10 Freeway that a collision further down towards Los Angeles on the intersection with the 625 has created a complete log-jam. This knowledge is new to me, so we already have a demonstration of media effecting a change in cognition. The bulletin goes on to identify two alternative routes. Since I want to get to downtown Los Angeles I weigh up the two alternatives, and make a decision in favour of one of them. This decision takes into account personal preference, consideration of time pressure, even driving style. None the less, we have a clear-cut case of the media effecting or at least contributing to a change in behaviour. Do the media help to change affect? Of course they do. The Hollywood motion picture industry is superbly skilled at eliciting intense emotional reactions to fictional narratives, and there can be scarcely anyone who reads this who cannot quickly recall a recent instance of being moved emotionally by the power of film.

So what is all the fuss about with 'media effects'; why has this label attracted such a negative image in a great deal of writing on media theory? The problem begins whenever there is a desire to attribute to the media causal responsibility for a specific good or bad effect, to say that a particular event, act or feeling is the result of a particular kind of media content. This is problematic whether responsibility is attributed historically, in explanation for some past incident or event, or predictively, in reference to things that it is thought will happen as a result of exposure to specific kinds of media content. Such discourses tend to elicit deeply felt passions or touch on controversial concerns such as the levels of criminal violence in society, the school performance of children, male and female role-modelling, the norms that govern sexual behaviour, racism, and so. As it turns out, it is very difficult to predict with certainty just what effect a particular message will have, in what way, and for whom.

If we look at the entirety of the effects tradition we see a movement away from a view of media audiences or readers as passive, towards a view of them as active users and interpreters of all kinds of media text. Simultaneously, there has been an increasing sophistication in what is understood by the term 'text', be it a novel, a campaign message, a television broadcast or film. This is not the kind of progression where later advances entirely cancel out everything that has gone before. From the earliest days of media research this intellectual journey has contributed to a rich pool of empirical research, conceptual resources and insight that is permanently available, that offers potential points of departure, building blocks and links in the development of new research, theories and explanations.

The first principle advance in the study of media effects was the discovery of intervening variables – that is, extraneous factors that influence in some way the relationship between text and audience, and that thus work to 'mediate' the impact of the effect of the media. There are a great many intervening variables; of the most important, some pertain to the technology itself (e.g. the complexity of semiotic systems available – film is a more complex semiotic system, in this respect, than traditional print). Others pertain to prevailing social perceptions of certain kinds of text (e.g. that some newspapers or media are more 'authoritative' than others). Others pertain to the viewer (including ascribed characteristics of sex, age and ethnic identity, and achieved characteristics such as education, marital status and income). Some refer to the social and cultural context within which the encounter between text and reader occurs (e.g. the formality of context – at work or at home; the presence or absence of other people, the motive – to solve a problem, perhaps, or for relaxation).

In as much as 'effects studies', especially from their early years, acquired a bad image among 'critical' media researchers, it was because they tended to ask the 'wrong' questions, used inappropriate methods, and therefore solicited wrong or irrelevant answers. The limitations of the tradition relate principally to the following sets of problems. This is particularly true of the early years of **effects research**, when the tradition was dominant by psychologistic approaches; as we shall see, this tradition has yielded more fruit as it has taken more account of sociological factors. In the points focused on below, I have drawn to some extent on the work of Gauntlett (1995) in identifying the major problems of the psychologistic approach to media effects.

- *Problems of range.* The early media effects studies were generally psychologistic. They focused on the effects of media on individuals at the expense of asking questions about the ways in which media impact on society as a whole, or on institutions, or on cultural practice. Thus an appreciation of 'effects' in this tradition could scarcely deal with the case of the arrival of print and its general social, political and economic consequences for fourteenth-century Europe. Nor could it handle the impact of mass broadcasting on the organization of the political process in democracies. Nor did it have a research vocabulary that could examine the impact of media on the social organization of time. Furthermore, if we ignore questions at the levels of society, institution and culture, then we are even less likely to achieve satisfactory answers to questions we ask about the impact of media on the individual level.
- *Problems of linearity.* The underlying model of media effects studies has been transmissional, the assumption that some kind of message or impact travels through some kind of delivery system from the producer to the receiver. Yet precisely the opposite may occur. Viewer characteristics, reflecting political, social, religious and cultural identities, may determine how and when media are used, and for what kinds of content, thus influencing what producers produce, and the kinds of effect they will anticipate in their structuring of texts.
- *Problems of cause–effect.* The transmissional model is a causal model. It gives insufficient space to intervening variables, as we have seen, or to third-party causes that may account for both the media message and its alleged 'effect'. If a television documentary about starvation in Ethiopia provokes a massive response to charitable campaigns, is this a media effect? Or should we not say that a certain western ethic, nurtured in part by the influences of organized religions and charities, widespread perceptions of the history of colonialism, and facilitated by western economic prosperity, accounts for both the documentary and for the audience reaction to it? A media-centred analysis that looked only at properties of the documentary as a likely 'cause' would have poor predictive value.
- *Problems of methodology.* The principal kinds of method employed in classical effects studies have included correlational studies of media content (e.g. television violence

measured against social indicators such as criminal violence), natural experiments, laboratory studies, experimental field studies, longitudinal surveys. All of these are associated with difficulties of one kind or another. Laboratory studies have caused the most controversy, perhaps best exemplified by Bandura's (1973) invention of the 'bobo doll', an inflatable plastic doll, about 1 metre tall. This has been well critiqued by Gormley (1998), as follows. The research team showed experimental groups of young children a film of another person (the model) beating such a doll with a baseball bat. The children were then 'frustrated' by having their favourite toys removed, and left in a room with a bobo doll and bat similar to the one they had seen represented in the film. This research, Gormley notes, failed to take account of the difference between beating a doll with a baseball bat, on the one hand, and actual violence on the other: its conceptual model could not distinguish between 'violence' and 'play'. Those who had been shown the model being slapped, the research demonstrated, were less 'aggressive' subsequently. Yet those exposed to such 'punishment' were the only experimental groups to have witnessed actual violence portrayed on screen. Cumberbatch (1995) has observed that this kind of research does not focus on what subjects think when they take part in laboratory experiments, nor does it engage in normal talk with children in a natural and humanistic way about their experiences of television.

- *Problems of definition.* Concepts such as 'violence', 'aggression', 'arousal' (sometimes confused with aggression) and 'frustration', are elusive and require careful operationalization (i.e. the finding of physical indicators that are precisely reflective of concepts that have been precisely defined). Is representation of an actor striking a doll with a bat as violent, or violent in the same way, as representation of an actor being slapped? It is not so much a given kind of behaviour in a text that should be our focus, perhaps, as the significance that the text, through narrative and style, invites us to attribute to that behaviour. Are incidents of violence in a television crime genre necessarily more important or as important, for example, as other features of the text, such as strong camaraderie and teamwork between policemen, or retribution for wrong-doing? Texts typically represent socially positive as well as socially negative attributes, and to isolate only one kind of feature out of the overall textual context invites misinterpretation as to semantic significance. It has been suggested that entertainment output in general (i.e. not just violence) may cause frustration. Cumberbatch (1995) quotes Gadow and Sprafkin (1989) who observed that while aggressive film content often produces elevated levels of anti-social behaviour, the control (non-aggressive) material produces sometimes even greater amounts of aggressive behaviour. Even television programmes that are specifically produced with the aim of encouraging pro-social behaviour in children may actually encourage aggressive behaviour. These findings should not be taken to be conclusive – they certainly are not – but they indicate that researchers working in this tradition have often failed to ask the right questions; they have failed to ask questions that take account of the nuances of content (see below), viewer experience and context, or whose vocabulary of 'effects' is subtle enough to capture the nuances of behaviour and their social significance.
- *Problems of content.* In the effects tradition, the approach to content has typically been crude. There is little attention to the relative contributions of music, speech, natural

sound, shading, camera movement, montage and so on to the way in which a text is experienced. Equally there is little attention to narrative structure and characterization.

- *Problems of research support.* This touches on the reasons why research gets carried out in the first place. In the field of effects, especially, research has been driven by groups with special agendas or interests. These include advertisers and political campaign managers, who want to demonstrate a predictive knowledge of 'what works'. Broadcasters and film-makers want to show politicians, advertisers and the public that what they do has no harmful impact on society or individuals. Certain consumer or citizen groups want to demonstrate that the media have strongly negative impacts on morality and behaviour.

- *Problems of focus.* The early field of media effects was captured by an absurdly limited research agenda, mainly to do with violence and advertising – especially in relation to young people – and political campaigns. A broader portfolio of issues over time has extended the list to sexual behaviour, representations of women and ethnicity, etc.; but, overall, the range is still narrow. The emphasis has also been on the cognitive and behavioural, and less on the affective dimension, including pleasure.

- *Problems with models of personal identity and 'effect'.* There is an understandable modernist tendency to accept the integrity of the 'self'. This reduces our capacity to understand how the significance of media experiences may be negotiated between different identities of a single self. More fundamental, however, is the common presumption of a 'one-off' media effect, within the broader context of lifelong projects of meaning-making, and this presumption is a travesty of the dynamics of how human beings engage, intellectually and affectively, with their world.

At worst, therefore, the media effects tradition narrowed the field of media research to issues of effects on individuals. It asked an absurdly limited range of questions that touched on a tiny fraction of the range of possible effects (focusing mainly on issues of violence and political or commercial persuasion). It employed dubious methods, used concepts that were ill-defined, and demonstrated an equally ill-defined grasp of the key dynamics of the nature of the 'stimulus' (media content) that was thought to induce the supposedly observed effects.

Though it has deservedly suffered a bad press in the critical tradition of media theory, effects research has also on many occasions seemed to ask the right questions, or at least it has asked questions that by common consent have seemed to move the field forwards in important respects. This is particularly true where effects studies have incorporated sociological methods. To the media effects tradition, therefore, we should acknowledge the important contribution of the concept of 'intervening variable'. This, as we have seen, posits that any influence of media content on a given individual, group or institution is likely to be mediated by factors relating to consumer or reader characteristics and the whole context in which texts are consumed. The concept of 'two-step flow' (Katz and Lazarsfeld, 1955) has also been fruitful even if the research on which the concept was first posited was problematic (Gitlin, 1978). This posits the likelihood that media and non-media communications are sometimes interrelated. One of the intervening variables of media influence of which account needs be taken has to do with the personal information networks in which individuals are situated. Media influences may be conveyed indirectly through such networks, and networks also form part of the whole context in which media content is read or consumed. A related and fruitful line of enquiry (Rogers, 1955) explored the different rates of adoption of different innovations ('diffusion research'), and attributed these in part to the intervention of interpersonal networks. In the 'spiral of silence' theory, Noelle-Neuman (1974) argued that a propaganda message achieved greater power the more that its message was presented as something with which the majority of people were in agreement, thus raising the social cost to individuals who wished to express alternative views.

The concept of 'agenda setting' (McCombs, 1974) pointed to a new level of effect, relating less to *what* people think than to what they think *about*. It engaged researchers in a productive evaluation of the relative importance of the media themselves as origins of media messages, as against significant and powerful sources of information on which the media depend. Who sets the agenda, and what is the agenda they set? Readers or consumers may resist the invitation to share a particular opinion or position on a subject, but if the agenda of information the media provide simply does not include certain issues or topics of which readers may have no direct experience, what does that say about the leverage the media hand to the powerful to determine currents of thoughts in society? 'Cultivation analysis' (Gerbner, 1973) focused on relationships between prevailing forms of representation of the world on television, and the beliefs and behaviours of people who are heavy consumers of television product. On the subject of media violence, cultivation theorists threw a cat among the pigeons when they suggested that the most likely consequence of media violence was not one of aggressive behaviour but one of fear. This line of research argued that media violence was a form of social control that favoured the interests of 'legalized violence', namely the forces of law and order. The 'uses and gratifications' school (McQuail, 1984) reversed the classic question of media effect from 'what effect do the media have on people' to 'how do people use the media' and thus helped to turn around or modify previous assumptions of linearity and cause–effect in thinking about media and audiences.

Uses and gratifications was one of several steps in media research towards defining the audience as having an active rather than a passive relationship with media (although the dichotomy between 'activity' and 'passivity' does not stand up to too much scrutiny). Empirical research did establish that viewers were conscious agents in choosing when and what to watch, in the case of television, and that typically they were far from 'glued' to the set. Extending the notion of 'active reader', Hall introduced the concept of 'critical reader', identifying the major different ways in which viewers could react to political or social documentary, from acceptance of a programme's basic premise to outright rejection or indifference. Hall's (1980) contribution to cultural studies as a whole has been to set it against the crude economic reductionism of some of the early political economy work. He developed a theory of ideology which allows that texts are 'polysemic', which is to say that they offer the possibility of a diversity of readings, even if a 'preferred reading' is inscribed within the text by its producers. Through the work of Morley (1980; 1986), in particular, this crucial insight has been further explored to reveal the divergent meanings that different groups, whether defined in terms of social class, gender or ethnicity, could draw from texts.

At this juncture the study of media effects moved from the notion of critical individual reader to that of the 'ethnographic reader', which is to say the reader as representative of a social and cultural context who responds to media content through frames and categories of thought, language and social practice. This movement took audience research from the level of cognition, political opinions and ideas, to a far more inclusive level, commensurate not just with sentiments of feeling as well as thought, but of everyday behaviour. Moss (1995) turned her attention less to the *what* of the interpretation of media text, than to the *how*, the processes whereby people take meaning from texts. She proposed that people construct their meanings of media experiences in part through conversation with others.

Thus we see that the tradition of media effects has undergone a number of transformations, above all in the past two decades. These transformations may be summarized as movements away from 'transmissional' models of effect towards the study of media within contexts of the making of meaning, of culture, of texts and of literacy, in the interaction between media texts and media readers. Those who have asked how people make meaning from texts have had to look both at the ways in which texts are structured, and at the readers themselves, their backgrounds and previous media experiences. Previous media experiences lead to 'inter-textual' readings – that is to say, readings that draw on previous exposure and memories of other texts and values.

The process of meaning-making therefore has increasingly been seen to be a cultural property, as Shirley Brice Heath (1983) observed in her study of print in the lives of children in three communities of South Carolina. Middle-class children, for example, were enveloped in a very special kind of experience through the ritual of the bedtime story, an experience that brought together parent and child in the context of reading a book, looking at its pictures, and talking about the story and about its pictures in a very special kind of way. The nature of the talk lost some of its conversational properties and turned into something that was itself more 'bookish' in its grammar and mode of address, anticipating no less the kinds of talk about books that these children would encounter in the school system. At the same time, however, the talk was more exploratory and inviting of imaginary worlds than was the case with the use of books in a working-class white community, where books were principally regarded as functional repositories of information. In the working-class black community, no special attention was given to children to help them decode literary texts; this was a community with a strong oral tradition that prized the skills of oral story-telling, and in which even private letters were read out, discussed and exclaimed upon. Through studies like this, therefore, we come to an understanding of 'media effects' also in relation not just to culture, but to the skills of literacy, as defined very broadly to refer to 'the making of meaning from texts'. Heath (1983), Radway (1984), Morley (1980) and others have all helped us understand the important interplay between roles, relationships, kinds of media content and literacy practices. Literacy practices include not only preferred ways of decoding texts, but ways of displaying and utilizing the texts. Where the television is, what it looks like, who turns it on and off, when it is turned on and off, all these things convey meanings about such things as identity, wealth, textual experience and preference, relationship and power.

The effects trajectory
- Hypodermic needle
- Intervening variable
- Two-step flow
- Diffusion of innovations
- Spiral of silence
- Agenda setting
- Cultivation analysis
- Uses and gratifications
- Active reader
- Critical reader
- Ethnographic reader

CULTURAL STUDIES

Following the trajectory of media effects therefore, as it has moved from psychological through to sociological and social anthropological premises, we find we have moved well into cultural studies and the position within it of 'new audience research'. But cultural studies is much more than the study of meaning in relation to practices of consumption, reception and text. It is about meaning in and through the text itself. Throughout the time of the effects tradition, there developed a growing sophistication in our understanding of textual construction. In summarizing approaches to the question 'How are texts structured to make meaning possible?', Cook (1992) begins with the work of F.R. Leavis (1952), for whom there was 'great art' and the rest. Great art was either mimetic/realist (imitating life and experience), or pragmatic/legislative (art as moral exemplar), or expressive/creative (the work of special creators). The rest was merely mass-produced and of 'only sociological interest'. The Leavisite endorsement of the separation of high and low art in effect endorsed an art created largely by the wealthy for the wealthy. This separation of great art and the rest has been undermined by the growth of interest in popular culture – spearheaded by Hoggart (1957) and Williams (1960), among others – and the growing acceptance that both elitist and popular cultural forms are available for sociological and aesthetic analysis.

In film analysis, an important debate developed in the 1970s. On the one hand there were those for whom the presence of a 'special creator' (usually the director) was the key to great work – auteur theory – and who considered that judgements about art were judgements about life. On the other hand, there were others who were uncomfortable with the critic's assertion of personal value judgements in assessments of film quality, and who looked for more systematic and transparent methodologies to determine the structures and mechanisms in any work that enable meanings. Arising from this second point of view there developed an interest in 'genre' studies that focused on the conventions of iconography, narrative and theme, and that clustered films into recognizably similar groups such as western or gangster movies. Interest grew in industry studies, which provided insight into how the conditions of production (financing, technology, distribution) influenced content.

Cook (1992) discusses debates around key concepts that in the interpretative tradition help to account for how texts are enabled to represent the world meaningfully to audiences. His narrative shows that in this tradition, too, there has been a discernible movement from a focus on the text itself to a focus on the reader and the act of reading. There is also a movement from a view of meaning as something immanent, or fixed within a text, to a view of meaning as residing in the psyche, in history or in culture. These debates he identified as follows.

- *Realism.* Realist narrative employs techniques that create an illusion of coherence and plausibility. Some critics, following Brecht, argued that illusion distracted audience attention from the artificiality of textual construction, and therefore called for anti-realist, self-reflexive texts, 'which would draw attention to their own constructedness and hence become resistant to easy identification with character, freeing the reader to reflect on the underlying causes of, for example, a character's situation' (Cook, 1992: 158). Others contended that such devices were not necessary, that what mattered were reading strategies, not textual constructions. Lovell (1980) distinguished between realist intentions (properties of the text) and realist effects (properties of the reading).
- *Semiotics, 'the science of signs'.* This aims to explain how it is that signs work to convey meaning. Signs work denotatively as representations of specific things and actions, but they also acquire more profound levels of meaning through the accumulation of usage within a culture and the associations they thus acquire (i.e. when they begin to function connotatively) (Eco, 1973). Meaning only occurs in the act of audience decoding of the signs, and is dependent on readers' abilities to recognize what is being constructed.
- *Rhetorical devices.* These refer to ways in which a text is structured to create the illusion of a plausible and coherent visual world – for example, editing cuts are 'always motivated by the ongoing cause/effect chain of narrative' (Bordwell and Thompson, 1976). Barthes (1972) proposed that meanings are produced through five 'codes of intelligibility', which the reader recognizes. For example, the cultural code invokes common sense or social knowledge to enhance the plausibility of the narrative.
- *The reader.* If texts are structured in certain ways to cue certain kinds of meaning, then the 'success' of a text depends partly on the 'competence' of individuals to read texts, and such competence is not evenly distributed in any society. Unevenness of competence yields the possibility of multiple meanings, the possibility that some people may choose to read against the grain of the text (i.e. against a preferred meaning that has been inscribed by the producers).
- *Readings.* Some alternative or oppositional readings are in part inscribed in the text by the text's own inability to reconcile its internal contradictions, sometimes the inconsistencies of a dominant ideology, which prompt audience resistance to positions (towards characters, for example) with which they would otherwise feel invited to identify. Hall (1980), as we have already seen, distinguished between dominant, opposition, negotiated readings. Mulvey (1975) argued with specific reference to gender that, both through

narrative and visual organization, film has rendered women as the passive and inferior objects of a 'male gaze', which it invites of male and female viewers alike. Cook (1992) distinguishes between three different kinds of reading: ideological (e.g. 'a feminist politics applied to an understanding of how films work produces re-readings', p. 163); cultural historical (these readings seek to connect the cultural artefact with the culture within which it was produced, and which is thought to be essential to a full interpretation of a text); and critical radical, which addresses the relationship between artefacts and national identity, in particular the heterogeneity of positions within national identity that takes account of divisions between classes, gender, regions, ethnicity and so on.

POLITICAL ECONOMY

In assessing the distinctive characteristics of the political economy tradition, Mosco (1995) has emphasized that it foregrounds:

- social change and historical transformation – current changes are seen within much longer-term frameworks
- the 'totality of social relations', in particular taking into account the interrelationships between politics, economics and ideology
- a commitment to moral philosophy – that is to say, to the values that help to create social behaviour and the moral principles that ought to guide it; various authors in this tradition have addressed values of self-interest, materialism and individual freedom, the acknow-ledgement of individual and social value in human labour, the extension of democracy to all aspects of social life
- social praxis – the unity of thinking and doing.

> **The principal characteristics of political economy**
> - Analysis of media in historical, social and political context
> - Addresses media relations to politics, economics and ideology
> - Has a moral purpose
> - Its end point is social action

The epistemology (or way of knowing) of political economy Mosco argues, is *realist*, in that it accepts as real both discourses and social practices. It is *inclusive*, in that it explains the present with respect to historical trends and broader social formations. It is *moral*, in that it is interested in moral issues. It is *constitutive*, in that it rejects economic explanations as sufficient for understanding. It is *critical*, both because it is interested in possibilities for improvement, but also because it recognizes and negotiates tensions between different intellectual positions.

In its approach to media, Mosco's political economy focuses on processes as much as on structures, as the following points demonstrate.

- *The processes of commodification* involves the transformation of measuring value in terms of use, to measuring value in terms of exchange on the market. Communication practices contribute to the commodification of all goods and services (e.g. by ceding greater control to producers over the entire process of production, distribution and exchange). Commodification, as a response to global declines in economic growth in the 1970s, also affected the media, leading to increased commercialization of programming, privatization of public media, and liberalization of communication markets. This has implications for the commodification of the consumer, whose time spent viewing or reading is sold by media institutions to advertisers.

- *The process of spatialization* refers to the process of overcoming the constraints of space and time in social life. Communications contribute to capitalism by reducing the time it takes to move goods, people and messages over space. They expand the resources of time and space that are available for those who can make use of them; and they contribute to the redrawing of the space of flows according to boundaries established by flows of people, goods, services and messages. Within the media industries themselves, the transformation of space is structured by global horizontal and vertical integration strategies, and by patterns of both globalization and localization in the origination and distribution of media products.

- *The process of structuralization* reminds us of the Marxist dialectic that people make history but not under conditions of their own making. This introduces into political economic analysis ideas of agency, social process and social practice. This includes the relationship between class and labour, gender and race, and the construction of hegemony, defined as 'what comes to be incorporated and contested as the taken-for-granted, common sense, natural way of thinking about the world' (Mosco, 1995: 160).

Both political economy and cultural studies are concerned with power in society, and regard power as something that is distributed very unevenly. In contrast with political economy, cultural studies, says Mosco, has been open to a more radical contestation of positivism, it has foregrounded the subjective and social creation of knowledge. It has demonstrated that culture is an activity in which all human beings are engaged, not just a privileged elite (hence Williams' notion of culture 'as a whole way of life'). In addition, it has gone further beyond issues of social class to embrace issues relating to gender, race and other social divisions. While it recognizes the importance of power, power is not the 'only game in town' for modern cultural studies, which has a broad agenda of issues and topics that contribute to its basic mission of elucidating the many dimensions of human expression in society. Political economy's strengths have been its firm hold on a realist epistemology, the value that it attributes to historical research, a mode of thinking in terms of concrete social totalities, a moral commitment and the goal of unification of thought with practice. Its moral commitment may be a problem, because it seems to lower resistance to at least some sources of ideology; proponents of political economy will argue that they offer transparency of value where classical scientific method obscures sources of ideological bias. In its favour, political economy has maintained a strong interest in the role of labour in media research. Cultural studies is particularly strong in the determination of what it is about texts that renders them capable of being meaningful, and of the strategies that real-life readers deploy to take meaning from texts. Political economy is strongest in its determination of the industrial production of culture and, therefore, the production and distribution of meaning.

Conclusion

Having got this far, the reader will not be surprised by the assertion that no introduction to media theory is a neutral or pure narrative. This section is no exception. It is intended to provide a reasonably comprehensive overview of the major different approaches and theories of the field. But within any given area on which this section touches there is a great deal more material and complexity that can only be appreciated via a more thorough search of the literature pertaining to particular theories, issues and topics. This section is inevitably selective. The reader need not feel that it should be digested completely in a single sitting or indeed in any particular period. It is something to turn back to from time to time, particularly upon completion of other sections in this volume that will help place some of the content of this section in a broader context. Above all, this section should be followed up by further reading, reading that is hopefully structured by a sense of the reader's own research priorities. Remember that all good theory, like life itself, is in a constant state of development.

SUMMARY

- In this section my purpose has been to identify the general purposes of theory in media research. I have considered the relationship and boundaries between theory and ideology, while noting that to some extent the very definition of the 'field' of media research is ideological.
- I have looked at some of the major different theories in media research, both over time and in the present period, and have considered how the fortunes of different theories are in part related to significant changes and developments in the very world that theories attempt to grasp and explain.
- Among the many different theoretical traditions, I identified three that I argued have been particularly productive and influential, namely the media effects, cultural studies and political economy traditions.
- I have noted that while these are in some senses cumulative movements, they do not necessarily abandon earlier iterations. These often live on in the literature contributing to a resource bank of thought, perspective and data.

Further Reading

Boyd-Barrett, O. and Newbold, C. (eds) (1995)
    Approaches to Media. London: Edward Arnold
Curran, J. and Gurevitch, M. (eds) (1996) Mass
    Media and Society. London: Edward Arnold
Dickinson, R., Harindranath, R. and Linne, O.
    (1998) Approaches to Audiences. London:
    Edward Arnold
McQuail, D. (2000) Mass Communication Theory
    (fourth edn). London: Sage

References

Adorno, T. and Horkheimer, M. (1979) The
    culture industry: enlightenment as mass
    deception. In The Dialectic of Enlightenment.
    New York, NY: Herder & Herder
Althusser, L. (1971) Ideology and ideological
    state apparatuses. In Lenin and Philosophy and
    Other Essays. London: New Left Books
Alvarado, M. and Boyd-Barrett, O. (1992) Media
    Education: An Introduction. London: British Film
    Institute
Bandura, A. (1973) Aggression: A Social Learning
    Analysis. Englewood Cliffs, NJ: Prentice Hall
Baran, P. and Sweezy, P. (1968) Monopoly
    Capital. Harmondsworth: Penguin
Barthes, R. (1972) Mythologies. London:
    Jonathan Cape
Bazalgette, C. (1992a) Key aspects of media
    education. In Alvarado, M. and Boyd-Barrett, O.
    (eds) Media Education: An Introduction.
    London: British Film Institute
Bazalgette, C. (ed.) (1992b) E555 Media
    Education: an Introduction – Workbook, Milton
    Keynes: Open University/British Film Institute
Bell, A. (1991) The Language of News. Oxford:
    Basil Blackwell
Bennett, T. (1982) Theories of the media,
    theories of society. In Gurevitch, M. et al.
    (eds), Culture, Society and the Media. London:
    Methuen, 30–55
Bordwell, D. and Thompson, K. (1976), Space
    and narrative in the films of Ozu. In Screen
    17(2), Summer
Bourdieu, P. (1986) Distinction: A Social Critique
    of the Judgement of Taste. London: Routledge
Boyd-Barrett, O. (1998) Media imperialism refor-
    mulated. In Thussu, D.K. (ed.) Electronic
    Empires. London: Edward Arnold, 157–76

Boyd-Barrett, O. (1999) Trends in world communi-
    cation. In Global Dialogue 1(1), Summer,
    56–69
Boyd-Barrett, O. and Newbold, C. (eds) (1995)
    Approaches to Media: A Reader. London:
    Edward Arnold
Cook, J. (1980) The interpretive tradition. In
    Alvarado, M. and Boyd-Barrett, O. (1992),
    Media Education: An Introduction. London:
    British Film Institute, 155–67
Cumberbatch, G. (1995) Media and Violence. Unit
    46 of the MA in Mass Communications, Centre
    for Mass Communications Research, University
    of Leicester
Curran, J., Gurevitch, M. and Woollacott, J. (1982)
    The study of the media: theoretical approaches.
    In Gurevitch, M. (et al.) Culture, Society and the
    Media. London: Methuen, 13–29
Curran, J. and Park, M.-J. (eds) (2000) De-
    Westernizing Media Studies. London:
    Routledge
Dijk, T. van (1985) Discourse and
    Communication. Berlin: De Gruyter
Dijk, T. van (1998) News as Discourse. Hillsdale,
    NJ: Lawrence Erlbaum
During, S. (1995) The Cultural Studies Tradition
    of Media Research. Unit 5 of the MA in Mass
    Communications, Centre for Mass
    Communications Research, University of
    Leicester
Eco, U. (1973) Social life as a sign system. In
    Robey, D. (ed.) Structuralism: An Introduction.
    Oxford: Clarendon Press
Gadow, K.D. and Sprafkin, J. (1989) Field experi-
    ments of television violence. In Pediatrics 83,
    399–405
Garnham, N. (1979) Contribution to a political
    economy of mass communication. In Media,
    Culture and Society 1(2), 123–46
Gauntlett, D. (1995) Moving Experiences:
    Understanding Television's Influence and
    Effects. London: John Libbey
Gerbner, G. (1973) Cultural indicators – the third
    voice. In Gerbner, G., Gross, L. and Melody, W.
    (eds) Communications Technology and Social
    Policy. New York, NY: Wiley, 553–73
Gitlin, T. (1978) Media sociology: the dominant
    paradigm. In Gouldner, A.W. et al. (eds) Theory
    and Society 6. Amsterdam: Elsevier Scientific
    Publishing Company, 205–53

Gormley, T. (1998) 'Ruination Once Again' – Cases in the Study of Media Effects, from www.theory.org.uk

Gramsci, A. (1971) *Selection from the Prison Notebooks*, London: Lawrence & Wishart

Habermas, J. (1989/1962) *The Structural Transformation of the Public Sphere.* Cambridge, MA: MIT Press

Hall, S. (1980) Encoding/decoding. In Hall, S. *et al.* (eds), *Culture, Media, Language*. London: Hutchinson

Halloran, J. (1995) *Media Research as Social Science*, Module 1, Unit 2 of the MA in Mass Communications, Centre for Mass Communications Research, University of Leicester

Hamelink, C. (1994) *Trends in World Communication.* Penang: Southbound Publishers

Heath, S.B. (1983) *Ways with Words.* Cambridge: Cambridge University Press

Hoggart, R. (1957) *The Uses of Literacy.* London: Chatto & Windus

Holmes, J. (1992) *An Introduction to Sociolinguistics.* London: Methuen

Innis, H. (1950) *Empire and Communication.* Oxford: Clarendon Press

Katz, E. and Lazarsfeld, F. (1955) *Personal Influence: The Part Played by People in the Flow of Mass Communication.* New York, NY: Free Press

Klapper, J. (1960) *The Effects of Mass Communication.* New York, NY: Free Press

Kornhauser, W. (1968) The theory of mass society. In *International Encyclopedia of the Social Sciences* 10. New York, NY: Macmillan/Free Press, 58–64

Kress, G. (1995) *Language in the Media*, Unit 49 of the MA in Mass Communications, Centre for Mass Communications Research, University of Leicester

Kress, G. and Leeuwen, T. van (1996) *Reading Images. The Grammar of Visual Design.* London: Routledge

Lazarsfeld, P. (1941) Remarks on administrative and critical communication research studies. In *Philosophy and Social Science* 9 (2)

Leavis, F.R. (1952) *The Common Pursuit.* London: Chatto & Windus

Leavis, F.R. and Thomson, D. (1948) *Culture and Environment*. London: Chatto & Windus

Lovell, T. (1980) *Pictures of Reality.* London: British Film Institute

McCombs, M. (1994) News influence on our pictures of the world. In Bryant, J. and Zillman, D. (eds) *Media Effects: Advances in Theory and Research*. Hillsdale, NJ: Lawrence Erlbaum, 1–16

McKenna, J. (1995) *Politics, Participation and the Public Sphere*, Unit 10 of the MA in Mass Communications, Centre for Mass Communications Research, University of Leicester

McLuhan, M. (1964) *Understanding Media.* London: Routledge & Kegan Paul

McQuail, D. (1984) With the benefit of hindsight: reflections on uses and gratifications research. In *Critical Studies in Mass Communication* 1(2). Annandale, VA: Speech Communication Association, 177–93

McQuail, D. (2000) *Mass Communication Theory: An Introduction* (fourth edn). London: Sage

Marcuse, H. (1964) *One-Dimensional Man.* London: Routledge & Kegan Paul

Marx, K. (1992) *Capital: A Critique of Political Economy.* London: Penguin Classics

Mills, C.W. (1956) *The Power Elite*. New York, NY: Oxford University Press

Merton, R. (1957) *Social Theory and Social Structure.* Glencoe, IL: Free Press

Morley, D. (1980) *The 'Nationwide' Audience: Structure and Decoding.* BFI TV Monographs 11. London: British Film Institute

Morley, D. (1986) *Family Television.* London: Comedia

Mosco, V. (1995) *The Political Economy Tradition of Media Research*, Module 1, Unit 4 of the MA in Mass Communications, Leicester, University of Leicester

Moss, G. (1995) *Media, Talk and Literacy*, Unit 43 of the MA in Mass Communications, Centre for Mass Communication Research, University of Leicester

Murdock, G. (1982) Large corporations and the control of the communications industries. In Gurevitch, M. *et al.* (eds), *Culture, Society and the Media.* London: Methuen, 118–50

Mulvey, L. (1975) Visual pleasure and narrative cinema. In *Screen* 16(4), Autumn

Newbold, C. (1995), Approaches to cultural hegemony within cultural studies. In Boyd-Barrett, O.

and Newbold, C. (eds), *Approaches to Media: A Reader*. London: Edward Arnold

Noelle-Neuman, E. (1974) *The Spiral of Silence*. Chicago, IL: University of Chicago Press

Parsons, T. (1949) *The Social System*. Glencoe, IL: Free Press

Pool, I. de Sola (1983) *Forecasting the Telephone: A Retrospective Technology Assessment*

Radway, J. (1984) *Reading the Romance*. Chapel Hill, NC: University of North Carolina Press

Rogers, E. (1955) *Diffusion of Innovations* (fourth edn) New York, NY: Free Press

Schiller, D. (1999) *Digital Capitalism*. Cambridge, MA: MIT Press

Schiller, H. (1969) *Mass Communication and American Empire*. New York, NY: Augustus M. Kelly

Smythe, D.W. (1977) Communications: blindspot of western Marxism. In *Canadian Journal of Political and Social Theory*, 120–7

Steinfield, C. (2000) Dispelling common misperceptions about the effects of electronic commerce on market structure. Paper presented to the 35th anniversary conference of the Chinese University of Hong Kong

Tunstall, J. (1971) *Journalists at Work*. London: Constable

Tunstall, J. (1977) *The Media Are American*. London: Constable

Weber, M. (1965) *The Protestant Ethic and the Spirit of Capitalism*. London: Allen & Unwin

Williams, R. (1958) *Culture and Society*. Harmondsworth: Penguin

Williams, R. (1961) *The Long Revolution*. London: Chatto & Windus

Winseck, D. (1995) *Canadian Telecommunications: New Technologies, Déjà vu and the Potential for Democratic Communication*, Unit 36 of the MA in Mass Communications, Centre for Mass Communications Research, University of Leicester

Tools for Studying the Media

Hilde Van den Bulck

Introduction

Media studies are obviously not just about theoretical discussions. There is also a wealth of factual studies being carried out on media actors and institutions, content and reception. Studying one of the aspects of the media, though, is not a wet-finger exercise: just as there are different theoretical approaches to media studies, there is a range of tools available to media scholars. Using these tools, moreover, requires a certain methodological rigour. Every method has its own rules of the game, which the media researcher is required to follow. Here I will give the main tools for media research, and their most important dos and don'ts. This should help the reader in his or her attempts to come up with a 'scientific' piece of media research.

First, in Chapter 8, we will try to come to terms with what 'scientific' is all about. When is a piece of research scientific? Is there only one (best) way of being scientific? Can we distinguish different views in the world of (media) research? What traditions are to be found?

These general considerations are then followed by a discussion of the main research methods and tools that can be used by a media scholar. The first two approaches concentrate on studying people, sometimes media professions, more often media audiences. In Chapter 9 we will discuss quantitative survey research as a way to arrive at an overview of a population by means of a systematic study of (part of) that population. Alternatively, if one wants to do a more in-depth analysis of a limited number of cases, a more qualitative survey may be more appropriate. In Chapter 10, therefore, we will look at individual and focus group interviewing. An even more in-depth approach to the understanding of people in relation to media is to study them 'in the field', that is in their daily dealings with the media. This will be discussed in Chapter 11, which talks about ethnographic field research.

After that, in Chapter 12, we will turn our attention to the analysis of media content. First, we will look at what is probably the oldest form of media research: systematic-quantitative content analysis. As the most widely used tool for a long time, it has also been open to a lot of criticism. Therefore, we will also look, in Chapter 13, at alternative, qualitative content analysis, particularly semiotics. This will be followed, in the final chapter of this section, by a look at the tools available to media scholars who want to carry out policy or historical research. In both cases use is made of documents: how to find them, how to treat them and how to evaluate them will be discussed. Finally, in the section summary, we will try to come up with a general 'list of things to do', which should be taken into account by anyone trying to come up with a thorough piece of media research.

CHAPTER 8

The Nature of 'Scientific' Research

THE NATURE OF (SOCIAL) SCIENCE AND SCIENTIFIC RESEARCH

The popular image of science is that of European Galilean science with its emphasis on material experimentalism in search of universal, physical laws (Anderson, 1987: 3), with Newton as the prototypical scientist. Scientific method in this view is considered to be public or generalizable, universal and thus objective, empirically systematic and rational, **holistic** and **cumulative**, and predictive (see Wimmer and Dominick, 1994: 9–12; MacLennan, 1992: 330). This is an image that, even today, stretches to social sciences and humanities, and thus to mass communication studies. The birth of this conception of (social) science goes back to what MacLennan (1992: 330) calls, the 'Enlightenment Project' of the eighteenth-century intellectuals (Philosophes). They considered science as the epitome of Reason, as different from – and superior to – 'distorted' forms of thinking such as religion, common sense or ideology. They worked towards the acceptance of scientific method as the basis for an understanding, and thus betterment, of human nature and humanity. This love affair of intellectuals with science was important in the emergence of the social sciences (Hamilton, 1992). It led to a rationalist and empiricist conception of social sciences that is still prominent today and that has extended its influence to media and communication studies. Anderson (1987: 15–17) refers to this as 'scientism', the doctrine of science as complete knowledge. It assumes that the product of good science is truth – the result of the search for universal generalizations that describe the order of phenomena. The discovery of these generalizations is often seen as the only purpose of science. This position clearly assumes that there is an underlying order, which is unitary, stable and knowable, and will therefore provide validation of the truth of scientific description. Scientism also proposes the thesis that science is progressive by definition, that the products of scientific discoveries have made life easier and better.

This traditional, 'ideal' model of social knowledge and science has been challenged in recent years. As the structures of society have started to change, so too have the funda- mentals of modern thinking become dogmatic and out of date. As Van Poecke (2000) explains, in recent years society has moved to multiplicity, plurality, decentralization, arbi- trarity and non-cumulative structures of knowledge. The state, culture, economy and finance – helped by rapid developments in information technology – have all melted together into a complex and untransparent system within which the practices of everyday life are formed. In this way, the binding parameters of the experiences and values of vast masses of people are produced unnegotiably by powers that escape any form of questioning, let alone con- frontation. These changes challenge the Enlightenment model of knowledge and science. For Foucault (1980) there is no longer room for the traditional view of knowledge as a privileged and unified whole of 'thoughts' that exists in the collective mind, and that is guarded with the utmost care by an elite of scientists, philosophers and academics.

The nature of science is not fixed in time for all cultures; it is rather a practice that shows regular and sometimes spectacular change. Referring to Kuhn, Priest (1996) underlines that scientific thinking changes in revolutionary leaps and bounds, not just evolutionary incre- ments. What is seen as scientific truth today may be thought of as illusion or prejudice tomorrow. What is more, science is also a reflection of a wider societal context. Social and political factors influence the choice of research topics and of the instruments and tech- niques applied to study those topics, and thus have powerful effects on what kind of know- ledge is created (cf. Halloran, 1981). For instance, in communication research, concern with propaganda during the Second World War set the research agenda for much early work; concern during and after the 1960s with the effects of television violence became more important as society's interests shifted toward understanding domestic unrest. Finally, science is also influenced by its micro-context, i.e. the scientific community in which it is being practised. All this, according to Lyotard (1984), leads to a reality of knowledge today as a vast group of 'movements' within pragmatic 'discourses' or 'language games', treated like an economic good that can be bought and sold according to the market principles of demand and supply. This leads to the virtual destruction of the aura of knowledge and science.

Taken to its extreme, this radical abandoning of the traditional notions of 'good science', creates a situation where no research is worthwhile. As such it almost inhibits any scientific research. As Halloran on several occasions has warned, we must be careful not to jump out of the frying pan into the fire and reduce knowledge to mere perspectivalism. Still, regard- less of how social and political factors influence the choice of research problems and of what methodological approach is used to study those problems, there is something like good (social) science and good mass communication research. Good researchers, whether positivist or interpretative, whether using qualitative or quantitative methods (see below), can follow the same principles. Anderson, following Leahey, sees as the goal of good science, 'to make sense out of human experience within authoritative, empirically grounded explanations to serve some human purpose' (Anderson, 1987: 3). Definitions abound, but all seem to stress the importance of a form of empirical 'evidence', accuracy and the purpose of enhancing knowledge and thus society itself.

Science then – as the explanation of human experience – aims at the best description of characteristics (ontology), methods and practices (praxiology), and causes and consequences (epistemology) of phenomena for the purpose of prediction, control and understanding. This explanation is based on empirical observation and is a public way of knowledge.

ON THEORY AND RESEARCH, PARADIGMS AND TRADITIONS

Despite this definition, science (even 'good' science) is not one-dimensional. As Anderson (1987: 3–5) explains, science is a human activity conducted within a community of practitioners. This scholarly community is not singular, but in fact consists of several communities claiming to be scientific. As such, there are separate communities for the physical and human sciences, allowing humanities to free themselves from their former ties to the systems of logic, the methods and the type of evidence of the physical sciences. But the community of the human sciences, too, is not homogenous: 'Loud arguments are heard over the propriety of different methods of study, the character of knowledge claims, the worth of those claims, who holds rightful membership and so on' (Anderson, 1987: 23). Finally, mass communication studies consist of different schools that look for 'evidence' in different places and that employ different criteria to assess validity (Halloran, 1991: 23; see also Halloran, 1981). Institutions, departments, journals and individual scholars adhere to different perspectives and methods of science.

To understand the forms that mass communication research can take within these different 'schools', there are a number of important distinctions to be made. The problems confronted in the communication field, as Melody and Mansell (1983: 106–7) note quite rightly, lie not with empirical evidence as such but with the decision as to what questions will be asked, what kind of data will be sought, how it will be gathered, and to what use it will be put. This refers to the different paradigms scholars can comply with. According to Smith (1988: 299), following Kuhn, a paradigm is a worldview or conceptual model shared by members of a scholarly community that determines how enquiry within the community should be conducted. In other words, a paradigm is a *Weltanschauung* that structures research within a scholarly community. Paradigms determine what questions are worth asking and what kind of data are required to provide acceptable answers to these questions. Below, we will identify a few key paradigms in communication research.

Qualitative Versus Quantitative Methods

Particularly since the 'qualitative turn' (Jensen and Jankowski, 1993: 1) in mass communication studies in the early 1980s, the distinction between quantitative and qualitative research has become central in the discussion on 'good' communication research. The debates between scholars on this topic are often antagonistic and fuelled by exaggerated oppositions. The differences can be situated at a conceptual-theoretical, methodological and analytical level.

Scholars within the quantitative tradition support the positivist notion that there is something like an objective reality (social facts) 'out there' that can be observed, measured, analysed and thus understood. For them, it is possible to abstract social phenomena from their social and cultural context, and from specific conditions, to identify and select as an outsider variables for analysis and to attribute (causal) relations to variables (Silverman, 1993: 21). Decontextualization and selection are thus central issues (cf. Sayer, 1992). Advocates of quantitative methods are convinced that these facts should be measured as accurately as possible, thus a strong belief in mathematical/statistical precision with its unambiguous character and its black-and-white validity. As such there is a heavy reliance on numerical analysis and measurement, and the accuracy and adequacy of scientific measurement instruments is a central focus of concern. The improvement of the tools is expected to provide 'an exact value for anything we might want to measure – a number we could all agree on' (Priest, 1996: 6).

The main objectives in quantitative research are generalization, explanation and prediction. It starts from existing theories to state hypotheses, which are tested by means of one out of a range of standardized and formalized tools such as survey, quantitative content analysis or the experiment. The analysis of data is by means of (now almost always computerized) statistical analysis. The results consist of charting surface patterns, trends and correlations in graphs and tables.

Qualitative research is grounded in the interpretative tradition, stating that there is no such thing as an objective social reality, but instead that 'reality' is a social and cultural construction (Denzin and Lincoln, 1994: 5), that can only be approximated, never fully apprehended. It is thus concerned with meaning attribution, with how the social world is produced, experienced and interpreted. Qualitative methods are designed to explore and assess things that cannot easily be summarized. The tools for data collection therefore are flexible and sensitive to the social context in which data are produced, aiming at compiling 'rich' data (Manson, 1996: 4). For qualitative data analysis there is a reliance on interpretation and analysis of what people do and say without making heavy use of measurement or numerical analysis. Understanding of complexity, context and detail is crucial. Qualitative researchers look for conclusions in the form of consistent descriptions of how something works, not mathematical equations. Stress is on a holistic approach with rounded understandings.

Rather than starting with a theory or hypothesis, qualitative media research will use a combination of methods to come to a hypothesis leading to 'grounded' theory (cf. *infra*). This constant interaction between theory and data collection makes qualitative research very flexible. To this end, mass communication studies can borrow from many different qualitative, interpretative traditions including phenomenology, ethnography, cognitive anthropology, symbolic interactionism, linguistic discourse analysis and semiotics. The main methodological tools are participant observation, in-depth interviewing and semiotic analysis of content.

Deductive Versus Inductive Methods

The traditional model of scientific research, according to Priest (1996: 8–9), is primarily a deductive one in which the researcher reasons from the general to the specific. In this 'theory comes first' approach (Manson, 1996: 143), the researcher starts with a theory, an exploratory idea that can be generalized to predict what will happen in a new situation. From this theory, or general proposition, the researcher derives one or more specific propositions (hypotheses) that can be tested by collecting and analysing a certain kind of data. The new data can either confirm the hypothesis so that the theory is upheld, or they can refute the hypothesis, so that questions are raised about the adequacy of the theory. The inductive or 'theory comes last' approach, on the other hand, adheres to a logic that reasons from a specific case to a general theoretical conclusion. As Huberman and Miles (1994: 431–2) explain, at the heart of analytic induction is the idea that there are regularities to be found in (the physical and) social worlds. The theories that we derive express these regularities as precisely as possible. For example, in exploratory research, a scholar who wants to study a certain problem will have no theory to guide the development of specific questions. The researcher, in other words, begins with just a question, not with a clear, well-defined theory or hypothesis. If at the end of the research, no general conclusions can be drawn that might apply to other research populations, it remains just another descriptive study without making contributions to general theory. Often, however, the study of a particular case will stimulate thinking that will result in the formation of new theory. The new theory could then be tested in additional communities – deductively. Sayer (1992: 157–8) refers to two problems with induction. The 'big' problem of induction is that social reality itself may change so that past arrangements, and thus theories, no longer hold. This does not mean though, still according to Sayer, that everything in the world is only contingently related and that no knowledge can be relied upon. If things in social life change, this will be observed and acted upon. Until then, making inferences about infinite sets of events on the basis of finite sets of observed events, can be risky but is justified. The 'little' problem of induction is that all our knowledge is, in principle, fallible. As such, this is a problem that stretches out to other areas.

In general, deduction can be considered as typical of quantitative methods, whereas qualitative research most often is inductive. A 'compromise' – originated from qualitative research traditions such as ethnographic field research – are the procedures known as 'grounded theory approach' (Glaser and Strauss, 1967). Here, inductive and deductive analysis are mixed. Once a theme, hypothesis or pattern is identified inductively, the researcher moves into a verification mode, trying to confirm or qualify the finding. This then kicks off a new inductive cycle.

Administrative Versus Critical Research

As Halloran (1981: 22) stresses, research is not carried out in a vacuum but must be considered in the context of its relations with economic, political and social factors. Yet an important distinction in communication research is made according to (the interpretations of) the ties or alignments of theory and research with economic and political factors. A very deep cleavage thus exists between administrative and critical research. According to

Smythe and Van Dinh (1983: 118), mass communication studies can be located in one of either category on the basis of three characteristics. First, they can be distinguished according to the type of problem selected. While administrative research is aimed at bettering an existing organization (e.g. research into the effectiveness of advertising), critical studies are looking at how to reform or create institutions according to the needs of a community (e.g. research into the importance of an independent African news agency). The second distinction is based on the research methods employed. Administrative research is said to apply positivist, behavioural theories, putting the individual at the centre, whereas critical research centres on the community and the socio-cultural dimension by providing historical material analysis. Finally, and most importantly, both approaches differ in their ideological perspective. Administrative research is aimed at linking problem, method, data and interpretation of results with no reference to issues regarding structures of societal institutions and power relations, and the influence of vested interests. Critical research, on the other hand, focuses on interpretation that involves (to a more or less extent radical) change. By calling into question asymmetrical political and economic relations, and the uneven power structure of society, the research effort is essentially geared to enhancing societal change.

Both schools have been seriously criticized and are quick to criticize one another. Administrative research is attacked for supporting the status quo and vested interests by providing simple, predictive models for the analysis of a limited number of discrete variables. It is said to limit itself to discrete static relations among individuals or atomistic organizational units (Melody and Mansell, 1983). Critical research, on the other hand, is said to overemphasize theory and substance at the expense of proper research design and methodology, of relevant empirical data and of thorough analysis. Whereas administrative research simply ignores issues of power and structure, critical research tends to make existing institutional structures the problem 'by definition' and change as equally necessary 'by definition'.

Paradigms and approaches

As this overview indicates, one can study a certain topic from within very different paradigms and points of view. Some very basic examples from the field of advertising can illustrate this.

For instance, to investigate the relative position of men and women in magazine advertisements (content analysis), one can decide on a quantitative approach. In this case, a considerable sample of magazine advertisements will be taken. This sample will be used to 'count' the number of men and women in the ads, which gender is more to be found in which type of ad, and so on. Alternatively, one can decide to carry out a more qualitative analysis of one, or some, prototypical example(s) of ads, and study semiotically the relative position of men and women. For instance, the denotative picture of a woman sitting at the feet of her husband, or of a man putting his hand on the shoulder of his – slightly shorter – wife can be interpreted as connotating male dominance in a family.

Research into advertising and its audience can also be administrative or critical. An advertising company can do a market study to find out the impact/success of one of its campaigns. For instance, it can send to a sample of consumers a standardized questionnaire asking: Did you see the ad? Did you identify the product? Did it lead you to buy the product? The results inform the industry whether or not it is on the right track. Yet the impact on the audience can also be studied critically. For instance, one can study the impact of an increasingly advertising-driven market on the materialism of the citizens. It implies a critical analysis of the advertising industry's influence on contemporary society. Often this type of research will work inductively.

CHAPTER 9

Quantitative Survey Research

The survey has always been a very important tool in mass communication studies (as in social sciences in general). Definitions vary but we will consider a piece of research as a quantitative survey when it is an empirical research, relating to a multitude of objects and when the data are collected in real-life situations and statistically processed (cf. Hüttner, Renckstorf and Wester, 1995). By means of a survey, researchers try to get an overview of a population through systematic observation, description and analysis of (part of) a population. Quantitative survey research can have different objectives: exploratory, descriptive or explanatory (Adams, 1989: 19–25). The basis of the research is usually reported behaviour (attitudes, etc.) as it is related to all sorts of characteristics of the population. The questionnaire is the main research tool here. In this type of research, every nerve is strained to come up with an experiment-like situation. Considerable effort therefore goes into sampling the respondents, designing the right (perfect?) questionnaire, training the interviewer and refining the statistical analysis instruments. Statistical aspects such as validity and representativeness are considered crucial. The aim is to come up with correct propositions based on quantitative data.

In communication research, survey is used most often in descriptive research to provide information on socio-economic status (SES), behaviour, attitudes, etc. of groups of people. Before (and even after) the so-called qualitative turn in the 1980s (cf. *infra*), survey was the central method to study the audience. Both fundamental audience studies – such as uses and gratifications research (for a prominent example, see McQuail, Blumler and Brown, 1972), agenda setting, cultivation analysis – and more applied and administrative audience research (size and profile of audiences for media institutions) make heavy use of standardized questionnaires to find out about groups of viewers. The result is either a structural description of the audience in terms of its compositions and its relation to the social structure of the population as a whole, or more behavioural, related to the influence of media content on the attitudes, motives, values and behaviour of audience members. The fact that audience research has moved to qualitative reception analysis, does not mean that survey research has become out of use either, in audience research or in mass communication studies in general (cf. Gunter, 1999). If anything, it has widened its scope – for instance, as a tool to study the use of new media. (For a recent example, see Roe, 1998.)

POPULATION AND SAMPLING

As Adams explains, sampling is used to create a 'miniature replica of the population, reflecting the range of its characteristics' (Adams, 1989: 46). It allows the researcher to study a population with great accuracy and at reduced cost. There are several ways of sampling that allow for representative results.

- With *random sampling* every element of the population under study has the same opportunity to be part of the sample and thus to be interviewed. To obtain such a sample one can use an electoral register (unless one wants to include the under-aged), a telephone book (although there are pitfalls here) or a similar source. Tables of random numbers as well as computer programmes generating random numbers have been developed to compose a sample.
- A *stratified random sample* will limit the variance within the population. The population is pre-ordered according to certain characteristics (e.g. age, sex) after which a random sample is taken from the different strata. In this way allowance is made for differences that may exist across the population.
- A *quota sample* (often used in commercial research) can be considered a stratified sample with sampling within the strata. The interviewer will have to find a certain quota of a particular strata (e.g. 50 DVD owners). One way of achieving this is through random walk sampling where the interviewer will start at a certain point (say a certain street) and will start collecting data according to a certain method.
- Finally, though not much used in survey research, one can opt for *purposive sampling*. Here the sample is not representative of the total population but rather consists of cases rich in information with an eye to study them in-depth rather than to generalize to the entire population. It could thus be a sample of typical, crucial, extreme non-conformist or homogenous cases.

Which type of sampling to use will depend on the topic of research as well as on the available resources.

TYPES OF SURVEY RESEARCH

Before drawing up the actual questionnaire, one has to decide on the form in which the survey will be conducted. One can distinguish three types of survey: written, telephone and face to face.

Written, Self-completion or Mail Surveys

In this case the respondent is given (often through the post) a questionnaire for self-completion. This method has several advantages: it is cheap and requires comparatively little organizational effort and time; the respondent can fill in the questionnaire in his/her own time and environment; it reduces the risk of socially acceptable answers – as the absence of an interviewer creates extra 'anonymity' – as well as the risk of interviewer bias. On the other hand, there are certain negative consequences of using the self-completion question-naire, especially when sent through the post: the fact that the interviewer is not there at the time of completion, requires that the questionnaire is very clear and simple as to prevent confusion or annoyance on the part of the respondent. The main problem with this type of survey, though, is the low return rate. Even though it is dependent on the topic of research, the organizing institute/sponsor, the follow-up contact and the way of approaching respon-dents, on average the response is as low as 30 per cent. Even though there are methods to increase response – see, for example, Dillman's Total Design Method' (Dillman, 1978) – up to 70 per cent, this still means that around one-third of the sample did not answer.

Telephone Interviews

Telephone interviews are relatively cheap and quick. With only a few interviewers (super-vised by a researcher) one can go through the sample in a few days. Yet, there are several limitations. The main problem is to keep going – both interviewer and respondent lose concentration and thus accuracy. The questionnaire has to be relatively straight-forward and short, with simple questions (e.g. a question with seven answer options would be impossible). What is more, the representativeness can be endangered as the sample is limited to people with a telephone and then often to those who actually answer the phone: housewives, the elderly or the sick, more than outdoor working people (see Lavrakas, 1993). In recent years, more and more use has been made of computer-based telephone interviews whereby the interviewer can read the questions from the screen and input the answers directly to the computer.

Face-to-face Interviews

Finally, one might decide to conduct face-to-face interviews. The considerable expense/investment required by this method, in terms of time, organization and money, is complemented by the advantages of the physical presence of the interviewer. The ques-tionnaire can contain more complex questions, can be more extensive, can be less struc-tured, etc. This approach requires well-trained and well-informed interviewers. The length of the questionnaire is also partly determined by the location – for example, a street inter-view will have to be based on quite a short questionnaire, whereas in a respondent's home one can take up to 45 minutes (Hansen et al., 1998: 239). The decision as to which approach to use is mainly based on the type of research question and the available resources.

QUESTIONNAIRE DESIGN

A questionnaire is not just a gathering of questions on a topic – quite the contrary. The designers of a questionnaire have to take into account several elements, such as the sequence/order of questions, the phrasing and length of questions, the types of question, and so on.

General Structure of the Questionnaire

Of course, every specific piece of research will bring specific requirements to the questionnaire. Yet there are certain general rules for questionnaire design. After the title page (including the name of the project, of the researcher and the number of the respondent), a questionnaire should start with a general introduction including the identity of the organization, the topic and goal of the research, the selection procedures, the protection of the respondent's privacy, the approximate time of the interview, the possibility of refusal, the possibility to ask questions and a general task description. With regards to privacy, it is important either to stress the anonymity of the respondent or, if the research requires identification, offer the assurance of confidentiality. Official privacy laws and regulations should be referred to. The actual questions regarding the research topic should be grouped by theme, with every section headed by a short introduction. Almost every questionnaire will contain general questions, which seek out the basic SES data of the respondent (age, marital status, etc.). As these data can sometimes be of a sensitive nature (e.g. income), such questions should come at the end of the questionnaire. The questions are followed by a report from the interviewer regarding the progression of the interview. The questionnaire will typically contain instructions for the interviewer allowing him/her to conduct the interview and complete the questionnaire in the form required.

Types of Question

According to *form*, one can basically distinguish between two types of question: i.e. closed and open. With closed questions, the answer categories are predetermined. There are several options: the respondent can only choose between two answers (e.g. yes/no; male/female); the respondent can choose between three or more answers in which case s/he is to be given a card with all possible answers; the respondent has to make two or more choices from a range of possible answers; the respondent indicates to what degree s/he agrees on a range of statements. Open questions allow the respondent to decide on the phrasing as well as the length of the answer. The interviewer should write down the answer as completely as possible and, if necessary, enquire further. According to *content*, a distinction can be made between factual and opinion questions. Factual questions stress the accuracy and completeness of the answer, whereas opinion questions stress the fact that the answers should conform to the honest and personal opinion of the respondent.

Question Wording and Order

When drawing up the part of the questionnaire with the actual research questions, careful attention should be paid to the *wording* as well as the *order* of the questions, as these aspects can have a serious influence on the answers given. One such element is the persuasiveness of the question: by including arguments the question can point the respondent in a certain direction (e.g. 'Do you think violent programmes can be broadcast before 8pm?' versus 'Do you think violent programmes can be broadcast before 8pm where it is easy for children to watch?'). Another is the influence of the use of 'no opinion': research has shown that not adding the 'no opinion' option to the answers of a closed question, can seriously influence the 'no opinion' of respondents. The frame of reference provided is again of significant influence. As such, the order of questions can determine the outcome of the results. The previous question can seriously influence the meaning of the following question or sharpen the attention of the respondent. (e.g. general and specific question). Question order can actually change a minority into a majority and visa versa (cf. Billiet, 1991; Billiet et al., 1992). To check sincerity and consistency, one can build-in control by asking the same question more than once (be it in a different phrasing).

Other things to think of when drawing up a standardized questionnaire are:

- keep hold of the actual research questions
- rely on previous research
- keep questions simple and clear
- formulate the questions in standard language
- questions – with certain exceptions – should be kept short
- questions must be one-dimensional and unambiguous
- avoid double negatives
- with closed questions, all possible answers have to be made clear
- one should not presuppose certain facts
- distinguish between questions about facts and questions about opinions
- define central concepts
- take special care of the design and lay-out of the questionnaire.

DATA GATHERING

Before going off to collect the data, it is important to pre-test the questionnaire on a small – not necessarily representative – sample of respondents. By means of this pilot, the researcher can find out whether all of the pitfalls mentioned in the above list have been avoided in his/her questionnaire. A lot of time, effort and money can be saved by testing out the questionnaire before feeding it to the entire sample.

Once the quality of the questionnaire has been established, the actual data-gathering can commence. Using telephone or face-to-face interviews, the researcher can conduct his/her own interviews (in the case of a relatively small piece of research) or s/he can rely on interviewers. In the latter case, the researcher can make use either of his/her own staff of interviewers or rely on the interviewers provided by a commercial market research company (Carton, 1995: 145). In either case, special attention should be paid to training the interviewers. When ringing a doorbell, the interviewer should know how to treat the respondent (to avoid 'door in the face'), to enhance perfect interview conditions (to secure the goodwill of the respondent, to avoid influence from a third person present, etc.), to secure a standard procedure for all interviews, and so on (cf. Billiet and Loosveldt, 1988; Van den Bulck, 1999).

DATA ANALYSIS

The statistical analysis of the material provided by a questionnaire is typically done by means of computer as the information is (usually) too extensive and too complicated to be handled manually. Therefore the questionnaire will be designed so that the data can easily be converted to computer-ready data. To this end, there will be a coding box with every question, and every possible answer will be given a 'code' (number). For data input to a computer, these numerical scores are brought into a data file. This data file will then be cleaned (removing input errors) so that it is ready for analysis. Several user-friendly statistical packages are available to help the communication researcher in his/her data analysis (these include SPSS (Statistical Package for the Social Sciences) or SAS (Statistical Analysis System).) A lot of the analysis of survey research is descriptive. By means of frequency and cross tables, a population will be described as having certain characteristics (e.g. 'How many Brits watch football more than twice a month?') or according to the co-occurrence of certain characteristics (e.g. relationship between age and watching current affairs programmes). At a more advanced level, survey data can be used to investigate potential causal relationships. The decision as to which statistical technique to use will depend on several elements, such as the theoretical model, the types of variable (nominal, ordinal, interval) and the presumed type of relations (linear, curvilinear, etc.).

Quantitative variables

One can distinguish between different variables according to the level of measurement (Billiet, 1995: 83–6; see also Wimmer and Dominick, 1994).

- *Nominal variables.* May be defined as 'the level of measurement at which arbitrary numerical or other symbols are used to classify persons or objects'. In the case of nominal variables there is only a 'relationship of identification' between the elements that are measured on the basis of a characteristic. Examples would include the characteristic of the variable 'gender'. Possible values are 'man' and 'woman'. The units that are distinguished on the basis of this characteristic can only be said to be similar or dissimilar. Other examples include nationality and colour of eyes. The numerical codes that are given to the values (e.g. 1 = male, 2 = female) are arbitrary and have no mathematical value.

- *Ordinal variables.* May be defined as 'the level of measurement at which items are ranked along a continuum'. There is a 'relationship of a certain order'. On the basis of the values given, the units of analysis can be ranked from low to high, few to many, first to last, etc. The distance between the points on the scale is not exactly the same, but there is a certain order. Examples of an ordinal characteristic include the order of birth in a family (first, second, third child), social background (low, middle, upper class), attitude towards violence on television (very much against to very much in favour). The numerical codes awarded have no mathematical value but indicate a certain order (e.g. degree of selfishness: a person scoring 4 is not twice as selfish as a person scoring 2, but is more selfish than the latter).
- *Interval (metric) variables.* May be defined as 'a measurement system in which the intervals between adjacent points on a scale are equal'. So here it is not only possible to rank the values according to a certain criterion, there are also fixed distances between consecutive values. A good example is age in years. The difference between a 15 and 16 year old is the same as the difference between a 72 and 73 year old, whereas the difference between 56 and 58 years old is double. Another example would be temperature.

The distinction between the different levels of measurement is very important for an adequate application of statistical methods. Every level has its own legitimate operations – compare and classify, sorting, mathematical – as well as its own validity and reliability tests.

CHAPTER 10

Qualitative Survey Research

Whereas a quantitative survey is aimed at mapping the distribution of certain characteristics and the degree to which they appear in a population, a qualitative survey is aimed at the description of individual cases and the discovery, formulation and typification of characteristics with a view to theory building. According to Jones (1985a), the best way to understand the actions and motives of people is to go and ask them in a way they can answer in their own words (rather than through a pre-set vocabulary) and with a depth that shows the context of meaning (rather than isolated fragments put on paper in a few lines). Central to this is the attempt to get an 'insider's view'.

TYPES OF QUALITATIVE SURVEY RESEARCH

The main research tool is the in-depth, semi-structured or open interview. It is the means by which the researcher can gain access to and, subsequently, understand the private interpretations of social reality that individuals hold. Michiello *et al.* (1992: 87) refer to the in-depth interview as a 'conversation with a purpose'. Some of its main characteristics are explained by Manson (1996). Crucial is its relatively informal style rather than a formal question-and-answer format. Second, it has a thematic, topic-centred, biographical or narrative slant. The researcher usually does not have a structured list of questions but a range of topics, themes or issues, which s/he wishes to cover. Finally, the data are generated via interaction, because either the interviewee(s) or the interaction itself, forms the data source.

Qualitative interview-based research can be divided into two broad categories:

- with single respondents (known as in-depth interviewing or individual interviewing, with oral history as a special case)
- with groups of respondents (known as group discussions, focus group interviews).

Even though the recent growth in popularity is undeniable, the qualitative interview has always had its place in mass communication studies as a tool in explorative and descriptive research.

Individual In-depth Interviews

These have been, and are, used in the study of communicators (see e.g. Morrison and Tumber, 1988) and audiences (see e.g. Gunter, 1999 for an early example). In policy research, oral history has taken a prominent place as a necessary addition to documentary evidence (cf. Das, 1998; Van den Bulck, 2001). It involves the reconstruction of meaning, beliefs or patterns of action, and is used to study the differences between groups regarding meaning attribution in dealing with media.

Focus Group Interviewing

As a research technique, this dates back to the Second World War where it was used as a tool to study the effectiveness of propaganda. Merton, among others, can be considered a key name here (see e.g. Merton and Kendall, 1946). Nevertheless, for a very long time it was mainly used in marketing research and was looked down upon by communication (and other social science) scholars. The renaissance of this technique came with the turn in mass communication studies in the 1980s and 1990s towards an interest in meaning creation and interpretation of media contents and technologies (cultural studies, reception analysis). The works of Morley (1980) and Katz and Liebes (1990) provide some insightful examples.

INDIVIDUAL IN-DEPTH INTERVIEW

Even though it may seem no more than a 'conversation with a purpose', the preparation and actual conduct of an in-depth interview is a very complex and exhausting task, which requires a lot of planning, effort and considerable expertise. The interviewer not only has to prepare the structure and flow of the interview, s/he also needs a particular set of social and intellectual skills.

As every interview takes place in a specific socio-political context and with a specific purpose, there are no set rules, no fixed scenarios for its organization and conduct. The amount of people to interview will depend on the research topic and the available resources but the precise number will be limited. The interview itself cannot be conducted according to a strict scenario as with a questionnaire, yet there are several elements worth considering in preparing/carrying out the interview.

First, a researcher needs to make a number of choices as to the degree of structure, the amount of control, the level of focus, etc. Michiello *et al.* (1992: 112–19) distinguish three alternatives. In *recursive* interviewing – the least structured form of interviewing – the structure is limited to the natural flow of the conversation, i.e. the interaction. To prevent the conversation from going off at a tangent, the interviewer can use transitions to link what the interviewee says with the research topic. Instead of recursive interviewing, the researcher can opt for *funnelling*. In this interview the researcher starts with the most general and broad questions and will then narrow down the area of enquiry. *Story-telling* is a model of interviewing in which the researcher elicits a story.

Even though the interviewer has no pre-set questions, s/he will use an *aide-mémoire*, or interview guide. This is a menu of general issues, ideally to be covered, which serves to jog the memory of the interviewer. Hansen *et al.* (1998: 273–6) suggest that the guide should indicate:

- the sequence of topics/issues to be covered
- the nature and extent of prompting and probing
- the nature and use of visual or verbal aids, and the points during the interview where these should be introduced.

With this aid at hand, the researcher can start the interview. Obviously it is important to start off on the right foot. This means that one has to try and set the tone of the interview early on and to establish a rapport, so that the interviewee feels at ease and comfortable enough to speak freely. Once the rapport is established, the actual interview can get under way. There are many different types of question that one can ask. Often used to start an interview are *descriptive* questions, asking descriptions about events, people, places and/or experiences. *Background demographic* questions can be asked here or – if sensitive – at the very end of the interview. *Structural* questions are aimed at finding out how the interviewee organizes his/her knowledge. Then there are *knowledge, feeling, opinion/value, sensory* questions, asking about these issues respectively. *Contrast* questions basically ask about differences, whereas with *devil's advocate* questions the interviewer takes the 'other side'. The interviewer can also solicit an opinion by asking a *hypothetical* question ('Say you had children, would you let them watch this?') or by *posing the ideal*. To elicit information more fully then the original questions that introduced the topic, one can ask *probing* or *follow-up* questions.

Throughout the interview it is important that the interviewer shows continued interest in what the interviewee is saying. This can be demonstrated through a *nudging probe* ('Is that so?'), a *reflective probe* ('She said that to you?') or via *mirror* or *summary* questions. Near the conclusion of the interview, it is important to leave some space for *loose-end* questions about things the researcher could not ask in the flow of the interview, and to allow the interviewee to add anything s/he feels is important.

The centrality of the interviewer presents the most important potential pitfall of this type of research. The interviewer can endanger the quality of the research through a non-representative sample, biased questioning, prejudice towards the interviewee or the use of interviews as a replacement for reading documents. Further problems – outside the interviewer – lie with the time-consuming and expensive aspect but also with the non-verifiability of oral evidence, and the dependence on 'survivors' and those willing to be interviewed (see also Feldman, 1995; Holstein and Gubrium, 1995; Jones, 1985b; Kirk and Miller, 1986; MacCracken, 1988).

Interviews are usually (and ideally) audio-taped and transcribed (although sometimes they are video-taped). Usually one also takes notes during the interview to include elements that cannot be registered from the tape (non-verbal behaviour such as facial expressions). Together, the transcripts and notes form the (considerable amount of) textual data to work with. These rough data need to be categorized and labelled. The schedule will depend on the research topics and objectives. After the first – rudimentary – classification of the content according to research topics, the material will be read and re-read to give all segments a thematic code (open coding). After that, the segments with the same code will be compared, subcoded and analysed. Eventually these will be interpreted. Nowadays, this process of coding and analysis is strongly enhanced by means of computer software (e.g. KWALITAN), ranging from simple indexing programmes to elaborate network analysis programmes.

Elite Interviewing: Oral History

A special case of in-depth interviewing is (life) oral history. Here one tries to elicit and understand significant experiences in the life of the interviewee. This can be done in the course of biographical research, but in mass communication studies it is more commonly used in policy research of which interviews with privileged witnesses – that were part of the policy-making process – make up a vital part. Interviews with privileged witnesses have several advantages. First, they can provide facts about events, people and relations that are not registered in documents. Second, they provide a background for the interpretation of people and events as well as of documents (Seldon and Pappworth, 1983: 36–52). For instance, the interview with a former head of television can provide a very useful insight into personal elements influencing programming policy at the time. However, there are some serious flaws in the method of oral history. Some of these are related to the interviewee.

S/he can provide false information because of a failing memory, but also because of deliberate deceit (a broadcaster may over- or underemphasize his or her role in the policy process). The deception can also be based on revenge (e.g. when the interviewee was aggrieved by a colleague or superior) or on exaggerated discretion (e.g. when the interviewee is too careful not to give away what might be confidential information). When interviewing people less centrally involved in the policy-making or the event under study (e.g. announcers rather than policy-makers) one may end up with only a superficial or over-simplified picture, based on secondary knowledge and hearsay. A lack of perspective, influence of personal feelings, self-consciousness, the influence of hindsight and repetition of published evidence can equally influence the interview in a negative fashion (Seldon and Pappworth, 1983: 16–33; see also Dexter, 1970). This is why interviews with privileged witnesses should be combined, not only with the study of written sources (see below), but also with in-depth interviews with external experts. The term external experts refers to people not directly involved in the actual policy-making, but with a clear view on the matter from their professional background (journalists, media experts, national policy-makers, politicians, cabinet members, etc.). They can point out holes or misinformation.

FOCUS GROUP INTERVIEW

Apart from the most obvious advantage of cost and speed, there are several other elements supporting the use of focus group interviews. First, they are of particular use for research topics in which social context is relevant: people have to be understood partly in their relationship with others; when understanding and insight are required; when new ideas are needed or in action research. Nevertheless, before deciding to bring respondents together in groups, one should consider some of the disadvantages of the method. First, in groups, personal positions can only be known quite superficially. Second, group pressure can affect responses. Dominant characters often influence and intimidate others. Third, the composition of the group can influence responses as bringing together people of a different gender and age, ethnic and social status, and heightens the possibility of violating cultural norms of proximity and speech rights. Fourth, because of face-work, groups are less useful for sensitive, 'private' or controversial topics such as watching porn or the like. Finally, group discussions are unfit for checking knowledge or awareness. In conclusion, it is important to always bear in mind that data obtained from focus group interviews are not identical to individual interview data. Focus group data are group data (Berg, 1995: 78).

A difficult question relates to amounts. How many participants to a group? How many groups? There is no clear-cut answer to these questions. Even though it may be more cost- and time-effective to have large groups, the quality of the discussion suffers under large numbers as the group becomes more difficult to control and individual group members may 'disappear' in the crowd. An 'ideal' number is considered six to seven – with more people it becomes difficult to handle, with fewer it is hard to keep the dynamic. In terms of how many groups, their number can be relatively small in qualitative research. Again there are different options but the minimum would be four to six (fewer will provide atypical information) whereas the maximum would be about 12 (more would be too costly). The overall sample would thus be about 20 to 100 people. The actual sample – as it is small – should be composed with the utmost care, not only along the traditional social-scientific SES dimensions, but more so according to specific dimensions relevant to the topic of research (cf. purposive sampling in Chapter 9 of this section).

The key figure in group interviews is the moderator. His/her role is to facilitate, moderate and stimulate discussion among the participants, not to dominate, govern or unduly lead such discussion (Hansen *et al.*, 1998: 272–3). Usually the moderator is the researcher him/herself. At the start of the discussion s/he has to get participants relaxed and confident enough to speak freely. S/he will explain the aim of the research and of the session, and will go round the group with simple unembarrassing and non-controversial questions, to get everyone in the mood. The moderator has a complex task: not only does s/he have to handle questioning (which questions to probe further, which topics are still to come . . .) that cannot just be solved by a guide or manual, but s/he also has to handle group dynamics, controlling dominating respondents and encouraging others to talk.

Data recording can be on audio tape, which can be transcribed later. This transcription can prove complicated, as it is not always easy to identify the different participants solely by voice. Therefore, audio-visual taping of focus-group conversations can prove more useful; it also allows a better study of the group dynamics and the interaction between the different group members. As the data in focus group research are of a considerable amount, the use of computer software for the analysis of the transcripts has become more and more standard procedure with this type of research.

CHAPTER 11

Ethnographic Field Research

Developed with(in) anthropology (by Malinowski, Evans-Pritchard, Mead and Boas) where they are now the standard research procedures, ethnographic field research and participant observation have also gained importance in other disciplines (including mass communication studies) as a preferred method for certain types of research. Even though different disciplines have different opinions about the 'art of participant observation', there is a consensus on the core of ethnography as a practice that puts the researcher in the midst of whatever s/he wants to study, thus enabling him/her to examine phenomena as perceived by the participants (Berg, 1995: 86–7). Ethnographic field research is a form of qualitative research in which the researcher takes part in the situations to be studied. The project is conceived as a learning process that enables the researcher to get to know the ideas, values, habits, ways and action patterns of the community in the field. It focuses on human interaction and meaning viewed from an insider's perspective in everyday-life situations and settings. Participation is a strategy for gaining access to otherwise inaccessible dimensions of human life and experience. Direct observation and experience are primary tools for data collection, but the researcher may also conduct interviews, collect documents and use other means of gathering information. A good general description of what participant observation is all about can be found in Jorgensen (1989: 23), and its history in Thomas (1993).

There are basically three types of research question that benefit most from the method of participant observation (Jorgensen, 1989: 12–13; Hüttner et al., 1995: 500–2). First, in exploratory studies, when little is known about the phenomenon under study or when one wants to get a grip on changes in social attitudes and (inter)actions. Closely related to this is action (policy) research when there are important differences between insiders' and outsiders' views. The second area of ethnography is the description of social relations and attitudes, i.e. of the meanings provided within the community under study. Finally, ethnography can help to provide an explanation for certain phenomena. Here research can generate theoretical interpretations and can thus lead to new theories. It can also be used, in a complementary way, to test a new theory.

In mass communication studies, ethnographic field research has become the standard procedure used to study the working of media institutions and, more recently, has gained ground in audience research. In the study of media organizations, participant observation has been the key method of enquiry for several decades, particularly in the area of news production. Ever since the early work on gatekeepers (see e.g. White, 1950, for an early example), the study of news production as an organizational activity has been profiting from field research. The influence of journalistic professionalism and news policy, as well as of news producers' dependency on only a few institutions of organized power, has thus been studied extensively. As both media theories and institutions change, new studies remain inevitable and relevant, securing the ongoing success of this type of research (for recent examples see Cottle, 1993; MacManus, 1994; Schlesinger and Tumber, 1994).

The other major strand of communication studies in which participant observation has taken a prominent position is audience research. The aforementioned shift away from the effects model to an interpretative approach has led to the use of ethnographic field research in cultural studies and reception analysis. The way in which families watch television in general, as well as particular programmes, has been a central topic of attention (cf. Lull, 1988; Morley and Brunsdon, 1999). Recently, it has also been applied to the study of the introduction and use of new media with individuals and families (cf. Tukle, 1996), as well as other fields of interest.

RESEARCH DESIGN

What is taken to be the problem for research by participant observation is the result of a flexible, open-ended ongoing research process of identifying, clarifying, negotiating, refining, and elaborating precisely what will be studied. (Jorgensen, 1989: 32–3)

Research begins with some 'foreshadowed problems' (Malinowski, 1922: 8), i.e. problems or issues obtained from reading through literature and information on the research area.

Although the research can be based on hypotheses drawn from an established theory, more often ethnography is concerned with developing theories through data collection. The first step, then, is to turn the foreshadowed problems into proper research questions. This is the aim of pre-fieldwork and early data collection. These questions will be continuously re-addressed, refined, elaborated and focused further through data collection. As such, **ethnographic research** is cyclical in nature: data collection, analysis and interpretation are a continuously interrelated and inseparable process. As the research problem becomes more defined, it is important to formulate key concepts. Concepts are derived from the meanings people use to make sense of their daily existence. In other words, a central objective is to formulate the key concepts in terms of the insider's perspective. As such, the data usually take the form of detailed descriptions and definitions. The problems will be studied in a specific setting. According to Hammersley and Atkinson (1983) the selection of a setting is contingent on:

● whether or not you can obtain access to the setting
● the range of possible participant roles you might assume
● whether or not this role (or roles) will provide sufficient access to phenomena of interest.

Next, within the setting the researcher will decide on the study of one or some cases. Within the case(s) a further selection will be made according to time, people and context.

Access

The way to gain access is, to a certain extent, dependent on the type of setting. Settings can be visible or invisible, open or closed.

● *Visible or invisible.* The visibility of particular aspects of human life depends on where you are located, as well as on your previous knowledge and experience. A setting is visible when information about it is available to a general public. Some settings are visible but less observable. Some human settings are almost entirely invisible from an outsider's perspective. Within almost every complex organization, there are cliques of people whose activities are obscure or inaccessible to non-members.
● *Open or closed.* A human setting is more or less open if access to it requires little negotiation. Some settings are almost entirely closed to an overt research approach, leaving the participant observer with a decision either to forego investigation or to find some way to negotiate access. Basically one can distinguish between open access, negotiated access, illicit or undercover access and no access. Whether or not a setting is open or closed to participant observation is only partly related to visibility. Simply because a setting is highly visible, this certainly does not mean that it is open to public inspection. Likewise, because a setting is only partly visible to outsiders, this does not mean that it is closed to participant observation. Goffman (1959) distinguishes between 'frontstage' as opposed to 'backstage' regions of human settings. While some settings, like restaurants, are almost entirely frontstage, other settings, such as bathroom or bedroom at home, are largely backstage regions. Most human settings, however, are neither entirely visible and

open (frontstage), nor entirely invisible and closed (backstage). Most human settings instead contain both frontstage and backstage regions.

In ethnographic field research, the stage of gaining access is a very laborious and complicated one, requiring a lot of imagination. In gaining access there are two basic options to choose from: overt or covert strategies. In general the overt, straightforward, open approach is preferred because it raises few ethical problems, is easier than other approaches, and provides the best and most effective access (Jorgensen, 1989: 45). Under most circumstances, overt access is gained by seeking permission from the highest possible authority (head of the production unit, head of the family). In doing so, the researcher should offer the authority a copy of the research proposal. It may be useful to refer to the prestige of the researcher and the prestige of the subject matter or discipline. It is important to understand that access should always be negotiated (Lindlof, 1995: 110–12); sometimes the researcher will have to modify his intentions in order to be able to gain access.

Some authors stress the ethical necessity of informed consent from participants in the research (e.g. Lindlof, 1995), whereas others accept alternative (covert) strategies as possible means of entrée (cf. Berg, 1995). Indeed, sometimes it is not possible to negotiate overt entrée or the strategy does not provide access, so the researcher is forced to go 'under cover' (e.g. to study a deviant subculture such as snuff movie watchers). The choice of strategy is a delicate one: if the direct approach fails, it may subsequently be difficult to enter the site covertly. It is also a complicated matter. Usually, even when an overt strategy is employed, not everyone is informed of the research interest. Conversely, even when a setting is approached covertly, it is likely that at least a few people will eventually be provided with information pertinent to the research aim. Hence, covert strategies may be applied in order to gain access, and afterwards the people may be told of the research interests.

Crucial in the process of negotiating access is the role of gatekeepers. These are people in a setting who police the boundaries of the setting and who are crucial in granting access. Yet there are some problems with this. The relevant gatekeepers are not always obvious. Even in formal bureaucratic organizations it is not always obvious whose permission needs to be obtained, or with whom it is crucial to have a good relationship. Lindlof (1995: 110–11) also refers to sponsors. Whereas a gatekeeper usually remains detached from the research(er), the sponsor will take a more active interest. S/he is an ally and will help to introduce the researcher to members of the community and to provide information.

Field Relationships

In ethnographical research there are different degrees of involvement in the setting. Often the dichotomy observation–participation is used. Some authors (Gold, 1958; Junker, 1960; see also Lindlof, 1995) distinguish four possible roles according to the degree of participation in the community under study, from complete observer, over observer-as-participant to participant-as-observer, and finally complete participant. The role of the researcher determines his/her social location in the community/group under study. His/her position can generally be conceptualized on a continuum between complete outsider to complete insider.

As an outsider looking in, one can get an overview of a scene, and gain a good impression of major and distinctive features, relationships, patterns, processes and events – a critical viewpoint lost by an insider. But the outsider role can also present problems. People interact with you as an alien. This may result in negative attitudes towards the researcher, ranging from friendliness (and even deference), to hostility and even contempt. At the same time, there are important aspects of human existence that simply cannot be known except from the inside, making a high level of involvement necessary. Throughout the research project, the participant observer may perform a variety of roles, introducing him or her to different perspectives that will lead to a more comprehensive and accurate picture.

Researchers conducting participant observation should always be aware of the danger of crossing the line. When the researcher does 'go native', or 'become the phenomenon', s/he may be contaminated by 'subjectivity' and personal feelings. The scientific status of the researcher may be spoiled. According to Jorgensen (1989) objectivity in the traditional view is like 'virginity' – once lost, it cannot be recovered.

As participant observation requires the establishment of a certain identity, a great deal of care and attention must be given to impression management. Even though certain aspects of one's identity cannot be altered (age, gender, ethnicity), others can be manipulated to facilitate access and good relationships with the members of the community. The researcher must judge what sort of impression s/he wishes to create, and manage appearances accordingly.

The growth and persistence of good field relationships are largely based on trust. Deceptions (both intentional and unintentional) in all respects will lead to negative sentiments. The quality of data is improved when the participant observer establishes and sustains trusting and co-operative relationships with people in the field. Field relations involve negotiation and exchange between the participant observer and insiders.

COLLECTING AND RECORDING DATA

Data collection in ethnographic field research can take the form of (unfocused and focused) observation, (solicited and unsolicited) insider accounts, and documents and artefacts. On entering a new setting, the researcher will observe the setting unfocused, to get a 'feel' for the place and the people, so that the researcher can then fit in almost unnoticed. Once in, the researcher can focus the observations on specific areas of interest. This is usually combined with a growing involvement and growing sociability with the community members. This in turn will result in solicited and unsolicited insider accounts. The researcher must rely on informants to get to know the less 'visible' aspects of the community and to double-check his information obtained from observation. Finally the researcher will come across a wide range of documents and other human artefacts that can help clarify and explain things.

Data can only be of use when they are recorded in a systematic way. Memory – no matter how good it may appear – is unsuited as a data recorder as memories always fail, and are tainted by previous knowledge and later experiences. *Scratch notes* and *head notes* can be of preliminary use – that is until one has the opportunity to make proper notes – but should remain what they are: a temporary solution. *Field notes* are the crux of the matter; they should be written immediately after each field experience. Field notes should be chrono- logical. Nothing should be left out, even if it doesn't seem important at the time of obser- vation. Observations should be described in detail, conversations should be transcribed verbatim. Names, locations, times should all be mentioned. One should try not to fall into the trap of summarizing. Usually the researcher will also keep a *diary*, providing room for more personal and emotional reactions. Researchers can also keep *thematic notes*. These notes will be complemented by transcripts from interviews, photos, documents and artefacts.

DATA ANALYSIS AND INTERPRETATION

As we have already seen, more than any other form of research, in participant observation the analytical stages are not chronologically separate. Rather, analysis should be seen as a process, 'with fieldwork, data-text translation, coding and conceptualizing all go ahead at the same time, albeit at different stages of progress' (Lindlof, 1995: 215). Nevertheless, analysis is definitely more than simple 'wet-finger' theorizing. Analysis implies breaking up the research material into separate units, then searching for patterns, categories, wholes. Jorgensen (1989: 108–10) suggests several analytic strategies:

- identify the basic components of a phenomenon
- look for patterns and relationships among facts
- compare and contrast
- ask different questions and rephrase them
- consult existing literature.

This attribution of meaning to the material leads to theorizing, i.e. the organization of facts in the shape of an explanation or interpretation. The methodology of participant obser- vation involves several different forms of theory, including analytic induction (Znaniecki), sen- sitizing concepts, grounded theory (Glaser and Straus), existential theory and hermeneutic theory.

CHAPTER 12

Quantitative Content Analysis

As Hüttner *et al.* (1995: 135–6) explain, the systematic-quantifying content analysis in its overall outset can be compared to the quantitative survey. Here, too, the research is aimed at gathering a relatively large amount of data from a large amount of units by means of an observation instrument that is used in the same way on all units. Different from survey research is the research material. The researcher is not concerned with the selection of people but with the selection of content of media products for systematic analysis. Content analysis can be and is used for descriptive research, but often it obtains an evaluative character when the results are set against a standard of measurement (e.g. rules of objectivity or moral standards).

Content analysis is probably the oldest way of studying the media and is an answer to the age-old concern with media content. Even the ancient Greeks worried about the potential – negative – impact of story-telling on children, and this concern has been expressed in varying forms ever since. Particularly in the twentieth century, books, press, comics, cinema, radio and television in its informative, entertaining or dramatic functions all became topics of attention (see Holsti, 1969; Krippendorf, 1980). The basic concern was, and is, with how media contents reflect or interpret social, cultural and political norms, attitudes, beliefs and values. As such many sociologists throughout this century (starting with Max Weber) were interested in content analysis as a means of 'monitoring the "cultural temperature" of society' (Hansen et al., 1998: 92). As an elaborated methodology it did not develop until the inter-war period, when it was introduced as a tool to study propaganda (e.g. Lasswell, 1927). Throughout the years, the method has been refined, and – since the second half of the twentieth century – has been used increasingly next to other forms of data collection in wider research projects.

Quantitative content analysis is now used for a variety of research problems. Next to specifically text-oriented analysis (for a recent interesting example, see University of California (CCSP), 1998), it can also be sender/production-oriented to study the influence of ownership, organizational routines and rules when it becomes integrated into studies of international media flows, media organizations, professionals, production of media content. Conversely, it can be receiver/consumption related in order to analyse the influence of media content on individuals' opinions or on wider socio-cultural, economic or political processes. Probably the most well-known and comprehensive example of the use of systematic content analysis as a means to compare (changes in) the cultural and socio-political climate with (changes in) attitudes and behaviour, is Gerbner's long-term cultural indicator project (see e.g. Gerbner, 1972; Gerbner et al., 1980). Despite the increased significance of qualitative content analysis (cf. infra), the systematic quantitative approach remains popular in both academic and administrative research, as can be witnessed from the countless examples in journals up to this day.

DEFINITION

As a method, content analysis became best developed in its systematic quantifying form. The definition par excellence of this type of content analysis was provided as early as 1952 by Berelson, who defined content analysis as a 'research technique for the objective, systematic and quantitative description of the manifest content of communication' (Berelson, 1952: 18). Even though the definition is short, almost every term in it has – over time – become a bone of contention. The claim of objectivity is probably the most contested, as it is – at best – an ideal state of affairs that can in no practical way be reached. To claim objectivity is to ignore the entire hegemonic process of meaning production. As such, the term cannot refer to more than reliability. The systematic character of content analysis becomes clear (as in survey) from the central process of data production with its sampling techniques and its elaborated registration instrument (the coding schedule), which frames the 'reading' of the material. The general idea is to gather a relatively extensive amount of data via a research tool that will be used in exactly the same way for all units of analysis. This systematic character, too, has been criticized over the years. The most important – yet much questioned – aspect of this method, though, is its quantification. This can be considered in two ways. First, it refers to the scale of the material considered necessary and a preference for (increasingly computerized) statistics. But also – and most problematic – it refers to the quantitative reading of the material. The aim is to identify and count units of analysis, thus trying to say something about the material as a whole. The problem is the extent to which the quantitative indicators are interpreted as intensity of meaning, social impact and the like. There is no simple relationship between media texts and their impact, and it would be far too simplistic to base decisions in this regard on mere figures obtained from a statistical content analysis. What is more, figures resulting from the analysis do not say anything about the context in which the units were placed.

So, content analysis has been heavily criticized for its number-crunching, positivist approach. Yet, as Hansen *et al.* put it:

> rather than emphasizing its alleged incompatibility with other more qualitative approaches (such as semiotics, structuralist analysis, discourse analysis) we wish to stress . . . that content analysis is and should be enriched by the theoretical framework offered by other more qualitative approaches, while bringing to these a methodological rigour, prescriptions for use, and systematicity rarely found in many of the more qualitative approaches. (Hansen *et al.*, 1998: 91)

SAMPLING IN CONTENT ANALYSIS

Systematic quantification analysis allows for large-scale research. So large bodies of text (media content) can be analysed. Nevertheless, if one wants to study, for instance, 'violence in US media', one cannot possibly study all violence in all US media. In other words, sampling/selection is necessary. The researcher has to select a sample that is both practical, feasible and theoretically/methodologically adequate. Following (and updating) Berelson (1952), one can distinguish three main steps in sampling.

The first step is the *selection of media or titles depending on the research topic*. The researcher must decide what type of medium (radio, television, newspaper, weekly, monthly) and – within the type – which specific channels (e.g. public or private, home or foreign, general or thematic, pay television or open channels), newspapers or magazine titles to analyse. Depending on the research topic, one can also decide to analyse across different media.

The second selection consists of the *sampling of issues or dates*. Once decided on the specific media to be studied, one has to settle on what issues of a paper or journal or what dates of broadcast to select. The main concern here is whether to sample for the analysis of a specific event or to study a more general aspect of media content. In the former, the sampling period is relatively 'natural' (e.g. the Gulf War on British television, the Dutroux case in the Belgian press, etc.). Yet one may want to include a before and/or after sample for reasons of comparison. In the latter case, the sampling requires sufficient knowledge of the selected media and channels/titles, taking into account the influence of time of publication/ broadcast on the content, such as more sports on television during the Olympics, the silly season in summer, more sport in Monday editions of newspapers, etc. Taking into account variations in media coverage inherent to production and seasons, one will want to compose what Hansen (1998: 102–3) calls, a 'reasonably representative' sample. Often, use is made of a composed week (or weeks) taken every day of the week randomly out of a different week of the period under study. Or one can randomly pick a starter date and then take the 'nth' day after that throughout the period under study. This can be done for both print and audio-visual media.

The third step is the *sampling of relevant content*. Eventually one also has to sample types of content or genres and, within these genres, sample articles/programmes 'relevant' to the research topic. So, if one wants to study the portrayal of gays on television, one can, for example, decide to study fiction rather than non-fiction and then to study sitcom rather than soap or drama. Then one should decide to take all sitcoms or only those with a gay character in them.

Finally, one must decide on the unit of analysis or recording unit – that is, the elements to count. These can differ from research to research. Following Krippendorf (1980), we can compare research units to the extent that they have been 'constructed'. Sometimes the unit can be determined 'naturally', on 'physical' grounds, but more often the researcher needs to 'compose' research units on the basis of more theoretical considerations, which are then analytically defined. Weber (1990), concentrating on written/spoken text, distinguishes six commonly used basic units of text, but when incorporating audio-visual material, one can distinguish the following nine units:

- word
- word sense (e.g. idioms like 'taken for granted')
- proper nouns ('the British Prime Minister')
- sentence
- theme
- paragraph
- entire article/programme
- individual character/actor/source
- scene/incident.

Defining the recording unit is vital as it would otherwise not be possible to use the above as proper, meaningful quantitative indicators.

DEFINING CATEGORIES

Before defining the categories, it is important to remember that one should avoid the temptation of counting for the sake of it, just to show that everything can be measured. Too often the researcher gets carried away in that sense. Instead, one should always choose characteristics to study according to the general theoretical framework and the specific research hypotheses. This makes it difficult to describe in general the categories required. Yet there are certain more or less standard categories, such as identification categories, which situate every unit of analysis in time and place. Hansen *et al.* (1998) also refer to the identification of the style/genre as a typical category. Next to these standard categories, the specific research aim and material will determine what other categories to include (categories defining actors/sources and their characteristics, defining subjects/themes/issues, indicating vocabulary/lexical choice, describing dimensions of values and stance). It is important to have a good knowledge of the research topic, material and aim so that one can construct categories that show in analysis the specifics of the text. As mentioned above, categorizing just for the sake of it is useless.

According to Weber (1990: 23), two important decisions need to be made when constructing analytical categories. First, one has to decide whether the categories should be mutually exclusive, so that a unit of analysis cannot be classified in more than one category. Otherwise in factor analysis, analysis of variance or multiple regression analysis, results will become dubious. Second, the researcher has to decide on how narrow or broad the categories should be. For instance, for news content one can either take a general category – say 'politics' – or use more specific and narrow categories such as 'home affairs', 'parliamentary' and 'local'.

THE CODING SCHEDULE

These steps should then lead to the construction of the coding schedule in which the categories are ordered and designed in an easy-to-handle fashion. The schedule contains all variables to be measured, as well as the possible values to be assigned to them. The schedule should ideally be accompanied by a code book, which will be used as a guide to the proper use of the schedule. This coding schedule can first be used on a pre-test (e.g. a pilot or sub-sample of the material) to check the clarity of the categories (so as to facilitate the removal of ambiguities) as well as the quality of the schedule as a practical research instrument. Inconsistencies, overlap or gaps in categories as well as over- or under-differentiation within categories can thus be detected. Piloting should also check *reliability*, here to be understood as consistency. One can distinguish three types of reliability with regard to content analysis: *stability* refers to consistency with one coder over time; *interreliability* refers to consistency between coders; *accuracy* refers to the extent a coding fits the norm set out by the researcher in the code book. Here it should be stressed that a detailed yet clear and unambiguous code book can go a long way towards securing reliability.

DATA ANALYSIS

In its most rudimentary form, the data can be studied and analysed 'by hand', though in practice it proves more productive to use a computer programme. The coding schedule (like questionnaires) will have been given coding boxes to put in the value given to the variables. These can then very easily be brought into a computer data file as the raw material to be analysed.

All these data, after being checked for errors (data cleaning), can then be analysed using the appropriate statistical programme (SPSS, SAS, Excel). Sometimes new and complex variables – constructed from the existing (basic) data – are developed at this stage, turning nominal data into quantitative material, or constructed through scaling techniques. Analysis can start with simple frequency tables but can go as far as factor analysis, analysis of variance, multi-level analysis, cluster analysis, etc. All main techniques are potentially applicable (see also quantitative survey). The data analysis needs to address the hypotheses set out at the start. On the other hand, one needs to be flexible: it is quite possible that throughout the analysis elements, relationships and trends can become apparent that shed new light on the research.

Developments in computer hardware (text scanners) and software have greatly enhanced the possibilities of computerized content analysis. Several advanced programmes exist that can automatically read and process texts (selection and interpretation) (see, for example, Tesch, 1990). This can range from relatively simple contingency analysis and frequency of occurrence (e.g. textpack) and key-word-in-context as well as key-word-out-of-context analysis, to more complicated (pre-programmed) procedures through which inferences are made by computers autonomously. In its most advanced form, computerized content analysis is related to research into artificial intelligence, even though this is not yet widely used in media studies.

CHAPTER 13

Qualitative Content Analysis

For a long time (social science and) mass communication studies were dominated by the quantitative paradigm, resulting in an underdeveloped theory of qualitative textual analysis. In the study of media texts, quantitative content analysis has always ruled, particularly since it could be facilitated through the use of computers, thus enhancing the analysis of huge bodies of texts.

Quantitative content analysis has come under serious criticism, though, some of which we have already discussed. A central problem is the issue of exactly what is meant by 'content'. For Berelson (cf. *supra*), the aim of content analysis is to study the 'manifest' content of a media text. Yet the opposition manifest/latent can be considered a false distinction. The content of a message is, in principle, an *open* quality of the text and it is only through specification of the researcher that it becomes apparent. The 'objective analysis of manifest content', in this view, is impossible (cf. Lisch and Kriz, 1978). As such, according to Manning and Cullum-Swan (1994: 464) and many others, this systematic approach to content analysis has not been able to capture the *context* within which a media text becomes meaningful.

This concern has become central with the paradigm shift to qualitative analysis, as it is oriented precisely toward the relationship 'between the "text" as a social construction and its form or its imputed audience-derived meaning' (Manning and Cullum-Swan, 1994: 464). Qualitative, interpretative content analysis, then, is aimed at the reconstruction of what could be termed the 'meaning structure' of the text or content. The problematic in this kind of research usually refers to the relationship between characteristics and patterns within the 'text' and the context of the material. As Newbold (Hansen *et al.*, 1998: 131) underlines, the methodology relies heavily on the reading of the text by the researcher, so on his/her interpretation. As such, the skills of description and classification are vital to a good researcher. Computer support in this type of research is not relevant, as it is concerned with *Verstehen* rather than numbers. Compared to the quantitative approach, qualitative content analysis is usually concerned with smaller bodies of material to be analysed.

It is hard to speak of one research tradition when referring to qualitative content analysis. From the broad hermeneutic tradition concerned with textual analysis, there are mainly two strands of specific importance in the field of mass communication studies. *Narratology*, on the one hand, concentrates on the structure of the story within a text and thus stresses the narrative or story-telling character of the text. Here stress is on how meaning is produced structurally within the text, rather than the relationship between text and reader, or text and industry. Although this approach is most widely used for the analysis of films, it can be used to study any media (written or audio-visual) and any media content ranging from news and current affairs, through talk shows, television series and serials, to advertising, pop songs, content pages of teen-girl magazines and even cookery programmes (cf. Ellis, 1992; Fiske, 1990; Silverstone, 1981; Strange, 1998; Taylor and Willis, 1999). All these media products are structured by narratives, as they are, in the words of Taylor and Willis (1999: 66), 'all packaged into coherent story sequences'. One of the important elements here is the concept of binary oppositions (Lévi-Strauss, 1966), which can be linked to the idea of function and myths (Propp, 1968). Other variants include Greimas's semiotic square (cf. Greimas, 1966; see also Lotman, 1990) and the work of Todorov (1977; see also, Berger, 1996; Strinati, 1995). (For an in-depth look at narratology, see Section 3, on the moving image). *Semiotics*, on the other hand, studies communication as a system of meaning-attribution by the reader to the text. It is concerned with signs and sign systems. Semiotics has different research strands. Both in mass communication and cultural studies, the tradition is now widespread (as is illustrated in other sections in this book).

Discourse analysis

A much-(ab)used term in qualitative content analysis is 'discourse analysis'. Particularly in gender and cultural studies, the term is widely applied to label all kinds of non-quantitative discussions of all kinds of texts. It is a flag covering many loads, sometimes more than it actually should.

To study the working of discourse, we must agree on what discourse is. A useful definition can be found in Fiske (1995: 14):

> Discourse is a language or system of representation that has developed socially in order to make and circulate a coherent set of meanings about an important topic area. These meanings serve the interests of that section of society within which the discourse originates and which works ideologically to naturalize those meanings into common sense.

Discourse is, in fact, the story of reality as it is presented to us through media or other cultural texts. Discourse analysis therefore starts from the given that reports on events and objects always construct these objects in a certain way and that this constructedness is inevitable (Wetherell and Potter, 1992: 62). There is no such thing as 'version-less' reality and discourse analysis tries to lay bare this constructedness. On the basis of this, a media or cultural text can be analysed by identifying the main discourses out of which it is structured. In this way we can look for a capitalist (or socialist) discourse of economics, or a patriarchal (or feminist) discourse of gender, a Euro-centric (or other) discourse of race. Such discourses frequently become institutionalized. This does not mean that there is only discourse. Indeed, Hall warns quite rightly that one should not expand the territorial claims of the discursive infinitely.

Discourse analysis has been applied to a wide range of different texts: interviews, newspaper reports, official memoranda, television commercials, sitcoms, weather reports, computer manuals and even the text on a box of cornflakes. Throughout the 1970s and into the 1980s a lot of attention was paid to sexist discourse (cf. Lee, 1992 for some interesting examples), but racist discourse, too, has initiated a lot of research (cf. Wetherell and Potter, 1992). An interesting contemporary example is the analysis of the discourse of national identity underlying the weather report. As Billig illustrates with reference to the press (Billig, 1995: 116–17): 'A homeland making move transforms meteorology into *the* weather. And *the* weather – with its "other places", its "elsewheres" and its "around the country's" – must be understood to have its deictic centre within the homeland.' 'The weather' appears as an objective, physical category, it is contained within national boundaries. At the same time, it is known that the universe of weather is larger than the nation: there is 'abroad'; there is 'around the world'.

SEMIOTICS

The second main approach to qualitative content analysis relevant to mass communication studies is semiotics. In its broadest and simplest definition, semiotics is the study of signs. As Manning and Cullum-Swan, (1994: 466) explain, for semioticians, social life and all socio-cultural values, beliefs and practices – as well as the content of group structures and relations – are all organized in the same way as the language system. So all human communication can be understood and thus studied as the use of a sign system. As semiotics is concerned with the study of all signification or meaning creation in all sorts of 'texts' (or communications), it is, according to Van Zoonen (1994), in a way no more than a formalized version of the continuous interpretative activities of all human beings.

From the 1950s and particularly the 1960s onwards, semiotics gained more and more ground in the study of media texts. Starting with Roland Barthes' ground-breaking application of semiotic principles on French popular culture (see e.g. Barthes, 1967; 1972), this approach was quick to gain currency among academics and has grown into a major research tradition in the field of media and cultural studies. One of the reasons of its success is that it can be applied to almost any form of text or medium. As such, it has not only proven suitable to study how meaning is produced in a diverse range of media texts from a variety of media, it has also been extended to the study of all sorts of aspects of popular culture, including architecture to name but one.

Even though their starting point (and results) are quite different, both the Swiss linguist Ferdinand de Saussure (1916–72) and the American pragmatist Charles Peirce (1931–66) are considered the founding fathers of semiotics. Starting from language, semiotics studies all sorts of sign systems 'of varying degrees of unity, applicability, and complexity' (Manning and Cullum-Swan, 1994: 466). As such all human expression and communication is a display of signs: a 'text' to be 'read'. According to Fiske (1995: 40) semiotics has three main foci of attention: the sign itself, the codes or systems into which signs are organized and, finally, the culture within which these codes and signs operate.

The Sign

A sign can be defined as *aliquid stat pro aliquo*: something that represents or stands for something else. Whereas Peirce sees a sign within a triadic relationship (object–representation–interpretant), Saussure sees a sign as composed of a *signifiant* (signifier: word, sound, symbol) that stands for a *signifié* (signified: that which the expression stands for – the content). The word 'chair' is symbol: it stands for the object to sit on. The smile on the face of a model in an ad stands for happiness, while her clothes, hairstyle, etc. stand for a certain lifestyle. In other words, a sign combines a material, physical element that we can perceive or sense with a meaning this has for us (Selby and Cowdery, 1995: 42).

Peirce distinguishes between three types of sign. *Icons* are signs that resemble the things they represent. Iconic signs replace reality on the basis of a similarity: they represent certain characteristics or qualities of the object. This is most explicit in a photograph, but also maps, diagrams or the signs indicating a disabled toilet, say, can be considered and thus studied as icons. As Selby and Cowdery (1995: 45–6) explain, a lot of the signs one is confronted with in mass communication studies are iconic, as they are inherent in (audio-) visual and photographic material. Peirce's second type of sign is the indexical sign. An *index* refers to what it signifies not through resemblance (as icons), but through some direct relationship between signifier (index) and signified (what the index stands for): for example, no smoke without fire, no blushing without shame, no waving of the flag without wind. So there is some existential tie, some natural relationship between the object and the sign. Finally, Peirce distinguishes *symbols*: these signs refer to their objects on the basis of a convention, a law. So they have no logical connection to the ideas or things they refer to. One cannot know the signified through the signifier unless one has learned the convention.

As Fiske (1995), and Selby and Cowdery (1995) explain, these signs can be found in all media texts. Particularly in the field of advertising, the different elements of an advertising message can quite easily be interpreted as a collective of signs that produce a certain meaning.

Code System

Saussurians underline that signs do not have a meaning on their own but in relation to other signs. Meaning thus becomes relational. Signs are organized into a code that puts them in a relationship to one another following a certain system that creates meaning. So codes are recognized systems of signs (Selby and Cowdery, 1995: 47).

Codes are organized along two axes: *paradigmatic* (based on choice) and *syntagmatic* (based on combination). A paradigm is a set of signs from which one (and only one) needs to be chosen. The signs that make up a paradigm have something in common (e.g. 0, 1, 2, 3, 4, 5, 6, 7, 8 and 9 are all numbers) and at the same time have a *distinctive feature* that distinguishes one from the other at the level of both signifier and signified: the symbol for six is different from that for seven and also has a different meaning (Fiske, 1990: 56–7). The combination of the different signs chosen from the paradigm then is a syntagm. Important are the conventions, rules, grammar on the basis of which the combination is made. In a syntagm the meaning of a sign is determined by its relationship with others in the syntagm. So, in summary, Van Poecke (1991) – following Greimas and Courtés (1979) – explains that while the paradigmatic system is characterized by an 'or . . . or' relationship, the syntagmatic process is characterized by an 'and . . . and' relationship. Meaning production, then, is a mechanism of rule-bound selection and combination.

Ground-breaking and still much-referred-to examples of the structuralist analysis of semiotic codes are Roland Barthes' (1967) *Système de la Mode* and Leach's (1976) study of vestimentary codes in his book *Culture and Communication*. Both illustrate how the meaning of what people wear is derived from, on the one hand, the meaning signifiers (vestimentary objects) have, based on their paradigmatic opposition to others (a turtle-neck versus a v-neck jumper, say) and, on the other hand, the rules by which these signifiers are syntagmatically combined – for instance, a black bow tie takes up a different meaning depending on whether it is combined with a black dinner jacket (a guest) or a white jacket (a waiter).

So in studying media texts, too, we can use these ideas as they can provide a way of assessing the meaning production in a text. Van Zoonen (1994) explains how one should start the semiotic analysis of the media text by looking for the relevant signs in the text and their dominant characteristics. These signs can then be analysed as the result of selection and combination whereby, following Selby and Cowdery (1995: 58), 'the syntagmatic axis describes the choices that actually were made (combination), and the paradigmatic axis describes the choices that could have been made (selection)'. This again can be applied to the vast area of media texts, from magazine front covers, through photo-journalism to television fiction.

Signs and Culture

Typically, these codes become naturalized. As Taylor and Willis (1999: 22) state: 'Human beings, as highly skilled users of signs, whether linguistic or iconic, their use becomes so normative that there is a danger of believing that signs are the most natural, most "correct" way to represent our environment.' Yet the relationships between signs and their meanings are conventional. They are created socially and historically and can also be changed socially.

The relationship between the signs, the systems in which they are organized and the culture in which they operate are vital and multiple. The connections among signs are variable, and the resultant meanings are variable as well. Basically, following Barthes and others, there are different levels of signification: first-order signification or *denotation* (meaning produced and understood merely on the basis of the immanent rules of the system); second-order signification or *connotation* (based on the interaction between the sign and the feelings and values of the culture); and *myths* or *allegories*. In a simple example, denotation is *what* is photographed, connotation is *how* it is photographed.

Typically, these connections between the expression and the content are shared and collective, and provide an important part of culture. Manning and Cullum-Swan (1994: 467) – following Bourdieu (1977) – explain that 'culture is sedimented in institutions that "pin down" and stabilize the link between expression and content and contain the codes that anchor the potentially migratory expression'. As meanings collect under an ideological canopy, unpacking them becomes more complex and problematic, and knowing the culture becomes essential.

These observations are important in the (semiotic) analysis of media text. Television news provides a good example. As Taylor and Willis (1999: 22) explain: 'Even while there exists a belief that a camera gives us access to highly objective accounts of the world, its images are as subject to codes of signification as drawings are.' Semiotic analysis enables us to realize that all media texts are mediated, using the codes and conventions of the sign systems in which they communicate. They can therefore never simply be transparent mediums through which we have access to a 'truth'. Examples abound but some interesting ones can be found in Hartley (1982), Fiske and Hartley (1978) and Page (2000).

CHAPTER 14

Document Analysis for Historical and Policy Analysis

Sometimes the aim of a piece of research in the area of mass communication studies does not require, or is not even helped by, the production of new data. So, there are several research topics that do not benefit from or cannot be studied via one of the methods outlined in this section, be it qualitative or quantitative, content or receiver oriented. Within mass communication studies there are mainly two research areas that make it very difficult to rely on the research methods described above: media history and media policy analysis. In both instances it will not suffice or not even be possible to interview people or to study some form of media content. A central method in these areas is documental research. As Tosh (1984: 56) explains, documents, records and the like – traditionally the staple diet of historical and policy researchers – have most often been studied from one of two angles: 'first, how did the institution which generated the documents and records evolve over time, and what was its function in the body politic? And second, how were specific policies formulated and executed?'

One strand in mass communication studies that relies for a very significant part on the study of (archives and) documents is *media history*. According to Dahl (1994: 339), media history can be defined as 'a branch of history dealing with institutions of a particular type that are distinguished by much more specific purposes than the overall quality of 'communication'. Both Dahl (1978: 131) and Hsia (1988: 281) observe that media history has established itself as a branch in mass communication studies. Broadcasting history in particular has become the focus of attention in many scholarly works. Probably the first proper example of a historical study of broadcasting is the extensive work of Asa Briggs, describing the history of the BBC in four volumes. Briggs set out to write a total, definite history – that is, one as accurate and as well backed by evidence as possible. Yet he did not want to fall into the trap of writing the 'official' history. This example, has been followed by many others in subsequent years, in many different countries. There are basically two types of broadcasting history (Dahl, 1978: 132–3), determined by the subject. Some are written as a collective work (several authors each treating their own subject), others are written by one historian, who writes several volumes. Each approach has its own pros and cons (cf. Dahl, 1978; Branston, 1998).

The second area of media research relying mainly on (archival and) documentary research is media and communication policy research. According to Hansen *et al.* (1998: 67), *communication policy analysis and research* seeks to 'examine the ways in which policies in the field of communication are generated and implemented, as well as their repercussions or implications for the field of communication as a whole'. Policy research can be both historical and contemporary, and can be either about the policy of a particular media institution (see e.g. Scannell, 1993; Cardiff and Scannell, 1987; Van den Bulck, 2001) or about a media policy in the field at large, such as governments cable policy (see e.g. Negrine, 1985), trans-European PSB (cf. Collins, 1998) or EU broadcasting policy (Schlesinger, 1991; 1994).

It is important to note from the outset that, even though document analysis is the main research approach for historical and policy studies, the researcher should always be aware that the approach can be complemented by oral history or other approaches.

DEFINING DOCUMENT ANALYSIS

Document analysis, then, according to Altheide (1996: 2), refers to: 'an integrated and con-ceptually informed method, procedure, and technique for locating, identifying, retrieving, and analysing documents for their relevance, significance and meaning'.

As the definition makes clear, the 'art' of document analysis is just as much concerned with the access to and acquisition of the right documents, as with the actual analysis and interpretation of these documents. As with any research, good documentary analysis is determined by a good demarcation of the research problem. Historical studies are by defi-nition broad ones, requiring a wide range of variables for their explanations. At the same time, though, it is important to delineate exactly what period and what topic to study (see, Altheide, 1996; Startt and Sloan, 1989). The same applies to media policy research. Not only does one need to determine which aspect of what area of communication or of which medium to study, one also has to be clear about exactly what policy analysis implies. Often policy is thought of as a coherent set of ideas and implementations concerning a well-defined area, set out by a single body. In truth, though, it is much more complicated and less straightforward (cf. Hansen et al., 1998: 67–8), involving different agents, different strands and different interpretations. It is important to identify all these different agents and aspects beforehand so as to be able: (a) to clearly select and define the research problem to be studied; and (b) to know what documents to obtain and from which agents to obtain them.

TYPES OF WRITTEN SOURCE

Documentary research is basically concerned with written sources. In trying to identify different types of written source, several categorizations and labels can be, and have been, applied. A common distinction is made between primary and secondary sources. According to Startt and Sloan (1989: 114), *primary* sources are original documents as well as con-temporary records, or records in close proximity to some event. *Secondary* sources, on the other hand, are based on primary sources. Fundamental though this distinction is in research, this categorization is not as clear-cut as it appears at first sight, and the precise demarcation varies from one research(er) to another. A simple example can illustrate this. Primary source refers to evidence contemporary with the event or thought to which it refers, but how far can the definition of contemporary be stretched? In hindsight, an account of the inclusion of the 'freedom of the press' in the Belgian constitution written 10 years after the event is considered contemporary, whereas a description of the introduction of British satellite television 10 years after, is not. Time is relative. 'Primary' or 'original' also suggest reliability or freedom from bias. Yet, often these sources are inaccurate, based on uncertain facts or even intended to mislead (cf. *infra*).

Alternatively, written sources can be categorized as a *published* or *unpublished* (manuscript). One can also make a distinction between written sources produced by governments and those produced by corporations, associations, or private individuals (Tosh, 1984: 29). In the end, any categorization of written sources reflects one's own perceptions of usage and involves some matters of choice.

For the study of (media) policy, the most useful distinction is between documents and reported evidence. A *document* is:

> one which is drawn up or used in the course of an administrative or executive transaction (whether public or private) of which itself formed a part; and subsequently preserved in their own custody for their own information by the person or persons responsible for that transaction and their legitimate successors. (Seldon and Pappworth, 1983: 234)

In other words, 'document' refers to material that was produced as part of a policy process. Such material offers a rich source of (quasi-)direct information about the policy. This includes policy memos, internal reports, background papers and reports, general messages (telegrams, letters, directives, memoranda, etc.) and reports on communications between people within the institution and from outside the institution. Next to the actual policy documents, a lot of information on issues of policy can also be obtained from so-called *reported evidence*. This comprises material that was abstracted from the continuous policy process and that either remained inert (as in a private diary that remains confidential for a long time), or was given to a third party that has no immediate relationship with that process or that community. Reported evidence refers to a variety of publications that paint a picture of an era, such as publications of government personnel, biographies, etc. These offer a lot of background information that helps to gain an insight into the context in which the policy was conducted and into the motives and reasons behind the policy.

HOW TO GET THEM

The study of documents has been fundamentally influenced by context, particularly *retrievability* and *access* (cf. Altheide, 1996: 4–7). In both historical and policy research, the documents have often been limited by their own physical availability and existence. While some documents can be obtained from libraries, special attention should be paid to the retrieval of documents from archives. Particularly when we are concerned with policy research, a lot of the relevant sources can be found in archives. Archives provide a specific set of structural constraints including: access to materials; the uniqueness of archival

materials; the non-circulation of materials; property rights; and the 'closed stacks' organization of archival repositories (Hill, 1993: 20–6).

As Tosh (1984: 57) explains, knowledge of administrative and archival procedures is vital
for any researcher to be able to get to the material. Yet these techniques are not only important in getting access to the material and retrieving it in the most 'economical' and effective
fashion, they are also essential if the researcher is to be alerted to one possible distortion
at this stage of the research – namely distortion in the surviving records. On the one hand,
this can be due to the deliberate removal of evidence from the researcher's reach (e.g.
embargoes on public office documents). On the other hand, it is possible that records were
pushed into the limelight. In several fields of recent history, collections of records published
soon after the time of writing can be consulted. It is important that these sources should
not be given extra weight just because they are so accessible.

In the past 20 years or so, a lot has changed due to the exponential growth in information technology. These new technologies for storage, consultation and retrieval of information
have had an influence on documentary analysis in terms of both access and retrievability.
Whereas documents for analysis were often quite limited, information technology has
opened up a potentially enormous source of new documents for investigation. Yet, this
entails adjusting views of documents and their significance.

Research into broadcasting history and policy is dependent to a large extent on archives.
Studies of broadcasting history have shown that the archives of broadcast institutions have
proved much more comprehensive than anticipated. As Dahl (1978: 130–1) explains, every
broadcast and programme is backed by an extensive written procedure, and the account-
ants and administration department, as well as the governing bodies, have left an abundance
of archive material. Of course, the source bases of the various histories vary according to
the size of the broadcasting institutions. This puts the broadcasting historian in a very
different position from the press historian, who often has to go without even the most rudimentary archive material concerning his/her paper.

Despite this abundance, a researcher using broadcasting archives is confronted with
problems of retrievability due to the (lack of) organization of the archives. For instance, as
Briggs (1980) explains, when he worked on his history in the 1960s, the BBC archives were
not formally separated from the BBC registry, and so before he could start work it was
necessary to list all relevant materials in the possession of the BBC. The result was that the
BBC put its archives in order (see also Briggs, 1985). A more recent, but striking, example
can be found in Burgelman (1988; 1991).

DOCUMENT EVALUATION

The evaluation of a document is a process consisting of two main types of criticism.
External criticism is concerned with determining whether a particular document is genuine,
whereas internal criticism is aimed at establishing credibility and understanding of content.
The questions to be asked are varied, and depend on the types of source and the topic

under study. Yet, there are certain basic procedures for external and internal criticism that have become standard practice in the study of documents.

On the one hand, one has to determine whether a document is authentic through external criticism. Startt and Sloan (1989: 117), distinguish three aspects of external criticism. The first and most important step in evaluating a document is *identification*. The researcher has to attribute the document to its proper author and fix it in its correct time. If the name of the author or other data that can identify the document are missing, the researcher must try to find them. If author, date and place of writing have been indicated, the researcher should check whether they are what they profess to be (Tosh, 1984: 51–2). At worst, the researcher will have to detect a forgery, but at a more simple level s/he will have to detect ghost writers or pseudonyms. Second, there is the process of *collation* (Startt and Sloan, 1989: 117) in which various texts are compared. A document needs to be examined for consistency with other texts as well as with known facts. Where needed or possible, one should try to compare the document to original records. Third, the genuineness of a document can be examined through *textual verification* (Startt and Sloan, 1989: 118). The form of a document can yield vital clues. As Tosh (1984: 52) explains, official documents usually conform to a particular ordering of subject matter and a set of stereotypical verbal formulae. But reported evidence, too, can be verified: letters can be compared to other authentic letters by the same author, diaries can be judged against the usual opinions and ideas held by the author. Questionable terms or references to chronological setting can give rise to doubts about the source.

All this is only preliminary to the more demanding stage of internal criticism. This deals with the interpretation of a written source. Still according to Startt and Sloan (1989: 121–2), internal criticism has two main aspects: examining the credibility of the author and interpreting the content. *Establishing credibility* of a source (be it a public document or a personal record) is concerned with evaluating the extent to which the source is telling the truth and involves a number of questions regarding someone's ability to report the truth.

- How near (in time and space) to the event was the source?
- How available was evidence to the source?
- How competent was the source to understand the event?

Competency can involve experience, class and cultural differences, and even physical fitness. Regarding willingness to express the truth, one can fall back on the basic proposition of intent. In the end, this step is to ascertain reliability of the source. What most affects the reliability of a source is the intention and prejudice of the writer. Was the purpose of producing a record to describe, to interpret, to condemn, to praise, to promote, to propagandize, to publicize, or to persuade? Documents written for posterity are suspect. A good example is distortions in autobiographies; Briggs was confronted with several difficulties in this area. For instance, most of the accounts of the BBC during the years covered in Volume II of the history (Briggs, 1965), were written by 'rebels', by people who were forced to leave, who did not like its ethos or who criticized its organization. According to Briggs (1980), even Reith ended up being a rebel.

Having established the reliability of the source, the final step is to *understand the content*. Without going into textual analysis, it is important to note that a source can be difficult to understand. Records can be 'misted' by archaic language, once-fashionable expressions and technical jargon. They might contain political or journalistic terminology. Perhaps they include references to ranks, grades and other terms of social, political, economic or administrative gradation. Moreover, some words change in meaning over time (e.g. imperialism, gay, correspondent, printer, broadcast, etc.), or according to how and by whom they are used (e.g. freedom of the press, democracy, entertainment, protest). Words can also have a more restricted meaning than they literally imply (e.g. public service, culture, social order, discipline). In dealing with historical documents, it is also important to take into account culture-bound assumptions and stereotypes of the day.

According to Tosh (1984: 56), in studying policy documents, *reliability* is hardly an issue, for in this type of research, documents and records are studied not as reports (i.e. testimonies of events 'out there'), but as part of a process (policy-making) that is itself the subject of enquiry. They are the creation of an institution, and therefore need to be examined in the context of that institution – its vested interests, its administrative routine and its record-keeping procedures.

Conclusion

It will have become obvious in this section that carrying out your own piece of media research is not a simple endeavour. Trying to turn a simple question about media production, content or reception into a proper research question and applying the right tools in an appropriate way to come up with a 'scientific' answer to your original question has been shown to require considerable effort.

I have tried to make clear that there is more than one way of going about it. Media studies have been shown to have both qualitative and quantitative traditions, concentrating on media producers and institutions, media content or media audiences. Certain approaches are based in a critical tradition, whereas other are more favoured in administrative research. Also, some tools may be more suited for studying unknown fields of interest, whereas other will be more rewarding when used to test an existing theory or research result. All different tools (quantitative or qualitative content analysis, surveys, individual or focus group interviews, ethnographic field research, document analysis) can be effective means of studying a research topic, provided that you follow the rules of the game set out in this section. This implies that you should consider whether you think a method is actually the most rewarding tool to come up with a proper answer to your question and, having established this, that you take care to use your tool in a rigorous way.

The most important 'message' throughout this section has been to show that there is not just one, ideal model of knowledge, science and scientific research but, at the same time, that there is something like good and bad science, and that as media scholars, we should aim at the former.

SUMMARY

Throughout this section, it has become clear that there is more than one way of carrying out 'good' communication and media research. Quantitative or qualitative, content or audience centred, inductive or deductive . . . all approaches have their own procedures, tools, protocols and rules of thumb to come up with a 'good' piece of research. This makes it very difficult to describe a single route to be taken in all types of media and communication research. Still, it can be interesting to try and work out some sort of 'list of things to do', with certain steps to be taken in the research process. Wimmer and Dominick (1994: 11) indicate eight steps in the research process, as do Hansen et al. (1998: 2). These have provided a good starting point for my final guidelines.

STEPS IN THE RESEARCH PROCESS

- *Select an area of research and a research problem.* Here one should try to combine academic, industrial or societal relevance with personal interest. It is very hard to study a research topic that one is not really interested in. Alternatively, studying something for totally idiosyncratic reasons, with no importance outside personal interest, can prove a waste of resources. The availability of these resources will often have a determining influence on the whole research project. The definition of the research problem takes the form of statements about a presumed occurrence or relationship.
- *Review existing literature and research relevant to the research problem.* When relevant, one should make a *status questionis*, i.e. a state of the research in that area so far. What is already known about the research problem? What results have been found yet? What questions still need to be asked? It is extremely important to make sure you are aware of what has and has not been done in the area you are interested in. This not only prevents you from re-inventing the wheel, it also helps to give you a better understanding of (the position of) your own research. This review should result in a revision and fine-tuning of your research problem and question(s).
- *Decide on one or more appropriate methods to collect your data.* This is a crucial stage in the research process. First, you should resist the temptation to simply use the method you like best or find most easy to use. It is very important to choose a method that will provide you with the right kind of data to answer your research question. This seems a very simple thing to do, but too often researchers opt for a method they feel most comfortable with, but that does not provide the right kind of data. Second, you should always consider the strength of triangulation. The weaknesses inherent in any one single method can be counterbalanced by using a complementary one. For instance, in policy research, the analysis of policy documents can be complemented by in-depth interviews with privileged witnesses. In this way, findings from one source can be triangulated with others. Consistencies as well as discrepancies can be identified, interpreted and pursued further.

- *Identify and select research material or subjects, and develop research instruments, protocols and parameters.* This means that you collect and prepare all the material and instruments necessary to collect your data. The actual steps to be taken here depend on, and differ according to, the method(s) chosen. These can include sampling, drawing up questionnaires, developing code books and so on. Here it is important to consider matters such as validity, reliability and relevance.
- *Pilot and fine-tune instruments, protocols, parameters.* Before analysing the entire corpus of research material, it is important to try out the research tools on a small sample. Often, this will lay bare some unforeseen problems and pitfalls. It will prevent massive reworking of the complete data collection.
- *Collect relevant data.* Once the instruments have been tested and fine-tuned, they can be used to collect all the data.
- *Analyse data.* As has been demonstrated in the chapters in this section, every method requires its own specific procedures to analyse the data. Still, it is always important, when analysing, to keep a firm eye on the original research question. It is very tempting to analyse all sorts of aspects but one should be careful not to do this just for the sake of it. The analysis should reflect on the original research question and should lead to a better understanding of the area of research.
- *Write up the research report.* Although this seems simple, it is in fact a laborious task that demands a great deal of time. It requires a clear exposition on the questions that were set, on the research that was done, on the results that were found, on what can be done further. In the case of triangulation, the different sources should be brought together and evaluated. Your own results should be reflected on in the light of other findings and theory.

Finally, it should be noted that the quality of the work will depend to a large extent on the sincerity of the researcher. Findings based on misguided respondents or sloppy coding will always backfire on you. For this reason, a high deontological standard is probably the most important research tool.

Further Reading

Altheide, D.L. (1996) *Qualitative Media Analysis*, Qualitative Research Methods Series 38. London: Sage

Gunter, B. (1999) *Media Research Methods. Measuring Audiences, Reactions and Impact.* London: Sage

Hansen, A., Cottle, S., Negrine, R. and Newbold, C. (1998) *Mass Communication Research Methods.* London: Macmillan

Wimmer, R.D. and Dominick, J.R. (1999) *Mass Media Research: An Introduction.* Belmont, CA: Wadsworth

Useful Websites

Useful websites that focus on quantitative methodology are:
http://www.statsoft.com/textbook/esc1.html
http://davidmlane.com/hyperstat/index.html
http://spps.com

Whilst useful qualitative sites are:
http://carbon.cudenver.edu/~mryder/itc_data/semiotics.html
http://www.ship.edu/~cgboeree/qualmeth.html

References

Adams, R.C. (1989) *Social Survey Methods for Mass Media Research.* Hillsdale, NJ: Lawrence Erlbaum

Altheide, D.L. (1996) *Qualitative Media Analysis,* Qualitative Research Methods Series 38. London: Sage

Anderson, J.A. (1987) *Communication Research: Issues and Methods.* New York, NY: McGraw-Hill

Barthes, R. (1967) *Système de la Mode.* Paris: Seuil

Barthes, R. (1972) *Mythologies.* New York: Hill & Wang

Berg, B.L. (1995) *Qualitative Research Methods for the Social Sciences.* Boston, Mass.: Allyn & Bacon

Berger, A.A. (1996) *Narratives in Popular Culture, Media and Everyday Life.* London: Sage

Berelson, B. (1952) *Content Analysis in Communication Research.* New York, NY: Free Press

Billiet, J. (1991) Research on question wording effects in survey. In *Graduate Management Research,* 66–80

Billiet, J. (1995) *Methoden van sociaal-wetenschappelijk onderzoek: ontwerp en dataverzameling.* Leuven: Acco

Billiet, J. and Loosveldt, G. (1988) Improvement of the quality of responses to factual survey questions by interviewer training. In *Public Opinion Quarterly* 52, 190–211

Billiet, J., Waterplas, L. and Loosveldt, G. (1992) Context effects as substantive data in social surveys. In Schwarz, N. and Sudman, N.M. (eds) *Context Effects in Social and Psychological Research.* New York, NY: Praeger

Billig, M. (1995) *Banal Nationalism.* London: Sage

Bourdieu, P. (1977) *Outline of a Theory of Practice.* Cambridge: Cambridge University Press

Branston, G. (1998) Histories of British television. In Geraghty, C. and Lusted, D. (eds) *The Television Studies Book.* London: Arnold

Briggs, A. (1965) *The Golden Age of The Wireless.* London: Oxford University Press

Briggs, A. (1980) Problems and possibilities in the writing of broadcasting history. In *Media, Culture and Society* 2, 5–23

Briggs, A. (1985) *The BBC: The First Fifty Years.* Oxford: Oxford University Press

Burgelman, J.C. (1988) Problemen voor de consultatie en wetenschappelijke relevantie van het, door de BRT en RTBF bewaarde omroearchief in België. In *Bibliotheek- en Archiefgids* 64(3), 211–20

Burgelman, J.C. (1991) *Omroep en politiek in België: Het Belgisch audiovisuele bestel als inzet en resultante van de naoorlogse partijpolitieke machtsstrategieën (1940–1960).* Brussels: BRT

Cardiff, D. and Scannell, P. (1987) Broadcasting and national unity. In Curran, J., Smith, A. *et al.* (eds) *Impacts and Influences.* London: Methuen, 157–73

Carton, A. (1995) Towards an effective evaluation of interviewers working within the context of a permanent network. In *Proceedings of the International Conference on Survey Measurement and Process Quality.* Alexandria, Virginia: American Statistical Association

Collins, R. (1998) *From Satellite to Single Market: New Communication Technology and European Public Service Television.* London: Routledge

Cottle, S. (1993) *TV News, Urban Conflict and the Inner City.* Leicester: Leicester University Press

Dahl, H.F. (1978) The art of writing broadcasting history. In *Gazette: International Journal for Mass Communication Studies* 14, 131–7

Dahl, H.F. (1994) The pursuit of media history. In *Media, Culture and Society* 16(4), 551–63

Das, S. (1998) Pictures of a native land: television producers and notions of Indianness. In Melkote, S. *et al.* (eds) *International Satellite Broadcasting in India: Political, Economic and Cultural Implications.* Lanham: University Press of America

Denzin, N.K. and Lincoln, Y.S. (1994) Introduction: entering the field of qualitative research. In Denzin, N.K. and Lincoln, Y.S. (eds) *Handbook of Qualitative Research.* London: Sage

Dexter, L. (1970) *Elite and Specialized Interviewing.* Evanston, IL: Chandler

Dillman, D.A. (1978) *Mail and Telephone Surveys. The Total Design Method.* New York, NY: Wiley

Ellis, J. (1992) *Visible Fictions: Cinema, Television, Video.* London: Routledge

Feldman, M.S. (1995) *Strategies for Interpreting Qualitative Data*. London: Sage

Fiske, J. (1990) *Introduction to Communication Studies*. London: Routledge

Fiske, J. (1995) *Television Culture*. London: Routledge

Fiske, J. and Hartley, J. (1978) *Reading Television*. London: Methuen

Foucault, M. (1980) Truth and power. In *Power/Knowledge: Selected Interviews and Other Writings*. Brighton: Harvester Press

Glaser, B.G. and Strauss, A.C. (1967) *The Discovery of Grounded Theory: Strategies for Qualitative Research*. Chicago, IL: Aldine

Goffman, E. (1959) *The Presentation of Self in Everyday Life*. Garden City, NY: Doubleday

Gold, R.L. (1958) Roles in sociological fieldwork. In *Social Forces* 36, 217–23

Gerbner, G. (1972) Violence in television drama: trends and symbolic functions. In Comstock, G.M. and Rubinstein, E.M. (eds) *Media Content and Control: Television and Social Behaviour* 1. Washington DC: Government Printing Office

Gerbner, G., Gross, L., Morgan, M. and Signorielli, N. (1980) The 'mainstreaming' of America: violence profile 11. *Journal of Communication* 30(3), 10–29

Greimas, A.J. (1966) *Sémiotique Structurale: Récherche de Méthode*. Paris: Larousse

Greimas, A.J. and Courtés, J. (1979) *Sémiotique. Dictionnaire Raisonné de la Théorie du Language*. Paris: Hachette

Gunter, B. (1999) *Media Research Methods. Measuring Audiences, Reactions and Impact.* London: Sage

Halloran, J.D. (1981) The context of mass communication research. In McAnny, E.G., Schnitman, J. and Janus, N. (eds) *Communication and Social Structure. Critical Studies in Mass Media Research*. New York, NY: Praeger

Halloran, J.D. (1991) Mass communication research: UK obstacles to progress. In *Intermedia* 19(4/5), 22–6

Hamilton, P. (1992) The Enlightenment Project and the birth of social science. In Hall, S. and Gieben, B. (eds) *Formations of Modernity*. Cambridge: Polity Press/Open University

Hammersley, M. and Atkinson, P. (1983) *Ethnography: Principles and Practice*. London: Tavistock

Hansen, A., Cottle, S., Negrine, R. and Newbold, C. (1998) *Mass Communication Research Methods*. London: Macmillan

Hartley, J. (1982) *Understanding News*. London: Methuen

Hill, M.R. (1993) *Archival Strategies and Techniques*, Qualitative Research Methods Series 31. London: Sage

Holstein, J.A. and Gubrium, J.F. (1995) *The Active Interview*. London: Sage

Holsti, O.R. (1969) *Content Analysis for the Social Sciences and Humanities*. Reading, MA: Addison-Wesley

Hsia, H.J. (1988) *Mass Communications Research Methods: A Step-By-Step Approach*. Hillsdale, NJ: Lawrence Erlbaum

Huberman, A.M. and Miles, M.B. (1994) Data management and analytic method. In Denzin, N.K. and Lincoln, Y.S. (eds) *Handbook of Qualitative Research*. London: Sage

Hüttner, H., Renckstorf, K. and Wester, F. (1995) *Onderzoekstypen in de communicatiewetenschap*. Houtem/Diegem: Bohn Stafleu Van Loghum

Jensen, K.B. and Jankowski, N.W. (1993) *A Handbook of Qualitative Methodologies for Mass Communication Research*. London: Routledge

Jones, S. (1985a) Depth interviewing. In Walker, R. (ed.) *Applied Qualitative Research*. Aldershot: Gower, 45–55

Jones, S. (1985b) The analysis of depth interviews. In Walker, R. (ed.) *Applied Qualitative Research*. Aldershot: Gower, 56–70

Jorgensen, D.L. (1989) *Participant Observation. A Methodology for Human Studies*. London: Sage

Junker, B. (1960) *Field Work*. Chicago, IL: University of Chicago

Katz, E. and Liebes, T. (1990) *The Export of Meaning. Cross-Cultural Readings of 'Dallas'*. Oxford: Oxford University Press

Kirk, J. and Miller, M.L. (1986) *Reliability and Validity in Qualitative Research*, Qualitative Research Methods Series 1. London: Sage

Krippendorf, K. (1980) *Content Analysis: An Introduction to its Methodology*. London: Sage

Laswell, H.D. (1927) *Propaganda Technique in the World War*. New York, NY: Knopf

Lavrakas, J. (1993) *Telephone Survey Methods. Sampling, Selection and Supervision*. London: Sage

Leach, E. (1976) *Culture and Communication. The Logic by which Symbols are Connected: An Introduction to the Use of Structuralist Analysis in Social Anthropology*. Cambridge: Cambridge University Press

Lee, D. (1992) *Competing Discourses: Perspective and Ideology in Language*. London: Longman

Lévi-Strauss, C. (1966) *The Savage Mind*. London: Wiedenfeld & Nicholson

Lindlof, T.R. (1995) *Qualitative Communication Research Methods*. London: Sage

Lisch, R. and Kritz, J. (1978) *Grundlagen und Modellen der Inhaltanalyse. Bestandsaufname und Kritik*. Reinbek: Rowohlt

Lotman, Y. (1990) *Universe of the Mind: A Semiotic Theory of Culture*. Bloomington, IN: Indiana University Press

Lull, J. (ed.) (1988) *World Families Watch Television*. Newbury Park: Sage

Lyotard, J.-F. (1984) *The Postmodern Condition: A Report on Knowledge*. Manchester: Manchester University Press

MacCracken, G. (1988) *The Long Interview*. London: Sage

MacLennan, G. (1992) The Enlightenment Project revisited. In Hall, S., Held, D. and McGrew, T. (eds) *Modernity and its Futures*. Cambridge: Polity Press/Open University

MacManus, J.H. (1994) *Market-Driven Journalism*. London: Sage

McQuail, D., Blumler, J.G. and Brown, J.R. (1972) The television audience: a revised perspective. In McQuail, D. (ed.) *Sociology of Mass Communications*. Harmondsworth: Penguin

Malinowski, B. *et al.* (1922) *Argonauts of the Western Pacific: An Account of Native Enterprise and Adventure in the Archipelagoes of Melanesian New Guinea*. London: Routledge

Manning, K. and Cullum-Swan, B. (1994) Narrative, content and semiotic analysis. In Denzin, N.K. and Lincoln, Y.S. (eds) *Handbook of Qualitative Research*. London: Sage, 463–77

Manson, J. (1996) *Qualitative Researching*. London: Sage

Melody, W.H. and Mansell, R.E. (1983) The debate over critical vs administrative research: circularity or challenge. In *Ferment in the Field, Journal of Communication* 33(3), 103–16

Merton, R.K. and Kendall, L. (1946) The focused interview. In *American Journal of Sociology* 51, 541–57

Michiello, V., Aroni, R., Timewell, E. and Alexander, L. (1992) *In-Depth Interviewing. Researching People*. Melbourne: Longman Cheshire

Morrison, D.E. and Tumber, H. (1988) *Journalists at War: The Dynamics of News Reporting During the Falklands Conflict*. London: Sage

Morley, D. (1980) *The Nationwide Audience: Structure and Decoding*. London: British Film Institute

Morley, D. and Brunsdon, C. (eds) (1999) *The Nationwide Television Studies*. London: Routledge

Negrine, R. (1985) Cable television in Great Britain. In Negrine, R. (ed.) *Cable Television and the Future of Broadcasting*. Kent: Croom Helm

Page, A. (2000) *Cracking Morse Code: Semiotics and Television Drama*. Luton: University of Luton Press

Pattyn, B. (ed.) (2000) *Media Ethics: Opening Social Dialogue*. Leuven: Peeters

Peirce, C.S. (1931–66) *Collected Papers of Charles Sanders Peirce*, ed. Hartshorne, C.H., Weiss and Burks, A.W. (eight vols). Cambridge: Belknap Press of Harvard University Press

Priest, S.H. (1996) *Doing Media Research: An Introduction*. London: Sage

Propp, V. (1968) *The Morphology of the Folktale*. Austin, TX: University of Texas Press

Roe, K. (1998) Children and computer games: a profile of the heavy user. In *European Journal of Communication* 13(2), 181–200

Saussure, F. de (1916–72) *Cours de Linguistique Générale*. Paris: Payot

Sayer, A. (1992) *Method in Social Science*. London: Routledge

Scannell, P. (1993) The origin of BBC regional policy. In Harvey, S. and Robins, K. (eds) *The Regions, the Nation and the BBC*. London: British Film Institute, 27–37

Schlesinger, P. (1991) *Media, State and Nation*. London: Sage

Schlesinger, P. (1994) Europe's contradictory communicative space. In *Daedalus* 123(2): 25–52

Schlesinger, P. and Tumber, H. (1994) *Reporting Crime*. Oxford: Clarendon Press

Selby, K. and Cowdery, R. (1995) *How to Study Television*. Basingstoke: Macmillan

Seldon, A. and Pappworth, J. (1983) *By Word of Mouth. Elite Oral History*. London: Methuen

Silverman, D. (1993) *Interpreting Qualitative Data: Methods for Analysing Talk, Text and Interaction*. London: Sage

Silverstone, R. (1981) *The Message of Television: Myth and Narrative in Contemporary Culture*. London: Heinemann

Smith, M.J. (1988) *Contemporary Communication Research Methods*. Belmont, CA: Wadsworth

Smythe, D.W. and Van Dinh, T. (1983) On critical and administrative research: a new critical analysis. In *Ferment in the Field, Journal of Communication* 33(3), 117–27

Startt, J.D. and Sloan, W.D. (1989) *Historical Methods in Mass Communication*. Hillsdale, NJ: Lawrence Erlbaum

Strange, N. (1998) Perform, educate, entertain: ingredients of the cookery programme genre. In Geraghty, C. and Lusted, D. (eds) *The Television Studies Book*. London: Arnold

Strinati, D. (1995) *Introduction to Theories of Popular Culture*. London: Routledge

Taylor, L. and Willis, A. (1999) *Media Studies. Texts, Institutions and Audiences*. Oxford: Blackwell

Tesch, R. (1990) *Qualitative Research. Analysis Types and Software Tools*. New York, NY: Falmer Press

Thomas, J. (1993) *Doing Critical Ethnography*, Qualitative Research Methods Series 26. London: Sage

Todorov, T. (1977) *The Poetics of Prose*. Oxford: Blackwell

Tosh, J. (1984) *The Pursuit of History. Aims, Methods and New Directions in the Study of Modern History*. London: Longman

Tukle, S. (1996) *Life on the Screen: Identity in the Age of the Internet*. London: Wiedenfeld

University of California Center for Communication and Social Policy (CCSP) *et al.* (1998) *National Television Violence Study 3*. Thousand Oaks, CA: Sage

Van den Bulck, J. (1999) Does the presence of a third person affect estimates of TV viewing and other media use. In *Communications* 24(1), 105–15

Van den Bulck, H. (2001) Public service broadcasting as a project of modernity: the instance of Flemish television. In *Media, Culture and Society* 23(1), 53–69

Van Poecke, L. (1991) *Verbale Communicatie*. Leuven: Garant

Van Poecke, L. (2000) Media culture and identity construction: the shift from modernity to post-modernity. In Pattyn, B. (ed.) *Media Ethics: Opening Social Dialogue*. Leuven: Peeters

Van Zoonen, L. (1994) *Feminist Media Studies*. London: Sage

Weber, R.P. (1990) *Basic Content Analysis*, Quantitative Applications in the Social Sciences Series 49. London: Sage

Wetherell, M. and Potter, J. (1992) *Mapping the Language of Racism: Discourse and the Legitimation of Exploitation*. Hemel Hempstead: Harvester Wheatsheaf

White, D.M. (1950) 'The gatekeeper': a case study in the selection of news. In *Journalism Quarterly* 27(4), 383–90

Wimmer, R.D. and Dominick, J.R. (1994) *Mass Media Research: An Introduction* (fourth edn). Belmont, CA: Wadsworth

The Moving Image

Chris Newbold

Introduction

This section is concerned with one form of media and communication content: the moving image. It provides a critically and theoretically informed examination of moving image content, its development and the key theories through which it can be analysed. We will consider its structure, its component parts, codes and conventions, styles and movements, and the demands of modern visual culture that unite all moving image products. This is developed, first, through examining the language of the moving image; we will then consider the history of the moving image and look at the first film products and film artists; finally we will examine key theories such as genre and narrative, which so dominate our critical understanding of the moving image. This section illustrates these discussions with examples and case studies drawn from some of the most influential moving image products, their styles, concerns and contributions. Here, we stress the importance of an understanding, not only of the construction of the moving image, but also of its history and development, as it is through an examination of these that we can come to understand the many forms and styles of moving image that so dominate the contemporary world.

The term moving image is used in this section to mean all mechanically, technologically and electronically produced images that are in some way active, are used by an audience, and are mediated through film, television, video, or computer screen. In a world of multimedia digital production, the barriers between types of image technology may already have crumbled, however, the audience still consumes moving image through a range of home, work and leisure centre-based media.

CHAPTER 15

Understanding the Moving Image

INTRODUCTION

In this chapter we start our examination of the moving image by discussing moving image language and techniques. In particular we focus on the use of camera (movement and shot), lighting, framing and the arrangement of characters, combined with the use of editing, sound and music to construct the moving image as we know and experience it, both in its fictional and non-fictional guise. It is important to think in these terms, since the first step in understanding the moving image is to recognize its component parts, the fact that nothing is there naturally or by accident, that there is intention behind every thing we see and hear. It is the recognition of this construction that the first part of this section is concerned with.

MOVING   IMAGE   PRODUCTION   AND LANGUAGE

As I have stated elsewhere: 'the first step to be taken in any moving image analysis, has to be that of standing apart from the text or texts that you are approaching, and *stopping them dead'* (Newbold, 1998: 132).

It is essential in attempting to understand the techniques and language of the moving image that we separate ourselves from the seamless and constant flow of images and stories, and are able to start to dismantle the individual component parts that make up the whole, and thus deconstruct their meaning. A useful starting point is becoming aware that the production and language of the moving image is governed and constrained by codes and conventions that are understood by both the producers and the audience. These are an essential part of the communication process; without these 'rules' or 'short-cuts' the process of communicating through moving images would be a rather laborious one of constant re-learning. We have throughout our lifetimes' viewing been socialized into the way we see and read the moving image, this is taken-for-granted knowledge that we all share.

Codes are the rules that govern the construction of the moving image, and the way that language is produced and communicates (for example, the use of the reverse-angle shot in the filming of a conversation or interview between two people, or the 180° rule when filming such a conversation), while conventions can be seen as the established practices that have become associated with particular types of moving image production or genre. A narrative convention of the traditional gangster film is that after the gangster's rise he must always be seen to fall, often in a very brutal way (see *Scarface*, 1983). A visual convention might be the dark urban setting of such films. A convention of factual news television might be on-screen newsreader facing the camera, addressing the audience directly. These codes and conventions reveal themselves as such when we try to imagine these situations in any other way than the way they are presented to us.

Recognition of codes and conventions is an essential part of understanding the moving image. However, a thorough knowledge of the nuts and bolts of production is the key to unlocking the language and meanings that we all read in our day-to-day experience of television, film and video. Thus, we shall spend a little time examining what we shall call the signifying systems. These can be divided into the technical and symbolic. The technical being camera angles, camera movement, shot duration, lighting, **depth of field**, editing, sound, sound effects, music, special effects, framing, etc., while the symbolic can be seen as colour/black and white, costume, objects, stars, performance, setting, location, etc. That is, those features of moving image language that are contained within that which the audience sees rather than those that are part of its 'seamless' technical construction.

The technical signifying systems can be divided into four main areas: the camera, editing, lighting and sound. A knowledge of the technical terms and their use provides us with not only the vocabulary to discuss content but, crucially, an insight into how moving image meaning is encoded or constructed.

The Camera

As it is the visual imperative that drives the moving image, it is the camera that first of all concerns us. For the purpose of the discussion here, we can split this into three areas: type of shot, lenses and camera movement.

Types of Shot

The shot is the smallest unit of film construction, it is the time from when the camera starts until it stops, or it is the length of film from one edit to the next. There are many types of shot, but the most significant are listed in Table 15.1.

The extreme long shots and long shots are more prevalent in film production than in television and video simply because of the size of the medium; indeed it is often the power of these shots that is lost when the pictures are reduced for television use. It is the medium shot and the close-up that dominate television production.

Lenses

The variety of lenses used is important, in that different lenses alter the type of image seen on the screen, having different effects on the subject, as illustrated in Table 15.2.

Full zoom, however, has the effect of exaggerating any shakiness of the camera, thus most film and television producers prefer to physically move the camera itself. Camera movement is of central importance, for it is the ability to follow moving action, or scan around a scene that in part separates the moving image camera from the still camera.

Table 15.1   *Types of shot*

Type of shot	Description	Use	Example
Extreme long shot/ establishing shot or wide shot	A scenic shot, which shows the location. Usually a long wide-angle view of a particular, or familiar, location associated with the narrative.	Often used to relate a person to their particular environment, conveying a consider-able amount of information in one shot.	Essential in the western genre, where the open-ing sequence establishes the hero in 'their' land-scape, such as in *The Gunfighter* (1950), or the vulnerability of the stagecoach in *Stagecoach* (1939).
Long shot or full shot	Shot of a character that includes both head and feet. If more than one character is included this is called a cover shot.	An important shot in viewing the relative proportions of objects and people, their sizes, shapes and placement.	Used by television reporters standing at particular or recogniz-able locations. Akira Kurosawa uses the cover shot in *Yojimbo* to emphasize the two warring camps.
Mid- or medium shot	The typical shot in studio television, it emphasizes some detail on a person, usually taken from waist up and filling most of the screen. Close objects around the person can be seen.	Showing the person or object to some extent isolated from their overall environment. In editing, often used as a transition shot between a long shot and a close-up.	Newsreaders are, more often than not, filmed in mid-shot, as are tele-vision quiz masters.
Close-up	Provides a magnified shot of a part of a person (head, arms, legs, etc.) or object.	Close-ups bestow a high dramatic sense or great symbolic value. They provide emphasis. They also direct the audience's attention, and establish identification or empathy with characters.	In *film noir* filmes such as *Double Indemnity* (1944), objects such as Phyllis's anklet are emphasized and given meaning by the close-up, as are fragile objects in films such as *The Big Heat* (1953) and *Laura* (1944).
Extreme close-up or big close-up	Clinical detail, showing only parts of faces and objects filling the screen.	Serves to greatly heighten tension, drama and horror.	In Buñuel's *Un Chien Andalou* (1929) the extreme close-up of an eyeball being cut by a razor is one of the most disturbing shots in cinema history.
Point of view (POV)	We see the world from the central character's subjective view, seeing what he or she sees.	Promotes identification with the central character.	In *Peeping Tom* (1960) we see murder through the camera lens the murderer is holding to record the event.

The variety of lenses   Table 15.2

Lens	Description	Use	Example
Zoom	The standard lens in film and television production, this enables a shot to be changed without stopping the camera – it is the frame that alters.	The audience's attention can be directed to specific objects or people within a shot.	Modern docu-soaps such as *Big Brother, Castaway,* or *Shipwrecked.*
Wide angle	The wide-angle lens provides a large angle of view.	In long shots or establishing shots, it provides a large focus range – that is, good depth of field. Used for sense of distortion in close-ups.	At the beginning of westerns, establishing the hero in his land-scape. Psychological thrillers or horror films.
Telephoto	Compresses images from far away and close up.	Can be used from some distance in order not to disturb the subject being filmed.	Documentaries – especially wildlife documentaries.
Fish eye	Stretches the object, bending it at the edge of the screen. The fish-eye lens works against the conventions of standard lenses.	The image imbues the scene with the sense of tension and drama. Characters look isolated or disturbed in their surroundings.	The films of directors like Wong Kar-Wai who film the isolated individual in the claustrophobic Hong Kong streets. Also used in a lot of rap videos such as those of Missy Elliot or Mase.

Movement

Hand-held camera movement is very important for freedom of movement in documentary-making. It has become a convention of many realist fiction films, such as those of the British New Wave, or those who wish to parody newsreel or documentary footage, such as the attack on the airforce base in *Dr Strangelove* (1963), or *Man Bites Dog* (1992) or, more famously, *The Blair Witch Project* (1999).

Viewing position

Camera angle, or the viewing position of the camera, is its placement in relation to the object or person on view. Angle can be used both for aesthetic and psychological values; most importantly, it can add to the spatial relations and thus diminish the two-dimensionality of an image on the screen. The main use of the camera is in the straight-on position. Low angle is where the camera is placed below eye level and looks up at the subject, often ascribing to it power, stature and control. High angle is where the camera looks down on its

Table 15.3 *Camera movement*

Movement	Description	Use	Example
Panning	Movement of the camera on the horizontal plane.	Action, or a character can be followed. A locale can be scanned, as in an establishing shot.	In the Coliseum scenes in *Gladiator* (2000), the camera pans around the crowd after Maximus's victory.
Tilting	Movement of the camera on the vertical plane.	A tall building, or a character can be scanned from top to bottom.	At the beginning of *The Spy Who Loved Me* (1977) Bond skies off a cliff, the camera follows him down until his parachute opens.
Tracking	The camera is mounted on a dolly and pushed on tracks, or is on a moving object or crane.	Moving action can be followed either close up, or at a distance. The audience stays with the events as they happen.	In Jean-Luc Godard's *Weekend* (1966), the camera tracks along a traffic jam for 7 minutes. *Citizen Kane* (1941) has a spectacular crane shot entering a nightclub.

subjects, making them look small, insignificant and sometimes vulnerable, especially if it is an individual in a lonely street. Leni Riefenstahl's Nazi propaganda film *Triumph of the Will* (1934) uses camera angles to great effect. First, the low-angle shot is used to look up at Adolf Hitler, bestowing control, strength and presence on him. Second, the high-angle shot is used to look down on the mass ranks of his supporters, adding to the feeling of spectacle and power.

Duration of shot

Length of take, or duration of shot, can alter the audience's sense of time and space. Long takes tend to incorporate tracking and panning or tilting shots. Long takes are particularly favoured by some documentarists such as Robert Flaherty in films like *Man of Aran* (1934), since they relate real time rather than screen time. Length of shot, particularly of a close-up, can heighten the drama and intimacy or even disturb the audience.

Framing

Framing is important in moving image production, since it is the positioning of people and objects within the limits of what we can see that contributes to the development of the narrative. In films such as *The Big Sleep* (1946) the developing relationship between the Humphrey Bogart character and the Lauren Bacall character is portrayed through the space between them. The spatial relations help convince us of the reality of what we are watching as well as pushing the narrative along. The principal elements of framing relate to camera distance, lens choice, camera movement and camera angle. The recognition that what exists within the frame, what passes before the viewer is not on the whole there by accident but is deliberately selected and placed, is essential to any decoding or analysis. This is also true of the positioning of the camera, whereby each scene is shot according to the intention of the director.

Editing

As we shall see in the next chapter, it was the camera, and photography, that kick-started the moving image, however it was the development of editing that set it on the path towards narrative dominance. The splicing together of two pieces of film meant that the moving image could transcend time and space, and develop longer narratives composed of multiple scenes. The importance of the development of cutting or editing, and montage editing in particular, is in the understanding of the relationship between shots. The simplest form of early editing was the straight cut, where one shot was instantly replaced by a second (this was often done 'in-camera'), which might then be replaced by a third, or it might be cross-cut to another line of the developing story. Shots linked together become scenes – that is, a series of shots in one setting. Scenes become sequences, or self-contained blocks of dramatic action. These linked together become the plot and the narrative.

Perhaps above all other technical codes, it is the recognition of editing techniques that enables us to identify the apparently seamless quality of the moving image. Often seen as the most creative and intellectual part of the film-making process, it is the editor who, through creative techniques, is ultimately responsible for the construction of the scenes into the plot and narrative. The editor's role can also affect the tempo, and thus the dramatic effect, of the product. Editing plays a key role, through the construction of space and time, in the realism, or the **verisimilitude** of the film. In most moving image products, the construction of time and space is subordinated to the logic of the narrative and, in particular, its cause–effect chain.

In Sergei Eisenstein's version of montage editing, it is the relationship between the shots that not only drives the narrative and creates meaning, but is also the source of film art, in that the shots are arranged creatively by the editor/director in order to generate emotional and intellectual impact by their juxtaposition. In *Battleship Potemkin* (1925) Eisenstein juxtaposes shots of a crucifix, a sword and the Russian imperial crest, thus creating the association of the church, the military and the Tsar with the oppression of the sailors on the battleship.

Sergei Eisenstein
Eisenstein's (1898–1948) contribution to film was as a director and a theorist. He was also at the forefront of what Lenin called the 'first revolutionary art': Bolshevik film. Eisenstein was a pioneer of Soviet cinema, in particular he took Lev Kuleshov's conception of montage editing as an expressive and symbolic process and developed it into concrete

practice in films such as *Strike* (1924) and *Battleship Potemkin.* Eisenstein considered that there was a bond between art and revolution – for him, art came through revolution, and revolution came through art. To this end he supported a move to a more intellectual cinema, built not only on the montage of attractions, but also through:

- symbolism
- experimental film
- the use of typage
- rejection of orthodox stage acting
- use of non-professional actors
- emotional engagement, not sentimentality
- the mass as hero.

His films had an eyewitness character. Footage from *October* (1928), for example, often appears in documentary films about the Russian Revolution masquerading as actuality film.

In a chequered career, disrupted by disagreements with the communist regime, Eisenstein made some of the great films of moving image history, *Ivan the Terrible* (Parts 1 and 2) being one of the most important.

Lighting

Lighting and the control of light is central to all moving image production, not only in terms of exposure and artistic use, it is also important in terms of visual perception, since bright objects automatically attract the eye. Light for moving image production comes from either available/natural light or artificial light. A great deal is made of the use of natural light for 'realist' films and documentaries. Artificial light is used in two main senses: for set lighting and for actor lighting. Artificial lighting can be used not only to create the sense of time and place, but also mood and character.

The terms high-key lighting and low-key lighting generally refer to the quality of lighting; thus high key describes an equal amount of lighting across a scene, while low key indicates that there is less light on the entire scene, creating greater contrasts and areas of light and shade. The convention of lighting is that high key will usually be used in musical or comedy products and television studio programmes where everything is open to viewer scrutiny, while low key occurs in horror films and, say, film noir mysteries and thrillers.

Film noir

The term film noir is used to describe a particular kind of dark suspense/thriller/melodrama. Although *The Maltese Falcon* (1941) is seen as being the first Hollywood film noir, the majority of the classic films of this type were made between 1945 and 1955. These include titles such as *Double Indemnity* (1944), *The Big Sleep* (1946), *Gilda* (1947), *They Live by Night* (1948), *In a Lonely Place* (1950), *The Big Heat* (1953) and *While the City Sleeps* (1955).

All these films are characterized by a strong visual style, relying heavily on extreme lighting contrasts in order to evoke mood, character and a sense of place. Character lighting can imbue actors with unknown depths, giving them a sense of mystery, offering hints at hidden dangers and the two sides to their characters. Light illuminating various aspects of the frame can help with the claustrophobic framing and the sense of a world off-balance that is so important to film noir. While back-lighting, especially through venetian blinds, staircases or window frames, can produce shadows of bars cast across characters, indicating entrapment. The plethora of shadows, bright and dark lines cast across walls, neo-lights, and the hidden alleyways and doorways hint at the night-time world inhabited by the film noir hero. This world is predominantly urban, with typically rain-soaked streets, bounded by bars, motels and speakeasies. The film noir hero is usually a police detective, or private eye; he is usually drawn into a murder by a *femme fatale* 'dressed to kill' in a long, tight-fitting black dress with a plunging neckline, stilettos, long gloves and a cigarette waiting to be lit by an unsuspecting male victim.

This visual style owes a great deal to the look of **German expressionism** imported into Hollywood by émigré directors such as Billy Wilder, Fritz Lang and Otto Preminger. Film noir remains a popular style today with neo-noir films, or film noir in colour, still being made.

Sound

Sound codes can be split into two kinds. First, diegetic sound, which is sound that emanates from the scene such as sound effects and dialogue. Non-diegetic sound is sound that does not emanate from the scene we are watching, and is essentially music or a voice-over. Sound effects are often used to create realism, but these can, similarly, be divided into two kinds: first, atmospheric sounds, background noises such as the wind, or birds singing and so on; and, second, sound effects that are justified – that is, they are sounds relating directly to what we are seeing, explosions or gunshots, etc. Music can be diegetic in that it may be part of the drama of a film based on a musician: *The Glenn Miller Story* (1953), for example. Most often, music is functional – that is, it is there to help direct the mood of the audience, to reinforce the pace of the screen action, or to provide a musical motif, such as the James Bond theme, behind the moving image.

Dialogue

The dialogue in narrative film is going to be of crucial importance, most often it is done in lip-sync, but can also be heard as a voice-over. Dialogue is most often scripted speech. However, many film-makers in the 'realist' tradition look for their actors, be they professional or non-professional, to improvise speech so as to heighten the realism of the product they are trying to create (as in the bedroom scene between Jean Seberg and Jean Paul Belmondo in Jean-Luc Goddard's *A Bout de Souffle* (1961)).

Special effects

Special effects exploit the qualities of the moving image medium in ways during the production and post-production phases so as to persuade the audience of the reality, verisimilitude, or sheer spectacle of the product. Production techniques might involve pyrotechnics, optical effects or trick photography. Post-production might include animation, superimposition or computer graphics. Other special effects might involve the use of chromakey or a matte (or masking) shot, in order to insert or combine images. Special effects not only dominate action films such as the *Die Hard* series, and television programmes such as *Buffy the Vampire Slayer* or *Roswell High*, but are food and drink to the music video business, from David Bowie's negative effects in the *Ashes to Ashes* (1980) video to Michael Jackson's *Thriller* (1983) and Will Smith's *Men in Black*.

Symbolic signifying systems

Colour, and black and white film

The use of colour and/or black and white film can convey both realistic and expressive messages. Each can convey atmosphere and underscore the theme of a moving image product. Warm colours are red, yellow and gold, while cold colours are blue and green. For example, in Jean-Jacques Beineix's *Betty Blue* (1986), changes in colour as the film progresses indicate changes in the relationship between the two central characters, as well as changes of mood within the film itself. The use of sepia in moving image products is often a code for the past or old film.

Costume and objects

Costume has been the mainstay of both genre and narrative production since the beginning of moving image history. It is used not only to connote time and place, but also to provide spectacle to products. Objects are also a key symbolic source of information in moving image products. They can have both connotative and mythic resonance. For example, the sheriff's badge in the western genre ties him to the community he serves as well as marking him out as the 'good' guy. Hence, sheriff Will Kane's action at the end of Fred Zinnemann's *High Noon* (1952) in throwing down the sheriff's badge, has particular meaning and significance within the film and the genre.

Stars

Stars are particular icons who carry symbolic power, and are identified with particular genres and personality traits. Arnold Schwarzenegger is associated with action/adventure films and portrays hero/anti-hero-type figures. Through the star system, film in particular depends on the popular appeal of star personalities to keep the audience coming back for more. Typecasting and genre recognition can become a problem for certain big-name stars; Schwarzenegger, for example, has tried to combat his *Terminator* (1984) image with films such as *Kindergarten Cop* (1990).

Performance

An actor's *performance* is also a symbolic element, being tied not only to the narrative, but to the generation of meaning within the film. The notion of performance is best understood and analysed by considering its physicality. That is, that the attention of the audience is drawn in by the movement, physique, facial features and personality displays of the actor. Because the large screen exaggerates movement, restraint is a central part of an actor's performance. Subtle emotional and character shadings reveal the quality of a performance as well as the verisimilitude of the character.

Mise-en-scène

Mise-en-scène, which literally means 'putting into a scene', can be understood as everything that is placed within the frame – the total picture: the content of the frame, the image, set design, costume, objects and their placement, the spatial relations (those who are dominant within the frame, the relationship between characters seen in terms of the distance between them). It is through *mise-en-scène* that all the above technical devices combine and work, and are thus understood by the audience. *Mise-en-scène* also points us towards understanding the role of the director in the construction of the moving image (we will look at in more depth in Chapter 18).

Setting and location

Mise-en-scène relies heavily on two important symbolic elements: the setting and the location. The setting establishes the time and the place of the narrative, be it historical, contemporary or futuristic. Many of the symbolic elements mentioned above are essential to helping establish the setting and thus the wider *mise-en-scène*. Setting, as we shall see later, is key in assisting our generic memory, developing expectations of the type of narrative we might expect. Specific genres in particular are tied to specific settings: westerns such as *The Searchers* (1956), for instance, with their wilderness landscapes; or gangster films such as *Once Upon A Time in America* (1984) with their predominantly urban settings. Location work is also important since it is the shooting of a scene outside of the totally constructed studio situation. Realist film- and programme-makers in particular endeavour to use location shooting much more than studio work, in order to establish a feeling of authenticity; the work of Italian neo-realism in films such as *Rome Open City* (1945), and British New Wave film-makers in films such as *Saturday Night and Sunday Morning* (1961) are good examples here.

The technical and symbolic devices we have discussed do not work in isolation, in any one scene many of these codes will have been working together in order to create the encoded meaning. The technical and symbolic elements, and the codes and conventions discussed in this first chapter of this section contribute to the opacity of much moving image production – that is, its need to conceal its own construction. It is only in taking these elements and *stopping them dead* that we can begin to understand their role in the construction of the moving image, and how it communicates its meaning.

CHAPTER 16

The Early Moving Image

PRE-MOVING IMAGE

In this chapter, we will consider the early pioneers of film-making and their contributions to the development of film technologies and film production techniques. An understanding of early conventions and film **aesthetics** is important in that these lay the foundations for the moving image we recognize today; indeed one might go so far as to say that, within the first decade of film production, all the codes, conventions and techniques we are familiar with as being part of moving image language, aesthetics and composition, had already been established.

Moving images did not suddenly jerk into life in Paris on 22 March 1895, with the creation of Auguste and Louis Lumière's Cinematograph, as popular mythology would have it. The moving image has a long prehistory. People across the globe had witnessed images moving on screens in one form or another for many centuries. If desired, it is possible to trace a linear history of moving images, from the multi-legged wild boar of the prehistoric Altamira cave paintings in Spain, to the magic lantern, such as Kirchener demonstrated in Rome in 1640, the camera obscura first developed in the sixteenth century, the various optical toys of the nineteenth century such as the Thaumatrope or the Zoetrope, finally to the invention of photography in 1839 and then the Cinematograph. All of these are concerned with the construction of images in order to recreate in one form or another 'real' images and 'real' movement. However accurate this linear history might be, it is inevitably somewhat reductionist.

A number of inventions, concerns and sciences need to come together in order for the moving image as we know it to emerge. There are four key areas, or prerequisites that are essential for the development of moving images: the scientific enquiry into the persistence of vision and of movement; the development of photographic reproduction; the construction of mechanisms of projection; and, finally, the emergence of visual culture and pre-existing forms of visual entertainment.

The first of these is the science of the persistence of vision. This is concerned with the physiological phenomena that the optic nerves retain an image for about a third of a second after the observation has ceased; these observations then merge into one. Persistence of vision was seen to be achieved at about 16 frames (or photographs) per second. This principle was first observed by the ancient Greeks, but published as a theory by Joseph Plateau in 1829. Both the Thaumatrope and the Zoetrope mentioned above illustrate this, in that both have spinning visual images that merge into one moving image when they are rotated. In modern cinema, 24 frames per second are projected, giving the illusion of movement.

Much of the work in the scientific study of motion is characterized by Eadweard Muybridge. Having been asked by Central Pacific Railroad president Leland Stanford to photograph the motion of his favourite racehorse, Muybridge developed a shutter system whereby a battery of still cameras would photograph the horse as it passed by on wooden boards triggering each shot. Coming under the patronage of the University of Pennsylvania, Muybridge extended his work producing not only moving images, but a large number of publications, for both scientific and popular consumption.

The second important area in the development of moving images was the development of photography. Louis Daguerre in France and William Fox Talbot in England were both working around the period of 1839, and are both hailed by their respective nations as the inventors of photography. The daguerreotype developed by Daguerre in 1839 fixed a positive image on to silvered sensitized copper plate with an exposure time of just less than 30 minutes. Bought by the French government, this development was made freely available and thus popularized the 'new art' of photography. William Fox Talbot had been experimenting with fixing images on to paper since about 1834. In 1840 he developed calotype, which made possible the reproduction of prints, through his use of the negative/positive principle. This initial exposure time was 3 minutes, but by changing from silver chloride to collidon, Talbot reduced this time to one-hundredth of a second. With the discovery of the plastic base of cellulose in 1855 by Alexander Parkes, the use of celluloid in photography was a logical step, the first photographic film being produced by Ferrier in 1879. Ten years later Kodak marketed celluloid roll film developed by George Eastman.

Alongside the developments in the sciences of vision and movement, and the development of photography, the mechanics of projection is the third important development we must consider. The origins of much of the work on projection lie in the development of the magic lantern, which had its antecedence in shadow theatre. By the end of the nineteenth century, however, the complexity and ingenuity of magic lantern displays were certainly an influence on, if not a rival to, the emerging cinema. As we shall see, people such as Georges Méliès were not only magic lantern theatre owners, but used many of their techniques in their own film productions. First clearly enunciated by Athanasius Kircher in 1646 and first illustrated by him in 1671, magic lanterns became popular entertainments, not only at public venues but also at private home showings during the eighteenth century. It was this century and the nineteenth that saw the emergence of what might be described as the first mass audiences for optical entertainments. Thus a great many techniques and devices were built upon the early mechanisms in order to make them more exciting, more vivid and to some extent more realistic. By sophisticated management of shutters, blinds and other light-controlling mechanisms, lighting transformations could be achieved. By using two separate (or even three) lanterns, dissolves and superimpositions could be achieved. By mechanical devices used on images pushed slowly through the projector, the illusion of movement could be reproduced.

The fourth and final strand in the development of film might be called the emerging visual culture – that is, the demand from a wide-ranging audience for optically based entertainments. To some extent visual illustrative entertainments had been confined to religious subjects throughout the world, be they in the form of sculpture or paintings. There were also visual entertainments linked to folktales and traditional myths, illustrated by shadow theatres, puppet shows or magic lanterns. Other pre-existing forms of visual entertainment ranged from the special effects toys (of interest to adults as much as children) already mentioned, to the age-old forms of public exhibition and spectacle, ranging from fairgrounds and magical shows to music halls, Vaudeville, puppet shows, shadow theatre and, as we have seen, sophisticated magic lantern shows. The nineteenth century is important here, not necessarily because of industrialization or urbanization, or even increased leisure time (although this is entirely relative), but due to the rise of professional entertainments at every social level, ranging from libraries to concert halls, and public houses to theatres in the widest sense. The audience desire for simple sensation and visual spectacle had become a major part of the entertainment of the urban masses in the second half of the nineteenth century. The interest in mechanical and natural curiosities was one inherited from the fairground tradition, which found a home in the moral and intellectual crusades of the later nineteenth century. Not only was literacy and education on the agenda but celebrations of national achievement such as the Great Exhibition, held in London in 1851, provided ample uplifting entertainment courtesy of the wonders of the age. The fair tradition also continued, with showmen like Barnum and Bailey, and Buffalo Bill, who had rapidly realized the showbusiness potential of the idea of the American West. Indeed, Buffalo Bill's wild west show was translated directly to film in 1894, when the Edison Kinetograph (see below) recorded the show.

These four broad areas, or lines of enquiry and development, were by the 1880s being recognized and followed, producing a myriad of ways of recording and projecting moving images. Frenchman Louis Le Prince used paper roll film and a single lens camera with a take-up spool and an electromagnetic shutter in 1888. William Friese Greene and Mortimer Evans, working through magic lantern technology, developed a camera that could produce photographic slides at a rate of four or five per second. In America the work of Thomas Edison and William Kennedy Dickson led to the development of the Kinétograph to record moving images and the Kinetoscope to view them (both 1891). Here, a perforated band of film 35mm wide was electronically pulled through the Kinetograph at 48 frames per second. The 50 feet of film lasting 20 seconds ran on a loop and was viewed in the Kinetoscope by individual fee-paying patrons in Kinetoscope parlours. The first parlour opened in New York in 1894. The topics of these short films were mainly comedy sketches such as *Fun in a Chinese Laundry* (1894), historical vignettes (*Execution of Mary Queen of Scots* (1895)), sports topics and dancing, all based on the popular entertainments of the time, such as boxing and vaudeville. These films were largely recorded in their own studio, *Fred Ott's Sneeze* (1894) reportedly being the first ever copyrighted film.

Simultaneously in 1895 a number of systems for recording and projecting moving films were devised. In Britain R.W. Paul developed the Theatrograph (first public performance 20 February 1896 in London); in America Thomas Armat and Francis Jenkins invented the Vitascope – often accredited to Edison (originally for box-office reasons) who manufactured it – (first public performance 23 April 1896); in Germany Max and Emil Skladanowsky produced the Bioskop (first public performance 1 November 1895 in Berlin). The most famous, though, is the Cinematograph designed and built by Auguste and Louis Lumière.

The importance of the Lumière brothers was in the first showing of films to groups of fee-paying people rather than single viewers as was the case with Edison's Kinetoscope (although the Kinetoscope films themselves were first projected on 23 April 1896). Auguste and Louis Lumière achieved a satisfactory system for taking, printing and projecting moving pictures made on a celluloid strip. It combined a hand-cranked camera and projector, which used 35mm film at a speed of 16 frames per second. Because it was hand-cranked it was lighter than the other inventions and, crucially, this made it portable, thus helping its rapid transit around the world. The first public presentation was on 22 March 1895 in Paris, and the first for the general fee-paying public on 28 December 1895. This cost 1 franc for the 30-minute show – the first day's takings were 33 francs and, in the third week, close to 2,000 francs were taken per day, thus persuading people of the economic viability of this form of entertainment. Lumière shows were rapidly demonstrated by their agents across the continent and indeed around the globe. The first London show was at the Polytechnic Regent Street, on 20 February 1896, in Rome on 12 March 1896 and in Austria on 20 March. Facil-itated by empire trade routes and railways linking major urban conurbations, the first Lumière show in India was in Bombay on 7 July 1896; previously there had been a show in Moscow on 19 May 1896, and in Shanghai during August of the same year. There were shows in Brazil and Argentina in July and September 1896.

Developments in what became known as *cinematographie* initially shared many visual attributes with its precursor, photography; it was, however, only a short time later that the moving image created its own language and art form. The first common genres were actu-ality films as pioneered by the Lumières, fantasy/science fiction by Georges Méliès, and narrative entertainment films by British and American film-makers. The development of narrative film production led to the predominance of the financially motivated, industrially organized and star-based film from America; this genre rapidly came to dominate European and world markets.

EARLY FILM CONTENT

The relationship between the development of technique and content is very important in con-sidering early film. For instance, the use of editing and, in particular, continuity editing, had a great influence on the advent of narrative film. As the novelty value of the usual bill of fare, a series of unconnected scenes, wore off, early films became predominantly narrative-led rather than merely skits or tableaux. This was aided by the development of techniques allow-ing the organization of space and time. These two leading dimensions of moving image representation created the causal logic, or narrative development, which is central to under-standing moving image language. The development of codes, of film language and mean-ing, emerged as a result of technical developments, of the industrialization of the film business and the related demands of audiences for more coherent film shows.

It is from these early building blocks that visual communication developed. We can see how film-makers such as D.W. Griffiths were able to express themselves so eloquently a mere ten years later. The diverse use of moving image language has developed from the fundamentals, as can be illustrated by the likes of the Lumière brothers and Georges Méliès in France, Edwin S. Porter in the USA, and R.W. Paul and George Albert Smith in England.

Put yourself in the late nineteenth century mind-set for these films. Nineteenth century people experienced film very differently than do twenty-first-century people. Not only do we carry a lifelong socialization into all aspects of moving image with us, we are also more widely experienced in terms of technology and travel, and perhaps a little more cynical about the world of magic and illusion. Tom Gunning goes further and sees the relationship between the spectator and the film as being one of 'the cinema of attractions' until about 1906–07. For Gunning this is the ability of cinema to '*show* something', as he says:

> The cinema of attractions directly solicits spectator attention, inciting visual curiosity, and supplying pleasure through an exciting – a unique – event, whether fictional or documentary, that is of interest in itself. . . . It is the direct address of the audience, in which an attraction is offered to the spectator by a cinema showman that defines this approach to film-making. (Gunning, 1990: 58–9)

The difference between this type of cinema and the modern narrative-led moving image can be characterized as the difference between centrifugal and centripetal forces in nature: a centrifuge throws outwards towards the spectator, rather than the centripetal forces that pull the spectator inwards towards the actions and motivations of character-associated narratives. It is in this spirit, then, that we should consider the early film-makers and their products.

Auguste and Louis Lumière

Through the Lumière brothers, cinema and film originated as a mechanical device for recording moving images of reality, not necessarily as a narrative medium. This does not imply that they were plotless slices of life, indeed commentators such as Deutelbaum (1979) have rightly pointed out that there is structural patterning within the range of Lumière films. The Lumière products were single-shot films, not a tableaux, as in some of Edison's Kinetograph films. Not entirely convinced of the future for film, the Lumière output largely consists of demonstration pieces for their roving operators to use in order to gain sales.

The earliest film techniques, particularly the framing of the shot, were a direct inheritance from the codes and conventions of still photography. The Lumière films used a fixed, stationary camera recording what passed in front of it in a continuous take. A static point of view shot is achieved, fixing the audience as observers, as voyeurs. The first film on their show reel *La Sortie des Usines* (*Workers Leaving the Factory*, 1895) illustrates this. Obeying rules of 'good' composition, the framing of the front of the factory allows us to see not only the main door but also the smaller door opening from across a road, providing us with a sense of depth and space, which will very soon be filled. This film also illustrates the active decision to structure a film, through the opening and closing of the factory gates. Providing us with anticipation at the start of the film (what is behind the doors?) and narrative closure at the end as the doors draw to, allowing the final few workers and a dog to scurry out. With the film completing a full circle, as the film visually ends where it began, it is undoubtedly the ultimately minimalist complete plot.

Repas de Bébé (*Feeding the Baby*, 1895), like many of these films, is to some extent a home movie featuring the Lumière family performing for the camera. Again the framing of the image and the sense of performance persuade us that we are not simply witnessing the reproduction of reality. Indeed, what is often remarked on as the audience's reaction to this film is the movement of the leaves in the background. Vaughan (1990) offers an interesting explanation for this that takes us beyond mere fascination with the real. He contends that the audience accepted movements of photographed people because they were perceived as being performers but, given their previous experience of static theatrical sets, it was the movement of inanimate objects that they found intriguing. .

Full performance, this time for comic effect, was achieved in *L'Arroseur Arrosé* (*Watering the Gardener*, 1895), generally considered a landmark in narrative cinema. Here a piece of classic music-hall slapstick was played out in front of the camera. Sneaking up behind the gardener, a boy steps on the hose pipe the gardener is using to water; as the flow stops the gardener peers down the nozzle, at which time the boy releases the pressure and the gardener gets sprayed. This is the gag, but to some extent it is what follows that is of particular interest here, emphasizing the staging of action, the extent of the frame, and movement towards the camera and audience. The gardener pursues the boy around, and off, what is the designated frame of the shot, and returns him to centre shot to chastise him.

Movement and flow towards the camera, and thus the audience, is a key element of many of these early films. We saw it with the flow of people from the factory in the first film, and again it occurs with the *Arrivée des Congressistes à Neuville-sur-Saône* (*The Arrival of the Congress*). Here the delegates at a photographic congress are disembarking from a steamer and pass either side of the static camera, fully aware of what is taking place; they smile and lift their hats to the camera. This was a demonstration film for the congress itself, as the film was then printed and later re-shown to the delegates. The most famous of these movement-towards-camera shots is *Arrivée d'un Train en Gare à La Ciotat* (*The Arrival of a Train at the Station*, 1895). The composition and framing of the shot again echoes still photography, and emphasizes the industrial icon of the steam train in the diagonal movement across the screen with the engine getting closer and larger. The well-known legend around the first showing of this film is of people ducking and diving to get out of the path of the train. This does seem improbable, as Vaughan (1990) points out. Audience reaction of this sort was certainly not the norm, and one can only agree with Christie (1994) that this was, more likely, a few (well-inebriated) people playing to the crowd, and 'striving for effect' (Christie, 1994: 15).

Vaughan is more intrigued by *Barque Sortant du Port* (*Leaving the Port*, 1895), on the surface another Lumière home movie, where Madame Lumière and two children watch, presumably, one of the brothers row a boat out of a tranquil harbour, only to return when rough sea is met. The key for Vaughan is that this final simple act represents the harnessing of spontaneity in the cinema and signals its potential more than any other of the Lumière films. As he says:

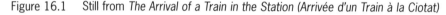

Figure 16.1   Still from *The Arrival of a Train in the Station (Arrivée d'un Train à la Ciotat)*

> The unpredictable has not only emerged from the background to occupy the greater portion of the frame; it has also taken sway over the principles. Man, no longer the mounte-bank self-presenter, has become equal with the leaves and the brick-dust – and as miraculous. (Vaughan, 1990: 65)

In the short 30-minute show of 12 film subjects, the Lumière Brothers presented, probably unwittingly, the potential of cinema, from the observational cinema of *La Sortie des Usine* to the staged performance of *L'Arroseur Arrosé*, and the spontaneity of *Barque Sortant du Port*. However, the excitement of all these potentials is epitomized, and given another layer of meaning through suspense, in *Démolition d'un Mur (Demolition of the Wall*, 1896). Here, Auguste is seen supervising the demolition of a wall in the factory grounds. Again there is initially a fairly classical framing of the subject, with strong, straight lines dissecting the picture reminiscent of the geometric design of Renaissance painting. Narrative suspense is generated as the workmen, moving in and out of the frame, chip away at the base of the wall with pickaxes and use a jack to push it over. As the wall collapses and the dust clears, a new vista emerges and depth of vision is provided by a house in the distance. More than the other films, *Démolition d'un Mur* is spectacle, with tension and suspense building to the dust-filled climax.

Technology becomes part of performance when time and space are altered by the nineteenth-century projectionists showing this particular film backwards for comic effect. Thus, what is now a classic visual joke, usually featuring the demolition of chimney stacks, is perpetrated by the wall being visually reconstructed as the workmen go about their tasks in reverse.

Georges Méliès

Georges Méliès is often seen as being the father of narrative film. He was already a magic lantern theatre proprietor, an illusionist and a magician before he became interested in film. He was present at the Lumières' first showing of the Cinematograph and recognized the potential of film not only to record his magic performances but also to be an integral part of them, creating his own fantastic worlds. As a creative, artistic person he was involved in all aspects of production, from design and directing to scripting and acting. From his film studio he was able to develop the techniques of multiple exposure and stop-action or sub-stitution, which were the building blocks of much of his work. He experimented with, and used, hand-painted colour frames. The key to Méliès' success was the production of fictional narratives consisting of multiple scenes; this made his films many times longer than previous productions. The earliest known example of this is *La Lune à un Mètre* (*The Moon at One Metre/The Astronomer's Dream*, 1898), which was based on one of his previous theatre shows and ran for 195 feet as opposed to the previous standard of 65 feet (or 48 feet for many of the Lumière films).

    La Lune à un Mètre consisted of three scenes. The first presents us with the observatory in which an aged astronomer looks at the moon through a telescope and then falls asleep. The second scene, 'the moon at one metre', has the moon descend from the sky and swallow him up. In the final scene he meets Phoebe, the goddess of the moon, but she disappears as he is chasing her, at which point the astronomer wakes up. The goddess's disappearance is achieved by stop-camera effect. Simply, the camera is halted mid-filming and the person removed before filming recommences. Stop-camera was a mainstay of much early filming, since not only could people be made to disappear, but inanimate objects could appear or metamorphose in some way. As with magic lantern shows, Méliès' early films were accompanied by commentary from the showman.

    Méliès' films are distinctive and characterized by vitality, experimentation, invention and humour. They are truly 'magical' in their quality and themes. Films such as *Escamotage d'une Dame Chez Robert-Houdin* (*The Vanishing Lady*, 1896) and *L'Homme à la tête de Caoutchouc* (*The Man with the India Rubber Head*, 1902) are more than simple magic tricks recorded by the camera – they required the intimate involvement of the camera and photography. In *The Vanishing Lady*, for instance, stop-camera was the 'trick' used to replace a woman with a skeleton.

    Méliès' most famous production, *Le Voyage dans la Lune* (*A Trip to the Moon*, 1902) is 825 feet long, lasts for 14 minutes and consists of 30 scenes or 18 separate tableaux. It tells the story of a group of astronomers who plan a trip to the moon in a projectile fired from a cannon. The projectile lands in the eye of 'the man in the moon'. They explore the moon's surface and its exotic wonders, like giant mushrooms, and are then captured by

Figure 16.2   Still from *A Trip to the Moon (Le Voyage dans la Lune)*

moon creatures. Later, they climb into their projectile, return to earth landing on the seabed, are rescued and proclaimed heroes. A statue is then erected to their leader, Barbenfouillis.

Le Voyage dans la Lune was shot at his studio stage in Montreuil, which was set up to utilize natural sunlight, and produced by his own company, Star Film. As with many of his films, Méliès himself plays the central character (Barbenfouillis), more often than not a person whose role is akin to that of a magician or scientist. As part of the cast he utilized dancers from the Théâtre Municipal du Châtelet, and acrobats from the Folies-Bergère. Many of the 'special effects' – such as the rising and lowering of the stage, the use of scenery to give a three-dimensional effect, and the use of backdrops – crown this relationship with theatre. Other out-of-camera tricks include the movement of the moon on a dolly, extensive scene movement and backgrounds on rollers. He also used pyrotechnics. Some of the in-camera work was directly inherited from photography, with background photography and double exposures, while stop-camera filming and dissolves were definitely part of the armoury of the new medium.

Méliès made a similar film in 1904 called *Voyage à Travers l'Impossible* (*An Impossible Voyage*), this time about a trip to the sun. These films betrayed their origins in three areas: first, the narrative construction followed the conventions of theatrical production; second, they were greatly influenced by the stories and visual style of the science fiction worlds of

Jules Verne and H.G. Wells; third, the production values were derived from magic lantern shows, pantomime and *scènes burlesques*. The multiple scenes were composed of single fixed shots, which positioned the audience in the centre aisle, with Méliès heavily directing actors entering and exiting stage left and right. The sense of performance *for* the camera is important. Indeed, there is a similarity with the Lumières here, in that the camera records the events played out before it, be they fictional or non-fictional – the camera plays little or no part in the construction of the performance.

Robert W. Paul

Robert William Paul was a scientific instrument maker and electrical engineer who spent a relatively short time working in film production and the mechanics of cinema. Given that the Edison-manufactured Kinetoscope was not patented in Britain, several attempts were made to copy it. Paul's was undoubtedly the most successful, manufacturing 60 examples in 1895. When the Edison company refused to supply films, Paul in conjunction with photographer Birt Acres produced a camera which produced films that could be shown on the Kinetoscope. Films produced in 1895 were *Oxford and Cambridge University Boat Race*, *The Derby*, *Rough Sea at Dover*, and a fictional piece called *Arrest of a Pickpocket*.

The Kinetoscope business was, however, in decline and, with the arrival of the Lumière films in France, Paul turned his attention to the projection of films on to a screen. Paul's first performance of what he called the Theatrograph was on 20 February 1896 at Finsbury Technical College of English. This coincided with the first Lumière presentation.

For Paul, the film production side of the business became more important to him as he realized that the potential and profitability of the new industry depended on a regular supply of new films on varying topics. In 1897 he created a production company called Paul's Animatograph Limited. Although he began with actuality films, recording what we might call news/sports events such as *The Derby* (1896), he moved on to fictional topics and humorous films. The most famous of the latter is probably the cinema's first piece of self-reflexivity – *The Countryman and the Cinematograph* (1901). Here a country bumpkin is seen reacting, much as earlier audiences were fabled to do, to the sight of a train coming towards him on the screen. He is also seen reacting to a dancer and recognizing himself in a courting couple.

The studio Paul built in London in 1899 enabled him to develop special effects photography. The stop-motion effect was a crucial development used by Paul, in that it allowed the film-maker to edit in the camera simply by stopping the film going through the camera, altering whatever scene was being worked on, then starting filming again. The upshot of this technique was that objects or people appeared to metamorphose or change in some way. The best example is Paul's *Extraordinary Cab Accident* (1903) in which a man is run over by a horse and cab, pronounced dead and then is miraculously seen to come back to life. In this film, a man is seen talking to a woman by the side of the road; he tips his hat to take his leave of her and steps back off the pavement as a cab approaches. The camera is then stopped and a suitably dressed dummy takes his place, the camera is restarted and the dummy then gets run over. The camera is stopped again and the man replaces the dummy. The camera restarts and the man is seen to miraculously recover. Other special effects

developed by Paul were the use of miniatures and superimposition, such as can be seen in
The (?) Motorist (1906). (The full title of this film has been lost in the mists of time.) Much of
his work is similar to that of Méliès in its use of complex trick photography in order to tell
short comic tales.

George Albert Smith

George Albert Smith, like many other pioneers of film production, had interests in many
aspects of those four prerequisites for moving image production that we discussed earlier.
He was an impresario, with interests in showbusiness at the booming seaside resort of
Brighton, where he was a prominent member of what became known as the Brighton School
of early film-makers. Smith was also a portrait photographer and a magic lantern lecturer.
He was a member of the Royal Astronomical Society who also used his magic lantern skills
to illustrate his lectures on scientific subjects. He built his own camera in 1896 and then
began producing films, building his own studio in Brighton in 1900.

It was his background in magic lantern performance that led him to become a pioneer of
trick photography, in particular double exposure, producing superimposition films like *The
Corsican Brothers* (1897), *The X-ray Fiend* (1897) and *Photographing a Ghost* (1898), or
parallel, side-by-side action films, such as *Santa Claus* (1898) where a boy and girl have a
dream about Santa Claus climbing down their chimney; this dream is shown alongside a shot
of the children asleep. He also pioneered the reverse action, or reverse motion, shot in films
such as *The House that Jack Built* (1901). Here, any motion in a shot can be seen to go in
reverse; hence the house that a little girl builds is seen to fall down when a boy knocks it
over and then it is magically 're-built' before our eyes. The effect is the same as the Lumière
brothers' projectionists reversing the demolition of the wall except that the effect, for Smith,
was achieved on the editing table.

Smith can be seen as the originator of the point of view (POV) shot and the extreme close-
up. He also made a significant contribution to the development of film continuity, dividing up
scenes into shots by cutting within a scene. The best example of all of these developments
is *Grandma's Reading Glass* (1900). In this short film a young boy uses a magnifying glass
to examine a series of objects in his grandma's parlour. We see the series of objects in
close-up from the boy's point of view, each one emphasized by a black circular mask around
the object reproducing his field of vision. We start with a close-up of a newspaper and scan
across the columns to rest on an advert. We then have a mid-shot of the grandma sewing
and the boy rummaging through the objects on her table; he finds a watch and lifts the
magnifying glass to his eye; we then see its workings from his point of view. He then has a
look at a bird in a cage, grandma's eye and a kitten. The film finishes with a mid-shot of the
boy examining grandma's sewing. This film, then, not only involves the viewer in the act of
looking, but directs the audience to see the world from the boy's point of view – the point
of view of a film character.

George Albert Smith's other pioneering work was in the development – with the American,
Charles Urban – of the first commercially successful colour process in 1908. Kinemacolor
was a two-colour process that used two rotating filters between the film and the lens, one

coloured red and one green. Although initially a commercial success this later ran into both patent and technical difficulties because of the specialist equipment needed.

Edwin S. Porter

Porter is possibly the last of the innovators of the early years of cinema; he is most noted for evolving the principles of continuity editing. He is also the epitome of the 'cameraman' principle of production in that he wrote, photographed, directed and edited his films. Initially a manufacturer of cameras and projectors, he had also been a projectionist at the Eden Musé. In 1900 he joined the Edison Company as a director and cameraman.

Although influenced by the films of his peers, such as Méliès' *A Trip to the Moon* (1902) and the Sheffield Photographic Company's *Daring Daylight Robbery* (1903), it was Porter himself who clearly conceived of the importance of continuity editing in the creating of a story of more than one or two shots. Necessity being the mother of invention, Porter saw longer films as a way of attracting the dwindling audiences back to the moving picture houses. Two key films in a film-making career of 15 years are *Life of an American Fireman* (1903) and *The Great Train Robbery* (1903).

Life of an American Fireman emerged out of an existing series of one-shot films, held by the Edison Company, about the fire service. Porter filmed some dramatic scenes and then edited the two things together to created a 20-scene film that lasted just over 6 minutes. With the exception of a close-up of a hand pulling the lever on a fire alarm box, the entire film is in long shot. The film opens with the fire chief asleep at his desk; a piece of parallel action shows us a dream bubble in which his wife and child appear. He has a premonition of danger and the next scene shows us the fire alarm box and the hand pulling the lever. This is followed by scenes of the fireman's dormitory, the interior and exterior of the fire station, and two street scenes as the engines rush to the house. On arrival at the burning house we get the famous cross-cut section, in which exteriors are cut with the interiors of the build-ing, thus simultaneous events are shown and the linear flow of time disrupted for the first time in cinema. After the family has been rescued, the final scene is an interior of the fire being extinguished.

The Great Train Robbery lasts about 10 minutes and contains 14 shots. It is undoubtedly the first narrative western-genre film, and exploits its violent action in a highly dramatic and very modern way. As with *Life of an American Fireman*, Porter cross-cuts between interior and exterior shots.

The film starts with an interior of a telegraph office, two robbers enter the office and hold the clerk at gunpoint; a train is shown pulling into the station on back-projection through a window. While the robbers hide, the clerk hands a paper to somebody through a hatch. The robbers then knock the clerk out and tie him up, exiting as the train is seen to leave the sta-tion. The next shot shows the train arriving at a water tower, taking on water and members of the gang furtively boarding the train, followed by its departure. The next shot is the interior of a mail car with the countryside rushing by as seen through an open door, again on back-projection. The robbers enter the car and, after a short gun battle, kill the guard; they blow open the strongbox, steal the money and exit the mail car. An interior of the engine

Figure 16.3   Still from *The Great Train Robbery*

cab now shows a struggle with the fireman, who is then shot and his body thrown off the train. A short exterior shot of the engine follows, where the driver is forced at gunpoint to get down and uncouple the engine from the rest of the train. The next shot is also an exterior one: the passengers, with their hands in the air, are disembarking the train on to the track. One of them is shot in the back as he runs towards the camera trying to escape. The rest of the passengers are then robbed of their valuables. The robbers run off, shooting in the air, and the passengers run towards the dead man holding him in their arms. The engine of the train is now seen at an angle and some distance from the carriages, the robbers run towards it, carrying sacks, mount the engine and it pulls off into the distance. The next shot, again at an angle (this time to the tracks), shows the engine pulling up and the bandits jumping off and disappearing down a ravine. In the next shot, the robbers pass through some trees, cross a stream to their horses and ride off. We then return to the interior of the telegraph office; the clerk wakes up struggles and passes out again, a young girl enters, unties him and helps him to his feet. We then move to the interior of a building where a dance is being held. The ladies and gentlemen are bowing to each other and dancing around. This continues for some time, with the men shooting at the feet of one man as he dances centre stage. The telegraph clerk then enters, gesticulates about the robbery and they all exit stage left. The next shot is looking down a wooded track. The robbers ride towards the camera and past it, shooting at the posse pursuing them. One of the robbers is shot and falls off his horse. As the posse ride past the camera, one of them stops and gets off to check the fallen robber. The penultimate camera shot is of a clearing: the three remaining robbers are dividing up the loot; the posse, however, are seen in the distance among the trees. A gun battle ensues and all three robbers are shot. The posse retrieve the stolen money. The final shot is of the robbers' leader looking straight at the camera and firing his pistol.

The Great Train Robbery, as with Life of an American Fireman, is largely filmed in long shot from a stationary camera. There are two very notable exceptions to this: first, there is a pan and tilt as the camera follows the robbers off the engine and down a ravine, and again another pan as they reach their horses and ride off; second, the film ends with an 'emblematic' mid-shot of the robbers' leader firing point blank at the audience. Both of these represent breaks with the established tradition of film construction and led the way to a more inventive and artistic use of the film medium.

With The Great Train Robbery, a number of crucial aspects of early film-making came together to create what was undoubtedly a 'modern' film. First, there is the idea of events that share the same simultaneous time being shown in linear continuity – that is, where the emphasis is on the continuity of shots and action, not the sanctity of time. This development may indeed have been inevitable when films began to move away from the single- or double-shot films. Second, a number of shots could impart the same meaning: you were not restricted to one shot one unitary meaning. Finally, each scene does not necessarily have to be complete before you move on to the next scene. By the same token, you could start a scene after its logical beginning. Meaning and narrative language, then, reside in the shot itself, and it is the arrangement of these shots that creates the moving image as we know it today.

WOMEN SILENT FILM-MAKERS

In 1914 one of the pioneers of film-making, Alice Guy-Blaché, stated that: 'There is nothing connected with the staging of a motion picture that a woman cannot do as easily as a man, and, there is no reason why she cannot completely master every technicality of the art' (quoted in Slide, 1977: 32).

Alice Guy-Blaché's optimism is understandable since in the first 20 years of the twentieth century there were about 150 women who had directed films. Most production companies, large and small, employed women in all aspects of production, not simply the performance or creative sides, but technical as well, from camera to editing and, of course, directing. The importance of women's contribution to early film has for most of film's history been forgotten, it is only in the last two decades or so that the names of Alice Guy-Blaché, Lois Weber, Germaine Dulac and Dorothy Arzner have been given the recognition they deserve. The explanation for this lack of recognition is not simply down to the fact that most histories of early cinema are written by men, but due to the very nature of early film-making, which was controlled by small 'cottage' industries. Early films were credited to the production company itself, not to individual directors. Early films were also short and produced in vast numbers, and the majority of these have simply been lost.

Women featured in the development of film-making across the globe, Elvira Notari was not only Italy's first woman film-maker, she also headed Dora Film in Naples from 1906. Anna Hofman was not only Sweden's first woman director, but also the world's second female director. Fatma Begum was the first woman director in India with her own production company Fatma Film. Among many others were: Edith Batley in Britain, who directed propaganda films during the First World War; Olga Preobrazhenskayain in Russia, who made *Noble-peasant Girl* (1916); Lotte Reiniger in Germany, who pioneered animation; while, in America, Gene Gauntier, Kathlyn Williams, Nell Shipman, Mabel Normand and Marguerite Bertsch all played major roles in the early development of American film-making.

Alice Guy-Blaché was the first woman director, indeed one of the first film directors. In her career she made over 600 films. Her first film was made in 1896. She wrote, directed, photographed and starred in *La Fée Aux Choux* (*The Cabbage Fairy*), which is possibly the first ever fiction film, the story of a woman who grows children in a cabbage patch. Alice Guy-Blaché had been at that very first demonstration of the Lumière Brothers Cinematograph. At the time she was secretary to Léon Gaumont, a photographic equipment manufacturer. Gaumont saw filmed stories as trivialities; he believed films were for scientific and educational purposes. This attitude can be seen as one of the reasons for so many women

Figure 16.4   *Photograph of Alice Guy-Blaché*

being accepted in the new industry. Another reason was that women had for some time been involved in the arts, music, drama and performing, thus it seemed natural that they would progress into the new art of motion pictures. Women were actively recruited into all aspects of the industry, especially production and exhibition. The new industry courted respectability, as the status afforded film-making was very low and cinemas were seen to attract a low-class audience. The new industry was egalitarian, because there was a great deal of pressure to meet production targets, and artists moved freely between trades and roles; thus women were able to work in all aspects of production, not just acting, directing and writing, on the same and between different projects. Two women, Mary Pickford and Lillian Gish exemplify this. Though better known as actresses, both produced and directed films. Mary Pickford formed her own studio – United Artists – in 1919 with Douglas Fairbanks and Charlie Chaplin. Alice Guy-Blaché had also formed her own company in 1910; called Solax Productions, it produced 325 films between 1910 and 1914, 35 of which could be identified as being directed by Alice Guy-Blaché herself.

America's first woman director, Lois Weber, started working for Alice Guy-Blaché and her husband Herbert Blaché in 1907. By 1916 Weber, working for Universal Pictures, was one of the highest-paid directors of the silent era. Her films tackled controversial issues such as abortion and birth control (*Where are My Children*, 1916), capital punishment (*The People vs John Doe*, 1916), adultery and promiscuity (*What Do Men Want*, 1920), capitalism and religion (*Hypocrits*, 1915). Because of their subject matter, her films were often subject to heavy censorship and closure. *Where are My Children* dealt with issues of abortion and class conflict; its success convinced her that audiences wanted serious intellectual and socially committed films. Women who had started off by directing domestic or 'emotional' dramas, comedies or features for children, gradually moved into documentaries and feature films dealing with social problems, as well as the more mainstream fare. The liberation of the jazz age and the extension of the franchise to women, were significant in that 'women's rights' films were becoming more central to female productions and more acceptable to audiences.

In France, Germaine Dulac was one of the first film-makers to focus specifically on female subjects in an avant-garde style. In particular, she focused on the invisible world of women's dreams and unconscious desires in films such as *The Smiling Madame Beudet* (1922). Dulac was not only a film-maker but also a film theorist, lecturer and member of the influential cinematic impressionists movement in France in the 1920s. She wrote essays on light, movement and composition, and opposed the dominance of narrative in content. Her films, such as *L'Invitation au Voyage* (1927) and *Thème et Variations* (1928), became surrealist visual symphonies, as she moved away from narrative cause and effect to very abstract camera work concerned with portraying women's interior world. As a women's activist her films make a clear distinction between objective reality and subjective point of view (POV) shots. In *The Smiling Madame Beudet*, for instance, the POV shots dominate the film, as Madame Beudet fantasizes about escaping from her ordered humdrum household life, the tyranny of her husband and the clock.

During the late 1910s and early 1920s the growing commercialization and industrialization of film-making had the result of removing women from their roles as directors, and maintaining them in positions of actresses and writers. In the early 1920s both Lois Weber and

Figure 16.5   Still from *The Smiling Madame Beudet (La Souriante Madame Beudet)*

Alice Guy-Blaché found themselves in financial difficulty. Alice Guy-Blaché retired to France in 1922 and did not make another film. Lois Weber made three talkies, but they were all failures.

The impact of commercialization on women in the film industry lay in several related areas:

- the industrialization of cinema meant that it was no longer a cottage industry and the birth of the studio systems meant that only financial giants could survive
- standardization and the imposition of rigid hierarchies made movement between studios and skills impossible; this was aggravated by trades unions and their restrictive practices, one of which was all-male membership
- commercialization also meant that film was no longer seen as a trivial or disposable product; it became serious business – i.e. a 'man's' world rather than a 'woman's', as it had started out.

The new Fordian approach to film-making was exacerbated by the technology associated with the coming of sound. The coming of sound also provides us with a more complex explanation of the failure or loss of women film-makers; this can be found in language and communication itself. The films of Guy-Blaché, Weber and Dulac reflected their concern with the exploration of emotion; they relied heavily on symbolism. Dulac deals with dreams and fantasies, and – as in *The Smiling Madame Beudet* – the piano is seen as related to the feminine, as are other symbols. The effect of such aesthetic symbolism is to liberate viewers from the normal relationships between time and space in conventional works of art, and locate them in a different kind of consciousness not controlled by rigid cause and effect narrative relationships. The coming of sound removes the emphasis in silent films on symbolism to communicate its meaning, and imposes on film the tyranny of dialogue, and thus narrative, and the cause–effect chain of events.

Anthony Slide feels that, 'During the silent era women might be said to have virtually controlled the film industry' (1977: 9) and he goes on to say that, 'many of these women were the equal of, if not better than, their male colleagues. All of them, without doubt, pioneers in the true sense of the word' (1977: 13). Of Hollywood's women silent filmmakers, only Dorothy Arzner survived into the sound era, and it is not until the 1980s that we begin to see anything like the same numbers of women in film-making as there were in the silent era.

CHAPTER 17

Narrative Theory and the Moving Image

INTRODUCTION

Narrative and genre theory are now at the forefront of the study of the moving image, having long held a prominent place in both the study of literature and film. The approaches of both narrative and genre are tools for opening up texts, they are key devices for examining meanings in all moving image products, and provide structures that can be used to analyse a wide variety of content, from news and current affairs, through advertising and situation comedies, to blockbuster films and music videos. The classic studies in these areas have tended to be applied particularly to fictional products such as gangster movies (Warshow, 1964) and westerns (Wright, 1975) in film, with soap opera (Ang, 1985) and drama (Berger, 1992) prominent in the study of television. More recent studies have applied them to news, (Helland, 1995), documentary (Winston, 1995), road movies (Cohan and Hark, 1997), body genres (Williams, 1991) and even cookery programmes (Strange, 1998).

Narrative and genre are all-pervasive in modern moving image products. That is, every moving image product is constructed around the demands of narrative, and all moving image products can be classified and understood in terms of genre. The examination of these two areas is central to our understanding of how the moving image operates and is understood. Being as though narrative is also an essential component of the understanding of genre, we shall also examine the relationships between these two areas within this chapter.

NARRATIVE

As we saw in the first chapter of this section, very quickly the audience found that the novelty of the early tableaux style of films soon wore off. There was a desire to find out more, to discover 'what happened next'. Early film-makers realized this and began to create simple, and then more complex, narrative structures. The moving image became dominated by narrative and great story-tellers such as Edwin S. Porter, Alice Guy-Blaché and D.W. Griffith with his films such as *The Birth of a Nation* (1915) and *Intolerance* (1916).

D.W. Griffith

David Wark Griffith (1874–1948) was a pioneering American director and producer. Often called the Father of Hollywood Narrative, it was Griffith who was largely responsible for the transition of film from the production of basically filmed stage plays to the birth of the moving image art form. His major development was to produce films that could express ideas and arouse emotion. Central to this was camera movement within a scene and close-ups, not only of actors' faces, but of objects as well. Griffith mastered the filming of the chase and rescue, which became his trademark in the early films he made with Biograph, such as *A Drive for Life* (1909) and *The Massacre* (1912). Of particular importance in these films is his developing of techniques of intercutting and parallel action. Pictorial beauty was also key to Griffiths work; locations were everything and, with his equally gifted camera-man Billy Bitzer, he produced some of the most memorable photography of cinema. The mass leaves blowing in the wind at the beginning of *The Beast at Bay* (1912) is a stunning example of this. This new kind of filming demanded new kinds of actor – those who had not previously been schooled in theatre acting. Griffith is credited with having got the star system under way, with actors such as Mary Pickford, Lillian Gish, Mabel Norman, Mae March and Robert Harron. Griffith is best remembered for his controversial masterpiece *The Birth of a Nation* (1915). Taken from the Thomas Dixon novel *The Clansman*, Griffith produces a spectacle that traces the history of one family through the American Civil War and the Reconstruction. In it he brings together all his directorial techniques, and his love of realism and photographic beauty, with a climactic rescue. Among his other films, the epic *Intolerance* (1916) told four stories simultaneously, spectacularly and at such a pace that Griffith himself described the ending of the film as being like 'one mighty river of expressed emotion'. *Intolerance* was a box office failure, some felt because the audience found it too overwhelming.

As a starting point, the concept of narrative in moving image is best understood as being the events, both inferred and presented, that are told through the actions of characters, in a linear cause and effect structure. This structure connects a beginning, middle and end, and is conveyed through the signifying systems. Narratives can be long and complicated, drawn out over weeks and years, or short and punchy, told in minutes or seconds. They emerge not only in fiction material such as drama productions, music videos and adverts, but also within non-fiction products such as news and documentaries, or even sports coverage. As we shall see, all of these have a relationship to narrative through their use of openings, conflicts and resolutions, and through their central use of characters.

Story-telling is a central form of communication, it is all around us. The world is revealed to us in the form of stories – they may be the stories we tell each other when asked questions about our lives, they may be the ways we spend our leisure time, or they may even be the way that we relate to and understand other societies. Story-telling can be seen as universal. We experience some narratives in our everyday lives and contact with individuals, others we experience through the process of education; however, it is through the mass media that we experience the majority of stories.

Narrative as we know it today emerged out of the folktale tradition and the nineteenth-century novel. Novels, as with magazines and newspapers, adapted the content and structures of stories from the oral and face-to-face traditions to more permanent and continually reproducible formats. Mechanical and electronic technologies in the twentieth century took these same structures and delivered them to mass audiences through the mediums of film, television and video. The twenty-first century is seeing the production of all of these into the digital format, allowing their delivery on a worldwide scale through the Internet and many other interconnected digitally based mediums. The larger the audiences these technologies reach, the more similar and familiar the narratives and their structures have to be. Thus, we can talk of a universal narrative structure, which all peoples can understand, regardless of their language or level of moving image literacy. Fiske (1987) refers to the universal narrative structure as the *langue*, of which specific narratives make up the *paroles*. This is a useful classification as it points us towards an examination of what narratives share in terms of common features, and how these can be present in individual texts.

The understanding of narrative structures is central to our task here. There are two basic approaches. The first is the syntagmatic approach, which considers the sequential development of the narrative. This is best represented by the **formalist** work of Vladimir Propp (1968). The second approach is the paradigmatic approach associated with Lévi-Strauss (1966), which is concerned with the patterns of opposition that exist and are created within a narrative. This approach is a structuralist one, in that it allows us to examine the underlying structures of narrative. This approach to narrative allows us to consider the ideological meanings underlining stories – for instance, soap operas can be seen to reflect the dominant view of the family, while advertising can be seen to reinforce the role of women in society. We will start with this latter approach to the study of narrative.

Types of Narrative Structure

The creation of meaning in moving image products is not the result of a random process, it is the result of the construction process used by a producer and the reading processes of an audience. Narrative structures are seen as the organization of plot into coherent sequences that convey meaning. It is the organization of the plot, that provides the fascination, or entertainment, for the audience. The plot is part of the narrative – it is its construction. For example, Orson Welles' film *Citizen Kane* (1941) has a simple narrative in that a boy inherits a fortune, runs a newspaper empire, becomes a recluse and dies. The narrative told through the plot is much more complex than this as the film begins with Kane's death and, through shifts in time and space, explains his life and the events that contributed to his unhappy existence before his demise.

It is often the case in fictional material that we already know the end, thus the pleasure derives from following the process of the story through to its conclusion. Many narratives that exist in non-fictional material are ostensibly about the process rather than the end, since there can be no discernible conclusions to 'stories' such as the Middle East crisis or the economy. In such ongoing news stories, we are aware of the characters, we have know-ledge of past events, and the daily news item simply feeds us more information on the story.

Contemporary moving image productions utilize many different forms of narrative struc-ture. The most common are the closed structures that are often associated with films, television plays, or even sports events, where all questions posed are answered by the end of the allotted time span, and the open structures of television narratives, such as serials or series. The open structure is limited to a small number of central characters, whom we follow through a trauma or number of events for the duration of the story. This may continue through several episodes over a number of days or weeks. Crucially there may not neces-sarily be a resolution to the narrative.

Narrative structures can also be single strand, revolving around the adventures of a single central character, such as Dirty Harry, Superman or Ripley in the *Alien* films, or multi-strand, where several characters form the focus of the narrative. This is particularly apparent in soap operas and some television series, such as the *Buffy the Vampire Slayer*. Narrative structures can also be linear, where events progress in chronological order, one following another, or non-linear with stories often being told in flashback, such as *Citizen Kane*, for example, or some of the classic film noir examples, such as *Double Indemnity* (1944).

Films such *Double Indemnity* illustrate how narrative structures can also be tied to particular genres. The investigative narrative relates to the structure of a plot whereby we follow the investigation of a crime. It might also concern a mystery that is being solved, an event that is being explained, or a quest being pursued. The *X-Files* is a good example of this. Realist structures relate not only to non-fiction products, but also to fictional ones, in that they refer to the fact that the world presented should not only appear plausible and coherent, but should also be structured around 'real' time, Italian neo-realist films such as *Bicycle Thieves* (1948), or British new wave (also called British social realism) films such as *Saturday Night and Sunday Morning* (1961) are good examples of this. Anti-realist structures attempt to challenge the readers' expectations and make them aware of the narrative struc-ture. These might be experimental films such as Maya Deren's *Meshes of the Afternoon* (1943), or surrealist films, such as Luis Buñuel's *Un Chien Andalou* (1928). A great many music videos are also anti-realist in their construction; the first ever pop video, Queen's *Bohemian Rhapsody* is a classic example. There are very few moving image products that do not contain narratives – even alternative narratives exist in relation to, or because of, our knowledge of narrative structures. Non-narrative only really exists in abstracts, clips or trailers, these being on the whole representations of full products.

Narrative structures can best be described and analysed by considering their component parts, and the elements from which they are constructed. ('Component parts' refers to the particular ingredients of narratives.) Classical Greek theatre is usually seen as the origin of modern drama; it was usually organized into acts, the standard being three acts. The act is a structural unit or component of the drama, usually containing more than one scene, which develops the plot. The three acts are divided into quarters, the first being the set-up, the middle two for the confrontation, and a final quarter for the resolution.

In the modern world of the moving image the dominant form of closed narrative is provided by the institutional mode of representation or the standard Hollywood narrative structure. In this narrative structure the key segments are the beginning, the middle and the end (also described as opening, conflict and resolution), as illustrated below.

opening	hero villain community	**conflict**	problem quest battle	**resolution**	victory recognition marriage

Within each of these segments we can see how a chain of events develops to produce the overall narrative. We can also begin to see how the audience moves through a narrative, starting with the introduction to the main characters, moving through the various components of action to the finale.

Narrative structures are a chain of events – a cause and effect relationship. That is, that the hero and the villain meet in a community, a problem emerges caused by the villain, there is a quest or journey, a battle between the main characters, victory for the hero, recognition of the hero by the community, and marriage. One event has caused, or led to, another. We may follow this in a linear pattern as illustrated above, or in a non-linear fashion, referring back in time to find the cause or identify the protagonists. The key to the narrative may well be a central question, problem or enigma. In the film *Jaws* (1975) the shark is the enigma; *Guns* in a murder mysteries such as the *Inspector Morse* series the crime is the enigma to be solved; in *The Full Monty* (1997) unemployment is the enigma to be overcome.

The standard Hollywood narrative structure is best described through the following features.

- There is a single diegesis – that is, one main storyline, although there may be a limited number of subplots.
- The chain of events should follow a logical sequence, and have an inner logic.
- The chain of events should be governed by the actions of central characters.
- The audience should empathize with central characters (drawn in by close-ups and POVs, as well as the use of the star system).
- The focus is on individuals rather than on the societal or collective level.
- There is a pattern of enigma and resolution, where all questions established during the narrative are answered.
- Narratives are dominated by verisimilitude – that is, they should be believable.
- The technical and symbolic elements in media texts are subordinated to the construction of the narrative and the need to drive it along.

In considering the domination of the Hollywood style of narrative, narrative transitivity is an essential feature. This is the movement through the narrative. Todorov (1977) has identified this movement from the opening to the closing of a narrative, as being a movement from one state of equilibrium to another. This process draws our attention to the dynamic movement in a text from equilibrium to disequilibrium, and then to the establishment of a new equilibrium. Todorov's formula establishes the following pattern.

- A state of *equilibrium* and *plenitude* exists.
- This is challenged by the arrival of an *opposing force*.
- This creates a situation of *disruption* and *disequilibrium*.
- A *unifying* and *equalizing force* arises.
- A *quest* takes place.
- The *opposing* and *equalizing force* meet.
- *Disequilibrium* continues as battle is joined.
- A *new equilibrium* and state of *plenitude* is achieved following the victory of the *equalizing force*.

If we apply this to Akira Kurosawa's film *Seven Samurai* (1954), remade as *The Magnificent Seven* (1960) by John Sturges, the formula is seen to work thus:

equilibrium and plenitude	=	peaceful village
opposing force	=	bandits
disruption/disequilibrium	=	bandits attack village
unifying/equalizing force	=	samurai/gunfighters
quest	=	search for samurai/gunfighters
opposing and equalizing forces meet	=	skirmish
disequilibrium battle	=	a series of engagements takes place
new equilibrium and plenitude	=	victory but changed situation for all

The same model can be modified, and applied to non-fiction products, such as television news magazine programmes, in the following way:

equilibrium and plenitude	=	familiar setting of news programme
opposing force	=	headlines and stories revealed
disruption/disequilibrium	=	negative events reported
unifying/equalizing force	=	official/national response
quest	=	report of events
opposing and equalizing forces meet	=	both sides are explained
disequilibrium battle	=	studio debate takes place
new equilibrium and plenitude	=	equalizing forces win
		back to presenter

It is often the case that what registers as a newsworthy event is indeed one that can be accommodated within the narrative framework of disequilibrium and equilibrium.

Ideology in narrative structures can then be revealed via Todorov's formula, by considering not only the fact that the status quo has been re-established, but also *how* the new equilibrium has been reached. Is this achieved through officially sanctioned, and thus legitimate, violence (as in police or military action)? Is it achieved by democratic means through the will of 'the people', or through social conventions such as marriage?

Todorov's formula, when applied to narrative, points up several key aspects of structure. First, there is a clear linear cause–effect relationship within the narrative. Second, there is a positive narrative closure: the mission is accomplished, the world is saved (or at least is returned to its normal condition). Third, there are positive character roles, and these roles fit the cause and effect chain of events. Narrative transitivity is also of interest in that it refers to the ways in which the audience moves through the narrative, witnessing the various stages of the story.

Binary Oppositions

The structuralist work of Lévi-Strauss (1966), concentrates on the *langue*, and introduces the notion of binary oppositions as a useful way to consider the production of meaning within narratives. As we shall see later, this approach has been used very successfully by Will Wright (1975) in his analysis of the western genre. Lévi-Strauss was interested in the production of myths in societies. He had studied cultures and believed, as did Propp, that there were common structures that could be found in the myths of many societies including the modern world. Crucially, myths were used to symbolically understand the contradictory elements of the real world. Myths provide explanations that resolve the incongruities between man's existence and the natural world. Thus, myths could explain the existence of drought by the eternal battle of good and evil.

Examples of binary oppositions found in some moving image narratives might be:

good	vs	evil	e.g. *End of Days* (2000)
male	vs	female	e.g. *Roseanne*
humanity	vs	technology	e.g. *Metropolis* (1926)
nature	vs	industrialization	e.g. *Walkabout* (1971)
East	vs	West	e.g. *From Russia With Love* (1963)
dark	vs	light	e.g. *Buffy the Vampire Slayer*
dirt	vs	cleanliness	e.g. soap powder advertisements

In binary oppositions, we know and understand what one thing is because of our knowledge of its opposite. We know what hot is because we know what cold feels like. We can understand what black is because we know what white is. In narratives we know what the villain is like because we understand what the hero is like. Binary oppositions also provide categories that allow us to define areas by what they are not. Blue is not red or is not green, for example. Most importantly, each category then supplies us with other sets of oppositions. Graeme Turner does this particularly well when he is discussing gender differences and feminist criticism (Turner, 1993: 73). He says:

Assuming male and female are opposites means that, automatically, women *are* what men are *not*; if the male is strong, then the female must be weak, and so it goes:

male	female
strong	weak
rational	irrational
reliable	unreliable

Oppositions are central components of all moving image narratives; they are the key to our understanding of the modern world and its myths. The analysis of myths through binary oppositions allows us to examine the deep structures of narratives, to tease out their hidden messages about our society.

Character and Functions

Characters are central components of all narratives. Vladimir Propp's (1975) formalist work on Russian fairytales, first published in 1928, isolated structures common to all fairytales. Crucially, he demonstrated the relationship between characters and the structure of the narrative. Fairytales are useful to analyse because they contain stock characters and structural ingredients. After studying 115 fairytales, Propp was able to identify seven main character 'roles', as he called them:

1 the villain
2 the donor (or provider)
3 the helper
4 the princess (or sought-for person) and her father
5 the dispatcher
6 the hero
7 the false hero.

These roles represent the building blocks of narratives, it is their actions, in what Propp calls 'functions', that construct the narrative. Propp states that several roles may well be filled by the same character and that some may also be filled by more than one character. The most often-used example of this is the *Star Wars* trilogy (Turner, 1993; Berger, 1992); this is because *Star Wars* makes an interesting point of comparison between the tradition of the fairytale structure and the classic Hollywood moving image product:

1 the villain = Darth Vader
2 the donor = Ben (Obi-Wan) Kenobi
3 the helper = Han Solo
4 the princess = Princess Leia
5 the dispatcher = R2-D2
6 the hero = Luke Skywalker
7 the false hero = Darth Vader.

If we were to apply this to a more recent example of a moving image product such as *Buffy the Vampire Slayer*, then we would be able to develop the following analysis. The hero in this case is a heroine, Buffy, a young woman who is the 'chosen one', the one who will fight the vampires. The hero, for Propp, acts in what he calls a sphere of action – that is, what he or she actually does. Buffy's role is to oppose evil, to go out on quests (patrols), to fight, to respond to the donor, and to desire romantic love. For the category of villain, there might be the various demons or vampires that are the focus of each episode, or a vampire like Spike, whose role continues across many episodes and series. The villain, for Propp, has a sphere of action that involves committing acts of villainy (in our example, killing people). The villain acts against the heroine, opposing her, fighting her and forming a focus for the action. In *Buffy* there are many helpers – people who aid and assist the hero in many ways, ways that often make up for some lack in the hero. Willow's interest in witchcraft is often used to aid Buffy. Helpers such as Zander or Cordelia, can be motivating factors, or indeed may be on hand to rescue Buffy from difficult situations. The princess and her father is an interesting role in *Buffy*, one that may well be filled by Buffy's mother. A person to be protected or sought for, but also someone whose sphere of action includes recognizing the hero, exposing them and punishing them – a role of authority that Buffy acknowledges in her schoolgirl and daughter, rather than 'slayer', persona. We have mentioned that, for Propp, a character might fill more than one role. Giles is a good example of this in *Buffy*, for he is not only the donor, but also the dispatcher. In the role of the dispatcher, it his he who sends Buffy out on her quests, but in the role of the donor, he provides a vital edge over her opponents with his vast knowledge of the forces of evil. He is a magical agent that Buffy can use to defeat the villain. The final role is that of the false hero, who may make claims on the hero's sphere of action. This role in *Buffy* is filled at various times by Angel (a vampire with a soul who is also a helper), Oz (a helper who is also a werewolf) and occasionally by Spike, who is also the villain. As the episodes and series progress, the roles, as we have just seen, can be fairly fluid – however, the important point is that they always exist in one form or another.

Berger (1992) expands Propp's rather static notion of roles by emphasizing the opposing actions of characters and their relationships. He says:

> Every time we think of a villain, we must think of a hero (or if we think of villainess we must think of a heroine) because concepts gain their meaning by relationships. In the same sense, every time we follow some action by some character, we interpret this action in terms of counteractions by opposing characters. (Berger, 1992: 18–19)

Propp's work allows us to consider character as one of the principle components of narrative structure. Characters are central to the development of the narrative. They have to be individuals with specific personality traits, desires and motivations. Very few moving image texts have been able to move away from the need to have individuals as central to the narrative. Sergei Eisenstein, the revolutionary Soviet director, tried to make the mass a collective hero, rather than making the individual the source of action and narrative development, in films such as *The Battleship Potemkin* (1925) and *October* (1927).

Roles, then, cannot be understood in isolation from each other, nor can they be separated out from what Propp calls 'function'. Functions are elements that constitute the plot.

The function is the act of a character, defined from the point of view of its significance for the course of the action. Propp identifies 31 functions; these can be separated into broad groupings of preparation, complication, transference, struggle, return and recognition.

Graeme Turner (1993) provides us with the most usefully abridged version of these narrative functions:

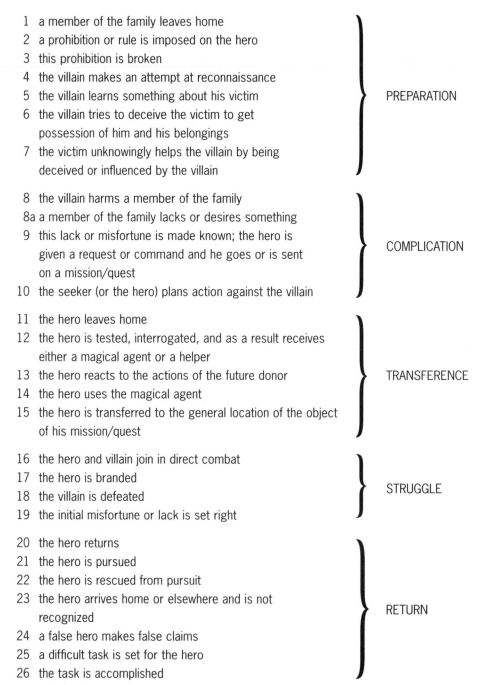

1 a member of the family leaves home
2 a prohibition or rule is imposed on the hero
3 this prohibition is broken
4 the villain makes an attempt at reconnaissance
5 the villain learns something about his victim
6 the villain tries to deceive the victim to get possession of him and his belongings
7 the victim unknowingly helps the villain by being deceived or influenced by the villain

PREPARATION

8 the villain harms a member of the family
8a a member of the family lacks or desires something
9 this lack or misfortune is made known; the hero is given a request or command and he goes or is sent on a mission/quest
10 the seeker (or the hero) plans action against the villain

COMPLICATION

11 the hero leaves home
12 the hero is tested, interrogated, and as a result receives either a magical agent or a helper
13 the hero reacts to the actions of the future donor
14 the hero uses the magical agent
15 the hero is transferred to the general location of the object of his mission/quest

TRANSFERENCE

16 the hero and villain join in direct combat
17 the hero is branded
18 the villain is defeated
19 the initial misfortune or lack is set right

STRUGGLE

20 the hero returns
21 the hero is pursued
22 the hero is rescued from pursuit
23 the hero arrives home or elsewhere and is not recognized
24 a false hero makes false claims
25 a difficult task is set for the hero
26 the task is accomplished

RETURN

27 the hero is recognized
28 the false hero/villain is exposed
29 the false hero is transformed   } RECOGNITION
30 the villain is punished
31 the hero is married and crowned

Not all narratives will have all these functions, as Propp freely admits. They will have some, and those they do have will appear on this list, and occur in the order he outlines.

As we shall see later, Will Wright (1975) uses and develops Propp to analyse the functions of four varieties of western films. In differentiating the four varieties, he takes some liberties with Propp's original functions, but retains their spirit. From Propp's lists of roles and functions, we can describe and analyse almost any moving image. For instance, we can produce the following shorthand framework, which could be applied to almost any product:

- hero leaves home and sets out on a quest
- villain acts against hero and/or community
- hero and villain join in direct combat
- villain is defeated
- hero is married and/or crowned.

Inevitably there will be variants on this framework. The latter function, for instance, is probably better seen as the hero receiving some kind of reward, in modern moving image products. Some narratives will not finish with a traditional happy ending. The beauty of Propp's work, however, is that he provides a description of our narrative expectations and any change will be recognized simply because we have those expectations to start with.

Alternative Narrative Structures

Alternative narrative structures have to be examined as counter to, or as a reaction to, dominant narrative styles – that is, the components of narrative, as discussed above, are applied in a non-standard way.

James Monaco in 1981 stated that Hollywood film was a dream, while dialectic (alternative or oppositional) film could be a conversation. Hollywood narrative film set out to soothe and please its audience; it worked to meet their expectations and reinforce their ideologies. Alternative narratives in moving image products set out not only to challenge the codes and conventions of production, but also to challenge the audience – that is, to remove the audience from its passive position of spectator, observer and voyeur, and to get it to be active, critical and even alienated from the film or programme it is watching. This is attempted by altering the mode of address.

The key theorist and practitioner here is Brecht. His theories on epic theatre sought – through a style of writing, acting and production – to alienate the audience from the production and performance. This *verfremdungseffect* was designed to disengage the audience from its emotional involvement with the action. The audience should still be entertained, but should remain detached and critical. Such devices to achieve this were direct address to the audience and actors standing on the side of the stage waiting to act, or taking multiple roles, thus showing that they were merely performers in a performance. Audience expectations and concentration should be constantly disrupted by use of technical devices, such as jump-cuts, so that the episodic nature of construction seems unnatural. Technical devices should also be used to emphasize the process of construction. The audience should be directly involved in the performance, so that they are aware that they are not witnessing reality, but an arbitrary construction of the real.

In particular, the theories of Brecht were influential on some of the film-makers of the French new wave in the 1960s. Jean-Luc Godard saw film production in terms of weaving a tapestry upon which he embroidered ideas rather than told stories. He felt that it was particularly important to show the mechanisms of film production, and to draw attention to the artificial nature of the medium. The writers of *Cahier du Cinéma* in France (Truffaut, Godard, Chabrol, *et al.*), felt that establishment products of French cinema were too ornately staged, heavily plotted, over-scripted and unspontaneous. All these elements they attempted to challenge in their urban style of 'guerrilla' film-making in the French new wave. Other directors, such as Ingmar Bergman, have called for unresolved ambiguity in film, to challenge the classic realist text and to stimulate the audience.

The empathy and identification of an audience with a character led, according to Brecht, to a feeling rather than a thinking audience, an accepting not an interrogating one. The dominant narrative form was ideological because its structure suppressed socio-political meanings in favour of individualistic narratives. Film and theatre strategies for Brecht should provoke intellectual involvement: people need to think and decode signs, rather than follow narratives.

Peter Wollen (1985) developed an interesting analysis of the work of Jean-Luc Godard and 'counter cinema'. This analysis is constructed in terms of binary oppositions. By schematizing it, we can create a table (see Table 17.1) that we can usefully apply to all moving image products.

Oppositional moving image products can, basically, be constructed in two ways. First, you can alter the content, you can make critical or politicized products such as Jean-Luc Godard's *Weekend* (1966). Critical products might work to alter or challenge the images or representations of minority groups in society, such as in Rose Troche's film about lesbians, *Go Fish* (1994). The second way you can create oppositional moving image products is by altering the form – that is, through changing the structure of narrative as in Alain Resnais' enigmatic *Last Year in Marienbad* (1961), or by developing techniques of production that consciously draw attention to themselves, such as the *mise-en-scène* created by the video camera in *The Blair Witch Project* (1999).

Narrative forms have been developed in new technologies, and have been epitomized by the growth of post-modern narratives such as video and computer games. Here the aim is often to complete a narrative, through various levels of Propp's 'functions'. Games often involve quests, fights and goals, with very specific 'roles' provided by the game. Of specific interest is the interactive nature of these sorts of narratives where, given a specific frame-work, the audience can develop its own particular version of the narrative.

Conventional narrative vs alternative narrative   Table 17.1

Conventional narrative	Alternative narrative
Narrative transitivity Chain of events, cause and effect, central enigma	*Narrative intransitivity* Gaps, interruptions, espisodic, digression, break-up of narrative
Identification Empathy and emotional involvement	*Estrangement* Direct address, multiple divided characters
Transparency Window on the world, seamless editing	*Foregrounding* Making the technical overt and explicit
Single diegesis Homogenous world	*Multiple diegesis* Heterogeneous world
Closure Self-contained, resolution of central enigma	*Aperture* Open-ended, overspill, intertextuality
Pleasure Entertaining, satisfying and confirming	*Unpleasure* Dissatisfaction, provocation and alienation
Fiction Actors wearing costume, doing a performance	*Reality* Real life, non-professional actors, breaking up representation

Multi-media moving image production is increasingly very important in the development of new narrative styles, combining computer graphics, animation, music, film and video all in one product. The director Peter Greenaway, has used multi-media packages to stunning effect in such films as *Prospero's Books* (1991) and *The Pillow Book* (1995). Computer animation first developed for *Star Wars* (1977) has been used extensively in films such as *Jurassic Park* (1993) and *Terminator 2* (1996), while *Toy Story* (1995) was the first film completely generated by computer. The effect of multi-media production on narratives is that it develops story-telling away from the domination of language and scripting, more towards visual and sign-based forms of communication.

Technologies such as satellite and digital communication create two possibilities for narrative. The first is that they will become increasingly multi-cultural, drawing on cross-cultures for their meaning and style. Second, narratives will become more and more universalized and similar, most probably dominated by the Hollywood style of narrative and appealing to the lowest common denominator of audience interest. Questioning narratives brings to the fore discussions of the role of the moving image in society generally. Questions such as 'Whose interests do they serve?' 'What are they saying?' We also have to ask ourselves, and our society, to what extent we have become narrative junkies. That is, is it the case that we cannot accept information, concepts and ideas unless they come to us in a mass-mediated narrative form?

CHAPTER 18

Genre Theory and the Moving Image

The term genre derives from the French word meaning 'type' or 'kind'. It is a term whose meaning is implicitly understood, by both audiences and producers, as being a way in which moving image products can be grouped and classified together. Genre is best seen as a set of principles by which we are able to associate a film, a television programme, or a style of music video with others of its kind. In genre analysis we are especially concerned with how similar products within a genre are constructed and relate to each other, and indeed how genres work across mediums. That is, what elements they have in common, and then how audiences recognize and respond to them. Genre products have been the staple diet for television for a long time now; the demands of the schedule and advertisers have meant that television companies have tended to play safe with the production of genre products that can guarantee an audience. Hence television's bill of fare consists of soap operas, quiz shows, chat shows, news, situation comedies and, lately, hospital dramas.

Two accepted definitions of genre might prove useful at this point:

A genre film is one in which the narrative pattern, or crucial aspects of that pattern, is visually recognizable as having been used similarly in other films. (Solomon, 1976: 3)

Genre is a system of codes, conventions, and visual styles, which enables an audience to determine rapidly and with some complexity the kind of narrative they are viewing. (Turner, 1993: 83)

Genre theory has its roots in literary theory, theatre and art criticism. Genre theory in film studies emerged in the late 1950s as a response to the growing dissatisfaction with the *auteur* debate. This was seen to privilege the film director as artist – that is, as the sole creator of meaning for the audience through the film text. Genre critics argued that an audience watches films within the context of other films, and generates its understandings of these films from the similarity and relationships between them. We might add that this is not only the case for the films that they have seen, but also other media products in the same genre, such as books, radio plays or magazines. For genre critics, meaning is essentially intertextual, residing in the relationship between many texts, not embedded in a single text or product. Genre critics argue that by drawing upon a predefined set of tools and conventions, both producers and audiences categorize media products into particular genres; communication is then achieved between the encoder and the decoder. The producer constructs the text with reference to the genre, and the audience 'reads' the text with reference to the genre.

Genre is also part of moving image marketing in that it allows moving image products to be packaged and clearly labelled for an audience, which is then able to select products for consumption according to its previous experience of that genre. It is in this way that the audience, and audience taste, can influence the types of genre available in any one period. There are, for instance, very few musicals made these days as compared to their heyday in the 1930s and 1940s. There are more soap operas available than ever before, and a glimpse at television schedules will show you that the western genre is as popular as ever.

Particular genres become associated with particular people or organizations. Actors or actresses become associated with particular film genres: John Wayne with westerns, Arnold Schwarzenegger with action/adventure, Christopher Lee with horror. Film genres become associated with particular directors: Alfred Hitchcock for thrillers, John Ford for westerns, and Wes Craven for horror. Companies become associated with certain kinds of product: CNN with news. Particular film studios made particular kinds of film: Ealing made comedies, MGM made musicals, Hammer made horror films.

The study of genre is largely based on description and classification. Any analysis may begin with an exploration of the largest categories of genre, such as fiction and non-fiction, move through various popular genres, such as soap operas or horror films, and finally consider the smallest divisions of what are called **subgenres**, such as body horror or the road movie.

GENRE IDENTIFICATION

Genres are not an imitation or representation of the real world, but rather of other media products. Thus, news may be about world events, but its format is constructed along particular lines – lines that are similar even across mediums. Genre works through, and depends on, intertextuality (that is, how one text relates to and is understood in terms of others). We recognize news in any medium because of its structure, its mode of delivery and its language. The idea of generic cores is of use here, in that all genres have a central element or series of elements around which they are constructed. The generic core of news is the listing and reporting of events. That is the essence or central point around which the news genre revolves. The generic core of a private investigator film is the occupation of the central character; for the western it is often the landscape against which the narrative is played out.

An audience's understanding of a genre will be dependent on its experience of it elsewhere, its familiarity with it, and its recognition of elements in its construction, be that people, objects or storylines. In this way the audience is able to make sense of what it is seeing. We all call upon and use our 'generic memories' in such situations. Generic cores, codes and conventions – such as headlines in news, thunder and lightning in horror films, and the cliffhanger in soap operas – will organize the audience's expectations of the specific genre. For instance, if we go to see a comedy film, we expect to laugh; at a horror film, we expect to be scared; watching a current affairs programme, we expect to be informed; and watching a romance, we expect to shed a tear.

Genre products continue to be made because they are popular, and there is thus a guaranteed audience and revenue for the product. The industry, then, uses the notion of genre when deciding which products to finance, and then publicizes those products via generic ideas and images in order to appeal to the audience. The key relationships in the production of twentieth-century genres are those between the genre, the industry and the audience. This is best seen as a triangular relationship, as shown in Figure 18.1.

Genre is so important to the media industries that they have developed and constructed themselves along generic lines. The BBC is still constructed by departments of, drama, current affairs, light entertainment, etc.

As we have said, genres rely on the audience's knowledge and experience of them in order for a process of understanding, or intertextual 'reading', to take place. However, genres actually work, and become recognizable, through their formal characteristics. These are essentially codes and conventions; they include stylistic characteristics (camera work, lighting, sound effects, speech, writing style, music, graphics, etc.), iconography, *mise-en-scène* and narrative structure.

Formal characteristics will obviously alter between media. We will examine the stylistic ones first. For film and television, camera work, lighting, sound and editing are all important in providing the visual codes and conventions by which we recognize the genre we are dealing with. In television news, for instance, the mid-shot of the newsreader addressing us directly is a crucial visual code; we may then order our expectations of the type of programme we are viewing simply upon that one shot – that is, that this is a serious programme and that the information we are being given is important and 'true'. The use of high-key lighting, minimal editing of newsreader and sound (especially lack of background sound and music), are all important to the 'look' or 'feel' of the genre of news on television.

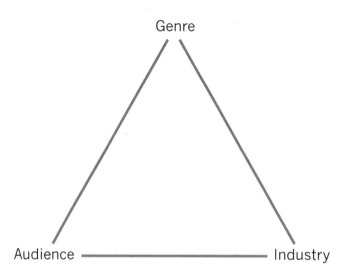

Figure 18.1   *Genre/audience/industry triangle*

Mockumentary

Mockumentaries are parodies of the documentary genre. They are fictional stories that work largely because of the audience's understanding of the codes and conventions of the documentary genre itself. The first mockumentary was probably *David Holzman's Diary* (1968) by Jim McBride, followed by *No Lies, No Lies* (1973) by Mitchel Block. The last 20 years have seen a steady stream of mockumentaries, from the famous rocku/mockumentary *This is Spinal Tap* (1984), through *Leningrad Cowboys Go to America* (1989), *Bob Roberts* (1992), *Man Bites Dog* (1992) and *CB4* (1993) to *The Blair Witch Project* (1999).

The key documentary influences on mockumentaries are Direct Cinema and Cinema Vérité. Both have a very strong visual style. The use of hand-held cameras, natural sound and lighting, are all central to the style of mockumentaries, at times even being taken to the extreme. The critical narrative structure draws its power from the documentary point of view, the investigative/questioning approach. Mockumentaries, as with documentaries, intrude into the lives and attitudes of the rich and famous. One of the most famous Direct Cinema films was D.A. Pennebaker's *Don't Look Back*, covering Bob Dylan's 1965 tour of Britain; the narrative and visual style of this is heavily covered by both *This is Spinal Tap* and more overtly by *Bob Roberts*. *Man Bites Dog*, which follows the career of a serial killer, clearly follows the conventions of Cinema Vérité, in that the crew are a visible part of the construction of the documentary.

Iconography

Iconography is very important in generic recognition. An icon is a type of sign, and resembles the object for which it stands. An icon is also an image with a meaning beyond its physical form. A stetson hat, for example, is an icon for the western genre. A horse in a western implies power, masculinity, control, independence and survival. The icon of the six-gun attains a mythic, quasi-religious meaning in the hands of an avenging sheriff out to rid the west of lawlessness.

The icon, be it a person or an object is significant in that we associate it with other films or media products in which it has appeared, and thus ascribe to it value and meaning according to that previous experience of it. An icon, then, provides a form of shorthand for both the producer and the audience – it saves them having to laboriously fill in the background to each person, image or object.

If you look at the images from western genre films presented in Figure 18.2 – *The Gunfighter* (1950) and *Unforgiven* (1996) – even though they are from different eras, your generic memory will immediately tell you much about the central figures and the objects that surround them. You will be able to guess what has occurred before the pictures were taken, you will have expectations of what is going to happen next and how each will act.

Mise-en-scène, as we seen earlier in this section, can be understood as being everything

(a)

(b)

Figure 18.2   Clint Eastwood in *Unforgiven* (a) and Gregory Peck in *The Gunfighter* (b)
Source: (a) Warner Bros; (b) Twentieth Century Fox Film Corporation

within the frame, location, image, set design, costume, placement of objects, spatial relations (those characters who are dominant/frightening), the interplay of light and shade, as well as the camera's position and angle of view. All these elements are important in the generation of mood, atmosphere and the feeling of a genre. *Mise-en-scène* is crucial for genre, since it gives us visual clues to the genre we are involved in. The two stills taken from westerns illustrate this well. We have the iconographical image of the central cowboy figure; his body language tells us a great deal about him. We also have the associated props. Period costume, too, is central to the *mise-en-scène*, as is the saloon with its wooden walls. The *mise-en-scène* here, combined with iconography, does two things: it provides us with visual cues, which nudge our generic memories, and it gives us a sense or feeling from the scene.

Ideological Themes

The ideological approach to genre concerns itself with the use of myths, meanings and values in society. Ideological themes are best understood through the identification of representations in genre media products. Genres tend to rely heavily on rigid stereotypes as part of their shorthand style of story-telling. For instance, in the western the roles for women are limited to mother/daughter, saloon girl (whore), or squaw. Later films, such as *Bad Girls*

(1994) and *The Quick and the Dead* (1995), have sought to challenge these representations, but to some extent have merely become parodies of the genre, because of the engrained nature of the stereotype of women in the western (this is also a reason why the western is a gendered genre being largely preferred by men).

The social, cultural and political significance of genre texts lies in their re-representing of existing social relations. That is, the use of recurrent themes, solutions, attitudes, situations and characters, reveals the way people think about society, and tends to reinforce the status quo. Genre viewing is a reinforcing and comforting experience. Unlike the alternative narratives we were discussing earlier, genre viewing closes down alternative meanings and ways of acting, in favour of the maintenance of the status quo. Hence, gangster films will always end with the gangster character being killed, as in *White Heat* (1949); this continues even in the more modern gangster-rap versions such as *New Jack City* (1991).

For writers such as Thomas Schatz it is in the resolution of the genre product that the ideological dimension becomes apparent. He provides the following analysis of the typical genre structure:

- *Establishment* (via various narrative and iconographical cues) of generic community with its inherent dramatic conflicts.
- *Animation* of those conflicts through the actions and attitudes of the genre's constellation of characters.
- *Intensification* of the conflict by means of conventional situations and dramatic confrontations until the conflict reaches crisis proportions.
- *Resolution* of the crisis in a fashion which eliminates the physical and/or ideological threat and thereby celebrates the (temporarily) well-ordered community.

(Schatz, 1981: 30)

For Schatz, genre films eliminate symbolically any opposing value systems; they portray our culture as stable and our value systems as inviolate. He also sees the Hollywood star system as playing a major role in the way that the resolution of genre films is precipitated by the hero's actions. The ideological attributes of a society can be seen as embedded in stars such as John Wayne (who, incidentally, was only 'killed' in one of his westerns – *The Cowboys* (1971) – and had to think long and hard about accepting that role because of the effect his demise might have on the audience).

Ideological themes can be found in even the most apparently neutral programmes. Animals in wildlife documentaries, which dominate television schedules, are nearly always given human attributes – that is, they are anthropomorphized (a process that contains many ideological lessons). The actions of the animal kingdom are commented on in terms of the way that we humans organize our societies. Male and female child-rearing roles are often emphasized, as are battles over territory. In this way, the same human activities are ideologically underpinned, in that they are seen to be part of the 'natural' world.

Ideologies of nationalism play a key role in many fictional genres, such as – obviously – war films, spy films and westerns. It has to be remembered, in the case of film and television products in particular, that these ideologies now play not only to a national but also to an international audience.

Genre Development

Christian Metz (1975) draws our attention to the process of the development of a genre throughout its life span. If we adapt his ideas we can suggest that genres pass through four phases of existence:

1 the experimental
2 the classic
3 the parody
4 the deconstruction.

The experimental phase of the western would include the early years of the genre's development with such films as *The Great Train Robbery* (1903) and *The Virginian* (1914). The classical phase would be once the genre was established and its conventions widely used and recognized; this would include films such as *Stagecoach* (1939) and *Red River* (1948). Parody would be film that mimicked the genre, such as *The Professionals* (1966) or *Blazing Saddles* (1974). Finally in deconstruction we find the generic elements of the western calling attention to themselves by being placed out of context; *Outland* (1981) does this by remaking *High Noon* (1952) but within the science fiction genre. Post-westerns also deconstruct the genre, by placing the western hero in a contemporary, and usually urban, American setting; *Midnight Cowboy* (1969) and *Coogan's Bluff* (1968) both do this.

The same schema can be applied to film noir. The experimental period might be seen as German expressionism, with films such as *The Cabinet of Dr Caligari* (1920) or *Nosferatu* (1922). The classical era is the period from 1941 to 1958, including such films as *Double Indemnity* (1944) and *The Big Sleep* (1946). Parody is undoubtedly provided by *Dead Men Don't Wear Plaid* (1982), while deconstruction can be seen in *Blade Runner* (1982), which mixes film noir and science fiction, or *Near Dark* (1987), which mixes film noir with horror.

This schema allows us to consider the development of genres, their genesis and their possible future directions. It also illustrates how genre categories can be flexible, and allows us to consider how the various moving image industries adapt to, or create, public taste.

The post-western

Evolving in the period after the Second World War, and finding their true expression during the 1960s and 1970s, post-westerns are essentially about the modern-day American west – that is, a west haunted by old myths and ideals. But they are also about how the westerners are now incongruous figures, not only in their natural setting but elsewhere in America. Films such as *Bad Day at Black Rock* (1954), *Lonely are the Brave* (1962), *Coogan's Bluff* (1969) and *Midnight Cowboy* (1969) show the westerner to be either vulnerable and pathetic or dangerous and anarchic. The traditional values he represents are seen as being out of place, misguided, threatening, simply belonging to another era or only to the world of film itself. According to Philip French the central characteristic of post-western films is that the people in them are 'influenced by, or are victims of, the cowboy cult; they intensify and play on the audience's feelings about, and knowledge of, western movies' (French, 1977: 140).

Coogan's Bluff places Clint Eastwood as an Arizona deputy in the middle of New York attempting to extradite a prisoner in a world much more complicated than his own simple western life. Constantly referred to as 'Texas', his western attire and forthright attitude soon call into question his place in the modern world. However, unlike Joe Buck the westerner in *Midnight Cowboy*, Coogan maintains his dignity throughout, and by the end of the film some compromises have been reached that have enabled 'right' to prevail in a world of drug users, hippies and social workers.

At a generic level, all post-westerns use iconography to manipulate audience knowledge of the western genre. Thus in both the above-mentioned films, stetson hats, cowboy boots and shoestring ties form aspects of the visual references that are part of the play within the film and intertextually within the western genre.

In *Lonely are the Brave* (1962), Kirk Douglas plays the last real cowboy in a world dominated by the internal combustion engine. This is perhaps the 'out of time' western *par excellence*, as Douglas struggles to maintain his cowboy lifestyle in the face of an ever-encroaching modern world. *Lonely are the Brave* sets up an interesting antithesis with the truck driver who will ultimately become Douglas's nemesis. For it is the truck driver who becomes the modern cowboy figure in later post-westerns, such as Peckinpah's *Convoy* (1978) or *Smokey and the Bandit* (1977).

The road movie

The development of the post-western is linked with the development of subgenres such as the road movie. The road movie can be seen as a subgenre of the western since it has at its core many of the same elements, conventions and themes. Paramount among these are movement, landscape, individualism and freedom.

Mark Williams draws some clear connections between the road movie and the western, not simply the obvious replacement of the horse and stagecoach by the motorcycle, car and truck, but the very nature of the landscape in which they take place:

> In the western this huge natural stage saw hackneyed themes of love, greed, friendship and revenge revitalized by picaresque characterizations, figures that were dramatically enhanced by the uncertainty and raw challenge of the pioneer era. The simple struggles of a disparate people trying to normalize life and scratch an income in a massive hostile landscape was, in itself, often enough to carry such a film. Road movies involve plots of a similar nature, the problems and choices are still made pretty plain, and the protagonist remains the common man trying to make it against easily identifiable odds. (Williams, 1982: 7)

One can add to this the position of women in road movies, the use of guns, and a sense of male chauvinism and camaraderie. The road movie casts many of the same themes of the western out on to the open road. Among the most interesting examples are *Easy Rider* (1969), *Electra Glide in Blue* (1973) and, more recently, *Thelma and Louise* (1991).

Dennis Hopper's *Easy Rider* is a film that takes its western heritage and symbolism very seriously. Two drifters Wyatt and Billy (Earp and the Kid!), after completing a drug deal, travel from west to east in order to attend the New Orleans Mardi Gras. On route they travel through familiar desert landscape, and stop off at a farming community where their bikes are compared visually with horses as forms of freedom and machines controlled by men. The film, once it has established these icons, begins to show the degeneration of the American dream through the attributes and behaviour of the people who now occupy the west. The film ends with the destruction of the central characters – and thus the destruction of the individualism and freedom they represent – by some 'redneck' farmers.

Thelma and Louise (1991) is Ridley Scott's rewriting of both the male western and the road movie to fit female specifications. The story of two women whose lives are changed by the attempted rape of one of them, constantly alludes to the western. The most striking scene is set in 'John Ford's' Monument Valley where a leather-clad cop is symbolically castrated (through the loss of his gun) by the two women and locked in the trunk of his car; later a Rastafarian cycles by, stopping only to breathe some of his 'joint' through the air holes shot in the trunk of the car. Thus we see that in the centre of the western heartland, the genre no longer belongs to the white male. Men are relegated to the periphery of this film, even the final freeze-frame sequence, which recalls *Butch Cassidy and the Sundance Kid* (1969), tells us that there are now two more western legends – women – to stand alongside the men in the genre's mythology.

James William Guercio's *Electra Glide in Blue* (1973), also filmed in Monument Valley, is a vision of the corrupt and degenerating west, where decay is all around. Here he places Robert Blake – the last straight motorcycle cop, John Wintergreen, who is constantly compared with Alan Ladd. *Electra Glide* is a parody of the western hero, whose values are now out of place and struggling against a tide of corruption from all angles. History has passed the west by; the road brings trouble and death from the outside world, but it also provides a means of escape and freedom.

Genre Criticisms

Before considering other relationships with genre study, it is worthwhile considering some criticisms of the notion of genre itself. There are four main points of attack, which can be summarized as follows.

- *Circularity*: the problem is that, to establish a genre, you first of all need to isolate its content, and you can only do so, if you already have a pre-existing set of criteria; this then presupposes the existence of the genre.
- *Linearity*: the generalized nature of descriptions may prove too static to accommodate adequately generic developments and diversity.
- *Labelling*: are the generic systems too large? We have to subdivide into sub- or post-genres – such as the crime genre into police drama, private eye, thriller, film noir, etc. – and there is some disagreement as to whether some of these are genres in their own right.
- *Repetition*: whether genre is merely repeating the same worn-out formulae to an audience lacking a variety of non-generic products to choose from.

Genre and Narrative Structure

Narrative structure is a key formal characteristic of genre – fictional genre products in particular, have typical and recognizable stories and plots. Narrative form or narrative structure should here be taken to mean all the elements used in a story to progress that story in a cause and effect chain. Genre, as we have seen, relies heavily on convention. We can list these conventions and apply them to the western genre:

- conventional central characters – cowboy, sheriff, Indian, bandit, etc.
- conventional representations or stereotypes – cantankerous 'old timer', saloon girl/whore, savage Indian, etc.
- conventional locations – the plains, the western town, the Indian encampment, etc.
- conventional settings – inside the saloon, the covered wagon, the jail, the tepee, etc.
- conventional objects – six-guns, saddles, bow and arrow, sheriff's badge, etc.
- conventional costume – gingham dresses, stetson hats, leather chaps, feather head-dresses, etc.
- conventional dialogue – 'head 'em up and move 'em out', 'Yee-ha', 'this town ain't big enough for the both of us', etc.
- conventional sounds – cavalry bugle, gun shots, saloon piano, stampeding cattle, yelping Indians, etc.
- conventional music – western ballad ('High Noon' by Frankie Laine), western fiddle and guitar music, etc.
- conventional set-pieces – the gunfight on the street, the saloon poker game, the bank/train robbery, etc.
- conventional plots – gunfighter comes to town, gunfighter causes trouble, sheriff challenges gunfighter, sheriff wins gunfight, peace restored to town.

This set of narrative conventions can be applied to any story-based genres, even soap operas, quiz shows or news.

The last convention, the plot, is one that unites all genres and can be identified as being the 'classic realist' Hollywood text. As we have seen, this refers to the fact that all Hollywood films have a beginning, a middle and an end. This Hollywood narrative structure is particularly strong in genre products, providing as it does another recognizable trait of particular genres.

If we now apply the model of a narrative structure used earlier with the example of a western gunfighter story we get the following.

	Sheriff runs a peaceful town
Opening	Gunfighter arrives
	Town doesn't want trouble
	Sheriff asks gunfighter to leave
Conflict	Gunfighter refuses and continues to make trouble
	Sheriff pursues gunfighter and his associates

Gunfight

Resolution   Sheriff wins through superior skill

Peace is restored, sheriff and town have developed

This narrative model can be applied to any fictional genre product. Despite obvious differences in genre products, genres as diverse as westerns, musicals and horror products, share this common structure of the 'classic realist' Hollywood text.

It must be remembered, however, that each genre has its own particular elements, patterns and processes to which all of the above formal characteristics contribute. Some of these might be themes, subplots, non-central characters, additional locations, musical signatures, particular use of language, etc.

It is the combination of these narrative elements and the formal characteristics that creates the formula on which each genre is based. Genres are often described as formula products, this is because they appear to adhere to a set of rules that the genre must follow in order to be identified as such. Soap operas, for instance, utilize the same setting every week, there is a very slow turnover of characters (some stay for years), and they concern themselves with everyday people and events (especially soaps from Britain and Australia). In films, however, different formulae can be present within the same genre. In the western, for instance, there are gunfighter films, cowboy films, cavalry films and outlaw films.

By varying the formal characteristics of a genre, new stories and themes can emerge. Thus the use of formulae should not be seen as a constraint on the development of a genre product. For imaginative media producers, formulae provide the backbone, the framework or map, on which they can describe their own route, safe in the knowledge that their audience has an idea of the road being taken, but can be constantly surprised by the new route to an old destination.

The narrative structure of genres such as the western relies heavily on mythical structure, hence the victory of good over evil, society over wilderness and lawlessness, etc. Will Wright (1975) used this notion of binary oppositions to identify four basic oppositions that reoccur in the western genre:

- good vs bad
- strong vs weak
- civilization vs wilderness
- inside society vs outside society.

The relationship between each of these oppositions is dependent upon the society in which westerns are made. Wright links together westerns of particular eras in order to demonstrate this:

- the classical western – 1930–55
- the vengeance western – 1950–60
- the transition western – early 1950s
- the professional western – 1958–70.

In the classic western, the hero and society are closely aligned with the left-hand side of the oppositions, as opposed to the villain, who is represented by the right-hand side. By the professional western, the right- and left-hand side of the oppositions have altered and the hero is now opposed to society.

The hero is thus:		Society and the villain are thus:
outside society	vs	inside society
in the wilderness	vs	civilization
strong	vs	weak
good	vs	bad

This development in the genre over 40 years has to be seen in relation to the changing nature of society itself over that period. A particular catalyst was the 1960s and the Vietnam War, where the old certainties of the American dream were seen to be disappearing, society and particularly the government were not always seen as being in the right, hence the development and relevance of the professional western.

We can develop Wright's analysis into the 1980s and 1990s, perhaps calling the new phase the pastiche western. Here the emphasis would be on the blurring of the boundaries between the hero and the villain in an individualistic society. Both are aware of their own mythology and their role in society and the genre. This self-reflection and introspection is key to understanding the pastiche western. A form of pessimism and relativism has placed society both inside and outside both the hero and the villain. *Unforgiven* is a good example of this. In this version of the western, societal moral codes and values have disappeared in favour of individual action. The generic construction of the hero is more self-aware of its reflection of society, thus films such as *Posse* (1993) and *Bad Girls* consciously draw on American contemporary society and its values.

In films such as *Wild Wild West* (1998) the icons are subverted in such a way as to create a discontinuity within the genre. As the genre becomes obsessed with its own look and style, image becomes more important than content. A form of media hyper-reality has taken the place of the interplay between hero and villain. There is also a form of hyper-signification involved, whereby the sophisticated audience draws on the multiple intertextual and semiological references within the text. The pastiche western is bound up with the social and cultural milieu much more than any of its predecessors.

Given the above, the pastiche western, in terms of oppositions, looks like this:

The hero is:	The villain is:
relatively good within the narrative	relatively bad within the narrative
society inside or outside the individual	society inside or outside the individual
a reflection of contemporary society	a reflection of the traditional western
weak and strong	strong and weak
politically correct	politically incorrect

Genre and narrative work through the use of conventions, structure and, as we have just seen, binary oppositions. Narrative is part of the marshalling and organizing of the audience's expectations. It has a function for both the audience and the film-maker, since narrative is part of the codes and conventions that circulate between audience, text and industry.

Auteur Theory and Western Directors

This chapter started by stating that genre emerged out of the dissatisfaction with *auteur* theory. It is worthwhile ending with a consideration of how this major moving image theory can indeed complement our understanding of how genre works. *Auteur* basically refers to the director as the author of the film. The director is seen as being responsible for the look and style of the film. This might be achieved technically through camera work, performance, lighting, editing, or simply through subject area, themes explored and characterizations, all contributing to the construction of the *mise-en-scène*. *Auteur* states that the director is able to impose himself, or herself, on the material, and stamp his or her authority on a piece of work regardless of narrative or commercial pressures.

Auteur recognition was first discussed by Alexander Astruc in his 1948 article 'The birth of the new avant-garde: le Camera Stylo'. Astruc saw the cinema as gradually becoming a language – that is, a means of expression and a form by which an artist could express his or her thoughts. *Auteur* first appeared as a powerful force in film criticism through the influential French journal *Cahiers du Cinema*. François Truffaut's article in 1954 on the *'politiques des auteur'* sees *auteur* as a policy for the personal freedom of the director in film production – a role that was to be followed through by the film-makers of the French new wave. It was Andrew Sarris (1962/63) in America who saw *auteur* as a theory, and the director as the determining factor in the film's production, as the artist creating meaning within the film.

Auteur as a theory has been criticized for ignoring the fact that film-making is a collective process, and also because it tends to privilege the director as the sole creator of meaning for the audience. It was this final aspect of *auteur* theory that genre critics were objecting to. Genre conventions were seen as being utilized by both audiences and film-makers; these then exercise a determining power over what the director can or cannot do. The constraints of genre, it was felt, limited the ways in which the authorial signature could be inscribed or detected. There remained for some time a gap between the *auteur* and genre approaches until, as we shall see, the role of the director in the creation of original genre products began to be examined.

Originality in the western is often seen as dependent upon the originality and insight of the director. It is also dependent upon the film-makers' handling of basic narrative, environment and character development. This is especially the case for a studio system that tightly controls the script; the originality of the director to some extent emerges in the handling of the material that he or she is given and the production of the *mise-en-scène*. It is not surprising that Bazin (1971) rejects the genre's empiricist enumeration of icons, symbols and events in favour of what he calls the true life of the western being in its *mise-en-scène*, for it is here that genre meets *auteur*.

Concerns with aesthetics, the look, or the artistic nature of genre, unite the approaches of both genre and *auteur*. The aesthetic approach strikes at the very heart of the criticism of genre as repetition. Indeed, much early debate in film criticism saw genre as an inadmissible concept since aesthetic quality was seen to be associated, as in art, with originality. Originality was perceived to be unattainable in a mass production system such as Hollywood. Hence the emphasis of the aesthetic approach has been, as Feuer states, 'to define genre in terms of a system of conventions that permits artistic expression, especially involving individual authorship' (1992: 145).

Solomon (1976), while accepting some charges of the repetition argument, states that, 'to achieve genre art, film-makers must be committed to exploring new facets of the familiar setting, elaborating on their insights into the mythic structures of the genre' (1976: 7). Solomon identifies the best products of a genre as being those that incorporate generic elements to the fullest degree, never going beyond the limits of genre formula. However, the artistic and intellectual insights necessary for such products are stored, according to Solomon, 'in the minds of film-makers such as Alfred Hitchcock and John Ford' (1976: 2). Jim Kitses extends this view beyond the directors' contribution to the idea that genres can help crystallize their preoccupations. He argues that:

> rather than an empty vessel breathed life into by the film-maker, the [western] genre is a vital structure through which flow a myriad of themes and concepts. As such the form can provide a director with a range of possible connections and the space in which to experiment, to shape and refine the kinds of effects and meanings he is working towards. (Kitses, 1969: 26)

We can now illustrate this with a number of examples.

John Ford

Place states that:

> There is an intentionality behind a work of art, no one familiar with the body of his work could deny that John Ford's personal vision makes up the bulk of the intentionality of his movies. . . . There are many ways to approach that body of work which is John Ford's westerns. Although the great power of his films comes from his personal vision, it is significant that they are rooted in American history, and set in the genre of the western. (Place, 1974: 4)

Ford recreates in his western films those American myths and ideals that are most meaningful to him, such as individualism, the building of new communities, the struggle with the wilderness, and the role of the military. These are combined in his films with an eye for emotional involvement with traditions and rituals, particularly religious and military ones.

Jim Kitses' approach to the *auteur* is to 'honour all of a director's work by a systematic examination in order to trace characteristic themes, structures and formal qualities' (Kitses, 1969: 7). In the case of John Ford, this has most markedly been achieved by Place (1974) and Anderson (1981), as well as by those articles on Ford represented in Caughie (1981).

Drawing on these, it is possible to systematize the Fordian view, or Fordian values, represented in the western.

- Ford's films are about history, with a nostalgic and sentimentalized approach in films such as *The Iron Horse* (1924) about the building of the trans-continental railway, or in *My Darling Clementine* (1946) about the gunfight at OK Corral.
- Ford's films are about landscapes: their beauty as well as men and women's place within them, and their struggle with them. In particular, Monument Valley in *Stagecoach* (1939), *The Searchers* (1956) and *Cheyenne Autumn* (1964) epitomizes the struggle between wilderness, savagery and civilization.
- Ford's films are about communities and what binds them together: the community of the cavalry in the 'Cavalry Trilogy', the community of settlers in *Drums Along the Mohawk* (1939), of the stagecoach in *Stagecoach*, the wagon train in *Wagonmaster* (1950), the Cheyenne in *Cheyenne Autumn*.
- Ford's interest in community particularly manifests itself in rituals, rituals that bind communities and groups of people: the dance in *Wagonmaster* and *She Wore A Yellow Ribbon* (1949). The funeral of 'Trooper Smith' also in *She Wore A Yellow Ribbon*, and most importantly of Ethan Edwards' family in *The Searchers*, which he brings to an abrupt end with the words 'put an amen to it', symbolizing Edwards' move away from the community spirit in his individual search for revenge.
- Ford's films are about individuals and how they act in and outside of organizations. Ethan Edwards is an obvious example here, as is Wyatt Earp (Henry Fonda) in *My Darling Clementine* and also Nathan Brittles (John Wayne) in *She Wore A Yellow Ribbon*, Ransom Stoddard (James Stewart) in *The Man Who Shot Liberty Valance* (1962).

The Fordian view altered over his 47 years of making western feature films, although the themes themselves did not. Films such as *The Searchers*, *Two Rode Together* (1961), *The Man Who Shot Liberty Valance* and *Cheyenne Autumn* all became more cynical and self-referential. In the first example, for instance, Ethan's obsessions have led him to rebuild a community, but the final shot reminds us that he is forever outside it. In *Two Rode Together* the hero and the woman he rescues flee into the wilderness at the end, in order to escape any kind of organized community. *The Man Who Shot Liberty Valance* is about the death of the old west, and the birth of the relationship between politics and the media. In his final film the fate of the Cheyenne represents the loss of ritual, victory, glory, honour and the ability to control one's own destiny, as Place states, 'The myth is exposed as inadequate. The search for meaning in life has become absurd' (Place, 1974: 246).

Sam Peckinpah

Although Sam Peckinpah made fewer western films than John Ford (six in all), there are some interesting connections between them, as Kitses states:

> Peckinpah is deeply rooted in and, like his heroes, oppressed by the American past. Here, as in so much else, he recalls John Ford; though where the older figure began by printing

the legend and ended by bitterly trying to print the facts, Peckinpah's vision incorporates at once myth and reality, romance and tragedy. (Kitses, 1969: 168)

Peckinpah makes very strong use of the western genre, but he does so to unmask America through its cinema. For him, the western film was a universal frame within which it was possible to comment on contemporary society. He wished to make judgements on social configurations both past and present. Criticism of Peckinpah accuses him of nihilism; his films reflect a breakdown in American values and a general loss of faith. Peckinpah insists that the values were sick and twisted in the first place, and that his films only reflect that: 'Peckinpah sees American history in terms of the emergence of a civilization whose main feature is wanton destructiveness' (Butler, 1979: 23).

In *Ride the High Country* (1962), society is corrupt, religion is corrupt, only nature represents escape. There is a moral complexity in the characters' interaction and their different relationships with society: the good guy, played by Joel McCrea, dies and the bad/good guy, played by Randolph Scott, lives. We know that Randolph Scott's character will return the gold he stole earlier in the plot at the end of the film – not through any sense of duty to society, civilization, God or law, but simply to honour his friend.

In *The Wild Bunch* (1969) there is no difference between civilization and the bandits. Nothing is what it seems: the soldiers turn out to be outlaws and the children are torturers. Kitses feels that, 'Properly understood, the film is criticism: of the American idea of the male elite, of the professionalism and incipient militarism of a Howard Hawks' (Kitses, 1969: 164). Or, one might also add, of a John Ford. The central characters in *The Wild Bunch* live in extremes, especially extremes of violence. Peckinpah uses a great many intertextual references, from characters to settings, even hymns such as 'Gather at the River', which was a much-used anthem in Ford and others, usually representing the coming together of community. Peckinpah, though, used it as a prelude to the destruction of a community. None of the violence in Peckinpah's films is seen as protecting a community, it is rather the last resort of individuals who live at the very edge of society, or completely outside society.

In Peckinpah's films, unlike those of Ford, the heroes are saddled with an internal conflict: as we saw in *Ride the High Country* (1962), the Randolph Scott character is torn between loyalty and his desire to steal the gold. In *Major Dundee* (1964) both the major himself and his Confederate prisoner Tyreen are uncertain about their lives in the post-Civil War world. Pike Bishop in *The Wild Bunch* is a tortured man on the verge of madness.

Pat Garrett and Billy the Kid (1973) was Peckinpah's last western, and can be seen as an addition to what might be called a minor branch of the western genre: the Billy the Kid film. Peckinpah adds his own layers of meaning, not only in the exploration of the two characters' motivation, but more importantly, and perhaps self-reflexively for the genre, their growing awareness and commitment to their own legend. At the end, for instance, Billy chooses to remain in the United States and face certain death, and thus immortality, rather than face Mexico and obscurity.

Terence Butler (1979) marks out many themes which indicate that Peckinpah is an *auteur* of the western genre, not least his concern with America's past, and with challenging issues such as: women, in *Ride the High Country* and *The Wild Bunch*; America's relationship with

Mexico, in *The Wild Bunch* and *Pat Garrett and Billy the Kid*; the military machine, in *Major Dundee* and *The Wild Bunch*; the government, in *Major Dundee* and *Pat Garrett and Billy the Kid*; and violence, sex and death, in *The Wild Bunch* and *Pat Garrett and Billy the Kid*.

As we have seen, genres are never static – if they were they would die. They change and develop according to the social and cultural climate of the time of their production. In the same way that science fiction films are not about the future but about the present, westerns – although set in the past – are ostensibly about contemporary America and its values. This is why a study of the western, as the longest-running genre can be most fruitful, as it can reveal the prevalent ideologies of any particular period of production. Given this, genre can be a liberating force in the hands of creative directors, who can use the codes and conventions to comment on contemporary society. *Auteur* also serves to remind us that film generally, and genre films in particular, are the result of creative minds, works of art, as well as being entertainment and subjects for academic study, and should be considered by students of the moving image through all of these criteria.

Conclusion

This section has examined the construction, early history and key theories associated with the study of the moving image. It has illustrated these with examples of cinema styles, films and the work of directors. It has been important to do this since any thorough analysis of the contemporary moving image has to be built on examples of moving image products and protagonists. It is important to remember that films, television and video are not only products of the moving image industry, but also of the artists who work in that industry, and the culture and society that surrounds them. Hence our study of women silent film-makers draws together not only the influence of women in the silent era, but also considers the reasons for the rapid decline in their numbers as film developed into the massive industry we know today.

In aesthetic and production terms, the work of all the early silent film-makers, as we have seen, can be said to have established most, if not all, the codes, conventions and techniques of production that we recognize today, and all this happened in just a 10-year span. A great deal can be learnt about the building blocks of modern moving images by studying the development of film over its first 10 years.

When studying the moving image it is important to understand the technical side of construction in order to be able to thoroughly decode the content of any given product. This is a demystifying process, one that enables us to consider the component parts of production not only in isolation from the seamless flow of images, but also to appreciate the role of each component in relation to the whole. The metaphor of the wardrobe is a useful one, in that it allows us to consider how the encoding process can be one of construction, combining and creativity.

In the final chapters of this section, the discussion of the two dominant theories of the moving image enabled us to consider not only the classification of all moving image products through genre, but also the construction of all moving image production through narrative. Both of these theories enable us to understand the relationships between content, industry and audience. This, after all, is the crucial relationship in understanding how the moving image creates and conveys its meaning. That is what this section has been about: how one form of media and communication content communicates meaning to us, the audience, what we communicate about ourselves as people and, increasingly, about our global cultures and societies.

SUMMARY

- In order to understand the language and techniques of moving image production we have to stand apart from the seamless flow of pictures and images and *stop them dead*. This is done not only by understanding the codes and conventions of production, but also the technical and symbolic signifying systems.

- A consideration of *mise-en-scène* allows us to look at the total picture, the feeling and understanding we gain from what we see. It also reminds us that nothing is there by accident, there is to a lesser or greater extent intentionality behind everything. Indeed, as we saw with the *auteur* theory, that intentionality is a result of the intervention of the director.

- There are four key prerequisites for the moving image to emerge: scientific enquiry, particularly into the persistence of vision and movement; the development of photographic reproduction; the construction of means of projection; and, finally, the emergence of a visual culture and pre-existing forms of entertainment. Without any of these, the moving image would not have developed as it did.

- The pioneers of film production, such as the Lumière brothers, Georges Méliès, R.W. Paul, George Albert Smith, and Edwin S. Porter, along with many others, developed and established in the first 10 years of film production nearly all the codes, conventions and techniques we use today.

- The role of women, such as Alice Guy-Blaché, Lois Weber and Germaine Dulac, in the development of film has been largely forgotten, although their role was central to the development of an industry that, ultimately, destroyed them and belittled their contribution.

- Narrative dominates and structures all forms of moving image production, from the obvious fictional products to non-fictional ones such as news and documentary. Within this domination it is the Hollywood narrative structure that is all-pervasive, with its single diegesis, its subordination of everything to the chain of events, events that are governed by empathy with central characters (or stars), all tied to a pattern of enigma and resolution.

- The work of Todorov, Lévi-Strauss, and Propp provides theoretical schemas by which we can seek to understand and decode these narrative structures.

- A consideration of alternative narrative structures, although few in moving image production terms, does help us reveal the taken-for-granted nature of existing narrative structures by providing an alternative.
- As all moving image products are classified by genre, a consideration of the theory of genre allows us to consider what the various genres have in common, and how genre contributes to our understanding of the relationship between industry, content and audience.
- Considering generic construction through icons, *mise-en-scène* and narrative structure allows us to discuss not only the intertextuality of content, but also how genre works in terms of marshalling the audience's expectations and triggering its generic memory.
- Genre and *auteur* brings us back to a consideration of the production of moving image texts, and illustrates how directors can use genre, and audience expectations of genre, to develop their own themes, ideas and, indeed, the genre itself. *Auteur* serves to remind us that moving image is indeed an artistic and creative endeavour.

Further Reading

Cook, D.A. (1996) *A History of Narrative Film* (third edn). New York and London: W.W. Norton & Company

Cook, P. (1999) *The Cinema Book* (second edn). London: British Film Institute

Hill, J. and Church Gibson, P. (eds) (2000) *Film Studies: Critical Approaches*. Oxford: Oxford University Press

Monaco, J. (2000) *How to Read a Film* (third edn). Oxford: Oxford University Press

Useful Websites

The most useful place to start is with the two major film associations:
www.bfi.org.uk
www.afionline.org/

For information on specific film directors, many have dedicated websites (as, of course, do specific films). See for instance:
http://www.davidlynch.com/
http://www.davidlynch.de/

For Kevin Smith's film *Dogma* see:
http://dogma-movie.com/

For John Ford see:
http://www.inforamp.net/~jzalken/johnford.html

For Sam Peckinpah see:
http://www.geocities.com/Hollywood/Academy/1912/

Articles and reviews can also be found. For an excellent article on the *auteur* theory see:
http://www.wga.org/writtenBy/1997/1097/possessory.html

For general information on historical film see:
http://www.bksts.com
http://www.reelclassics.com/
http://www.filmsite.org/

References

References

Anderson, L. (1981) *About John Ford*. London: Plexus

Ang, I. (1985) *Watching 'Dallas'*. London: Methuen

Bazin, A. (1971) The Western, or the American film *par excellence*. In *What is Cinema* (essays selected and translated by Gray, H.). Berkeley, CA: University of California Press

Berger, A.A. (1992) *Popular Culture Genres: Theories and texts*. London: Sage

Butler, T. (1979) *Crucified Heroes: The films of Sam Peckinpah*. London: Gordon Fraser

Caughie, J. (ed.) (1981) *Theories of Authorship*. London: Routledge & Kegan Paul/British Film Institute

Christie, I. (1994) *The Last Machine*. London: BBC/British Film Institute

Cohan, S. and Hark, I.R. (eds) (1997) *The Road Movie Book*. London: Routledge

Deutelbaum, M. (1979) Structural patterning in the Lumière films. In *Wide Angle* 3(1)

Feuer, J. (1992) Genre study and television. In Allen, R.C. (ed.) *Channels of Discourse, Reassembled: Television and Contemporary Criticism* (second edn). London: Routledge

Fiske, J. (1987) *Television Culture*. London: Methuen

French, P. (1977) *Westerns* (revised edn). London: Secker & Warburg/British Film Institute

Gunning, T. (1990) The cinema of attractions: early film, its spectator and avant-garde. In Elsaesser, T. (ed.) *Early Cinema; Space Frame Narrative*. London: British Film Institute

Helland, K. (1995) *Public Service and Commercial News Contexts of Production, Genre Conventions and Textual Claims in Television*, Report 18. Bergen: University of Bergen Press

Kitses, J. (1969) *Horizons West*. London: Thames and Hudson/British Film Institute

Lévi-Strauss, C. (1966) *The Savage Mind*. London: Wiedenfeld & Nicholson

Metz, C. (1974) *Language and Cinema*. The Hague: Mouton

Monaco, J. (1981) *How to Read A Film* Oxford: Oxford University Press

Newbold, C. (1998) Analysing the moving image: narrative. In Hansen, A., Cottle, S., Negrine, R. and Newbold, C. *Mass Communication Research Methods*. London: Macmillan

Place, J.A. (1974) *The Western Films of John Ford*. Secaucus, NJ: Citadel Press

Propp, V. (1968) *The Morphology of the Folk Tale*. Austin, TX: University of Texas Press

Sarris, A. (1962/63) Notes on the *auteur* theory in 1962. In *Film Culture* 27, Winter

Schatz, T. (1981) *Hollywood Genres: Formulae, Film-making, and the Studio System*. Philadelphia, PA: Temple University Press

Slide, A. (1977) *Early Women Directors: Their Role in the Development of the Silent Cinema*. New Jersey: A.S. Barns & Co

Solomon, S.J. (1976) *Beyond Formula: American Film Genres*. New York, NY: Harcourt Brace Jovanovich

Strange, N. (1998) Perform, educate, entertain: ingredients of the cookery programme genre. In Geraghty, C. and Lusted, D. *The Television Studies Book*. London: Arnold

Todorov, T. (1977) *The Poetics of Prose*. Oxford: Blackwell

Turner, G. (1993) *Film as Social Practice* (second edn). London: Routledge

Vaughan, D. (1990) Let there be Lumière. In Elsaesser, T. (ed.) *Early Cinema: Space Frame Narrative*. London: British Film Institute

Warshow, R. (1964) *The Immediate Experience*. Garden City, NY: Anchor

Williams, L. (1991) Film bodies, gender, genre and excess. In *Film Quarterly* 44(4), Summer

Williams, M. (1982) *Road Movies: The Complete Guide to Cinema on Wheels*. London: Proteus Books

Winston, B. (1995) *Claiming the Real: the Documentary Film Revisited*. London: British Film Institute

Wollen, P. (1985) Godard and counter cinema: vent d'est. In Nichols, B. (ed.) *Movies and Methods 2*. Berkeley, CA: University of California Press

Wright, W. (1975) *Six-guns and Society*. Berkeley, CA: University of California Press

Media Industries

Roland Van Gompel, Hilde Van den Bulck and Daniël Biltereyst

Introduction

The new 'media millennium' could not have had a symbolically more meaningful start than with the announcement in January 2000 of the largest business **merger** in the history of the communications industries. The mega-deal between Time Warner, one of the largest multi-media conglomerates in the world, and America Online (AOL), the biggest US Internet service provider, by its very nature and grandeur has been greeted as if constituting a new milestone in the development of the global media market. Together with the mere size of the deal and its coincidental outing at the eve of the twenty-first century, the joining of forces between Time Warner and AOL indeed has something metaphorical: a sort of ultimate confirmation, at industry or company level, of the integration of the traditional world of the mass media within the new, globally Internet-linked communication order. Whether the Time Warner/AOL alliance will actually acquire this symbolic status or, as is more likely to be the case, is simply noted as just another basic fact in the records of modern media life, is something over which time will be the judge. At present, though, the mere scale of operation and co-operation of these leading communication firms offers new ammunition for proponents of both optimistic and pessimistic assessments of current transformations in the world's media industries. On the one hand, such a coalition of economic forces may be considered the necessary institutional basis for the innovation and diffusion of information technologies and their diverse applications that will form the offspring for real democracy in the global village. On the other hand, such a coalition of economic forces may be considered part of the process whereby the oligopolistic power and market dominance of a very select group of transnational multi-media conglomerates is consolidated and reinforced. Whatever interpretation is attached to it, the Time Warner/AOL construct takes its place in the long list of cases pinpointing the process of international media concentration as one of the predominant tendencies in modern media industries.

This introductory section takes a closer look at these and other trends that have provoked dramatic shifts in the outlook and structures of the media industries in contemporary western societies. Apart from presenting basic facts to illustrate the significance and structural impact of media concentration, transnationalization and other related processes, the focus will be on the key factors of change and the underlying rationales that are highly responsible for these developments. At the same time, the implications of these shifts for society will be discussed, starting from the general perspective that the study of media and communication as an industry or an industrial process is not only important to understanding the material organization and control over these crucial agents of public communication, it also helps to explain key trends in the content, aesthetics, ideology, reception and social functions of media messages, as media industries to a large extent set the constraints within which these are generated.

MEDIA INDUSTRIES, PRODUCTS AND MARKETS

In this section the media are basically addressed as an industrial sector, as a particular economic activity of production and distribution, subject to the laws and workings of the market. Such a perspective implies that the media in their common everyday form are likely to be approached as products in the narrow sense of the word. When talking of the media, however, it is essential to acknowledge their fundamental ambivalence, at least in two different ways (McNair, 1998). First, the media can be approached as public services, having a cultural 'use value' that takes many forms on different occasions for different groups and individuals. The media may be used by citizens for psychological, social or political ends, as a source of information, opinion, education or entertainment. At the same time, however, the media are consumer goods, having an economic 'exchange value' that is used to fulfil many other purposes, most notably making profits. The media are commodities, offered for sale in an economic market-place, and thus subject to various pressures and constraints arising from market competition. It is precisely the tension between these cultural and economic values, and especially the potential primacy or dominance of the latter, that inspires the ongoing discussions and different normative positions taken regarding the societal role and performance of the media.

Second, and further complicating the ambiguous nature of the media industries, in a free market economy the bulk of the media cater for two different markets. In the consumer market media companies sell their products to the audience, while in the advertising market they sell media time or space to advertisers, or, stated in more critical terms, they are selling the audience itself to advertisers (i.e. the audience as commodity). The relation of sales to advertising revenues is conventionally used as a measure of the degree to which the media depend on advertising. It should be clear, however, that the media in many instances – such as with newspapers being sold at a price below their cost per unit – are totally dependent on advertising in order to break even or to make a profit. Furthermore, both the consumer and the advertising market are highly interdependent, as advertising revenues depend on the size and configuration of the audience reached, while the latter is (partly) determined by the financial resources at hand to invest in the quality or attractiveness of the product offered to the public. As such, the nature of most media as 'joint commodities', serving two economic markets, implies a spiral in which the success or, as it happens, failure of reaching audiences of high quantity and 'quality', and of attracting advertisers, is each reinforced by the other. Structural dependence on advertising, therefore, is a basic fact of most media life, while attending to both the advertising and the consumer market inevitably influences the form, style and content of media products.

In approaching the advertising and consumer market media corporations are subject to the hidden – although sometimes politically corrected – hand of the market, obeying the fundamental laws of economic trade and competition. Still, some important features seem to delineate the media as a sector with a proper industrial logic. This is especially the case with the combination of high fixed and initial production costs on the one hand, and the potential of large-scale reproduction at a relatively low cost on the other hand. Producing a newspaper, for instance, requires large capital investments and high fixed costs (printing facilities, distribution infrastructure, marketing activities, administrative departments) as well as substantial first copy costs (of journalistic work and editorial preparation), which are relatively independent from the number of copies eventually printed and sold. The higher the level of reproduction (circulation), however, the more these fixed and initial costs can be spread over a large number of units produced, or the more the average production cost per copy of a newspaper declines. This logic is perhaps even more important in other media sectors such as the film industry. Here it is vital to distribute as many copies of a film as possible, to heavily promote the film and to cash in on distribution rights for video and television, in order to 're-win' and exploit the very expensive and risky business of producing the first copy. When these production costs are already covered to a sufficient extent by sales in one's domestic market, highly competitive prices can furthermore be set in order to compete successfully in the international market.

This particular feature explains the strong imperative present in all media industries to take advantage of economies of scale and scope, by increasing company size and production output. Together with the mere desire to increase revenues and to gain higher profits, it urges media corporations to apply various commercial tactics and strategies in order to maximize audiences and sales. Together with the need to meet the advertising business with strong market positions, it pushes them to expand their markets, on a local, national or international scale, and within as well as across different media sectors. This fundamental economic logic, then, is highly responsible for processes of media concentration, and this the more so because the market advantages of large media companies and the high costs of entering most media markets ultimately put severe restrictions on market penetration and competition. Economic factors and motives of this kind, in short, explain to a large extent the predominant tendencies apparent in contemporary media industries, both on the level of media ownership and structure (concentration and internationalization) and on the level of media production and content (commercialization or 'commodification').

The major developments and shifts, which, significantly, have changed the outlook of the communications industries in recent years, however, cannot be fully accounted for on economic grounds alone. Rather, they are the result of a complex interplay or intricate web of technological, political and cultural as well as economic factors and constraints. This we will try to demonstrate throughout this section, although our main concern will be with media policy and regulation (Chapter 20) and the economic media environment (Chapter 21); for more in-depth accounts of technological developments, and of the social contexts and cultural factors impinging on media workings (e.g. audiences and reception), we may refer to other sections in this volume. In Chapter 20 we adopt a more historical viewpoint in schematizing the transition from an old to a new media order, for which the radical changes in the European television sector since the 1980s serve as a model. In Chapter 21 we will take a closer look at the structures of this new media order and at the dynamics at work in its industries. The larger part of this chapter deals with the issue of media ownership and control, and focuses on the common tendencies of media concentration in general and on the growth of transnational multi-media conglomerates in particular. The impact of the economic environment on media production and content will also be addressed in terms of the effects of market competition and commercial exploitation. The aim is to describe these processes and developments, to clarify the rationales behind them, and to illustrate their scope and impact on media structures and operations with some basic facts and figures. Their wider social, cultural and political implications, however, will also be discussed, as the processes of globalization and commercialization in particular seem to put a definite but ambivalent strain on the output and functions of the media (Chapter 22). Recent trans-formations in the media sector seem, together, to have produced a shift in the central struc-tures of control from the (nation) state, the government and the political sphere to the market, the (transnational) industry and the economic sphere, and thus indeed throw up renewed questions about the democratic role of the media and the contours of the public sphere. As this discussion is informed by the main interpretations given from different theoretical and ideological points of view, we do however start off with an overview of these paradigmatic frameworks.

CHAPTER 19

The Power of the Media Industries:
Theoretical Positions

Media industries do not operate in a social vacuum, but in a close relationship to society, characterized by various mutual influences. On the one hand, many theories, models and classifications can be applied to approach, and structure the impressive field of internal and external influences on media organization and functioning. In their comprehensive review of influences on media content, for instance, Shoemaker and Reese (1991) built up a hierarchical model consisting of five interdependent layers: on a system level these include ideology and the influence of wider cultural values, knowledge structures and consensual norms; on an extra-media level of influences from outside of media organizations, they further deal with pressures and constraints within the immediate social, political and economic media environment (media regulation, market competition, advertisers, news sources, audiences, etc.); on an organizational level they incorporate the internal structures, policies and dynamics of media institutions, such as ownership patterns, management strategies, and institutional means and objectives; while on a subsequent level they are locating media production practices and the influence of professional (news) values and routines; on an individual level, finally, the impact of the individual background, attitudes and beliefs of journalists and media workers is addressed. Within this broad field of influences on media production, this section will especially address those factors of a technological, political, economic or cultural nature that provide the context for the media industries to develop in and adapt to a continuously changing social environment.

As for the influences of the media on society, on the other hand, the mere extent of the research domain clearly shows the historical preoccupation of communication studies with audience reception and media effects, most often in individual, behavioural terms. In this section, however, a more aggregate, societal level of media influence will mainly be focused upon, largely conceived in terms of the political functions and significance of the media in modern liberal-democratic societies. The basic questions at the heart of debate and studies of the media's relationship to society deal with this civic, democratic role and with the way in which the media should be organized in order to perform it. As these questions ultimately revolve around the power and autonomy of the media, and their social responsibility and accountability, the striking historical tendencies and most recent developments in the communication sector have mainly been interpreted and commented upon within the framework of localizing power in society. As a result, divergent, ideologically more or less coherent, views of society have given birth to many theoretical and normative perspectives regarding the role, organization and functioning of the media.

Conventionally these heterogeneous schools and traditions have been located in either one of two polarized paradigms, which in general correspond with differentiated media empirical approaches, research agendas and techniques. These 'two models of media power' – the 'dominant' paradigm of liberal-pluralist perspectives and the 'alternative' paradigm of radical, Marxist-critical approaches – have been summarized and schematized (as shown in Table 19.1) by McQuail, who immediately noted, however, that 'mixed versions are more likely to be encountered' (1994: 70).

As both of these interpretative frameworks will be used in the following chapters to discuss the impact of various tendencies within the media industries, it is important first to look at their main theoretical assumptions and contrasting conceptions. Still, following McQuail's careful but important note, it is also useful to look at how both of these 'mainstream' traditions have developed, internally and in relation to each other. It is also important to address those 'mixed versions' that can be situated in the vast grey area that extends itself between these two classical functionalist positions and that, therefore, in an amalgamated form,

Two models of media power Table 19.1

	Dominance	Pluralism
Societal source	Ruling class or dominant elite	Competing political, social, cultural interests and groups
Media	Under concentrated ownership and of uniform type	Many and independent of each other
Production	Standardized, routinized, controlled	Creative, free, original
Content and worldview	Selective and uniform, decided from 'above'	Diverse and competing views, responsive to audience demand
Audience	Dependent, passive, organized on a large scale	Fragmented, selective, reactive and active
Effects	Strong and confirmative of established social order	Numerous, without consistency or predictability of direction, but often no effect

Source: McQuail (1994: 70)

seem to constitute a kind of alternative 'third route' (Curran, 1991a; for a useful 'guided tour of media sociology', see Curran, 1996).

THE DOMINANT PARADIGM: LIBERAL-PLURALIST PERSPECTIVES

Within the liberal functionalist tradition, society is seen as a dynamic system that continuously strives for unity and harmony, for cohesion and stability. Institutionalized mechanisms of negotiation and co-operation exist to resolve conflicts between competing groups and interests, and to achieve a shared, collective agreement or consensus. In fact, as McQuail indicates:

> the underlying, though rarely explicated, view of society in the dominant paradigm is essentially normative, [presuming] a certain kind of normally functioning 'good society' which would be democratic (elections, universal suffrage, representation), liberal (secular, free-market conditions, individualistic, freedom of speech), pluralistic (institutionalized competition between parties and interests) and orderly (peaceful, socially integrated, fair, legitimate). (McQuail, 1994: 42)

According to liberal democratic theory, the media play a crucial role, as channels of information and communication, between social groups, by stimulating collective debate, by fostering social integration – in short, by facilitating this 'normal' functioning of society. Provided that they are free and independent institutions, the media will reflect and represent all the important views circulating and competing interests present within society. In doing so, they will respond to changing social circumstances and adapt to shifting relations of power. This reflection thesis, considering the media as a mirror of reality, or, in more qualified terms, as a social index or cultural indicator of major importance, is underscored by three key assumptions, as the liberal tradition 'emphasises popular control of the media through the market, stresses the importance of "professional" mediation, and tends to see the media as organizations autonomous from the power structure of society' (Curran, 1996: 138). The autonomy of the media, its independence of the state and of vested social, political and economic interests, as well as journalists' autonomy and self-willingness within media organizations, is perhaps the most central premise of liberal media theories. Together with the professional orientation, values and procedures of journalists, which involve the accurate, objective reporting of news events and the balanced, disinterested representation of views and opinions, media autonomy ultimately ensures that the wider public interest is served. Even excessive control of the media by its proprietors and the potential abuse of their power for personal, political or ideological ends, will eventually be countered or mitigated, according to this view, by competing interests within media institutions as well as by external forces, most notably the sovereignty of the consumer. Indeed, from a liberal point of view, in competitive, free market conditions the media most strongly respond to the needs, tastes and preferences of the audience, which is believed to be highly fragmented, selective and rather rational in its behaviour. In other words, liberal approaches tend to see the media not as dominating or even strongly influencing the (mass) audience; the media, rather, are continuously challenged by an active, powerful audience, but one whose wishes and demands are only properly registered through the market system.

In order to fully understand the liberal-pluralist view of the relationship between media and society, it is necessary to trace its historical roots in relation to the eighteenth- and early nineteenth-century development of the press and its struggle for freedom. Indeed, as Curran (1996) indicates, it was in this period that liberal thought scripted the dominant form in which it traditionally has conceived the role of the media – that is, in terms of the political system and the media's contribution to the democratic functioning of society. It is in the wake of the Enlightenment (with the rise of rationalism, liberalism and new ideas on the nature of man, the relationship between the individual and the state, and intellectual and economic freedom) and in the historical context of developing capitalism (marked by scientific and technological progress, economic expansion and the rise of a new middle class) that the now all-too-familiar, quintessentially liberal, concepts of 'the free market-place of ideas', 'the fourth estate' and 'the watchdog of democracy' are rooted. With reference to Habermas's classical concept of the public sphere, Curran describes this crucial role of the press as follows:

> They [the media] distribute the information necessary for citizens to make an informed choice in election time; they facilitate the formation of public opinion by providing an independent forum of debate; and they enable the people to shape the conduct of government by articulating their views. The media are thus the principal institutions of the public sphere or, in the rhetoric of nineteenth-century liberalism, 'the fourth estate of the realm'. (Curran, 1991a: 29)

As complete independence of the state is the principal prerequisite for the media to provide a check on government and a forum for public debate, liberal democratic theory
regards the free market as the only, or at least the best, possible way to organize the media
system in a democratic, pluralistic society. Since the winning of press freedom from state
control in the mid-nineteenth century, which itself marked the start of an extremely expansive phase of growth in the history of the press, the liberal-market approach thus has been
the dominant model of organizing the (newspaper) press in modern western democracies.

There is, however, a different kind of historical account of the press, of the same
processes of its freeing as well as of its further twentieth-century development. These revi-
sionist accounts sometimes brutally expose the mythical nature of the concept of the fourth
estate, as it is said to obscure both the economic and political realities of newspaper life
(see e.g. Boyce, 1978). In what he calls 'the ugly face of reform' (Curran and Seaton, 1991),
Curran argues that the attainment of press freedom from the state in the nineteenth century
was not a transition to popular, democratic control of the press, rather it was a (deliberate)
replacement of the state 'taxes on knowledge' by the more sophisticated and effective
control system of the market, which served the political and economic interests of the new
bourgeoisie and ultimately eradicated the British nineteenth-century radical press. Referring
to the profound transformations of both the media and society since that particular historical
moment, Curran goes on to describe the classic liberal conceptions, which in the nineteenth
century 'were framed partly in order to legitimate the "deregulation" of the press, and its full
establishment on free market lines' as 'a legacy of old saws' (1991b: 82); but which have,
nevertheless, been repeated continuously in the twentieth century to justify the capitalist,
free market-based organization of the press; and also, in an updated but still familiar discursive form, are most frequently brought to the fore to underscore the recent tendencies
of privatization and deregulation in the broadcasting sector.

THE ALTERNATIVE PARADIGM: MARXIST-
CRITICAL PERSPECTIVES

Critical arguments like these fit into a totally different, radical view of society as being
dominated by a ruling class or political-economic elite, which has a privileged hold on
material resources and economic power and, as such, also controls cultural and ideational
production. Society, according to classic Marxist-critical definitions, is characterized by:

> wider historical conflicts between dominant classes and groups who wish to maintain and
> reproduce the inequalities of existing social and political relations, and subordinate or
> oppositional groups who may wish radically to transform them. (O'Sullivan et al., 1994: 60)

Refuting all key premises of liberal thought, radical-critical perspectives traditionally
portray the media as agencies or instruments of social control and ideological reproduction,
subordinate to and serving the interests of the ruling class or dominant elite. According to
these views, the media are not independent institutions, but inextricably linked to or

integrated within the hierarchical structures of power in society. Particularly their close ties with and the privileged access of both state institutions and corporate businesses pre-dispose the media in favour of dominant social interests, at the expense of oppositional voices and progressive forces for change. The media, then, are not neutrally reflecting social consensus or change, nor channelling diverse views and interests into a meaningful collective debate. On the contrary, through their 'constructions' of reality, directed or deter-mined by powerful influences from above, the media have a manipulative function. They are mystifying the true nature of power and concealing the real inequalities and conflicts of interest in capitalist societies, and, by doing so, they are producing false consciousness and consent, and ultimately legitimizing and sustaining the established social order. It is precisely this role – of domination instead of reflection, by an 'ideological state apparatus' (Althusser) instead of a 'fourth estate' – that is said to be both disguised and reinforced by classical liberal rhetoric and its canons of market competition and media professionalism. It is accom-plished by delivering standardized, uniform products, transferring the dominant ideology to a passive, alienated mass audience.

The radical Marxist view on media and society, mainly elaborated in the critical theories of the Frankfurt School, has found in the political economy tradition its most adept con-temporary variant and research component. This tradition explains the workings and output of the media industries primarily in terms of their political and economic organization, processes and relationships. Thereby it pays foremost attention to the structures of media ownership and control in general and, in particular, to the powerful role of transnational media conglomerates within the global information and culture industry. Radical political-economic accounts of national and international media structures thus traditionally describe how commercial and political imperatives and constraints (imposed by advertising, high capital investments and economies of scale, audience and profit maximization, etc.) lead to increased control by powerful financial and industrial corporations, concentration of owner-ship, restricted market entry and monopolistic market dominance; how, as a consequence, market processes do not ensure public control and sovereignty, but allow media controllers to manage public demand and further their agendas; and how these market distortions limit media diversity, exclude subordinate groups from the public domain and align the media with the dominant views of the elite; how, in short, reality has come to deviate from the idealized picture of the media as, collectively, an independent agent of popular demo-cratic representation.

The alternative paradigm, however, comprises a very heterogeneous set of approaches, and this up to the point where, especially since the mid-1980s, different explanations for the media's skewed orientation in favour of the dominant and the powerful have engendered a growing 'internal' division. Contrary to the rather media-centric approach of political economy, indeed, 'another, structural-culturalist strand of radical functionalism sees the media as shaped by the dominant culture and power structures of society' (Curran, 1996: 129). Through the development of this tradition, among others, it has become convincingly clear that, historically, critical media theory has extended its horizon far beyond classical Marxism and radical materialism. Actually, the reductionist argument of economic deter-minism underlying its domination thesis has been wiped out almost completely in contemporary critical accounts. So, stirred by the writings of Stuart Hall and the Birmingham School, and their adoption of Althusserian and Gramscian insights, the idea of one dominant ideology, perpetrating through all levels of a static society in a unrivalled way, has given way to a view of a more dynamic and complex society where different, opposed groups and coalitions of interest are engaged in a continuous struggle for hegemony. From this point of view, and especially in culturalist revisions of journalism studies, the media have been reinvigorated with a relative degree of autonomy, and re-conceptualized as a site of contest, as 'a battleground between contending forces' (Curran, 1991a: 29; Curran, 1990; Schlesinger, 1990; Schudson, 1989). According to the initial views of Hall and his associates (1978), the hegemony of the powerful is, nevertheless, consistently and systematically supported by the media, since their privileged access and accredited status as news sources lend them the power to define the primary interpretation of a situation and to set the terms of reference for all subsequent coverage and debate. Other views and criticisms, however, have increasingly distanced themselves from this perspective, acknowledging still the existing inequalities of access to the media, but at the same time emphasizing the internal differences within and between elites, the competition between sources, and the strategies used by both dominant and subordinate groups to gain media access (see e.g. Schlesinger, 1990). As such, a move towards more liberal conceptions of a pluralist society, in which (definitional) power is more widely diffused, has become apparent.

THE THIRD ROUTE: MIXED VERSIONS

Culturalist views of the media's relationship to society have already, then, to a certain extent undermined the conventional representation of media studies as a field sharply divided into two ideologically opposed camps. The wider intellectual movement of revisionism currently sweeping through mass communication research, however, has left its deepest traces in the way the relationship between the media and their audiences came to be re-assessed. What is now commonly referred to as the critical cultural studies tradition, where the focus of enquiry has generally been on the concrete ways in which ideology is transferred through media culture and language – and where this focus has also, clearly, shifted from class conflict and bourgeois domination towards emphasis on other forms of social cleavage, notably (youth) subcultures, race and gender – has played a prominent role in re-invigorating the power of the audience. In general terms, members of the audience are believed to bring their own social and cultural experiences to confront, select and decode, quite possibly in an aberrant or oppositional manner, the polysemic texts offered by the media. Again, and especially when taken to the extreme in some post-modernist accounts, such a view implies a crucial break with classical Marxist assumptions; and, again, it can be seen as a further retreat from traditional radical positions and as a parallel act of increasingly embracing liberal-pluralist arguments (Curran, 1996).

Seemingly in correlation with the rise of (neo-)liberal thought in the media practices and policies of the 1980s and 1990s, then, liberal-pluralist conceptions seem to have strengthened their hold as the 'dominant' paradigm in media theories. Still, it should be stressed that the liberal tradition itself is heterogeneous and full of internal criticism and debate, dividing for instance adepts of economic *laissez-faire* liberal principles from more socially oriented liberal democrats. As a result, refinements on the side of liberal theory as well seem increasingly to have bridged the gap. A considerable body of sociological studies of media organizations, for instance, has pointed out how news production is influenced and constrained by organizational procedures, resources, policies and objectives, and thus indirectly has stressed the relative degree of journalistic autonomy. Other liberal accounts, some of them of a quite respectable age, acknowledged how market pressures may induce sensationalist tendencies and excesses, and started a plea for the media to take their social, democratic responsibility within a commercial market environment. Although still claiming freedom for the press and basically calling for responsible conduct and self-discipline, the theory of social responsibility in the 1950s even opened up legitimate ways for the government and regulatory bodies to intervene and to correct market mechanisms (e.g. in order to downsize the effects of media concentration). Its propagation of freedom, together with notions such as responsibility, pluralism, balance and objectivity – notions that also are to be found in the basic philosophy underlying the public service (broadcasting) model – can be seen as illustrative of a general concern neither to give up the benefits of a market-based media system, nor to disregard its (economic) deficiencies.

What seems to arise from all this is a kind of 'third route', as Curran (1991a) labels it: a hard-to-define theoretical position situated between conventional liberal-market and Marxist-collectivist approaches, which tries to capitalize on their strengths while, at the same time, trying to avoid their flaws and their rigid one-sidedness. Common to this range of liberal-, social- and radical-democratic perspectives is that they neither, in a deterministic way, limit their focus to economic substructures and material matters of ownership and control, nor uncritically adopt the beneficial workings of the hidden hand of the market, the self-corrective model of media professionalism, or the powerful image of the sovereign consumer. Rather, by considering a multitude of, often contradictory, forces and pressures on the media, from above as well as from below, they try to account for the dynamic nature, the ambiguity and complexity of things. Subject to a crossfire of influences, the media, according to this view, may act as a top-down agency of social control, or as a bottom-up agency of popular empowerment, or as both at the same time; but to which side the balance will sway ultimately depends on the specific configuration of a society and its media system at any particular moment in time.

CHAPTER 20

Media Systems, Policies and Industries in Transition

In this chapter we will focus on the related organization of society and the media, and on the main shifts that have recently occurred in the policy framework and the overall configuration of media systems and industries in western, liberal-democratic societies. Starting from the central idea that media systems to a large extent are determined by the specific socio-political structure and culture of society, many attempts have been made to come to concise, global typologies or classifications, some of which will first be presented as general models of media organization. While the relationship between the media and the state or the political system in general comes up as one of the most crucial elements of distinction between different kinds of media system, it also forms, as we have seen, a focal point around which the main media theoretical and normative positions are organized. This relationship is, however, also amenable to change in close connection with profound transformations in the media sector. This will become clear as, in the main part of this chapter, we will concentrate on the historical traditions and changing frameworks of media policy and regulation in western (European) countries.

MEDIA MODELS: FOUR AND MORE THEORIES OF THE PRESS

One important typology of world media systems has become known as the 'four theories of the press', named after the classic work of Siebert, Peterson and Schramm (1956). These authors started from the idea that 'the press always takes on the form and coloration of the social and political structures within which it operates' (1956: 1). Media organization, in other words, departs from the basic philosophical assumptions and political tenets a society holds regarding the relationship between the state and the individual. In practice, Siebert et al. saw four such overall societal frameworks, each with its corresponding media system (see Table 20.1).

On the one hand, Siebert et al. describe the authoritarian media theory, a model primarily referring to the absolutist monarchies of (post-)medieval Europe, but also to Nazi-totalitarianism and many military and/or dictatorial regimes in the world at present. In such authoritarian systems, the media, whether privately or publicly owned, are strictly controlled, through patents, licenses and permissions, and through censorship and repressive measures, by the government in power whose interests, policies and ideologies they have to serve. The Soviet-totalitarian media theory, referring to Marxist-Leninist thought and the practice in (former) communist states, is regarded by the authors mainly as an extension or

Table 20.1 *Four theories of the press*

	Authoritarian	Libertarian	Social responsibility	Soviet-totalitarian
Developed	In sixteenth- and seventeenth-century England; widely adopted and still practised in many places	Adopted by England after 1688, and in the USA; influential elsewhere	In USA in the twentieth century	In Soviet Union, although some of the same things were done by Nazis and Italians
Out of	Philosophy of absolute power of monarch, his government, or both	Writings of Milton, Locke, Mill and general philosophy of rationalism and natural rights	Writing of W.E. Hocking, Commission on Freedom of the Press, and practitioners; media codes	Marxist-Leninist-Stalinist thought, with mixture of Hegel and nineteenth-century Russian thinking
Chief purpose	To support and advance the policies of the government in power and to service the state	To inform, entertain, sell – but chiefly to help discover truth, and to check on government	To inform, entertain, sell – but chiefly to raise conflict to the plane of discussion	To contribute to the success and continuance of the Soviet socialist system, and especially to the dictatorship of the party
Who has the right to use media?	Whoever gets a royal patent or similar permission	Anyone with the economic means to do so	Everyone who has something to say	Loyal and orthodox party members
How are media controlled?	Government patents, guilds, licensing, sometimes censorship	By 'self-righting process of truth' in 'free market-place of ideas', and by courts	Community opinion, consumer action, professional ethics	Surveillance and economic or political action of government
What is forbidden?	Criticism of political machinery and officals in power	Defamation, obscenity, indecency, wartime sedition	Serious invasion of recognized private rights and vital social interests	Criticism of party objectives as distinguished from tactics
Ownership	Private or public	Chiefly private	Private, unless government has to take over to ensure public service	Public
Essential differences from others	Instrument for effecting government policy, though not necessarily government owned	Instrument for checking on government and meeting other needs of society	Media must assume obligation of social responsibility; and if they do not, someone must see that they do	State-owned and closely controlled media existing solely as arm of state

Source: Siebert *et al.* (1956: 7)

further development of the authoritarian model. Here the media are owned by, and under the close surveillance of, the state or the Communist Party in order for them to serve socialist revolutionary ideals.

On the other hand, from a far more normative perspective, the authors discuss the libertarian media theory. This theory is mainly based on the freedom of the press, its independence from the state, and a free market approach, as necessary conditions for the press to fulfil its crucial role in the public sphere between the state and the citizens (check on government, forum of opinion and public debate, etc.). Here the controlling mechanism is assumed to be the 'self-righting process of truth' in the 'free market-place of ideas', which ultimately aligns the media with the needs of citizenship. Aware of the conflicts arising between economic market laws and commercial media exploitation on the one hand, and various norms and standards of media performance (diversity and pluralism, quality and pro-tection of private rights, open access and fair representation) on the other – based on actual experiences, mainly within the US press – Siebert *et al.*, however, took care of refining this normative theory. Within the theory of social responsibility the freedom of the press (rights) is complemented by its responsibility towards society (plights). The media 'must assume obligation of social responsibility', which mainly is to be ensured through mechanisms of self-control such as professional codes of conduct; as such, the social responsibility theory reinforces the liberal belief in professional commitments as a restraint on market-induced excesses. Nevertheless, with the phrase 'if they do not, someone must see that they do', this line of thinking also includes possible regulatory involvement or active state intervention to correct market mechanisms and to ensure that the public interest is being served.

Apart from serious doubts about the extent to which this last normative scheme of the media assuming responsibility is really applicable in the context of market competition, the classification of Siebert *et al.* has been criticized on many grounds (Nerone, 1995). Indeed, one can point at the underlying rationales of this work, produced in the cold war climate of the 1950s. Apart from legitimizing western liberal media systems and practices in general, by opposing them to authoritarian and totalitarian approaches, the work overtly intended to support and promote the social responsibility approach. Not only the collapse of the com-munist system at the end of the 1980s has undermined the model, but also many other (changed) social realities have not been properly accounted for. While, generally speaking, the dichotomy of the authoritarian and the libertarian (market, commercial) model, as well as the existence of many possible gradations in between, has been commonly accepted, two other models in particular, developed in the 1960s and 1970s, are worth noting in this respect (McQuail, 1994).

On the one hand, the development media theory refers to the current situation and prac-tice of the media in many developing or advancing countries of the world. This theory acknowledges the fact that in many post-colonial states the media are not only working in totally different conditions, but often are also enclosed in broader projects of education, social and economic development. On the other hand, the democratic-participant media theory reflects a general disenchantment regarding the structures and operations of the established communication systems and professional media organizations in liberal-capitalist societies, and ultimately goes far beyond the moderate alterations of the social responsibility theory. In fact, not only libertarian as well as authoritarian approaches are lamented, even the social responsibility model, which is said increasingly to lead to central-ism, bureaucratization, politicization and paternalism, is strongly denounced. This model, then, can at best be defined in opposition to each of the former models or forms of media organization, whether they are controlled by the state, by the market or by some political or cultural elite. Williams, rather eloquently, puts it like this:

> It [the democratic system] is firmly against authoritarian control of what can be said, and against paternal control of what ought to be said. But also it is against commercial control of what can profitably be said, because this also can be a tyranny. (Williams, 1976: 133)

By 'paternal control', Williams is mainly referring to the established forms of public service broadcasting, which are based on monopoly exploitation and the classic Reithian philosophy, and which are embedded in an official climate of political control and cultural elitism. Against authoritarian, commercial and paternal media systems, he places the project of democratic communication systems providing public service in the true sense (free access and active participation of all citizens). Inspired by critical theory and neo-Marxist thought, the democratic-participant theory stresses egalitarianism, political emancipation and democratic participa-tion as its key values. These values are translated in a democratic community model of media characterized by independence, openness, participation and interaction, or, in short, by actual communication rather than mere distribution. The model applies in practice to alternative, small-scale ('grass roots') media forms, such as the underground press, local community or minority television, alternative music labels, and the pirate (Caroline, Veronica) and amateur local radio scene, which boomed in the 1970s. Still, in practice, in order to be economically viable, many of these 'community media' in the end turn to or are obliged to seek refuge in commercial ways of functioning, ultimately leading to their incorporation into large franchising systems and commercial networks. Other ones, resisting the economic logic of the market, are often confined to marginal positions, if not forced to close down.

Many further attempts have been and are being made to update, revisit or go beyond the 'four theories of the press' (for a recent and concise overview of media typologies, see Nordenstreng, 1997), mostly trying to avoid its deterministic rigidity. It is indeed clear that, apart from the general political structure of society, many other factors are influencing the out-look, functioning and development of media systems; and also that most national media sys-tems, in practice, show a definite mixture of media philosophies, organizations and structures.

TRADITIONAL APPROACHES: 'THE OLD MEDIA ORDER'

When focusing on media/state relationships in western, liberal-democratic societies, it should indeed be clear that, historically as well as at the present moment, the role of government and the state, and of media and communication policy in general, can take many forms, at several levels and along different dimensions. Not only the government can determine the basic principles or general framework in which the media operate (e.g. by inscribing press freedom in constitutional law), in general it has two basic functions or pack-ages of tasks. The first implies policing and control, in terms of correcting and/or stimulat-ing the free market via content and/or (common) carrier regulation. The other involves active intervention and participation, especially through state or public ownership; active involve-ment of other political actors and institutions, such as with the political party press, may also be considered in this respect. It is of the utmost importance to stress how actual prac-tices may differ: (a) temporally, accounting for historical phases and changes in the relation-ship between media and politics; (b) geographically, depending on wider cultural and political traditions; and (c) sector-wise, in terms of different approaches to the press, to broadcast-ing and to other communication sectors. Although it seems rather trivial, it should also be emphasized that (media) politics is not the exclusive domain of governments, but a complex process of negotiation to which many different sorts of actors, at different geopolitical levels, bring their own logic, objectives and strategies.

As pointed out earlier, the (newspaper) press in western European countries for more than a century and a half has been organized in accordance with the liberal-market model, installed after the abolition of authoritarian state control in the nineteenth century. In some countries at that time the freedom of the press has explicitly been taken up in constitutional law providing for a parliamentary democratic system; from the start, however, limitations have often been formulated in order to protect the individual rights of citizens (privacy, libel) and vital social interests (national security, democratic institutions). Nevertheless, free market competition and private economic initiatives have been the key terms of press development, corresponding with a kind of non-intervention plight on the part of the state. Still, especially in the 1960s and 1970s – in the context of increasing press concentration, growing concerns about media pluralism, economic crisis and a general social-democratic upheaval – many countries swept away from *laissez-faire* liberalism towards a corrective, interventionist approach. While some countries, like Sweden, developed a subsidy system to support newspaper diversity – a policy that often also extended to other media sectors such as national film industries – debate on the feasibility of anti-trust legislation was quite widespread. Measures of this kind, however, nearly always provoked criticism and opposi-tion from the liberal 'camp', as they were said to increase (the danger of) political dependence as well as disrupt normal market conditions.

From the beginning, the libertarian model of press organization has been extended to radio and television broadcasting in the United States, where, historically, the media have been overwhelmingly market-based, and state involvement has been minimized. As a matter of fact, the US broadcasting system is often referred to as the archetype of the private com-mercial broadcasting model, which regards radio and television foremost as (free) market commodities. Central characteristics of this commercial model of broadcasting are private ownership (with a minimal role for government, mainly concerning the granting of licences and the setting of standards for technical components and equipment), private means of financing (advertising, sponsorship, merchandising), and mainly popular content. Typical for commercial television is also that production, programming and distribution are highly flexible and strongly based on external services and competition (independent production companies, syndicated programmes, much imported and externally purchased material). Apart from independent TV stations, networks are often built up with local affiliated stations, such as is most notably the case with the US television networks NBC, ABC and CBS.

In western Europe, broadcasting followed a totally different path of development in relation to the American broadcasting scene, as well as in relation to its own press industries. Initially, in the 1920s, radio was privately exploited, mainly by industrial manufacturers of technical equipment and powerful suppliers of electricity. In many European countries, however, a tradition of either pragmatic liberalism or outright collectivism, applied to strategically important telecommunication infrastructures (mail, railway, telephone, telegraph), was soon transferred to radio broadcasting. Depending on local policy traditions (e.g. a high degree of state centralism in France), these sectors were often nationalized for technical, economic and political reasons or to comply with wider geopolitical and military aspirations. For comparable reasons, including the possibilities offered by radio as a powerful means for propaganda and information in political, war and trade affairs, national broadcasting monopolies under state or public ownership were installed in most western European countries, in which, later on (1930–50), television was incorporated. At the same time a set of public service responsibilities was attached to these national broadcasting systems, giving birth to the public service broadcasting (PSB) model, which would become the dominant model in western Europe for nearly half a century.

This PSB model was established and legitimized on several grounds. One of the most important rationales or arguments for PSB monopolies was one of a technical nature, meaning the overall scarcity of frequencies for terrestrial transmission. Other pragmatic reasons underlying its establishment implied economic motives such as the high exploitation costs and capital investments demanded from private investors. Then there certainly were various political and ideological reasons to closely guard broadcasting, going hand in hand with the politically sensitive position and the firm belief in the power of the medium. The interests and motivations of state and party-political actors to control information and/or to demand fair representation stimulated the build-up and development of PSB. Or, as McQuail in his explanation for the monopoly privilege of PSB rather bluntly put it, the argument of technical scarcity merely served as 'a pretext that concealed a determination not to let this potent communications medium slip out of government control' (1995: 149).

Above all, the PSB model was, however, justified on more theoretical, cultural and philosophical grounds, demanding that the audience was not to be served as market consumers but as private citizens. This basic philosophy proclaimed the need of broadcasting to be a universally available and accessible public service. It should cater for the nationwide audience and respond to the needs, interests and tastes of all groups, including those of minorities. This presumes internal pluralism, in terms of a politically balanced approach in news and current affairs, and diversity in programming, in terms of offering a broad and balanced mix of information, education and entertainment. It also presumes content meeting high standards of quality and performance (accuracy, objectivity, impartiality), and reflecting national cultural identity. Indeed, in its most thoroughbred version – that is, according to the ethos of Lord Reith, the first Administrator-General of the BBC, which gave PSB its rather strong paternalistic and elitist etiquette – public broadcasting should be in the first place 'an instrument of a unified national cultural project bringing the same high-quality pro-grammes nationwide to everybody' (Siune and Hulten, 1998: 23). Finally, public accounta-bility and independence *vis-à-vis* political and economic interests, two other core principles of PSB, were assumed to be guaranteed, at best, by systems of public sponsorship, most notably in the form of a mandatory licence fee.

All this, it was argued, could only be provided by licensing a legal monopoly to a public, state-linked corporation under some form of representative control. It is perhaps in terms of political representation and control at the structural level that the traditional PSB institutions most strongly differ across individual European countries. While, for instance, in The Netherlands there exists a rather unique 'pillar model', with broadcasting time and control being allotted to different political, social and religious groupings in proportion to their number of members, Germany also stands out as a rather peculiar case, mainly because of its federalized structure. In general, public broadcasting has usually been either 'highly politi-cised or politically neutralised' (McQuail, 1995: 150). Traditionally, a significant degree of autonomy has been conceded to the PSB corporations and their professional administrators in the Nordic countries and in Britain, where the general aim has been to shield public broad-casters from direct political involvement. In continental Europe, on the contrary, public broadcasting has been rather highly politicized. Especially in France and southern European countries like Italy and Greece, PSB institutions have been firmly under government control or strongly colonized by political parties in proportion to their electoral strength. Tendencies of politicization and bureaucratization, however, have been quite common characteristics of all PSB institutions, just like a high degree of internal centralization of production (facilities), programming and control over distribution.

Basic features of the 'old order'

Taking into account the differences in the actual configuration of PSB due to historical circumstances and local political or cultural traditions, in general, then, one can distil from this picture the following basic features of the 'old order', common to the national broad-casting systems in western Europe until the 1980s (Brants and Siune, 1992: 102; McQuail, 1995: 148–51; Siune and Hulten, 1998: 24–5):

- a public service commitment – with close regulation of content and high standards of quality and performance
- a universal service – of a national (territorial and cultural) scope and of a diverse, pluralistic nature
- public accountability – some form of accountability to (political representatives of) the public, achieved not through market forces, but through regulatory bodies and parliaments, and through some form of public administrative organization
- non-commercialism – not dominated by the search for profit, but shielded from commercial pressures through some element of public finance (commercial revenues are not excluded – mixed systems of financing are in fact quite common – but only allowed under strict conditions)
- a licensed monopoly – or at least protection from competition (regulated or limited market entrance).

PARADIGMATIC SHIFTS: 'THE NEW MEDIA ORDER'

Since the 1980s far-reaching developments have, however, radically changed the media structures in all western European countries (and also, of course, in many other parts of the world, not least in eastern Europe). Key terms describing this nearly paradigmatic shift are deregulation, liberalization, privatization and commercialization, as well as a significant process of internationalization. These developments occurred hand in hand with important shifts at the political level itself. On the one hand, nation-states are confronted with the internationalization of (media) policies and regulations, corresponding with the rise of a transnational economy, the internationalization of (media) industries and trades, and the accelerated development of global (media) markets. The process of European integration in particular has transferred many legislative tasks and roles to a level above governments of individual EU member states. On the other hand, a gradual withdrawal of national political decision-makers, institutions and organizations as active participants in the media sector seems to characterize this new epoch. Although part of a long-standing, cumulative histori-cal process in many countries, for instance, political parties and trades unions have given up their traditional hold of newspapers in favour of larger press chains controlled by financial/industrial corporations or international media conglomerates, and managed by 'market-led pragmatists'. This gradual shift from (party-)political control towards stronger market patron-age has refuelled the time-worn debate about the political role of the press between liberal apologists and critical media watchers (Curran, 1991b).

It is in the broadcasting sector, however, where this withdrawal has taken the true form of a paradigmatic break with the past, in terms of the overall abolishment of the PSB monopolies, and the introduction and expansive growth of privately owned, commercial tele-vision. As this new commercial television sector did not replace, but developed alongside, the existing public channels, dual broadcasting systems were established all over western Europe. In some larger countries – like the UK, where the Independent Television Authority (ITA) in 1954 started its commercial ITV network of regionally affiliated TV stations, and Italy where, apart from the RAI since the mid-1970s, a private television sector developed in a rather chaotic manner – such dual broadcasting systems already existed. But it was clearly in the 1980s and 1990s that private, commercial television expanded and became an indis-pensable component of national TV systems. Symptomatic of this is the fact that since 1989 – the year the EU announced its famous 'free trade' policy directive on 'Television without Frontiers' – the number of private channels exceeds the number of public channels in the European television sector.

Various coinciding and often mutually reinforcing factors should be taken into account when searching for the basic rationales underlying this paradigmatic shift. First, techno-logical developments clearly played a key role, as the growth and expanding capacity of cable and satellite distribution technologies devalued the traditional argument of scarce terrestrial frequencies and gradually created a multiple channel environment. In smaller countries, particularly those with a high degree of cable household penetration (such as Belgium and The Netherlands), public broadcasters already faced strong competition from foreign channels long before their monopolies were ended. Satellite transponders serving the cable networks provided the means for such flows across national borders on an international or even global scale, while digitalization and the convergence of different information technologies are currently further extending this potential range of choice to seemingly unknown limits.

The technology factor

Technologies perfect the ways in which the media function and contribute to the development of new media services and infrastructure. As such, the communication industries are witnessing a fundamental technological change with significant implications for their organization.

Central to these developments is *digitalization* – the shift from analogue to digital coding. In analogue systems, the shape in which information is stored and transmitted carries a certain continuous and recognizable relation to the original form (e.g. tones on a black and white negative, and the play of light in the photographed scene). Digital systems translate all information – image, text, data or sound – into a universal computer language so that everything can be reproduced in binary codes. This digital revolution has important consequences for the future development of communication industries. Because they used very different ways of coding information, analogue systems helped to maintain the boundaries between industrial sectors – every sector had its own technologies for information storage and transmission. Now that all information can be kept and sent in digital form, these historic boundaries are being dismantled, causing a convergence between formerly distinct communication sectors. The result is that we live in a multi-media environment in which ever more diverse symbolic data can be stored, transmitted and consulted by consumers at the same time. This process of convergence is organized around the most important communication industries, which are becoming ever more closely intertwined: the computer industry (storage and processing), the telecommunications industry (transmission); and the screen industry (display).

Second, these changes must be seen in the light of the formation of the European common market and the general political climate of neo-liberalism in the 1980s that provided the conditions for the liberalization of the European television market. Of particular importance in this respect was certainly the fact that, as McQuail rightly notes, 'the "Europeanization" of broadcasting policy supported the logic of commercial development as a way of fighting off the increased competition in both hardware and software markets from the United States and Japan' (1995: 153). Political support for private competition, however, also came from national governments: they generally redirected their media policies towards the national economic benefits related to technological innovation and improvement, thereby rather deliberately leaving the accompanying investments and risks with the private sector. Other political motives also played a role in breaking up the traditional PSB monopolies, such as growing discontent, from all or some political parties and groups, with the way the PSB corporations performed their tasks and failed to comply with the legal or statutory requirements of impartiality and fair representation of all political views and interests.

Third, apart from technological and political rationales, various economic motives from different sorts of actors stimulated the privatization and commercialization of television. The expansion of commercial television did not only meet the interests of the advertising business, it also provided favourable conditions for the whole audio-visual industry – including independent TV production companies and film distributors – to flourish. For the established, national and international press and media groups, private commercial television offered vast and lucrative opportunities for expansion and diversification. Most often newspaper and magazine publishers acted as powerful lobby groups, developing strategies to ensure their economic interests were taken care of. Indeed, the challenge of facing new, fierce competition for advertising revenues has in most countries led to an anxious involvement of the press in the whole debate. The argument that the economic viability and, indirectly, the pluralism of the press was at stake, often inspired a regulatory framework providing for participation of press companies in commercial television. Ultimately this has stimulated patterns of cross-ownership between press and broadcasting companies.

The process of deregulation, however, has had many more implications, of which one could only try to pinpoint some of the most important. First, the most obvious consequence has undoubtedly been the proliferation in the number of TV channels, all in all giving an important impetus for the European audio-visual industry to develop. Apart from many generalist TV channels, we have witnessed the introduction of many international and pan-European thematic satellite TV channels, TV channels targeting specific audience groups, communities and minorities, and various pay-TV channels, also often in thematic packages. In fact, one could reasonably state that the term 'dual system' no longer adequately describes the complex situation that came into being in all western European countries. Broadcasting systems now consist of a broad mix of channels that can be categorized in all sorts of ways, depending on transmission modalities (terrestrial, cable, satellite), financing systems (advertising, subscription), reach (local, regional, national, international), audience segments, programme schedules and content (generalist or mixed, as opposed to thematic or specialized). Nevertheless, in one way or another, the private commercial model of broadcasting currently stands out as fairly hegemonic in the structures of European broadcasting. (For details on broadcasting structures in individual western European countries, see Euromedia Research Group, 1997; also Weymouth and Lamizet, 1996; d'Haenens et al., 1998).

In addition, while most TV stations in Europe are still nationally oriented in their specific, linguistically or culturally bound offerings, at a structural level (ownership, financial structure, organization) television has increasingly become a transnational sector. One has only to point at the role, scale and scope of media empires such as those of Murdoch, Bertelsmann, CLT, Canal Plus and other powerful groups with channels, subsidiaries and participation in different countries, to illuminate this phenomenon. The liberalization of the European telecommunication sector, the digitalization and upgrading of cable networks, and the rise of pay-TV and all sorts of new multi-media services, furthermore stimulates powerful alliances between traditional broadcasting companies and telecommunication operators. Still, television seems to remain strongly embedded in local cultural contexts, and viewers' preferences for domestic productions are high. Not surprisingly, then, home markets remain central to transnational media conglomerates, while penetration of foreign markets with programmes in their own national language (e.g. RTL in Luxembourg, Belgium, Germany and The Netherlands) on the whole seems to be a more successful strategy than catering for one transnational audience market (with the exception of some well-known examples, such as CNN or MTV).

While growing competition extended the range of choice, it also increased the weight of commercial pressures. Not only for all private initiatives, but certainly also as far as PSB is concerned, which has been obliged to confront the challenges and pressures posed by a wholly new competitive context of television production. This has affected its programme schedules, in so far as many national and international comparative studies have pointed out diverse strategic reactions to commercial competition, going from relative opposition, resistance or purification (e.g. BBC) to adaptation, imitation or convergence (e.g. RAI) (Hulten and Brants, 1992). In one way or another, PSB institutions have been forced to deal with the tension between attending core values of public service and attracting a share of an increasingly fragmented audience, in order not to be confined to a cultural 'ghetto' or to lose public and political support (Mitchell et al., 1994; McQuail, 1995; Siune and Hulten, 1998). In general, therefore, public channels have responded to competition and changing viewing patterns by adopting new scheduling styles and programme formats ('infotainment'), and by increasing domestic fiction and entertainment (in prime time) often as well as the amount of news and current affairs. As competition has inflated prices on the international television market, this has also affected financial budgets and increased the need for higher efficiency as well as alternative systems of financing (advertising, sponsorship, merchandising). More generally and structurally, commercial competition provoked a (identity) crisis situation for many PSB corporations, whose legitimate aims, inert bureaucratic organization, public financial resources and often highly politicized, hierarchical structures have been severely criticized and questioned. On the other hand, many pleas could and can be heard, directed at media policy-makers at both a national and European level, to safeguard the public service component of national media systems, to restore the decisiveness of the institutional framework, and to protect its ideals and the vulnerable values at stake (see e.g. Blumler, 1992). This plea largely arises from the fear that the basic role of (public) television, defined in terms of its contribution to the democratic functioning of the political system, has come under serious threat by the transition from the old to the new media order (see Table 20.2).

In this respect, finally, it is also important to signal how, ultimately, media policy itself, its basic principles and rationales, have changed. Murdock (1990) stated how one should better speak, not of deregulation, but of re-regulation, implying also a re-orientation of political concerns. Although political support for PSB still exists, one cannot deny that the radical changes in the structures of European broadcasting towards predominantly commercial systems have, to a large extent, been engineered by political decisions, both on a national as well as a European level. As many critics are arguing, in the course of this process the economic logic has come to dominate the cultural logic in media policies as well as in media practices. McQuail, for instance, calls it a shift in emphasis 'from cultural and political issues to economic and industrial ones . . . from public service and the needs of citizens to the supposed interests of consumers and entrepreneurs' (1995: 161). In any

Table 20.2   *Old and new media structures*

	Old media structure	New media structure
Broadcasting	Monopoly	Competition
Goals	Democracy	Survival/success/profit
Means	Programme production/ selection of material	Selection of material/programme mix
Logic	Responsibility	Market/economic
Criteria for selection	Political relevance	Sale
Reference group	Citizens	Consumers
Focus on	Decisions taken/power structure	Processes of policy-making/new conflict dimension
Perspective	Nation/system	Individual and global

Source: Siune and Hulten (1998: 36)

case, over the last two decades, tensions between the economic options of liberalization and privatization on the one hand, and various social values and national cultural interests on the other, have continuously been felt. Here one can, for instance, refer to the discussions about content regulation concerning advertising and the protection of children. One can also be reminded of the important problems linked with conditional access (pay-TV), limiting choice for those who do not possess the necessary economic power (the have-nots); and the problems concerned with exclusive programme rights (e.g. for international cultural and sporting events), especially when obtained by subscription channels, in relation to free news-gathering and the public's right to know. And, of course, there is also the matter of globalization and (local) cultural identity, a problem mainly raised in relation to the large import of TV fiction programmes from the USA. On an international level, the harsh GATT negotiations over free trade between the EU and the USA in the mid-1990s, dealing with economically and culturally inspired quota and subsidies for domestic audio-visual production, showed how deeply rooted fears of economic and cultural imperialism remain. But also within the EU there are 'differences of opinions regarding the nature of television . . . as part of the cultural sphere of individual countries and thus in the domain of national sovereignty . . . [or] as just another sector of the free and common market of goods and services' (Siune and Hulten, 1998: 34). As such, smaller European nation-states have been trying to confront and ward off penetration of their markets by foreign TV companies by way of various regulatory provisions. These mainly intended to anchor their indigenous media industries, to shield their own regional markets from foreign, multi-national conglomerates and, ultimately, to protect their national languages and cultures. These and many other problematic issues illustrate how media policy is bound continuously to face the hard task of finding a balance between cultural interests and economic processes like those that will be described in the next chapter.

CHAPTER 21

The Structures and Dynamics of the Media Industries

As indicated in the previous chapter, particularly since the 1980s a new mass media environment has developed. In this chapter our aim is to show why this 'new order' can best be described as a 'transnational oligopolistic media market', with new central players and principles, and with new problematic issues largely dealing with economic strains placed on cultural values (see Albarran and Chan-Olmsted, 1998; Blumler, 1991; Mazzoleni and Palmer, 1992; Murdock, 1992; Pilati, 1993; Skovmand and Schrøder, 1992; Van Poecke and Van den Bulck, 1994). First, we will look at the main structural forces and imperatives at work in this new media market, showing how the 'old problem' of media concentration acquired 'new dimensions' (Meier and Trappel, 1998: 38) by its increasing occurrence across media sectors and across national borders. The result has been the forming of transnational multi-media conglomerates, which, as we shall see, through various processes and strategies are able to consolidate their powerful positions on the global media map. Next, we will give a short overview of this new media market and its main players, as some hard facts and figures provide us with a more clear idea of the present scale and scope of the media industries. Finally, we will discuss some of the major implications of these developments; basically, that is, we hope to shed some critical light on the tendencies of concentration, commercialization and internationalization of the media, starting from the different theoretical frameworks presented earlier.

MEDIA CONCENTRATION: THE STORY OF THE MULTI-MEDIA MULTI-NATIONALS

Concentration of ownership and control is undoubtedly one of the most prominent features and developments, in history and up to the present, of the communications industries in the West. The process of media concentration can be defined as 'an increase in the presence of one (monopoly) or a few media companies (oligopoly) in any market as a result of acquisitions and mergers or the disappearance of competitors' (Meier and Trappel, 1998: 41). It should be clear, however, that media concentration is a very complex and multi-dimensional phenomenon. It would actually lead us too far to discuss the rather confusing use of terms and the concrete differences between concentration and related concepts such as media integration. (For an overview of frequently used notions and definitions, see Sanchez-Tabernero, 1993.) Still, one of the most relevant distinctions in this respect is, conventionally, made between horizontal, vertical and diagonal types of concentration, respectively – depending on whether the concentration process involves two or more media corporations offering the same or a substitutable final product, whether it involves enterprises or activities on a different level in the media production chain (most notably production and distribution) or whether it involves actors from different economic sectors, such as financial holdings buying into the media market. Media cross-ownership (which refers to a situation in which a media company operates and controls outlets in different media sectors) is sometimes considered as a special form of horizontal concentration, while in other instances this form of cross- or multi-media integration is seen as a concrete example of diagonal concentration. But, however conceptually defined, media concentration processes occur in many forms and gradations. Various corporate strategies are involved, ranging from product diversification and all kinds of co-operative agreements, strategic alliances and joint-ventures, to actual mergers and acquisitions, resulting in the formation of ever larger and economically more powerful entities.

Some examples can clarify this trend, whereby almost the entire communication and information sector is witnessing a concentration movement leading to oligopolistic situations, in which the economic market is concentrated in the hands of only a few providers. A striking example can be found with the British ITV franchises (regional network stations), where the decentralized principle is thus undermined. In November 1996 Carlton (already controlling Carlton Television and Central) bought Westcounty Television; in June 1997 Scottish Television acquired Grampian and took an 18 per cent stake in Ulster (to be bought out completely in due course); and in August 1997 Granada bought Yorkshire/Tyne Tees Television. Concentration is not limited to buying or taking over single companies, though. Another European example of the intricate web into which the audio-visual market has developed, can be found with CLT/UFA. This company – with one of the largest audio-visual turnovers in Europe – is the result of the merger of Bertelsmann's audio-visual activities (UFA Film und Fernseh GmbH and Co KG) with CLT (Audiofina) and with Havas as a committed partner. So, as a result of such takeovers, mergers and similar ventures, only a few (but very large) corporations and conglomerates – such as Walt Disney, Viacom, Time Warner, Sony, News Corporation, Bertelsmann and CLT – control the market (cf. *infra*).

The basic economic rationales behind media concentration have already been referred to when talking of the fact that the high production costs, as opposed to the relatively low reproduction costs of most media products, urge companies to increase their operating scale and capacity and, accordingly, to expand their markets. While, especially in rather small or saturated media markets, a takeover is one of the most direct ways to achieve such an increase in size and output, it also allows one to penetrate quite easily into new media markets without the expensive, time-consuming and risky business of setting up a wholly new business. More generally, mergers and acquisitions, as well as co-operative agreements and diversification strategies, allow for further growth and increased profitability, as important economic and financial benefits can be derived from larger-scale, joint or more diversified operations at both the cost and the income side of media companies (Meier and Trappel, 1998). On the one hand, concentration tendencies are motivated by the search to take advantage of **synergies**, and economies of scale and scope, and to cut costs and raise efficiency in general. By joining forces or by controlling different outlets in different media sectors, for instance, production and distribution facilities can be shared, as can other costly resources such as manpower, know-how and management skills, or market research activities and expenditure. On the other hand, it is the general aim to strengthen market positions and to maximize audiences, sales and advertising revenues that leads media firms to deploy a vast array of expansive corporate strategies. Vertical integration of production and distribution, for instance, provides a higher degree of market autonomy: by controlling important distribution channels media production companies are capable of pushing their products through the market; similarly, by taking over production houses or acquiring the (exclusive) rights of programme software, hardware producers and tele-communication operators are able to push their hi-tech products. The search for new, lucrative markets and fields of operation has likewise furthered the process of media cross-ownership, from which many other market advantages are to be derived. For one thing, diversification enables media firms to spread company risks, which further contributes to their economic strength. Control of different media outlets in different sectors also offers possibilities of cross-promotion and, in particular, of sharing and recycling existing media content, programme software and successful talent: 'synergies result from control of the content or the performer's fame, and the capability of spreading the costs of the contract or content over multiple outlets, while at the same time deriving revenues from multiple sources' (Meier and Trappel, 1998: 52–4). The marketing of *Pocahontas*, and many other animated characters, by Walt Disney (the film, the dolls, the books, the jigsaw puzzles, lunchboxes, etc.) is but one of many examples of this (worldwide) exploitation of one product in as many markets as possible. Finally, strong and dominant market positions also pay off in terms of advertising, as advertisers are attracted by large market shares, pack-age discounts and diversified portfolios. Moreover, concentration in the media sector recently has been pushed to a certain extent by similar trends towards the centralization of market power in the advertising industry itself.

Apart from these economic incentives, it is clear that media concentration has also been stimulated by other environmental factors, and in particular by both technological and political developments and opportunities. Technological innovation contributes to the process of media concentration in at least two respects. On the one hand, small media com-panies may be forced out of the market or into the hands of larger media entities, as they generally lack the necessary capital resources required to upgrade production technologies or to install new production equipment; at the same time, the high level of capitalization associated with technological innovation establishes high barriers to market entry for new entrants and potential competitors. On the other hand, new markets and opportunities for expansion and diversification are opened up by new information and communication tech-nologies, while the economic logic of digitalization requires the formation of multi-media groups that can operate in previously separate sectors and can gain maximum advantage from technological convergence.

Examples abound of the fact that the convergence of technologies seems naturally to have found an economic counterpart in the formation of highly integrated multi-media conglomerates. Many of the companies in the top ranks of the audio-visual market are multi-media companies (e.g. NewsCorp) or diversified companies with interests in electronic goods (e.g. Sony) or in transmission and programming (production, distribution, broadcasting, cable, video and sound recording). Sony, for instance, has its main business (¥4.355 billion in 1999) in electronics (audio equipment, video equipment, television, computers, electronic components) followed by games (consoles and software, ¥760 billion), music (¥719 billion), pictures (¥540 billion), insurance (¥339 billion) and others (credit card businesses, satellite distribution services, Internet-related businesses, etc., ¥81 billion). The most spectacular (and expensive) example yet is the recent merger of the multi-media giant Time Warner with the young Internet company America Online (AOL). This is an example of the integration of almost all old (film, radio, television, publishing) and new (IT, Internet) media. Time Warner was already involved in cable television networks through Turner Broadcasting (merged in 1996) and HBO, publishing through Time, Inc. and New Line Cinema, entertainment through Warner Bros and Warner Music Group, and cable systems through Time Warner Cable. Each of these companies in turn has several subsidiaries (Warner Bros, for instance, has 18 different subdivisions). Its merger with AOL gives it the crucial Internet link that can turn it into the most important multi-media company in years to come.

Recent changes in national and international media policies and regulations have also had a substantial impact on media concentration. Mainly as a result of the widespread development of cable and satellite technologies in the 1980s and 1990s, all western European countries saw their public broadcasting monopolies collapse. The pressure towards European integration and the development of a free internal market further contributed to the deregulation of the audio-visual media sector, enabling established press groups and investors from outside the media to enter the broadcasting market. As a result, cross-ownership between press and broadcasting on the national level has been given a strong impetus, sometimes even quite deliberately by governments and regulative bodies in order to protect national media industries from acquisitions or market penetration by foreign enterprises. According to Meier and Trappel, national media policies have thus generally operated in favour of media concentration:

> The common policy of privatization and deregulation all over Europe has aggravated the very problems [it was] intended to solve. In other words, state and administrative bodies in charge of media regulations have willingly stimulated – and not reduced – the concentration process. (Meier and Trappel, 1998: 39)

This contention also applies to media policy on a European level, where the complex and paradoxical nature of the problem of concentration has probably most been felt. While concentration and transnational integration can be considered as quite natural tendencies when a free internal market is established, they threaten to distort the very same process of free market competition and can therefore be considered incompatible with the internal market. At the same time, however, it is commonly argued that 'European media groups have to become more integrated in order to be competitive in the global market' (Meier and Trappel, 1998: 44) *vis-à-vis* their mainly American (and Japanese) counterparts.

As a result of these economic, technological and political currents and developments, clearly the issue of concentration is no longer confined, as in earlier times, mainly to national newspaper markets: 'the dimensions of media concentration have grown both in terms of geographical scope and media fields affected' (Meier and Trappel, 1998: 43). As a matter of fact, the trend of multi-media integration has largely been part of that other important trend in the industrial organization of the contemporary communication system, meaning the transnationalization whereby the main corporations operate across frontiers on a global scale. These transnational multi-media conglomerates state that the way in which the production, distribution and consumption process is currently running pushes them towards a global policy. Since the initial costs of programme production make up the main investment, and since the further costs of reproduction or transmission for wider audiences are comparatively low, there has always been an expansive dynamic within the media. Since audiences are spread geographically, this dynamic has always had a geographic dimension, pushing towards a wider 'audio-visual space'. What we seem to witness now is the ultimate fulfilment of this logic by organizations whose aim it is to compete on world markets and whose priority lies with economies of scale that enable this. Rupert Murdoch, with his News Corporation, is a prime, perhaps even archetypal, example of such a global multi-media mogul. Of Australian origin, Murdoch obtained American citizenship in order to expand his Australian businesses with American takeovers. He bore fruit of his friendship with Margaret Thatcher to take control of British satellite television (set out to be British) and was quick to (successfully) enter the new market of the Far East. Thus, NewsCorp has dominant interests in at least three continents, and as such proves to be a typical example of current market trends.

THE SCALE OF THE NEW MEDIA MARKET: KEY PLAYERS

At this point it is necessary to turn to some basic facts and figures, showing the real contours of the transnational media market and the oligopolistic position of its key players. After all, a clear indication of the size and shape of the market can only be obtained by looking at some hard data. Who are the main economic players in the field? How many of them are there? How big are they? Such data can be simple but very revealing. To ensure internal and external validity, all basic quantitative data are taken from the same source (European Audiovisual Observatory, EAO); they are complemented by more in-depth material. Following the EAO's example, the nationality of a company is determined by the country in which its head office is located. The size of a company is indicated by its yearly turnover in US$. The total turnover represents all the activities of a company; the audio-visual turnover represents all the audio-visual activities of a company.

The World's Leading Multi-media Companies

Multi-media companies must be understood here as 'companies or groups involved in at least two different branches: press, cinema, broadcasting, sound recording industry, video-games industry, etc.' (European Audiovisual Observatory, 1995). This means that these companies can have subsidiaries (or even their main activity) outside the media and communication sector (e.g. General Electric/NBC). Here, the turnover figures refer only to their media and communication aspect (see Table 21.1).

The 12 rankings listed in Table 21.1 have witnessed some significant changes over time. Rankings can differ considerably from one year to another, due to continuous merging and changes of ownership. Comparing the top versus the bottom of this ranking, it becomes obvious that even between the 12 biggest companies – which already hold a more than significant part of the world market – there is a serious discrepancy in turnover. The market can thus be seen as dominated by only a few (but gigantic) companies. The places of origin of these mega-companies are not very surprising. In 1998, the ranking included nine US, seven European, two Japanese, one Australian and one Canadian corporation. Whereas in 1993 the USA had only one company in the top five, by 1998 it dominated in terms of turnover with three out of five. Still, the fact that there are three European companies in the top 12 seems to indicate a certain future for the continent's media industries. The fast-moving aspect of this business can be illustrated by the turnover of Bertelsmann, which went from US$8.682 in 1993 to US$12.534 two years later. The reason it lost its 1996 top position to the US Walt Disney Group – also the world's leading audio-visual group (cf. *infra*) – lies with the merger of its audio-visual operations with CLT (in CLT/UFA). The merger of Time Warner and America Online (in January 2000) will increase its turnover dramatically, thus pushing Walt Disney Group from its number one position overnight. On average, the top 12 companies have seen a yearly increase in turnover.

It is interesting to see how the activities of these companies are spread over different media sectors. Some, like Viacom or Time Warner, have spread their activities roughly evenly over different sectors, whereas others are less balanced. Even though the press sector is often considered to be part of the 'old media', publishing houses represent a strong industrial power. This becomes clear from the position of companies such as Hachette or Gannett. Similarly, communication groups such as Havas may not be heavily involved in audio-visual, yet they do have considerable interests in other media. As such, these printing and communication companies have a secure financial base and, often, a strong worldwide presence. These may prove to be the prerequisites that enable them to develop into the leading market players of the future. The distinct growth in multi-media supports (combining sound, image, print and computer software) will make the consumption of both entertainment and educational products more and more common, and thus more profitable. Again, this will influence the rankings in years to come.

The World's Leading Audio-visual Companies

In both academia and industry, the bulk of attention in the last two decades has been paid to the audio-visual market. This is not to say that press corporations have been banished to the fringes of the media market; groups like Bertelsmann and NewsCorp prove different. Yet an important part of their growth and a great deal of the growth in the market in general is situated at the audio-visual level. Hence, it is worth studying the world-leading audio-visual groups (see Table 21.2).

Table 21.1 The world's top 12 multi-media companies (1993–98)

	1993			1995			1997			1998		
	Company	Country	Turnover (US$ mill.)	Company	Country	Turnover (US$ mill.)	Company	Country	Turnover (US$ mill.)	Company	Country	Turnover (US$ mill.)
1	Matsushita	JP	22.723	Time Warner	USA	14.375	Walt Disney	USA	17.459	Walt Disney	USA	17.444
2	Philips	NL	10.008	Bertelsmann	D	12.534	NewsCorp	AU	13.566	Time Warner	USA	13.618
3	Bertelsmann	D	8.682	Viacom	USA	11.689	Viacom	USA	13.206	NewsCorp	AU	13.002
4	Time Warner	USA	7.963	Havas	FR	9.107	Time Warner	USA	12.412	Viacom	USA	11.824
5	Sony	JP	7.305	NewsCorp	AU	9.028	Bertelsmann	DE	11.840	Bertelsmann	DE	11.235
6	NewsCorp	AUS	7.129	Sony	JP	8.619	Sony	JP	9.872	Sony	JP	10.492
7	Matra-Hachette	F	5.214	Fujisankei	JP	7.457	Time Warner Ent	USA	7.531	Time Warner Ent	USA	8.373
8	Havas	F	4.938	Capital C/ABC	USA	6.879	Havas	FR	6.517	Matra-Hachette	FR	7.137
9	Capital C/ABC	USA	4.663	Matra-Hachette	F	6.269	Matra-Hachette	FR	6.448	CBS Corp	USA	6.805
10	Paramount	USA	4.434	Walt Disney	USA	6.002	ARD	DE	6.295	Seagram	CA	6.682
11	Times Mirror	USA	3.714	Polygram	NL	5.479	Polygram	NL	5.686	ARD	DE	6.327
12	Walt Disney	USA	3.676	MCA (Seagram)	CA	5.325	Seagram	CA	5.455	Cox Enterprises	USA	5.355

Source: adapted from European Audiovisual Observatory

The ranking of the audio-visual companies in Table 21.2 differs considerably from that of the top 12 multi-media companies listed in Table 21.1. The exclusion of press and publishing operations alters the top 12 world ranking, with Europe losing ground to the USA. The ranking of the leading audio-visual groups has also changed dramatically over time and offers an excellent illustration of the move to a 'transnational oligopolistic media market'. In 1987, nine of the top twelve companies were terrestrial broadcasters, including the three major American networks (Capital Cities/ABC, NBC and CBS), NHK, Fininvest, BBC, ARD and RAI. By 1995, only four of these companies were included in the ranking. Other companies witnessed a dramatic growth. Viacom, a minor player in 1992 and only 14th in 1994, in 1995 suddenly moved up to top position after taking over Blockbuster and Paramount. The year after that, with a growing but similar turnover, it lost top place to Walt Disney. The sale of Polygram by Philips to Seagram in December 1998 will possibly go on to push this company into the top three, although the fickle market of video games (vital for these companies) makes their position unstable.

As in the multi-media rankings, there are serious and still growing discrepancies in corporate turnover of audio-visual media. A look at the top 50 audio-visual companies confirms this disparity in corporate turnover. The ratio of the top company's audio-visual turnover to that of the 50th company is 1 to 13 in 1998, as against 1 to 10 in 1993. Some holdings – particularly American groups such as Viacom – have seen spectacular growth in audio-visual turnover. In part, this can be ascribed to the numerous mergers and acquisitions in recent years. It should be noted, though, that not all of these increases result from takeovers. They can also be due to internal growth within a group. NewsCorp, for instance, provides an interesting illustration of the latter as its growth in audio-visual turnover is due to the success with the audience of its broadcasters in the USA (Fox Broadcasting), Britain (BSkyB) and Asia (Star TV). There is also a considerable difference in the percentage of audio-visual turnover in the total turnover of the companies in the ranking. Whereas a lot of companies have a majority stake in the audio-visual sector, there are companies – even though they are key players in the audio-visual market – whose main activity lies elsewhere. Good examples are Sony and General Electric/NBC: only 19 per cent and 5 per cent, respectively, of their total turnover comes from audio-visual activities. Time Warner's merger with America Online will re-define its percentage of total turnover generated from audio-visual activities.

Finally, when looking at countries of origin within the world's top 50 audio-visual companies, the European industry is the most heavily represented with 23 companies in 1997, against 15 US, 8 Japanese and 4 other (Brazilian, Mexican, Canadian and Australian) companies. It might seem, then, that the future of the European industry is quite rosy, but in terms of turnover, the picture is somewhat different. The average size of the European companies listed in these rankings (US$2.435,8 million in 1998) is noticeably smaller than that of the American (US$5.050,1 million) and Japanese (US$3.622,6 million) companies, and is increasingly growing at a much slower rate than the American and Japanese companies. Compared to 1997, for instance, in 1998 there was only a 2.9 per cent increase for European, while there was a 5 per cent increase for American companies.

Table 21.2　*Ranking by audio-visual turnover of the 12 world-leading groups (1992–98) (US$ million)*

Rank	Company	Country	1992	1993	1994	1995	1996	1997	1998	1998 Av. turnover
1	Walt Disney	USA	4.197	5.089	6.591	8.150	14.237	17.459	17.444	76%
2	Viacom	USA	1.454	2.028	5.171	8.772	9.818	9.997	11.254	93%
3	Sony	JP	6.659	7.320	7.945	8.619	9.087	9.872	10.492	19%
4	Time Warner	USA	9.975	3.334	3.986	4.196	5.084	7.892	9.267	64%
5	Time Warner Ent	USA	–	5.755	5.997	6.718	7.498	7.531	8.373	68%
6	NewsCorp	AU	3.115	3.534	4.190	4.881	6.200	7.328	8.265	61%
7	ARD	DE	5.587	5.611	5.824	6.601	6.450	6.295	6.805	100%
8	Polygram	NL	3.763	3.993	4.525	5.479	5.628	5.686	6.682	54%
9	Seagram/Universal Studios	CA	–	4.606	4.744	4.876	5.417	5.455	6.327	100%
10	Gen Elec/NBC	USA	3.363	3.102	3.361	3.919	5.232	5.153	5.269	5%
11	NHK	JP	4.437	5.254	5.744	6.043	5.617	5.091	4.964	100%
12	CBS Corp	USA	–	–	–	0.931	3.952	5.061	4.674	36%

Source: adapted from European Audiovisual Observatory

The European Audio-visual Market

To complete the picture, we will take a look at the European audio-visual market (see Table 21.3).

In the first instance, the European audio-visual market shows a less dramatic picture of change. In 1998, up to one-third of the market is still taken up by PSB. What is more, two of the top five companies are public service broadcasters, with ARD in top position and BBC third. The financial health of certain PSB corporations does seem to be improving, with a general increase in turnover, coupled with mostly positive net income figures for 1998. The other positions in the top six companies are mainly taken up by three groups whose business is music: Polygram, Bertelsmann and Thorn-EMI. However, the positioning strategy of these three companies differs. While, for Bertelsmann, music and video make up only 38 per cent of its turnover, with Polygram these sectors account for 84 per cent. Thorn-EMI is exclusively involved in the music and video business. These companies also score well on the world ranking of audio-visual groups, giving Europe a stronghold in the world market.

A country-by-country breakdown of the European top 50 audio-visual groups shows the

Table 21.3   *The European top 16 audiovisual companies (1998) (turnover in US$ million)*

Rank	Company	Country	Av. turnover	Total turnover	Growth Av. turnover
1	ARD	DE	5.653,8	5.564,6	1.6%
2	Bertelsmann	DE	4.176,0	11.659,0	11.9%
3	BBC	GB	3.812,6	4.187,1	9.5%
4	KirchGruppe	DE	3.544,0	3.544,0	10.5%
5	EMI Group plc	GB	3.510,7	3.510,7	−3.2%
6	Polygram	NL	3.293,7	3.293,7	−34.4%
7	CLT-UFA	LU	2.742,8	3.061,6	6.2%
8	RAI	IT	2.654,4	2.654,4	4.3%
9	Carlton	GB	2.493,7	2.727,7	−2.7%
10	BSkyB	GB	2.257,1	2.257,1	7.4%
11	CANAL+	FR	1.988,4	2.457,1	10.7%
12	Mediaset	IT	1.879,8	1.879,8	8.0%
13	TF1	FR	1.662,3	1.662,3	5.8%
14	ZDF	DE	1.448,7	1.448,7	0.6%
15	Granada	GB	1.406,0	6.016,4	41.3%
16	The Rank Group plc	GB	1.379,1	3.070,1	6.3%

Source: adapted from European Audiovisual Observatory

importance of German and British companies (28 per cent each of the combined turnover of the top 50 companies). Dutch companies take third place (13 per cent). The Netherlands provides a good example of successful European enterprise with Endemol (a merger between JE Entertainment and De Mol) featuring in the top 50 for the second year running as one of the main producers and exporters of TV programme formats in the European markets.

Yet as far as the European industry is concerned, some of these optimistic remarks need to be modified. First, despite the survival of PSB, it is walking a tightrope. The public radio and television sector still makes up one-third of the market, yet its overall share seems to be decreasing, due to a slower rate of growth (9.2 per cent from 1996 to 1997, against 12.3 per cent for the 50 top companies taken as a whole). Several PSB institutions are still experiencing severe structural problems. Second, several of the major audio-visual companies are not, in fact, European but the affiliates of American companies (e.g. The Rank Group, Viacom International Netherlands and Time Warner Entertainment's British affiliate). Polygram, acquired by Seagram in December 1998, will for this reason no longer feature in the most recent rankings.

Bertelsmann takeover

A typical example of the relentless concentration movement can be found if we look back to February 2001 when Bertelsmann acquired a majority stake in RTL Group/GBL. As the company proudly announced on its website:

Aside from its existing 37 per cent stake, Bertelsmann AG is taking over another 30 per cent of the shares in Europe's largest and most successful TV, radio and film production group, 'RTL Group', from Groupe Bruxelles Lambert SA (GBL). At the same time, GBL – the majority of which is held by the entrepreneurs Albert Frère and Paul Desmarais – will take over 25.1 per cent in Bertelsmann AG, with 0.1 per cent of the shares being without voting rights. This share swap was announced by Bertelsmann CEO Thomas Middelhoff today in a Press Release. He spoke of an important move in terms of strategy and corporate history. As a result of this move, Bertelsmann now holds 67 per cent of the shares in the RTL Group, 22 per cent remain in the hands of Pearson, 11 per cent are publicly traded on the stock market. The new partner of Bertelsmann AG, GBL, will be represented with two seats on the Bertelsmann Supervisory Board. GBL has the right to go public with part of its participation in three to four years' time. Bertelsmann Chairman and CEO Thomas Middelhoff declares: 'From both a strategic and a historic point of view, this is a significant step that will lastingly shape the company's future. It will strengthen Bertelsmann's position as the driving force in television, a future growth market. The RTL Group has a central meaning in Bertelsmann's corporate strategy. The brand's magnetism can be leveraged and developed for many media consumer communities throughout the various sectors and product lines. We have longstanding friendly ties with GBL and welcome them as a new shareholder. Bertelsmann's unique corporate culture will remain intact even in the event of a possible IPO in about three years from now.'

ECONOMIC FORCES, CULTURAL VALUES AND PUBLIC INTERESTS: NO NEED TO WORRY?

By now the global picture should be clear. Communication systems have, on a worldwide level, witnessed a transformation whereby the traditional boundaries between media markets have increasingly been broken down. On the one hand, as information technologies have converged, the boundaries between different media sectors have blurred, resulting in a level of industrial organization in highly integrated multi-media firms. On the other hand, media are no longer predominantly a 'national affair', developing within a market context that is geographically confined to national territories; the scale and scope of media markets, industries and regulations have increasingly become inter- or transnational. In this new market environment, extending across media sectors and national frontiers, economic power is, to a high degree, concentrated in the hands of a limited number of transnational multi-media giants. These conglomerates consolidate their market position, not only through mergers and acquisitions, but also simply by taking advantage of the logic of commerce (e.g. marketing strategies based on synergies). The potential problems and/or benefits associated with these processes are manifold and have been much discussed. Starting from the main schools of thought described earlier, we will focus here on some of the most relevant implications of these market tendencies.

Concentration and Multi-media Integration

From a critical perspective, concentration is fiercely criticized and considered as a logical consequence, or even a downright demonstration or proof of the fact that the production and distribution of media and cultural products is dominated and controlled by the economic and political elite. According to these views, powerful groups are using, or able to use, the media they own to promote their own economic and political interests. In the economic field, concentration increases the structural power of the main corporations, their potential to determine the rules of the game, which smaller and weaker competitors need to abide by. At the societal level concentration increases the possibility for media owners to use their control over the communication markets for political purposes. The way the Italian **media tycoon** Silvio Berlusconi used his media power to ascend to presidency is often referred to as a prime example of this dangerous situation. More generally it is argued that the mono-polization of control over information-gathering and distribution by only a few large suppliers further jeopardizes the free flow of information and the free circulation of opinion. This holds true for local press barons as much as for international media moguls, as well as for those global news agencies that, from their western home-based market, control large parts of the international traffic of news and information. Media diversity and pluralism, and ultimately democracy, are at stake, then, both in terms of the rights of the public to be adequately informed as well as in terms of all interests and views in society to be properly represented. And since the economic factors previously described (e.g. the high capital needs for media production) also imply high barriers for (under-capitalized) newcomers to enter the market, certain groups and minorities face the risk of being under-represented or even of, literally, being excluded from the public domain. In his historical review of the British press Curran (1991a), for instance, followed this basic interpretative scheme to account for the decline of the left-wing press and the gradual but significant conservative, rightward drift of the newspaper press.

From a liberal point of view, however, such critical arguments about political-economic forms of dependence and control are countered, in particular, by the argument that one should not too hastily identify ownership with actual control over media content. According to this view, the power of media owners is counterbalanced by many other actors and interests at stake, and not least by the consuming audience, whose tastes, needs and demands, in a free market environment, ultimately prevail over any incentive of media owners to abuse their power and influence. Both possible direct forms of influence through editorial interventions, as well as inevitable indirect forms of influence through the setting of objectives and the allocation of resources, are in other words subject to a necessary kind of market-led pragmatism. One might go further and argue that concentration processes such as takeovers are sometimes the only way for loss-making media with a proper identity and democratic voice to continue to exist, although their future configuration then largely depends on the policies and arrangements of the 'over-taker' to ensure editorial autonomy. More generally, large and economically strong media companies, through strategic investments, cross-subsidization and the like, might best provide the fertile soil and means required for media to ensure professional work, editorial quality and audience responsiveness.

Market Competition and Commercialization

Different interpretations of this kind can also be given for other phenomena linked with the workings of the market and the commercial exploitation of the media, such as the role of advertising, the implications of competition, and processes of commercialization and depoliticization. In general, from a liberal-pluralist point of view, competition is considered to be a necessary condition for media diversity and consumer choice, while further also inspiring innovation and adaptation, creativity and originality. It urges media to invest in the quality of their products, while forming the backbone of their responsiveness to (changing) audience tastes and preferences as well as to broader social developments. Media that fail to do so are likely to disappear, as a result of the natural selection process implied by free market competition. As such, the theoretical assumptions of social reflection and consumer sovereignty underpin the socially beneficial values of the market mechanism in media industries.

From a critical perspective, exactly these assumptions are considered to be false, to be myths continuously used to justify or legitimize both the dominant way in which media systems are organized and structured in contemporary (late) capitalist societies, and the everyday practices and routines of journalists and other professional media workers. One area of criticism, stressing the detrimental effects and deficiencies of the free market mechanism, deals with the important role of advertising. On the one hand, there are the consequences of the structural dependence of the media on advertising. To give but one example, in his account of the British press, Curran (Curran and Seaton, 1991) explains how the lack of advertising was a structural handicap – or mechanism of capitalist, market control – that the nineteenth-century radical press was not able to overcome. Furthermore, advertising stirred up a polarization between downmarket popular papers (more heavily dependent on sales in the lower, working-class sections of the market) and the quality press, which as a result of its upmarket profile and audience of '(big) spenders', drained away advertising without being urged to popularize. One interpretation of this economic weighting by advertising is that it acted as a prime instrument in dividing media along social class lines and in further breeding a cultural or knowledge gap. On the other hand, and following the essential role of advertising at a structural level, there are the more direct effects of adver-tising on the form and content of media products. As the need for advertising income and the drive for audience maximization go hand in hand, examples abound of the preponder-ance of audience ratings affecting TV programme strategies and schedules. With its high demands of attracting consumer attention, advertising also, to a large extent, determines the volume, form and layout of newspapers and magazines, and might even induce all sorts of editorial adaptations as far as the actual content is concerned (e.g. content-wise parallelism between editorial pieces and advertised products). Ultimately this brings us to more far-reaching forms of dependence on the media vis-à-vis the advertising business: the sometimes nearly invisible mixtures of advertising and editorial output or programme con-tent in terms of product placement, 'advertorials' and 'infomercials'; all kinds of editorial pieces or media products produced by advertisers themselves (cf. soap opera), and the mostly hard-to-detect forms of self-censorship of the media inflicted by advertising interests.

An even more fundamental criticism has not only to do with the role of advertising, but with processes inherent to the 'normal' laws and workings of the market in general – includ-ing media concentration – dictating media form and content. So, cultural homogeneity and ideological uniformity are said to be promoted as 'intense competition between a limited number of producers encourages common denominator provision for the mass market' (Curran, 1991a: 47), or as 'the mass media are rather like political parties in that they tend to gravitate towards the centre in response to competitive pressures' (Curran, 1996: 140). This common denominator theory involves many aspects. In political or ideological terms, it implies a further breakdown of media pluralism as the media refrain from taking radical, oppositional or non-conformist positions in order not to scare off potential consumers and advertisers. It also implies, as many content analyses tried to show, a gradual depoliticiza-tion of media content. When the quantity of politics and serious information has to give in to entertainment as the dominant ingredient of media offerings, or has to adapt to its styles and formats (cf. infotainment, reality TV, etc.), this undermines, so it is argued, the political knowledge, conscience and engagement of citizens. More generally, the common denomi-nator theory argues that news articles, documentaries, fictional programmes or films, or any other media product, which, regardless of their social-cultural use value for any kind of minority, do not pass the test of their economic trade value, are destined to be sacrificed in a commercial and highly competitive media environment. According to this view, then, competition does not stimulate innovation, creativity and originality – on the contrary, it breeds standardization, imitation and convergence. In the context of multi-media integration, for instance, one might indeed question whether cultural diversity is being promoted by bringing on to different markets mere variations of one theme (cf. *Pocahontas*). Thus, consumer choice and autonomy are not only limited by social-economic conditions – the distribution of economic and cultural capital in society – but already by the real offerings of the media industries themselves.

Finally, and linked to all this, a large body of criticism focuses on the impact of competition and commercial pressures on media form and content via the consequences they have for the practices and procedures employed by media workers in their everyday occupation. Most of these criticisms focus on news production, journalistic values and professional routines, and involve problems of a predominantly ethical nature associated with the public responsibility of the media. As such, commercialization is often said to imply a lowering or 'tabloidization' of journalistic standards. Most of the time one refers, then, to the sensationalist compulsion of the media, their obsessive search for exclusive material, sensational scoops and nasty scandals, and the dubious practices used in this respect (e.g. 'cheque-book journalism'). However, even apart from such extreme phenomena, competition and related working conditions such as tight time schedules and deadlines are said to induce an approach to news and information that, in general, is marked by superficiality and fragmentation. By focusing on isolated events, and neglecting or being compelled to neglect background information and explanation of causes, processes and effects, political ignorance and indifference are said once again to be stimulated. The widely used strategies of personalization and dramatization, which to a considerable extent have influenced the communication of politics, even further enhance this effect. Then, of course, there is also the traditional criticism of the widespread preoccupation of the news media with negative events (the 'bad news syndrome'), often implying that minorities, oppositional and deviant groups only are pictured or represented in the news in the context of negative acts and events (crime, strikes, demonstrations). According to critical theory, in the end, all these (routine) practices and strategies, by obscuring the real social relations, problems and conflicts and by excluding or misrepresenting certain groups and interests, do legitimize the status quo.

Transnationalization and Globalization

By way of conclusion, one might consider these implications more specifically in the context of the formation of a global media market. Here as well, these consequences have been discussed extensively in the recent past in both academic and public forums, and also quite often from a 'doomsday' perspective. Other contributions in this book discuss several of these matters, from different points of view, but we would like to draw attention to two important issues.

One area of concern is the consequence of the above-mentioned evolution on the functioning of the media in the public sphere and thus on civil society (for an interesting discussion, see Braman and Sreberny-Mohammadi, 1996). In Habermas's ideal of the public sphere as 'that space of social life determined neither by market nor by the state in which the formation and reformation of public opinion through open debate is deemed possible' (Sreberny-Mohammadi, 1996: 9), the mass media have always been given a prominent position. Even though this public sphere in its ideal form never has been, nor will be, realized, it has always had a strong position (implicitly or explicitly) in both media theory and practice. A central position in this was always given to the press, but PSB too was set out and has always striven to provide a forum for democratic ideas. The transnationalization of the media, as well as the growing hybridization of different media (e.g. transnational news media, news on the Internet), has been heralded by some as the basis for a global mediated public sphere and thus for worldwide political democracy and participation, for a 'true' civil society. Yet, the political economy of the media provided above, should at least caution an over-optimistic analysis. First, the media becoming an economic commodity – rather than a part of culture – seems to imply an 'economization' of the public sphere in which ideas have to prove economically viable. Equally, access to the civil forum increasingly carries a price tag. Finally, but most importantly, one must ask whose ideas are being brought to the worldwide forum when this forum is owned by only a handful of western companies (see e.g. Verstraeten, 1996).

The second area of concern is related to collective identities. Here the discussion in recent years has been particularly sweeping and rife with strong but often simplistic statements. Starting point is the perceived shift in identities. As Hall states:

> The old identities which stabilised the social world for so long are in decline, giving rise to new identities and fragmenting the modern individual as a unified subject. This so-called crisis is seen as part of a wider process of change which is dislocating the central structures and processes of modern societies and undermining the frameworks which gave individuals stable anchorage in the social world. (Hall, 1992: 274)

The exponential growth in international media and the mediation of culture in general is seen to undermine these vested identities or, in the words of Price (1995), the 'plethora of changing signals, floating, then raining from space, poses impressive problems of belonging, identification, nationalism and community'. Terms such as coca-colonization, Americanization and the like are often used to describe the processes caused by the aforementioned shifts in media structures. Concentrating the media (content) in the hands of only a few transnational (and often American) corporations is seen to lead to homogenization of culture with a distinct American signature, depriving people and local communities of their (national) roots. This bleak picture needs modification, though. First, the main 'problem child' in this story is national cultural identity, which is seen to be eroded by the internationalization of the media. Yet, this reasoning ignores the fact that national culture is itself 'a site of contestation on which competition over definitions takes place' (Schlesinger, 1991: 174) and is thus itself a power-related construct. Second, it is important to realize that, still according to Hall (1992), identity is a matter of becoming as much as being, a continuously constructed and reconstructed category. Identity is not an essence, not fixed and unchangeable over time. The identities now under threat through internationalization were themselves in the past replacing older identities. Finally, even though the internationalization is undeniable, there are also counter-forces, such as the clear localization that seems to have accompanied the globalization of culture. This seems to indicate that the dreaded homogenization will not be total.

This is not to argue that the economic developments in the media are of no cultural consequence – on the contrary. But it does warn against a media-centric view of cultural homogenization, implying that the media in themselves are strong enough to change the distinctiveness of complete regional or national cultures and identities. **Collective identity** formation in all its aspects is a much wider process than simply the part that is established through the media.

CHAPTER 22

News, Technology and the Paradoxes of Globalization: a Case Study

In this final chapter the potential impact of the current state of the media industries in all its complexity will be discussed on the basis of a case study. We will try to illustrate, on the one hand, how the structural processes and changes that have been taking place, influence both media content and audiences, but also, on the other hand, how this influence cannot be seen as straightforward.

The case focuses on the way in which those developments described above gave rise to a powerful 'discourse of globalization' (Dahlgren, 1995: 88; Tomlinson, 1999). This means that we are all convinced of the fact that in our rapidly changing world we cannot understand our culture and society without taking into account the international and global dimensions. Even on a local or domestic level of personal experiences, we have to consider the global dimensions in the flows of capital, technology, people, ideas, images and so on. Globalization clearly is not only a material reality, though – changing the ways in which industry, finance, economy, policy, culture and media operate. As Silverstone (1999: 144) states, globalization is also a 'state of mind', meaning that we know that we undoubtedly live in a global age in which we have our own maps of the world and maps of our own place in it.

To a large extent the current shifts in the media sphere are a result of these overall globalizing tendencies, of which the media themselves are part, but there is more to it. Indeed, we all seem convinced of the centrality of communication technologies in this momentum of globalization. We know that 'global economies and global finance cannot work without a global information infrastructure' (Silverstone, 1999: 106). We know that globalizing tendencies in the political, economic, financial and other spheres have their stimulating counterparts in the world of information, communication and the media. In this respect we can refer, once again, to the emergence of ever-stronger global multi-media alliances, whereby traditional media companies and huge telecommunication operators collaborate and use new interactive technologies in order to improve and expand their global services; or to transnational media conglomerates in general that are trying to target and create international and even global audiences. For some euphoric communication scholars (e.g.

Volkmer, 1999), services such as CNN and BBC World, as well as the Internet, might succeed in creating a sense of global community or even build an alternative, global public sphere. Whether or not we actually share such optimistic views, we seem strongly convinced of the fact that communication technologies play a crucial, catalytic role in mediating, representing and stimulating wider globalization processes. We are reconfirmed in these beliefs by the works of leading social and cultural theorists such as Anthony Giddens, Manuel Castells, Nicholas Luhmann and others, who tend to reserve a special place to communication technologies in the processes of globalization.

In this respect it is not surprising that, in recent years, many research efforts in the field of media and communication have been driven by this powerful 'discourse of globalization'. However, this discourse has not been unchallenged. Many critics have warned against the extensive use and abuse of these ideas, while many contradictions emerge. In a recent review of the literature on the analysis of global communication, for instance, Tomlinson (1999: 235) even suggested abandoning the terms 'global', 'globalization', and other concepts stimulating the ultimate 'academic G spot'.

One of the most intriguing contradictions deals with international and foreign news. As society has become more 'global', it is clear that the media, and the news media in particular, compress the world and make unknown cultures more available than ever. This follows from the simple, obvious observation that 'each time we turn on the television we are caught up with . . . the life-worlds of others who are all distant from the places in which we live' (Stevenson, 1999: 11). However, one might be surprised at what various researchers called the paradox of the shrinking news coverage of foreign and international events in these times of globalization. It is indeed amazing that 'as the technological capacity and sophistication of the global media expand, news coverage of foreign events seems to be shrinking' (Tomlinson, 1999: 171). The issue has been taken up more recently by many commentators and critics, denouncing the tendency towards journalistic parochialism and, more broadly, the West's growing indifference, isolationism and inward tendency. The paradox of the shrinking foreign and international news output is also a frequently used argument in debates on how news media are swamped by entertainment and commercialism, thus undermining the myth of their central democratic role (Bird, 1997; Kimball, 1994; McLachlan and Golding, 2000; Moisy, 1997).

As Moisy claims, 'the share of foreign news in the US fell from 35 per cent to 23 per cent between 1970 and 1995, while the average length of those stories dropped from 1.7 minutes to 1.2 minutes' (1997: 82). According to Utley (1997), the foreign news coverage by the leading American networks has been halved over the past decade. A similar narrowed news agenda has been observed by Hallin for US newspapers too, where international news 'has declined from 10.2 per cent of the news hole in 1971 to 2.6 per cent in 1988' (1996: 255). Talking also of the USA, Tomlinson states that 'network coverage of foreign affairs has fallen by two thirds in two decades . . . and by 42 per cent between 1988 and 1996' (1999: 171). And he adds that similar trends can be observed in other developed countries, such as the UK, where 'documentary output on international topics across all British terrestrial TV channels fell by 40 per cent between 1989 and 1994' (1999: 171).

This tendency is not limited to tabloids or widely consumed, commercial news media, as a recent analysis of leading British quality newspapers indicates. Using 'less international news coverage as a possible indicator of tabloidization', McLachlan and Golding (2000) found that both *The Times* and the *Guardian* showed a gradual decline. The results for *The Times* showed a continual decrease from a high of 3.7 stories per page in 1957 to a low of 0.4 per page in 1997. The *Guardian* showed a 'general downward trend . . . from 2 international news stories per page in 1962 to a low of just 0.6 per page in 1992' (McLachlan and Golding, 2000: 79). Similar, though less alarming, findings can also be found for some other European countries, such as Germany, France and The Netherlands.

In addition, this hypothesis concerning the quantitative degradation of foreign news has a qualitative turn too, more specifically in the way foreign and international news items are treated. This can go from scheduling ever-shorter foreign news items at the end of news programmes, to putting them into a carousel format accompanied by a repetitive musical tune. Also the use of upbeat stories before the foreign news carousel (i.e. announcing an upcoming story as a teaser) can be seen as a marginalizing technique in scheduling foreign items (Zillmann et al., 1994). Another technique for softening international news items has to do with domestication. This widely researched practice refers to rendering foreign events comprehensible and relevant to domestic audiences (Gurevitch et al., 1991). Given the importance of cultural proximity as a news value, it seems to be necessary that international and foreign news items are, more than ever, domesticated in order to catch the audience's attention. These techniques all serve the purpose of softening the (often) hard character of foreign and international news, or of making it relevant and comprehensible to the public. So, it seems that not only the amount of foreign news is shrinking. Faced with increasing competition for ratings and with declining audiences for news (Moisy, 1997; Bird, 2000), foreign items seem to be marginalized and, as much as possible, domesticated, personalized and 'made relevant'. They are presented in a much more fragmented way than local news, often treated without any broader interpretation or context.

These pessimistic voices on the shrinking foreign news output are indicative of, and reinforced by, a powerful lament regarding the audience's shrinking interest in foreign issues. The paradox of the narrowed news agenda, with considerably less international news in this age of globalization, is mostly treated as a structural case of how a market conception of the media transforms vital 'hard news' into softer, more sensationalist formats. In a competitive media landscape with commercially driven journalism, many foreign news items are seen as too complex and/or uninteresting for audiences.

From this perspective, the whole paradox fits not only into the debate about barriers to McLuhan's 'global village' and the cosmopolitan idea in general, but the paradox also throws up questions about the functions of the media in organizing and disseminating public knowledge. Referring to public sphere theories (Habermas, 1989; Garnham, 1992), the paradox seems to be illustrating the declining potential for a free, democratic communication system. It relates to the social responsibility of the media and to the civic ideal of making it possible for citizens really to have access to all relevant and diverse forms of information and experience.

The question, however, is whether these alarming analyses of the paradox between globalization and the degradation of international news coverage are indeed legitimate. Looking more closely at the issue at stake, it seems that many of the arguments about the shrinking foreign news output do not take into consideration many of the technological and other fundamental shifts that are occurring in the wider media and news ecology. The lament over the narrowing news agenda and the consequences for the role of the media in society is powerful indeed, but there may be some weaknesses in this analysis.

So, one can seriously question whether international and global news has degraded, or is degrading (in such an alarming sense). For one thing, even if the overall share of foreign and international news in most of the traditional, national news media has declined over a shorter or longer period of time, one cannot easily escape the simple observation that, especially since the 1990s, there has been a tremendous growth in daily news output. The proliferation of TV channels, the emergence of 24-hour radio and television news channels, the extension of broadcasting time (including breakfast news programmes), the explosion in newspaper supplements, are examples that most directly come to mind, but there is more. Looking at the wider news ecology in which we currently live, one should also take into account the emergence of all kinds of subgenres at the boundaries of traditional news and information, such as various forms of reality TV, readily indicating the manner in which contemporary television is obsessed with actuality (Corner, 1996; 1999). Traditional news, therefore, seems to have changed into such a rich variety of cultural forms, continuously surrounding us, that one could reasonably argue, as Cottle does, that 'for those living in advanced, late-capitalist societies news has become an all-pervasive and an inescapable part of modern existence' (2000: 20).

Still, one can have doubts as far as the real variety or diversity of this extended news diet is concerned. One can also cling to the arguments that 'hard' news and 'serious' information in general are softened or eroded by various techniques and new formats ('infotainment'), and that foreign and international news in particular is being pushed aside. The debate on whether commercially attractive formats such as infotainment have detrimental effects for a rationally informed citizenship, or have democratizing effects by broadening access to and understanding of relevant public information, will certainly not fade out in the short term. Nevertheless, one should not reject too hastily the potential benefits of processes inherent to a highly competitive, commercial media context. Processes of market differentiation and segmentation, for instance, extend to news and current affairs in general, and to foreign and international news in particular. Although the uplift of the quality press, which has recently been seen in several countries, may largely be the result of their giving in to 'tabloidization', for any quality newspaper, foreign and international news remains a commercially vital element of distinction and market positioning vis-à-vis popular papers as well as other competing quality papers. Instead of all relying mainly on the same national news agency filter to fill in the blank newspaper spots with foreign items, then, the increasing need to differentiate oneself from one's competitors may urge newspapers to invest in their own special correspondents, continually to look for new 'proper' angles from which to approach foreign news items, to look for different news sources and so on. More research on these potential aspects is needed, though, and, as many a critic has argued, commercial pressures, tight schedules and deadlines, dependence on similar authoritative sources and the like, certainly may have the opposite effect of leading to more homogeneous, little diversified media products. Still, and this is not only the case for (quality) newspapers, a clear and distinct profile is, more than ever, vital to competing successfully in a crowded media market; and although most media product definitions nowadays seem to cherish a kind of journalistic parochialism, there will always be others choosing a more global line of sight.

Furthermore, when speaking of the all-pervasive news environment in which we live, and of the rich variety of cultural forms in which traditional news and information has changed, one of course also has to include online technologies. Nearly everywhere a growing number of newspapers, news agencies and other news providers offer new, interactive services. In the UK and the USA, for instance, virtually all newspapers and the vast majority of regional titles are represented on the World Wide Web, while the major broadcasters (e.g. BBC) and news agencies (e.g. Reuters) offer comprehensive Internet services too. As it further grows into a mass medium, the Internet in general, and these news services in particular, will influence the way people receive and use the bulk of their news information, including those on foreign societies. It will also change the role, content and presentation of the traditional foreign and international news on television and in newspapers – a process of transformation that should be high on the current news research agenda (Hjarvard, 2000). Whatever developments are to be expected, one cannot see the evidence on the shrinking international news agenda as conclusive without taking into account the huge 'alternative' technological routes and the many customized online forms by which news and information from and about different countries and cultures is spread.

A final problematic issue in pessimistic accounts of international news coverage in these times of globalization, is of an overall conceptual nature, dealing mainly with defining what foreign and international news was, is and will be about. Not only the new Internet news services 'will gradually make the boundaries between national, foreign, and international news media less clear and obvious' (Hjarvard, 2000: 17); in view of the tendencies of globalization, the reconfiguration of the state and the national, and the formation of a new geography of power, it has become hard to define what precisely is local, national, foreign, and inter- or supranational. One has only to think of the process of European integration and its impact on the policy and the economy of EU member states, to realize how difficult it has become to try to distil clear-cut definitions of these geopolitical notions. When analysing newspapers or other news media and services, more than ever one is bound to have similar problems of adequately delineating news stories with a local, national and foreign or international angle or scope.

In the end, then, it is difficult to conclude that foreign and international news coverage is sufficient, good, better or worse than it was in previous times. Notwithstanding the 'all-pervasive' news environment that has developed, for example, it remains hard to deny that the foreign and international news agenda of many of the most popular mass media has narrowed. One should, however, not become nostalgic or underestimate the emergent possibilities of the widening media and news culture, stimulated and changed by the new information technologies. While it poses new challenges to the traditional mass media and possibly leads to a further fragmentation and perhaps disappearance of the national audience, the new technological news environment certainly creates new opportunities for journalists and citizens to be better informed about what happens elsewhere. To understand the paradoxes in the process of globalization, then, one should acknowledge how technological, cultural and economic or commercial factors interact in a complex manner, at times synchronized, but quite as often contradictory. Or, more generally, when evaluating the consequences for the central role of the (news) media in national or global political democracy, one should always recognize the complexities and contradictions inherent to developments in the media industries.

Conclusion

The aim of this section has been to describe some of the most important processes and developments that can be witnessed in the media industries. We tried to clarify some of the rationales behind them and to illustrate their scope and impact on media structures and operations. Facts and figures were provided to illustrate the significance and structural impact of media concentration, transnationalization and other processes. The main emphasis, though, was on the key factors of change and the rationales that were responsible for these developments. At the same time we tried to provide a link with society as well as with other aspects of media such as content, aesthetics, ideology, reception and the social function of media messages.

The communication systems have been shown to have been subjected to transformations whereby traditional boundaries between media markets were broken down. As information technologies merged, boundaries between media sectors blurred, leading to integrated multi-media companies. National boundaries, too, have broken down as the scale and scope of media markets, industries and regulations have become inter- and transnational. Economic power is concentrated in the hands of only a limited number of multi-national multi-media holdings, consolidating their position through mergers, acquisitions and taking advantage of the logic of commerce. The potential problems and/or benefits accompanying these processes have been discussed.

Throughout this section it has become clear that there are always at least two sides to a story. Both the dominant (liberal-pluralistic) and the alternative (Marxist-critical) paradigms provide an account of the processes and structures to be witnessed in old and recent media industrial trends and, most importantly, of their impact on society. For liberal democratic theorists, media play a crucial role in the 'normal' functioning of a democratic society, responding to changing social circumstances, adapting to shifting power relations and used by an active and powerful audience.

Critical thinking, on the other hand, though it comprises a heterogeneous set of approaches, stresses how the media are not independent institutions, but inextricably linked to or integrated in the hierarchical structures of power in society. As media are closely related to the dominant socio-economic and political interest, they tend to favour these at the expense of oppositional and progressive voices, a picture far removed from a neutral reflection and/or open forum for debate. Whether the 'truth' is somewhere in the middle, as the contemporary 'third route' of thinking seems to indicate, is yet to be seen. A multitude of often contradictory forces and pressures on the media, from above as well as from below, seem to be at play, leading to a dynamic, complex and often ambiguous situation. As we said at the end of Chapter 19, whether media act as a top-down agency of social control, or as a bottom-up agency of popular empowerment, to a very large extent depends on the specific configuration of a society and its media system at any particular moment in time.

S U M M A R Y

This section looked at the main trends that have provoked dramatic shifts in the outlook and structures of the media industries in contemporary western (and, increasingly, global) societies. It discussed both the causes and consequences of fundamental developments in media. A lot of important lessons can be learned here.

- Media operate in close relation to society, being both product and producers of societal developments. Even though, today, the economic aspect of the media seems to dominate industrial affairs as well as academic discussion hereof, technology, politics and culture, too, provide central dynamics in the developments in media industries.
- In looking for the bigger picture behind the complex web of contemporary media, it is important to remember that, on the one hand, there are certain general trends to be found, but, on the other, actual practices differ according to time, place and sector.
- Even though the classical 'four theories of the press' put too much stress on the political aspect and thus painted a too politically deterministic picture of media structures, it is important to see how government and politics are one of the core determinants here. Governments provide two basic functions: first, policing and control; and, second, active intervention and participation. These functions have been defined and redefined according to time and place.
- Economically, media industries are dominated by a double ambiguity: they have both a 'cultural value' (psychological, sociological, political, educational) and an 'exchange value' (economic, aimed at making profit). They also cater for two different markets: the audience/consumer market and the financers/advertisers market. These basic rules determine many of the structural developments and varied problems discussed with regards to media industries.
- The 1980s witnessed the rise of a 'new media order' as technological, economic, political and cultural changes brought about a paradigmatic shift in the way the media were treated. Processes of liberalization, transnationalization and the increase in commercial pressures led to what seems a definite shift from political control to market patronage.

- An overview of the main players in this new media market shows that it is increasingly dominated by only a few key competitors: gigantic American, European and Japanese companies spread over different media sectors, with increased attention to the audio-visual sector and with a growing discrepancy between the very few mega-holdings and the rest of the field.

- The main trends this new media rationale brings about are concentration, competition and transnationalization, which for liberal thinkers provide increased possibilities for plurality, diversity and consumer choice, whereas for critical voices this is exactly what is being endangered. Does concentration restrict the media supply to an elite or does it help to 'save' loss-making media and thus plurality? Does competition lead to lowest-common-denominator media or does it increase consumer choice?

- Of central concern is the transnational and even globalizing tendency that can be witnessed. National identities are losing ground to 'imaginaire' communities at world level. Civil society itself seems under threat from globalization as the public sphere seems to lose its original power and purpose. As the case of international news coverage illustrates, though, the matter is not straightforward.

Further Reading

Albarran, A.B. and Chan-Olmsted, S.M. (1998) *Global Media Economics: Commercialization, Concentration and Integration of World Media Markets*. Ames, IA: Iowa State University Press

Dahlgren, P. (1995) *Television and the Public Sphere*. London: Sage

McQuail, D. and Siune, K. (eds) (1998) *Media Policy: Convergence, Concentration and Commerce*. London: Sage

Sparks, C. and Tulloch, J. (eds) (2000) *Tabloid Tales. Global Debates over Media Standards*. Lanham: Rowman & Littlefield

Tomlinson, J. (1999) *Globalization and Culture*. London: Polity Press

Useful Websites

Interesting data on European media can be found on the website of the European Audiovisual Observatory:
http://www.obs.coe.int

Information on ownership can be found on the sites of the major media companies, such as:

http://www.world.sony.com/index_eng_nn.html
http://www.cltmulti.com

Some interesting information regarding the theoretical aspects can be found at:
http://www.aber.ac.uk/media/sections/gen.html

References

Albarran, A.B. and Chan-Olmsted, S.M. (1998) *Global Media Economics: Commercialization, Concentration and Integration of World Media Markets*. Ames, IA: Iowa State University Press

Bird, E. (1997) News we can use: an audience perspective on the tabloidization of news in the United States. In *Communication Research* 5(3), 33–51

Bird, E. (2000) Audience demands in a murderous market: tabloidization in US television news. In Sparks, C. and Tulloch, J. (eds) *Tabloid Tales*. New York, NY: Rowan & Littlefield

Blumler, J.G. (1991) The new television market place: imperatives, implications, issues. In

Curran, J. and Gurevitch, M. (eds), *Mass Media and Society*. London: Edward Arnold, 194–215

Blumler, J.G. (ed.) (1992) *Television and the Public Interest: Vulnerable Values in West European Broadcasting*. London: Sage

Boyce, G. (1978) The Fourth Estate: the re-appraisal of a concept. In Boyce, G., Curran, J. and Wingate, P. (eds), *Newspaper History: From the 17th Century to the Present Day*. London: Constable, 19–40

Braman, S. and Sreberny-Mohammadi, A. (eds) (1996) *Globalization, Communication and Transnational Civil Society*. Creskill, NJ: Hampton Press

Brants, K. and Siune, K. (1992) Public broadcasting in a state of flux. In Siune, K. and Truetzschler, W. (eds), *Dynamics of Media Politics: Broadcasting and Electronic Media in Western Europe*. London: Sage, 101–15

Corner, J. (1996) Editorial: changing forms of 'Actuality'. In *Media, Culture and Society* 18(1), 5–9

Corner, J. (1999) *Studying Media. Problems of Theory and Method*, Edinburgh: Edinburgh University Press

Cottle, S. (2000) New(s) times: towards a 'second wave' of news ethnography. In *Communications* 25(1), 19–41

Curran, J. (1990) Culturalist perspectives of news organizations: a reappraisal and a case study. In Ferguson, M. (ed.), *Public Communication: The New Imperatives*. London: Sage, 114–34

Curran, J. (1991a) Rethinking the media as a public sphere. In Dahlgren, P. and Sparks, C. (eds), *Communication and Citizenship: Journalism and the Public Sphere in the New Media Age*. London: Routledge, 27–57

Curran, J. (1991b) Mass media and democracy: a reappraisal. In Curran, J. and Gurevitch, M. (eds), *Mass Media and Society*. London: Edward Arnold, 82–117

Curran, J. (1996) Rethinking mass communications. In Curran, J., Morley, D. and Walkerdine, V. (eds), *Cultural Studies and Communications*. London: Arnold, 119–65

Curran, J. and Seaton, J. (1991) *Power Without Responsibility: The Press and Broadcasting in Britain* (fourth edn). London: Routledge

Dahlgren, P. (1995) *Television and the Public Sphere*. London: Sage

D'Haenens, L., Saeys, F. and Alvarez, M. (eds) (1998) *Media Dynamics and Regulatory Concerns in the Digital Age*. Berlin: Quintessenz

Euromedia Research Group (1997) *The Media in Western Europe: The Euromedia Handbook* (second edn). London: Sage

European Audiovisual Observatory (1995) *Statistical Yearbook: Film, Television, Video and New Media in Europe 94/95*. Strasbourg: Council of Europe

European Audiovisual Observatory (1997) *Statistical Yearbook: Film, Television, Video and New Media in Europe 97*. Strasbourg: Council of Europe

European Audiovisual Observatory (1998) *Statistical Yearbook: Film, Television, Video and New Media in Europe 98*. Strasbourg: Council of Europe

European Audiovisual Observatory (1999) *Statistical Yearbook: Film, Television, Video and New Media in Europe 99*. Strasbourg: Council of Europe

European Audiovisual Observatory (2000) *Statistical Yearbook: Film, Television, Video and New Media in Europe 00*. Strasbourg: Council of Europe

Garnham, N. (1992) The media and the public sphere. In Calhoun, C. (ed.), *Habermas and the Public Sphere*. Cambridge, MA: MIT Press

Gurevitch, M., Levy, M.R. and Roeh, I. (1991) The global newsroom: convergences and diversities in the globalization of television news. In Dahlgren, P. and Sparks, C. (eds) *Communication and Citizenship: Journalism and the Public Sphere*. London: Routledge

Habermas, J. (1989) *The Structural Transformation of the Public Sphere*. Cambridge: Polity Press

Hall, S. (1992) The question of cultural identity. In Hall, S., Held, D. and McGrew, T. (eds), *Modernity and its Features*. Cambridge: Polity Press/Open University

Hall, S., Critcher, C., Jefferson, T., Clarke, J. and Roberts, B. (1978) *Policing the Crisis: Mugging, the State and Law and Order*. London: Macmillan

Hallin, D. (1996) Commercialism and professionalism in the American news media. In Curran, J. and Gurevitch, M. (eds) *Mass Media and Society*, London: Arnold

Hjarvard, S. (2000) *News Media and the Globalization of the Public Sphere.* Copenhagen: Working Paper No. 3

Hulten, O. and Brants, K. (1992) Public service broadcasting: reactions to competition. In Siune, K. and Truetzschler, W. (eds), *Dynamics of Media Politics.* London: Sage, 116–28

Kimball, P. (1994) *Downsizing the News: Network Cutbacks in the Nation's Capital.* Washington DC: Woodrow Wilson Center Press

McLachlan, S. and Golding, P. (2000) Tabloidization in the British press: a quantitative investigation into changes in British newspapers, 1952–1997. In Sparks, C. and Tulloch, J. (eds) *Tabloid Tales: Global Debates over Media Standards.* Lanham: Rowman & Littlefield

McNair, B. (1998) *The Sociology of Journalism.* London: Arnold

McQuail, D. (1994) *Mass Communication Theory: An Introduction* (third edn). London: Sage

McQuail, D. (1995) Western European media: The mixed model under threat. In Downing, J., Mohammadi, A. and Sreberny-Mohammadi, A. (eds), *Questioning the Media: A Critical Introduction.* Thousand Oaks, CA: Sage, 147–64

Mazzoleni, G. and Palmer, M. (1992) The building of media empires. In Siune, K. and Treutzschler, W. (eds), *Dynamics of Media Politics: Broadcasting and Electronic Media in Western Europe.* London: Sage, 26–41

Meier, W.A. and Trappel, J. (1998) Media concentration and the public interest. In McQuail, D. and Siune, K. (eds), *Media Policy: Convergence, Concentration and Commerce.* London: Sage, 38–59

Mitchell, J., Blumler, J.G. and Mounier, P. (eds) (1994) *Television and the Viewer Interest: Explorations in the Responsiveness of European Broadcasters.* London: John Libbey

Moisy, C.L. (1997) Myths of the global information village. In *Foreign Policy,* Summer

Murdock, G. (1990) Redrawing the map of the communications industries: concentration and ownership in the era of privatization. In Ferguson, M. (ed.) *Public Communication: The New Imperatives.* London: Sage, 1–15

Murdock, G. (1992) Citizens, consumers and public culture. In Skovmand, M. and Schrøder,

K.C. (eds), *Media Cultures: Reappraising Transnational Media.* London: Routledge, 17–41

Nerone, J.C. (ed.) (1995) *Last Rights: Revisiting Four Theories of the Press.* Urbana, IL: University of Illinois Press

Nordenstreng, K. (1997) Beyond the four theories of the press. In Servaes, J. and Lie, R. (eds), *Media and Politics in Transition: Cultural Identity in the Age of Globalization.* Leuven and Amersfoort: Acco, 97–109

O'Sullivan, T., Hartley, J. and Saunders, D. (1994) *Key Concepts in Communication and Cultural Studies* (second edn). London: Routledge

Pilati, A. (ed.) (1993) *Mind: Media Industry in Europe.* London: John Libbey

Price, M.E. (1995) *Television, the Public Sphere and National Identity.* Oxford: Oxford University Press

Sanchez-Tabernero, A. (1993) *Media Concentration in Europe: Commercial Enterprise and the Public Interest.* Dusseldorf: European Institute for the Media

Schlesinger, P. (1990) Rethinking the sociology of journalism: source strategies and the limits of media-centrism. In Ferguson, M. (ed.), *Public Communication: The New Imperatives.* London: Sage, 61–83

Schlesinger, P. (1991) *Media, State and Nation: Political Violence and Collective Identities.* London: Sage

Schudson, M. (1989) The sociology of news production. In *Media, Culture and Society* 11(3), 263–82

Shoemaker, J. and Reese, S.D. (1991) *Mediating the Message: Theories of Influences on Mass Media Content.* White Plains, NY: Longman

Siebert, F.S., Peterson, T. and Schramm, W. (1956) *Four Theories of the Press.* Urbana, IL: University of Illinois Press

Silverstone, R. (1999) *Why Study the Media?* London: Sage

Siune, K. and Hulten, O. (1998) Does public broadcasting have a future? In McQuail, D. and Siune, K. (eds), *Media Policy: Convergence, Concentration and Commerce.* London: Sage, 23–37

Skovmand, M. and Schrøder, K.C. (eds) (1992) *Media Cultures: Reappraising Transnational Media.* London: Routledge

Sreberny-Mohammadi, A. (1996) Globalization, communication and transnational civil society: introduction. In Braman, S. and Sreberny-Mohammadi, A. (eds), *Globalization, Communication and Transnational Civil Society*. Creskill, NJ: Hampton Press, 1–20

Stevenson, N. (1999) *The Transformation of the Media: Globalisation, Morality and Ethics*. London: Longman

Tomlinson, J. (1999) *Globalization and Culture*. London: Polity Press

Utley, G. (1997) The shrinking of foreign news. In *Foreign Affairs* 76(2), 22–34

Van Poecke, L. and Van den Bulck, H. (eds) (1994) *Culturele globalisering en lokale identiteit. Amerikanisering van de Europese media*. Leuven: Garant

Verstraeten, H. (1996) The media and the transformation of the public sphere: a contribution for a critical political economy of the public sphere. In *European Journal of Communication* 11(3), 347–70

Volkmer, I. (1999) *News in the Global Sphere*. Luton: University of Luton Press

Weymouth, A. and Lamizet, B. (1996) *Markets and Myths: Forces for Change in the Media of Western Europe*. London: Longman

Williams, R. (1976) *Communications* (third edn). Harmondsworth: Penguin

Zillmann, D., Gibson, R., Ordman, V.L. and Aust, C.F. (1994) Effects of upbeat stories in broadcast news. In *Journal of Broadcasting and Electronic Media* 38, 43–66

The Analysis of Popular Culture

John Lough

Introduction

In the contemporary western world, our lives are inextricably intertwined with popular culture: it is our source of role models, pleasures and information, from holidays to car design, TV news to bars, rock music to fashion. Popular culture has become *the* dominant form of culture for most. However, defining 'popular culture' and 'culture' itself is not simple, for what it is depends on how you define these terms.

WHAT IS POPULAR CULTURE?

Unfairly, most discussions surrounding the merits of popular culture have focused almost exclusively on popular media in the last 50 years, just as cultural studies has (arguably) maintained its trajectory as dominant analytical paradigm over this period. It has become one of the dominant epistemologies for understanding popular culture within most of the English-speaking world and beyond, and has entered into common parlance – unlike the US-influenced 'mass communication research' and 'communications theory', which have, by and large, remained within academic circles – while every teenager obsessed with style has internalized many of the key aspects of it without the accompanying jargon. We arguably now have the most semio-literate generation in history, able to semiotically deconstruct artefacts like trainers, scooters or jeans, at a level only dreamt of a few years ago. Many of the central concepts have become crucially influential in the production of popular culture. One only has to listen to contemporary pop, or see shows such as *South Park* or *Eurotrash*, to appreciate the influence of post-modernism or queer theory. Cultural studies rapidly achieved a position as *the* interpretative paradigm for the majority of courses within education in classes on media/film studies, communications, literary theory and many other disciplines within Britain, and much of Europe. It is rapidly gaining ground in the USA and the rest of the world; it is informing school curricula on 'media literacy' and affecting the media itself, for many of today's practitioners were media students. One has only to see the intertextual nature of most contemporary media to observe the concrete representation of cultural theory.

It is, however, a field, not a discipline, for, above all, it is inter-disciplinary. Often, it is easier to say what culturalism is *not*, taking approaches and terms from fields as diverse as semiology, literary theory, feminism, Marxism, philosophy and political theory. One of the most difficult things for newcomers to grasp is that, unlike other disciplines, there is no consensus on the merits of one methodological tool over another – many texts and concepts that were seen as seminal until recently are now derided as risible. Indeed, one of the criticisms levelled at culturalism is that it is more prone to the whims of academic fashion than subject areas like the natural sciences; imported methodologies such as psychoanalysis have all waxed and waned in popularity. There is, however, a tendency against positivism, for much cultural theory has been established in opposition to more conventional paradigms of media sociology, which traditionally focused more on the structuralist. None the less, it is a measure of its success that many traditionally oriented projects have included aspects of culturalist methods, and some culturalist work has made a nod towards empiricism (e.g. David Morley and his culturalist contextualizing of 'uses and gratifications').

It can be argued that *culture* has replaced *society* as the object of study for much social science, and this has had ramifications in unexpected fields, such as the introduction of culturalism into engineering, the law and anthropology, among others. This traffic in epistemologies has been exceptionally useful, and can be seen as a movement towards a 'big science' of holistic explanations. The central problematic is the *definition* of 'culture'. The British anthropologist E.B. Tyler believed that 'culture is that complex whole which includes knowledge, belief, art, morals, law, customs and other capabilities and habits acquired by men as a member of society' (Sardar and Van Loon, 1997: 4).

This contrasts with the definition of 'culture as the best of what has been thought and said', which was the choice of the 'culture versus civilization' tradition of Matthew Arnold, F.R. Leavis *et al.* This view was not amended until Raymond Williams and Richard Hoggart in the 1950s, for the term 'culture' is polysemic, and arguments over its meaning reflect larger power struggles within society; for example, Williams claimed that elites impose their definition of culture on the rest of us. Richard Johnson coined the term 'culturalism' to describe the work of E.P. Thompson, Raymond Williams and Richard Hoggart, which breaks with past traditions and is united by an approach enabling an understanding of ideas and behaviours of those within a culture, a perspective emphasizing *human agency* – the ability for the individual or social actor to make their own choices, rather than being simply unthinking cogs in a societal machine.

How, then, can the field be defined? It *is* its history, so we must see its roots and developments as inseparable. It is an anti-discipline (Sardar and Van Loon, 1997: 8) which,

cuckoo-like, depends on borrowing methods from everywhere, but any list of its characteristics would have to include:

- the relating of cultural practices to power relations within society, and highlighting these
within a capitalist socio-political context
- culture as both the object of study and the location of political struggle.

It was, and is, still largely a *political* project, primarily Marxist in approach, committed to
progressive/radical action, which seeks to understand and change structures of dominance;
although this may be less so today, as the incorporation of culturalism into the academy
may lead to accusations of diluting this progressive trajectory. It examines how meaning is
socially created within a social context, viewing culture as the sphere in which class, race
and other stratifications are represented and naturalized in ways that seek to hide real power
relations, so notions of ideology are central to cultural studies.

For early cultural critics, culture indisputably concerned morals, art, aesthetics and maintaining standards; today, cultural studies rejects easy definitions of value, but rather analyses
in *whose interest* such judgements are made. It encompasses ways in which groups resist
cultural domination, so culture is the site of struggle over hegemony (hence the focus on
reception/ethnography). Of course, popular culture consists of far more than TV viewing, yet
the majority of work centres on this. At the time of the founding of the field in the 1950s,
electronic media were achieving dominance over older forms of entertainment such as the
pub, cinema and music hall. TV is also easier to study than topics like evenings out, holidays
in Blackpool and shopping; yet areas of everyday life *deserve* more study – from gardening,
messing with cars, to shopping – as cultural activity. Although TV dominates, or at least connects with, popular culture today as a primary factor; it communicates fashions, knowledge,
ways of thinking about current events and phenomena, and so much more. As a subject,
cultural studies is still young, and has been in a state of flux. In order to give some narrative
to this stew of competing and opposing arguments, I will set out its development in a roughly
chronological format.

CHAPTER 23

Origins

In a field as debated as this, it would be simplistic to declare an undisputed founder, but
Matthew Arnold (1822–83) has a claim. Arnold, the headmaster of Rugby School, was a
poet and literary critic, whose most influential work was *Culture and Anarchy* (1869). In
common with later writers, Arnold saw popular culture as opposed to 'real', *serious*, culture.
He propounded an early version of the 'mass society thesis' (a homogenized dumbing down)
and is probably best known for setting one of the key definitions of culture as 'the best of

what has been thought and said in the world' (Storey, 1993: 21). Arnold made explicit the connection between the health of the social order and its cultural artefacts, developing concepts from romanticism, such as criticisms of industrialization (Storey, 1993: 25) and its ability to corrupt 'true' culture. Along with many of those in cultural studies, Arnold was a highly influential educationalist; and his notion of education being the spread of a hierarchical, canonical 'culture' still exists today.

Mass society thesis

Mass society thesis is the belief that society is, or has become, homogenized, dumbed down as result of industrial society and the growth of relativism, globalization and other elements of (post-)modern culture.

Often opposed to the individual and synonymous with 'mob', this term still has resonance in concepts like the different epistemologies of mass communication research, which tends to hypothesize a unified mass audience, as opposed to 'media studies' or 'cultural studies', which see a complex nexus of individuals all acting on their own specific social forces and personal agency (see Swingewood, 1977).

Arnold popularized the 'culture versus civilization' argument. Observing the nascent democratic movements (mass suffrage, socialist parties, trades unions etc.) as representing a threat to the civilized/'cultured' status quo, by constructing an inherently destructive urban 'philistine' culture (Turner, 1992: 39) and representing anarchy, as opposed to the intelligentsia's civilization. He believed that materialism had corrupted the middle classes, just as the working classes had been soiled by industrialization, which had destroyed a golden era of folk culture.

Today, Arnold represents aspects of unconscionable elitism. Implicit in his œuvre is a thread of anti-Americanism (Strinati, 1995: 23), which has been a dominant theme in cultural criticism. He said 'in things of the mind and in culture . . . America, instead of surpassing us all, falls short' (1995: 23). This view was rooted in a view of America as representing massification at its most threatening and vulgar. For Arnold's is a discourse *from above*, an elite 'us' looking down on 'them', making no attempt to connect with the pleasures or mechanisms of reading that others might gain from texts he dismissed as worthless and culturally harmful. Arguing that 'knowledge and truth will never be attainable by the great mass' (Storey, 1993: 24), Arnold contrasts the two concepts of civilization (the nation as a whole) and cultivation (an elite). He felt that the only thing that could save culture was an elite 'remnant' consisting of the uncorrupted remains of the intelligentsia of each class. Arnold's was a deeply conservative analysis; he envisaged the aristocracy as being further up the evolutionary ladder (Storey, 1993: 24), and his concept of 'the great tradition' proposed an unarguable canon of great works (still current today), embedded in the high/popular culture debate. He prescribed a cultural absolutism, and the concept of 'the touchstone', i.e. an unquestioning (inadequately described) benchmark of great literature (Barry, 1995: 27). Yet his criteria are undefined, based on 'close reading' and, like Leavis's ethereal criteria of 'life', there is no *methodical* textual analysis.

In the British tradition of cultural critics, F.R. Leavis (1895–1978) looms over the 1930s and 1940s. A literary and social critic, Leavis was part of the influential 1920s Cambridge group of academics with William Empson, and I.A. Richards. In 1932 Leavis founded the influential journal *Scrutiny*, together with his wife Q.D. (Queenie) Leavis, Denys Thompson and L.C. Knights. This group was to achieve the power to *make* literary reputations for decades. Leavis, the ideologue of *Scrutiny* and T.S. Eliot were central to the development of the 'culture versus civilization' debate throughout the 1930s. The key texts that emerged from the movement were *Fiction and the Reading Public* by Q.D. Leavis (1932), an analysis of popular fiction; and *Culture and Environment* by F.R. Leavis and Denys Thompson (1933), concerned with the deleterious effect and content of contemporary advertising. Leavis and *Scrutiny* were politically ambiguous and, though not progressive, did address the cultural issues ignored by the left, and broke new ground despite being 'evaluative and moralising' (Turner, 1992: 173). In common with both left and right, Leavis was a cultural pessimist who saw decline, homogenization and levelling down; he gave his name to a school of thought synonymous with the concept of an elite minority maintaining cultural standards against massification. Like Arnold, Leavis argued that British popular culture had been 'American-ized', a theme raised by many later critics. This massification thesis, inherently elitist, was based on a canonical view of a great tradition, a fixed pantheon of literature. In *Culture and Environment*, Leavis and Thompson argued that popular fiction offers addictive forms of 'compensation' and 'distraction' (Storey, 1993: 29), leading to 'the refusal to face reality at all'. They refused to engage in the analysis of popular culture; even though Queenie had done her doctoral thesis on popular fiction, she described a 'drug addiction to fiction . . . [that] leads to maladjustment in actual life . . . gets in the way of genuine feeling and respon-sible thinking' (Storey, 1993: 29). Leavis dismissed cinema as a serious cultural form (Strinati, 1995: 46) and Queenie felt Hollywood film was 'largely masturbatory' (Storey, 1993: 29). He especially hated advertising, since, in its non-standard language, it repre-sented the quintessence of vulgarity, but his work neither attempted to explain *why* we consume popular culture so enthusiastically, nor the reasons why mass culture was created by post-industrial society. In reality, boundaries between folk, popular and high cultures are constantly shifting and contested (Strinati, 1995: 46).

This tradition of literary analysis was evaluative and anti-theoretical, and Leavis was reluc-tant to codify his criteria, preferring vague concepts, such as a text having *life* in it (Barry, 1995: 16). As part of the 'practical criticism' tradition, which included Eliot and others, Leavis's 'close readings' were paraphrasing, rather than real analysis. He did not put texts into their socio-political contexts, and assumed that the reader read a text as he did. He developed Arnold's justification of elite culture – a common culture, based on language, as essential to support the elite. Although not a leftist, he engaged with the left in debates over popular culture from a liberal humanist position. Until the 1960s, his was the dominant paradigm, and is still evident in conservative journals worldwide, as well as in much political thought on issues such as education and culture. Though flawed, his attempted analysis of popular culture utilized methods previously only applied to high culture; criticizing middle and high-brow forms, and questioning canonical hierarchies. As Mulhern points out (Turner, 1992: 174), '*Scrutiny* did much to shape and sustain England's cultivated politically philistine intelligentsia.' Leavis set agendas for English and cultural studies, and professionalized both subjects, which would be developed by his successors. The role of education was said to be to instil resistance to mass culture, and Leavis suggested that the state did not do enough for the arts or culture.

Leavis was nostalgic for an idyll of a shared culture based on authoritarian power and cultural hierarchies, with the last remnants of this in rural villages (e.g. folk songs and handicrafts). Of course, in the real 'organic communities', life had been very different (Strinati, 1995: 44). Like most genuine popular culture, working-class culture had actually revelled in the vulgar, crude, and Rabelaisian. This 'folk culture' never existed: it was a hard and dirty life for most, with few material or cultural rewards. This ideological **myth** recurs in the work of Thomas Hardy and William Morris. Although he could not specify when the golden age was, Leavis saw the growth in leisure and popular culture as the consequence of the loss of the nobility of labour, and 'compensation' was taken in tawdry entertainments instead.

Leavisism was overtaken by the re-definition of culture as encompassing *lived experience* by Williams and Hoggart in the 1950s and post-1968 structuralism. Despite crystallizing many existing ideas, Leavis's influence was based on his charismatic personal power, yet in his later years, he was increasingly marginalized by the Cambridge hierarchy. Unfortunately, work such as Leavis's isolated literary critics from cultural criticism, sociology and other fields, whereas the growth of much 1960s theory made inter-disciplinary links.

A major influence on the field has been the Frankfurt Institute of Social Research ('the Frankfurt School'). Attached to Frankfurt University, the School flourished in the 1930s, yet many of its central concepts reverberate today. Its foundations were sociological, rather than literary, Marxist, rather than liberal. The School was primarily composed of a group of Jewish humanist intellectuals, who described themselves as *critical theorists*. Founded on socialist triumphalism following 1917, and influenced by the Russian formalists, it became part of the Weimar theoretical movement. Among its most influential members was Theodor Adorno (1903–70), who was committed to the study of culture, notably music, psychoanalysis and aesthetic theory. Though a Marxist, he considered the role of individual agency in opposition to a simplistic 'mass communication' model; and he was crucial in forming the cultural criticism element of the School's doctrine of critical theory with *The Dialectics of Enlightenment* (1944), which saw post-Enlightenment rationalism, science technology and positivism contributing to new barbarism, echoing perhaps for different reasons Leavis's fears of massification; this view brought him into sharp opposition to the anti-elitism theories of the aura propounded by Benjamin.

Other members included Max Horkheimer (1895–1973), who was a social philosopher with a particular interest in critiquing empirical positivist methodologies within social science. His position as Director of the Institute, and his influence on critical theory, were crucial factors in the making of the School. His *Traditional and Critical Theory* (1937) was, in many ways, a founding text of the field. Herbert Marcuse (1898–1978) joined the Institute in 1933 and went on to become a significant model for the 1968 generation, suggesting alliances between various groups such as blacks, hippies and others, mixing Marxist politics, philosophy and psychology in his *Eros and Civilisation* (1955) and *One Dimensional Man* (1964). Walter Benjamin (1892–1940) was sidelined by his peers for his maverick approach. He is known today for his ideas on the effects that reproduction of art has on our perceptions of it, which many have suggested has contributed much to discussions of the merit of popular culture, and even foreshadowed post-modern theory. He claimed that destruction of the 'aura' of art (the connotations of high culture) allows a cathartic release of energy in the viewer. Benjamin's *Art in the Age of Mechanical Reproduction* (1936), the most anthologized work of the School, raised issues of high and popular culture in a way that has more relevance today than much of their cultural pessimism.

Lesser figures within the School were: Paul F. Lazarsfeld, a major influence on American mass communication research in the 1940s; Erich Fromm, who became involved with the school in the early 1930s, synthesized Marxism and psychoanalysis, but was ultimately alienated from the School in 1939 due to his increasing reliance on empirical and positivist approaches (Bottomore, 1984: 20) – this reliance on Enlightenment rationality was derided by much of the school as ideologically reactionary; and Jurgen Habermas (b. 1929), who represents perhaps the most famous of the School's second generation of theorists – he became Adorno's assistant in 1956 and went on to be one of the pre-eminent thinkers in post-war Europe. Well known for his ideas on the crisis of legitimation in modern society, which, in keeping with so much of the work of the School, served to alienate him from much contemporary thought, which saw it in opposition to post-modern theory. He has written extensively on many aspects of cultural theory – from psychoanalysis, action theory (discussions of change stressing human agency) and hermeneutics, to ideology from a Marxist perspective, yet keeping a humanistic view of positive human agency – if there is to be social progress, it must be through reason and communicative action on the part of the people. He has also significantly developed the School's critiques of positivism. Wilhelm Reich was also on the fringes of the School; one of the most famous, or perhaps infamous, of those associated with the School, the controversial psychologist, political philosopher and seer went on to achieve infamy with his 'orgone boxes' (for which he was jailed for fraudulently claiming them as miracle cures), theories of how to cure short-sightedness, the value of the orgasm, the mass psychology of fascism, how to produce rain, and many other devices and theories. Like so many of this group his work reverberates through 1968 to the oppositional cultural politics of today. Key works of the School included *The Dialectics of Enlightenment* (1947), a volume of cultural criticism by Adorno and Horkheimer, which although written during the war, was based on their pre-war experiences. It raised the idea of 'cultural industries', critiqued positivism, and discussed science and technology. The School's founder, historian Carl Grunberg, set a Marxist agenda by focusing on class struggle. In 1930, Horkheimer replaced Grunberg and moved towards cultural criticism. Horkheimer and others migrated to the USA in 1933 to escape Nazism, and he directed the School in absentia until Hitler closed it in 1941. He re-established it in 1950 and it continues to this day.

The output and methodology of the Frankfurt School can be separated into four eras:

1 from 1923–33, it produced a wide variety of work, much of which was empirical

2   1933–50 was its most historically significant era, from which emerged 'critical theory'
    and a new interest in psychoanalysis
3   in 1950, it returned to Frankfurt, but many stayed in the USA; *'Les eventements'* of 1968
    re-popularized their work, as it had anticipated the mixture of the personal and the
    political
4   from the 1970s, a new wave of theorists, such as Jurgen Habermas, emerged.

Theirs was a totalizing discourse, examining every aspect of an issue. Importantly, they saw
language as transmitting the status quo (whereas Leavis saw language as transmitting
tradition), and so there existed a need for the modernist, defamiliarizing language of Joyce,
Beckett *et al.* They developed Marx's 'ruling ideas' thesis, employing a massification-
influenced view of self-reproducing mass culture, considering US capitalism and mass
culture to be as great a threat to the working classes as Nazism; they believed that the
'possibility of radical social change has been smashed between concentration camps and
TV for the masses' (Strinati, 1995: 54).

   Critical theory was significantly different from traditional 'political economy' Marxism, as
it examined culture rather than economics. It both developed and critiqued Marxist thought,
and extended the concept of commodity fetishism (i.e. social relations embedded in goods
and their perceived value) into cultural forms. In their terms, the cultural industries impose
culture on the masses, forcing together high and popular forms, and creating an illusion of
different products. In reality, standardization, homogenization and banal mass culture hides
a manipulative ideology in which conformity replaces consciousness. This model
presupposes an audience as powerless dupes, with all constituents making the same
readings.

Political economy

Often perceived as the *bête noire* of culturalism, the political economy (PE) school of
thought derives from media sociology, often from American-oriented mass communication
research, and sees the economic base having a direct effect on the ideological forces
maintaining control in societies.

   Texts such as *Cultural Studies in Question* (Ferguson and Golding, 1997, London: Sage)
take a political economy-based critique of culturalism, and much early culturalism, notably
from the Centre for Contemporary Cultural Studies (CCCS), tended to criticize the PE
stance as simplistic and mechanistic, writing much of it off as 'vulgar Marxism'; ignoring,
for example, oppositional readings and the complex networks of ownership and allegiances
within the media (e.g. the western capitalist media and other industries made strategic
links with communist bloc countries when necessary, and the likes of Murdoch and Maxwell
were only too happy to publish magazines, books and other products highly critical of
capitalism as long as they made money from them).

   However, in recent years the antagonism between the two schools seems to have been
thawing as both realize that neither has the monopoly on useful analysis.

The Frankfurt School was influential for many reasons.

- An institute, not an individual, produced a coherent body of work, paving the way for later groups like the Centre for Contemporary Cultural Studies (CCCS), *Screen* etc.
- It set the terms of reference for future cultural criticism, establishing what to study (popular culture, music etc.), and *how*, specifically inter-disciplinary work using wide-ranging methodologies.
- Like cultural theory today, critical theory was a political project aimed at interpreting and changing social reality.
- The concept of 'the cultural industries' and their being agents of mass deception was, in large measure, a precursor of the study of ideology and the media that was to boom in the 1960s.
- Their critiques of Enlightenment rationalism contributed to the scepticism towards positivism, leading to interpretative methodologies (e.g. semiotics) and can be seen as forerunners of post-modern scepticism, Adorno seeing scientific thought as 'false clarity' (Bottomore, 1984: 19).
- It developed Marxist concepts, such as the 'ruling ideas' theory, into a cultural dimension; and the 'cultural industries' are a short step from theories of cultural domination propounded by Althusser.

There are also, however, serious critiques to be made.

- They remained part of the 'culture and civilization' tradition, and although they placed less emphasis on a past idyll, still prioritized high culture and the avant-garde, rather than the culture produced by the working class.
- This cultural pessimism remained the dominant model for many decades, until the advent of a more active picture of the reading process.
- Their argument against the 'cultural industries' as creating formulaic products was problematic, as it can be argued that *everything* is formulaic: from TV genres to Renaissance painting.
- From a modern perspective, they did very little work involving either women or class, and actually focused on a remarkably narrow range of concerns.
- Perhaps one of the major criticisms of the School concerns elitism and methodological laxity. Adorno's opinion that the 'truth is known by small groups of admirable men', indicated that only a (male) elite can see this deception. They argued the need for an art that would subvert – i.e. avant-garde and modernism – and believed high art to be inherently oppositional, the 'cultural industries' tainting all art, and mass culture was merely 'bad consciousness of serious art'.
- They failed to develop rigorous analysis. Theirs was a subjective damning of capitalism in rhetorical, moralistic and apocalyptic terms in an impenetrable writing style: Adorno's modernist-influenced work was especially episodic and rambling.
- Critical theory was, deliberately, a vaguely defined concept. It was critical, negative and existed to subvert anything that did not further socialism; it did not deal adequately with the economic or historical forces that shape cultural practice.

In conclusion, the Frankfurt School attacked the same things as the 'culture and civiliza-tion' tradition, but for different reasons. While, in retrospect, their theories can be seen to be flawed, their legacy is a major body of cultural criticism remaining to be fully explored.

E.P. Thompson (1924–93) was, according to Stuart Hall, the single most significant influ-ence on post-war social history. Unusually, Thompson was a historian, not a literary critic or sociologist. A Marxist of the post-1956/Hungary generation, rather than the 1968 variety, Thompson was, like Williams and Hoggart, an extra-mural lecturer at Leeds University. His biography of William Morris (1955) became an icon of socialism and the early culturalist wave, although his most famous work was *The Making of the British Working Class* (1963), on the radical working-class resistance to utilitarian philosophy in the late eighteenth cen-tury, from the perspective of the marginalized tradesmen who had been replaced by new practices. Thompson contended that the working class *made itself*, and that the period around 1780–1832 was 'the most distinguished popular culture that England has known' (Storey, 1993: 58). He did not, however, prioritize one form of culture over another, neither did he propose some past golden age. This celebratory **epistemology** of the book was, in part, a reaction to the functionalism of Talcott Parsons.

His next major work, *The Poverty of Theory* (1978), focused on a perceived divide between culturalism and structuralism, and was seen at the time as an anti-Althusser diatribe, with Thompson claiming that reason had been sacrificed in the pursuit of a fashionable ideal. In fact, he was *not* anti-theory, rather he claimed that such theory demanded a level of empirical support and should instead engage in dialogue, instead of simplistic positivism. Some followers of structuralism saw culturalism as rigid, abstract and mechanical, while culturalists viewed structuralism as over-theorized, abstract and alienated from 'real' cultures. He opposed mechanistic, 'vulgar Marxism'. Seeing class as a process produced by social relations, Thompson argued against a simplistic focus on the economic *base*, but saw human agency and free will as the force behind historical change, and it was this socialist humanism that marked him out in the field. He did not elevate high culture over popular culture, but saw the two as distinct and different, and demonstrated that popular culture has a *history*, and that this offers possibilities for progressive social change.

A major presence in the fields of both cultural theory and history, Thompson shifted the paradigms of history from being the study of 'the great and the good', to 'history from below': the small people whose everyday lives make up history. Unlike Williams, who became a Marxist after he was a writer, Thompson had been a Marxist before he became a historian and had been on the board of *New Left Review* with Williams. He has influenced disciplines as diverse as history, anthropology, sociology and cultural theory, and proposed culture as not solely a way of life, but rather a struggle between ways of life. This conflict of class – and competing interests – drives social change, and this thesis has been developed and elaborated by others such as the CCCS (notably Richard Johnson) ever since. In his latter years, Thompson made a second reputation by becoming a leading light in the anti-nuclear movement.

Arguably, the study of popular culture originated with Raymond Williams (1921–88), Hoggart and Thompson in the 1950s. In 30 years as writer and teacher, Williams made an immense contribution to theories of culture, communication, TV, press, cultural history and more. Williams studied under Leavis and, after being adult education tutor at Oxford University (1946–60), became Professor of Drama at Cambridge. As he moved away from adult education, his writings moved from 'lived experience' to studying the media. *Communications* (1962) reflected the current paradigm of American functionalist 'mass communication research' and, initially anti-Marxist, Williams became gradually influenced by it (a progression apparent in *Culture and Society* – a work that established his reputation) and throughout the 1960s, was involved in the left/Leavisite journal *Politics and Letters*. Williams re-defined cultural studies, seeing it as 'the study of relationships between elements of whole way of life' (Strinati, 1995: 52). By making possible a democratic analysis of popular culture, the emerging culturalism could be seen as a British answer to contemporary French structuralism (which explained the world in a new theory of all things being socially constructed of signs, codes and hidden meanings – notably popularized by Barthes in the mid-1950s with the accessible and revolutionary 'mythologies'). He shifted the paradigm away from Leavisism, rejecting elitism, while agreeing with the need for textual analysis and the relevance of *culture*; and arguing that art is not inherently great or magical, but rather is only one cultural practice among many. Williams questioned 'massification', believing, like Thompson, that *people* make history. His major works encompassed projects as varied as *Culture and Society 1780–1950* (1958), which focused on literature and its relation with culture. *The Long Revolution*, published in 1961, was a historical study of culture, its mechanisms of reproduction, social opposition and media. This was written at a time when structuralism had yet to arrive in Britain, and Marxist approaches were in their infancy. In *Television, Technology and Cultural Form* (1974) the previous 'mass communication' paradigm was replaced by elements of technological and historical determinism. It introduced the concept of 'flow' (an evening's TV watching, rather than discrete shows) and Williams dismissed (the then hugely famous) McLuhan as ignoring cultural, economic and historical forces. *Marxism and Literature* (1977) defines Williams' view of ideology, takes Althusser and Gramsci on board, embraces semiotics and foregrounds culture over 'base and superstructure'.

Williams' work is important for a number of reasons, including the rejection of the simplistic base and superstructure of Marxism prevalent in the 1950s. He showed that popular culture is valuable in its own right, and is vital to culture *as it is lived*. He codified the – now commonly accepted – three co-existing definitions of culture (Storey, 1993: 52) as a 'way of life', 'the best of what has been thought and said' and 'the body of work produced by a culture'. 'A culture,' he wrote, 'is not only a body of intellectual and imaginative work, it is also and essentially a whole way of life' (Milner, 1994: 38); he saw culture as always related to its historical context; 'the traditional culture of a society will always tend to correspond to a contemporary system of values' (Milner, 1994: 38). He did not envisage a past golden era, but rather a possible future socialist common culture, involving a long revolution uphill to a common culture. 'Structures of feeling' are a central concept of his work, set out in *The Long Revolution*. They are vaguely defined and arguably constitute little more than the current ideology or 'zeitgeist'. They *are* the culture of a period – common across classes, yet representing interests of the dominant class. Perhaps they are best described as the collective unconscious, ideology or shared values of a group. Structures of feeling (Barry,

1995: 184) that oppose dominant ideology are often found in literature, e.g. the characters in Brontë's novels actually oppose the prevailing Victorian values. The concept shows that popular culture can survive and prosper, despite the elite's attempts to stamp it out as worthless. Williams was part of the cultural movement that politicized a breakdown in British life, which marked a shift towards consumption of media and popular culture as never before. Finally, *Culture and Society* was important as it relates debates over meanings of the word 'culture' to historical and social processes, allowing the connection of social relations to cultural artefacts.

Richard Hoggart (b. 1918) is known as the first major figure in the British field to study the media; he brought an inter-disciplinarity to the subject, drawing on sources such as sociology (notably *the embourgeoisement thesis*, the idea that the values and mores of the working class were disappearing in the new post-war affluence, to be replaced by a new privatized, more middle-class homogeneity; a view popularized by the sociological research of Goldthorpe and Lockwood such as the 1968 publication *The Affluent Worker*), Leavisian literary criticism and American 'massification theory' such as that propounded by Shils, Lazarsfeld and Bell. Although none of these methodologies was pursued rigorously enough for his reputation to be monumental, his most famous work, *The Uses of Literacy* (1958), was influential on the left. The book, which was the first culturalist work to take a working-class perspective, applied literary methodologies to interconnected social processes, acknowledging popular culture, if not accepting it as equal to high culture. Perhaps its most significant ramification is that 'it reveals a network of shared cultural meanings which sustains relations between different facets of culture' (Turner, 1992: 48), and this emphasis on shared meanings was instrumental in developing our understanding of popular culture. He introduced new objects of study, such as youth, popular culture and class. From 1960 to 1964 Hoggart was English Professor at Birmingham University and, in 1964, founded the Centre for Contemporary Cultural Studies (CCCS) at Birmingham University. He was Director until 1968, when Stuart Hall took over, and their work expanded on many of Hoggart's interests, specifically culture and social change (Turner, 1992: 70).

The Uses of Literacy and *Culture and Society*, were both in a tradition of literary and social criticism, but both used methods of literary analysis on other forms. This new movement was 'a methodology which stresses culture (human agency, human values, human experience) as of crucial importance of a given social formation' (Storey, 1993: 60). *The Uses of Literacy* discusses the 'full rich life' of the pre-war working class. It discusses and connects cultural activities such as pubs, clubs, sport, music, magazines etc. It is, however a nostalgic recollection of an organic community, and he fails to deal with issues such as women's roles, male violence, work or unions. Modleski points out the phallocentrism of much of cultural studies from Williams and Hoggart onwards (Barker and Beezer, 1992: 171) and, undeniably, their books are about men's lives. Though perhaps not as influential as *Culture and Society* or *The Popular Arts*, *Uses of Literacy* was vital. It was an indictment of the effects of 1950s mass culture – milk bars, film, jukeboxes, and American film and crime magazines. These were seen as phoney artefacts and practices, which displaced 'real' popular culture, which Hoggart believed was truly connected to the social conditions of participants.

Despite Hoggart's proletarian stance, his book is actually about 'discrimination' – in both producing and consuming culture – and high culture values. Although part of the 'culture and civilization' tradition, it also acknowledges Williams' concept of culture as 'way of life'. These two contradictory perspectives are evident; the first half is a fond account of past working-class culture, while the second is a harangue against massification (Storey, 1993: 44). His work found echoes in many forms: films made by the 'British social realists' in the late 1950s, such as *Saturday Night and Sunday Morning* (1961), also reflected this feared disappearance of working-class culture in the face of privatized, home-owning workers and the disappearance of the old tenements. Hoggart's book seemed to be part of the predominant *Zeitgeist*, despite the fact that much of it was written in the early 1950s, when the embourgeoisement thesis, and debates on the changing nature of the working class were common, as had been so even in Hardy's time. In common with Williams, adult education was crucial to Hoggart's understanding of culture – that is, the non-traditional adult education student that Hoggart met may well have influenced *Uses of Literacy*, for there had been a huge post-war growth of working-class students going to universities.

There is an uncomfortable elitism in Hoggart's work. In *Speaking To Each Other* (1966), he argued that, 'we must understand good literature to understand the nature of society; literary criticism analysis can be applied to certain social phenomena other than academically respectable literature' (Turner, 1992: 46). Hoggart's ideas of taste were still based on traditional literary criticism and, like Arnold, he used the concept of remnants – Leavis's elite – and talks about (Hardyesque) 'Judes': outsiders capable of judgement because they *are* outsiders. Scathing in his criticism of post-war youth, he considered 'jukebox boys' to be 'a portent . . . directionless and tame helots . . . less intelligent than average' (Turner, 1992: 46). Hoggart saw the possibility of a passive working class consuming the new mass media culture, yet he also saw workers' culture continuing the old ways of 'dominoes, working men's clubs, brass bands, working class ways of speaking' (Storey, 1993: 50). Despite work continuing this trajectory of popular culture encompassing social life, pastimes *et al.*, this is an area yet to be studied fully, as most culturalist work since Hoggart focuses almost entirely on the media. Criticisms of the book include its selective use of evidence and examples to support his views, while ignoring anything that might question them. For instance, Hoggart's 'proof' that literature is not as good as it was consists of parodies devised by him, rather than real examples. His work is ahistorical, in that it does not see class transformations over time. He employed an anecdotal style, not factual evidence – rejecting rigorous sociology for its failure to show true meanings, yet happy to accept concepts of embourgeoisement and classlessness – while *Uses of Literacy* offers no real evidence for the alleged debasement of the proletariat or youth.

Hoggart's idealistic emphasis on morality came from Leavisian literary criticism, but was equally an anti-theoretical position, contradictory and incoherent. Like Leavis, he saw education as crucial to establishing resistance to mass culture, but while Leavis looked back to the eighteenth century, Hoggart looked to the 1930s, celebrating what Leavis had despised. His fear of Americanization was a common reaction to changes in popular culture; Both left and right despised American cultural imperialism and its spreading mass culture. Turner (1992: 12) claims that neither *Uses of Literacy* nor *Culture and Society* could show

how social pleasures and mechanisms operated, as neither had a constitutive notion of ideology and society, indicating the need for Marxism and semiology, which was to emerge in the 1960s. While Leavis at least began questioning 'culture' and 'the canon', Hoggart and Williams took up these issues from a working-class perspective; yet both have aspects of the 'culture and civilization' tradition, so both *Uses of Literacy* and *Culture and Society* can be seen as left-Leavisism (Storey, 1993: 43). Hoggart, however, does not claim a moral decline of the workers, but rather a decline in the moral seriousness of the culture provided for them. He optimistically stressed that they can resist and assimilate aspects of mass culture while simultaneously dismissing this mass culture. Hoggart was a guiding light to later academics, like the CCCS, who proposed understanding connections between popular culture and social relations. Williams' review of *Uses of Literacy* (Storey, 1993: 47) points out that the new generation of working-class people progressing to the middle class through education consistently derided the hopeless vulgarity of the people they had left. Similarly, Hall believed that Hoggart 'continued a tradition while seeking in practice to transform it' (Storey, 1993: 51).

In the 1950s the early rumblings of radical popular culture began, and the 'independent group' at the ICA and sections of the Young Communist League – then a cultural force – did much to question the automatic superiority of high culture fed into the early *Screen* magazine. A powerful thread in the 1970s – comparable to the CCCS and Open University Popular Culture course (U203), which was to go on to become so influential on the field in the 1970s – was *Screen*, the premier British film theory journal, comparable to the French *Cahiers du Cinema*. There was no monolithic *Screen* party line, but it generally spoke with a coherent voice, publishing Laura Mulvey, Stephen Heath, Colin McCabe, Ros Coward, John Ellis, Richard Dyer and others. *Screen* originated as *The Society of Film Teachers Bulletin* in 1950, and was associated with the Society for Education in Film and TV, a British Film Institute (BFI) offshoot. Taking its present form in 1971, *Screen* was a ragbag mix of film theory, drawn from French writers like Christian Metz, semiology, psychoanalysis, Althusserian subjectivity, post-Freudian, Lacanian psychoanalysis, and feminism, and focusing on themes such as **scopophilia** and identification. Its growth in the 1970s was due to many factors: the declining fortunes of *Movie*, its only competitor; the paucity of other British theoretical outlets; and the burgeoning European influence (Alvarado *et al.*, 1987: 27). *Screen* played a significant role in the acceptance of film theory by British academe at a time when 'English literature' was declining in popularity. This decade was the high water mark for *Screen*, after which it descended into intellectual tail-chasing and obscurity through its intellectual arrogance and failure to take on board new developments. Despite its name, its base was a mix of British-centred film and cultural theory, though it sold widely in America and Australia. *Screen* had a streak of Barthesian structuralism and, from the late 1960s onwards, was increasingly Althusserian, playing a large part in popularizing him. While most of the culturalist field took on Gramscian 'opposition' and 'alternate readings', *Screen* remained in an elitist textual determinism that focused solely on their unisemic readings of the text, without taking into account industrial or personal reading conditions. (In other words, did the audience decode these films in ways differently to the *Screen* writers, or what was the effect of the international film industry on the production of these images?)

Many contributors, such as Colin McCabe, were from English studies and, in the mid-1970s, this led *Screen* to move from a semiology-based, Barthesian epistemology, which took the hidden meaning of a text from its sign content, to become influenced by the post-structuralist theories of Derrida *et al.*, which raised questions as to whether there were fixed meanings at all. Central to *Screen* theory was Althusser's concept of *interpellation* – how we are 'sutured' into the text (literally, sewn into the picture by the film language showing us a world, with us, the viewer, firmly at its centre) and therefore into the dominant ideology (cf: Steven Heath, 'Notes on Suture', *Screen* 18(4), 1977/78) through language and film language. This assumes that no differential decoding is possible (i.e. the monosemic view, that we all get the same meaning from a given text whereas, as Morley was to show, we actually decode signs very differently depending on our social position) although, more recently, the influence of post-structuralism has shifted *Screen* theory towards multiple possible reader positions.

Among other long-running disputes was a discussion of film realism in the 'Days of Hope' debate, developed by McCabe, who explored the problems of realism in his much-anthologized 'Notes on Some Brechtian Theses' (Easthope, 1993: 53–67). In their search for the ideal 'progressive text', *Screen* contributors imbued obscure films with non-realist devices, allowing an anti-capitalist ideology. They could not bring themselves to like popular texts.

Mulvey's 1975 'Visual Pleasure and Narrative Cinema' piece (*Screen* 16(3), Autumn 1975) is probably the single most collected and cited article in film studies, and is important because it shows how ideology positions the viewer, and the relation of pleasure to ideology is vital. Although there is not an infinite range of possible reading positions, the concepts of the 'male gaze' and the feminine/feminized spectator began a whole new sub field of 'spectatorship'. However, Mulvey's work did not allow for variations in reading practice. Like most *Screen* work, Mulvey favoured the avant-garde, This methodology was not conducive to analysing popular texts. *Screen* was a positive progression, in that it attempted to build an overarching theory for the field, and made a significant contribution to discussions of subjectivity. Heath and McCabe looked at ways in which texts position the viewer, attacking 'Hollywood realism', while developing Brechtian critiques of realism (conveniently ignoring the fact that Brecht recommended accessibility). *Screen* was also valuable for incorporating a wide range of methodologies, and for critically recuperating Hitchcock, Ford and Huston. The influence of *Screen* theory is also evident in U203, and OU readers brought many *Screen* articles to a wider audience. 'Realism' was seen as an essentially conservative part of the cinematic code, an Althusserian 'ideological state apparatus', thereby unable to show the contradictions of capitalism (Milner, 1994: 95). 'Progressive texts' were necessarily modernist, avant-garde (e.g., Godard, Straub *et al.*), and it is significant that *Screen* looked at art film, while the more successful CCCS studied popular TV. Like the Frankfurt School, *Screen* was politically pessimistic, an elitist cadre isolated from the masses, and its shrinking readership found it increasingly hard to read. There are many reasons for *Screen's* decline; there was a loss of interest in Marxism after 1979, and a number of notable critics, such as Morley and Stuart Hall, began to throw stones at their glass house and it was widely criticized as being 'parochial, punitive, and grim' (McGuigan, 1992: 65). *Screen* theory was a conscious opposition to much 1970s work and, in fact, the CCCS established a discussion group to address *Screen* theory; history shows *Screen* to have lost decisively.

The next step in the development of the field was to be the Open University U203 course team, which team included Janet Woollacott, Stuart Hall, Colin Mercer, James Curran, Michael Gurevitch and Tony Bennett. Its evolution was partly due to the appointment of Stuart Hall as Professor of Sociology in 1979. Their readers (e.g. *Culture, Ideology and Social Process*, 1981) and course texts played a role in disseminating culturalism, and were used as set texts for many media/cultural studies courses. Bennett found the concept of 'popular' problematic, believing that the 'concept of popular is virtually useless', and defining it in four ways: well-liked; what remains after high culture; a synonym for mass culture; and cultural practices rooted in creative impulses of the people (1981: 65).

In the 1980s, the course also popularized Gramsci over Althusser, employing the concept of hegemony as structurally imposed dominance *and* form of opposition. An offshoot of the influential Mass Communication and Society course, which ran from 1977, U203 ran from 1982 to 1987; 5000 students registered for it and it involved over 50 lecturers, many of whom went on to become pre-eminent in the field. Its appeal lay in its textual analysis, which was more concretely theorized than *Screen*'s. It was wide-ranging, covering topics as diverse as Christmas, radio, TV cop shows, sitcoms, reception practice, Blackpool and holidays, rock music, James Bond, science, language and schooling. In an attempt to reconcile the CCCS's culturalism, and the structuralism of the Society for Education in Film and Television/*Screen*, U203 developed *Screen* textual analysis using concepts such as visual pleasure, drawing on Mulvey's work, modernism and Barthes' concepts of texts of bliss/pleasure. It also produced seminal TV programmes exploring the 1970s show *Gangsters*.

Although there was relatively little on race and gender, and it could be accused of celebrating the popular simply because it *was* the popular (Barker and Beezer, 1992: 51), U203 was an early example of the 'cultural optimism' and focus on oppositional readings that expanded in the 1980s. It brought together history and political theory; attempted to link the development of TV cop shows with shifts in post-war hegemony and, although this endeavour to read texts and history simultaneously might be over-ambitious, it was an effort to cross under-explored territories.

Meanwhile, on the continent, the French were again producing work that was to redirect the subject; The French sociologist Pierre Bourdieu (b. 1930) is primarily known for his work on taste and class. Proposing that the consumption of culture is 'predisposed consciously and, deliberately or not, to fulfil a social function of legitimating social differences' (Storey, 1993: 8), Bourdieu submitted that the dominant culture sees popular culture as mass trash produced for profit and simple entertainment; while high culture is individual and creative, showing that 'taste' is distaste for others' culture. He should be more important within cultural studies, as he addresses central issues – that is, the relationships of popular entertainment/activities, and the axis of class, power and hegemony. In common with most theorists in the field, he has a political agenda and played a significant role in re-establishing the status of French sociology.

Bourdieu's work illuminates the ways in which the economic reproduction of inequalities is achieved through the cultural sphere, and is an example of growing links between cultural studies and sociology. His concept of 'symbolic violence' refers to the meaning systems that legitimize social inequalities (i.e. 'natural discrimination' asserts primacy of dominant cultural forms), and establishes their difference from others, while making it appear that the elites have 'natural' taste.

Another idea credited to Bourdieu is that of habitus: a set of acquired patterns of thought, behaviour and taste, which constitute the link between social structure and social action. Habitus stresses the importance of agency, so is the consciousness that is structured by – and structures – consumption; we learn it through exposure to social conditioning, and these values are shared by those with similar experiences. This idea is, however, vaguely defined and it is unclear how it differs from ideology, or 'structures of feeling'.

Bourdieu's name is often linked with cultural capital: as with economic capital, social institutions naturalize economic inequality by making constructed hierarchies (of value) of learned cultural competencies. The collection of competencies allows us to take part in the culture of various classes and groups. Such knowledge and qualifications serve to exclude others, and to include an elite. Bourdieu points out and criticizes the 'scholastic fallacy' (Stevenson, 1995: 56) whereby critics assume that the audience makes sense of popular texts in the same way as academics. Though he has written about TV, his studies include a range of practices – clothes, food, furnishings and art. TV is problematic, as mass TV necessarily merges diverse class audiences (for instance, the popular British soap opera, *Coronation Street*, could not achieve huge ratings without appealing across classes and genders), however, perhaps the growth of 'niche' TV will return such class/consumption-based audiences to more specific forms of consumption. Through education, familial and other social methods, we learn the cultural competences, i.e. we become competent in a wide, or narrow, range, depending on education and family background; so access and disposition to 'the dominant aesthetic', or, the 'official arts' (Stevenson, 1995: 95) depend on class position.

For Bourdieu, all societies are characterized by a struggle between 'groups and/or classes and class fractions to maximize their interests in order to ensure their reproduction' (Storey, 1993: 188). Praising the positive, life-affirming aspects of popular culture, Bourdieu argues that 'the popular aesthetic affirms the continuity between art and life' (McGuigan, 1992: 13). Within this system, taste and discrimination become weapons used to mobilize hatred of certain forms (for instance, both left and right used anti-Americanism to vilify popular culture). Taste is very much about what *not* to like – that is, we understand our social position as much by knowing what is not acceptable. Bourdieu's influence can be seen in the work of Fiske, although Fiske overextends Bourdieu's ideas into an extreme 'cultural populism'. His thought can be seen as effectual upon post-modernism (Lash, 1990: 237) as related to new forms of social formation related to consumption rather than simplistic class stratification. It is perhaps difficult, though, to translate some of these cultural activities across national boundaries – for example, do the French have different relationships to art from, say, the British?

The influence on the field of Professor Stuart Hall (b. 1932), cannot be underestimated for a number of reasons: he consistently developed Marxist thought in engagements with key thinkers such as Althusser, Gramsci, Barthes, de Saussure, Lévi-Strauss and Volosinov; As Director of the CCCS from 1964 to 1979, he created some of its most important work, such as *Resistance Through Rituals*, and *Policing the Crisis*; after moving to the Open University, he played a key part in establishing another major school of culturalist thought in the U203 course team; he reflected a pluralism within sociology, opening up areas such as signification, representation, hegemony and modernity to serious interrogation in ways – and on a scale – never previously achieved. Hall played a pivotal role in the early formation of the field by critiquing the 'culture and civilization' tradition with *The Popular Arts* (Hall and Whannel, 1964); and, as editor of *New Left Review* until 1962, he established the study of ideology – and its relationship to socio-cultural domination – as central to the field.

His work has shifted the focus from deterministic textual analysis towards the significance of reception of media texts – i.e. though the dominant ideology may be encoded into the preferred reading of texts in the production process, there are oppositional readings possible in the decoding. In 'Encoding and Decoding the TV Discourse' (During, 1993: 90), he develops Parkin's proposed reception model into a workable picture of reception, which others at the CCCS, like Morley, developed and evidenced, both empirically and theoretically.

To oversimplify, this model sees three possible forms of decoding the *preferred reading* – that favoured or produced by the dominant ideology.

1 *Dominant*: accepting, uncritically, the desired message.
2 *Negotiated*: whereby the message is partly accepted, e.g. we may enjoy a TV ad, yet not wish to purchase the product, or we may agree with the preferred reading that 'unions are rabid communists holding the country to ransom', yet except ourselves from this formulation, as our union is moderate and sensible!
3 *Oppositional*: the message is rejected outright.

These forms of decoding will be affected by our position in class/gender/race hierarchies. Hall's focus on the concept of communications as *process*, or a cultural circuit, is more holistic, whereas his predecessors had studied the elements discretely. As Michele Barrett says: 'it is no exaggeration to say that cultural studies as a discipline is now far more influential than sociology's attempts to study either art or the media . . . and was definitely established in the encoding/decoding model' (Stone, 1998: 270).

Hall produced some of the most trenchant, and indeed prescient, work on Thatcherism; and, as a Jamaican who came to Britain as a Rhodes Scholar in 1951, he brought a new dimension to debates on race and post-colonialism, and introduced methodologies such as post-modernism, psychoanalysis and Foucauldian ideas of identity, in raising questions concerning the black diaspora.

Since the 1970s, Hall has popularized Gramscian notions of hegemony and shifted the central paradigm of cultural studies by swinging the pendulum firmly away from the 'cultural pessimism' of cultural dopes passively accepting the dominant ideology of the text, to a more active reading model, elaborated by Fiske and others. A great communicator, Hall regularly appears on TV as a cultural commentator on innumerable topics, and recently has shown enthusiasm for films from the black avant-garde.

Although many distinguished names have been associated with the CCCS at the University of Birmingham, it is inextricably linked to Stuart Hall, and it is commonly held that some its best work occurred under Hall's leadership. It is the institutional home of British cultural studies, and a multitude of graduates, such as Dorothy Hobson, Charlotte Brunsdon, Phil Cohen, Iain Chambers, Paul Willis and Stuart Laing, have gone on to promulgate the Centre's approach, through their teaching and writing. CCCS has remained a tiny department since its establishment by Richard Hoggart in 1964, using money from Penguin Books. It is a mark of the reaction against Hoggart's anti-populism that much key work on popular music has come out of the Centre, including Iain Chambers' *Urban Rhythms* (1986) and Hebdige's *Subculture and the Meaning of Style* (1979).

Richard Johnson took over the directorship from Stuart Hall in 1979 and adopted E.P. Thompson's social history perspective. When Jorge Lorrain replaced him in the 1980s, the Centre was losing ground in the light of contemporary educational and political shifts including the rise of Thatcherism. In its early days, the centre was confronted with French structuralism, and Althusser and Gramsci's developments of Marxism. It played a central role in establishing the serious academic study of popular culture by looking at the ways in which pleasure and meanings are constructed, not solely in texts and in their production, as before, but also by the members of a culture themselves. When CCCS launched its journal, *Working Papers in Cultural Studies*, in 1971, it refused to define 'cultural studies', rejecting a narrow culturalist approach and claiming that it was embarking on 'a sustained work of theoretical clarification' (Turner, 1992: 4). Under Hall's leadership, it moved away from the American-influenced, empirical 'mass communication research' perspective, towards media and ideology. These two elements played a part in introducing structuralism to Britain and moved media studies away from the identifiable behavioural effects of the media, to effects of *ideology* (i.e. the production of ideologies of domination). An indicator of this was the seminal paper by Hall, 'Culture, Media and the Ideological Effect' (Curran *et al.*, 1977).

The CCCS studied histories of everyday life, influenced by E.P. Thompson; and ethnographic methods from anthropology and sociology, as seen in Hobson's 'Housewives and the Mass Media' (in Hall) and work by David Morley. Members of the CCCS produced work on subcultures, and their symbolic methods of resistance to the dominant ideology, focusing on the urban youth that Hoggart had dismissed as 'jukebox boys'. Writing such as Hebdige's *Subculture and the Meaning of Style* opened up theory to include fashion, cultural practices and behaviours, with formative influences as diverse as Barthesian semiology (e.g. 'bricolage' in punk fashions), French cultural theory journal *Tel Quel* and literary criticism. The impact of Phil Cohen's subcultural theory, *Folk Devils and Moral Panics*, which linked class, leisure and cultural opposition, was widely evident. In *Hiding in the Light* (1988), Hebdige retracted the importance of subcultures, seeing little oppositional ideology in current youth subcultures. The CCCS was also in the vanguard of British feminist research, notably in the writings of McRobbie and Hobson, who discussed women's lives, use of media and involvement in subcultures.

Under Richard Johnson, the Centre moved away from textual analysis and towards social history, specifically the historical construction of subjectivity. Johnson was sceptical of previous ethnographic work as possibly under-theorized elitist paternalism (Turner, 1992: 73).

It provided the main British opposition to *Screen*'s textual determinism, with Morley's view of TV signs as polysemic being in the foreground of the CCCS's 'optimistic' position.

David Morley's main achievement was to re-introduce the element of audience uses to the media process. Taking Parkin and Hall's propositions concerning the projected differential decodings of the audience being affected by social factors, Morley applied aspects of classical mass communication theory, ethnography and culturalism to produce two seminal works: *Everyday Television – 'Nationwide'* (1978) and *The 'Nationwide' Audience* (1980). The former showed how preferred readings (that is, those possible readings that reflect the dominant ideology of the text) were encoded into a TV show, while the latter explored the extra-textual determinants of reception. More than any other CCCS member (from 1975–79) Morley shifted the emphasis from the text and its presumed ideological effects on an undifferentiated audience, to a view of decodings and the uses/pleasures a frag- mented audience makes of it. In *Everyday Television – 'Nationwide'*, Morley employs Althusserian concepts such as interpellation to show how the text constructs a preferred reading. He followed this up in *The 'Nationwide' Audience* by showing episodes from the then current British magazine show, *Nationwide*, to 26 different socio-economic focus groups, comprising members from differing age, gender, ethnic and class backgrounds. This book illustrated the relationship between whether the audience read the text in an oppositional, negotiated or dominant mode, according to factors related to their social position, such as class, race, age, gender or ethnic background; in addition to 'cultural identity' – that is, involvement in subcultures, political parties etc. (all of which will be informed by class, gen- der and so on) – the viewers' experience of the issue involved access to relevant technology (e.g. VCRs), and the context in which the decoding occurs – home, school, workplace. For Morley, then, reception became a combination of the discourses of the text and of the audience.

Looking back at his ground-breaking work, there are faults: it was little more than a new slant on 1940s' 'uses and gratifications' theory in a fashionable guise, and many empiricists felt it was under-researched and methodologically flawed. (This approach and much con- temporary work was trenchantly critiqued by James Curran, cf. Curran, 1990) By modern standards, it was vague as to the precise extent to which other factors beyond race, age, class and gender affect decoding practice. He suggests that there is a close relation between, for example, subcultural affiliation and reading practice, yet this is – perhaps necessarily – not given further explanation, and most importantly, he cannot show how, or why we decode differently.

Brunt and Jordin (cited in Price, 1998: 121) criticize the work, arguing that it does not show any connection between social position and decoding, because Morley insists on categorizing audience responses into the tripartite bands. It may be more useful, then, to see all readings as negotiated, explore issues like 'pleasure', and look at *how* resistance to the text may be encoded into the text.

This is not to oversimplify Morley's findings; it was not suggested that a mechanistic decoding existed – for, he says, 'social position in no way directly correlates' (Turner, 1992: 125) – but rather that what organizes reception is social position *plus* the possession of certain discourse positions (i.e. knowledge, prejudices etc.), which, as Bourdieu says, are connected to culturally predisposed hierarchies (habitus). Morley stresses that readings are neither arbitrary nor subject to an infinite number of possible readings, but are structured by the text itself, as well as the nexus of social and discursive factors. He has gone on to develop this empirical/theoretical approach in books like *Family Television* (1986), which took the *Nationwide* project to task for its methodology. In addition, he examined the social and familial power relations within the context of viewing and audience-focused research in *TV, Audiences and Cultural Studies* (1992). The *Nationwide* project can be criticized: the samples were limited; reactions were interpreted inconsistently; many of the participants would never normally have watched the show; the setting was not the normal viewing environment; and Morley's subsequent research took place in the less artificial setting of the home.

There have been too few large-scale studies evidencing the complex nexus of taste, social position and other factors that impinge upon the decoding process. Morley set himself an impossibly complex task to map these 'shared orientations' and their impact on reception, but his contribution to the field has been to illuminate that the relevant discourses – and range of discourses – available to the audience do structure decoding.

More than any other piece of work from the CCCS (except possibly Hall's *Encoding and Decoding the TV Discourse*), the *Nationwide* project legitimated the focus on the reception of media. It mixed cultural approaches with mass communication research and ethnography. Other key CCCS work includes Hall and Jefferson's *Resistance Through Rituals* (1976). This viewed subcultures as distinct patterns of life making up a mosaic of cultures, so the CCCS looked at subcultures rather than cultures, the oppressed rather than the dominant, and their work was typified by a focus on the social underdog. Why, then, was the CCCS so influential? Apart from the sheer breadth of the work, its teaching methods stimulated the field. It encouraged students to publish, and developed small reading and research groups, rather than formal courses; it functioned as a collective, which does not easily translate into mass undergraduate teaching in these days of large classes and managing courses on a more conventional – and cost-effective – basis.

CHAPTER 24

Dominant Theories: Marxism and Ideology

Although currently less fashionable, Marxism has consistently been a major element in cultural theory, particularly the role of ideology within culture, and the post-Marxism of Gramsci and Althusser. Ideological analysis within the study of popular culture has two foci: first, how the dominant ideology is inscribed within textual practices (which promoted semiology, the commonest method of getting at these ideological meanings); and, second, the role of the media in social control.

The study of ideology has its origins in Marx's *The German Ideology* (1845), and specifically his edict that 'the ideas of the ruling class are, in every age, the ruling ideas' (Strinati, 1995: 131). This, together with his concept of 'phenomenal form and real relations' (exploitation is hidden behind a mist of obfuscation), pointed towards a theory of ideology as a device of social control, expressly, the concept of a dominant ideology, which serves to subjugate the proletariat by making the artificial, socially constructed appear natural (cf. Abercrombie, Hill and Turner, 1980).

Ideology ensures the acceptance of societal values, and this thesis has been the dominant 'effects' paradigm since the late 1960s, in opposition to the sociological 'behavioural effects' models. Texts that reflect this view include Stuart Hall's *Culture, Media and the Ideological Effect* (in Curran *et al.*, 1977), which was widely reprinted and has arguably been the model for understanding the interaction of media and ideology since.

Another perspective on Marxism and media analysis has been the political economy thesis; however this has been more popular within a mass communication research context than a culturalist one. This approach is exemplified by the work of Golding and Murdock (Strinati, 1995: 139), who propose that the factors of ownership (the economic base) and, thereby, the needs of a capitalist class, are more important than the cultural factors (the superstructure). Culturalism, on the other hand, tends to suppose the reverse; indeed, it could be argued that the schism between economic/empiricism versus cultural/phenomenology is at the heart of the chasm between culturalist and 'mass communication' paradigms. Golding and Murdock contend that:

> by concentrating on the economic base we are suggesting that control over material resources and their changing distribution are ultimately the most powerful of many levers operating in cultural production. But clearly such control is not always exercised directly, nor does the economic state of media organisations always have an immediate impact on their output. (Strinati, 1995: 139)

In *Culture and Society* (1958), written when Marxism was in the doldrums as a result of Stalinism and the Russian invasion of Hungary, Williams scoffed at it. In terms of cultural theory, Marxism had been seen as redundant since the 1930s; and, although the New Left emerged in the 1950s as a reaction to these events, it was not until 1968 that Marxism enjoyed a renaissance.

The 'psychedelic left', or new Marxism of 1968, is often represented as being influenced by Louis Althusser (1918–90). As Hall says, 'Althusser's interventions and their subsequent development are enormously formative for the field of cultural studies' (Storey, 1993: 107). In fact, it is hard to find a journal or text of the 1970s, such as *Working Papers in Cultural Studies, Screen, New Left Review, Decoding Advertisements* by Judith Williamson (1978) etc. that does not contain pro- or anti-Althusser articles.

Many of Althusser's concepts have become central. For instance, interpellation, defined as the idea that ideological subjects are constructed by specific terms of address. A heavy metal fan, for instance, will know that s/he is being sought by a magazine employing gothic typography and iconography that includes leather, long hair, 'babes', demons etc. This not only creates the subject, but incorporates them in an imaginary community of consumers – the text literally hails them: 'Hey, you there! I'm talking to you!'

Althusser's re-reading of Marxism mixes it with structuralism, seeing society as a structure consisting of legislative, political and other levels. He focused on cultural and ideological determinants, rather than the political economy thesis. His most influential concept was that of 'ideological state apparatuses' – institutions such as the family, education, religion and media, which enforce social stability without recourse to the 'repressive state apparatuses' (army or police) that use force to control. In addition, his concept of 'cracks and fissures' was central in the areas of cultural optimism and active decoding. This thesis proposes the notion that media with a pro-capitalist worldview inevitably allows oppositional moments of social criticism to leak through. This is exemplified in many shows, from overtly political texts, such as Ken Loach films, to commercial shows like *Miami Vice*, *Cops* and *South Park*, which may have ground-breaking moments while asking serious questions about the family, society etc.

The other key player in the study of ideology has been Antonio Gramsci (1891–1937). He propounded the theory of hegemony – that is, the way in which, despite being an exploitative relationship, the subjugated classes permit themselves to be ruled. There is, apparently, constant give and take, the dominated classes are offered sufficient incentives to avoid direct confrontation (e.g. parliamentary democracy, consumer goods) and the illusion of possible change is maintained. This aspect of social exchange and compromise can be seen in arenas as diverse as the roles of women, classes, ethnic groups, geographical areas and so on. Hegemony has been crucial to many aspects of culture, principally within the cultural optimist camp. The 'culture and civilization perspective' portrays a mechanistic notion of a culture imposed from above, whereas the political economy school argues that there exists a crushing economic determinism. Gramscian hegemony, however, allows for a negotiation of struggle between groups and classes, in which territory is in permanent dispute – that is, in some ways, a text may clearly support the dominant view, and in others question it.

Of course, the dominant ideology shifts over time: today we are allowed to do things that would once have been taboo; for instance, we have more sexual freedom, and there is increased equality in areas of gender and race. New social changes are incorporated into the dominant ideology; advertisements may, for example, feature single mothers, who were, until recently, portrayed as 'folk devils'.

Rarely, such as in time of war, do those in power deliberately manipulate the media for political ends. The mechanisms of ideology are far simpler, as the reproduction of ideology is perpetrated by work practices and occupational ideologies, the very visual language we read, training and many other methods. Why, then, has this perspective become so important to culture today? It is taught as part of media courses to enable students to interpret and create texts with an ideological dimension, so that they can deal with the social power of texts, be they pro- or anti-dominant ideology. Awareness of issues such as ideology and 'news bias' may cause the media to gradually take such concepts on board, and there may be a shift in representation – not necessarily towards an anti-capitalist/'neutral' stance, but perhaps towards an incorporative liberal encoding practice. Of course, one of the critiques of the dominant ideology thesis is that if it is so invisible, yet all powerful, how is it that some critics can see it all? Can we escape ideology now we know about it?

The analysis of popular culture in America took a very different path, which has only recently converged with the European perspective. It arrived later because of the hegemony of the functionalist sociology model – which still holds far more power – although a few writers prefigured developments in culturalism. For example, Shils' relatively optimistic concept of 'taste cultures' transcending socio-economic classifications, rooted as they were in the massification theory and functionalism of the early 1960s:

> The present pleasures of the working classes . . . are not worthy of profound aesthetic, moral or intellectual esteem, but they are surely not inferior to the villainous things which gave pleasure to their European ancestors . . . mass culture is now less damaging to the lower classes than the dismal and harsh existence of earlier centuries. (Storey, 1993: 37)

In this, Shils sees the problem as being partly of massification, but diverges from Leavisism in feeling that mass society has brought benefits to make up for the loss of 'genuine' folk culture. In the 1970s, Daniel Bell's critical view of a coming post-industrial society ('the end of ideology' thesis) preceded the post-modern theory espoused by Lyotard *et al.*, which foresaw a grim future, rather than a liberating freedom. Like McLuhan, Bell was also too mired in Conservatism, so focused entirely on continental US concerns, which blinded him to the international context of globalization. Much of what passes for cultural studies in the USA today has origins in the 'critical communication studies' thread of media sociology (cf. Hardt, 1992), which had a liberal theoretical basis, acknowledged the influence of European thought and is exemplified by the work of Horace Newcomb and others. Just as British culturalism had roots in literary criticism, so American critics, such as Dwight MacDonald, Gilbert Seldes, William K. Wimsatt and Monroe C. Beardsley – who were part of the 'new criticism' of post-war America – and, later, Stanley Fish, influenced the American field.

There is an undisputed boom in American cultural theory today, yet the apolitical trajectory of most work distances it from the European form; and it is often accused of being hideously self-referential, self-indulgent, and over-theorized. There are problems transferring culturalism to America. Many European examples are unfamiliar and there have not been the same struggles over culture, or such an organized labour movement. Given that culturalism has a short history in America – perhaps 20 years in the academic mainstream – there exists the entirely possible thesis that the international field may come to be dominated by US theory, because not only have many European academics migrated there but, perversely, much of the most interesting and revolutionary recent thought has emanated from that country, from Lawrence Grossberg to bell hooks and Richard Rorty.

Pivotal to the 1980s recuperation of 'low culture' or hegemonic, reactionary texts, has been the folkloric concept of carnival, originated by the Russian literary theorist and social philosopher Mikhail Bakhtin (1895–1975). This emerged from his work on Rabelais and the ramifications of his thought – and the concomitant pleasures – in literature. 'Carnival' enabled the celebration of texts such as the 'Carry On' films and other British sex comedies of the 1970s (Hunt, 1998: 98), as laughter is central to carnival, which Bakhtin himself saw delegated to 'low genres'. Debasement, degradation, centrality of the body and carnival figures (such as the clown and the mask) recur throughout carnivalesque texts. The mask is 'connected with the joy of change and reincarnation, with gay relativity and the merry negation of uniformity and similarity' (Lechte, 1994: 9). The archetypal characters of the fool and the satirist in comedy are clearly visible; but whether this theory is popular solely to permit the justification of the writer's personal taste, as has been alleged, is debatable. Such texts have also been claimed as camp/kitsch post-modern pleasures, in which ideas of a 'world turned upside down', where social truths and realities are contested to their limits, thus demystified and shorn of power. This anthropological pleasure of reversal of status and communal Rabelaisian excess is seen in many cultures (All Fools Day, for example, when the highest is subservient to the most humble). In the Middle Ages, there was no difference between spectators and participants, as it was not a performance, as we would understand the term. Today, carnival can be seen as a societal safety valve, sanctioned by the dominant class. It is not a simple spectacle or a permissible release, for the rulers are also subject to the laws of carnival.

> The laws, prohibitions and restrictions that determine the structure and order of ordinary life are suspended . . . what is suspended first is hierarchical structure . . . all distance between people is suspended and a special carnival category goes into effect; free and familiar contact among people. (Bakhtin, in Storey, 1997: 130)

This anarchic clash of the sacred and profane, the lord and the beggar, is marked by laughter. The fool plays a special role, with humour illuminating the disappearance of limitations and authority. One can perhaps see these oppositions existing between carnival and official culture as illustrated in Table 24.1.

These Straussian binary oppositions can be seen in popular comedies, which have touched a paganistic nerve with the public. Films like *The Blues Brothers* have moments when officialdom is mocked and the communal experience of pleasure becomes the focus, notably in a scene in which a whole city block sings and dances outside Ray's Music Shop for no real narrative reason.

The subversion of authority and taste is the basis of comics and, similarly, most sitcoms revolve around this systematic opposition to – and subversion of – authority. From *Sergeant*

Table 24.1   *Carnival culture vs official culture*

Carnival culture	Official culture
laughter	seriousness
body	mind
profane	spiritual
unofficial	official
horizontal	vertical
open	dogmatic
contingent	immutable

Bilko to *The Simpsons*, moments of carnival promise a better, more egalitarian future. The focus on bodily functions (birth, eating, defecation etc.) and sexuality is often connected to a comedy of excess and vigour, encompassing parodies of our social betters, as seen in *Beavis and Butthead et al.*

Carnival can be viewed as a threat to capital, as it supports a proletarian, scatological taste for ridicule and coarse laughter. Such pleasures can be found in nineteenth-century broadsides, full of *double entendres* (such as 'The Bonny Black Hare'), and this poses an egalitarian threat to modernism and its view of a improving, universal culture. Bakhtin wrote (in Hunt, 1998: 35) that he was unequivocal about the noble vulgarity of 'the people'. His longing for peasant folk culture sometimes recalls a populistic Leavisianism. The raucousness of carnival has allowed the post-modern rehabilitation of non-politically correct shows like *Are You Being Served* and *The Benny Hill Show*, which are hugely popular worldwide. It is possible to criticize Bakhtin, whose work is overly central in the writing of Fiske, whose *TV Culture* (1987) has become the set text for many TV courses, and who, in the 1980s, did most to popularize the active decoding, optimistic, view. Fiske has recently been criticized for his naïve celebration of 'lowest common denominator' culture: 'Carnival celebrated temporary liberation from the prevailing truth and from the established order; it marked the suspension of all hierarchical rank privileges, norms and prohibitions' (Fiske, 1987: 241). Citing Bennett, Fiske sees that 'the value of excess associated with carnival formed part of an image of the people as a boundless, unstoppable material force, a vast self regenerating and undifferentiated body surmounting all obstacles in its path' (Fiske, 1987: 249). He views surveillance/reality shows – like *You've Been Framed/America's Funniest Home Videos* – as 'according to the logic of the inside out' (Fiske, 1987: 242). Such shows reverse the natural order of reality, and place the viewer in the powerful position of being a possessor of knowledge, rather than the powerless one: they know the joke of the show, and are aware that the fall into the mud will surely come.

CHAPTER 25

Main Areas of Cultural Studies Today

POST-MODERNISM

Defining post-modernism is problematic. There are many uses of the term, and, like 'culture', there is struggle over its meaning. Generally, post-modernism applies to cultural products such as media, art etc., while post-modernity exists in a social science context. Perhaps it is best seen as being:

- a *practice* within the cultural industries – that is, one can be a post-modern film-maker, artist, writer etc.
- a *sociological condition*, which many believe that the western world is moving into, or may already be in
- a set of *philosophical ideas* concerning the shifting, transient nature of reality in a post-industrial society
- a *combination* of the above, and more.

Certainly Jean François Lyotard's concept of 'incredulity towards metanarratives' is central. He introduces a rejection of the certainties of modernism, favoured by Darwin, Freud, Marx *et al.*, which marks popular scepticism to systems of explanations and institutions such as science, the law, the family, democracy, work etc. Just as, under modernism, the Enlightenment and industrialism replaced faith and feudalism, so a post-modern era has post-modern philosophy, and a global information society; it is a new social form in which consumption replaces production.

Post-modernism is evident everywhere, from car design and TV shows, to film and scientific theory. It questions the foundations of western metaphysics and, in its aims of defining and knowing the world, one even has post-modern physics, with concepts such as charm, strangeness and fuzzy logic, which are on the borders of 'new age' (another post-modern phenomenon) philosophy. Habermas sees a 'crisis of legitimation' (Sim, 1998: 268), but interprets the current cultural flux as 'high modernism' rather than post-modernism; he sees post-modernism as inherently conservative, refusing its social responsibilities, arguing that new communications will not shift social paradigms, any more than the telegraph did.

With post-modernity, history disappears under a welter of representations of the past as an idealized 'heritage'. Time and space become meaningless; most of us have grown up lacking any organic relation to the public past. Paul Fayerabend (in *Against Method*, 1975) believes that science needs sloppiness, chaos and opportunism to progress (Sim, 1998: 243), as there are no knowable truths simply waiting to be discovered by science, which is itself seen as no more than another discourse whereby elites exercise power. Doubt and scepticism are aspects of the post-modern condition, as exemplified in the representation of science in TV series like *The X-Files*. This anti-science can be seen merely as a development of C.P. Snow's 'two cultures' debate (art versus science), for much post-modernist theory originates from the arts rather than the empirical sciences, but it is more useful to see post-modernism as transcending modernist concepts of science.

One of the central characters within post-modernism is Jean Baudrillard (b. 1929), a hugely eclectic thinker who, like many post-1968 theorists, shows the influence of situationists such as Guy Debord in his work. In common with Barthes, and other French sociologists and writers, Baudrillard is interested in the minutiae of everyday life. In a European extrapolation of McLuhanism, he saw the possible effects of 'cyberblitz' on society – that is, an information technology overload, which has transformed existence for many in the West profoundly. As with many post-war French writers, Baudrillard opposes simplistic meaning, so his work can be impenetrable and ambiguous. His confrontational style has outraged feminists and Marxists alike, but his concept of the simulacrum has been central to post-modernism. This is an image generated when commodity and sign combine in a self-referential loop to form a sign (whose reality is wholly illusory) perceived as an external referent (a reality), which is vastly preferable to the sum of its parts (Sim, 1998: 358). An example of this might be the – probably entirely mythical – event in which tenants in an apartment block chose to watch the TV news coverage of a murder in the block rather than walk into the corridor and see the real thing. Examples of the simulacrum can be found commonly in popular narratives, e.g. the false world that is so much better than the real one in *The Truman Show*, or perhaps the world of *The Matrix*.

Baudrillard is apocalyptic. Infamously he questioned whether the Gulf War actually happened. We prefer television that is hyper-real – a theme taken up by Umberto Eco in *Travels in Hyper-reality* – since this reality is the real that has disappeared completely into the process of 'simulation' (i.e. mass reproduction, echoing Benjamin's thesis) and has become its own pure simulacrum (Sim, 1998: 193). This recurring concept suggests that we only accept reality through TV and other simulacra of reality, as we become increasingly sceptical about TV news, and genres like docu-soap replace documentaries as knowledge. By pronouncing these trends of disappearing value and alienation through information technology and television, welcoming Disneyland as being America's true reality, and propounding an apolitical surrender to capitalism and a lack of rigorous thought, Baudrillard is seen as the post-modern prophet.

Second to Baudrillard in the field is Jean-François Lyotard (b. 1924), whose *The Post-modern Condition* (1984) defined 'incredulity towards metanarratives'. He believes that intellectuals can no longer explain the world, but only interpret it, leading to a serious crisis for knowledge and certainty. Science led us to Hiroshima, so we believe in fantasy instead. God is dead and we have 'new age' end-of-the-world doom and gloom. Politics failed so anarchy rules, and scepticism of any political order (e.g. *The X-Files* and its paranoia concerning government conspiracies) and issue politics is rife.

Breaking from conventional Marxism, Lyotard put his faith in the 'little narrative' of the individual human being (Sim, 1998: 271), and this libertarian anti-authoritarian figure has been responsible for originating many of the central debates today. Though Francis Fukayama sees the end of history (Sim, 1998: 27) with the end of the cold war, there are no more major ideological confrontations – although Daniel Bell (possibly erroneously) saw similar events with his 'end of ideology' thesis in the 1960s. Derrida takes up this theme, arguing that 'never has the horizon of the thing being celebrated been as dark, threatening and threatened'.

Post-modern cultural products

Music: the minimalist 'systems music' of Philip Glass; nihilistic grunge for the 'slacker generation'; sampling; fragmentation into innumerable genres that replace musicians with technology and randomness; and the reclaiming of 1970s camp trash culture.

Animation: Manga, with its transgressive sex and violence; apocalyptic, post-holocaust futures; and human metamorphosis (e.g. men into machines and machines into other forms of machines). Manga proposes a Japanese centre rather than the usual American ethnocentrism. *Ren and Stimpy*; *The Simpsons*; *South Park* are all self-referential; *The Simpsons* breaks boundaries by including 'Itchy and Scratchy' cartoons within a cartoon, and continually makes reference to other TV shows, as well as its own fictional existence, and has 'real' guest stars playing themselves.

Design: post-modernism is exemplified by the trend towards retro (a fond looking back to the past) and pastiche. Cars like the Mazda Miata/MX5 is a 1960s Lotus with upgraded technology; and the Plymouth Prowler is a 1950s hot-rod filtered through 1990s design. Almost every modern car has aspects of such design. Equally, in architecture, one can see in new structures, like the Lloyd's building, Charing Cross Station and the Pompidou Centre – and perhaps most of Las Vegas – a trend towards stylistic eclecticism, retro and fore-grounding its own construction. Malls are the typical post-modern shopping experience: temples of consumption, with identical stores throughout the world, in artificial 'heritage' settings. One of the key originators of post-modern theory, the architectural critic Robert Venturi, argued that the public wanted Disneyland, not modern architecture.

Fashion and subcultural styles: these provide a multiplicity of representations of post-modern culture today. Post-modernism is evident in tribalism: subcultures transcending class and more usual markers, to reclaim neo-Celtic imagery; and new primitivism – tattooing, body modification and piercing, which show the body as the last personal area of control. In addition there has been a move towards infantilism – fashions based on a regression to a sexualized childhood, as seen in the 'kinderwhore' style of Courtney Love, and the ambiguous, sensual child look of Manga.

Film and TV: post-modernism is ubiquitous in these media; transgressive, popular parodic TV blurs the barriers of time and space, as seen in the retro styling of *Happy Days* and *Heartbeat*. Hyper-real shows like *Homicide – Life on the Street* break film language in the style of cinema verité. Deconstructive devices abound – characters in *Wayne's World* look into camera and offer multiple-choice endings. MTV rock videos and many commercials utilize montage and repetition, and are self-referential (e.g. Coke ads play on past Coke ads). Texts are increasingly hyper-conscious, self-aware and cognisant of their place in popular culture. *The Simpsons* and *South Park* both refer to their existence as shows with an audience. Post-modern readings allow recuperation of past shows, like *The Avengers* or *Thunderbirds*, for camp, oppositional decodings and pleasures. The style-conscious, reflexive documentaries of Michael Moore and Nick Broomfield are common; these centre on the process of making a documentary, and one only learns about the designated subject by inference. Many shows become increasingly populist and reactionary – daytime talk shows, and home video shows focus on voyeurism; control and surveillance have become cultural themes, building on concepts from Jeremy Bentham (e.g. the Panopticon) and Foucault's notions of surveillance and control.

There has been a boom in media shows: TV about TV and film about film. Films such as *Get Shorty* mix a proposed film with events in the film we are watching, and make references to real movie stars. The divisions of reality/fantasy become more blurred, with simulacra a major theme in films like *The Truman Show*; and 'neo-TV', such as *Seinfeld/Alan Partridge*, is everywhere.

'Generation X', or the 'slacker generation', is visible in such films as Kevin Smith's *Clerks*; and queer families and the otherwise alienated are seen regularly in popular TV like *Friends* and *Ellen*. Arnold Schwarzenegger has been described as the ultimate post-modern film star (Appignanesi and Garratt, 1995: 147) because he is a blank slate, a non-actor upon whom we can project any meaning. His films, notably *Total Recall* and *Terminator*, offer themes of lack of reality and the pleasures of spectacle, rather than narrative closure.

What are the causes of post-modernism? Increasingly remote from the processes of production since the Industrial Revolution, we are allegedly more reliant on televisual experience over reality, which is fundamentally altered. As our ability to deal with time and space is lost, it seems that schizophrenia has become the post-modern condition. Computers are part of everyday existence, and new technologies such as VCRs and satellites cause us to lose contact with more traditional forms of interpersonal communications and the institutions, such as the family and work, that supported them. The rise in education, semiology and interdisciplinary fields such as media studies led to semio-literacy, industrial trends (including post-Fordism) and a move to a service economy. Both new age philosophies and their mirror image, fundamentalism, have profited from a crisis in more traditional belief; our heroes are heroes of consumption rather than production: Elvis and Madonna are famous for their excessive spending in addition to their production of artefacts.

Post-modern media possess several key characteristics.

- *Transgression and excess*: breaking accepted boundaries of taste. Scatological, overtly offensive, designed to shock, all can be related to a focus on the body as a site of cultural struggle (e.g. an interest in sexuality, body piercing etc.).
- An *eclectic approach*, whereby multiple styles and influences are thrown together, is inherent in post-modern culture.
- *Parody*, pastiche, self-referentialism, intertextuality, quotation: *The Simpsons* refers to *The Flintstones*; *Due South* mimics buddy cop shows like *Starsky and Hutch*; *Reeves and Mortimer* parodies 1970s British game shows such as *The Sale of the Century* and science fiction shows, such as *Third Rock from the Sun*, a 1950s sci-fi sitcom. While many museums and zoos suffer from the rise of VCRs, video games and the Internet, we are often accused of becoming more passive, expecting culture to come to us.
- *Reception* alters in a fragmented world, for as technologies like VCRs allow different reading strategies, zapping through many channels offers options of constructing a unique 'flow' of television.
- *Originality is dead*. The use of samplers/remixes in music demonstrates that many, if not most, texts are re-makes. Film generates a television spin-off show, and vice versa; *The X-Files* combines elements of cop show, sci-fi and horror, while revisiting 1950s sci-fi/ horror films such as *The Thing*, and *Dracula*.
- *The blurring/destroying of barriers* between genres. *Twin Peaks* was a film noir soap opera, and *Homicide – Life on the Street* mixes documentary, cop show and soap opera styles.
- *Reality/fantasy*: philosophers like Rorty argue that our definition of reality is only composed by our understanding of sign systems. In subgenres like docu-soaps, it is

often hard to see whether a show is a fiction shot in a documentary style (*Homicide – Life on the Street*) or a documentary shot like a drama (*Driving School, Airport* etc.).

- *Texts showing their own construction*: *South Park* (Terrance and Philip) and *The Simpsons* (Itchy and Scratchy) employ the device of framing cartoon stories to comment upon/reflect on the main story. The films of Peter Greenaway, such as *Drowning by Numbers*, and Nick Broomfield's documentaries *The Leader, The Driver, and the Driver's Wife*, display their internal form as well as excess.
- *High and popular culture merge*: popular film uses art film narrative structures and devices (e.g. David Lynch), and art forms use popular culture (Nigel Kennedy, for instance, plays classical versions of Jimi Hendrix and Philip Glass composes symphonies based on the work of David Bowie). One no longer needs to be a maestro to be a star or artist – Brian Eno does not claim to be a musician, and much modern music is made on a sampler, rather than through musical dexterity. Bugs Bunny and Greek tragedy are seen as both merely sign systems, and so are of equal merit.
- *Distortion of time and space*: in what year(s) are *Heartbeat* and *Happy Days* set? The same might be asked of *Rumblefish, Blue Velvet, Delicatessen, Brazil* or *Hellraiser*. There is no time and no geographical place, only an eternal present exists.
- *The McDonaldization of the world*: led by standardization and globalism, world culture is accused of becoming homogenous, as multi-national conglomerates take over every-thing through vertical integration. Conglomerates shift virtual money around the world, only impinging on our personal experience when this puts us out of work; yet, paradoxi-cally, we also see a move to fragmentation and dispersal in the break-up of previously monolithic nation-states.
- *Fragmented audiences* cause the emergence of multi-layered readings; wildly differing *pleasures* can be gained from texts. *South Park* can be seen as a children's show *or a* sophisticated parody for adults. Post-modernism allows new pleasures, so camp or tacky shows (the likes of the 'Carry On' films or *The Brady Bunch*) are fashionable again, and are enjoyed for reasons not originally foreseen. This has resulted in much cult TV, such as *The Prisoner, The Clangers et al.*
- Allied to this is *hyper-signification* – that is, the ability to read texts, which is now at an unprecedented level. Most teenagers can decode the significance of Doc Martens, PlayStation games or Nike Air Jordans at a level superior to that of literary critics inter-preting Shakespeare.
- *Post-modern realism* has replaced conventional verisimilitude: the audience may discover what is real through watching TV shows, rather than from experience; borrowing from art film conventions, such as Tarantino's *Pulp Fiction*, with its Godardian elliptical narratives. Many do not want elucidation any more, just enjoyable, ephemeral gloss and easy expla-nations. Technique is less important than surface (the animation in *South Park* is terrible, but it is a transgressive text), and the pleasure of cinema becomes pure spectacle (e.g. *Star Wars* and the French '*cinema du look*'). As image becomes inseparable from expe-rience, there is no difference between surface and depth, and *The Big Breakfast* (and other 'zoo TV' or tabloid TV/infotainment) is shallow, more interested in bad puns than

political analysis; yet, by its very shallow nature, manages to make points about society that might be excised on more 'serious' shows.

- *Retro is ubiquitous*: 'cyberpunk' films like *Blade Runner* look like a 1930s view of what the twenty-first century will look like, as does *Batman*. These use past styles, such as film noir, to recreate an imaginary past/future; and museums are about 'heritage', an idealized past that we prefer to the harsh reality of history. Perhaps the past returns because the present and future are too terrible. ABBA, 1970s clothes, remakes of 1970s music/television, and other cult phenomena are common.

There are many criticisms to be levelled at post-modern theory. Much of it is culturally pessimistic, foreseeing a homogenized, industrialized 'mass' culture, though this may simply be *fin de siècle* gloom. While it portends the end of metanarratives, it is itself one! It is primarily of concern to first-world states; most developing nations aspire to such industrial or cultural conditions. Historically it can be argued that there has *always* been mixing of genres and transgression, from Shakespeare and Rabelais to the Marx Brothers.

Then there is the debate over value, in that although hierarchies of merit may be undesirable, they may be necessary; i.e. can we, or must we, unequivocally claim that *The Teletubbies* are equal to *Citizen Kane*, or can we still establish some criteria that transcend multiple personal readings and pleasures?

Within the field, there is little agreement over terms and ideas, with both left and right claiming it as their own; post-modernism is often contradictory and paradoxical, with literature as difficult and jargonistic as structuralism. Debates over retro may well be as much informed by pure nostalgia as anything else and, as TV consumption takes place in a social setting, it is more than possible that the readings we get will still be influenced by social factors, rather than some vague, anti-realist post-modernist mode.

The Canadian duo McLuhan and Harold Innis have been posited as the originators of post-modernism, in that they foresaw a globalized culture made possible by new communications, producing a standardized world culture. Yet its roots can also be seen in Nietzsche and the Frankfurt School, since it shares their concerns over homogenization and cultural pessimism. Table 25.1 may illuminate some of the key oppositions between modernity and post-modernity.

Queer Theory

A collision of post-modern ideas with gay activism, queer theory is elusive to pin down. As it is such a new and developing field, there is no overall coherence as to methods or subjects. However, since the 1980s, growing out of gay studies, and triggered by developments in post-modern theory and the HIV crisis, there has been a plethora of books, articles, art and work in other media that can be called 'queer theory'.

The majority is overwhelmingly theoretical and philosophically oriented, rather than empirically based, and this has attracted criticism from the sociologically inclined. Queer theory uses inter-disciplinary methodologies from sources like Foucault, post-structuralism, feminism, film theory and Lacanian psychoanalysis, to illuminate areas such as desire and

Table 25.1 *Modernism vs post-modernism*

Modernism	Post-modernism
taste	excess/anything goes
forward-looking	retro
presence	absence
paradigm	syntagm
authorship/purpose	play
selection	combination
centring	dispersal
closed	open
distance	participation
primitivism	existential
elites	mass
progress	nihilism
possible utopia	likely dystopia
planned	random
serious	fun
beliefs	cynicism
design	chance
dehumanizing	anti-elite
hierarchy	anarchy
genital	polymorphous
hetero versus homo	queer
art object	process
inventing	recombining
originality	referential
rational	anti-rational
eternal	ephemeral
urban	global village

sexual instability. The dominant paradigm tends towards a 'social constructionist' view, that (sexual) identity is non-essentialist, created in a reality mediated through discourse alone. It is about rehabilitating, and celebrating, the marginalized; such as queer history – pre- and post-*Stonewall* (1968) – encompassing the entire historical sweep of gay/lesbian figures from Oscar Wilde to Rock Hudson, films by George Cukor and Dorothy Arzner, to the social history of gay communities and individuals. It celebrates the confrontational, sexually explicit pleasures of the camp/kitsch, stylish and transgressive, through *Eurotrash*, Derek Jarman, Madonna, Julian Clary and Lily Savage. In post-modern theory, the traditional nuclear family is doomed as a metanarrative (or institution), so symbolic, reformed, transgendered 'queer families' emerge, such as those seen in shows like *Seinfeld*, *Friends*, *Ellen* etc.

Queer media transcended 'politically correct' roles, and in the films of Pedro Almodovar, and the indefinable 'new queer cinema' of the 1980s and 1990s (such as Todd Haynes, Greg Araki, Jarman and others) a wider and more complex problematic arena was addressed.

Most queer theory addresses issues of identity and its transcendence, rather than equality or difference, but proposes instead a new pan-sexual state of being, focusing on the relation of sexuality to social control and cultural politics. According to Judith Butler (Sim, 1998: 345), the purpose of queer theory is to 'destabilise the entire system of sex regulation that undoes binary oppositions such as gay/straight'.

Queer media and theory examined **transgressivity** or, as Sinfield calls it 'dissidence' (for 'transgressive' suggests that it has happened, while the cultural process of queer is ongoing). This transgressivity is represented by celebrations of excess, like sado-masochism and role-playing. The very 'sexiness' of the field, a radical chic for the 1990s, makes it attractive to critics and students alike. The fact that it is a previously under-researched area, and offers opportunities to gay writers (although many of those who have written on it are not gay) must also be factors in its remarkable recent exponential growth.

Themes of rebellion and pluralism abound, i.e. there is no one stable gay identity or community, but a multitude of shifting elements linked loosely by an indeterminate, polymorphous perverse sexuality. There is no homosexual subject within queer theory, intending to be inclusive by this vague, transient non-categorization. Though primarily an area that has grown out of academe, it makes links with radical queer groups such as Act Up and Queer Nation. It connects with post-modernity on many levels, notably investigations of the body, blurring boundaries, rejection of metanarratives such as the family and identity, centrality of difference not integration, and a focus on analysing texts, not prescriptive theory.

Queer texts include films such as Kenneth Anger's *Scorpio Rising* (1964), Fassbinder's *Querelle*, 'new queer cinema', and television celebrating perverse (another term reclaimed in queer culture) sexuality and the shallow, e.g. *Eurotrash*. Although queer television in the USA and Europe is in its infancy due to the institutionalized nature of most media, there are signs of growth on outlets with more access to the marginal, including US cable channels, literature such as Gore Vidal and Armistead Maupin, and the whole academic industry of Madonna as queer icon.

Though issue-specific in recent years, queer theory has links with wider social/cultural criticism and politics – that is, some queer theory now connects with discussions of hegemony. Critics submit that it is indicative of the demographics of academe that, while such areas as queer theory grow, subjects such as representation of ethnicity remain almost totally unresearched. As with other aspects of queer culture, queer theory can be seen as exclusive, for body fascism excludes those who do not conform to an Adonis physique and those who do not live in a metropolis. Queer theory can, therefore, often be spectacularly incomprehensible, wildly suppositional, often relying on examples from relatively obscure cultural texts. In these aspects the field harks back to some of the culturalist writings of the 1970s.

Those who have contributed towards this burgeoning discipline include: Alan Sinfield (*Cultural Politics – Queer Reading*, 1994), who incorporates Foucault's theories into discussions of marginality and cultural relativism; B. Ruby Rich; and Jonathan Dollimore (*Sexual Dissidence*, 1991), who challenges perceptions of barriers between dominant and subordinated groups, and explores the cracks and fissures of texts. In addition to other film theorists, like Teresa De Lauretis and Alexander Doty, Richard Dyer has done much to popularize theories of gays in film, particularly *Now You See It*. Other major names in the field include Diana Fuss (*Inside Out*) and Eve Kosofsky Sedgwick (*Epistemology of the Closet*).

The influence of Lacanianism was significant, as it was only psychoanalysis that had developed a sophisticated language to deal with sexuality, while sociology had virtually ignored the issue. Giddens and Habermas did not mention *any* sexuality; and it is argued that Foucault became the unknowing father of queer theory by showing how sexuality is socially constructed. It could also be said that other progenitors of this movement in the 1970s include Jeffrey Weeks with works such as *Sexuality* and *Coming Out – Homosexual Politics*. In recent years there have been attempts to put queer theory on a more solid theoretical footing, making connections with sociology – as seen in *Queer Theory/Sociology* (ed. S. Seidman, 1996).

Post-colonialism

Another paradigm linked to post-modernism is post-colonialism: an elastic term covering many contradictory discourses. It centres on the exercise of power to subjugate, within a post-colonial context, either by a direct repressive power or an ideological cultural imperialism of language, consumer culture, or ideology, focusing on interrogating relationships between peoples, texts and institutions within the context of post-colonial rule. Above all, it is the social, political, economic and cultural practices arising in response to colonialism and Eurocentrism, and is a *critical* perspective, originating largely from literary and cultural studies, through which to view colonialism and its legacy. It excluded the subject culture from definitions of 'real' culture, seeing the 'other' as radically different, and hopelessly inferior; so the focus of post-colonialism has been on how nations and groups have been marginalized to a European centre of 'civilization'.

Post-colonialism concerns the work of those from nations forcibly colonized by European countries, including Africa and the Indian subcontinent, and from countries settled relatively peacefully (or whose natives were quelled quickly and quietly, such as Australia and Canada). There is a third category of nations combining the two (e.g. South Africa).

The post-colonial trajectory encompasses the manner in which European thought and power achieved ideological control (before *and* after direct Imperial control) through knowledge production, education and ways of thinking. Earlier this century, European empires covered 85 per cent of the globe, and their legacy has caused vast repercussions in the cultural field, which have yet to be worked through. The cultural production of the formerly colonized – previously called 'Commonwealth literature', or 'black' or 'Asian' – has been transformed into the post-colonial by ideas imported from post-modernism and post-structuralist thought, such as the importance of language, subjectivity, gender and race. In so far as post-colonialism supersedes one condition, rejecting the Enlightenment concept of metanarratives, it is a development of post-modernism. It displaces, and transcends, an existing condition and is in flux. Just as post-modernism originated in theory then manifested in media, so post-colonialism began in literature, but is likely to become expressed in popular culture, especially in terms of *representation of race* in media.

Post-colonialism and post-modernism de-centre and historicize the subject, recognizing race, class and other issues as constituting the subject. Both use textual strategies, such as irony and pastiche, to subvert the dominant discourse. Both are de-constructive strategies within texts – that is, they challenge metanarratives such as western notions of history, rationalism etc., and reject notions of the essential or universal.

Post-colonialism has its literary roots in writers such as Salman Rushdie, Anita Desai, Rohinton Mistry and Derek Walcott; and historians C.L.R. James and Henry Louis Gates. It was widened by a growth in media reflecting post-colonial concerns in the 1980s – for example, Hanif Kureishi's *The Buddha of Suburbia*, Isaac Julien's *Young Soul Rebels*, and in the work of film-makers like Mira Nair, Horace Ove and Pratibha Parmar.

Central themes of the field include: the centre versus the margin; the language one should write in; national identity; and women and post-colonialism. It interrogates the relationship between issues such as gender, homophobia and emerging cultural identities; and inscribes race, second languages, and the problematics of language and linguistics, hence the growth of forms such as West Indian dialect poems and overtly political texts.

The characteristics of post-colonialism are varied, but many texts incorporate culturally specific details without offering explanations of 'alien' cultural practices, often reducing white characters to nameless ciphers who exist only to exert colonial power. The founding moment of the movement may either be 1947, with the beginning of European withdrawal from empire, especially India and Africa; or the 1978 publication of Edward Said's *Orientalism*. Said (b. 1935) found 'Europe's deepest and most recurring image of the other, a western style for dominating, restructuring, and having authority over the orient' (Sim, 1998: 336). His text was influential on the reconsideration of literature from post-independent nations, and allowed post-modern readings of earlier writers such as Frantz Fanon. Said argued that the imperialist powers needed to create an other – an orient – in order to define themselves as the centre. 'Orientalism', the image of the orient, or the other, expressed as an entire system of thought and scholarship, encouraged a westernized ideology and, consequently, hegemony.

Although he has been criticized in recent years for verging towards occidentalism (Sim, 1995: 348), Said is generally seen as a seminal figure. Another key player is Chakravorti Spivak (b. 1941), who is one of the most subversive of post-colonialist critics. A translator of Derrida, she aims to go beyond reclaiming Indian history for its own sake, to destroy the western metanarrative of traditional historical reasoning itself. Spivak is part of the Subaltern Studies Group at Delhi University. Taking this term from Gramsci and the imperial terminology of rule, it is used to refer to the growth of class consciousness within the dominated group; and although criticized in India for importing elitist western methodologies to analyse eastern conditions (Sardar and Van Loon, 1997: 81), Spivak's post-structuralist, and sometimes difficult, writing has been crucial in the development of the field.

One of the most prolific post-colonialist writers is Homi Bhabha (b. 1949), whose work draws on psychoanalysis and on a central pillar of post-colonialism: 'hybridity'. This third space, beyond Marxism or liberalism, can not only displace the history that creates it, but can set up 'new structures of authority, and generate new political initiatives' (Sardar and Van Loon, 1997: 120).

Key debates of this broad field include: negritude; ethnicity; representations; pastiche; essentialism; difference; slavery; resistance; displacement; migration; and the diasporic experience in relation to western metanarratives of science, literature, philosophy and history. It problematizes the established concept of nation, focusing on new definitions of identity and diaspora, and promises to become, like post-modernism, influential beyond academe.

CHAPTER 26

Semiology and Beyond

What is today considered to be 'semiology' is based on a work by the Swiss linguist Ferdinand de Saussure (1857–1915), entitled 'A Course on General Linguistics', written from the lecture notes of his students, circa 1912. (In the USA, the philosopher C.S. Pierce (1839–1914) came to comparable conclusions, but used different terminology.) The next major development was Roland Barthes' 'Mythologies' (1956), which combined Marxism, the study of ideology, popular culture (such as photographs in newspapers, car design, wrestling etc.) and semiology.

Though popular in France from the 1950s, it did not find favour in Great Britain until the late 1960s, when magazines such as *Movie* and *Screen*, and the newly translated writers, including Barthes, were rapidly taken up by the CCCS, Williams and others. Although often used interchangeably, there are differences between the meanings of 'semiology', 'semiotics' and 'structuralism': semiology is that devised by de Saussure; semiotics is the preferred term in America and among those following the work of Pierce; and structuralism focuses on the structure that produces meaning, rather than the sign within.

Many theorists have incorporated semiotics into their work: Foucault in philosophy and history; Christian Metz in film theory; and Lacan in psychoanalysis. Since the 1960s, Umberto Eco has done much to popularize semiology in academic texts, novels, newspaper columns etc., and in anthropology Lévi-Strauss employed de Saussure's theory to look at myths and symbolic systems of 'primitive societies'. In *Sixguns and Society*, Will Wright's use of Lévi-Strauss's oppositions for narrative analysis proved to be influential (e.g. cowboys/Indians, civilization/wilderness, men/women etc.).

Semiology achieved rapid popularity as a research method, although today there has been opposition from more traditional critics from the 'culture and civilization' tradition. It countered the positivist empiricism of much American content analysis, and also acted as a complementary methodology, especially with the new theoretical bases such as feminism, Marxism and psychoanalysis. Much modern semiology is theorized with Marxism, showing how ideology is inherent within the sign through myth. In the USA, C. Wright Mills picked up the work of Pierce, although mainly in a relatively obscure sociological context, rather than the general cultural arena of semiology within Europe.

There are criticisms of semiology to be addressed. Although designated the 'science of signs' by de Saussure, it is not a science, as it depends on a subjective reading, rather than scientific objectivity. While it is unlikely that there will be huge differences in most readings, for we must share meanings if we are to communicate, modern semiology attempts to take other possible readings into account, and deals with the intentions of the author, as well as those of the readers. Semiology is not in itself inherently theorized, so some meaning has to be added, be it Marxism, feminism or whatever. The original pre-Barthesian version of semiology was extremely limited, with no theoretical base for meaning. Textual interpretations shift over time, and across cultural boundaries, thus analysis must be diachronic (across time) as well as synchronic (an instant frozen in time). Unfortunately, much semiology was purely synchronic, and it is easy to imagine that most texts will mean something entirely different 20 years after their appearance; this ahistoricism can limit analysis. The logic of deconstructing latent meanings, and privileging them over the more obvious 'manifest' ones, is questionable, for the audience may not see this latent dimension; the analysis may be longer than the text. The task is time-consuming, and often tells us what we already know in a language we don't understand.

The scientific validity of semiology is questionable – in comparison with traditional positivistic science, at least – for it is not replicable (it is impossible to repeat with exactly the same results). It is not easy to show that semiology examines the subject it sets out to study, i.e. it is a scatter-gun approach, analysing what it hits. There are advantages of using semiology as a tool, however. It exposes the ideological, latent meaning behind the surface of texts, allowing us to grasp the power relations within them.

POST-STRUCTURALISM

This is an extrapolation of structuralism, together with deconstructionism and post-modernism, yet its influence has not travelled far beyond academe. Even then, it can be seen as rather *passé* today (in company with '*Screen* theory' and its ilk), while structuralism itself has had tremendous ramifications and continues to do so.

Post-structuralism affords human agency more import (marking a move away from Marxism), together with chance and randomness in the construction of events and their 'meaning'. This method largely derives from linguistics and originates with the French deconstructionists, such as Jacques Derrida, Roland Barthes, Jacques Lacan and Jean-François Lyotard, most of whom are better known for their accomplishments in other areas.

The basis of post-structuralism is that meaning is not fixed, as semiotics suggests, but rather is constructed by the speaking subject and, as philosophical and ideological discourses construct meaning by marginalizing certain terms, there is no fixed nature of truth and knowledge. We therefore have to deconstruct the text, and any reading of the text is as valid as any other. The role of the reader, then, is not to ascertain the objective meaning of the text (as with structuralism) but to uncover the ideological power relations within the meaning system of the text, and to illuminate the linguistic contradictions inherent within. The text contradicts structuralist accounts of meaning, but also contradicts itself!

Post-structuralism is an umbrella term, used to refer to developments in structuralism, such as post–feminism, post-modernism and deconstructionism. 'Post-structuralism' and 'deconstructionism' are interchangeable, although it is better to see post-structuralism as a developing aspect of deconstruction. Equally, it can be seen as a progression of structuralism, rather than a successor or a replacement for it: it is certainly a significant shift away from a fixed conception of the subject, heralding many post-modern ideas of the shifting nature of reality as representation. Within post-structuralism, there are no hierarchies, or essentialist metanarratives such as truth, identity or certainty. It is rooted in the premise that one may shape the world through the use of language, but that language, likewise, shapes us (that is, the meanings of words are so embedded in how we use language that the language itself largely determines what we say).

In *Writing and Difference* (1978), Derrida criticized the western 'logocentric' notion of an ever-active, transcendent centre. The semioticians showed that language has no fixed centre, and the sign is always arbitrary and socially agreed, not naturally fixed; language is unstable, prone to 'slippage', so meaning can never be fixed or understood.

Post-structuralist tendencies can be seen in the work of recent European writers, such as the ideological analysis of Gilles Deleuze and Foucault; and the feminism of Luce Irigaray and Helene Cixous. Although it does not truly offer a methodological form of analysis of texts in the same way that semiology and other methods do, it does provide an impetus to critically, and more thoroughly, examine the meaning systems in play.

Unfortunately, as with many of the post-war European theorists, the texts themselves are often impenetrable, since they play with the meanings of the texts themselves. This insinuation of no ultimate reading may suggest an (anti-social) anarchic individualism – yet, if taken with a pinch of salt, it can be useful.

POST-FEMINISM

Post-feminism can be seen as either a backlash against 1960s feminism, or a post-modern development of it, representing the interests of a younger generation of women who want equality, but also a 'feminine' sexuality.

Popular culture of the 1990s has produced many examples of the latter – 'laddettes', such as the Spice Girls, and the plethora of girl bands following on their coat tails; the short-lived Riot Grrrl movement; Courtney Love; and Madonna; to name but a few. These new role models are empowered, yet vulnerable, young women taking charge of their own sexuality and careers.

TV has produced many shows that can be seen as post-feminist, in that their central characters are successful in their profession, while remaining traditionally 'feminine', their lives incomplete without serial monogamy. The hunt for men is key to the narrative in shows like *Ally McBeal*, *Veronica's Closet* and *Grace Under Fire*. These could be seen as representing a new feminism or as hegemonic tokenism, whereby the dominant ideology offers women the opportunity to have it all (looks, career, family, sexuality) yet, in reality, the gulf between the experience of them and most women is huge. These shows fulfil 'politically correct' requirements, while still providing the voyeuristic pleasures of 1970s 'jiggle shows' like *Charlie's Angels*. It could be argued that women *are* playing central roles, but with little difference between these new feminist heroines and older shows like *Cagney and Lacey* and *Police Woman*. Ultimately, these women work for men within a patriarchal system, and crave 'normal' lives of heterosexual family consumption. The assertive, well-dressed, ambitious women of contemporary TV may be admirable role models, but post-feminism has difficulty addressing most women, who do not have these advantages.

Post-feminists have demonized 'second wave' feminists as 'sex negative', bra-burning, hairy lesbians; of course, this is no more representative of the range of feminist thought than the Spice Girls are representative of post-feminism. There is a fundamentally essentialist element to post-feminism, that significant biological, 'natural' differences exist between genders and transcend 'social constructionist' arguments (i.e. in direct opposition to the majority of feminist theory, which is rooted in sociology and psychology, and proposes a social construction of gender). Post-feminism can be seen as an outgrowth of post-modernism, as it is playful, inconsistent, confrontational and transgressive, unafraid of sacrificing sacred cows in order to confront texts with elements of pleasure, sexuality and shallowness. Its pre-eminent theorist is Camille Paglia (b. 1947), whose contentious personal attacks on many feminist theorists has brought her a greater notoriety than is common for academics. She brings a rock'n'roll sensibility to cultural theory, and with her charismatic personality, overt lesbianism and championing of causes like pornography, sado-masochism and paganism, she has rattled the cages of many in the field. Her essentialist argument conflicts with many second-wave feminists; her writing on pre-Christian goddess worship poses a link between the burgeoning female paganism of much recent feminism and a tribalistic, magical emphasis on culture, which has become popular.

Like many post-feminists – notably the anti-censorship movement – Paglia is sex-positive. Unlike many of the second wave, who advocated lesbianism as a way of escaping patriarchy, Paglia suggests that the pleasures of living with men outweigh the dangers. Paglia opposes French structuralist thinkers, such as Lacan, Foucault and Derrida, deriding them for their 'rigid foreign ideology' (Sim, 1998: 331).

Although post-feminism is often perceived as exciting, challenging and argumentative, it can be reactionary. As Sim argues, 'if there is any lesson to be learnt from post-feminism it is that the openness and celebration of post-modern relativism can be co-opted into its opposite, an uncritical and absolutist stance' (1998: 337). At times, Paglia's combative style spills over into an unbridled conservative stance: 'happy are those periods when marriage and religion are strong. System and order shelter us against sex and nature. Unfortunately we live in a time when the chaos of sex has broken into the open' ('Sexual Personae', cited on www.camillepaglia.com).

Like Leavis, some of Paglia's reputation emanates from personal charisma. Her 'rockist' approach to theory is clear in that her 'idol is Keith Richards, the Rolling Stones guitarist who made menacing music out of the Dionysian darkness never seen by the society-obsessed Foucault. The thunderous power chords of the hard rock smash the dreary little world of French theory' ('Sex, Art and American Culture': 228, cited on www.camillepaglia.com). Not only is her comparison invidious, but the Rolling Stones are very much part of the 1960s she so despises, rather than the sampled house/electro scene of the post-modern 1990s.

In a rant against her *bête noire* – second-wave feminists who oppose pornography – she pronounced '[Catherine] MacKinnon and [Andrea] Dworkin are victim mongers, ambulance chasers, and atrocity addicts. They are fanatics, zealots, and fundamentalists of the new feminist religion. Their alliance with the reactionary antiporn far right is no coincidence' (cited on www.camillepaglia.com). It is hard to see *whom* she admires, except herself: 'at this point I'm the leading woman intellectual in the world, there's no one else' (cited on www.camillepaglia.com).

As with post-feminism generally, her work is contradictory, obtuse and angry; multidisciplinary; amusing yet maddening. Post-feminism is too new and diverse to represent a comprehensible philosophy as yet, and may appear as little more than a quirky footnote in feminist history, although its offering of a wider ranges of female roles may be progressive. Post-modern feminists, such as Paglia and Julia Kristeva, propose a challenging notion of gender roles, rather than binary oppositions; while Andrea Dworkin and other more traditional feminist theorists deal with metanarratives of gender.

CHAPTER 27

Criticisms of Cultural Studies

Despite, or possibly because of, the boom in the field, it has attracted criticism. The leftist 'political economy' perspective, taken by Golding and Murdock, sees the subject as over-theorized and under-evidenced, while its relativistic, anti-canonical stance is guaranteed to enrage conservatives. Some of the critiques include the following.

- It is centred on popular film and TV, with little about other media – for example, newspapers – which remain popular and influential in western culture.
- Little exists on other aspects of life as it is lived – 'culture' is about pastimes, not life. Williams saw culture as 'ordinary', but little has been written about conditions of work or life. We spend less time in front of the TV and more time online, yet the field has little to say about education, pubs and other activities; and much appears to be so deliberately anti-empirical that it is in danger of cutting off its theoretical nose to spite its face.
- It has become as canonical as the Leavisian tradition that it rails against; the pantheon of Hall, Williams, Althusser *et al.* are constantly cited in the majority of texts, creating 'an emergence of an orthodoxy, a canon of founding fathers which was beginning to ossify an intellectual and academic community that insistently advocated openness, dialogue and inter-disciplinarity' (Ferguson and Golding, 1997).
- Cultural studies has not engaged with media policy. Despite the growth of the subject, coinciding with trends like worldwide erosion of public service broadcasting, media globalization, concentration of ownership etc., no coherent opposition, theory or research to

facilitate organized opposition has been offered. In its celebration of populism, cultural studies has, effectively, put its head in the intellectual sand; as its subject is, almost by definition, the consumption of texts, not their industrial production.

> Students emerging from cultural studies programmes are able to offer the most elegant and detailed discourses on Derrida or Lacanian theory, yet are seemingly unaware of current threats to public service broadcasting or legislative and industrial trends, eroding media plurality and democratic diversity. (Ferguson and Golding, 1997)

- It does not effectively use history, and ignores the rigorous study of archives etc., in favour of subjective anecdotes (Ferguson and Golding: xix).
- Value matters: it is one thing to show phone books and Shakespeare as being equivalent sign systems, but some absolutism is essential. If all things are of equal merit, then what is to be taught? What criteria must be established in order to understand or evaluate cultural products? There is a subgenre of theory, which is struggling to define value; no one would seriously suggest a return to rigid canons, but their lack raises serious problems for the discussion of culture.
- The exclusive focus on popular culture often serves to justify the writer's taste; and cultural theory can also be accused of crude populism, since it seems to ignore middle-brow and high culture.
- Mulhern points out that 'populism . . . insists on the active and critical element in popular cultural usages . . . tends to overlook the overwhelming historical realities' (Ferguson and Golding: xxiv).
- Cultural studies is virtually always represented as emanating from Britain and, to a lesser extent, France (and, in recent years, a little from the USA). This neglects traditions from other countries, such as Australia, and American 'material culture studies'.
- The post-modern retreat into defeat and meaninglessness can be seen as symptomatic of cultural studies having lost its way and its direction, with increasing numbers of books interpreting other culturalist texts, writing histories of the field, and relatively few doing anything new.
- Although the field does not value class power relations as much as gender, sexuality etc., it originally emerged from class-based analysis. Golding points out that it does not clearly elucidate how the means of production affects representation (Ferguson and Golding: 70). It has defined itself as opposing 'base and superstructure' Marxism and the 'political economy' debate by focusing – though not exclusively – on the 'cultural optimism' per-spective of subordinate groups actively decoding the hegemonic media in an opposi-tional, resistive manner.
- In the post-Thatcher era there has been a considerable reaction against relativism and post-modern concepts of value, multi-culturalism and so on, primarily from the right, yet no theorists of equal stature or rigour have come forward to challenge the hegemony of the left. It may be that the epistemological criteria established by culturalism would auto-matically exclude any political opposition; and, although ostensibly a leftist project, it is similar in many ways to right-wing 'end of ideology' paradigms. The common culture of

semiotic democracy proposed by Fiske and Bell, with pick-and-mix decoding, is closely related to the precepts of conservative free market choice.

- The scourge of the culturalist left has been Roger Scruton. This successor to Leavis is a pro-hunting, religious traditionalist, in whose vision the next generation is culturally doomed, due to a surfeit of shallow, meaningless mass culture. 'Their social aspirations are derived from adverts and pop, and no gratification is forbidden or postponed for long enough to offer a vision of the higher life' (Appleyard, 1998: 2–3). This ideologue of the British right considers that the devil's work is to destroy high culture and, thereby, religion, belief and criticism. Modern popular culture – which Scruton admits to knowing virtually nothing of – is dismissed as false, echoing the 1930s massification theorists. To Scruton, pop music is seen as the inept art of 'a new human type . . . it is an unreal ecstasy which also penetrates and pollutes what is real . . . current high art is not a new form of art, but an elaborate pretence at art' (Appleyard, 1998: 2–3). He made sweeping criticisms of the content and style of cultural studies, while simultaneously rejecting its politics and its sweeping away of canons: 'Theory repeats, in opaque and solidified prose, the assault on bourgeois values, patriarchy and the "official" culture that was led by the soixante-huitards. To encounter theory is to enter the literary equivalent of a socialist-realist museum' (Scruton, 1998: 131).

- Cultural theory is jargonistic, and often wilfully obscure. Due to the influence of French structuralism, in which the tyranny of language was to be solved by deliberate obscurantism, there is little work that does not reduce a keen undergraduate to tears of frustration with its 'psychobabble'. This can lead to vague concepts being taken as proven, with extensive use of metaphor and simile, e.g. 'Spirit of the Times' in 'Policing the Crisis' (Ferguson and Golding, 1997: xxii), and similar obfuscating terminologies.

- Relevant is the *cause célèbre* perpetrated by Alan Sokal who, in 1996, published an article in *Social Text* purporting to be a learned culturalist work, but which was actually a meaningless parody. He followed this with a book on the failings of post-modernity and many aspects of cultural theory, specifically its pretentious grasp of the physical sciences and its incomprehensible style. Sokal's stated aim was to 'make a . . . contribution to the critique of the admittedly nebulous zeitgeist that we have called postmodernism. To draw attention to the abuse of concepts . . . from maths and physics' (Sokal and Bricmont, 1998: 4). Unfortunately, Sokal's hoax was taken up by the right, as a general damning of theory as non-scientific or invalid, and their work has been held up as a case against anything relativistic or interpretative (Ree, 1998). Although the philosophy of science as propounded by Irigaray, Debray and others may lapse into prolixity, it is an area that cannot simply be dealt with on a positivistic, empirical level.

- Culturalism has represented a male history, especially in its origins. Williams, Hoggart and Thompson only made passing reference to women – it has largely been post-feminism that has attracted significant writing – and it has seldom focused on issues that impinge on the condition of women today, such as lack of child care, inequalities of employment, the virtual slavery of women in developing countries and so on, but rather has dwelt on Lacanian analyses of Madonna or, as Hall said about the late arrival of feminism to cultural studies, 'as a thief in the night it broke in, interrupted, made an unseemly noise, seized the time, and crapped on the table of cultural studies' (Sardar and Van Loon, 1997: 140).

In defence of cultural studies, however, it must be conceded that it introduced qualitative methods that 'mass communication research' perspectives had not been capable of dealing with. It has since been forced to take on many interpretative concepts – for example, culturalism questioned the long-standing middle-class biases of traditional media research, while working-class cultural history was sometimes seen by more traditional communication researchers as one of unimportant vulgarity.

Conclusion

Today, we live in era of 'culture wars' as the concepts made familiar by cultural studies enter everyday discourse. Key debates are foregrounded in diverse cultural arenas (schools, museums, media and politics) and the field becomes more consequential to the generations of semio-literate students who, without realizing it, have seen 'the death of the author', with the shift from modernist music made by creative individuals, such as the Beatles, to anonymous, technology-driven dance music.

Leavisian arguments over the increasing Americanization of European culture have, to an extent, been marginalized as 'American' and 'popular' culture have become synonymous. One can see how European culture has adapted US cultural products for its own specific needs and decoding practices, yet it is a subject that would stand disinterring. As eastern Europe increasingly consumes MTV culture, and American multi-nationals achieve increasing economic power with an unspoken cultural imperialism, it is an aspect of post-modern surrender that the European left rarely critiques this 'McDonaldization'.

A tendency is the reclaiming of previously unconsidered cultural artefacts. In *British Low Culture*, Leon Hunt deconstructs topics as varied as *On the Buses* and 1970s British sex-exploitation films, making the point that, today, 'it is the middlebrow . . . which has been recast as the low, the indefensible' (Hunt, 1998: 160). Madonna, 'Carry On' films and the Spice Girls *et al.*, have been recycled as cultural heroes of the workers, yet Celine Dion and Andrew Lloyd Webber have yet to be similarly heralded. Hunt also makes the point that, apart from a minority of academics, the world does not treat popular culture with the respect that it might deserve; in reality, popular culture is actually treated with a distinct lack of seriousness – at least on its own terms. It becomes, rather, 'a source of populist credibility, self-serving nostalgia . . . and of intellectual idleness' (Hunt, 1998: 160) – that is, though aspects of culturalism have trickled down into the wider consciousness, we are still some way from dealing with the lived experience of the majority adequately, or equally, to that of high culture. As critics of post-modernism suggest, it is possible that the old barriers of class, cultural capital and 'value' are still firmly with us.

As for the future, research promises closer links between culturalism and sociology.

> Much audience theory remains over concerned with the microscopic worldview of
> socially dispersed viewers . . . the semiotic focus upon the production of meaning was

inadequately appreciative of the social function . . . media theory should seek to inter-relate consumerist rights to private pleasure, and wider, more public forms of rights and obligations. (Stevenson, 1995: 113)

Moves exist within cultural theory to rediscover more empirical and positivist method-ologies (Ferguson and Golding, 1997: xxiii).

It is widely considered within education that it is only a matter of time before cultural studies is offered at school, for it (together with media studies) has been one of the most popular and successful degree options. There has been exponential growth throughout Britain, and to a lesser extent in Europe and the USA. Cultural studies is the dominant paradigm for analysis of media, literature and a myriad of aspects of culture, and both agreement and dissent co-exist within a field still in flux. It is increasingly used in debates about national culture, and is appearing in many contexts under a variety of guises.

With competing streams of post-feminism, post-modernism, post-post-modernism . . . ad infinitum, there is increasing fragmentation within cultural theory. Yet there is also a growing consensus; practitioners may not agree on *what* it is, but arguments about it are producing some of the most interesting work on culture within western societies today, and it is affect-ing every aspect of those societies. The culturalist approach has advantages and dis-advantages, for there is a necessity for both positivist and phenomenological methods of media analysis.

Admittedly, there are serious lacunae, which are only likely to be addressed if funding becomes available for a subject still not taken totally seriously by the academy. For example, why has there been virtually no serious interpretation of phenomena like rave culture and Ecstasy, or even pleasures like modern evenings out? Cultural studies must address new areas away from popular TV. One also has to pose the question that, if the field is so popular, why are there so few significant associations or journals devoted to the analysis of popular TV? Cultural studies remains a political project with a socialist focus, centred on ethnic minorities, women, gays, the working class and other groups seen as oppressed. It studies *popular* culture above all; however, a gap exists, for little research on the class/taste rela-tions of high art has been undertaken. Yet the field will undoubtedly continue to go on boom-ing for the foreseeable future.

SUMMARY

- **Cultural studies is inherently political – specifically Marxist – dealing as it does with social relations within and outside texts.**

- **It has grown rapidly out of literary theory to become a major force within European/US media/cultural analysis.**

- **It has given rise to highly influential critical offshoots, such as post-modernism, post-feminism and post-colonialism.**

- In recent times, concentrating on readings and social uses of media texts, it has focused on the role of ideology within society and the texts it produces.

- Today, it is inter-disciplinary and increasingly variegated in its approaches; and, although it has methodological failings, continues to be highly influential in all spheres of culture.

Further Reading

Barker, C. (2000) *Cultural Studies*. London: Sage

Brooker, P. (1999) *A Concise Glossary of Cultural Theory*. London: Edward Arnold

Connor, S. (1997) *Postmodernist Culture*. Oxford: Blackwell

Edgar, A. and Sedgwick, P. (eds) (1999) *Key Concepts in Cultural Theory*. London: Routledge

Story, J. (1993) *An Introduction to Cultural Theory and Popular Culture*. Hemel Hempstead: Prentice Hall

Strinati, D. (2000) *An Introduction to Studying Popular Culture*. London: Routledge

Useful Websites

Daniel Chandler's MCS site (perhaps the best media studies site) is at:
http://www.aber.ac.uk/~mcswww/functions/mcs.html

An excellent cultural theory site:
www.theory.org

Voice of the shuttle (cultural studies-based site):
http://vos.ucsb.edu/shuttle/media.html

University of Iowa communication studies site:
www.uiowa.edu/~commstud/resources/cultstdy papers.html

Study of popular culture:
www.popcultures.com/articles.htm

More culturalist resources:
www.cultsock.ndirect.co.uk/muhome/cshtml/index.html

References

Abercrombie, N., Hill, S. and Turner, B. (1980) *The Dominant Ideology Thesis*. London: George Allen & Unwin

Alvarado, M., Gutch, R. and Wollen. T. (eds) (1987) *Learning the Media*. London: Macmillan

Appignanesi, R. and Garratt, C. (1995) *Postmodernism for Beginners*. Cambridge: Icon

Appleyard, B. (1998) The truth about the philosopher. *Sunday Times* 12 December 1998, 2–3

Barker, M. and Beezer, A. (1992) *Reading into Cultural Studies*. London: Routledge

Barry, P. (1995) *Beginning Theory*. Manchester: Manchester University Press

Bottomore, T. (1984) *The Frankfurt School*. London: Routledge

Curran, J. (1990) The new revisionism in mass communication research. In *European Journal of Communication* 5(2)

Curran, J., Gurevitch, M. and Woolacott, J. (eds) (1977) *Mass Communications and Society*. London: Edward Arnold

During, S. (1993) *The Cultural Studies Reader*. London: Routledge

Easthope, A. (1993) *Contemporary Film Theory*. London: Longman

Ferguson, M. and Golding, P. (1997) *Cultural Studies in Question*. London: Sage

Fiske, J. (1987) *Television Culture*. London: Routledge

Hall, S. and Whannel, P. (1964) *The Popular Arts*. London: Hutchinson Educational

Hardt, H. (1992) *Critical Communication Studies*. London: Routledge

Hunt, L. (1998) *British Low Culture From Safari Suits to Sexploitation*. London: Routledge

Lash, S. (1990) *Sociology of Postmodernism*. London: Routledge

Lechte, J. (1994) *Fifty Key Contemporary Thinkers*. London: Routledge

McGuigan, J. (1992) *Cultural Populism*. London: Routledge

Milner, A. (1994) *Contemporary Cultural Theory, An Introduction*. London: University College London Press

Price, S. (1998) *Media Studies*. Harlow: Longman

Ree, J. (1998) The storm is put back in its teacup. *Times Higher Education Supplement* 10 July, 22

Sardar, Z. and Van Loon, B. (1997) *Cultural Studies for Beginners*. Cambridge: Icon Books

Scruton, R. (1998) *An Intelligent Person's Guide to Modern Culture*. London: Duckworth

Sim, S. (ed.) (1995) *A–Z Guide to Modern Literary and Cultural Theorists*. Hemel Hempstead: Harvester Wheatsheaf

Sim, S. (ed.) (1998) *The Icon Critical Dictionary of Postmodern Thought*. Cambridge: Icon Books

Sokal, A. and Bricmont, J. (1998) *Intellectual Impostures*. London: Profile Books

Stevenson, N. (1995) *Understanding Media Cultures*. London: Sage

Stone, R. (ed.) (1998) *Key Sociological Thinkers*. London: Macmillan

Storey, J. (1993) *An Introductory Guide to Cultural Theory and Popular Culture*. Hemel Hempstead: Harvester Wheatsheaf

Storey, J. (1997) *An Introduction to Cultural Theory and Popular Culture* (second edn). Hemel Hempstead: Harvester Wheatsheaf

Strinati, D. (1995) *An Introduction to Theories of Popular Culture*. London: Routledge

Swingewood, A. (1977) *The Myth of Mass Culture*. London: Macmillan

Turner, G. (1992) *British Cultural Studies*. London: Routledge

Representation, Identity and the Media

Alina Bernstein

Introduction

Media **representations** have been the focus of much scholarly attention within media studies. This section opens with a discussion of theoretical aspects of the concept of 'representation', emphasizing the relationship ideology–reality–representation (Chapter 28). One of the most widely studied and discussed areas of media representation is that of **gender** and this constitutes a large proportion of my discussion in Chapters 29–30. The following chapter (Chapter 31) discusses the less studied, but by no means less important, topic of **race** representation. These discussions are linked to television genres and accompanied by examples from a variety of television programmes.

Identity, and the media's role in relation to this concept, is intertwined into the discussion in all the chapters of this section, since representations are assumed to affect the formation of identity. However, in the final chapter (Chapter 32) of this section, this complex concept becomes the focus of discussion, linking it mainly to the impact of television portrayals on identity as discussed in the literature dealing with gender (especially women) and race.

CHAPTER 28

Representation and the Media

DEFINING REPRESENTATION

Much academic attention has been paid over the years to the concept of representation. In essence, representation refers to the process by which signs and symbols are made to convey certain meanings. Importantly, this term refers to the signs and symbols that claim to stand for, or re-present, some aspect of 'reality', such as objects, people, groups, places, events, social norms, cultural identities and so on. These representations may be constructed in any medium (see, for example, Hall, 1997) and are an essential feature of social life; they allow us to communicate and make sense of our surroundings. The focus of the discussion in this, and the following chapters, however, will be on their construction in the mass media, an area that has been central to media studies.

In this respect, it is important to stress that underlying these discussions is the theoretical assumption that contemporary mass media preserve, transmit and create important cultural information. According to Gerbner's Cultivation Theory, for example, the more a viewer watches television, the more s/he will form expectations about reality based on the represented world rather than the experienced world. Thus, the assumption is that how members of society see themselves, how they are viewed, and even treated, by others is determined to a great extent by their media representation (Dyer, 1993). Such ways of thinking attribute a great – in many cases harmful – influence to the media, although nowadays it is clear to most media researchers that these effects must be studied and not assumed. However, the perceived power of representations is in fact the reason why it is important to study this aspect of the media (see Dyer, 1993).

The focus for media research in this context is the ideological role of representing and representation – the ways in which representations are made to seem 'natural'. Thus this chapter includes a discussion of the relationship ideology–reality–representation.

Media representations can be approached from various angles. For instance, representation can be discussed in relation to wide themes such as class, race, ethnicity and gender. In fact, one of the most widely studied and discussed areas of media representation is that of gender, women in particular, and this will constitute a large proportion of my own discussion in Chapters 29 and 30. However, not only wide themes have been studied in relation to representation, more specific ones such as the representation of politics, environment, war and conflict, childhood, old age, occupations and so on have also been explored.

An alternative approach is to study different media, such as television, film and newspapers. In my discussion, television will be the medium most referred to as it is considered to be the most widely consumed and most influential mass medium of our times. Referring to this medium means looking at a variety of television contents (see the discussion of fiction and non-fiction below). A possible further approach to the study of representation is generic – namely, studying gender in sitcoms or soap operas, race in advertisements and so on.

Before focusing on particular issues of representation, a discussion of several related concepts – such as 'reality', 'realism' and stereotyping – is required.

REALITY AND REPRESENTATION

Representational theories offer a critique of the media's construction of reality; they refer to the relationship between the ideological and the real. According to these theories, it is necessary to draw a clear distinction between reality and its media representation, and to realize that by mediating for their audiences the 'real world', the media create a version of reality for them. (In fact in every respect – not only when it comes to media representations – 'reality' can only be 'known' through ideology.)

Television is a medium in which representations appear to resemble reality more closely than in any other (see Corner, 1999) and yet audiences, in fact, consume images that stand in place of real things and people. As Fiske (1991) puts it:

> The core argument in theories of representation is that, despite appearances, television does not represent (re-present) a piece of reality, but rather produces or constructs it. Reality does not exist in the objectivity of empiricism, but is a product of discourse. The television camera and microphone do not record reality, but encode it: the encoding produces a sense of reality that is ideological. What is re-presented, then, is not reality but ideology, and the effectivity of this ideology is enhanced by the iconicity of television by which the medium purports to situate its truth claim in the objectivity of the real, and thus disguise the fact that any 'truth' that it produces is that of ideology, not reality. (Fiske, 1991: 55–6)

Different writers emphasize different aspects of this process, but what seems obvious to them is that representations are selective, limited or framed, and mediated (McQueen, 1998; see also Baker, online; Dyer, 1985; Grossberg et al., 1998). Representations are selective simply in the sense that, out of a large amount of information, very little is being actually presented by the media. In the much-studied case of television news, for example, only very few stories are selected to become part of a given news programme and even these items are edited down from many hours of footage to several minutes. Thus, a large amount of alternative information is being excluded. Indeed, the question of what of all possible, and conflicting, perspectives is being represented and/or what has been left out needs always to be asked. In most audience consumption it is safe to assume that these questions are generally forgotten. Related to this is the fact that representations are limited or framed as, for instance, the very fact a television camera is positioned in front of 'reality' means that only a fraction of it is being focused on.

Representations are mediated; this is a fact that audiences of fiction programme are assumed to be aware of (as with the case of 'canned laughter' being added to sitcom soundtracks). However, when it comes to non-fiction programmes, like documentaries and news, it is more likely that audiences believe the information they are getting is 'true' and are less aware of these programmes being mediated, for example, by the elements of a news story being organized to introduce a coherent narrative (see the further discussion of fiction and non-fiction below).

Thus, it should be evident that 'reality', as it is represented by the media, is an interpreted and constructed reality. This, as mentioned above, links into the concept of ideology, which in essence means that every society maintains its continuing existence, its institutions and structures of power, by 'getting people to accept a particular way of thinking and seeing the world that makes the existing organization of social relations appear natural and inevitable' (Grossberg et al., 1998: 177). To this end, the defining of reality – indeed its representation – in a certain way is crucial as it is about social power. As in contemporary society the media are probably the most important producers of meaning, 'when they make claims about the way the world is, they become powerful ideological institutions' (Grossberg et al., 1998: 182) and thus also a site for social struggles.

Two further points should be made in relation to this discussion. First, that there is an underlying assumption that representations mean the same thing to all audiences – a notion that has been challenged by media studies. In fact, nowadays the question is being asked as to what texts, and representations within them, mean to audiences (I will look at this in more depth in the following chapters).

The second issue that has to be addressed is the question of what exactly 'reality' means nowadays. Discussing the representation of reality implies that an objective reality exists separately from its representations, which, in fact, is a paradox.

REALISM

A term often linked to the discussion of reality and representation is 'realism'. It is important, as the more the realism of a text is being accepted by audiences the less they are likely to question the representations it offers, and the more these representations will seem natural.

The term realism 'often refers merely to the extent to which representational details resemble or concur with the knowledge of the object (which may be an emotion, theme or idea as well as a thing) that we already have' (O'Sullivan et al., 1994: 257). However, this much discussed concept is 'a relatively controversial one, as is shown by the fragmentation of the concept into more and more subdivisions: classic realism, social realism, empirical realism, documentary realism, psychological realism, emotional realism, neo-realism' (O'Donnell, 1999: 215). (For a more complete discussion of various aspects of 'realism' on television see Fiske (1987). Indeed, O'Donnell argues (1999: 215) that 'any attempt to define "realism" is an attempt to define the evanescent'.)

What needs to be stressed in this context is that realism is merely a convention (see, for example, Abercrombie, 1996; Chandler, 1994). For example, for audiences, a musical soundtrack is accepted as part of a 'realistic' film or television programme, although in 'reality' there is no burst of romantic music when two people are about to kiss.

Within media studies, realism has been discussed much more in relation to fiction than to non-fiction programmes (see the further discussion of this below) as, in fiction, the feel of reality needs to be constructed. One genre referred to quite often in this context has been soap operas, especially British ones, as there are 'claims that they reflect "the everyday life" of their viewers and that they will deal with "highly topical" issues' (O'Donnell, 1999: 216; see also Abercrombie, 1996; Geraghty, 1995 and 1996). Contrary to American soaps or the Latino-American telenovelas, British soaps are perceived as being committed to the tradition of social realism, associated with the 1950s British kitchen sink films and dramas. Importantly, according to Chandler (1994): 'Social realism emphasizes "relevance" – a sympathetic portrayal of everyday social problems recognizable to the working class.' In a soap like *EastEnders*, 'trouble is taken to make characters and sets authentic so that the illusion is created that these are real people in a real east London setting' (Abercrombie, 1996: 27). There are many further elements that enhance this 'feeling' of being true to life, such as the passage of time, which appears to reflect real time (Geraghty, 1995).

Abercrombie (1996) suggests that the critical question raised by the 'convention of realism is then: is there a *systematic* exclusion of particular features of the world from television?' (1996: 28). Several writers argue that there is (see, for example, Tulloch, 1990), and that this has a particularly powerful effect since the realist convention seems to reflect the 'real' world. Some even go as far as suggesting that 'television presents one reality and audiences are persuaded to accept it as the only reality' (Abercrombie, 1996: 28).

FICTION AND NON-FICTION

From the above discussions it follows that there cannot be absolute 'reality' in any media text. However, the media include both fiction and non-fiction contents and although the clear distinctions between the two have been eroding, especially in television contents, the differences between them should be emphasized when discussing representations.

It seems common sense that audiences know that pictures shown on television, for example, are not 'real'. In fact, it can be argued that audiences decode mass-mediated images with, at least, some degree of understanding that much of television's content deals with the world of fiction and decode it as such, and yet it cannot be assumed that, while consuming fictional contents, audiences are necessarily aware of the ideological aspects of these texts, of what is represented, and how or what shared knowledge these texts rely on.

Furthermore, although it can be assumed that much of the time people know the difference between fact and fiction, this assumption is problematic. It becomes particularly problematic when television programmes are presented as non-fiction (for which, read 'real') as in the case of the American daytime talk shows of the Jerry Springer variety. Indeed, as Orbe and Cornwell (1999) state: 'tensions and contradictions emerge when "realistic" documentary-type television, fronting as accurate representations, contain codes and signifiers that reinforce stereotypes and negative images of diverse members of society' (Orbe and Cornwell, 1999: 1).

When discussing the media's claim on reality, on showing the world 'as it is', it is especially important to draw attention to the fact, mentioned before, that news, current affairs pro-grammes, documentaries and similar seemingly 'real' representations of reality can repre-sent but a version of 'reality'. Within media research, such issues have been widely studied in relation to news, proving from various perspectives that news is just as mediated and con-structed as any other content and, indeed, shows a particular version of 'reality' (see, for example, Cohen *et al.*'s 1996 study of the Eurovision News Exchange).

In discussing documentaries, Downes and Miller (1998) put it very clearly and amusingly:

> In making a documentary about lions, the programme-makers have done two things simul-taneously. They have brought lions to our living room, thereby extending our experience of the real world, and they have selected for us what they think it is important for us to know about lions, thereby restricting our experience of the real world. What is selected for inclusion in the documentary depends on the viewpoint being taken, and the points that the producers wish to convey to the audience. (Downes and Miller, 1998: 64)

Downes and Miller (1998) emphasize that other representations of lions may be presented to the audience at other times, as different programme-makers would produce different programmes about the same topic, be it lions or indeed any other theme. More-over, even if audiences are exposed to a variety of programmes (and representations), all of them put together can give only a selection of information.

Thus, in documentaries, or news and current affairs programmes, a selection is made of representations of places, ideas and people. Although these texts are not necessarily created with the explicit intent to promote certain beliefs and ideologies, they inevitably do so. For instance, news programmes can reflect certain viewpoints not as a result of a con-scious decision but because of the people who work for a given news organization (see further discussion of this in relation to representations of gender and race).

The point I wished to emphasize in this section, although these issues have already been mentioned and will be discussed throughout the following chapters, is that all media texts are constructed and that, to varying degrees, both fiction and non-fiction contents construct representations that can reinforce (and in some cases contradict) audiences' understanding of reality.

STEREOTYPING AND REPRESENTATION

In order to represent 'reality', codes and conventions of presentation have to be used (Dyer, 1993); without them, media texts can hardly be expected to be understood by audiences. One of the most referred to of these in this context is stereotyping, a much-mentioned con-cept in relation to representation (some, like Burton (1990), refer also to 'type' and 'arche-type' as levels of representation). Although a very familiar term, in both academic and public discourse, it is necessary to make clear what it stands for in media studies.

The word 'stereotype' was the name of a printer's metal plate that was used as an original from which to print exact copies (McQueen, 1998). Today, when the term stereotyping is used in relation to the media, and in fact society in general, it means that an assumption has been made that certain people are not individuals, but the same as each other. Within media studies it has come to mean 'the continuous repetition of ideas about groups of people in the media. It involves taking an easily grasped feature or characteristic assumed to belong to a group and making it representative of the whole group' (McQueen, 1998: 141). Thus, by a few strokes of simple descriptions, it is possible to invoke for audiences a 'type' of person that corresponds with pre-existing knowledge (see also Dyer, 1993). Importantly, as already mentioned, this simplified – or even oversimplified – representation becomes established through years of repetition in the media and thus also instantly recognizable.

Although, as should be clear by now, the discussion in this, and the following chapters, will focus on stereotyping in relation to the media, it is important to stress that it has been studied in other disciplines – such as social psychology – as well. Indeed, this simplification is part of our daily lives; we use it to make sense of real persons or groups, which are far more complicated. The 'Implicit Personality Theory', for example (see discussion in Baker, online), explains the way humans categorize people into types in order to simplify the task of person perception. Thus, stereotyping is something all humans do, indeed, people might even hold stereotypical views of their own social group (see Alvarado et al., 1987). Put simply, it can be argued, then, that the media stereotype because human beings stereotype.

Some groups view their stereotyped, negative media representation as harmful, and even destructive. As these images are repeated, and audiences are exposed to them in a multitude of texts, then according to those who attribute much influence to these representations, they can cause – or reinforce – negative tendencies towards certain groups, even leading to discrimination and racism. Moreover, when a perceived idea of a certain group matches the 'reality' of media representations a powerful stereotype is being reinforced. According to this view, audiences accept this limited picture of a group and do not question it.

At the other end of the spectrum, media professionals would probably argue – especially with regard to fiction – that production conditions, financial constraints or even particular narratives demand that some characters or people are drawn only with the broadest of strokes. Importantly, these are based on the assumption that the audience's attitudes and values are those of the mainstream.

In fact, some scholars believe that stereotypes are not, by definition, bad; the implicit value judgements they reveal depend on the way they are used (Burton, 1990). Furthermore, they would argue that stereotypes are not always 'false', necessarily about 'others', always concerned with oppressed or minority groups, or indeed unchanging (Tessa Perkins, 1979, as discussed in McQueen, 1998).

Yet, others do insist that stereotypes are 'simple, negative and inaccurate, and because they are so loosely related to the "real world", they are not easily changed by alternative evidence' (Alvarado et al., 1987: 203). Moreover, these attitudes express hostility towards minority groups, which, are usually in a weaker social position and thus work to the advantage of dominant groups, making their views seem 'natural' or 'normal' and not the result of a systematic process of construction. Indeed, 'stereotyping has been described as one strategy amongst many used to secure the power and influence of the dominant groups in society' (McQueen, 1998: 158). Put differently, stereotyping is an ideological process that works to the advantage of the more powerful groups in society (see the further discussion below).

This might mean that representations in general and stereotypes in particular will never change, and yet it can be argued that representations are changing over time and even that the media respond to changes in society (and do not simply reinforce beliefs and attitudes), and therefore that representations and stereotypes already have and will continue to change to some extent (see the discussion in the following chapters).

Overall, within media studies much attention has been paid to the stereotyping, in both fiction and non-fiction texts, of various categories. These, in most cases, use content analysis as their prime research method (McQueen, 1998). Among the most researched categories are gender (see Chapters 29–30), sexuality (see Chapter 30), class and race (see Chapter 31). Many further categories have also been examined in this context, such as age (both young and old – see McQueen, 1998), occupations and so on.

To further clarify the above discussion I would like to link it to one example that has been studied within the area of mediated sport, and that is national stereotypes and the coverage of sport.

National Stereotypes and the Coverage of Sport

As I have already mentioned, stereotyping is part of non-fiction contents as well as fictional ones. The coverage of sport can serve as an example in this case. Within the realm of sport, there exists an extremely thin line from generalizations to 'crude national stereotypes' (Whannel, 1992: 30). Moreover, according to Whannel, such stereotyping 'can make an easy transition into out-and-out racism' (1992: 30). To illustrate, he draws on the example of a British commentator who described the Indian hockey team as 'being on a bonus of 100 popadoms per man' (1992: 30). He proceeds to explain that, 'The underlying message is that people less competent than the British are comic, erratic and happy-go-lucky.'

Blain, Boyle and O'Donnell (1993) conducted several large-scale studies of the images of nations through the sports coverage in the European media (subsequent studies have been carried out by, among others, Wagg (1995), and Boyle and Haynes (1996)). In their studies of the press coverage of Italia 90, and the press and television coverage of Wimbledon 1991, they found many examples of stereotypical images of nations and athletes who participated in these competitions. In their interpretation of these findings, they conclude that the behaviour of both the participants and their fans, read like 'an index of the nature of national characteristics' (Blain et al., 1993: 57; see also Wagg, 1995).

The most extreme cases of stereotypical portrayal of nations may be found in the English popular press, which routinely expresses actual xenophobia, not only in relation to sport (Blain et al., 1993; Wagg, 1991). To give one example, 'while the press throughout Europe referred to the Egyptians as "the Pharaohs" . . . the English Sun is not willing to dally with the glorious days of Egyptian history. "Charlton's Heroes Stymied by Camel Men" it says acidly' (Blain et al., 1993: 63).

Although the English popular press is an extreme example, other European and North

American media were found to express a stereotypical view of other nations. For instance, they found that, throughout Europe, the German team was presented as the personification of 'discipline, dedication to work and reliability' (Blain et al., 1993: 69). Additionally, this team was described as a 'machine team'. However, their findings also showed that a 'problem' may arise when the stereotype 'does not fit', such as when the German team displayed much flair and individual skill. Journalists, however, have their solutions, and 'rather than simply throw overboard these ascriptions of national character' they find bizarre and revealing metaphors to explain such a phenomenon; for instance, 'Germany speaks Italian' (Blain et al., 1993: 69).

The Italia 90 Football World Cup provided the media with an opportunity to describe a successful African team, Cameroon. In this case, many stereotypes revealed themselves, most notably, the Cameroon footballers were described as 'joyful, uninhibited, enthusiastic' (Blain et al., 1993: 71), and like the Brazilians before them, the Cameroonians were also credited with bringing 'magic' to the game. Blain et al. (1993) see this as:

> . . . closely connected for European commentators with the magic of childhood, but it is not simply the childhood of the individual – this discourse connects with well-established European discourses of the childhood of Man, set in some idealized pre-industrial non-European society where people were free of the constraints of modern living and able to act in accordance with their instincts. (Blain et al., 1993: 72)

Moreover, their play was regarded in many newspapers as 'temperamental', 'inventive', 'creative' and, above all, as we have seen, 'joyful'. In extreme cases, the Cameroonian style of play was presented as 'irrational', 'as befits children below the age of reason' (Blain et al., 1993: 72). Indeed, the Cameroonians were described as football's version of the 'savage infant'. Not surprisingly, then, when Cameroon was eventually eliminated from the tournament, the coverage attributed this to the very same characteristics that made the team attractive in the first place – its 'ingenuousness . . . lack of professionalism and polish, even [its] lack of cynicism, in short, a style of football which had not yet grown up' (Blain et al., 1993: 76). This example also highlights the fact that the point of reference of the studied coverage is fundamentally a western one.

In a similar vein, the Latins (in this case, mainly the South Americans) were described with the aid of clichés like 'calypso-footballers' (Costa Ricans) and 'samba kings' (Brazilians). All these nations were presented as being passionate, a passion that 'binds the South Americans with their European Latin cousins, in particular the Italians, [and] shows how the same hot blood runs through their veins' (Blain et al., 1993: 70). The Italians, in turn, were portrayed by 'volcanic' metaphors.

This stereotypical portrayal was also found with regard to individual athletes, although it was less evident than in national-team sports. For example, in the European press coverage of Wimbledon 1991, Blain et al. (1993) found that newspapers referred to the tennis players as 'representatives' of their countries. Two main sets of discourses of national stereotypes were found here: the Swedes and the Germans. The major component of discourses of Swedishness was coolness; Bjorn Borg was always described as an 'iceberg'; several years on, Stefan Edberg was also referred to as a 'Swedish iceberg'. Interestingly, the Swedish newspapers themselves viewed this notion of 'Nordic coldness' as a foreign generalization. Similarly, the Germans were consistently described in accordance with the 'machine' metaphor, an important element of this being the notion of efficiency. In this case as well, the British tabloids represent the extreme; they were found to concentrate on 'notions of violence, aggression, greed and arrogance, pleasure in inflicting pain' (Blain *et al.*, 1993: 146–7).

From the examples discussed, it becomes evident that in both print and visual media coverage of sport, nations are portrayed in terms that can only be described as stereo-typical. In relation to sport, the effects of such coverage were studied over 30 years by Halloran, who addressed the specific question of the development in young people of images, knowledge and attitudes concerning other people and other countries in relation to the Olympic ideals. Halloran (1990) concludes that, among other issues, the media are more likely to play a part in the formation of attitudes about people from another continent than they are with regard to attitudes of neighbours, or even to people from another country they have visited or with which they have some connection.

This chapter has examined media representation, relating this much-researched and discussed area of media research to issues such as ideology, reality and stereotypes. As mentioned, a large body of theory and research in this context looks at the representation of gender by the media.

CHAPTER 29

Gender and the Media: the Representation of Women and Femininity(ies)

INTRODUCTION – GENDER AND THE MEDIA

Gender has been defined as 'the cultural differentiation of male from female' (O'Sullivan *et al.*, 1994). Thus, while the term 'sex' refers to the fact that women and men are born different in physiological and biological terms, 'gender' refers to the cultural meaningfulness attributed to these natural differences. Especially since the 1960s, much academic (and at times public) attention has been paid to the idea that the social definitions of 'femininity' and 'masculinity' are culturally constructed and have to do with ideology and power rather than being 'natural'. Indeed, as Craig (1993) emphasizes, the definition of the terms 'gender', 'masculine' and 'feminine' is based on cultural expectations of behaviour. This idea has been discussed from many perspectives, drawing attention to the macro level of the social powers at play to the micro level of the psychological construction of identity.

Beginning with early feminist writing, the media have been considered central social 'players' in this context. According to this argument, the media, and television in particular, present on a daily basis images of femininity(ies) and masculinity(ies) that do not simply reflect 'natural' sex differences, but actively participate in the symbolic discourse of gender, a discourse that is rooted in power relations. Importantly, based mainly on content analysis, these media representations – discussed particularly with regard to women – have been viewed as harmful images and as leading to sexist socialization, this although some writers have cautioned of these effects being assumed rather than studied.

Writers approaching the topic of gender and the role of the media in relation to it, tended to focus on the amount and type of the media portrayal of women and femininity. For a long while, studies that addressed issues relating to the representation of men and masculinity did so only when juxtaposing it with the representation of women. In recent years, it has become clear that such an approach might mean ignoring the full picture and that masculinity(ies) should not be perceived as unproblematic. That has been reflected by an emerging study of men and masculinity, clearly influenced by feminist thought (see further discussion in Chapter 30).

For the sake of discussion clarity, the current chapter directs attention to the arguments and literature focused on the media representation of women, femininity(ies) and the related issues of women's place in the media industry and the reception of media content by women. The following chapter will focus on the representation of men, masculinity(ies), gays and lesbians. It should, however, be emphasized that these discussions are in fact completely intertwined.

FEMINIST MEDIA STUDIES

As a consequence of the feminist movement, academic attention has been directed to the media's role in making women's place in society seem 'natural'. Over the years feminist media theory and research has become plentiful and has influenced media studies in general by, for instance, focusing on the private, domestic female sphere of television reception (see, for example, the discussion in Mumford, 1998).

From very early on, feminist analysis attempted to uncover the constructed messages behind the representations of women in the media, attributing to these images a crucial role in the perception of real-life women and thus the maintaining of a social status quo. In her pioneering work, Gaye Tuchman (1978) concluded that women are 'symbolically annihilated by the media through absence, condemnation or trivialisation'. Indeed, many of the studies that followed (see summary in McQueen, 1998) were content analyses which showed that women are relatively under-represented in the media – which, in feminist writing, is perceived as marginalizing them – and that the portrayal of women in the media trends to sexualize, commodify and trivialize them (for a detailed account of these studies see Gunter, 1995). Overall, these studies show clearly that women are not simply represented as different from, but as lesser than, men. Importantly, as Brunsdon *et al.* emphasize:

many of the initial feminist dealings with television were, in fact, calls to action growing out of a deep conviction that women's oppression was very much related to mass media representations and that change was not only urgent, but possible. (Brunsdon *et al.*, 1997: 5)

Over the years further content analysis studies have been concerned with the general notion that 'women are not being portrayed accurately, that representations of women in the media do not reflect real women and their roles in contemporary society' (McQueen, 1998: 146). In fact, to date, feminist research is still often engaged in content analysis – qualitative as well as quantitative – which, for instance, shows that although media representations of women have changed over the last decades – and much of US and UK television content features strong women, single mothers and other 'female types who are integral to feminist critique and culture' (Brunsdon *et al.*, 1997: 1) – in many cases women's ultimate goal continues to be portrayed as romance and marriage (see, for example, Ally of *Ally McBeal*). On the other hand – which in fact places television in a 'no-win' situation – some believe that 'the media, in a desire to be "politically correct", actually overcompensate for women and frequently allot them roles in the media that do not reflect the reality of male–female relations outside television studios' (McQueen, 1998: 149; see, for example, the character of Amanda in *Melrose Place vis-à-vis* the discussion of women's place in the advertising industry, below).

As 'some of the limitations of content analysis have been recognized by the researchers themselves, and in some cases properly addressed' (McQueen, 1998: 146), 'since the 1970s, feminists have become increasingly interested in television as something more than a bad object, something that offers a series of lures and pleasures, however limited its repertoire of female roles' (Brunsdon *et al.*, 1997: 1). This is related to a different methodology a 'hybrid of sociological, anthropological, and in some cases, historical method, and is generally concerned with the way women view television, how they interpret it, and/or how the context of domesticity relates to these modes of reception' (Brunsdon *et al.*, 1997: 8). This, it should be noted, cannot – and in recent years has not been – separated from the analysis of texts (see the further discussion in Chapter 32) as, indeed, is the production context (see discussion below).

Currently it is clear that feminist research includes a plurality of approaches and addresses issues that have been ignored in the past, such as representations of black femininity after years of being concerned mainly with white, middle-class, heterosexual, western women (for comprehensive discussions of the development of feminist media studies see Brunsdon *et al.*, 1997; Geraghty and Lusted, 1998; van Zoonen, 1994).

In the context of this brief general discussion it is worth considering some specific examples of media representations of women and femininity(ies). Since the study of television – perceived as a 'prime medium' for cultural representation (Mumford, 1998) – has generated a large body of work in this area, the discussion below will focus on some of the more widely studied television genres.

GENRE AND THE REPRESENTATION OF WOMEN

Two genres that have been identified, and in some cases defended, by feminist writers, as women-targeted genres are soap operas and situation comedies (sitcoms) (Brunsdon *et al.*, 1997). However, it can be argued that 'even genres that were once widely male identified have been touched by feminist sentiments' (Brunsdon *et al.*, 1997: 1). For example, in the past, police and crime series – such as *The Sweeney* – represented individualistic, active male protagonists whose qualities were contrasted with those of women. Those who were defined as good were 'typically passive and helpless, emotional and even hysterical' (Abercrombie, 1996: 72) and when they tried to help the hero they often ended up having to be rescued by him. On the other hand, women represented as active often turned out to be bad characters, thus the active, forceful qualities of the male hero were 'pointed up by the passivity of the women – or their evil activity' (Abercrombie, 1996: 72). However, in later years, series like the internationally distributed and successful *Prime Suspect* featured a very different action heroine in a detective role (Brunsdon *et al.*, 1997).

Prime Suspect Figure 29.1

Source: Pictorial Press Limited

Furthermore, it is worth noting that one of the most widely studied areas of women's representation has been and still is advertising. Indeed, as Alvarado *et al.* (1987) note, 'representations of women in advertisements have traditionally provided a "good way in" to media studies' (1987: 182) and 'advertising has been a focal point of concern in respect of sex-role portrayal in mass media' (Gunter, 1995: 33; for a comprehensive summary of these see Gunter, 1995: 33–50; for further discussion see Section 7 of this volume).

Further fiction, and indeed non-fiction (see van Zoonen, 1994), genres could be discussed here; however, the discussion of genres that have been identified as 'women's' reflects on subjects that are central to feminist analysis of television.

Soap Operas

Soap opera was one of the first genres feminist critics turned to and it has been dominant within this field ever since (for a comprehensive bibliography of women and soaps see Brunsdon, 1995; see also discussion in Mumford, 1998). This low-status, denigrated – and for a long while ignored – genre has been identified by feminist scholars as essentially dealing with women's world. The fact that the lion's share of its viewership are women further enhanced its identification as a 'women's genre' and thus as especially relevant for feminist critique. Indeed, although currently men constitute about one-third of the soap audience, 'there can be little doubt that the bulk of viewers continue to be women and girls – in some cases quite young girls' (O'Donnell, 1999: 220). Thus, as Brunsdon (1995) argues, soap operas are mainly attractive to feminist analysis because they are perceived as 'both for and about women' (Brunsdon 1995: 54).

There are various structure-related elements on which the notion that soaps deal with women's world is based (see Brunsdon *et al.*, 1997 and van Zoonen, 1994). However, in my discussion here I would like to highlight some content-related issues. For instance, one of the genre characteristics that has been discussed in the context of referring to soap as a woman's genre, is the fact that much of the action takes place in domestic settings, and even those scenes that do take place in work or public spaces centre on the relationships between the characters and thus are simply an extension of the private (Abercrombie, 1996). Indeed, as Alvarado *et al.* (1987) argue, even when the characters are presented in their working lives 'they are rarely seen to be working. Instead, work features as a space where women congregate to pass comment on each other, or events in the street' (1987: 189). Even in the prime-time American mega-soaps, such as *Dallas*, which do relate to business, 'the business dealings are personalized or heavily intertwined with family matters' (Abercrombie, 1996: 51). And yet, as Brunsdon *et al.* (1997) note, the 'romantic glorification of women's isolation at home' (1997: 6) has been challenged by some scholars, as this creates a division between the public (male) and private (female) spheres (Geraghty, 1991).

Related to this is the fact that the soap's narrative focuses on feelings, personal relationships and emotional life in general. This, as Geraghty (1991) argues is still the domain of women in our society. According to her, 'it is this engagement with the personal which is central to women's involvement with soaps' (1991: 42; and see also Mumford, 1995). Indeed, this deep involvement with emotions presumes an audience that knows and is able to judge personal life; moreover, the 'culturally constructed skills of femininity – sensitivity, perception, intuition and the necessary privileging of the concerns of personal life . . . are both called on and practiced in the genre' (Brunsdon, quoted in Abercrombie, 1996).

These are some of the main examples of the characteristics of soaps on which their categorization as a woman's genre is based, a notion – as mentioned – that explained the feminist academic interest in this genre. However, in the context of the discussion in this chapter the representation of women in this genre is of greatest interest. In fact, a very large body of work exists in this area relating to the representation of women in soaps. Most of these studies focused on American or British soaps, and to some extent on Australian soaps and Latino-American telenovelas. More recently, work has been done into soaps in other European countries (O'Donnell, 1999) and worldwide (Matelski, 1999).

As Gunter (1995) argues, 'numerically and on balance, the research indicates that women in televised fiction seem to get the best deal in soap operas. Such programmes are populated almost equally by women and men' (1995: 11). Although women are definitely not under-represented in soaps, some writers have argued that even here the range of roles female characters are given tends to be very narrow and emphasizes certain stereotyped characteristics of women (Gunter, 1995); although, as Gunter (1995) also concurs, women in soaps have been seen in a more positive light compared with, for example, action-drama. Others, like Abercrombie (1996), argue that soaps, and especially the British ones, are actually organized around very strong female protagonists whose actions or feelings drive storylines. This, in fact, is one of the reasons some feminist scholars embraced this genre (see Brunsdon et al., 1997). Overall, women who are active and dominant figures are a staple of soaps, and Peggy Mitchell of *EastEnders* can serve as a prime example in this context. However, as O'Donnell (1999) argues in conclusion to his extensive study of European soaps:

> . . . the matriarchal figures of so many soaps may be an expression of the structural weakness of women in contemporary European societies rather than of their personal strength. They are allowed to be strong when their strength has been depoliticized and others are struggling as they struggled before. The disappearance of the men is irrelevant since the structures which gave them power as individuals remain in place. If soaps are a women's genre, their initial message may be flattering, but their ultimate message would appear to be survival in a battle where the other side's troops may disappear or retire but whose generals and heavy artillery always remain primed for action off-screen. (O'Donnell, 1999: 224)

Feminist attention to soaps developed an interest, which is not confined to textual analysis but also to production and reception. Most importantly, reception in this case meant research focusing on the private, domestic female sphere of television reception (see discussion in Brunsdon et al., 1997 and van Zoonen, 1994). Studies on the reception of 'imported' soaps, mostly American, have also been conducted – for example, Miller's (1995) analysis of the consumption of *The Young and the Restless* in Trinidad, which showed that 'soap opera has the extraordinary appeal that is evident cross-culturally while still being able to discern the very particular imperatives that determine its consumption in specific communities' (1995: 232). Indeed, as mentioned, these types of work on soap opera have influenced the study of television in general (see Mumford, 1995 and 1998; and further discussion in Chapter 32).

In television programming the boundaries between the soap opera form and other genres are becoming blurred. Maltby (1983) noted in the early 1980s – before so many programmes have moved in this direction – that 'it is an undeterred truism that all television aspires to the condition of soap opera' (1983: 303–4). Abercrombie (1996) uses the British show *The Bill* as an example of the fusion of soap opera and police series, but the list of further possible examples is very long and includes even sitcoms, such as *Seinfeld* and *Friends*, which have moved from a state of series (episodic) to serial (continual) in many cases (see Mumford, 1998). In these programmes, 'gender roles are less stereotypically separated' (Abercrombie, 1996: 73) and although male and female characters continue to emphasize different qualities in them, they are not sharply differentiated and do not attract extremes of positive and negative evaluation. As Geraghty (1991) notes, this – and some further recent changes in the genre – may in fact put at risk the continuance of soap opera as a woman's genre.

Situation Comedies

As Brunsdon *et al.* (1997) note, 'much of the current entertainment output of television features strong women, single mothers, and female friends and lovers – that is, female types that are integral to feminist critique and culture' (1997: 1). This is very evident in the popular genre of situation comedies. Yet this is the same genre in which many exaggerated stereotypes – such as the 'dumb blonde' – have been, and still are, presented for what is perceived as comic effect (see also the discussion of humour below). In fact, as sitcom episodes are fairly short 'the identities of characters need to be established as quickly as possible', and thus it can be argued that in this television form 'characterization will tend towards the stereotypical' (Bowes, 1990: 134; see also Medhurst and Tuck, 1982). This has been the case with representations of men and women who for very many years retained traditional gender roles in this genre (for recent changes see the discussion below).

Importantly, although humour could be taken lightly, it arguably does reveal underlying, deeply rooted, social ideas, beliefs and views. More specifically, it is possible that 'humour is used as an 'excuse' for perpetuating certain myths about the ways in which men and women are expected to behave in our society' (Bowes, 1990: 136).

In the past women were under-represented in sitcoms and other genres. Gunter (1995) reports on several studies, up to the 1980s, which showed that in the American context men outnumbered women in sitcoms by two to one. In Britain, as McQueen (1998) argues, the great tradition of situation comedy has centred around men. In fact, sitcoms like *Steptoe and Son*, *Dad's Army* and *It Ain't Half Hot Mum* 'are remarkable for having virtually no female roles' (1998: 58). And yet, US sitcoms do have a long history of programmes with women as their main characters, including *I Love Lucy* (for an analysis of this forever re-run and much-studied sitcom see Mellencamp, 1997), *Bewitched*, *The Mary Tyler Moore Show*, *Rhoda* and *The Golden Girls*. Moreover, 1970s sitcoms like *The Mary Tyler Moore Show* and

Rhoda are regarded as shows that 'picked up and developed cultural concerns with shifting definitions of femininity' (Fiske, 1987: 112). These are also examples of the first kinds of programme in which single women were represented on American television, with the 1970s *The Mary Tyler Moore Show* being the first series focusing on a single professional woman with no plans for marriage (for further analysis see Dow, 1996).

Writing in 1990, Bowes argues that, 'sitcom rarely challenges any of these traditions through the characters and situations it uses. Even more "progressive" sitcoms . . . fail to present a challenge to traditional role models' (1990: 135) and further notes that in this genre, in contrast to soap operas, women rarely get strong roles. Importantly, he attributes part of the problem to the fact that most sitcom writers are men.

However, since the late 1980s and particularly in the 1990s, representations of women in sitcoms are much less stereotypical, more varied and represent more 'real' women (although, it should be noted, still primarily white), a shift that arguably came on the back of the feminist movement (see Andrews, 1998). In noting these changes, I do not argue that women's representations in this genre are no longer stereotyped. As comedy's appeal is indeed related to extreme characterization and stereotyping, stereotypical representations do persist in sitcoms. Indeed, in her analysis of issues of gender in popular British comedy in general, Porter (1998) shows how a strikingly narrow range of female comic stereotypes – most notably the 'ingenuous curvaceous bimbo', the 'nagging unattractive wife' and the mother-in-law – persist across time and a range of comic forms, including cinema, stage, television, radio and seaside postcards.

Yet changes did take place, and scholarly attention has been directed to them. Indeed sitcoms, in which – and similarly to soap opera – the narrative takes place predominantly in a domestic setting, have been of interest to feminist writers for many years (although to a lesser extent then soaps). Andrews (1998), for example, examines the shifts in the representations of the role of the housewife and notes an important shift in the late 1970s 'from texts within which women were portrayed as the objects of humour, or as merely in a supportive role' to what she calls 'housewives comedy' (Andrews, 1998: 50). In her view this shift reflects the same criticisms and concerns 'in relation to domesticity, housewifery and . . . child care as 1970s and 1980s feminism' (1998: 50). Explaining the contexts of the representations of housewives in sitcoms like the British *Butterflies* and *2.4 Children*, and the American *Roseanne* and *Grace Under Fire*, Andrews (1998) argues that these types of sitcom challenge male power and re-negotiate what it means to be a housewife. Through humour, she explains, these types of sitcom actually deconstruct the myths – very much perpetuated by television – of idealized family life and the housewife's role within it.

Sitcoms form a major part of television programming and, indeed, the representations of women in internationally successful American sitcoms of the 1990s like *Murphy Brown* (see Walkowitz, 1997), *Seinfeld*, *Friends* and *Frasier*, or recent British ones like *Game On* and *Babes in the Wood*, are very much worth considering. Following feminist literature I would, however, like to draw attention to two sitcoms that can be seen as pioneers of a new brand of comedy (Geraghty and Lusted, 1998) – especially in the context of representations of women and femininity(ies) – the American *Roseanne* and the British *Absolutely Fabulous*. Both, it is important to emphasize, created and scripted by women.

Figure 29.2   *Roseanne*
Source: Pictorial Press Limited

Roseanne

Generally speaking, *Roseanne* deals with the 'constant tension of working class existence, and, through humour, the absurdities and pain of living the American dream' (Lee, 1995: 470–1), consciously fracturing the myth of the happy suburban families of TV-land. Within this context, this sitcom, which is narrated from the perspective of its female protagonist, criticizes women's roles in society and the family in particular (Rowe, 1996). This is done while representing a 'realistic', blue-collar, strong and assertive woman – Roseanne – whom we see balancing the demands of home, work and society (Lee, 1995).

One central aspect of the representation of Roseanne's 'autonomous womanhood', as Lee (1995) argues, is the fact that she is a fat women in a society where 'thin is the norm', thus offering a feminist critique of 'fat oppression'. However, as Lee (1995) suggests, this representation can also be viewed as feeding the stereotype of the (unthreatening) fat jolly person. In fact, Roseanne Barr herself proclaimed on several occasions – before she lost dozens of pounds and underwent several plastic surgery sessions – that weight is a feminist issue.

Motherhood, which is 'one institution that has certainly been over-represented for women in the media . . . is the target for Roseanne's humour and thus a site for cultural interference' (Lee, 1995: 473). As Rowe (1996) suggests, Roseanne – both in her sitcom and in her star persona – replaces the 'perfect wife and mother' with a 'domestic goddess' whose sensibilities and physique challenge the norms of femininity. Apart from the relationships in the family, *Roseanne* also explores female relationships, particularly through her interaction with her sister and workmates, sending 'messages of female friendship and solidarity' (Lee, 1995: 473).

Absolutely Fabulous owes a debt to *Roseanne* specifically in presenting women who behave in vulgar and 'unruly' ways that break many unwritten codes of the television representations of women in general, and the appropriate female conduct of mothers and women over 30 in particular (Kirkham and Skeggs, 1998). Thus, several issues that have been mentioned above can also be related to this, by now, cult series.

In general, this sitcom 'draws on 1960s' hippydom, 1970s' hedonism, 1980s' Thatcherism and 1990s' righteousness' (Kirkham and Skeggs, 1998: 288), critiquing mainly Thatcherite political values. Indeed, the two leading characters, Edina Monsoon and Patsy Stone, represent aspects of 1980s' Thatcherism by being 'bullish, selfish and hideously materialistic' (Kirkham and Skeggs, 1998: 288), although this is set against their 1960s/1970s lazy and laid-back lifestyle. Kirkham and Skeggs (1998) analyse this sitcom in different contexts and from several perspectives, but in the context of this discussion I would like to emphasize their argument that:

... crucially, feminism of the 1960s and 1970s provides the context for much of the humour of *Absolutely Fabulous* ... handled through contradiction and contrast. The emphasis on women as best friends, the flirtation with lesbianism, the way in which Edina and Patsy pursue their own goals seem to stem from feminist positions of independence and female worth. (Kirkham and Skeggs, 1998: 289)

However, although it can be argued that the two heroines challenge ideals of beauty, in contrast to *Roseanne*, in their obsession with fat they 'continually fly in the face of the notion that "fat is a feminist issue"' (Kirkham and Skeggs, 1998: 289). Yet, this sitcom definitely does challenge prevailing ideals of motherhood, proper female behaviour and even female friendship. Regarding motherhood, for example, it is evident that Edina refuses maternal responsibility over Saffy and also ignores her 'duties' towards her own mother. Indeed, 'the traditional roles of mother and daughter are reversed in Edina and Saffy, and Edina's relationship with her mother is shocking in the lack of filial affections' (Kirkham and Skeggs, 1998: 292). Overall, as Kirkham and Skeggs argue, the disfunctionality of the family in *Absolutely Fabulous* is taken to an extreme, thus portraying the strongest relationship as the one between Edina and Patsy (although Edina is also an irresponsible friend).

Overall, both *Roseanne* and *Absolutely Fabulous* show unruly women who refuse the straitjacket of femininity. However, in concluding the discussion of sitcoms in general and of these two series in particular, it is worth considering the argument that although comedy certainly has the ability to be political, 'topics receiving attention within the sphere of comedy may consequently not be taken seriously outside that sphere and . . . this may therefore neutralise potential radicalism' (Andrews, 1998: 51). Also worth considering is the more general notion that the gains that have been made in the representations of women might only be a 'smokescreen, which disguises enduring inequalities' (McQueen, 1998: 150).

A last point that should be made here is that in examining the representations of women in situation comedies, as in other media texts, the representations of men should also be considered, 'particularly as comedy is often derived in the pairing of gender and sexual opposition' (Porter, 1998: 65). Indeed, many situations in sitcoms revolve around men and women who are set against each other (Abercrombie, 1996; the discussion of men's representations in this context will constitute part of the following chapter).

Production and Reception

As already mentioned, although feminist writers direct much attention to the content of the media, some have drawn attention to the importance of the production and reception contexts in analysing media representations of women and femininity(ies).

As for reception, it has been argued that any discussion of content is in fact also a discussion of reception, as the two not only cannot but also should not be separated. Indeed, quite a few of the more recent studies cited above make this very clear (see, for example, Kirkham and Skeggs, 1998; Rowe, 1996). Thus, a discussion that separates content from reception (and/or production), could be viewed, nowadays, as problematic. (Bearing this in mind, a more in-depth discussion of the literature dealing with media reception and gender will be part of Chapter 32.)

WOMEN AND THE MEDIA INDUSTRIES

One explanation for the portrayal of women being as it is, has been attributed to the gendered structure of media industries. Indeed, the – relatively few – studies of the 'sexism and economic equity in the mass communication . . . tell the same story of the Sisyphean journey for women in mass communication practice' (Creedon, 1993: ix).

The comprehensive anthology *Women in Mass Communication* (Creedon, 1993) includes several chapters on the status of women in the – mainly American – media industries relating, for example, to radio (Cramer, 1993), magazines (Johnson, 1993) and television (Sanders, 1993; Smith, Fredin and Ferguson Nardone, 1993). Importantly the television-related studies address the world of television news. The various studies approach this issue from different perspectives and employ a variety of methodologies, and yet they all challenge the notion of 'equal opportunity' for women in media industries (see also the discussion in van Zoonen, 1994).

One of the main arguments to arise from the literature is that women are under-represented in the media industries, especially at the top (the 'glass ceiling effect'). Thus, although evidence suggests that women's overall percentage has increased in media organizations, at least in western industrialized countries (see Creedon, 1993 and van Zoonen, 1994), they are still dominated by (white) men. The exceptions can be found in areas that can be seen as an extension of women's 'domestic responsibilities', such as children's and educational media, programmes or sections, and in consumer and domestic programmes (van Zoonen, 1994). Furthermore, figures show that 'it is hard to find women in senior management positions, even in women-dominated areas' (van Zoonen, 1994: 51). As advertising has been so central to the discourse of women's media representation, and as some view it as a 'pink collar' or 'velvet' ghetto, it is worth highlighting women's place in this particular case.

In fact, the notion that things might be improving is knocked whenever a closer look is taken. For example, in Britain, the Institute of Practitioners in Advertising (IPA), the advertising industry's trade body, conducted a survey into women in advertising, which examined the number of female employees, the nature of their jobs and how senior they were in that industry. This report showed that in 1990 women were noticeably absent from key senior positions and were almost totally unrepresented in many departments. This report was viewed by its author, Marilyn Baxter, as a 'wake-up call to the industry'.

Moreover, a follow-up article (Archer, 1999), almost ten years later in the 13 September edition of the *Guardian* found that:

> . . . the picture looks alarmingly similar. Despite the gender split in the industry still being around 50/50, *Media Guardian* has found, via a poll of the UK's top 20 agencies, enough evidence to suggest that ad-land has not progressed sufficiently as an equal opportunities employer. Out of the line-up of leading agencies, none today can claim a female chairman and only two have a woman in the position of chief executive. . . . Moreover, while there are only two chief executives, there are no female managing directors whatsoever: every top 20 managing director's position today is filled by a man. . . . More disturbing is the fact that there are still, as 10 years ago, no female creative heads.

Although there are female heads of departments, in all cases the ultimate creative directors are all male, whereas women fare better in the traditional support roles (like planning, PR and marketing, account management, etc.), but that was already true ten years earlier. Indeed, on the creative side, only 6 per cent of copywriters are women and only 15 per cent of art directors. According to Belinda Archer: 'This is surprising, if not downright wrong, given that over 80% of all TV advertising is said to be targeted at women, and indeed that women account for around 70% of all purchasing decisions in most households' (Archer, 1999).

The advertising executives interviewed for this article find it difficult to account for this situation, offering explanations like 'it must be because to be creative you have to be pig-headed and vain', 'women take rejection to heart too much, and rejection is a big part of being creative'. A different explanation is given by Archer who suggests that the 'blokeish' element in advertising might be putting women off, not least because images of women in ads do not tempt female creative talent into the industry. Furthermore, she states, the culture in most creative departments is alienating to women as it is 'laddish' and its currency is 'football, pool tables, *Loaded* and beer'. Related to that is the notion that many male bosses admit to 'hiring themselves', probably feeling more affinity with men than with women (see the further discussion of this argument in van Zoonen, 1994).

A further issue that inevitably comes into play in these discussions is related to having a family. Indeed, female directors interviewed for this article agreed that, as one put it, 'to hold a job down and have a life with their children, then we are talking Superwoman'. Yet, this article concludes that there are signs of hope for the future, as women have progressed and are successful in certain departments. However, it is clear that until 'predominantly male creative bosses actively promote women and boost their female intake' fundamental change will not take place, as indeed it did not occur during the 1990s.

The discussion in this section has highlighted the fact that, in most cases, women are not the producers of women's representations (for the reasons of this state of affairs and the various discriminatory practices taking place in the media industries, see Creedon, 1993; van Zoonen, 1994). However, according to existing studies, the answer as to what effect a larger proportion of female journalists, for example, would have is not clear. This is linked to the more general finding that workers tend to adapt to the organizations they work for; this, as van Zoonen (1994) argues, does not occur by the use of 'repressive force but by a subtle process of rewards and punishments' (1994: 56). This organizational and professional socialization means that, in many cases, women working in the media, in fact, adapt to the hegemonic male ideology.

WOMEN, MEDIA AND SPORT

One area of investigation that is particularly interesting and can clearly demonstrate most aspects of the discussions above, is that of women, media and sport. As sport is about physical activity, it offers an arena for reproducing concrete, everyday examples of male physicality, muscularity and, thus, superiority. Put differently, 'the very physicality of the female body represents subservience, frailty and weakness' (Kane and Greendorfer, 1994: 31). Hargreaves (1986), for example, argues that physical size or muscularity is an essential symbol of male power in western cultures. Ultimately, as this argument goes, 'this physical, biological, "natural" supremacy of males becomes translated into the "natural" supremacy of males in the larger social order' (Kane and Greendorfer, 1994: 31). Essentially this argument is based on the notion that, in sport, physical and biological differences interface with social and cultural interpretations of gender role expectations.

A feminist critique of sport emerged in the late 1970s, and began to flourish during the early 1980s. It viewed sport as a sexist institution, male-dominated and masculine in orientation. The feminist studies of the time explored the sex differences in patterns of athletic socialization, aimed at demonstrating how sport as a social institution naturalizes men's power and privilege over women. They concluded that the marginalization and trivialization of female athletes serves to reproduce the domination of men over women (Sabo and Curry Jansen, 1992). During the 1980s, a dialogue between critical theorists in sport sociology and the feminist theorists resulted in the recognition, by some scholars (Bryson, 1990; Hall, 1990; Messner, 1988), that the concept of hegemony should be employed to analyse gender relations in sport. A number of authors argued that, perhaps more than any other social institution, sport perpetuates male superiority and female inferiority (Hasbrook, 1988).

Although it is beyond the scope of this section to discuss at any length the issue of inequality in sport itself, a few remarks are required in order to contextualize the arguments regarding the media's role in this context. First, it is clear that over the last decades women have made many advancements in organized, competitive, high-performance spectator sport. The Olympic Games are a clear example both of the changes in attitude towards female athletes and of the increased numbers participating in sport. When the modern Olympic Games were revived they were meant to be reserved for the male sex only, as they had been in ancient times. Pierre de Coubertin, to whom the revival of the Games is attributed, through his whole life believed that women should not 'dirty' the Games with their sweat, but merely crown the victors (Leigh, 1974). Indeed, at the first modern Olympics, in 1896, there were no women participants. From the 1900 Games onwards, the number of women participants and the sports in which they participated, increased steadily although, for many years, women's sports remained marginal. Women were only allowed to compete in those sports that had no connection with visible effort, physical strength and body contact. The femininity of female athletes, so it was believed, should be preserved as far as possible.

Recent facts and figures show that in the 1992 Barcelona Olympics 2708 female athletes participated in the Games, this constituted 28.9 per cent of the overall number of participants. These figures grew at the 1996 Atlanta Games and the 2000 Sydney Games. Moreover, the Sydney Games incorporated more than 20 new women's events into its programme, including, for instance, water polo, and weightlifting. And yet women are still left completely out of a few sports, such as boxing and wrestling. In fact, at Sydney, there were 296 events, 166 of them specifically for men, 118 women's events (and 12 mixed), and with all the increase in numbers women are still but 30 per cent of the athletes participating in the Olympic Games.

Overall in sport, figures suggest a rise in women's participation, particularly in western societies and most clearly in the USA. Yet it should be stressed that these figures do not sustain the premise on which some of the feminist writers base their arguments, i.e. that there is a major social change in the participation of women in sports that is not reflected by the media. According to this argument, the media persist in covering mainly male athletes although female athletes have increased their presence in sport dramatically over the last century. This can be seen as one of the causes of the media's attitude towards women in sport, as will be discussed further below. However, it can also be regarded as one of its results. This vicious circle is clearly visible with regard, for example, to women's football in Britain; the growth of the sport is hindered by a lack of funds, which as for all organized sports nowadays, come primarily from sponsorship. Sponsors wish to invest in sports and teams that feature regularly on television and as women's football does not qualify as such, it doesn't get big cash injections.

This links in to the discussion of gender within the context of mediated sport. Similar to other media contents discussed in this chapter, the research into this area tends to focus on two main issues: the amount of coverage and the portrayal of female athletes in the media. Regarding the amount of coverage,

> [a] consistent finding well documented in the literature is the quite noticeable under-reporting (and thus underrepresentation) of female athletes and their sporting events throughout all mass media. This severe underrepresentation often creates the impression that females are non-existent in the sporting world. (Kane and Greendorfer, 1994: 34)

The view that sports programming is an almost all-male world is supported by a wide range of studies – like Woolard's (1983), which found that 85 per cent of newspaper coverage of sport was devoted to men's sports, or Coakley's (1986), which concluded that an estimated 95 per cent of all sports coverage dealt with males. More recent figures do not reveal a significant change; in 1994 men were found to receive 93.8 per cent of television coverage on US television (Duncan and Messner, 1998; see also Shifflett and Revelle, 1996). It is important to stress that this is not an American phenomenon, although many of the studies in this field are conducted in the USA; for example, Duncan and Messner (1998) cite an Australian survey, which showed an even lower percentage and, in the Israeli context, similar percentages were found (Dror and Starnel, 1995). As already mentioned, according to this argument, although women have increased their presence in sport, the media persist in covering mainly male athletes and, as the media reflect on what is important and has prestige, by hardly showing women the media send a message that female athletes have little value in society, especially compared to male athletes.

In some instances, changes in the amount of coverage can be traced, like the extensive and overwhelmingly successful (in ratings terms, especially in the USA) coverage of the 1999 Women's World Cup, the amount of coverage dedicated to women's tennis, or, within the Israeli context, the extended coverage of the European success of the Ramat Ha'Sharon basketball team. These could seem like major shifts – however, these are in most cases major, international sporting events in which it is safe to assume that any successful athlete will get extensive media attention in his or her home country regardless of their sex. When the routine, day-to-day coverage has been studied, the conclusion, towards the end of the 1990s, remained that female athletes were being 'symbolically annihilated'.

Furthermore, in a comprehensive look at the relationship between *Women, Media and Sport* (1994) it is suggested that a change has been taking place both in the world of sport (in the 1992 Olympics US women won all 5 gold medals and, in total, 9 of the 11 medals won by US athletes) and in the amount of coverage given to women. On the surface, it is suggested by Kane and Greendorfer (1994), that media coverage of the 1988 and the 1992 Olympics 'departed from past practices, as women athletes appeared finally to have achieved visibility in the national media' (Kane and Greendorfer, 1994: 28). But, as they go on to discuss, the focus remained on such sports as gymnastics, and the image of the female athletes remained feminized and sexualized. Thus sheer numbers are not the only important factor to consider.

The next step writers take from the exclusion argument is to question whether sports reports on female athletes are not only fewer but also different from those on their male counterparts. The answer emerging from literature (see, for example Creedon, 1994) is yes, although explanations as to how exactly this takes place and what should be done 'to eliminate it' (Creedon, 1994) differ slightly. The issues brought forth include, for instance, visual production techniques, language, terminology and commentary in women's sport that provide a highly stereotypical feminized view – one that tends to sexualize, commodify, trivialize and devalue women's sporting accomplishments.

Sabo and Curry Jansen (1992), for example, find that 'the skills and strengths of women athletes are often devalued in comparison to cultural standards linked to dominant standards of male athletic excellence, which emphasize the cultural equivalents of hegemonic masculinity: power, self-control, success, agency, and aggression' (1992: 176). Furthermore, whereas male athletes are 'valorized, lionized, and put on cultural pedestals' (1992: 174) female athletes are infantized by sports commentators who refer to them as 'girls' or 'young ladies' (male athletes are 'men' or 'young men'). Messner, Duncan and Jensen (1990) in their study of the coverage of tennis found that commentators referred to female tennis players by their first names 52.7 per cent of the time and men only 7.8 per cent of the time. This phenomenon is perceived, by them as well as by other researchers, as a display of a hierarchy of naming, i.e. a linguistic practice that reinforces the existing gender-based status differences. Duncan, Messner and Williams (1990), who examined the verbal descriptors applied to men and women athletes, found that 'men were framed as active subjects whereas women were framed as reactive objects' (Duncan et al., 1990: 21). Moreover, whereas male athletes tend to be described in terms of strengths and success, female athletes' physical strengths tends to be neutralized by ambivalent language.

Also, while the male performances are often linked with power metaphors (like war) the coverage of female athletes is often framed within stereotypes that emphasize appearance and attractiveness rather than athletic skill. Indeed, many researchers find that the media focus on the female athletes as sexual beings, rather than serious performers (see, for example, Kane and Greendorfer, 1994). According to this argument, the sexualization of female athletes 'trivializes' them and 'exploits the women's athletic endeavour' (Whitson, 1986: 104–5) and, in fact, robs female athletes of athletic legitimacy, thus preserving hegemonic masculinity.

While openly prejudiced expressions are becoming rare, they can still be found. For example, in the first rounds of Wimbledon 1996, a sports commentator on *Sky News* expressed joy at the advance of Anna Kournikova to the next round as she is a 'gorgeous blonde'. Indeed, women's tennis is getting no less, and sometimes even more, media coverage than men's, but that is not only because it seems more interesting in sporting terms but also, as many have noticed, due to the beauty of some of the new players. Indeed, the introduction to an eight-page spread in *Hello!* magazine featuring Anna Kournikova put it thus: '. . . the waist-length flaxen hair, endless legs, smooth tan and metallic silver-blue eyes which have undoubtedly helped her into the celebrity stratosphere' (*Hello!*, 1999).

Figure 29.3   Anna Kournikova

Source; Pictorial Press Limited

Generally speaking, a kind of ambivalence emerges every time a female athlete is covered in the media, not because of her sporting performance, but because she is glamorous and conveys sex appeal. The consequence of this ambivalent media portrayal is that it denies female athletes the power and prestige that is their due (Kane and Greendorfer, 1994). This ambivalence serves the function of allowing those in power to acknowledge (and therefore to accommodate) the social changes that have taken place within the last two decades, while simultaneously offering resistance through the maintenance of the status quo.

As Kane and Greendorfer (1994) conclude, by portraying female athletes as feminized and sexualized others, the media trivialize and therefore undermine their athletic achievements, and eventually this kind of media portrayal results in constructions of female athleticism not only as 'other than' but as 'lesser than' the male's. In western culture males are expected to be 'active, aggressive and spontaneous' whereas females are 'weak, passive and responsive', the hierarchy being that the former is superior to the latter. Furthermore, as sport is essentially an institution of male dominance and control, women's entry into this arena on a national and international scale represents, by definition, 'a fundamental challenge to male power and privilege' (Kane and Greendorfer, 1994: 32). According to

Kane and Greendorfer, the central mechanism for accommodating and resisting women's entry into sport has been through the messages socially constructed in the mass media.

The discussion in the literature about the gendered nature of media sport focuses, to a great extent, on the content of the media. However, as writers acknowledge (Cramer, 1993; Creedon, 1994), an analysis of the production and the audience is also required for an understanding of the issue at hand within a wider context. At the production end, the most obvious point is that there are very few female sport journalists and broadcasters (Creedon, 1994; Schmitt, 1996), which means that women's sports and female athletes are covered from a male point of view (Theberge and Cronk, 1986; Creedon, 1994). Indeed, writers suggest that one of the causes for the stereotypical portrayal of female athletes might be the lack of female sports journalists. Cooper-Chen (1994), for example, notes that, in England, the number of sportscasters is growing, but sports reporting remains a male preserve worldwide (see also Cramer, 1993).

In the literature it is sometimes assumed that having more female sports writers may change the amount and type of coverage women's sports and female athletes get and even the general mode of sports writing (Cramer, 1993). However, as with other media contents, to what extent having more female journalists and editors (viewed, possibly, as different gatekeepers) would change the picture is not clear, for various reasons. One reason might be that 'sports media organizations traditionally have determined that women's sports are an area where news is least likely to be made' (Cramer, 1993: 167). Moreover, as both scholars and media professionals seem to agree, sport is the prime means of attracting one of the most difficult demographic segments of the population: adult males. Adrian Metcalfe, former commissioning editor at Channel 4, and more recently chairman of API Television and director of venue production in the 1996 Atlanta Olympics, also believes that programming is not only up to sports editors, he attributes a semi-editorial influence to advertisers and said in an interview: 'They want a male audience to which they can sell men's products, traditional sports programming gives them that audience. They can get women at other times of day' (The Times, 22 April 1992). Thus, the 'blame' is being laid at the advertiser's door, by both theorists and practitioners (see also Jhally, 1989).

It seems a matter of 'common sense' to the media professionals that women watch at certain hours of the day and that, if they watch sport at all, it is particular sports they are interested in. Research reaches similar conclusions: 'in the United States and abroad, women watch more than men in every time and program category except one: sporting events' (Cooper-Chen, 1994: 258). Although the global counterpart of the United States story must be pieced together from television ratings data and anecdotal evidence, Cooper-Chen (1994) reports that, worldwide, more men than women watch televised sports. She also found that the sex-appropriateness of sports seems to hold across national borders. Individual sports, especially those with graceful movements and minimal body contact, appeal to female viewers. As in the United States, women elsewhere like to watch ice-skating, swimming, diving and gymnastics. According to data from Norway, for example, women are more likely than men to watch swimming and gymnastics.

As the media professionals aspire to large audience figures, and as women do not regularly constitute a high percentage of the sports audience, some writers conclude that the media are covering sports women do not want to watch. They also imply that what women would want to watch are women's sports; however, it is important to emphasize that there is no empirical evidence to support this notion.

Generally speaking, very little has been done to explore audience preferences for televised sports involving women. Creedon and Becker (reported in Creedon, 1994) began a research project in 1985. However, six years of experiments and surveys only reconfirmed, empirically, what has already been written in the literature: people do not like the unknown; female sports are perceived as inferior; and some sports are viewed as inappropriate for women. They went on to discuss theoretically what they could not find empirically, which is that 'we still don't understand why preferences exist for men's sports or why exposure did not alter them' (Creedon, 1994: 14). It should be noted that, to this day, the reality is that the media output of sports coverage consists mainly of men's sports and thus when women do watch sport it tends to be men's sport they watch.

Women football fans

Football in Britain spells men's football in the media: although it should be mentioned that in countries like Italy and Brazil women have been keen football spectators for many years. At British football grounds a change in female fanship has been evident in recent years; the reasons for a growing number of female spectators in Britain may be attributed to improvements in the quality of the stadia. The FA Premier League Survey 1995, produced by the Sir Norman Chester Centre for Football Research (University of Leicester) shows that 24 per cent of new fans are women. If women are interested in the sport as spectators at the stadium there is a good chance they are watching and reading about it as well.

The growing interest of female viewers in football in Britain may also be attributed to the fact that, after Italia 90, the game was portrayed as glamorous. To illustrate this, in the semi-final, a record 28 million Britons were watching the match on television and half of them were women. According to a popular women's magazine: 'Pavarotti sang, Lineker scored, Waddle missed, Gazza cried and women were hooked' (*Cosmopolitan*, September 1995). This quote – in itself very simplistic and sexist – reinforces the notion that women are only interested in sport when it is served with a large portion of melodrama.

Within the context of the discussion of gender and media – especially television – representations, this chapter has concentrated on the representations of women and femininity(ies) by referring in particular to soap operas, situation comedies and sport. It also linked the discussion of content to that of production (reception will be discussed in more detail in Chapter 32). However, as mentioned, a more rounded analysis of gender representation by the media should also address representations of men, masculinity(ies), gays and lesbians.

CHAPTER 30

Gender and the Media: the Representation of Men, Masculinity(ies), Gays and Lesbians

INTRODUCTION

The discussion of gender refers to the ways in which femininity(ies), masculinity(ies), sexuality(ies) – and even relationships – are constructed in any given society. Although, for a while, theorists and researchers writing about gender and the media tended to focus on women and femininity, this has meant that writers who did address masculine representation and identity, for example, did so by juxtaposing it with the feminine one. However, over the years academic interest in other aspects of gender representation and identity has grown – clearly influenced by feminist thought – and these will be discussed in this chapter.

MEN, MASCULINITY(IES) AND THE MEDIA

The fact that scholarly attention has not been paid to men and masculinity in the past should come as no surprise considering that it is consistent with 'the lack of attention paid to other dominant groups', as Katz (1995: 133) writes. This is also true for the discussion of race, which for a long while did not deal with whites and whiteness (see further discussion in Chapter 31). However, since the 1980s, a field of 'men's studies' has emerged (see, for example, Brod, 1987; Kimmel, 1987). A specific interest in the media's role in this context has also emerged, mainly in the 1990s (see Craig, 1992), making clear that media representations of men and masculinity (or, more precisely, masculinities) should not be perceived as unproblematic (or as less constructed), as might have been implied by early feminist writing. Thus this section will highlight the main arguments found in the literature focusing on the representations of men and masculinity(ies) in the media. Some of the work referred to here was, in fact, aimed at a discussion of media representation of women or gays and lesbians, but offers insights into the media representations of men and masculinity as well. Indeed, the discussion in the previous chapter, while relating mainly to the representation of women was also, in some respects, about the representation of men. This reflects the fact that the contemporary study of men and masculinity is not exclusive to men's studies (see also discussion in Fejes, 1992; Saco, 1992).

Masculinity(ies)

As the discussion in the previous chapter has related, societies ascribe different and distinct qualities to men and women. Being aggressive, autonomous, and active have been considered for a long while as male qualities (certainly in western societies), whereas being caring, warm and sexually passive have been, and many would argue still are, considered female qualities. These qualities, as discussed, are to a great extent socially determined and constructed, *and* maintain male power. In fact, as should be clear by now, the human race is not 'naturally' divided into male and female, nor is gender identifiable by such sets of 'immutable characteristics' (Kibby, 1997).

Moreover, nowadays, masculinity – which is the focus of the discussion here – is no longer perceived in society and by the media as a monolithic identity that relates to the above-mentioned qualities. There is a range of masculine identities (some of them contradictory) that are related to changes that took place in society over the years as well as to race, class and culture. However, some versions of masculinity are more accepted by society than others. It can still be argued that hegemonic masculinity – which provides normative attributes against which other forms of masculinity are measured – still means to a great extent avoiding feminine behaviour, focusing on success, being emotionally distant and taking risks (Kimmel, 1987). It should also be emphasized that hegemonic masculinity is, to a large extent, constructed in the image of white middle-class heterosexual males.

However, the discussion of the media representation of men and masculinity is grounded in the realization that, as a result of changes brought about by the feminist movement, the definitions of masculinity have undergone major changes in western societies, particularly in middle-class (and upwards), urban, secular parts of these societies. For example, displaying 'feminine' qualities, such as being sensitive and 'soft', are not necessarily perceived as a weakness in men. Anecdotal evidence of the fact that women no longer perceive John Wayne-type macho behaviour as the ideal is underlined by the fact that in recent singles columns in US newspapers some women advertised that they were looking for a 'gay acting straight man' (Lev-Ari, 1999).

Overall, the traditional views of man's role as 'bread-winner', protector and leader certainly continue to exist in today's society. However, values of a 'new' masculinity, such as expressing feelings, have become accepted in many western societies. This, however, has occurred in varying degrees; whereas in the USA and Europe it can be argued that is has been accepted to a large extent, in Middle Eastern countries (including relatively 'developed' ones such as Israel) traditional views still prevail (Lev-Ari, 1999). In fact, towards the end of the 1990s it has been argued by writers like Susan Faludi – in her controversial book *Stifled: the Betrayal of the American Man* (1999) – that American men are stifled, since their sense of what it is to be a man has been destroyed (this book is based on interviews conducted by Faludi).

Last, it should also be emphasized that the 'study of masculinity inevitably leads us back to issues of femininity and sexual orientations and the links between gender, and race, class and national identity, to the construction of individual subjectivities' (Kibby, 1997; see the further discussion in Chapter 32).

MEDIA REPRESENTATION OF MEN AND MASCULINITY(IES)

Many studies show that the media still tend to reinforce the dominant ideology of masculinity and fail to portray the changing cultural norms of masculinity. In this context it should be emphasized again that – as with all other representations discussed – the media do not simply reflect 'natural' gender difference, but are themselves part of their construction and a site for the struggle over their meanings.

Many studies of men's representations in the media in the 1980s were empirical and were conducted from a sociological functionalist perspective, examining the nature and effects of stereotyped male and female representations from within a sex-role framework (Fejes, 1992). Analysis of the 'new' male roles during these years has shown that softer images of masculinity did emerge, although it can be argued that these do not reflect a questioning of real gender inequities (see Kibby, 1997). Although, as Kibby (1997) notes, popular American shows of the time, such as *The A-Team*, defined masculinity as 'related to power, authority, aggression and technology' (for an in-depth analysis of this programme as a masculine text, see Fiske, 1987), men's representations did get more varied. Moreover, in series such as the American show *Magnum PI*, Tom Selleck, the star of the programme (which turned out to appeal to a female viewership), had increasingly been constructed as spectacle, as an erotic object playing off a variety of representations of masculinity against each other (see Flitterman's (1985) analysis, used here as cited in Fiske, 1987).

Indeed, it is, today, worth considering the changing representations of men and masculinity(ies) in similar programmes, belonging to genres that are perceived as male, most notably crime/police series (like the British *Cracker* and *The Bill* and the American *NYPD Blue* and *Homicide – Life on the Street*). In these, as well as other cases, it can be argued (see Kibby, 1997) that although the media representations, informed by cultural changes, have indeed changed and some gender differences have been blurred – not least through a construction of more 'feminized' representations of men – these are merely slight adaptations to contemporary social conditions. Thus, representations of hegemonic masculinity change simply in order to maintain the hegemonic status of masculinity and, no less importantly, to retain audiences. Moreover, it has also been suggested that some media representations reflect an 'ideal' of what it means to be a man in contemporary western society rather than 'reality'.

The discussion here will focus on two television genre: sport (which has been viewed as one of the last 'chances' of men to escape from what is perceived as the growing ambiguity of masculinity in daily life); and situation comedies (which are considered as a genre that has adopted, more than others, a representation of 'new' men and gender relations). (For a discussion of advertisements in this context see Section 7 of this volume.)

Masculinity, Media and Sport

Hargreaves (1986) claims that 'in sport "masculine" identity incorporates images of activity, strength, aggression and muscularity and implies, at the same time, an opposite "feminine" subjectivity associated with passivity, relative weakness, gentleness and grace' (1986: 112). In fact, masculinity and sport have been culturally equated in western cultures (Sabo and Curry Jansen, 1992) and yet in this context there has been relatively little research. In recent years, however, a handful of scholars have studied sport as a male preserve, and as a source of the production and reproduction of masculine identity.

In relation to the media, once attention is directed to masculinity it becomes quite clear that the 'dominant narrative structures in sports media construct and valorise hegemonic masculinity' (Sabo and Curry Jansen, 1992: 169). This, examining the literature, can be taken in two directions. The first relates to the coverage of male athletes as compared to that of their female counterparts.

Following this direction, several arguments emerge. For example, in the literature that does exist (see Duncan, Messner and Williams, 1990; and further discussion in Duncan and Messner, 1998) it has been noted that the sports media emphasize men who succeed, concentrating on success stories and, more specifically, on the theme of fighting back from adversity in the form of injury, drug addiction and so on. Indeed, 'the media do not ordinarily focus on men who fail to measure up in sports or life' (Sabo and Curry Jansen, 1992: 178); in fact, the media hardly ever tell the other side of the story – that of all the athletes who fail to succeed. In 1994 a surprise hit at the box office was the American documentary *Hoop Dreams*, the story of two young black Americans from the ghetto, struggling to make their way into basketball's big league (the NBA) and not finding success in their quest. The film enjoyed huge box office success in American cinemas and went down unexpectedly well around the world. This, however, is not the type of story one normally encounters in the media.

In cases of male athletes who fall from grace in the midst of a scandal, the coverage becomes a site for testing out the challenges a fallen hero poses to the legitimacy of dominant cultural values. But 'the net effect of the extended coverage is to rescue hegemonic masculinity by framing the transgressor as an anomaly, whether as a cheat, an impostor, a tragic victim of flawed judgment, or a compulsive personality' (Sabo and Curry Jansen, 1992: 178; and see, for example, the discussion of Mike Tyson in Sloop, 1997). Ben Johnson, the Canadian sprinter who was stripped of his gold medal when he tested positive for taking performance-enhancing drugs, can serve as an example. Once his story broke he was portrayed as a cheat and an anomaly. The American basketball player, Irwin 'Magic' Johnson is another example. The media coverage, after he announced that he was HIV positive, centred on him as 'Tragic Magic', who was flawed in terms of personal strength, 'accommodating' his female groupies and sleeping with (one) too many of them (Rowe, 1994).

In addition to the notion, found in the literature, that media sport concentrates on success rather than failure, when it comes to male athletes there is an argument that male athletes are represented in sports programming in relation to 'competition, strength and discipline' (Hanke, 1992: 191). More specifically, they tend to be described with metaphors such as 'pounds, misfire, force, big guns, fire away, drawing first blood, or battles' (Sabo and Curry Jansen, 1992: 175). Indeed, Duncan, Messner and Williams (1990) found, in their comparative study of the coverage of women's and men's basketball in the USA, that whereas male basketball players were described by commentators as 'attacking the hoop', female basketball players on the other hand 'went to' the hoop.

A second line of argument in relation to hegemonic masculinity turns from discussion about 'masculinity', to 'masculinities'. Examining the representation in the media, of the male in general and the portrayal of male athletes in particular, it emerges that non-hegemonic forms of masculinity are being marginalized. In fact, 'alternative or counter-hegemonic masculinities are not ordinarily acknowledged or represented by sports media' (Sabo and Curry Jansen, 1992: 177). Furthermore, the 'valorisation of a highly stylised version of traditional masculinity in sports media . . . expresses and reinforces hegemonic models of manhood while marginalizing alternative masculinities' (1992: 179). A clear example of this argument is the very minimal coverage of the Gay Olympics. Moreover, the fact that some male athletes are gay is ignored by the media, a contemporary illustration being Greg Louganis – the American Olympic gold medallist diver – who came forward with the disclosure that he had contracted AIDS. The coverage of this case of a gay athlete was much less sympathetic than that of the heterosexual 'Magic' Johnson when he announced that he was HIV positive. As noted in other programming (Hanke, 1992; and see further discussion below), gay men are largely viewed as 'a problem' and the perspective from which they are represented is that of straight men. This seems to apply equally in sport as well.

The discussion about masculinity and sport in the media context, touches on some further significant issues. For example, Katz (1995) points out that 'violence on-screen, like that in real life, is perpetrated overwhelmingly by males. Males constitute the majority of the audience for violent films, as well as violent sports such as [American] football and hockey. However, what is being 'sold' to the audience is not just violence, but rather a glamorized form of violent masculinity (Katz, 1995). Within this framework, it is important to note that the concept of the male sports hero as a role model was brought into severe doubt in both the cases of Mike Tyson and O.J. Simpson (see Sloop, 1997). With regard to the boxing heavyweight champion Mike Tyson, Rowe (1995) explains:

> . . . it may be argued that the violence, arrogance and contempt for women that he dis-played was consonant with a sycophantic culture of celebrity in masculine sport, where women are routinely regarded as 'groupies' and 'hangers-on' with nothing to 'trade' but their sexuality. . . . Rather they demonstrate the ways in which the economic structure and cultural complexion of professional sport interact in a manner that produces problematic forms of (especially masculine) sports celebrity. (Rowe, 1995: 116)

The case of Simpson – one-time American football hero and actor – brought the problem of gender violence to the forefront of America's social agenda (Lapchick, 1996) and also called the concept of sports hero into question, by placing it within a violent context.

Situation Comedies

Craig (1993) has observed that 'softer' male characters, so-called 'reconstructed males', began appearing in prime time a few years ago, coinciding with the general 'feminization' of prime-time programming. According to him, although some may have seen this as evidence that television had had its gender consciousness raised, television economics offers a better explanation. By this argument he refers to the notion that the motivation to produce 'enlightened' gender portrayals in prime-time programmes is driven by advertisers wishing to reach working women. Whatever the reasoning might be, it is clear that the television content nowadays (as discussed in the previous chapter) does include complex gender portrayals and a larger variety than in the past of representations of both femininity and masculinity, sometimes within the same programme. However, these portrayals, as Craig (1993) emphasizes, 'cannot be too far from the mainstream, lest the program alienate the more traditional viewers'. In his view the solution employed by television to solve this dilemma is in many cases making issues of gender identity the centrepiece of a programme. In this context it is worth considering the television genre that clearly manifests recent changes in gender representations: the sitcom. Through humour, sitcoms are able to deal with the discomfort of contemporary gender representations, the more so because this genre has traditionally dealt with relationships and the family.

As Craig (1993) has noted, much of the humour in such programmes involves conflict between the sexes, frequently involving the situations that question traditional masculine and feminine values. Relating to the American sitcom *Cheers*, Craig argues that the Sam Malone character 'is constructed as a parody of traditional male values', and in fact 'much humour in the show is predicated on his attempts to rationalize and justify his version of masculinity'. A similar argument can be made regarding the British sitcom of the 1990s *Men Behaving Badly* – rivalled in its success only by *Absolutely Fabulous* (discussed in the previous chapter) – and particularly the character of Gary Strang. (An American version of this sitcom was produced by NBC and ran from September 1996 to December 1997.) Lewisohn (1998) describes this sitcom as follows:

> The antidote to all that 1980s talk of New Man, *Men Behaving Badly* has made the New Lad into a *cause célèbre*, crystallising 'traditional' male behaviour that had certainly been out of vogue for a while. To be what the media categorised as a New Man, you had to care and share with your partner, and children if you had them, be responsible and recognise your place in the home and the community. To be a New Lad meant saying 'bollocks' to all of that, being self-centred, rude, crude and boorish, getting pissed on beer, swearing, bragging, belching, farting, fantasising, spewing and publicly rearranging the position of your genitals. (Lewisohn, 1998: 431)

Although this sitcom does indeed challenge the 'new man', the behaviour of the 'new lad' is being constantly ridiculed by the female characters, and in this case much of the humour is based on Gary's attempts to justify his version of masculinity.

However, the analysis of some sitcoms shows how representations of different masculinities in the same programme can in fact reinforce the status quo, positioning non-hegemonic masculinity as ridiculous. As already mentioned, in many cases one can find within the same sitcom different male characters manifesting different and in some cases contrasting masculinities. For example, in his examination of the American sitcom *Evening Shade*, Steinman (1992) shows how the two major male characters featured are constructed to signify very different masculinities. Wood Newton, played by Burt Reynolds, represents hegemonic masculinity in is role as a cigar-smoking football coach who is strong, athletic and muscular. His assistant, Herman, is thin, weak and clumsy, which makes him the archetypal 'nerd'. This pairing makes Wood's character seem more masculine by contrasting him with a feminized male. The text clearly prefers the former to the latter and thus, according to Steinman (1992), reinforces the status quo.

One issue sitcoms have been especially concerned with is the relationship between masculinity and family. In this context, the highly popular American sitcom *Home Improvement* (Craig, 1996; and see also McEachern, 1994) is an interesting example. This sitcom, according to Craig (1996), 'blatantly makes gender relationships, masculinity and male power its central themes'. Analysis shows how it highlights tensions and contradictions in the discourse and construction of masculinity (and femininity). For instance, Tim Taylor, the main male character (played by Tim Allen) 'exhibits several negative characteristics many people associate with masculinity. He is assertive, egotistical, and frequently insensitive to the feelings of others. His machismo is symbolized by his desire to own and use bigger and more powerful tools' (in his fictional cable home improvement show) (Craig, 1996). However, each week's episode shows his wife Jill's struggle to temper with his machismo, equalize her power in their relationship and reconstruct him as a 'new man'. This is done while representing Tim's version of masculinity as foolish and extreme, ridiculing his male chauvinism, although it should be emphasized that he is not represented as a villain but as 'a funny and generally likeable character'. This, in turn, means that the overriding message of *Home Improvement* is that men do have some 'bothersome traits' but they are fundamentally good, loving and – most importantly – changing for the better. Thus, according to Craig (1996), although the programme appears to challenge hegemonic masculinity, 'it actually co-opts any counter hegemony into the new 'modernized' version of hegemonic masculinity that seems to offer concessions, but ultimately winds up reinforcing the same patriarchal domination'.

Indeed, Craig (1996) argues that *Home Improvement* 'is constructed as a satire of traditional masculinity, yet still acts to reinforce patriarchy through a "modernized" hegemonic masculinity'. According to Craig (1996), in this case, as with other commercial television programmes, it is clear that the show is produced to appeal to a large audience and make a profit. Thus it is carefully crafted to offer pleasure to large numbers of both men and women viewers. This is made possible by the programme 'offering viewers . . . an extensive reservoir of raw material that can be used to construct meanings most useful to them'. For example, again according to Craig (and see also the further discussion of reception in Chapter 32):

> . . . despite the anti-macho satirical nature of the show, men may use *Home Improvement* to construct meanings that allow them to express their hostility toward women while at the same time resolving themselves to their accommodation, at least in the form of modernising hegemonic masculinity. (Craig, 1996)

The media representations of men and masculinity(ies) have, then, changed over the years; they are certainly more varied and include, for example, 'softer' images of mascul...

However, as discussed particularly in relation to sport and situation comedies, the representation of hegemonic masculinity as more acceptable in society still prevails in many media texts. This leads into a further area of investigation of media representations that has acquired prominence in recent years.

GAYS, LESBIANS AND THE MEDIA

Much recent scholarly attention has been directed, mainly in the USA, to gay/lesbian/bisexual/ transgender studies (GLBT studies, as they have come to be known) and the role of the media in this context (see Gross and Woods, 1999). The discussion in this section will focus mainly on media representations of gay and lesbian people.

The main argument in the literature is that gay and lesbian media representations have, for a long while, been minimal and, in most cases, highly stereotypical (see discussion in Gamson, 1999), thus perpetuating and reinforcing stereotypes of gays and lesbians. Gross (1989), for example, argues that when gay men are represented at all they are 'negatively stereotyped as villains or victims of ridicule' (quoted in Hanke, 1992: 195). Indeed, common stereotypes include homosexual men as having 'a mincing walk and camp voices' and of lesbians as 'butch, dungaree-wearing feminists' (McQueen, 1998).

It can be argued that the very fact that gay and lesbian characters have been rarely represented meant that programme-makers were all the more likely to rely on quickly recognizable, visible signs of 'gayness' in order to portray these character's sexuality. As with other stereotypes (see discussion in Chapter 28), these stereotypical representations draw upon what is perceived by programme-makers as commonly held impressions of gay and lesbian people in society.

After many years in which lesbian and gay people were almost completely absent from television, they now appear in many mainstream media texts (to name but a few American prime-time examples: *Melrose Place*, *Ellen*, *Dawson's Creek*, *Will and Grace*). This probably reflects the fact that as part of more general social and cultural transformations, homosexuality is more (although not fully) accepted in today's society. Furthermore, as Alvarado *et al.* (1987) note, 'the bedrock of common-sense assumptions as to what constitutes homo- or heterosexuality is fissured: ideas about sexuality are contradictory and changing' (1987: 178). In this context, I would like to draw attention to a selected number of issues and programmes that expose the complex issues related to the representations that do exist.

As already mentioned, one of the often used (and referred to in the literature) gay types ⟨…⟩n is that of camp, one clear example being the character of Mr Humphreys in the ⟨…⟩m *Are You Being Served?*. Some argue that this kind of representation was ⟨…⟩ 1970s, and yet it is still widely found in film and on television: Julian Clary's ⟨…⟩ammes on British television can serve as an example for the 1990s. Camp, ⟨…⟩g to Dyer is a characteristically gay way of 'handling the values, images and ⟨…⟩ dominant culture through irony, exaggeration, trivialization, theatricalization, ⟨…⟩nt making fun of and out of the serious and respectable' (Dyer, 1986), is ⟨…⟩ the least threatening and thus most acceptable representation of gay characters (see Steinman, 1992). This 'humorous' portrayal, which positions gay sexuality as 'being somewhere in the middle of male and female' (Wood, 1996), can be found mainly in television sitcoms (for a discussion of the 'dyke' and the 'queen' as 'in-between' representations, see Wood, 1996).

Apart from further common stereotypes (see the examples below), it has been argued that representations of homosexuals are constructed around a limited number of plots, such as stories concerning friendship between gay males and single, heterosexual female characters, or gay and lesbian characters coming to terms with their homosexuality. In the 1980s, 'most media attention to gay men was in the context of AIDS-related stories' (Gross, 1995: 65), framing homosexuality even more than ever before as 'a problem'.

Soap Operas

Interestingly, soap operas are a genre in which less stereotypical representations of gays and lesbians can be found. This is the case as in soap it is unnecessary for audiences to immediately identify a character as being homosexual since this ongoing dramatic form – which has regular audiences – allows for character development in a (slow) way which is not possible in many other media texts. One of the first examples in this context was the character of Steven in the American soap *Dynasty*. His character was not stereotyped in any particular visual way; in many ways, he was simply represented as an individual who happened to be gay. However, in this case too, he was mainly involved in storylines that centred on his father's homophobia and unwillingness to accept his son's sexuality, thus – as in other texts – reducing everything about the character to sexuality-related issues. Wood (1996) analyses the same point in relation to British soaps in which gay characters became part of several storylines in the 1990s. For example, one such story in *EastEnders* involved the gay couple Tony and Simon. Their characters were not portrayed as visually different from the heterosexual characters in this soap, furthermore, they were not confined to plots concerning their sexuality. However, plots that did centre on their sexuality portrayed homosexuality as a moral problem and, in essence, dealt with the issue of heterosexuals coming to terms with gayness. Wood (1996) further emphasizes that, although such programmes appear to be sympathetic to the portrayal of gays and lesbians on television, they still rely, largely, on the stereotypical plot conventions adopted by television programmes in portraying homosexuality to a mainstream audience.

Indeed, not only in the case of soaps, gay and lesbian media representations are not representing, in most cases, a gay/lesbian perspective – they are constructed from a heterosexual point of view and aimed at a heterosexual audience. One consequence is that, in many cases, media texts deal with storylines of tolerance and/or acceptance.

Talk Shows and 'the Price of Visibility'

'The price of visibility' has been an issue raised by writers like the American sociologist Joshua Gamson (1999), who studied the American popular tabloid talk shows – such as *Jerry Springer*, *Jenny Jones* and *Geraldo*. His book *Freaks Talk Back* is an analysis based on interviews, transcripts and focus-group discussions with viewers, as well as Gamson's own experiences as a gay audience member. In it he argues that these talk shows give a much-needed visibility to people outside of the sexual mainstream, often expressing a progressive, if fleeting, level of acceptance. In fact, the talk show hosts 'want you to talk about it publicly, just at a time when everyone else wants you not to'. Moreover, as these shows 'are about talk, the more silence there has been on a subject, the more not-telling, the better talk topic it is' (Gamson, 1995). However, this happens under a banner of freakishness, as many of these shows have more than a passing resemblance to freak shows, albeit on a psycho-logical level. Thus, as Gamson argues, sex and gender outsiders entering these shows 'arguably reinforce their inhuman, outsider status, by entering a discourse in which they are bizarre, outrageous, flamboyant curiosities'. However, anti-gay bigots are turned into 'freaks' by the show as well, often in ways 'that make the sex and gender outsiders look just fine'. Furthermore, although these shows are indeed exploitative spectacles, they are also, according to Gamson, opportunities. For example, he argues that the yelling, hooting, bickering and even displays of homophobia – which are very different from the 'pre-packaged, insincere tolerance that passes for discourse' in other media content – give rise to much more genuine discussions. Moreover, these shows include a much greater diversity of gay people than usually portrayed on television.

It fact, in most cases, gays are represented by the media as white, middle-class males, whereas a more 'realistic' approach would have to include a diversity of queer people includ-ing, for instance, in terms of race and class. This lack of diversity can also be linked to Gross's (1995) notion that 'the rules of the mass media . . . exclude and deny the existence of normal, unexceptional as well as exceptional lesbian and gay men. Hardly ever shown in the media are just plain gay folks' (1995: 65).

Drama: *Queer as Folk*

A programme that has been hailed by some as a step in the right direction is Channel 4's *Queer as Folk*, which had its first, highly controversial and critically acclaimed, season in 1999 (at the time of writing, an American version of this series was being filmed; see Hensley, 2000). In Britain's first gay drama series, it is heterosexuals who appear only now and then as support characters; the central gay characters in it are young, stylish and 'fuck in bath-rooms, fuck in threesomes (on video), fuck with minors and on the Internet – and that is just for starters' (Frid, 1999). The explicit gay sex in it included the initiation scene between a 15-year-old boy and a promiscuous man in his late twenties (which was cause for much com-plaint, see further discussion below). In the third episode, for example, one character died, not of AIDS (although condoms were nowhere in sight in this series) but after taking a suspicious drug given to him by an even more suspicious sexual partner. These gay people are far from perfect, they are not sensitive poets, noble victims or camp. Most of them are not even nice; worst of all is Stuart who is portrayed as a 'full-time' homosexual who 'fucks everything in sight', tempts married men and emotionally abuses his best friend who is secretly in love with him. He, in fact, is the lead character in *Queer as Folk*. As Frid (1999) puts it: 'politically correct it's not'.

Russell Davis, the creator of the series (and the only openly gay person associated with it) explained that gay culture:

> . . . has become part of the mainstream and every child knows its icons, but this is really the first time homos get centre stage and are not the next-door neighbour, the nice flat-mate or the best friend of the straight heroine.

According to him, this is the healthy stage of gay representation, since gays are represented as individuals and not as 'official representatives' of the gay community. This, in his view, is true social acceptance: 'we saw selfish, bad and problematic straights, now we will also see such gays' (quoted in Frid, 1999).

The controversy surrounding *Queer as Folk*

Not surprisingly, in 1999, this series accounted for more complaints to the Independent Television Commission (ITC) than any other drama (Gibson, 1999). In response, the ITC did not uphold the complaints about homosexual activity, although it expressed 'concerns about the celebratory tone' of the first episode, which it said 'left little room for any questions to be raised in viewers' minds about the rights and wrongs of the illegal under-age relationship'. Furthermore, Channel 4 was censured for failing to take the opportunity to provide educational back-up to the series on subjects such as safe sex, and young people and sexuality; according to the regulator, further episodes of the series should be 'enhanced by such responsible messages' (Gibson, 1999).

There is little wonder that such a series was produced by Channel 4, which has always aimed to be the channel for people who value 'freedom, permissiveness, hedonism, discernment, experimentation, ambition and individuality' (Jackson, 1999). Channel 4's director of programmes, Tim Gardam, claimed that the series 'epitomized our mission to put alternative viewpoints and voices on screen', and also that 'it broke new ground for television drama and provoked a huge response from viewers with the majority very supportive of its style and subject matter' (Gibson, 1999). As Michael Jackson, general director of Channel 4, said of *Queer as Folk*:

> It was funny, truthful and stylish. In the past, this subject would have been handled in a self-conscious manner. But in *Queer as Folk* there are no 'issues'. There are only emotions, unsympathetic gay characters and, shockingly, no safe-sex message. It's a programme no other broadcaster would have shown. (Jackson, 1999)

However, the complaints regarding this series were not confined to heterosexual audiences – the gay community also had its reservations, claiming, for example, that the use of a young character could harm the legalizing of 16 as the age of consent. More generally, there were voices that resented the portrayals of gays in *Queer as Folk*, to which the series' creator Russell Davis's response was:

> . . . you can't win, if you present nice gays they will say you are 'sucking up', if you show them gays who are not nice they will say you are a homophobe and if you present real gays they will complain these are stereotypes. (Frid, 1999)

Although in many respects it can be argued that this ground-breaking series represented gays in a (much) less stereotypical fashion than most media texts, it is worth noting that the public relations campaign promoting the series emphasized the fact that all the lead actors in it were heterosexual. This can be viewed as a directive to read the series as 'not real', thus 'boys can fantasize about the actors but girls will get them' (Frid, 1999). Furthermore, in this case too, the exploitative argument can also be made since 'the series is like a peep show which quickly turns into a freak show' (Frid, 1999), presenting the 'exotic' gays to a heterosexual gaze.

Reception by Gay and Lesbian Audiences

As far as reception is concerned, some work has been done into the reception of media texts by gay and lesbian audiences (see, for example, Gross, 1995; Steinman, 1992) suggesting 'several categories of response to the mainstream media's treatment of minorities; among them are internalization, subversion, secession and resistance' (Gross, 1995: 66). As Fiske (1987) argues, 'audience is composed of a wide variety of groups and not a homogeneous mass; and these groups actively read television in order to produce from it meanings that connect with their social experiences' (1987: 84). Thus, gay and lesbian audiences can read and make meaning of mainstream media texts in a way that connects with their own experience.

One of the examples often used is that of the American police series *Starsky and Hutch*, which can be read as a series that explored homosexual issues in an indirect, subtle way. As Fiske (1987) notes:

Starsky and Hutch exhibited many signs of a homosexual relationship, but their physical and emotional intimacy was not, in itself, a source of satisfaction and pleasure to them. Their fulfilment came from the goals that their relationship enabled them to achieve, not from the relationship itself. (Fiske, 1987: 213)

In fact, Starsky and Hutch's relationship was not a homosexual one and, as Wood (1996) notes, it is unlikely that the programme would have been so popular had a wide audience seen signs of homosexuality in their relationship (for further discussion of the representation of male friendship on television, see Spangler, 1992).

A more contemporary example, and indeed a more clearly 'polysemic' (Fiske, 1986) one in this context, is *Xena: Warrior Princess*. This series follows the exploits of Xena and her companion Gabrielle as they travel through time, history, myth and, as Meister (1998) argues, feminism. Importantly, 'the text of the show does not revolve in any way around Xena's interpersonal interactions with men. In fact, the show most directly revolves around Xena's interpersonal interaction with her travelling companion Gabrielle' (Meister, 1998). As a consequence, although Xena and Gabrielle have had male love interests in the programme, the series has a strong lesbian following, reading the extraordinarily close, loving relationship between the lead characters as a lesbian one. This is reflected in a multitude of Internet sites in which there is frequent discussion regarding the characters' sexual orientation. As Meister (1998) notes, there are some 600 stories published on the Internet that take their basis from the show, almost all of these 'revolve around Xena and Gabrielle's emotional connection with each other or with their emotional and sexual connection to each other'. Importantly, suggestions of a lesbian relationship are not unintended; in one interview Lucy Lawless – who plays Xena – said in regard to this, 'we are aware and we're not afraid of [the lesbian element]. This is a love story between two people. What they do in their own time is none of our business.' Rob Tapert, the programme's producer has also said that the relationship was 'whatever you want it to be' (see http://whoosh.org/faq/faq16.html). Thus, it can be argued that *Xena: Warrior Princess* is designed to appeal to many people in many different ways (see the further discussion of reception in Chapter 32).

Although these texts allow a gay and/or lesbian reading, it has been argued that 'the ultimate expression of independence for minority audiences . . . is to become the creators and not merely the consumers of media images' (Gross, 1995: 68). This indeed may be the case with *Queer as Folk*.

Xena Warrior Princess   Figure 30.1
Source: Pictorial Press Limited

CHAPTER 31

Representation, Race and Ethnicity

REPRESENTATION, RACE AND ETHNICITY

The term 'race' is problematic, not in the least as 'there is little or no biological evidence to support the use of the term at all' (McQueen, 1998: 155). In fact, it can be argued that 'there is no such thing as "race"', however 'there is racism' (O'Sullivan et al., 1994: 257). Put differently, 'race', is far from being an innocent term: it carries much ideological weight.

The history of racial ideology is long and by no means over. Indeed, a discussion of race representation by the media should be contextualized by a wider discussion of the histories that structured racial inequality, 'which used racial differences to mask social, economic and political oppressions' (Alvarado et al., 1987: 198). Thus, it must be stressed that prejudiced and stereotyped representations of race in the media – as is true in the cases discussed in previous chapters – are linked with much wider social assumptions and practices.

In fact, as McQueen (1998) puts it, 'there is a long and shameful history of representations of "race" in "Western" nations'. This includes, for example, the representation of Jews – particularly in films such as The Eternal Jew (1940) – by the propaganda machine of the Third Reich, which was meant to legitimize their extermination. Overall, the media, as discussed in previous chapters, is a central means of ideological production and has indeed been perceived as creating, reproducing and sustaining racial ideologies (see discussion in Hall, 1995; and Orbe and Cornwell, 1999). In fact, as Dyer argues, 'racial imagery is central to the organisation of the modern world' (1997: 1).

It is important to emphasize that much of the discussion of race in media studies literature, originating from Britain and the USA, refers to images of black people in the media; in fact, the term 'race' is actually assumed to refer to black people. However, in studying 'peoples of Afro-Caribbean origin', Alvarado et al. argue that their analysis 'in many cases will also hold true for any group which is outside the ethnic and cultural mainstream of Anglo-Saxon society' (1987: 200). In this respect, it is also important to note that studying the way the media represent different groups as 'other than ourselves' helps to inform an understanding of 'ourselves' and those that, as this implies, do not 'belong'.

Thus, although the discussion in this chapter, reflecting on the existing literature, will indeed refer mainly to the representation of black people, the arguments raised in it are relevant to other groups as well. Importantly, in recent years studies of representation of race and ethnicity have addressed further groups and have even pointed out the fact that, in this context, an analysis of the representation of whites and whiteness is also required (see the discussion below).

Studies into the representation of race, grounded in many cases in the tradition of British cultural studies, originated in Britain but can now be found in the USA, focusing on African-

American images in film and television (Orbe and Cornwell, 1999). In this context, it is important to note that the quantity, and according to Daniels (1998) quality, of studies in this field is much smaller than in the related area of gender representation. Many of the studies that do exist looked at the representation of black people in television texts, mainly 'in drama and light entertainment. There is very little information available on the coverage of black people in news, current affairs and documentaries' (Daniels, 1998: 133; although see discussion below). Much of this work has called attention to the ways in which black people in the media have remained largely invisible, marginalized to the point of insignificance, or have been limited to specific stereotypes (see, for example, Tulloch, 1990).

Alvarado et al., for instance, draw attention to the under-representation of black people and argue that any discussion of race should be 'a discussion of absence' (1987: 223). In fact:

> Relatively few black performers are employed by television, and when they appear on television it is predominantly in the traditional roles of sports people or singers and dancers. It is almost unknown for a black person to be consulted as an 'expert' on the EEC, on nuclear power or on science, for example. (Alvarado et al., 1987: 223)

As already mentioned, more qualitative studies have found that, even when black people are represented, their portrayal is stereotyped (this aspect is especially worth noting as it can be argued that, in recent years, black people have been more visible; see the discussion below). Most notably, as black people and other ethnic groups have been framed as a 'social problem' (see Hall, 1995; Tulloch, 1990), their images include criminals, gang members, drug addicts and, generally, trouble-makers (McQueen, 1998; see also discussion in Hall, 1995). This, according to Tulloch (1990), is also true of news and documentary programmes. For example, Alvarado et al. (1987), analysed what they identify as the four significant sets of media representation of racial difference: the 'exotic', the 'dangerous', the 'humorous' and the 'pitied'. I found these a useful starting point for my own discussion.

The 'exotic' refers to black people being represented as 'wondrous and strange', evidence of which is the British media coverage of international tours by the royal family. A related point raised by this study is that black people are 'allowed' by the media to be 'wonderful' only in certain areas such as music and sport. As others have also noted in relation to sport, this is also linked to a perception that black people are good at sport because it requires physical rather than intellectual qualities (Davis and Harris, 1998). Furthermore, when in comes to boxing in particular, the image of black boxers displays in many cases 'brute animalism' (see the discussion of Mike Tyson in Sloop, 1997; for further discussion of the stereotypes of African-American athletes, see also Davis and Harris, 1998). At such points, the 'exotic' becomes the 'dangerous'.

The 'dangerous' relates to the ideological framework of 'black equals danger', which in fact is less explicitly played out in recent media fiction programmes (although it can still be found in non-fiction content). However, an examination of the history of such representations reveals many such examples, as in the film genre of the western, which depicted the 'Indians' as wild, savage, primitive, dangerous and marauding, which also meant that they could be 'unthinkingly killed without a single moral or political qualm' (Alvarado et al., 1987: 214).

This links to the fact that black male sexuality is being represented – at least in the US context – as dangerous (see Orbe and Cornwell, 1999; Sloop, 1997). However, Alvarado et al., referring mainly to British television examples, state that 'black male sexuality generally exists as a barely discernible undercurrent, something that is *too dangerous* to allow to come to the surface except in pornography' (1987: 216), and suggest that the handling of the 'sexual' of 'racial otherness' is mainly played out through humour, particularly in sitcoms.

The 'humorous' set of representation includes the stereotyping of black people as 'cheerful, rolling-eyed simpletons' (McQueen, 1998: 155; see also Hall, 1995). The 'humorous' representation can be found mainly in sitcoms, a genre in which stereotypes of many groups are present, since this format 'demands easily recognisable characters and situations' (McQueen, 1998: 155). Such programmes, neutralize the 'threat' and 'danger' of the 'otherness' of black people by making them and their situation comic and laughable. This is also true for other ethnic minorities – Manuel, the Spanish waiter in *Fawlty Towers*, can serve as a prime example in this case. As McQueen (1998) also points out, some sitcoms include racist characters (as in *Till Death Us Do Part* and *Rising Damp*) assuming that audiences will 'laugh at these bigots for their foolishness'; however, 'some audiences . . . will enjoy the racial insults, producing an "oppositional", racially prejudiced reading' (1998: 156).

With regard to sitcoms it is important to note that this is also a genre in which 'positive' images of black people can be found. In fact, American sitcoms like *The Cosby Show* and *The Fresh Prince of Bel Air* – which present wealthy black families – have actually been accused of being 'unrealistically overpositive' (McQueen, 1998: 156). Jhally and Lewis (1992, discussed in Abercrombie, 1996) say in their study of *The Cosby Show* that this sitcom is worth considering because all its leading characters are black, but they emphasize that:

> . . . the increasing number of images of black upper middle-class, including and propelled by the Huxtables, do represent a reality of some sections of the black population. But they also crucially hide and distort how the majority of black Americans are understood. This distortion leads to the emergence of a new set of regressive racial beliefs. (Jhally and Lewis, 1992: 70, quoted in Abercrombie, 1996)

Moreover, this and similar sitcoms have also been criticized for (in most cases) simply ignoring racial discrimination issues.

Finally, the 'pitied' representation is to be found especially in non-fiction content, representing black people as 'victims', 'sufferers' and unable to help themselves. Images from countries like Ethiopia of swollen-bellied babies do not, however, 'offer an account of the virtual holocaust that led to this state of affairs' (Alvarado et al., 1987: 219). Still, in this case it can be argued that these images draw media attention and subsequently financial aid.

As already mentioned, in the 1990s there were indications that black people were being represented much more than in the past by the media, and appeared in television programmes, both non-fiction and fiction. Moreover, Tulloch (1990) believes that the situation has improved in series like the British soap *EastEnders*, in which black characters play a more balanced range of roles than the criminals, servants, singers or bus conductors they played in 1950s–1970s television content. In a similar vein, Abercrombie (1996) argues that in series such as *EastEnders*, *Brookside* and *The Bill*, black, as well as Asian, characters are no longer stereotyped but simply play 'ordinary' people. He further states that a similar process seems to be taking place in the US but, as in the case of *The Cosby Show*, the black characters on American television – unlike those on British television – have become steadily more middle class. This, as already mentioned, can be viewed as suppressing the fact that most African-Americans are not middle class. Indeed, such representations, as Jhally and Lewis (1992) argue, hide and distort the social reality of most African-Americans.

If, in fiction, representation of black people has become more varied and less stereo-typical (for further discussion of the changing images of blacks in the film industry and on television, see Grossberg *et al.*, 1998: 222–5), in news programmes they are still widely associated with drugs and other criminal or deviant behaviour in both Britain and the USA (Abercrombie, 1996). However, although scholars continue to conclude that representations of black people are in many cases stereotypical, there is an assumption that some progress has been made in the media against racist ideologies.

An interesting case to consider in the context of non-fiction representation is MTV's *The Real World*. In this alternative programme one would expect to find a reflection of change, if it has truly occurred. Orbe and Cornwell analysed this programme and argue that it represents a powerful source of influence because representations in it are 'presented not as mediated images, but as real-life images captured on camera' (1999: 12). Alarmingly, in their critical, semiotic analysis of *The Real World* they clearly show how, 'under the mask of representing reality', this programme actually 'reinforces stereotypical images of African-American men as angry, potentially violent and sexually aggressive' (1999: 2), thus con-tributing to the 'general societal fear of black men' (1999: 1). Thus, in this case too, it seems clear that deeply rooted racist assumptions still prevail when the representations that do exist are examined closely.

Finally, it is worth noting that the discussion in this section has dealt more with the rep-resentation of black men and masculinity than with the representations of black women. Although this reflects, to some extent, the existing literature, some writing does address more specifically the media representations of black women (see Bobo and Seiter, 1997).

White

Racism has been viewed as 'institutionalized policy of prejudice and discrimination which is directed towards minorities characterized by colour and other forms of supposed difference by more powerful and established groups' (O'Sullivan *et al.*, 1994: 256). Indeed, as the above discussion of 'race' shows, concepts like 'black' or 'Asian' have been used to describe 'race' as the 'other', while the notion of 'white' remained absent. However, it is very much present as being the 'mainstream' or 'us' in white-dominated societies or, as Dyer argues, 'white people's hold on privilege and power . . . is maintained by being unseen' (1997: 44).

In recent years the construction of 'whiteness' and the media's role in the naturalization of white privilege are no longer ignored (see, for example, Seiter's 1995 study of the racial representation in advertising).

Richard Dyer's *White* (1997) is a central text in this context. In it he examines the representations of 'whiteness' in relation to 'invisibility', 'opposition', 'privilege' and 'extreme whiteness'. According to Dyer, 'to apply the colour white to white people is to ascribe a visible property to a group that thrives also on invisibility' (1997: 42). As already mentioned, the very hold on privilege and power by white people is maintained by their 'invisibility'. The notion of 'opposition' refers to the idea that the symbolic connotation of whiteness is commonly represented as a 'moral opposition of white = good and black = bad' (1997: 58). Whiteness is also 'privilege', in fact 'white people are systematically privileged in Western society' (1997: 9) and 'being visible as white is a passport to privilege' (1997: 44). Lastly, Dyer argues that one of the key themes in 1990s discourse is the notion of whiteness under threat (in particular 'white masculinity'). Within this context images of 'extreme whiteness' co-exist with 'ordinary whiteness' and act as a distraction as whites can take comfort in not being marked as white.

Production and Reception

Orbe and Cornwell observe that, 'many critics . . . have posited that the vast majority of African American media images represent portrayal of Black life as European Americans see it' (1999: 3). As they go on to explain, this is due to the fact that, historically, black people have not had control over these images. This argument is clearly related to the finding in research that black people (as well as other ethnic groups) are under-represented in the media industries (Daniels, 1998), except in 'ethnic minority programmes' (Abercrombie, 1996: 70). Thus, as Tulloch (1990) in analysing the British case, argues, only when black people are equal in the media industries their representations in both fiction and non-fiction programmes will be more adequate (see also Bowes, 1990).

Within the context of this chapter, representation, race and ethnicity have been discussed in isolation. It should, however, be noted, as indeed has been pointed out in some of the above arguments, that a much more complex picture emerges when considering class and gender as well. Finally, it is important to emphasize that, whereas representation and gender is a well-researched area of media studies – particularly with regard to women – representation and race, as reflected even in the comparative length of my own discussions, has been studied much less and is very much required.

CHAPTER 32

Identity and the Media

INTRODUCTION

Inevitably, the issue of identity and the media's role in relation to this concept has been intertwined in the discussion in previous chapters. This has been the case as the discussion of representations is based, at least to some extent, on the assumption that media depictions affect the formation of identity. As Woodward puts it, 'representation as a cultural process establishes individual and collective identities, and symbolic systems provide possible answers to the questions: who am I? what could I be? who do I want to be?' (1997: 14).

Identity – as Woodward (1997) writes in the introduction to the book *Identity and Difference* – matters,

> . . . both in terms of social and political concerns within the contemporary world and within academic discourses where identity has been seen as conceptually important in offering explanations of social and cultural changes. . . . Identity can be seen as the interface between subjective positions and social and cultural situations. . . . Identity gives us an idea of who we are and of how we relate to others and to the world in which we live. Identity marks the ways in which we are the same as others who share that position, and the ways in which we are different from those who do not. (Woodward, 1997: 1–2)

Indeed, identity is a complex concept, which has become 'the subject of increased academic interest as a conceptual tool with which to understand and make sense of social, cultural, economic and political changes' (Woodward, 1997: 1). Scholars address these issues from diverse perspectives and on different levels including the global, national, local and personal ones. Importantly, this concept lies at the heart of current debates in cultural studies and social theory (see, for example, Hall and Du Gay, 1996).

From the literature addressing this concept, it has become evident that identity can best be understood as a fluid process, always in formation, negotiated and re-negotiated, 'at once defined and redefined' (Saco, 1992: 24); indeed, that identity is always unstable and temporary. Moreover, as 'identities in the contemporary world derive from a multiplicity of sources – from nationality, ethnicity, social class, community, gender, sexuality – sources which may conflict in the construction of identity positions and lead to contradictory fragmented identities' (Woodward, 1997: 1), this view recognizes the idea that 'modern self is composed of a multiplicity of identities, not just one' (Stevenson, 1995: 40).

Although the concept of identity (including 'self-identity', 'social identity' and even the notion of 'the crisis of identity') merits a much more in-depth discussion (see, for example, Grossberg *et al.*, 1998: 205–34), this chapter focuses specifically on the idea that:

radio, television, film and other products of media culture provide materials out of which
we forge our very identities, our sense of selfhood; our notion of what it means to be male
or female; our sense of class, of ethnicity and race, of nationality, of sexuality, of 'us' and
'them'. (Kellner, 1995: 5)

Thus, this chapter deals with the impact attributed to media representations – as discussed extensively in the previous chapters – on the formation of identity. In this context it
is worth noting that some view the 'media's ability to produce people's social identities, in
terms of both a sense of unity and difference' as 'their most powerful and important effect'
(Grossberg et al., 1998: 206) – a view that is also based on the notion that the strength of
the traditional sources of identity, such as religion, family and work, has declined in proportion to the growing power of the mass media (this although people clearly form and re-form
their sense of identity in the 'real' world).

More specifically, the following sections relate to the impact of television portrayals on
identity as discussed in the literature dealing with gender (especially women) and race. It is
worth noting in this context, as Geraghty and Lusted do, that:

. . . perhaps no approaches to the study of television have crossed disciplinary boundaries
so much as academic feminism and black studies. What they share is a founding concept
of representation and its relation to and impact on the formation of personal identity.
(Geraghty and Lusted, 1998: 90)

GENDER, IDENTITY AND THE MEDIA

As discussed in Chapter 29, early feminist writers looked at the media portrayal of women
and were concerned with the impact of these – viewed in many cases as 'negative' – representations. This type of content analysis, which was central to early feminist writing, still
exists and is viewed as necessary predominantly as scholars tend to agree that the media
representations play a significant role in maintaining the political and social status quo.
Feminist writers in particular clearly agree that television – and in this chapter, too, this is
the medium I will be focusing on – plays a central ideological role not only in reflecting but
also reinforcing existing ideas about gender.

It is worth mentioning that textual analysis itself has gone beyond analysing representations, most notably by looking at the ways in which 'women viewers are interpellated –
addressed and positioned – by the television text in terms of their cultural expertise, and to
the extent that they respond to this hail, they are positioned as female (rather than male,
ungendered, multiply gendered, etc.) spectators' (Mumford, 1998: 120).

Although, as already mentioned more than once, some scholars emphasize that the
effects of media representations in general, and in relation to the formation of identity in
particular, should be studied rather than assumed. Indeed, especially in recent years, the
impact of media representations has not gone unnoticed in feminist television studies. Moreover, as Mumford (1998) emphasizes:

The fundamental questions of feminism focus on issues of cultural identity and position: What does it mean to live as a woman or a man? How do we learn to do it in the first place? To what extent does gender – our own identities as male or female, our ideals about what that might mean – shape our experience of the culture around us? These questions neatly inflect the fundamental question of TV Studies – what are we doing when we watch television? – and prompt us to ask how television works to establish or promote not just specific gender identities, but existing cultural relations generally. (Mumford, 1998: 116)

Thus, beyond content analysis 'more sophisticated theoretical tools, a wider spectrum of interests, and the influence of Cultural Studies have gradually led feminist TV scholars to consider "images of women" in a new way' (Mumford, 1998: 121). This is related to the idea expressed by many current writers, that audiences actively, and even creatively, construct the meanings of media texts rather than passively absorb predetermined meanings imposed upon them (see, for example, Ang, 1996). Although this is the case, and writers do agree that meanings are negotiated by an active audience, they differ considerably in their view of how powerful audiences are in resisting or actually rejecting 'TV's ideas about gender, sexuality identity and other issues' (Mumford, 1998: 117). Some view the content as stronger than viewers' resistance, others attribute more power to the viewers, and some writers view this process as a struggle. Although these are very different views of the process of meaning-making, what they do share is an understanding that 'our viewing practices and our ways of making sense of what we watch are articulated within a particular political and social context' (Mumford, 1998: 118; however, for the dangers of taking the notion of an active audience too far, see Silverstone, 1994).

This, in turn, is related to the notion that identity is fundamental to the process of meaning-making. In this context it should be recalled that no one argues nowadays that identity is determined by a single component, but as the discussion that follows will focus primarily on women, it is important to note that studies in this field assume 'that at least some of the time, the viewing experience is inflected by a certain aspect of identity – in this case, membership in the social category "women"' (Mumford, 1998: 120; but see also further discussion below).

Importantly, feminist scholarship – along with cultural studies – has been central to the highlighting of the importance of looking into the interaction between text and its consumption (labelled by some 'the ethnographic turn'; for further discussion see Ang, 1996). For example, Radway's (1984) seminal work considered the reading practices of women consumers of romantic fiction. In her fieldwork she focused on a small group of romance readers in the USA and related their pleasures of reading to women's subordinate position within patriarchal households. Her study showed that the actual practice of romance-reading enabled women to negotiate a space for their leisure pursuits and in fact use the very act of reading romances as 'a "declaration of independence" from one position accorded them by dominant patriarchal discourse: the position of ever-available and nurturing housewife and mother' (Ang, 1996: 121). What was also evident from her study was that women interpreting these texts understood the romance as a symbolic female triumph, as – according to their reading – these were stories about cold, distant, isolated men who transform into caring, nurturing and feminized human beings. As Stevenson notes, 'one of the strengths of Radway's study is that it raises some difficult questions related to identity that have been ignored by discourse analysis and mainstream media studies' (1995: 107). Furthermore, Ang views this study as 'a good example of how some female persons inadvertently reproduce their gendered subjectivity through all sorts of positions they take up and identify with in the course of their lives' (1996: 121).

Following studies like Radway's (1984) and others (see, for example, Morley, 1986), feminist writers increasingly complicated the ideas about audience and its interaction with texts. What they make clear is that media texts, including representations, do not affect audiences in a simple and direct way, but rather that this process is complex, ambiguous and at times even contradictory. It also became clear that women derive pleasure from watching television by directly enjoying certain programmes but also by resisting their messages or even constructing alternative meanings from them. For example, some found that women viewers could turn representations to their own purpose and experience what can be described as 'negative' representations of women as 'positive' ones. This was, for instance, a central finding of Modleski's (1982) study of women viewer's identification with soap opera villainesses. A more complex understudying of the pleasures derived by the – predominantly female – audience of soap operas, was offered by Ien Ang (1985) in her classic study of *Dallas*; in this book, Ang's (1985) argument against the media imperialism thesis is that *Dallas* is a polysemic text whose construction is dependent on the social and discursive context of the viewer.

In this context it is important to stress that academic interest in the interaction between audience and text goes beyond the ways in which gender shapes meaning-making. For example, in their study of *Dallas*, Katz and Liebes (1985) show, like Ang (1985), that 'the audience is not a "sponge" which will automatically soak in Western culture for good or evil. Rather, it picks and chooses what it likes and interprets what it chooses' (Pack, 2000). What Katz and Liebes (1985) clearly show is that ethnic groups bring their own identities to the meaning-making process of television programmes.

These different studies of soaps show the merging of the concerns of feminism and cultural studies, which have 'jointly sought to map out the ways in which the self is fashioned out of contemporary cultural forms' (Stevenson, 1995: 102). This, among other things, resulted in the view that identity, including gender identity, is actually a constantly shifting set of positions created through various social and cultural practices. Indeed:

> Feminists, along with others concerned with identity issues, seek to establish gendered selves as discursively unstable constructions. The aim is to fruitfully deconstruct simple polarities between men and women, straights and gays, lesbians and gays, and unravel the complex ways in which identities are actually constructed. (Stevenson, 1995: 102)

Moreover, in recent the years there is a clear understanding that:

> Despite the force of hegemonic gender discourse, the actual content of being a woman or a man and the rigidity of the dichotomy itself are highly variable, not across cultures and

historical times, but also, at a more micro-social and even psychological level, amongst and within women and men themselves. Gender identity, in short, is both multiple and partial, ambiguous and incoherent, permanently in process of being articulated, disarticulated and rearticulated. (Ang, 1996: 125)

This is also related to the view that the very focus on women viewers is problematic since it assumes that '"women" exist as some objective, unified whole, rather than being a fragmented and polysemous category under constant construction by and through social and cultural practices' (Mumford, 1998: 126). Moreover, 'being a woman can mean many different things, at different times and in different circumstances' (Ang, 1996: 119). Importantly, one result of this understanding is that feminist scholars caution against generalizing from the experiences of western, white, middle-class, heterosexual women – who are the most widely studied – to 'all women' (see Bobo and Seiter, 1997; see also the further discussion in the following section).

Finally, I would like to make clear that although in this section 'gender' stands mainly for 'women' – as indeed is the case in much of the literature – some studies do address other gender categories in relation to the issues discussed. Feuer's work on gay viewers of *Dynasty* (1989), for example, looks at the ways in which specific audience factions make meaning through their own gendered and sexual identities (see also the discussion in Chapter 30).

RACE, IDENTITY AND THE MEDIA

Apart from directing attention to women – and gender in general – feminist theory with its high profile:

has helped to ensure that even scholars who are not explicitly committed to that area nevertheless pay at least lip-service, and in some cases serious attention, to gender, as well as to other crucial relationships of difference, such as those involving sexuality and (albeit somewhat less successfully) race. (Mumford, 1998: 116)

As mentioned in the introduction to this chapter, academic feminism and black studies crossed disciplinary boundaries to a large extent, and what they share is exactly the interest in representations and their impact on the formation of identity (Geraghty and Lusted, 1998). This brief section addresses the issue of race identity within this context.

Most notably, what became clear through feminist analysis of audiences is that 'other differences may stand in the way of watching primarily "as women"' (Mumford, 1998: 120). Indeed, several studies showed that women of colour do not make the same meaning of texts, which include representations of black people, as white women (see, for example, Jhally and Lewis's 1992 study of *The Cosby Show*). For instance, in her study of the television viewing habits of black women in London, Reid (1990) found that their criticism of the portrayal of blacks on British television revolved around the extent to which these representations were far from their own experiences. As an example, 'the black women largely disparaged *The Cosby Show* for depicting an idealized and thus unrealistic portrayal of blacks while similarly condemning documentaries because they reinforced negative images of blacks' (Pack, 2000; see also further discussion of this programme in Chapter 31).

However, as in the previous section, it is important to emphasize that black people (like women) do not share the same identity; racial identities are as specific, fragmented and contradictory as any other identity, and much more so than theories of stereotypes assume. Some (see the discussion in Grossberg et al., 1998) argue that the very thinking of people in terms of stereotypes only enables us to ask whether a stereotype is an accurate portrayal of a particular group (see Chapters 28 and 31). But asking this question 'already assumes that this grouping of people is inevitable and natural, that its identity is singular and stable and exists independently of how it is represented in cultural codes and the media' (Grossberg et al., 1998: 224–5).

Finally, it should be noted that the limited discussion in this section reflects to some extent, as already articulated in Chapter 31 (and see also Daniels, 1998), the fact that there is a relatively small body of published work about race in the areas discussed here and that what does exist deals mainly with black people. Thus, although some research has been conducted over recent years (see, for example, discussion in Bobo and Seiter, 1997) it cannot be stressed enough that much more work is required into media representations and identities when it comes to race.

Conclusion

The extent of the literature about media representations and struggles over them are indications of the social power attributed to them. However, 'it is too easy for some people to ignore that, for some people out there, the media are representing who they are'. In fact this 'raises one of the most important questions about the role of the media in people's lives, for it deals with how people come to understand who and what they are, to view their identities and identifications, the positions that they occupy in society' (Grossberg et al., 1998: 224).

Within the context of the discussion in previous chapters, the last one of this section focused attention on ideas that counterbalance the assumption that media representations have an automatic and/or direct effect over audiences, especially regarding identity issues. Although this has already been intertwined in the discussion in Chapters 28–31, what I tried to underline in Chapter 32 was that although representations most certainly do matter, their interaction with identity is very complex as indeed are all the relationships between media and reality (see the discussion in Chapter 28). As should be clear by now, this complexity has many faces and is related, among other things, to the fact that the media texts themselves (including television – the medium to which I dedicated most of my discussion) are not homogenous at any point in time and definitely change over time, in some cases corresponding with changes taking place in society. Put differently, representations are neither uniform nor isolated from 'reality'. Indeed, the struggle over what it means to be, for example, a 'women' – a category on which I focused much of my writing in this section – in today's society should not be limited to the analysis of media representations; it must be studied within a context of a complex array of other social practices.

Furthermore, identity – or more precisely identities – is another very thorny concept, which clearly cannot be viewed as being constructed by media representations alone. Indeed, as I have tried to show in this section, identity affects meaning-making, maybe even more than it is constructed by media texts. Importantly, as Grossberg *et al.* put it, 'the history of media representations is not a progression from stereotypes to truth but a struggle to constantly articulate the meanings of people's identities and the ways they can live those cultural categories' (1998: 231).

SUMMARY

- Contemporary mass media preserve, transmit and create important cultural information; media representations are attributed with affecting the way in which members of society see themselves, how they are viewed and even treated by others.
- Representational theories offer a critique of media's construction of reality; they refer to the relationship between the ideological and the real.
- Within media studies, the term 'stereotype' means a simplified – in many cases oversimplified – representation that becomes established through years of repetition in media texts. Audiences tend to accept these limited pictures of social groups and do not question them. Stereotypes work to the advantage of society's dominant groups.
- Feminist analysis attempts to uncover the constructed messages behind the representations of women in the media, attributing to these images a crucial role in the perception of real-life women and thus the maintaining of a social status quo. The most widely studied television genres in this context are advertisements, soap operas and situation comedies.
- In recent years, scholarly attention – clearly influenced by feminist thought – has extended to include men, masculinity, gays and lesbians in the study of gender representation and identity.
- The media offer a central means of creating, reproducing and sustaining racial ideologies. Much of the work in the area of the media representation of race – referring mainly to black people – draws attention to the ways in which for many years people who are not white remained largely invisible, marginalized to the point of insignificance, or were framed by specific and limited stereotypes.
- Although writers direct much attention to media content, some have drawn attention to the impotence of the production and reception context in analysing media representations.

> The study of media representations is based on the assumption that media depictions affect the formation of identity. Scholars address this issue from diverse perspectives and on different levels, including the global, national, local and personal. The concept of 'identity' lies at the heart of current debates in cultural studies and social theory, and is best understood as a fluid process, always in formation, negotiated and re-negotiated.

Further Reading

Dines, G. and Humez, J.M. (eds) (1995) *Gender, Race and Class in Media – A Text-Reader*. London: Sage

Dyer, R. (1993) *The Matter of Images – Essays on Representations*. London: Routledge

Gunter, B. (1995) *Television and Gender Representation*. London: John Libbey

Hall, S. and Du Gay, P. (eds) (1996) *Questions of Cultural Identity*. London: Sage

Woodward, K. (ed.) (1997) *Identity and Difference*. London: Sage/Open University

Useful Websites

http://www.aber.ac.uk/media/
http://www.theory.org.uk/
http://adam.ac.uk/index.html
http://www.popcultures.com/
http://carmen.artsci.washington.edu/panop/home.htm
http://www.post-gazette.com/tv/

References

Abercrombie, N. (1996) *Television and Society*. Cambridge: Polity Press

Alvarado, M., Gutch, R. and Wollen, T. (1987) *Learning the Media – An Introduction to Media Teaching*. London: Macmillan Education

Andrews, M. (1998) Butterflies and caustic asides – housewives, comedy and the feminist movement. In Wagg, S. (ed.) *Because I Tell A Joke or Two – Comedy, Politics and Social Difference*. London: Routledge, 50–64

Ang, I. (1985) *Watching 'Dallas': Soap Opera and the Melodramatic Imagination*. London: Methuen

Ang, I. (1996) *Living Room War – Rethinking Media Audiences for a Postmodern World*. London: Routledge

Archer, B. (1999) What's your problem? In *Guardian*, 13 September

Baker, A. and Boyd, T. (eds) (1997) *Out of Bounds – Sports, Media, and the Politics of Identity*. Bloomington and Indianapolis, IN: Indiana University Press

Baker, S. Representation. At: http://dspace.dial.pipex.com/steve.baker/Frame.htm

Blain, N., Boyle, R. and O'Donnell, H. (1993) *Sport and National Identity in the European Media*. Leicester: Leicester University Press

Bobo, J. and Seiter, E. (1997) Black feminism and media criticism: *The Women of Brewster Place*. In Brunsdon, C., D'Acci, J. and Spigel, L. (eds) *Feminist Television Criticism – A Reader*. Oxford: Oxford University Press, 167–83

Bowes, M. (1990) Only when I laugh. In Goodwin, A. and Whannel, G. (eds) *Understanding Television*. London: Routledge, 128–40

Boyle, R. and Haynes, R. (1996) The grand old game: football, media and identity in Scotland. In *Media, Culture and Society* 18. London: Sage, 549–64

Brod, H. (ed.) (1987) *The Making of Masculinities: The New Men's Studies*. Boston: Allen & Unwin

Brunsdon, C. (1995) The role of soap opera in the development of feminist television scholarship. In Allen, R.C. (ed.) *To Be Continued . . .: Soap Operas Around the World*. London: Routledge, 49–65

Brunsdon, C., D'Acci, J. and Spigel, L. (eds) (1997) *Feminist Television Criticism – A Reader*. Oxford: Oxford University Press

Bryson, L. (1990) Challenges to male hegemony in sport. In Messner, M.A. and Sabo, D. (eds) *Sport, Men, and the Gender Order: Critical Feminist Perspectives*. Champaign, IL: Human Kinetics, 173–84

Burton, G. (1990) *More Than Meets the Eye*. London: Arnold

Chandler, D. (1994) The TV soap opera genre and its viewers. At: http://www.aber.ac.uk/media/Functions/mcs.html

Coakley, J.J. (1986) *Sport in Society: Issues and Controversies*. St Louis: Times Mirror/Mosby

Cohen, A.A., Levy, M.R., Roeh, I. and Gurevitch, M. (1996) *Global Newsrooms Local Audiences – A Study of the Eurovision News Exchange*. Acamedia Research Monograph 12. London: John Libbey

Cooper-Chen, A. (1994) Global games, entertainment and leisure – women as TV spectators'. In Creedon, P.J. (ed.) *Women, Media and Sport – Challenging Gender Values*. London: Sage, 257–72

Corner, J. (1999) *Critical Ideas in Television Studies*. Oxford: Oxford University Press

Corner, J. and Harvey, S. (eds) (1996) *Television Times – A Reader*. London: Arnold

Craig, S. (ed.) (1992) *Men, Masculinity, and the Media*. London: Sage

Craig, S. (1993) Selling masculinities, selling femininities: multiple genders and the economics of television. In *The Mid-Atlantic Almanack 2*, 15–27. At: http://www.rtvf.unt.edu/people/craig/genecon.htm

Craig, S. (1996) More (male) power: humour and gender in *Home Improvement*. In *The Mid-Atlantic Almanac 5*, 61–84. At: http://www.rtvf.unt.edu/people/craig/hialmank.htm

Cramer, J.A. (1993) Radio: a woman's place is on the air. In Creedon, J. (ed.) *Women in Mass Communication*. London: Sage, 154–66

Creedon, J. (ed.) (1993) *Women in Mass Communication* (second edn). London: Sage

Creedon: J. (ed.) (1994) *Women, Media and Sport – Challenging Gender Values*. London: Sage

Curran, J. and Gurevitch, M. (eds) (1991) *Mass Media and Society*. London: Edward Arnold

Curran, J., Morley, D. and Walkerdine, V. (eds) (1996) *Cultural Studies and Communications*. London: Arnold

Daniels, T. (1998) Television studies and race. In Geraghty, C. and Lusted, D. (eds) *The Television Studies Book*. London: Arnold, 131–40

Davis, L.R. and Harris, O. (1998) Race and ethnicity in US sports media. In Wenner, L.A. (ed.) *MediaSport*. London: Routledge, 154–69

Dines, G. and Humez, J.M. (eds) (1995) *Gender, Race and Class in Media – A Text-Reader*. London: Sage

Dow, B.J. (1996) *Prime-Time Feminism – Television, Media Culture, and the Women's Movement Since, 1970*. Pennsylvania, PA: University of Pennsylvania Press

Downes, B. and Miller, S. (1998) *Teach Yourself Media Studies*. London: Hodder and Stoughton

Dror, N. and Starnel, E. (1995) The Israeli newspaper coverage of judo. Tel-Aviv: Tel-Aviv University, seminar paper (in Hebrew)

Duncan, M.C. and Messner, M.A. (1998) The media image of sport and gender. In Wenner, L.A. (ed.) *MediaSport*. London: Routledge, 170–85

Duncan, M.C., Messner, M.A. and Williams, L. (1990) *Gender Stereotyping in Televised Sports*. Los Angeles, CA: Amateur Athletic Association

Dyer, R. (1985) Taking popular television seriously. In McQueen, D. (1998) *Television – A Media Student's Guide*. London: Arnold

Dyer, R. (1986) *Heavenly Bodies: Film Stars and Society*. New York, NY: St Martin's

Dyer, R. (1993) *The Matter of Images – Essays on Representations*. London: Routledge

Dyer, R. (1997) *White*. London: Routledge

Faludi, S. (1999) *Stifled: the Betrayal of the American Man*. USA: William Morrow and Company

Fejes, F.J. (1992) Masculinity as fact – a review of empirical mass communication research on masculinity. In Craig, S. (ed.) *Men, Masculinity, and the Media*. London: Sage, 9–22

Feuer, J. (1989) Reading *Dynasty*: television and reception theory. In *South Atlantic Quarterly*. Durham, North Carolina, Spring

Fiske, J. (1986) Television: polysemy and popularity, edited from *Critical Studies in Mass Communication* 3(4), 194–204. In Dickinson, R., Harindranath, R. and Linne, O. (eds) *Approaches to Audiences – A Reader*. London: Arnold

Fiske, J. (1987) Television Culture. London: Methuen

Fiske, J. (1991) Postmodernism and television. In Curran, J. and Gurevitch, M. (eds) *Mass Media and Society*. London: Edward Arnold, 55–67

Flitterman, S. (1985) Thighs and whiskers, the fascination of *Magnum PI*. In *Screen* 26(2), 42–58

Frid, Y. (1999) They're not exactly Mr Humphreys. In *Ha'ir*, 19 March (in Hebrew)

Gamson, J. (1995) Freak talk on TV. In *The American Prospect* 23, Fall, 44–50. At: http://epn.org/prospect/23/23gams.html

Gamson, J. (1999) *Freaks Talk Back: Tabloid Talk Shows and Sexual Nonconformity*. Chicago, IL: University of Chicago Press

Geraghty, C. (1991) *Women and Soap Opera: A Study of Prime Time Soap*. London: Polity

Geraghty, C. (1995) Social issues and realist soaps: a study of British soaps in the 1980s/1990s. In Allen, R.C. *To Be Continued . . .: Soap Operas Around the World*. London: Routledge, 66–80

Geraghty, C. (1996) The aesthetic experience: soap opera. In Corner, J. and Harvey, S. (eds) *Television Times – A Reader*. London: Arnold, 88–97

Geraghty, C. and Lusted, D. (eds) (1998) *The Television Studies Book*. London: Arnold

Gibson, J. (1999) Gay programme upsets viewers. In *Guardian*, 22 June

Goodwin, A. and Whannel, G. (eds) (1990) *Understanding Television*. London: Routledge

Gross, L. (1995) Out of the mainstream – sexual minorities and the mass media. In Dines, G. and Humez J.M. (eds) *Gender, Race and Class in Media – A Text-Reader*. London: Sage, 61–9

Gross, L.P. and Woods, J.D. (eds) (1999) *Columbia Reader on Lesbians and Gay Men in Media, Society and Politics (Between Men–Between Women)*. New York, NY: Columbia University Press

Grossberg, L., Wartella, E. and Whitney, C.D. (1998) *MediaMaking – Mass Media in a Popular Culture*. London: Sage

Gunter, B. (1995) *Television and Gender Representation*. London: John Libbey

Hall, M.A. (1990) How should we theorize gender in the context of sport? In Messner, M.A. and Sabo, D. (eds) *Sport, Men, and the Gender Order: Critical Feminist Perspectives*. Champaign, IL: Human Kinetics, 223–40

Hall, S. (1995) The whites of their eyes – racist ideologies and the media. In Dines, G. and Humez J.M. (eds) *Gender, Race and Class in Media*. London: Sage, 18–22

Hall, S. (ed.) (1997) *Representation: Cultural Representations and Signifying Practices*. London: Sage/Open University

Hall, S. and Du Gay, P. (eds) (1996) *Questions of Cultural Identity*. London: Sage

Halloran, J.D. (1990) *A Quarter of a Century of Prix Jeunesse Research*. Munich: Stiftung Prix Jeunesse

Hanke, R. (1992) Redesigning men – hegemonic masculinity in transition. In Craig, S. (ed.) *Men, Masculinity, and the Media*. London: Sage, 185–98

Hargreaves, J.A. (1986) Where's the virtue? Where's the grace? A discussion of the social production of gender relations in and through sport. In *Theory, Culture and Society* 3(1), 109–21

Hello! No. 574, 24 August 1999

Hensley, D. (2000) Inside *Queer as Folk*. In *The Advocate*, 21 November. At: http://www.advocate.com/html/stories/825/825_cvr_queer.html

Jackson, M. (1999) Four the record. In *Guardian*, 5 July

Jhally, S. (1989) Advertising as religion: the dialectic of technology and magic. In Lan, A. and Jhally, S., *Cultural Politics in Contemporary America*. New York, NY: Routledge, 217–29

Jhally, S. and Lewis, J. (1992) *Enlightened Racism: 'The Cosby Show', Audiences, and the Myth of the American Dream*. Boulder, CO: Westview Press

Johnson, S. (1993) Magazines: women's employment and status in the magazine industry. In Creedon, J. (ed.) *Women in Mass Communication*. London: Sage, 134–53

Kane, M.J. and Greendorfer, S.L. (1994) The media's role in accommodating and resisting stereotyped images of women in sport. In

Creedon, J. (ed.) *Women, Media and Sport – Challenging Gender Values*. London: Sage, 28–44

Katz, E. and Liebes, T. (1985) Mutual aid in the decoding of *Dallas*: preliminary notes from a cross-cultural study. In Drummond, P. and Paterson, R. (eds) *Television in Transition: Papers from the first International Television Studies Conference*. London: British Film Institute

Katz, J. (1995) Advertising and the construction of violent white masculinity. In Dines, G. and Humez, J.M. (eds) *Gender, Race and Class in Media*. London: Sage

Kellner, D. (1995) Cultural studies, multiculturalism and media culture. In Dines, G. and Humez, J.M. (eds) *Gender, Race and Class in Media – A Text-Reader*. London: Sage, 5–17

Kibby, M.D. (1997) Representing masculinity. In *Real Men: Representations of Masculinity in the Eighties Cinema*, thesis submitted to the University of Western Sydney, Nepean, for the degree of Doctor of Philosophy. At: http://www.newcastle.edu.au/department/so/represen.htm

Kimmel, M. (ed.) (1987) *Changing Men: New Directions in Research on Men and Masculinity*. Newbury Park, CA: Sage

Kirkham, P. and Skeggs, B. (1998) *Absolutely Fabulous*: absolutely feminist?. In Geraghty, C. and Lusted, D. (eds) *The Television Studies Book*. London: Arnold, 287–98

Lan, A. and Jhally, S. (1989) *Cultural Politics in Contemporary America*. New York, NY: Routledge

Lapchick, R.E. (ed.) (1996) *Sport in Society – Equal Opportunity or Business as Usual?* London: Sage

Lee, J. (1995) Subversive sitcoms – *Roseanne* as inspiration for feminist resistance. In Dines, G. and Humez, J.M. (eds) *Gender, Race and Class in Media – A Text-Reader*. London: Sage, 469–547

Leigh, M. (1974) Pierre de Coubertin: a man of his time. In *Quest* 22, 19–24

Lev-Ari, S. (1999) Built for relationship. In *Ha'aretz*, 14 October (in Hebrew)

Lewisohn, M. (1998) *Radio Times Guide to TV Comedy*. London: BBC Worldwide Ltd

McEachern, C. (1994) Bringing the wildman back home: television and the politics of masculinity. In *Continuum: The Australian Journal of Media and Culture* 7(2). At: http://www.cowan.edu.au/pa/continuum/

McQueen, D. (1998) *Television – A Media Student's Guide*. London: Arnold

Matelski, M.J. (1999) *Soap Operas Worldwide – Cultural and Serial Realities*. Jefferson, North Carolina: McFarland & Company, Inc.

Medhurst, A. and Tuck, L. (1982) Situation comedy and stereotyping. In Corner, J. and Harvey, S. (eds) (1996) *Television Times – A Reader*. London: Arnold, 110–16

Meister, M. (1998) '*Xena: Warrior Princess*' Through the Lenses of Feminism. At: http://www.whoosh.org/issue10/meister2.html

Mellencamp, P. (1997) Situation comedy, feminism, and Freud: discourses of Gracie and Lucy. In Brunsdon, C., D'Acci, J. and Spigel, L. (eds) *Feminist Television Criticism – A Reader*. Oxford: Oxford University Press, 60–73

Messner, M.A. (1988) Sports and male domination: the female athlete as contested ideological terrain. In *Sociology of Sport Journal* 5(3), 197–211

Messner, M.A., Duncan, M.C. and Jensen, K. (1990) Separating the men from the girls: the gendering of televised sports. Paper presented at the meeting of the North American Society for the Sociology of Sport, Denver, CO

Miller, D. (1995) The consumption of soap opera: *The Young and the Restless* and mass consumption in Trinidad. In Allen, R.C. (ed.) (1995) *To Be Continued . . .: Soap Operas Around the World*. London: Routledge, 213–33

Modleski, T. (1982) *Loving with a Vengeance: Mass-Produced Fantasies for Women*. London: Methuen

Morley, D. (1986) *Family Television: Cultural Power and Domestic Leisure*. London: Comedia

Mumford, L.S. (1995) *Love and Ideology in the Afternoon – Soap Opera, Women, and Television Genre*. Bloomington and Indianapolis, IN: Indiana University Press

Mumford, L.S. (1998) Feminist theory and television studies. In Geraghty, C. and Lusted, D. (eds) *The Television Studies Book*. London: Arnold, 114–30

O'Donnell, H. (1999) *Good Times, Bad Times – Soap Operas and Society in Western Europe.* Leicester: Leicester University Press

O'Sullivan, T., Hartley, J., Saunders, D., Montgomery, M. and Fiske, J. (1994) *Key Concepts in Communication and Cultural Studies* (second edn). London: Routledge

Orbe, M.P. and Cornwell, N.C. (1999) *Contradictions of Television Reality: the Case of Black Men on MTV's 'The Real World'.* Paper presented at the annual meeting of the International Communication Association, San Francisco, Cal. Published (1998) in *Southern Communication Journal* 64(1), 32–47

Pack, S. (2000) Reception, identity, and the global village: television in the fourth world. In *A Journal of Media and Culture* 3(1). At: http://english.uq.edu.au/mc/0003/fourth.html

Porter, L. (1998) Tarts, tampons and tyrants – women and representation in British comedy. In Wagg, S. (ed.) *Because I Tell a Joke or Two – Comedy, Politics and Social Difference.* London: Routledge, 65–93

Radway, J. (1984) *Reading the Romance: Women, Patriarchy, and Popular Literature.* Chapel Hill, NC: University of North Carolina Press

Reid, E.C. (1990) The television viewing habits of young black women in London. In *Screen* 30(1), 115–21

Rowe, D. (1994) Accommodating bodies: celebrity, sexuality, and 'Tragic Magic'. In *Journal of Sport and Social Issues* 18(1), 6–26

Rowe, D. (1995) *Popular Cultures – Rock Music, Sport and the Politics of Pleasure.* London: Sage

Rowe, K.K. (1996) Roseanne: unruly woman as domestic goddess. In Baehr, H. and Gray, A. (eds) *Turning it on – a Reader in Women & Media.* London: Arnold

Sabo, D. and Curry Jansen, S. (1992) Images of men in sport media – the social reproduction of gender order. In Craig, S. (ed.) *Men, Masculinity, and the Media.* London: Sage, 169–84

Saco, D. (1992) 'Masculinity as signs – poststructuralist feminist approaches to the study of gender'. In Craig, S. (ed.) *Men, Masculinity, and the Media.* London: Sage, 23–39

Sanders, M. (1993) Television: the face of the network news is male. In Creedon, J. (ed.) *Women in Mass Communication.* London: Sage, 167–71

Schmitt, M. (1996) The state of women in sports media. In Lapchick, R.E. (ed.) *Sport in Society – Equal Opportunity or Business as Usual?* London: Sage, 234–6

Seiter, E. (1995) Different children, different dreams – racial representation in advertising. In Dines, G. and Humez, J.M. (eds) *Gender, Race and Class in Media – A Text-Reader.* London: Sage, 99–108

Shifflett, B. and Revelle, R. (1996) Gender equity in sports media coverage – a review of the NCAA News. In Lapchick, R.E. (ed.) *Sport in Society – Equal Opportunity or Business as Usual?* London: Sage, 237–43

Silverstone, R. (1994) *Television and Everyday Life: Towards an Anthropology of the Television Audience.* New York, NY: Routledge

Sloop, M.J. (1997) Mike Tyson and the perils of discursive constraints: boxing, race, and the assumption of guilt. In Baker, A. and Boyd, T. (eds) *Out of Bounds – Sports, Media, and the Politics of Identity.* Bloomington and Indianapolis, IN: Indiana University Press, 102–22

Spangler, L.C. (1992) Buddies and pals – a history of male friendship on prime-time television. In Craig, S. (ed.) *Men, Masculinity, and the Media.* London: Sage, 93–110

Steinman, C. (1992) Gaze out of bounds – men watching men on television. In Craig, S. (ed.) *Men, Masculinity, and the Media.* London: Sage, 199–214

Stevenson, N. (1995) *Understanding Media Cultures – Social Theory and Mass Communication.* London: Sage

Theberge, N. and Cronk, A. (1986) Work routines in newspaper sports departments and the coverage of women's sports. In *Sociology of Sports Journal* 3, 195–203.

Tuchman, G. (1978) The symbolic annihilation of women by the mass media. In Tuchman, G., Kaplan Daniels, A. and Benet, J. (eds) *Hearth and Home: Images of Women and the Media.* New York: Oxford University Press, 3–17

Tulloch, J. (1990) Television and black Britons. In Goodwin, A. and Whannel, G. (eds) *Understanding Television.* London: Routledge, 141–52

Van Zoonen, L. (1994, reprinted 1996) *Feminist Media Studies*. London: Sage

Wagg, S. (1991) Playing the past: the media and the England Football Team. In Williams, J. and Wagg, S. (eds) *British Football and Social Change*. Leicester: Leicester University Press

Wagg, S. (1995) The business of America: reflections on World Cup 94. In Wagg, S. (ed.) *Giving the Game Away: Football, Politics and Culture on Five Continents*. Leicester: Leicester University Press

Wagg, S. (ed.) (1998) *Because I Tell a Joke or Two – Comedy, Politics and Social Difference*. London: Routledge

Walkowitz, R.L. (1997) Reproducing reality: Murphy Brown and illegitimate politics. In Brunsdon, C., D'Acci, J. and Spigel, L. (eds)

(1997) *Feminist Television Criticism – A Reader*. Oxford: Oxford University Press, 325–36

Whannel, G. (1992) *Fields in Vision – Television Sport and Cultural Transformation*. London: Routledge

Whitson, D. (1986) Structure, agency and the sociology of sport debated. In *Theory, Culture & Society* 3(1): 99–107

Wood, M. (1996) *The Portrayal of Gays and Lesbians on TV, and How Viewers React*. At: http://www.aber.ac.uk/media/Functions/mcs.html

Woodward, K. (ed.) (1997) *Identity and Difference*. London: Sage/Open University

Woolard, H. (1983) *A Content Analysis of Women's and Girl's Sports Articles in Selected Newspapers* (Master's thesis). University of Iowa

Advertising and Marketing

Rachel Eyre and Michel Walrave

Introduction

This section on advertising and marketing is split into two main areas. First, we will examine the history and development of advertising, focusing on particular issues such as gender and regulation. Second, we will consider the role of the marketing communication mix, with particular reference to webmarketing.

The first chapter in this section will consider in detail the relationship between the move to industrial society in Britain and America, and the concurrent historical development in advertising. We will also demonstrate that it is important for students of the media to examine advertising, because of the importance of advertising revenue in shaping the modern communication industry.

The second chapter will tackle the theories and methods used to analyse modern advertising. Critical theory will be utilized to consider whether audiences are being socialized by advertising into an acceptance of the dominant consumer culture and reproduction of the capitalist society. An account of the semiotic tools used to read adverts or 'texts' will be provided, thus putting the theory of semiology into practice by a consideration of the visual and literal images used, as well as the location of adverts, in order to attract the viewer's attention. The second chapter also explores the use of gender in advertising and the overuse of body image, with its possible influence on the stereotyping of sex roles in society.

Chapter 35 offers examples from Britain and America of the regulations imposed on advertising to ensure that the public are protected from misleading information about products. The restrictions placed on the advertising community are interesting because they highlight how influential the medium is perceived as being and the necessary measures used in order to govern the industry. An example is given of a British advert that broke the rules. A brief assessment of the global nature of modern advertising is offered. An example of the type of advertising employed by one international clothing company is given.

We will finish this element of the section by considering some arguments in support of the advertising industry and its role in contemporary society. We ask whether advertising merely draws our attention to the varied products on offer, leaving the individual to make a well-informed choice while being entertained with attractive images and witty repartee.

The final chapter in this section is intended to present an overview of marketing communication in general and new forms of commercial communication through the Internet in particular. First, we sketch the instruments most commonly used to promote a product or to service a target group. We then focus on the types of communication used to develop a personal relationship between a business and individual **prospects** or consumers. One of the aims of this chapter is namely to provide an understanding of the place of new forms of marketing communication in the general marketing communication mix. We will also stress the possibilities for the integration of different tools; it is not our aim to provide an in-depth theoretical and practical perspective of marketing communications, but to lift the lid on some new tools marketers use. In the last chapter of this section we therefore narrow our focus to the possibilities and limitations of the promotion of products and services on the Internet.

CHAPTER 33

'We're Surrounded!' Advertising in Society

Rachel Eyre

INTRODUCTION

Advertising can be seen as a cultural commodity in that its popularity as a tool of communication is a consequence of our developing society. From pre-industrial, industrial to consumer and global society, advertising communicates to us the centrality of consumerism in the western world.

Such is the influence of advertising in the media that it engenders comments like: 'The persuasive nature of commercial TV and TV ads is such that [the] present industrial system could not survive without it' (Leiss, Kline and Jhally, 1997: 23). In addition, such is its influence that it is monitored by independent authorities that consider the moral and ethical issues related to advertising: 'All advertisements should be legal, decent, honest and truthful. All advertisements should be prepared with a sense of responsibility to consumers and society' (British Advertising Standards Authority, Advertising Codes 2.1, 2.2).

ADVERTISEMENTS IN CONTEXT

It could be said that, to take a historical look at advertising is to glance back at the development of western industrial society. It could also be said that the advertising industry presents, in written, visual or verbal form, ideas and values from society in any given age; it tries to capture the mood of a period and capitalizes upon it.

Where did advertising begin? In short, a basic form of advertising has existed as a vehicle of communication from the very start of civilization. Branston and Stafford (1996: 97) say that advertising is chronicled as far back as Greek and Roman times, when criers would alert the public to the services of tradesmen. Joseph Dominick (1987: 359) says that the first printed advertisement in Britain was a handbill during 1480. By the 1600s, adverts were frequently produced in newspapers.

In western societies the creation of the modern advertising industry was inspired by the transformation from an agricultural- to industrial-based economy. After the 1760s in Britain, and the 1860s in America, the dominance of rural, agricultural life was replaced by the onset of industrialization. The use of raw materials (i.e. coal) in manufacture, the invention of labour-saving machines, developments in transport for distribution and the move to urban cities sparked a new phenomenon of mass production. This meant that a surplus of goods could quickly be produced due to the new technology and concentration of people working in factories. In order to avoid overproduction more consumers were needed in a larger market.

Before this time, advertising was unnecessary because products were produced in local communities and were not '**branded**' by manufacturers. Adverts were simple, produced by local shopkeepers in the style of an announcement alerting consumers to the availability of goods. After industrialization, people were no longer in control of the production of their household supplies as goods were mass-produced. People had to adjust to their new role as consumers in society with their work being part of a large organized system.

Advertising also had a new role to play in alerting new consumers to the amount and diversity of goods available. Commentators argue that advertising had a social role in helping people accept their lives as city dwellers. Advertising would suggest that products could relieve social problems and thus reduce the stress of modern living. The relationship between consumer and producer in capitalist society was settled. Manufacturers produced a wealth of new products and the consumer was encouraged by advertising to buy. As Sean Brierley (1995: 8) says, advertising is born in the industrial period from the need to match the 'demands of mass production' with the consumers' desire for commodities. In other words, if industrial society based on mass production is to survive, then the population has to be encouraged to spend without limitation on the goods on sale.

Until the late 1800s adverts were limited to a written description without illustrations, and confined to tight newspaper column space. Many lacked literary flair due to being written by industrialists. Although produced in 1903 the front cover of *Country Life* (March 1903) provides a useful example of this classic style of advertising. The adverts are allocated a rigid column space. Compared to modern examples the adverts are informative, but unappealing due to the bold black type and heavy reliance on description.

The emergence of advertising agencies

During the 1890s advertising agencies emerged in America. With the wealth of brand products available at this time, an opportunity arose for a business that could offer sophisticated adverts of a higher quality than manufacturers could produce. Therefore, from the early 1900s in Britain and America, the role of advertising agencies has included the following:

- space brokers – buying space in the media in large quantities and selling to advertisers
- media specialists – producing words and illustrations in an attractive and sophisticated format
- market research – manufacturers need to know what the consumer is interested in and the advertising agency will produce market research for each client (as stated elsewhere in this chapter, advertising agencies have utilized the study of psychology in order to understand the desires of the individual).

Product-oriented Approach and Advertising

Leiss *et al.* (1997: 153) highlight four periods in the development of advertising. The first stage, referred to as the 'product-oriented approach', lasted from 1890 to 1925 and was concerned with the era in which *Country Life* magazine (in our example) was printed. Leiss *et al.* identify four other historical periods that we will return to throughout this chapter. In this approach to advertising, the product is sold by a rational explanation of its uses and benefits. The written description forms the main body of the advert. The page from *Country Life* offers another example of this style with Power's Whiskey: a straightforward description of the product is presented, followed by advice on where to purchase. In the opposite column, Borwick's Baking Powder is advertised, again providing a description of its authenticity followed by information on its uses. The audience is seen as able to make a rational choice and persuasive language is limited.

Developments in technology in the late 1800s meant that the use of illustrations in magazines and newspapers was first witnessed. Magazine adverts overtook the newspaper as a medium for advertising at this time. Up until the 1880s magazines had been proud to thrive without the need for advertising revenue. By the 1890s this had changed, with some entrepreneurs in the magazine world producing cheap lifestyle magazines supported financially by advertisers. These cheap magazines – with their new technology in the form of colour illustrations and photography – appealed to the public. As a result, by the turn of the century many magazines and newspaper publishers were considering readers as potential customers that could be sold to advertisers. The advertising business was influencing the material produced in print media as publishers produced articles directed at a **target audience**.

Figure 33.1   Front cover of *Country Life*, 28 March 1903

Product Symbols and Advertising

Stuart Ewen (1976) maintains that at the turn of the century there was a need to attract consumers from the working classes as well as the wealthier classes in order to counteract overproduction in industry. However, advertising focused on a description of the product and this failed to attract enough customers. The advertising industry developed a new style of campaign, concentrating on the consumer rather than the product. The selling point became what the product could do to enhance the life of the consumer. In Leiss *et al.*'s (1997: 153) second stage of advertising, this is recognized as a time of 'product symbols' (1925 to 1945). The discipline of psychology was employed in order to study what appealed most to the consumer. The consumer was seen as less rational and susceptible to buying on impulse. In order to succeed, advertising needed to concentrate less on the utilitarian value of a product and more on the attraction it had for the consumer. The aim became to sell the product on the premise that it provided the consumer with something they most desired. Advertisers used different techniques to encourage customers, developments in print technology bringing more attractive formats to magazines with illustrations.

The advert for Wright's Coal Tar Soap in Figure 33.2 (*Country Life*, March 1903), shows a clear example of Leiss *et al.*'s product symbol stage. The photograph of the children on the left-hand side immediately captures the viewer's eye. It says more to the viewer than had

Advertisement in *Country Life* for Wright's Coal Tar Soap   Figure 33.2

been possible from a reliance simply on written description. The picture is idealized with the garland of flowers surrounding the frame. The image of the naked boy holding the soap bar reinforces the message printed underneath: 'Is it good for baby?' The baby in the picture looks reassuringly healthy. There is also the mother's positive reply and the bold statement: 'Absolutely Pure'. The product name is printed in stylized writing with a white border to bring the letters jumping up from the page. All these images demonstrate the length to which the focus on the needs of the consumer (product symbol) have replaced the simple description of product. The advert tells the parent that the soap is of great use to the consumer by helping to prevent childhood diseases. We are told that the soap works as a 'preventive of measles, scarlet-fever [and] small-pox'. The use of a letter from a grateful mother adds the final stamp of authenticity and therefore acts as a powerful persuader.

Another technique is employed in the Cadbury's Cocoa advert (*Country Life*, March 1903) shown in Figure 33.3. Here consumers are encouraged to be familiar with a product by presenting a reassuring slogan – 'A Perfect Food' – written in bold black capitals. The little child in the illustration looks happy, healthy and middle class in his smart Victorian clothes: positive visual signs for the viewer that the product is of benefit to him. Again the advert is supported by education and advice, this time from medical and quality magazines. Positive words are used throughout: 'nourishing', 'pure', 'strength' and 'food'.

"A PERFECT FOOD."

CADBURY's COCOA is a valuable beverage for the Young,
being highly nourishing, perfectly pure, and very easily digested.

The *Medical Magazine* says of CADBURY's Cocoa: "For Strength,
Purity, and Nourishment, there is nothing superior to be found."

The *Lancet* says:—"The statement that CADBURY's Cocoa is an
absolutely pure article cannot be controverted in view of the results of
analysis which, in our hands, this excellent article of food has yielded."

Health says:—CADBURY's Cocoa has in a remarkable degree those
natural elements of sustenance which give the system endurance and
hardihood, building up muscle and bodily vigour, with a steady action that
renders it a most acceptable and reliable beverage."

CADBURY'S COCOA — ABSOLUTELY PURE, THEREFORE BEST.

Figure 33.3   Advertisement in *Country Life* for Cadbury's Cocoa

There was an enormous growth in national advertising in the period between 1890 and 1920. At this time the idea of a brand name was born, with manufacturers producing goods distinguished from those of other manufacturers by an image that appealed to the consumer. Through brand names, products could be easily identifiable and the consumer was able to influence production by calling for a demand in a specific brand. This brand image was sold through advertising. As social mobility increased with the move of large populations to urban areas, national brand products could be sold in the new department stores opening in England and America.

In America in the 1920s and 1930s advertisers launched into the medium of radio. They became absorbed in media production, with the organization of studios and shows. A good example of this is the advent of the soap opera. This type of radio show was written by advertising agencies and sponsored by detergent companies. In Britain, broadcasters had a more conservative attitude towards sponsorship through advertising: the BBC rejected the principle of advertising due to concerns over the influence advertising values may have on national culture.

Nevertheless, in the 1920s some musical concerts were given on BBC radio and sponsored by business. Although devoted to public broadcasting, which rejected the idea of sponsorship, support was accepted due to restricted funds. Murdock (in Strinati and Wagg,

1992: 208) says that the BBC could broadcast sponsored events and commercial informa-tion while forbidding **spot advertising**. Sponsored concerts were very popular at the begin-ning of the 1920s, but declined by the end of the decade as the BBC became more financially independent. As a result, in Britain the advertising industry moved towards commercial radio. Radio Luxembourg, launched in 1933, set a trend for the commercial radio stations of the future. It used brand-name publicity, first employed in America, and sponsors were able to put their names to shows. The 1930s and 1940s were decades when radio was the prime vehicle for advertisers.

Branston and Stafford say that 'lifestyle advertising' (1996: 98) was employed, linking the purchase of a product with a lifestyle to which the consumer would like to aspire. Advertising was directed at women, who were acknowledged as primary consumers. Men were perceived as working in the public sphere earning money, while women were seen as spend-ing it. New technology in the home sold as labour-saving devices accounted for a large percentage of advertising. This was marketed as releasing women from nineteenth-century domesticity, which had involved hard manual labour; again, the product is marketed by what it can do for the woman. An advert for gas cookers (*Daily Mail*, May 1937), see Figure 33.4, shows a photograph of a woman placing a dish in a bright new oven. Consumers are reassured by her domestic status, which is demonstrated by the clean kitchen, apron and oven gloves. However, she is a modern woman who (thanks to the cooker) has time to wear glamorous clothes, shoes and jewellery. The visual cues are supported by the written description provided: 'Gas cookers have knocked the guesswork out of cooking.'

Branston and Stafford (1996:99) maintain that, from 1912 onwards, the cinema became an important vehicle for advertising products. Hollywood films would prominently display labour-saving devices. This was even achieved humorously through sketches by renowned comics such as Laurel and Hardy. In the film *Unaccustomed As We Are* (1929) the comedi-ans are featured in a storyline where they accidentally blow up the new cooker of their next-door neighbour. The joke is concentrated on the incompetence of the heroes rather than the new technology, which is shown prior to their arrival as a smart addition to the woman's kitchen. With the inclusion of the new cooker, the kitchen would have looked bright and modern in its design to those watching the comedy. This was a contrast to the open ranges in Victorian kitchens. Cigarette companies also hired famous Hollywood stars by canvass-ing the actors to smoke in their films. At this time Hollywood was an important asset in the advertising world as audiences were captivated by the images they saw on the big screen.

Tremendous growth in advertising took place after the Second World War. Dominick (1987: 360) describes the change from a 'war economy', where people made do with what they already had, to a 'consumer economy'. This was created by a rise in affluence and mobility after the restrictions of the war years. In America, NBC demonstrated the first public television in 1939. However, it was not until after the war that the television industry really got started. In America in 1945 there were 8 television stations, by 1950 there were 38.

In Britain the BBC dismissed the idea of television advertising on the grounds that the service it provided was educational and informative and would not be sullied by the economic concerns of advertising. Nevertheless, the Conservative government proposed a

MAINSTAT - CONTROLLED
GAS COOKERS
have knocked the
guesswork out of
cooking

Figure 33.4   Advertisement in the *Daily Mail* for Main gas cookers

public authority that would operate a network of transmitting stations and rent these facilities to private television companies. These companies would finance their programmes by attracting advertising. The Television Act 1954 heralded the beginning of commercial television with the start of the Independent Television Service. By 1958 the number of TV licences had reached 8 million (Strinati and Wagg, 1992: 204), which encouraged advertisers to use the medium.

Subliminal Advertising

The progress of advertising on to television screens led to a moral panic among media commentators. The potential influence of advertising appeared more profound, with the sophisticated visual images that could be channelled directly into the home. Moral panics were heightened by the possibility of subliminal messages being used in television. Vance Packard defines this technique as 'getting visual or whispered messages to us below our level of conscious awareness. Visually they can be split-second flashes, or fixed but dimly-lit messages that stay on the screen for longer periods' (Packard, 1981: 232).

Not all advertising is criticized by Packard, only that which aims to deceive the public in the manner he describes. The concern was that while audiences were watching or listening to one message, another would be placed in their subconscious minds. In *The Hidden Persuaders*, Packard refers to the work of Wilson Brysan Key who claimed to have found examples of sexual imagery in American printed advertisements: the word 'sex' depicted in the organization of ice cubes and a glass was used in an alcohol advert.

However, it was never conclusively proved that the existence of subliminal messages altered the behaviour of audiences or increased product sales. Nevertheless, commentators at the time were concerned that subliminal messages could exploit the deep-rooted fears or desires of audiences. Vulnerable groups and children would be susceptible to messages that played on individual weaknesses.

Vance Packard's book is a critique of American advertising. American advertising has enjoyed greater freedom than its counterparts in Britain. Gillian Dyer identifies the difference (Dyer, 1982: 59) between Britain and America as follows: in Britain, advertisers were only allowed to buy airtime for their 'spot' adverts, which are broadcast in breaks during programming (since the publication of Dyer's book, to a lesser extent in Britain, advertisers are now allowed involvement in the production of television programmes); however, in America a majority of advertising pays for the production of television programmes or series and this could lead to it influencing programme content (for example, as Dyer says, by advertisers insisting that their product is treated favourably and not criticized in programmes).

The possibility of subliminal advertising led to a public outcry. Murdock (in Strinati and Wagg, 1992: 202–3) argues that, in America, the cold war with the Soviet Union influenced government attitudes towards advertising techniques. It was felt that subliminal messages would appear too much like thought control and that this would damage the image of America as a democracy. By the late 1950s, state legislation banning the practice was followed by a ban from the National Association of Television and Radio Broadcasters. Murdock says that, in Britain, events abroad were seen as a warning to protect our culture against becoming too Americanized. The practice of subliminal advertising was banned in Britain under the Television Act 1964. However, Murdock says that there were never any recorded uses of this practice in Britain.

Murdock argues that other techniques exist that work as 'embedded persuasions' in parts of television programmes themselves. Murdock (in Strinati and Wagg, 1992: 205–6) gives five examples. The first is of occasions when advertisers provide products to programme-makers free or at a lower cost than normal in return for acknowledgement on screen. For example, the car or holiday that is the main prize on a game show. Second, there is the advertiser who provides the money for a TV station to buy or produce a programme. (This is the particular character of advertising found in America, but to a lesser extent is witnessed in Britain today.) Murdock says that this does not give sponsors a direct editorial say in decisions but, their mere association with certain programmes, could affect what programmes are made in the long term.

The third of Murdock's examples is the sponsorship of sports or arts programmes, which are then broadcast with credit to the sponsors. The fourth example is paying to have a product or an advertisement placed in an appropriate part of a programme (for example, the star of a programme using a particular product). Murdock says that product placement works well when its existence appears to be completely natural. Finally, programmes can be used to promote a product range (for example, a cartoon based around a range of toys).

Personalization and Advertising

Many of the techniques used in radio adverts could be adapted to television (for example, the use of social dramas and characters with which the audience can easily identify). In their third period of the development of advertising (1945 to 1965), Leiss *et al.* (1997: 155) describe the 'personalization' that took place with the move from primary advertising in magazines and radio to television. Advertisements became more personalized, as products were associated with a desirable self-image. The medium of television was able to present effectively, for example, a glamorous image with the combination of verbal and sophisticated visual images. Advertising used consumer research to achieve a more thorough understanding of what motivated individuals to buy certain products.

Market Segmentation and Advertising

In the 1960s, with people looking forward as they moved further away from the war years, a comparative confidence was expressed in adverts of the period. In the 1960s, advertisements became more confident, with brand names being brought to the fore and paraded with the support of modern images and music. Leiss *et al.*, in their final account, refer to this period of advertising (1965 to 1985) as 'market segmentation'. In a market-place that had become increasingly competitive and saturated with products, advertising agencies needed profiles of consumer lifestyles in order to succeed. Research carried out on targeted audiences looked into groups such as class, gender and age. In order to capture a specific market, television advertising focused on the lifestyles and tastes of groups of individuals. Advertisers drew on the knowledge and culture of groups rather than appealing to consumers as a mass audience. As television advertising is directed at a selected audience, it challenges other media that offer local or specialized markets. Leiss *et al.* maintain that all four types of advertising technique are still utilized by agencies when required.

The advertising process
- A client and its marketing team approach an advertising agency for a one-off advertisement, a campaign, the development of an existing campaign, or the launch of a new product. They brief the agency, a timetable is agreed and a budget allocated.
- The advertising agency's team is assembled and meets to discuss the client's brief, including the aims of the campaign, the tone of the advertisement, the target audience and the medium to be used.
- Product research is carried out with potential customers. The target audience need is assessed, and the tone and language of the advertisement considered.

- The creative stage starts with a blank layout board and ends with an inspirational idea that, hopefully, meets the brief.
- The idea is presented internally first, usually to the creative director, then to the client for approval.
- The campaign is designed and the creative work completed.
- The client agrees to go ahead with implementation of the campaign and a final budget is agreed.
- The advertising space, in whatever medium, is purchased by the media buyer.
- The campaign then runs for the agreed duration in the specified medium.
- Consumer research is carried out to assess the success of the campaign.

CHAPTER 34

Theory, Method and Analysis

Rachel Eyre

INTRODUCTION

At the heart of advertising is the different interpretation by advertisers of what will appeal to audiences. In order to analyse the messages conveyed in advertising, students of the subject utilize different communication theories and methods. These include critical theory, neoliberal theory, semiotics and feminist theoretical perspective. A brief description of these will offer readers a useful guide for further work.

CRITICAL THEORY AND ADVERTISING

Advertising has been analysed by academics from a critical theoretical background. Critical theorists argue that the dominant ideas and values in a culture are reproduced for the benefit of an elite few. These opinions are conveyed as if they are the only possible, natural order of social relations. Capitalism, Marxists argue, is prone to self-destruction due to the very nature of its organization. Ideological control (i.e. that people see the organization of society as normal) explains its ability to exist when production is so great that it surpasses demand. At the heart of the critical theory is the unnecessary level of goods produced after basic needs have been satisfied. This leads to the exploitation of the mass of the population in order to continue such a system. Critical theorists argue that, in reality, only a very few of those in control of capitalist industries benefit.

Critical theorists maintain that advertising is one of a number of institutions that have an ideological control over the individual. Leiss *et al.* (1997: 31) suggest that this is achieved by the dominant concept promoted by advertising, of the individual as consumer rather than producer. Therefore, we accept our position in society as consumer and buy more goods than we can possibly need. People are reliant on others for goods and survival, and therefore they are open to coercion. Advertising, in practice, increases demand for products, which reduces the surplus of goods. It is this surplus of goods that could overload the capitalist society and lead to its breakdown.

Advertising presents a picture that supports the status quo and encourages the public to place a social value on products. We see advertising images of an affluent family life in the type of car that the father drives, or the popularity of a teenager in the type of clothes she wears. What is being bought is a package of product and improved lifestyle. However, critical theorists would argue that putting a social value on products is 'unhealthily'. For example, if we buy perfume we should do so because we enjoy the smell, rather than with the hope that wearing the product will make us more attractive to the opposite sex.

The critical theory of the Frankfurt School (Branston and Stafford, 1996: 103) argues that we are absorbed into overidentifying with products because of the power of persuasion. They are concerned with the increasing amount of advert-funded television. The criticism is that a concentration on advertising will break down the cultural values of a nation, which will become a society concerned only with consumerism. They are especially concerned about the amount of time children spend viewing television and the consequences this may have for future society. Finally, the School are concerned that, although in the western world there are authorities to govern advertising, developing-world countries are not protected by such bodies. For example, Branston and Stafford (1996: 103) argue that women in the West are encouraged to breast feed for health reasons; however, in developing countries, women are encouraged by incorrect information to buy formula baby milk.

For critical theorists, advertising encourages a fantasy world, achieved by buying consumer products. It is within this world that we are invited to exist. The power of consumer product dominates and influences the real world. The critical theorist Raymond Williams refers to this as 'the magic system' (Eldridge, Kitzinger and Williams, 1997: 107) or magical techniques of persuasion. These techniques ensure that we see goods as having an ability to enhance our lives to a greater extent than their real practical value. Our preoccupation with consumer products means that we, as a society, do not concern ourselves with trying to change or improve the structure of society itself. Advertising works within a framework of institutions ensuring the continuation of capitalist society, diverting our minds from real issues such as the quality of health or education institutions. The desire for certain non-essential products is created by advertising. Theorists argue that, in addition, advertising teaches us that happiness can only be achieved through purchasing.

The critical theorist Goldman (1992: 2) refers to reading the messages in adverts as a 'political act' rather than 'depoliticized diversion'. In other words, the process of decoding adverts is not a harmless distraction, but a socializing process for the individual into the dominance of the consumer culture. This culture has the power to dominate our lives because the individual is ruled by consumer values. In Goldman's account, advertisements are part of a 'cultural hegemony' (1992: 2), in which our view of the world is reduced to a consumer reality. The perimeters of reality shift as moments are taken from a 'lived context' (1992: 5) and placed in an advertisement to give the advert meaning. For example, the power of attraction between the sexes is a very desirable commodity. Most people want to feel the pleasure of attraction, love, friendship or sex, and advertisements co-opt these everyday emotions in order to sell products.

Marxist theorists argue that the only way to release the individual from exploitation by a dominant elite is to change the very structure of society itself. This is a very idealistic stance that relies on society having a class-consciousness and the desire or motivation to implement change. This is a particularly unlikely outcome seeing as changes in recent history have been confined to countries moving towards capitalist, rather than socialist, means of production.

Neoliberal Theory

Neoliberal theory offers a less radical approach to those of its critical contemporaries, by suggesting that changes can be made within the present economic system. John Galbraith (in Leiss, Kline and Jhally, 1997: 19) says that advertising inhibits **consumer sovereignty** because adverts are involved in the manufacturing of desire for goods. Therefore, the production industry, as opposed to the individual, has control over demand. In this respect the individual suffers from a similar sense of powerlessness as observed by critical theorists. However, rather than a change in the organization of society, neoliberal theorists call for a more constructive use of economic resources. Instead of the present 'blind support' (Leiss, Kline and Jhally, 1997: 20) of increased production, more money should be allocated to the important areas of society – for example, health and education.

Advertising and Semiotics

Semiotics, or the 'science of signs' as coined by Ferdinand de Saussure, was first applied to advertising by Roland Barthes (1973: 36–8) in his analysis of soap powder adverts. Semiotics is the meaning that we take from signs in the world around us. Van Zoonen says that 'Semiologists . . . analyse how particular combinations of sign systems construct particular meaning' (1994: 75). Signs can be words or visual images that convey a certain meaning. For example, a sketchy drawing of a male or female figure (usually differentiated by the appearance of a skirt or trousers) on doors in shops or restaurants tells customers where the appropriate toilets are to be found. It is a very simplistic example, but demonstrates that the sign – i.e. the male or female figure – has a meaning in our culture that most people would understand without the need for the word 'toilet' to be included. The female or male character on the door is the signifier, and the meaning (toilet) created by its presence is the signified. The two combined create the sign. All things that have a meaning are, by definition, signs.

How much we understand a sign depends on our knowledge and appreciation of the cultural environment in which we live. Meanings derived from signs are related to specific cultures. For example, in Britain the word 'pants' is a sign meaning underwear. However, in America the word means trousers worn over underwear. To tell someone to get their pants on would have two very different meanings in the two countries. Semiology has a central role in the analysis of advertising. Semiology owns the methodological tools with which to explore the visual and written texts of the advert. It does more than simply count the number of times a certain image appears (content analysis), but goes further by debating the construction of the message.

GENDER IN ADVERTISING

Adverts are only a few seconds long and, in order to get their messages across, advertisers need an instantly recognizable formula. The most successful is a cultural stereotype. If advertisers can recreate something audiences have been used to seeing, or socialized to believe in, then they will understand the message of the advert very quickly and most probably accept its meaning. The advert may be complex and sophisticated in nature, but if the audience can recognize a sign or meaning then it will understand the overall message presented. Advertisers are tapping into the very ideology of a society, ideology being the taken-for-granted norms that we unconsciously accept. As Goffman (1979) argues, men and women are represented in adverts in terms of their social gender. Therefore the societal constructions of femininity or masculinity (the way that society perceives the different sexes) is reinforced in advertisements.

Goffman (in Leiss, Kline and Jhally, 1997: 215) argues that a person's gender is the most basic means of identification. Goffman uses the representation of women and their relationship with the physical environment in the advert. He suggests that women lack control over this environment. They 'caress' rather than 'firmly grip' products or their male companions in adverts. Second, women tend in more cases than men to be seen lying down with a camera/audience looking down on them. Finally, Goffman suggests that in a woman's face there is the look of 'drifting away' when she is with a man. As if his physical presence in the advert is enough to send her into a dreamy trance. The whole effect promotes the cultural stereotype of women as the weaker sex.

The semiotic reading of the advert or text promotes the image of the woman as caring, nurturing and the gentler sex. When lying down, the meaning created is that she is vulnerable, subordinate and inviting sexual contact. As the woman 'drifts away' in a man's arms, the audience perceives her as romantic and dreamy. Finally, in many cases women tend to be dressed scantily and men appear more fully clothed. These images are not alien to us, as our culture has thrived on the basic differences between men and women, with men taking on roles in the public sphere and women taking control of the private, home environment.

The important point illustrated by Goffman is that women in adverts are always portrayed within the cultural stereotype for their sex. However, it could be argued that men are also subjected to cultural stereotypes, being portrayed in a majority of adverts as having a strong presence and dominant physical position.

What needs to be remembered is that the style of adverts does alter from product to product, and from one medium of communication to another. Magazines tend to be more guilty of reinforcing these images because they are targeted specifically at men or women. However, television advertising can be a little more adventurous in its portrayal of gender. Television adverts tend to use parody by turning around gender stereotypes – for example, the woman who has more knowledge about cars than her boyfriend, or the man who can cook. Nevertheless, by using parody, the underlying feeling is that the television advert is suggesting that this is not the norm.

FEMINIST THEORETICAL PERSPECTIVE

Drawing on a feminist theoretical perspective Van Zoonen (1994: 80) argues that the 'natural' differences between men and women are exploited to hide the true role of capitalist society. Women, due to biology, are the sex who bear children and therefore, over the years, have taken time away from the public domain of work to care for them. The fact that women work for no wage in the family is accepted as a cultural norm. Van Zoonen says that this sustains the present economic system, which exploits both men and women. Men have to work long hours to support the family, and women can rarely afford to juggle home life and a career outside. While people are preoccupied by worrying about how to survive financially they are subordinated to the system that exploits them.

Since the 1960s the feminist movement has seen advertising as a 'most disturbing cultural product' (Van Zoonen, 1994: 67). This is because the natural, biological differences between the sexes have been exploited for the purpose of advertising material. Women are the target of a majority of advertising due to their role as caretaker of the home. Therefore over the years women have been the central figure in domestic adverts. Women have always been seen as consumers of goods rather than involved in the public, masculine world of production. Before women began entering the workplace in larger numbers during the 1930s, freedom as it was defined by adverts came within the sphere of the home. This was provided by labour-saving devices such as the vacuum cleaner and the washing machine. It was suggested that women were released from the drudgery of housework and, as a result, their lives improved thanks to consumer products.

Van Zoonen (1994: 71–3) says that, from the 1950s to the 1980s, women were portrayed in adverts as working outside of the home, but that this did not exceed more than 25 per cent of adverts. She maintains that any images of economically independent women in adverts simply support the present economic system, in other words, by suggesting that women are not so exploited in real life. Van Zoonen would rather see fewer images of women in the workplace, because she is concerned that these token images will encourage women to believe that independent lifestyles are possible without social change.

In addition, it could be argued that the new career woman departs only marginally from the traditional image of homemaker. Although the woman is seen in the working environment she is still defined by her gender. Her level of femininity is still seen as the key to success with career and office relationships. Adverts tend to concentrate on the woman's appearance rather than her competence at work. Ad women are still preoccupied with finding the best lipstick, which stays on throughout the working day, tights that don't ladder in the office, hairspray that keeps your style in place and nail varnish that dries in the office lift.

Advertising and Body Image

Van Zoonen argues that advertising has an 'obsession' (1994: 67) with gender and sexuality. Advertisers present a narrow version of a woman's life experience by focusing heavily on only certain aspects of womanhood. In contemporary women's magazines the images portrayed are repeatedly focused on the female body. The connotation is explicit as well as implicit, with the message being that the female body can be used as sex object to attract and dominate men. The glossy pages, with their attractive, brightly coloured photographs, repeat images of the female body, accompanied by written suggestive titles and catch-phrases. The whole process creates a rolling effect of article to advert, where both are so similar in design and context that they merge and it is difficult to tell the two apart.

An example, from British *Cosmopolitan* (November 2000), see Figure 34.1, shows the importance of location in advertising. A great deal of effort is taken in placing an advert where its message will be reinforced by the communication surrounding it. The advert for Wonderbra is featured opposite an article on the 'The one-hour orgasm'. The topic areas, like the design of the magazine, tend to merge and therefore reinforce the message pre-

Figure 34.1   Advertisement in the *Cosmopolitan* for Wonderbra

sented. Such continuity in material benefits the advertising business because the magazine articles reinforce the advertising message. As described in the previous chapter, this is not coincidental – the magazine industry is delivering audiences to advertisers with the material it produces.

In the advert for the Variable Cleavage Wonderbra the main focus of the camera is the blonde, blue-eyed woman wearing a black Wonderbra. She stares directly at the viewer, drawing her into the picture and its message. She draws the viewer's attention to the bra, with her tantalizing hold on the strings below her cleavage. She dares the viewer to see further and discover her advertising message. We know immediately that her message is sexual from the semiotic signs with which we are familiar and which are used again and again by advertisers. For example, her breasts, which are covered only scantily by the Wonderbra; her full, red lips, parted in a gesture of arousal; her long slim fingers, teasing the viewer with their hold on the bra strings. The bra has a 'new' variable cleavage setting, identified by the three pictures on the right.

However, there is a much stronger covert message being presented by the advertisers. The message is one of power and dominance of the woman over her sexual attractiveness. If we do not get the message from the visual picture it is clearly stated by the writing on the top left-hand side. 'I pull the strings' – the idea of a woman in control of a sexual encounter with a man. For the woman there is the suggestion that if she can control the height of her bosom then she is in control of interpersonal communication with men and, as a consequence, her life. The woman is liberated by a bra. However, as usual the woman is defined by her sexuality. The amount of power she wields is influenced by her physical attractiveness. The more she can pout her lips and package her physical assets in attractive bras, the more attention she will gain.

With the continual representation of the female body as an object, critical theorists are concerned that reality is itself compromised. The fiction of advertising (based on a cultural belief) about the fascination of the female body exploits and overloads popular culture with such images. As a consequence, advertising is involved with creating a new reality whereby women focus on their bodies more as a means to achieving goals, whether these are a career in the workplace or a desire to find the right companion. The image varies from the suggestive female pose (as in Figure 34.1) to the explicit. A recent advert for the perfume Opium used body image and personal sexual gratification to sell the product. (Interestingly, these adverts are all designed to convey a message of the female in control of her environment.) In the Opium advert, the woman was seen to be giving herself sexual gratification. The connotation for the viewer is that the perfume smells so good that the very wearing of it could have an orgasmic effect. The name of the perfume is itself an important semiotic sign for viewers. Opium is a well-known drug and therefore the transference of this name to the perfume implies that the product has similar effects to taking the drug.

This advert works on many levels that may be appealing to potential customers. The advert is suggesting that the woman is in a position of power because she does not need a man to have an orgasm. She is finding pleasure independently and this gives her freedom. In addition, the woman is a positive image because she is shown enjoying sex for herself, rather than pretending to enjoy the moment for the sake of a man. All this is suggested to come from the very fact of wearing the perfume. The image presented in the Opium advert is one of the woman's independence and freedom. She is financially well off, which is demonstrated by her expensive shoes and jewellery. She has desirable physical attributes, with a beautiful, pale, womanly body and face. She could be the subject of a pre-Raphaelite painting with her smooth and flawless skin.

The woman is different because she wears Opium. Yet some signs in this advert mean that it can be perceived in a different way – a way in which the woman is transferred from power to powerless, with her as the object of the viewer's gaze. Unlike the advert for Wonderbra, the woman is not challenging the viewer by looking at the camera; instead her whole body language is one of submission. She is seen in a horizontal position on soft blue velvet, her eyes closed, her mouth tilting upwards as if ready for a kiss. She is different to other women, with her bright green eye shadow and her brilliant red hair. Behind her are dark blue stripes running vertically down the page. They look like bars. Perhaps she is in a cage? The suggestion is that this woman is wild and unique. Perhaps her wild nature (demonstrated by her actions) needs restraining, or maybe she is simply an object for voyeurs. She is reduced to an object for the viewer's gaze. The portrayal of the woman, as usual, reverts to stereotype. This leads to a criticism of the types of message that are presented to women in modern society. Advertising has been accused of not providing any useful information in its content. Much worse than this, in some instances advertising could be providing ideas that women are only valued if they look attractive. This could give women (especially young women) a negative impression of their personal value.

CHAPTER 35

Advertising, Regulation and Reputation

Rachel Eyre

INTRODUCTION

A poster billboard of the aforementioned Opium advert was displayed in Britain in over 500 locations in three weeks up until the middle of December 2000. At this stage it was banned by the British Advertising Standards Authority (ASA). During this time it attracted more complaints than the ASA had dealt with in 5 years (730 complaints overall). The ASA stated that the advert broke the British advertising code of 'likely to cause serious or widespread offence'. Concerns were expressed about its influence on young and vulnerable members of the population, as the poster could not be avoided when shown on the streets. However, in October and November of the same year, the advert had attracted very few complaints (only three) when it had appeared in women's magazines. It was argued that this was different because a magazine is seen only by a selective audience. This audience is familiar with other similar images in magazines, which could be described as 'porn chic'.

THE ADVERTISING STANDARDS AUTHORITY

The British Advertising Standards Authority (ASA) was established in 1962 as a self-regulatory body independent from both the government and the advertising industry. The ASA is one of three bodies that scrutinize commercial communication. The others include the Advertising Standards Board of Finance (in charge of funding for the ASA) and the Committee of Advertising Practice (responsible for reviewing, altering and enforcing codes). The ASA maintains that by policing the advertising community it prevents any one advertising company from bringing the whole industry into disrepute by unethical advertising practice. The ASA is responsible for advertising in non-broadcast media and maintaining the rules established by the British Codes of Advertising and Sales Promotion.

A majority of those working in the ASA come from outside the industry. The ASA estimates that over 30 million adverts are published each year in Britain. The authority responds to complaints made by the public and also conducts its own research into the types of advert available in each media. Only cigarette advertising has to be continually checked before publication. More attention is also paid to sensitive areas such as health and slimming products. The ASA does not regulate broadcast media, this is the remit of the Independent Television Commission (ITC) or the Radio Authority.

The ASA considers adverts that appear to be factually incorrect, misleading or likely to cause offence. The accompanying box-out describes the principles and codes of the authority. This definition will explain in more detail the system that removed the Opium advert from British billboards.

The main ASA principles and codes of advertising practice
- All advertising should be legal: advertisers have primary responsibility for ensuring that their adverts comply with the law and do not incite others to break it.
- All advertising should be decent: should not contain anything likely to cause serious or widespread offence, on the grounds of religion, sex, sexual orientation or disability. Advertisers must consider public sensitivities.
- All advertising should be honest: advertisers should not exploit the credulity, lack of knowledge or inexperience of consumers.
- All advertising should be truthful: no advertisement should mislead by inaccuracy, ambiguity, exaggeration, omission or otherwise.
- All advertisements should be prepared with a sense of responsibility to consumers and society.
- All advertisements should respect the principles of fair competition generally accepted in business.
- No advertisements should bring advertising into disrepute.

The ASA's rules, which govern advertising, are thorough, with advertisers having to hold documentary evidence to substantiate the claims made in their adverts. Whether these claims are direct or implied, the ASA's decision on an advert is binding and those responsible for 'commissioning, preparing, placing and publishing' an advert that is deemed unsuitable will be requested to amend or remove it. The ASA's codes do not carry the weight of British law, but if advertisers refuse to comply with them, they risk negative publicity through the ASA's monthly report. This may lead to a loss of support by media refusing to sell space to them and loss of trading privileges.

In law the ASA is supported by the Control of Misleading Advertisements Regulations 1988. If an advert continues to appear after the ASA has ruled against it the Director General of Fair Trading can intervene. If advertisers continue to ignore the ASA's ruling then they will be referred to the Law Courts by the Office of Fair Trading. After the event, pre-vetting of future adverts may be endorsed by the ASA. This has been the result of the ruling on Yves Saint-Laurent's Opium advert. For the next two years the company will, if requested, have to submit its billboard posters to be pre-vetted. Finally, the ASA was part of the move to establish the European Advertising Standards Alliance. Located in Brussels it is responsible for the promotion of self-regulation throughout Europe and offers advice internationally.

THE BRITISH INDEPENDENT TELEVISION COMMISSION

In Britain the Independent Television Commission (ITC), empowered by the Broadcasting Act 1990, is responsible for codes on standards and practice in television advertising. Under consideration when finalizing these codes were the Codes of Practice stated by the Broadcasting Standards Commission and the EU Directive on Television Broadcasting 1989. The ITC codes apply to three terrestrial channels, satellite television provided by broadcasters in Britain, cable channels and digital programme services. Any channel with an ITC licence has to uphold these codes, which are produced and monitored by the ITC. In common with the ASA, if the ITC investigates a complaint, it has the power to insist on an advert being withdrawn. Also in common with the ASA, ITC rules are established on some moral as well as legal principles: 'Television advertising should be legal (comply to law common or statute), decent, honest and truthful' (ITC Code of Advertising Standards and Practice, 1998: 1). The accompanying box-out describes some of the main standards set by the ITC (for a full list, refer to the ITC guidelines).

ITC code of standards on advertising in television
- Separation of advertisements and programmes: viewers must be aware of the difference between an advert and a programme. If an advert takes on the style of a programme it must be made very clear that the viewer is watching an advert. Adverts must not include extracts from recent or current programmes.

- Persons appearing in adverts and programmes: advertisements should not feature a person who appears in a programme that advertisers are not at liberty to sponsor. (Refer to ITC Code on Programme Sponsorship.) Advertisements cannot feature those who present real-life events, i.e. the news. If a person is featured in a programme they cannot appear immediately after it in an advert.
- 'Subliminal' advertising: messages cannot be relayed to the viewer without their full awareness.
- Captions and superimposed text: information produced as captions should be legible and presented long enough for the full message to be read.
- Noise and stridency: no advertisement should be excessively noisy or strident.
- Politics, industrial and public controversy: no adverts can be used if they are political in nature or on behalf of industrial disputes.

THE AMERICAN FEDERAL TRADE COMMISSION

In America, since 1938, the Federal Trade Commission (FTC), a Federal Government Agency, has had responsibility for preventing any deceptive advertising from reaching the general public. (The Federal Communications Commission (FCC) holds broadcasters accountable for any false or misleading advertising that might appear on television stations. The FCC takes into account FTC decisions concerning broadcast adverts.) The FTC has responsibility for deciding whether an advertisement is false or misleading. It has the power to issue trade regulations that suggest guidelines for advertising industry. Like the British authorities, the FTC is able to insist on advertisers proving claims. The FTC (see http://www.ftc.gov/: 1) oversees the following:

- consumer complaints in all advertising
- it assesses truth in advertising, fair packaging, labelling, product liability, direct mail advertising, etc.
- its guidelines cover the whole range of products, from environmental marketing claims to household and personal products.

The accompanying box-out lists the codes and practices established by the FTC to regulate the advertising industry.

FTC codes and practice
- There must not exist a representation, omission or practice that will mislead the consumer, false written or oral representations, misleading price claims or sale of hazardous or defective products.
- The FTC examines practice from the position of a consumer or group acting reasonably under the particular circumstances.

- Representation, omission or practice must be 'material'; in other words, if the practice influences the consumer's decision with regard to product. If so, the practice is material and consumer offence is likely because another decision would have been made without the misleading information.

A good example of what the FTC would consider to be a misleading advert can be found in its guidelines on environmental marketing (see http://www.ftc.gov/: 21). In this example, a product is advertised as 'environmentally preferable'. This claim suggests to the consumer that the product is environmentally superior to other products and therefore may influence their purchasing choice. If the manufacturer is unable to support this broad claim, it would be seen as deceptive.

ADVERTISING IN A GLOBAL CONTEXT

While manufacturers expand abroad, advertising agencies need to develop their business on a global scale. Since the 1940s established advertising agencies have set their sights on new markets abroad by taking over other advertising companies. Examples of globally advertised brands include Coca-Cola and McDonald's. Leiss, Kline and Jhally (1993: 169–71) have suggested three stages of globalization in the advertising industry.

1 1900 to 1950s: a small number of agencies opened offices abroad for certain manufacturing clients.
2 1960s to 1970s: American advertising agencies start international expansion with development of business across markets around the world.
3 1980s to present day: American, European and Asian advertising agencies have merged into global agencies for global clients. They buy advertising space from global media.

Some commentators on the global expansion of the advertising industry are critical of the possible decline in national and local cultures – the idea that global advertising is a form of cultural imperialism (Mattelart, 1991). Global advertising is absorbed into local culture and therefore influences and changes that culture. It is argued that adverts also hide the reality of capitalist production, i.e. the poor working conditions in those countries that produce the majority of products.

Since the 1960s Benetton has built a huge fashion industry producing clothes that are sold all over the world. However, the company's fame lies more in the global advertising campaigns that it has employed since the early 1990s. Before this decade the company produced advertising that stressed the harmonious relationship between culturally distinct groups. Young people in particular were seen dressed in Benetton clothes and holding hands in a union of friendship. The advertising slogan became 'United Colours of Benetton', i.e. bringing nations together. However, it was felt by the 1990s that this advertising campaign was too much at odds with the real world, which was characterized by human conflict.

A sharp contrast in the company's advertising style thus appeared at the beginning of the 1990s. Dramatic, emotive and purely shocking images were now employed in promoting the product. In an era of global advertising, such images were transmitted around the world. For example, visual images of a person dying of AIDS, a newborn child still bloody and attached to its mother and a man living on America's death row were all employed, accompanied simply by the Benetton slogan. The company claimed that this was part of a move away from the over-sweet images of most advertising, to a demonstration of concern for contemporary social issues. The company's claimed that it wanted to make people aware of what was happening around the world and to identify itself as part of a movement for social change. The reaction to such images was mixed, from Benetton winning awards in some countries (i.e. France) for its hard-hitting message, to a ban on posters by the British ASA in the case of the newborn baby advert.

Some British magazines banned adverts as they arrived from Benetton headquarters in Italy. This would sometimes occur at the last minute before the magazines went to press, meaning that the page allocated for the advert would have to be left blank. Benetton can be criticized for reducing serious and often very sensitive social issues to advertising material for commercial gain. In addition, although Benetton claimed to be making a social comment on important issues, the visual images that were produced (accompanied only by the Benetton slogan) were in reality divorced from any useful political, economic, social or cultural context.

ADVERTISING AS BAD GUY?

The advertising message is all-persuasive. We, as consumers, witness the advert, which is populated with bright, beautiful people coveting a product and using words that are positive and confident. We want to be them, and we go out and buy. As critical theorists would argue, advertising reinforces our subordinate place within society as it sells us happiness through consumer products. Or does it? People remember humorous dialogue or theme music used in adverts. Overall a significant impact has been made by the advertiser. However, ask that person what the advert was actually for and there is a chance that their knowledge is limited. They might know that it was a car advert, but not for which type of car, or that it was washing powder but not which brand. It is common for the individual to have no idea at all what the advert was advertising. The details of the advert have literally washed over them and their unconscious mind has only selected the parts that appealed to them.

This dilemma, which advertisers fully recognize, provides a strong criticism of critical theory. People become familiar with the techniques used in advertising because they are exposed to so many adverts throughout their lives. They are not, as is suggested by critical theorists, passive recipients of the message; they know that the advert is a fiction, created by an industry to sell a product. In a consumer society people are surrounded by adverts and they are far too experienced to be easily influenced.

It is argued that success lies in repeating the advertising message. By doing this some of the message becomes lodged in the mind of the consumer and is remembered when out shopping. As a result a new brand is tried and perhaps becomes regularly used. This scenario must occur, but the new brand must satisfy consumers or they will return to their original choice.

Critical theorists have argued that advertising makes people desire products that they would not otherwise think about or need. However, research has suggested that advertising is unlikely to influence a person to start using a completely new product. Where advertising is perhaps effective is in encouraging a person to try a different brand in a product they already utilize. For example, Schudson (in Leiss, Kline and Jhally, 1997: 36) says that although there was a huge growth in cigarette sales over the twentieth century, actual tobacco consumption increased at a slower pace. Schudson argues that any influence advertising has had has been to switch cigar and pipe smokers to cigarettes.

In a smaller, self-sufficient economy, communities would be in control of production and would know more about the products around them. Those in support of advertising would argue that, in our contemporary society of mass production, with an infinite amount of products available for the same purpose, the consumer needs a guide to products. The consumer has a product in mind and a need already exists. The advert helps him or her choose which is the most useful product.

Finally, to criticize advertising as a manipulating tool is to miss the important role that it plays in popular culture. Advertising is concerned with appealing to the consumer. Demands are not created as such by advertisers. Rather it is through our contact with others that the desire to have consumer goods increases. In a consumer society acquisition of goods is part of the process of identifying with others. We aspire with others to own certain possessions, and products influence how we perceive our social status or self-image, whether the product is an item of clothing or a new car. Products have a social value and they influence our happiness. Therefore the demand already exists and is created by the environment within which we live.

At any given time advertising taps into the attitudes, interests, opinions and style of a society and feeds back in an advertising format these familiar ideas. To criticize a vast majority of advertising is a bit like shooting the messenger for unwanted news. The reason critical theorists dislike advertising so much is because of their intolerance for the organization of capitalist society. Advertising condones consumer, materialistic happiness and presents in fictional form what it thinks people will most like to see. It is society rather than advertising that places a personal value on the consumer product. People place personal value on items – for example, the car for many people is a symbol of how they see themselves, whether this be the design of the vehicle, its colour or size. Advertising uses these existing feelings for cars and creates an emotive advert. By suggesting that advertising is the bad guy, critical theorists are in danger of missing the crucial point: people enjoy consumer goods and consumer lifestyles. As Leiss *et al.* argue:

> Human subjectivity and the need for symbolism is now part and parcel of the case for the defence (of advertising): we want and desire the symbolism of advertising. What is at stake here is a deeply felt human need. We never relate to goods only for their plain utility; there is always a symbolic aspect to our interactions with them. In fact, the need and desire for symbolism is one of the defining features of human nature. (Leiss et al., 1997: 45)

CHAPTER 36

Marketing Communications:
Possibilities, Limitations and Innovations

Michel Walrave

MARKETING: WHAT'S IN A WORD?

The aim of marketing is to offer products and services to a target group, and to develop the income of the business by satisfying customers' needs and wants. The marketer's philosophy nowadays consists less of just offering goods and communicating about them, but daring to adapt offerings to consumers. In other words, marketing is not just talking about the offerings in different words that appeal to different consumers, but is willing to change the product or service, or aspects of it (Kotler, 1987: 56–7). Therefore it is important to identify the needs of particular groups of consumers (or potential business partners) who share similar characteristics, to develop and communicate an offer that satisfies the identified needs and wants of the target group at an acceptable price, and that is easily available through well-organized distribution channels (Fill, 1995: 4).

A target group can exist of individual consumers or businesses/organizations. Targeting the former is called consumer (or business-to-consumer) marketing, targeting the latter is called industrial (or business-to-business) marketing. In this chapter, I will concentrate on consumer marketing.

To put the result of the activities of a business on the market-place, an organization needs a few key factors. First, there is the product or service a company wants to deliver. Then one has to decide about the price of the product or service, and the place where this article can be bought or service used. Finally, the characteristics of the product or service (including the place where a consumer can buy it, and the price) must be communicated to the target group (in other words, promotion). These four fundamental elements of every business – namely product, price, place, promotion – are known as the 'four Ps' or the marketing mix (as developed by McCarthy). The combination of these components are the building blocks of each company in its interaction with the market-place. To plan and combine this mix of ingredients is the main target of a marketing manager and his/her team.

Communication plays a vital role in getting consumers to buy products or use services. In the first place, consumers have to be informed that a product exists, what its essential characteristics are, what it will cost and where s/he can find it. Furthermore, communication about products and services wants to influence the attitude of consumers, creating a positive feeling about, and goodwill towards, the promoted product. Marketers have to persuade consumers of the quality of the product, its convenience, utility and other positive aspects; in other words, build a positive image of the product, which carries positive values and differentiates from its competitors. Actually this information and persuasion serves the attempt to get as many consumers as possible to cross the line and start a relationship with a business by buying a product. However, when a consumer has bought a product, his experience with the article, but also communication, can convince him that he made the right choice. A great- or poor-quality product says more than any amount of advertising. Therefore, the experience of a consumer will or will not inspire him or her to become a loyal customer, and maybe to become an advocate of the company, by disseminating positive word-of-mouth publicity.

Also, by reassuring customers, businesses wish to retain them and stimulate them to buy their product again. This is a very important growing trend in marketing – namely, not only investing in obtaining new customers, but also taking care of the relationship with each individual customer, in order to attain and retain their trust. This, in particular, is the reason why businesses are more than ever investing in satisfaction research, but also in scanning the attitudes and behaviour of consumers towards their own products and those of competitors. This information is not only interpreted in anonymous facts and figures: a growing number of companies are collecting information about individuals, stocking it in databases, and analysing consumers' personal characteristics and behaviour. By building profiles of consumers, they try to target offers to them based on their knowledge of each individual. In other words, businesses try to retain current customers by knowing their needs, wishes, remarks and actual buying behaviour, and try to give them a personalized offer. The use of direct and interactive media (i.e. mail, telephone, fax, e-mail) gives businesses the opportunity to start a dialogue with individual consumers. This is the basis of so-called relationship marketing, better known as direct marketing or database marketing. We will develop the amazing opportunities – but also the limitations – offered by direct marketing communication tools below, but first we will look at the bigger picture: the whole marketing communication mix.

The Marketing Communication Mix

The marketing communication mix is a schematic overview of the armoury of communication tools used to influence consumer attitudes, knowledge and behaviour towards a product or service. First, we have to emphasize that not only the promotion mix communicates about a product or service, aspects of the product are also communicated through the other 'three Ps' of the marketing mix. A high price for a watch, for example, might symbolize quality or exclusivity; the distribution of a toothpaste in a pharmacy instead of a supermarket communicates the 'medical' value of the product; finally, the design (size, shape, colour) of the product itself and its packaging communicate both explicitly (name, information on the label) and implicitly (colour, form) to the consumer who sees the product.

Marketing communication does not, however, exist in isolation from other forms of communication. The way in which a business communicates about itself – so-called corporate communication – can also influence the image consumers have of the products and services it develops. Moreover, the way in which management communicates about a company's business activities, products and services to its own staff is also important. A good internal communication makes a company's own employees the first ambassadors of its products and services. Therefore it is of the utmost importance to streamline corporate communication, marketing communication and internal communication, to send messages to consumers that re-affirm each other. In this chapter, I will concentrate on pure communication about products and services, namely the marketing communication or promotion mix. In this mix of communication tools (as depicted in Figure 36.1) we can distinguish two major types of marketing communication: thematic and action.

By using thematic marketing communication tools a marketer wishes, in the first instance, to influence the knowledge and attitude of a consumer, before the consumer is in a situation where he can buy the product. By using advertising (through commercials or posters), for instance, a marketer aims to give some information about a product and to create goodwill towards that product. Finally, the advertiser hopes that this will affect in a positive sense the behaviour of the consumer when s/he is confronted with the product in a shop. Action communication, on the other hand, wishes to influence consumer behaviour directly. By creating appealing packaging, by communicating discounts, marketers aim to stimulate buying behaviour, usually at the point of purchase (i.e. in a shop, supermarket or even an e-shop). We will see in the following overview of marketing communication tools that there is no strict separation between thematic and action communication. Marketers can create hybrid forms that integrate both types of marketing communication.

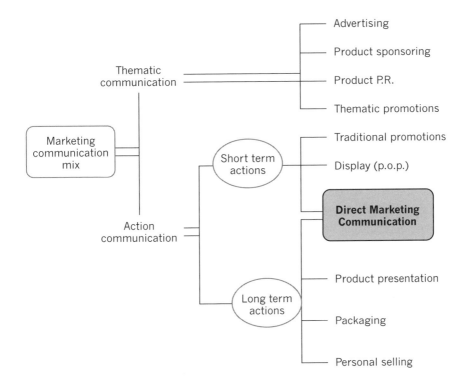

The marketing communication mix

Source: based on Floor and Van Raaij, 1998: 14; Walrave, 1996: 46

Figure 36.1

Advertising

One of the oldest and most visible forms of marketing communication is definitely mass-media advertising. It can be defined as a non-personal form of commercial communication, through paid mass-media space, by an identified advertiser, to influence a target group. Through posters, radio and TV commercials, and advertisements in newspapers and magazines, the receivers' curiosity is often stimulated by the use of rational or emotional arguments. Sometimes advertising does not contain a great deal of information about a product, but the marketer tries to stimulate some emotions by setting the product in an atmosphere that associates a product with certain values and builds the products image. On the other hand, advertising can also try to give the consumer rational arguments to convince him or her that the promoted article is useful, cheaper than a competitor's, etc. Most of the time advertising combines rational and emotional elements in its message. For example, one can promote a brand of mobile phone by showing how handy this particular phone is, by stressing a very competitive price, but also in the same commercial by showing the mobile phone used by a dynamic golden boy or girl, which implicitly bestows a particular image on that product and its would-be users.

However, it is not only the selection of arguments and the atmosphere that will be created in the advertisement that are important – the choice of mass media, the timing of the advertising campaign and the number of repetitions of the message are important too. Next to the creative side of advertising there is the planning of the communication of the message in specific mass media, known as media planning. By selecting TV or radio channels, or newspapers that have a national or international reach, or a specialized TV channel or magazine, the media planner targets the message to a broad and general audience or a more specific target group. Following the draft of the message and before the transmission to the target groups, the effectiveness of the message is tested among a restricted but representative audience (this is called the pre-test). After the commercial has been broadcast, its influence on consumer attitude and knowledge is again tested by means of a (telephone) survey, for example (this is called the post-test). The actual influence on sales is more difficult to measure, and this is one of the most persistent criticisms of mass-media advertising.

Sponsorship

The second instrument in our communication mix is sponsorship. We can distinguish between product sponsorship (which is part of the marketing communication mix) and corporate sponsorship (which is part of the corporate communication mix). In the former, a business pays another organization (cultural association, sports club, media) to be present at an event (and in the communication of that event) with the accompanying use of a brand name, logo and other information about a product or service. In the latter case, it is not a specific product that is associated with the event, but the company as a whole. For example, a producer of telephones can be present at a rock festival with a specific brand and model of cellular phone designed for young people (product sponsorship). This company pays the organizers of the festival to be present (with posters, displays, etc.) and visible to the audience. That same company could prefer to be present not by communicating about a specific product, but by communicating the name and other characteristics of the company (corporate sponsorship). Both types of sponsorship are in fact an exchange between two organizations. One organization (the sponsor) offers financial or logistic support to another organization in exchange for a presence at an event. The sponsor hopes to be visible during the event and that the audience will associate the values of the event with the product or company. In our example of the rock festival, the producer of the cellular phone hopes to reach young people and be associated with the young, dynamic, avant-garde atmosphere of the festival. Thus, by sponsoring an opera performance, rock festival or sports match, a company would try to reach a different audience and be associated with different values. It is clear that a sponsorship activity does not, in the first place, intend to boost sales of a product, but instead to increase knowledge of the product, create an image and stimulate a positive attitude. This is the reason why sponsorship is part of the thematic section of marketing communication.

Public Relations

Public relations (PR) aims to stimulate mutual comprehension between a company and its target groups (customers, shareholders, dealers, journalists, competitors, government, etc.). By analysing public opinion, government action and the decisions of competitors, PR officers try to get to know the image different groups in society have of a company and its products. They analyse the weaknesses and contradictions in this image, and try to fill any gaps by offering information to the mass media or directly to specific target groups. Journalists are free to use or alter that information as they wish, or indeed to discard it altogether. In fact, a PR officer aims to build trust by informing those groups in society that are relevant for the company about its evolution, events etc. S/he hopes that the media will cover the event or integrate the information in an article that reflects in a positive way the company as a whole (corporate PR) or a product or service (product PR). An example of product PR is the event organized when a new car model is launched on the market and journalists are invited to test the car; they receive technical information at a very attractive location where the guests are cosseted. This can lead to free positive publicity. This kind of communication about a product has one of the highest values. A favourable article in the press or in a commentary on radio or television is less surrounded by scepticism than advertising, for example. PR events and press meetings are, increasingly, organized because they lead to a message about a product being disseminated by a trusted third party: the mass-media journalist. PR also implies the acceptance of a risk, namely that a publicity stunt can result in negative communication in the media. But, still, there's nothing like free positive publicity.

A specific form of PR is public affairs or lobbying. This is the attempt of an organization to influence the decision-making process of (local, national or international) government by giving the decision-makers information that puts the interests of the company at the forefront. Again, the lobbier has to gain the trust of decision-makers by informing them in a professional way.

Sometimes the mission of the PR officer is to rebuild trust when it has been damaged by a crisis which has hit the company or a specific product. All professionally structured organizations should have a crisis plan in which, among other things, those aspects of communication are enumerated that are vital for the organization when hit by a fire, an unpopular restructuring plan, a fault in a product or some other calamity. In recent history there have been examples of problems with products that have had to be recalled, scandals or reorganization plans with drastic social and economical consequences for a company's personnel. The way in which a company reacts in a crisis can be a turning point in its history. Trust can be vitally damaged, but a professional, cool-headed way of dealing with a problem, and an honest communication about it, can rebuild trust.

Promotion

A kind of marketing communication that is sometimes, literally, stuck to the product is called promotion. One can discern two types: traditional sales promotion and thematic promotion. Sales promotion tries to stimulate selling by adding value to a product. This is possible by offering a discount on a product or more value for the same price. Sales promotion is often a short-term kind of marketing communication targeted at specific groups and accompanied by advertising that makes consumers aware of the promotions and where they can find them. This type of promotion is actually action communication, because it aims directly to stimulate consumers to buy a product. It does not claim to communicate values and create a positive image, but it certainly wants the consumer to grab the product in the shop.

More and more promotions are associated with electronic or magnetic loyalty cards. By buying specific products or being loyal to a supermarket, one can gain points and receive discounts or gifts. This builds the success of frequent buyer cards in supermarkets or even airline frequent flyer cards. By this means, companies wish not only to reward loyalty, but also to collect information about purchasing habits. This information can, as we will see in the next paragraph, be used for direct marketing. Thematic promotions, on the other hand, are not an incentive to buy a product by offering a discount or a greater amount of the product for the same price, they have a more thematic image-building, value. A customer is offered a gift that is connected with the product. An airline, say, will offer a travel bag; a brand of sun cream will offer a cap or beach towel; and a brand of perfume will offer a stylish make-up bag. These gifts are used not only to stimulate purchases but also to create an image around a brand. By using these objects (with the brand name marked on them) the consumer becomes an advertiser for the brand. A positive aspect of promotion is that it is temporary and can be targeted at specific groups (the supermarkets in one region, for example). In this manner a marketing manager can calculate the influence of a promotion on sales. It is clear that both kinds of promotion require the participation of shops and supermarkets. Furthermore, these promotions not only have to be communicated through mass-media advertising, but also by different means at the point of sale.

Point of Purchase Communication

The majority of items used to decorate a shop or supermarket have a communicative value. Light, posters, colours and music have to create an optimal atmosphere for shopping. Even the structure of the shop – namely the way the racks or shelves are organized – is the result of studies on what has a positive influence on buying behaviour. For example, have you noticed that, most of the time, food and other essential goods are presented not near the entrance of a supermarket, but at the back of the building? So a customer has to zig-zag with his or her trolley through a lot of other areas, noticing other products and perhaps being tempted by promotions, displays, demonstrations of new products by sales people, etc. If the essential goods, for which a majority of customers visit the supermarket, were displayed near the entrance, a lot of areas would have few visitors. Furthermore, a loyal customer who after some time has the map of the supermarket engraved in his head, could go automatically to those parts of the supermarket where he finds what he seeks. He's driving his trolley on automatic pilot. Designers of supermarkets want to disturb this automatism and to catch the attention of the shopper by means of moving displays and video screens. A lot of experimentation takes place into the point of purchase. New techniques are developed to catch the attention of the shopper and to stimulate him to grab a specific product. The 'videocart', for example, is a shopping trolley with a video screen and a small antenna; when the trolley passes a promoted product, the screen receives a signal and a commercial pops up on it.

An explicit manner of informing and influencing customers is the task of sales staff. In a personal face-to-face contact, a sales person informs, helps and influences, always keeping in mind that he is a representative of the shop or of a specific brand. The quality of the information and the effectiveness of his influence are based not only on talent but also on the way in which sales people are trained and motivated. This is why personal selling is long-term action communication. The strategies used by sales people to help and influence consumers do not change from day to day. Even the organization of the shelves and the design of a supermarket are only changed after some reflection. Also the packaging of a product cannot be changed very often, because loyal customers could not recognize their favourite goods. Sales promotions – specific displays for products – on the other hand, are short-term marketing stunts to boost the sales.

Personal selling is long-term action communication because one needs experience and training to perform well. It is not just verbal communication that is important in the interaction between the sales person and the consumer, but also non-verbal behaviour. The body language of the consumer informs a well-trained and experienced sales person whether or not the consumer is ready to buy. The strength of personal selling is direct communication with immediate feedback. It is an expensive way of selling goods, particularly when he or she has to travel to a prospect or customer. This is the reason why a growing number of businesses have put their sales people behind a desk and telephone. Such telesales people call consumers at home to propose products or services and, if they are interested, plan a personal visit to demonstrate the product, or send a mailing or catalogue. This leads us to direct marketing, which is an answer to some of the weaknesses of mass-media marketing communications and personal selling, which revolve around costs and the ability to measure the effectiveness of communication. Before paying more attention to direct marketing, I would like to summarize the strengths and weaknesses of the above-mentioned marketing communication tools. This will offer an insight into the gaps and weaknesses of mass-media marketing communication for which direct marketing tries to compensate.

Strengths and Weaknesses of Communication Tools

The above-mentioned tools of the marketing communication mix have a number of strengths and weaknesses. Each can be evaluated by looking at its capacity to move a consumer from unawareness, through product knowledge, a positive attitude towards the product and, finally, to purchase. Important in this evaluation is the difference we have established between action and thematic communication. Where the former wants to influence behaviour directly, the latter wants to build the product's image and create goodwill towards the brand. Advertising scores better on creating a product's image and sales promotion on directly influencing buying behaviour. Of course, both are interdependent: a sales promotion functions better when advertising is also functioning as a backcloth of facts about, and values around, the product. Awareness and a positive feeling help buying to take place. We can also evaluate the different marketing communication tools, using the following criteria: reach, trust, cost, control and feedback. A synthesis of this comparative overview of the strengths and weaknesses of marketing communication tools is displayed in Table 36.1.

As we have seen, advertising using mass media can both reach a large diverse audience or a more homogeneous target group, depending on the specific media selected in the media plan. A particular form of advertising, which overlaps with direct marketing, is direct response advertising, where individual feedback from the audience is made possible. The cost per contact (i.e. the cost of an advertisement per individual of the audience) is lower than the cost of sending a direct mail to an individual consumer or having a telesales person call him. The overall cost, on the contrary, of developing and disseminating the mass-media promotional message is a less attractive characteristic, especially when compared with other less expensive techniques such as PR, where – in the best case – the mass media put over for free the message of an organization. Moreover, this trusted third party contributes to the credibility of the message because the information has passed through the selective and critical hands of journalists.

Another weakness of mass-media advertising is the low level of interaction with the audience (except for direct response advertising). Furthermore, by spreading a message through mass media, 'wastage' could be important – namely communicating a message to those who are not part of the target group the advertiser wishes to influence. The amount of wastage is again dependent on the quality of the media plan. Reassuring the advertiser is the fact that he has a serious level of control over the content of the message, the moment of communication and other aspects of the communication process. This contrasts with PR, where journalists are free to discard or change the information they receive in a press release or at a press conference. Next to advertising, promotions, sponsorship, personal selling and other communication at the point of purchase, direct marketing offers a higher degree of control over the content and transmission of a message. Absolute

Table 36.1 Summary of the strengths and weaknesses of marketing communication tools

	Advertising	Sponsoring	Public relations	Sales promotion	Personal selling	Direct marketing
Reach						
Ability to reach a large audience	High	High	High	Low	Low	High
Ability to reach a specific targeted audience	Medium	High	High	High	Low	High
Ability to interact with individual consumers	Low	Low	Low	Low	High	High
Trust						
Credibility given to the message	Low	High	High	Low	Medium	Low
Irritation provided by the communication	Medium	Low	Low	Low	Low	High
Cost						
Absolute cost	High	High	Medium	Medium	High	Low
Cost per contact	Low	High	High	Low	High	Low
Possible wastage	High	Low	High	Medium	Low	Low
Control						
Ability to control the final message disseminated	High	High	Low	High	Medium	High
Feedback						
Possibility for the audience to individually give feedback	Low	Low	Low	High	High	High

Source: based on Fill (1995: 12) and Walrave (1999b: 59)

control is not achieved because an incident with a product or a crisis in the company or its sector, or some other unforeseen event, can give rise to rumours that interfere with the advertising message. This leads us to a less studied process of communication, which is almost out of the control possibilities of the advertiser: word-of-mouth communication, in the positive or negative sense, people becoming ambassadors for, or critics of, a product or service.

Depending on the objectives a marketer wants to achieve, depending on the target groups, the financial resources for marketing communication etc., a marketer selects one or several complementary tools to create a specific marketing communication mix for a product and a specific target group. The correct integration of these tools is important in maximizing the effect of the different messages and to avoid the spread of confusing and contradictory messages. Again, marketing communication does not operate in a vacuum, but must be streamlined with corporate communication and internal communication. In the marketing communication mix, direct marketing's place is growing because it combines a number of strengths and fills up a number of gaps between mass-media marketing communication and the individual consumer.

THE DIRECT MARKETING COMMUNICATION MIX

Direct marketing seeks individual communication by delivering a personal message, stimulating an individual response and trying to build a long-term relationship with customers. As the number of offers grows, consumers are confronted with an overload of mass-media advertising, and differences between competing products and services diminish; the differentiation of brands in the minds of consumers becomes confusing. This results in a hesitant consumer who falls prey to discounts and other promotions, resulting finally in brand switching, the breakdown of brand loyalty. For this reason, more and more companies are working to establish relationships, neither with mass groups nor with target groups, but with individual prospects and customers. The individualization of cocooning consumers (as a trend of post-modernist society), has played its part in this evolution (Walrave, 1999b: 29–44). This is why a growing number of companies wish to communicate directly with prospects and customers. One of the key issues facing marketers is namely the need to be more effective and more efficient in the use of their budget to influence consumers' attitudes and behaviour. Thanks to the possibility of measuring response to each direct marketing effort (telephone call, mailing, commercial e-mail etc.), a growing number of businesses are re-routing marketing funds and efforts into direct marketing. Moreover, marketers want to create synergy between the used tools; this means that the different messages (through mass media and direct media) reinforce each other.

Direct Mail

One might think this is a new marketing phenomenon, with all the current fuss about direct marketing tools. Some tools, though, have been used for centuries. Direct mail, for example, has been used since the start of the book industry to mail catalogues to libraries, universities and individuals. Some department stores have, since their launches, been sending catalogues of goods to people living far from the city, giving them the opportunity to pick up a product they could not find in their own region. The telephone has also been used for decades to make offers to individual consumers. However, there is now an intensification of the use of direct mail and the telephone for marketing purposes. For example, the last 10 years have seen a doubling of the number of mailings sent to European consumers, to 18 million items (FEDMA, 1999: 13). This is the number of personally addressed printed promotional communications delivered to the consumer via a postal operator, including mail-order catalogues. We can distinguish direct mail from direct non-mail, the latter being promotional material dropped in each letterbox (of a defined area) without any personalization of the message and without bearing the name and address of the receiver.

The use of direct mail requires a database of names, addresses and other personal data in order to target a group of prospects. For example, a direct mailing about a new sports magazine is likely to interest sports freaks. Therefore the marketing department will collect data by hiring or buying the database of sports clubs and, say, tour operators who organize sporting holidays. A promotion team from the magazine can also be present at sports events, handing out copies of the magazine or forms that allow consumers to fill in their personal data in order to receive a copy and/or participate in a contest. Another strategy could be the publishing of an advertisement in a newspaper (in the sports section, of course) with a coupon that can be sent to the company to request a copy of the magazine and a subscription offer. In the same advertisement a (toll-free) telephone number can be included; by calling and identifying yourself you are recorded in the database. This last strategy, namely using a mass media (in this case a newspaper advertisement) and stimulating an individual to contact the company (by sending in the coupon or phoning), is called direct response advertising. It is a mixture of mass-media advertising and direct marketing, namely the use of advertising on the mass media (TV, radio, the press, posters), which carries a response mechanism for the consumer to contact the advertiser directly (a coupon, freephone telephone number, a web or e-mail address). By responding to such an offer, those who are interested in the product or service identify themselves. The large audience of a mass-media commercial becomes less anonymous and the database built from these responses serves as a source for contacting consumers by direct mail, telephone or e-mail.

Thanks to the development of telematics or ICT (the integration of telecommunications and information technology), marketers are now able to reach more consumers and decision-makers in person, and not by using mailing strategies alone. The telephone makes targeted two-way communication possible between companies and their prospects or customers. We are also experiencing a fast evolution in other telecommunication media – for example, experiments with interactive teletext, the possibility of combining direct marketing tools, interactive television, CD-ROM and DVD with online connections and certainly the Internet. Figure 36.2 depicts the main direct marketing tools. As you can see, not only direct and interactive media are used, but also mass media, to stimulate personal contact between the prospect and company representatives.

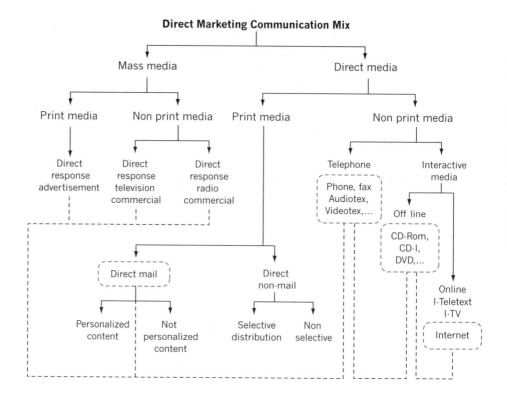

Figure 36.2　The direct marketing communication mix
Source: Walrave, 1999b: 74

Telemarketing

In recent years the commercial use of the telephone and of the Internet for prospecting, sales, customer services etc. has really taken off. The majority of big national and international companies have organized their telephone contacts with prospects and customers in a call centre. A call centre is a division in a company (or a company in itself) where operators (also known as call centre agents) communicate by telephone with prospects and customers of the business. A distinction is made between inbound and outbound calls. Outbound calls are the initiative of the call centre agents. They call consumers at home – for example, to ask some questions about their needs and wishes in a particular area – and propose a product or service that matches their needs. A telephone call can, however, also come from the consumer her/himself, encouraged by a direct response advertisement, to ask for more information about the product presented. Increasingly, companies are investing in such direct response communication and in so doing stimulate consumers themselves to approach the company if they are interested and at a time that suits them. However, besides reacting to a direct response advertising message, the consumer may have other reasons for phoning a company's call centre. When a consumer calls a helpdesk or complaints service, he can get information on, or help with, questions or complaints about a product. This is why 'hotlines' have become so popular. These are the kind of customer services that software and hardware manufacturers have started to provide, making themselves accessible to their customers by telephone so that, for example, when the customer has a PC application problem, he or she can get advice immediately.

These different commercial telephone practices are also often brought together under the umbrella term telemarketing. Information, complaint handling, advice and selling through the telephone help in building and maintaining a relationship between the company and each individual customer. The drawback, though, is essentially situated in outbound tele-marketing. Not every consumer likes to be called in the evening at home to hear a telesales person praising his wares. In different surveys in the USA, UK and Belgium, consumers com-plained about telephone selling. This is the reason why the types of inbound telemarketing are often more consumer- and privacy-friendly. (For a more comprehensive overview of call centre possibilities, and the attitude and behaviour of consumers towards outbound tele-marketing, see Walrave, 1999a: 138–56.)

There are also fresh combinations possible between direct marketing and other market-ing communication tools. When an event is sponsored, for example, direct marketing can be present, by distributing contest forms to win a product produced by the company. By this means, the business has also collected personal data (name, address, etc.) from those who were present at the event. In the future, the company can send them an offer by mail. Companies, though, have to respect the privacy rights of these consumers by informing them about the purpose of the collection of their name and address, and giving them the opportunity to practise their privacy rights, i.e. not to receive direct marketing messages from that company.

Crisis PR can use the call centre to interact with journalists, displeased or worried cus-tomers, or employees. A direct mailing can be sent out after a crisis in order to rebuild trust, and to inform about past problems and the ways in which they are resolved. PR officers can use e-mail to send press releases to journalists or other interested parties. As we have already mentioned, the loyalty cards used in supermarkets are a source of information about individual customers necessary to target personalized offers through direct marketing.

In Figure 36.2 you can see that there is more in the direct marketing communication mix than direct mail and telephone marketing. Interactive media are also used to communicate directly with individual consumers. Think of the electronic version of a mail-order catalogue on CD-ROM: it is cheaper to send to the consumer than the heavy paper version; customers can find specific goods and services using a search engine; they can change the colours of the clothes they like; finally, if they wish to order, the CD-ROM makes the connection with the database of the mail-order company and the order is registered. In some countries marketers experiment with interactive television or teletext. More than an experiment, how-ever, is the use of the Internet for marketing purposes, as we will see in the next section.

THE WEBMARKETING COMMUNICATION MIX

The Internet brings, thanks to its unique characteristics, new possibilities to communicate with target groups and individual cybernauts. In this section we will explore the opportunities offered by the Internet for the promotion of products and services. Marketing communication, through mass media, delivers a standardized message for a more or less large audience. Even direct mail has limitations in personalizing and targeting its message; on the contrary, the promotional message delivered by telephone marketing can be adapted to the remarks, wishes, needs and critiques a consumer expresses during their dialogue with the telesales person. The Internet goes a step further: the advertising message can be delivered on a one-to-one basis, but it is not limited to written words and standing images (like direct mail) or nothing but speech (like telemarketing). The different applications of the Internet bring together speech and sound, the written word, standing and moving images, to deliver a message that can be adjusted to the individual. This is made possible by means of two fundamental techniques: electronic forms and the monitoring of net-surfing behaviour.

When an Internet user fills in a form on a website to receive more information, to participate in a contest, or to subscribe to a magazine or e-zine (electronic magazine), the data are stored in the database of the company and analysed to compose the profile of the individual visitor. Moreover, the surfing behaviour of that individual on the website, what kinds of products he likes, which hyperlinks he clicks on, which search commands he inputs, can be scanned. The compilation of personal data (delivered in an electronic form) and the possibility of monitoring surfing on a website, builds a detailed portrait of individual prospects and customers. The data collected not only reveal the success of, or lack of interest in, specific web pages or products/services promoted on the website, they can be linked to individual visitors. One of the techniques that may be used to link information about website traffic and individual visitors is the cookie. (For a more comprehensive overview of tracking and personalization possibilities on the Internet, see Allen, 1998; Gelman, 1998; Peterson, 1998; and Walrave, 2001.)

A cookie is a text file generated by the server of a website you visit and sent to your browser. This little file is a kind of barcode stored on the hard disk of your computer; the cookie stays on your computer and is communicated to the server when you visit that website again. Originally cookies were meant to be time savers, leading you to the language you chose during your first visit or automatically accessing a site that requires membership or a password by recognizing the cookie stocked on your hard disk. Cookies, though, offer marketers the opportunity to track your visits, record the web pages you selected and, by so doing, to know what you like or dislike (analysing the clickstream as they call it). This helps cybermarketers to build profiles and to send offers to users that fit their profile, perhaps by means of a pop-up commercial displayed while surfing, a banner ad (electronic advertising 'poster') or an e-mailing (electronic direct mail). For this last purpose, the cookies stocked on a computer must be linked to the personal data (at least an e-mail address) that a user communicated on the website or in another website that commercializes this information. Browsers give the Internet user the opportunity to control this clandestine chatting between a computer and the server of a website. Users can block cookies or ask for more information about a cookie before accepting or rejecting it. Software has also been created to protect online privacy for cookies and to counteract online spying; these are called privacy enhancing technologies (PETs).

Now we have traced the opportunities offered for marketers to get to know the surfing behaviour of each Internet user and how this can be used to personalize commercial offers, let's look at the different communication tools used to seduce the online consumer. In this review, summarized in Table 36.2, we can distinguish two dimensions: on the one hand the distinction between inbound and outbound communication (as seen in the review of call centre applications); and, on the other, the communication processes that will mainly stimulate an order or support the selling process.

With inbound marketing communication on the Internet, the initiative of the communication process lies with the consumer him/herself. He or she contacts the organization, stimulated by one or another way of 'webvertising', namely an advertisement on a web page. For example, a marketer puts a banner on a website, but it is the Internet user who decides whether or not to click on this banner to receive more information about the promoted product. In other words, the marketer broadcasts an electronic poster on a web page and the individual consumer decides if s/he wants more information. By clicking on the banner they read the details of the offer and maybe they can leave their e-mail address and other personal data in an electronic form or coupon. This e-mail address is then, if necessary, used to send more information or a personalized offer. This last communication process is known as outbound communication: the initiative of the communication lies with the marketer. Now we will go through the most common Internet marketing communication tools used to incite a consumer to buy a product online, or to support the selling process and/or propose after-sales services.

The Banner: the Electronic Advertising Poster

One of the first, and until now, most used forms of webvertising is the virtual poster. This is mostly a rectangular advertising message (with text and graphic elements), linked to a web page where an interested consumer can find more information about an offer (the so-called target ad) and can be linked to the home page of the website of the company that proposes the product. If an e-shop wants to attract visitors, it must be promoted on other websites

The webmarketing communication mix   Table 36.2

	Sales	Sales support
Inbound	banners e-coupons call me button	banners promotainment e-zine discussion group/community call me button
Outbound	opting-in of opting-out mail intermercial push (webcasting)	opting-in of opting-out mail intermercial text preferred listing push (webcasting)

Source: Walrave (2000)

on the Internet; examples are websites with large amounts of traffic – search engines such as Yahoo! or Webcrawler – and websites visited by individuals who have the same profile as your target group. For example, if a cybermarketer wants to promote a sports shop on the Internet, the banner about this shop or a specific offer could be placed on the website of a sports magazine. Thanks to the pasting of a banner on this website, a reader of that online periodical can click on the banner in order to be connected to the home page of the electronic sports shop.

With banner advertising, a distinction is made between the banner ad, the target ad and the proper website of the company, as shown in Figure 36.3. The banner ad is a short message that tries to capture the attention of the Internet user while he is surfing. Through text and (moving) images, a cybermarketer aims to stimulate the viewer's curiosity to click on the banner and to be linked to the target ad. This advertisement will contain more in-depth text about the product or service that has been announced in the banner ad. In the target ad more arguments and illustrations are given to stimulate the consumer to decide to order the product. From this target ad the consumer can further explore the website of the company. This most commonly used structure of banner advertising is shown in Figure 36.3.

The strength of banner advertising is that the effectiveness of a banner ad can be measured, by calculating the click-through rate. This is the number of visitors of a website, where

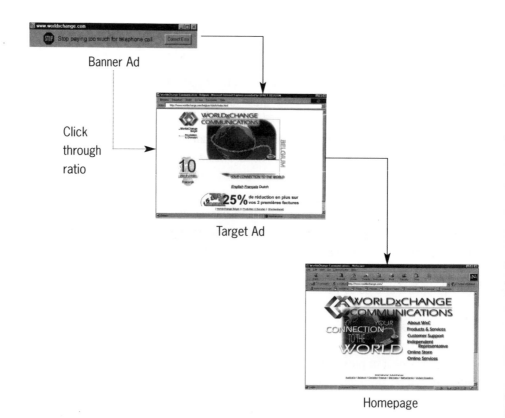

Figure 36.3   The structure of banner advertising

the banner is hosted, compared with the number of persons who actually clicked on the banner ad to be linked to the target ad. A click-through rate of 3 per cent means that 3 out of 100 people who have seen the banner ad on the website have clicked on it. This simple calculation can help to test the effectiveness of a banner ad when hosted by different web-sites. The marketer can compare the click-through rate obtained on different web pages where the banner ad is integrated and then decide whether to stop or continue to pay for the placement of a banner ad on a specific website. In addition, different versions of a banner ad for one product can be tested on the same website. After such a test, the marketer can choose to continue the advertising campaign with the banner ad that achieves the highest rate, because it is the most appealing electronic poster.

As we have already seen, the advertiser pays a fee to the host website for the insertion of his banner ad. This fee can be calculated on the click-through rate. The more people that click on a banner ad, the higher the fee paid to the owner of the website where the banner ad is inserted. The fee can also be a fixed amount paid for the space on the website during a certain time (the so-called flat fee). Finally, the fee can be calculated on the basis of the number of visitors to the website (the so-called CPM or cost per mille, a fee per thousand visitors to the website) or on the basis of the results obtained with the banner ad (a per-centage of the benefits of the sale, the so-called CPS or cost per sale). Another, sometimes less expensive method used for banner advertising, is the organization of a banner ad net-work. This is a co-operation between a number of companies to give one another some space on their web pages to host banner ads. This is especially interesting when the com-panies offer on their websites complementary products and services, and when their target groups are similar.

Companies that use banner advertising are increasingly confronted with the problem of how to attract the attention of the browsing consumer and get him/her to click on the ban-ner ad. The growing use of banner ads makes it more difficult to get noticed by the Internet user. Moreover, a banner ad must, on a small surface, not only attract the attention but also incite a visitor to a website to interrupt his/her browsing to click and receive more informa-tion about a product. As visitors to websites are sometimes overwhelmed with banners or other buttons (i.e. smaller messages from companies that lead the viewer, by clicking, to the website), marketers try to be innovative in their banner advertising and to surprise con-sumers with stimulating offers, moving images and sometimes sounds. In view of decreas-ing click-through rates, marketers have create new forms of banners. For instance, the e-banner or interactive banner ad. This is a dynamic banner, which allows an interested con-sumer to chat with a sales person using a little 'chatbox' integrated in the banner ad, or where the consumer can select a subject from a roll-out menu that is part of the banner ad. The click-to-video banner offers the opportunity to view on a pop-up screen a demo of the product in moving images. The roll-out banner changes in a larger advertisement, rolls out when you click on it or presents an electronic form where the user can fill in his or her per-sonal data and receive more information by mail or e-mail. Figure 36.4 shows an example of a roll-out banner.

Such roll-out banners compensate for the disadvantages of certain classical banners. When you click on certain banners, the target ad or home page of a website pops up in a

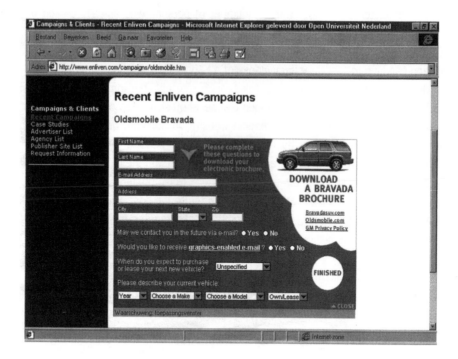

Figure 36.4   A banner ad rolls out in a form

Source: http://www.enliven.com

new window, but sometimes you have to leave the actual web page you were reading and the advertising occupies the whole screen. The roll-out banner, on the other hand, enlarges the space it occupies on the host web page without leaving this page. It can also be closed or shrunk to its original form. When this type of banner ad is provided with an electronic form, it incites the viewer to receive more information by e-mail. He can read that information whenever it suits him and does not have to interrupt his browsing through web pages right then in order to view the product information. By inputting his e-mail address on to a form, he receives a brochure in his mailbox.

A banner ad can also be linked to an e-coupon. This electronic coupon gives a discount. It can be printed and exchanged in a shop or can be used in a webshop. In this way the consumer is stimulated by a sales promotion to visit a shop on the Internet. Connected to the banner ad, but with other interaction possibilities, there is the 'call me button'. This is a button on the host web page, which is linked to a pop-up screen where a visitor can input his or her name, telephone number and a specific question about a product or service. By clicking on the send button the consumer requests to be called by a call centre operator to receive an answer to his question. The call me button is useful when a visitor to a website is searching in vain for certain information, has specific questions or complaints, or wishes to contact someone who can help him immediately.

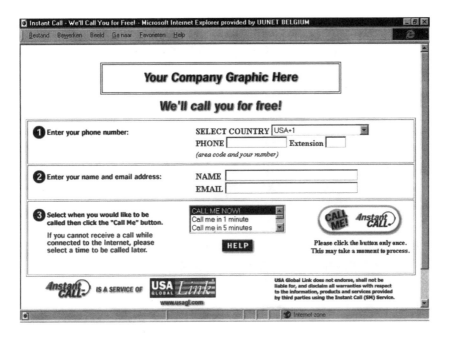

The form that pops up when an Internet user clicks on a call-me button   Figure 36.5

The conversation between the consumer and the call centre agent can be combined with what is called 'push technology'. This is the opportunity for the call centre operator, for instance, to push through the Internet specific content to the browser of an Internet user (when this person has installed the necessary software). When a consumer is interested in a product, but lacks some information about it, the web pages can be sent to his browser. Meanwhile the operator and the consumer can go through this information together, questions can be answered and orders taken.

As with the placement of traditional advertisements and posters and the broadcasting of commercials, the space needed for banner advertising must be selected carefully, taking into account the traffic on the website and the profile of the users.

The search for web pages where a banner can be seen by prospects is a crucial step in Internet advertising. Cybermarketing companies are, therefore, conducting more and more research into the profile of Internet users and visitors to specific websites. This information is needed in order to target a banner ad to a particular group. An advertiser can also collaborate with those responsible for a search engine. The deal is that, when a search topic is asked for by a visitor which is connected with the product or service offered by the advertiser, then the banner ad with a specific offer will appear. For example, when a user of a search engine enters the word 'house' or 'real estate' or 'building company',

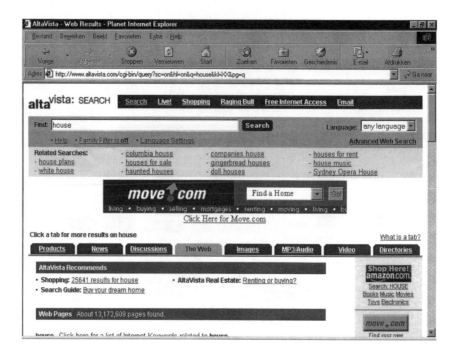

Figure 36.6   In this search engine the banner of an advertiser is shown when related search topics are entered

then the banner of a building company, which has a contract with the search engine, is shown.

This collaboration between a search engine and a company is interesting, because the advertiser gets a chance to attract more attention by showing his banner than the tens or hundreds of hyperlinks shown as a result of the search command. Another strategy is called 'text preferred listing'. In this case an advertiser hires one or several topics. When a visitor to a search engine enters one of these reserved topics, a hyperlink to the advertiser is shown at the top of the list of results.

The Intermercial: the Electronic Commercial

There is more to webmarketing than banner ads and buttons, however. Radio and television commercials also have their Internet versions. We can distinguish two types of Internet commercials or intermercials: interstitials and superstitials.

An interstitial is a commercial shown on a whole computer screen. This commercial (with moving images and sound) is presented while downloading a web page or software. Most of the time, the commercial is shown in between two web pages. The advertiser wants to attract attention to the advertising message, not only by using video and sound, but also by

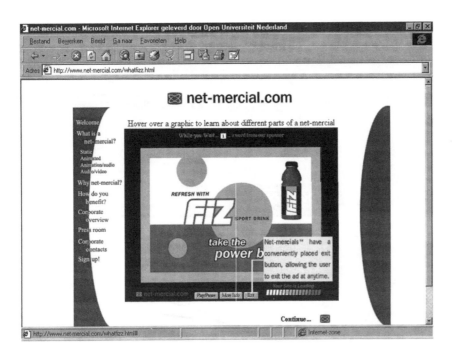

The interstitial uses the whole screen to catch the attention of the Internet user for the advertising message

Figure 36.7

seizing the whole screen. A banner ad or button only takes up a small part of a computer screen, an interstitial, on the other hand, is difficult to ignore. This is also the reason why interstitials are sometimes criticized. They fill up the whole screen without warning the Internet user or even asking his or her permission. The irritation this causes inspires some advertisers and marketers to provide their Internet commercial with a toolbar where a viewer can quit the intermercial, interrupt the commercial or request more information.

Another way of using intermercials, which aims not to irritate or bore the viewer, is to offer content or even entertainment (video games, quizzes etc.) linked to the topic of the website the Internet user is interested in. When entertainment is linked with the promotion of a product or service, this is called 'promotainment' (promotion and entertainment). A quiz can be linked to the promotion of a product in an intermercial, for instance. Again, the appearance of an intermercial can be triggered by the search command one has given to a search engine or it can be linked to the software one wants to download or the website one visits, or even the surfing behaviour connected with a cookie that identifies the user of a computer.

The superstitial does not occupy the whole screen of the computer because it pops up as a separate little screen, as shown in Figure 36.8.

This type of Internet commercial catches the attention of the viewer by appearing suddenly

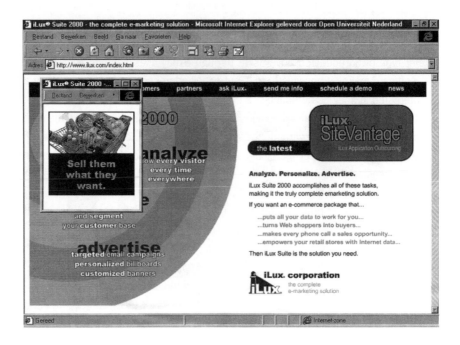

Figure 36.8   The superstitial is an Internet commercial that pops up in a separate little screen

and promoting a product by moving image and sound in a small screen that can be closed when the advertising message disturbs the viewer. Otherwise, if the consumer views the commercial until its conclusion, it is followed by a micro-site; this is a limited website of a few pages about a product or service on the pop-up screen where the commercial was shown. This screen can be enlarged to make the information more readable.

The E-mail: Electronic Direct Mail

E-mail is the oldest communication tool that uses the Internet as channel. E-mail is an interesting, though delicate, tool for online marketing communication. There are only about three ways of using e-mail for marketing purposes. Highly criticized is spamming, this is sending an unsolicited commercial e-mail (UCE). In this kind of UCE, we can discern two types: bulk e-mailings and segmented e-mailings. The former uses a database of e-mail addresses without segmentation based on the characteristics or interests of the individuals. Therefore the advertising message in the e-mailing is not personalized and it is likely that the message will reach a lot of people who do not have any affinity with the promoted product or service. This can be interpreted as a disturbing commercial communication and result in a negative attitude or behaviour on behalf of the receiver. Sometimes this can lead to what is called flaming: a lot of receivers of UCEs send angry e-mails to the company to stress that they do not want to receive commercial e-mails. If a lot of people send an e-mail in a short period of time, this could lead to technical problems for the Internet server of the company.

Another type of unrequested advertising through e-mail uses segmentation techniques. Specific software makes it possible to pick out e-mail addresses on web pages. If an advertiser is interested in specific companies, a cybermarketer can gather e-mail addresses and register them in a database that will be used for the e-mailing campaign. Again, the receivers of the e-mailing have not been warned, nor asked for permission to be sent advertising. This could also lead to negative feelings or behaviour towards the sender. There is less chance of wastage in sending the e-mailing to a segmented target group, because the marketer has selected the addresses of a group of users that share some characteristics and interests.

Finally there is a more privacy- and consumer-friendly type of e-mail campaign; this is called permission e-mail marketing. Before sending an e-mailing to an individual, a company asks for permission to send commercial information. For example, a consumer visits the website of a company and fills in a form to order a product. In that electronic form, the company asks explicitly if it can use the consumer's e-mail address to send them regular updates of their offers. Next to that question the consumer has to tick a box to indicate his or her choice. This form of permission e-mail marketing is also called opting in. Consumers are asked to opt in to the database used to mail offers. A lot of companies prefer the opting-out system. They send out an e-mailing and offer consumers the opportunity to be eliminated from their mailing list. In the European Union regulations have already been put into practice in several member states to offer the consumer at least an opting-out possibility.

Another opportunity for companies to find out the e-mail addresses of consumers without the risk of being flamed, is to use professional opting-in mailing lists. Some cybermarketing companies compile data from consumers who explicitly subscribe to a particular mailing list. When entering their personal data, they can also tick the subjects or product categories they are interested in. The company that manages such databases then hires out these e-mail addresses to businesses that correspond to the subjects or products the members of the opt-in mailing list are interested in.

Collecting e-mail addresses is a crucial phase in e-mail marketing. But the structure and style of the e-mailing, and the arguments enumerated, are also of paramount importance. An e-mailing consists of three distinctive parts: the subject line, the body copy and possible attachments. The subject line is the first impression the receiver has of the message. Therefore it is important to grab the attention by stressing a so-called unique offer, which will stimulate the receiver to read the actual message and not just press the delete button. Sometimes the purpose of the commercial e-mail is not quite clear to the receiver. Marketers use appealing words such as free, new, important without giving more information about the commercial purpose of the mail, in order to compel the receiver to open the mail and read more about it. In the actual message (i.e. the body copy), the advertiser can first of all stress the reason why he is contacting the recipient by e-mail. For example, because s/he has subscribed to an update or an e-mail newsletter about the company. Often the first sentence is a question or remark to stimulate curiosity. Further, the message is short, with a clear structure of arguments about the product, an invitation to open the attachment (with more information) or to click on the hyperlink, which will connect the viewer directly with the section of the company's website which deals with that specific offer. The use of colours, italics and underlined words helps the reader to scan the important parts of the message. Finally, the e-mail ends with the details of the person you can contact (by mail, phone, etc.) and the necessary opportunity to opt out of the mailing list.

A growing number of companies prefer to send an e-zine, an electronic magazine or newsletter, to prospects and clients who have subscribed to it on their website. This electronic periodical is often a wise and well-balanced mix of information and advertising. Sometimes the whole newsletter is made up of interesting content, preceded or followed by a short message from the sponsors. Hyperlinks are integrated for those who want to surf to the website of the sponsors. This kind of mixture of information and advertisement in mass media advertising is sometimes referred to as an 'advertorial' (advertisement and editorial) or 'infomercial' (information and commercial); it offers the consumer information about topics that interest him/her and gives regular visibility to the sponsors of the e-zine. Furthermore, banner ads are sometimes integrated into the e-mailing or e-zine, offering the opportunity for the advertiser to use colours and moving images to stimulate the reader to click on the banner ad and see the target ad or home page appear in his browser. In addition, some free e-mail services offer sponsors the opportunity to send advertisements to the owners of a free e-mail account. While a company can communicate directly and individually to consumers using e-mail, an advertiser can communicate with individuals and target groups using newsgroups or Internet communities. A business can develop its own newsgroup or community around specific topics, or sponsor existing discussion groups. In this way, a company does not only have an opportunity to communicate information about a product or product-related subjects, but also offers the participants the opportunity to exchange ideas and experiences with each other and with the company. It can be very instructive indeed for the company to hear positive and negative remarks about their products and services or questions about unsolved problems.

THE FUTURE OF INTERACTIVE MARKETING COMMUNICATION

After summarizing the different types of mass media, direct and Internet marketing communication, we have to stress that an increasing integration of different tools occurs. The integration of feedback possibilities for individual consumers to advertising messages becomes a priority of marketers. The use of direct and interactive media, moreover, offers an opportunity to scan the behaviour of prospects and clients. Knowledge about consumers is built, not only about their buying intentions or perceptions of and attitudes towards a company or product. Data on the actual behaviour of individual consumers is stored in databases and analysed in order to inspire personalized communication.

Marketing on the Internet is, at the moment, the pinnacle of this trend. Banners and intermercials cannot just, however, be broadcast on a website, where the visitors more or less have a similar profile as the target group of the advertiser. Advertising on the Internet can also be sent to the browser of an individual visitor to a website, depending on his profile, the web pages he has visited, the search commands he input and the electronic form he filled in. Besides, more individualized and detailed information can be sent by e-mail.

The communication process between the consumer and the website can be a learning process, in which the offers and services of the advertiser can be adapted in real time to the questions, hints and surfing behaviour of the prospect. These characteristics of the Internet, integrated with mobile telecommunications, offer new possibilities to marketers, as shown in the following example.

A consumer wants to order a ticket for a concert. On the website of the concert hall he first chooses the event and the date, and then looks at the map of the hall where it is indicated which seats are available. By clicking on a seat he gets a 3D view of the stage; he can then order a ticket. He can also make a reservation for a dinner table in the foyer of the concert hall, and even check the menu and place an advance order. When browsing the information before ordering, questions can arise and be answered by clicking on to a FAQ (frequently asked questions) page. A chatbox or call me button can help the user to receive an answer to his question from an operator. Finally, the order has been placed and the evening of the event arrives. While driving to the concert hall, a traffic jam occurs. Thanks to his onboard computer or mobile phone, the concert-goer can be informed of an alternative route so he can still get to the concert hall in good time.

Mobile telecommunications offer more possibilities than voice communication and some of the other services that offer to help travellers. The integration of mobile communication standards and the trend towards personalized marketing leads to so-called 'proximity marketing'. The mobile phone offers the opportunity to situate you geographically with a certain precision. This can be used by marketers to send you advertising messages based not only on your profile but also on your location. For instance, you possess a loyalty card for a specific supermarket and you are driving in the neighbourhood. A short message on your mobile phone can attract your attention to the promotions on offer. (Again, I would stress that such possibilities cannot be realized without the informed consent of consumers.)

Such new tendencies in marketing communication bring us to the conclusion that three main trends can be distinguished.

- First, there is the trend towards the personalization of commercial communication: so-called one-to-one marketing or relationship marketing, giving birth to the new term CRM (customer relationship management), namely following the needs, wants, behaviours, questions and remarks of consumers in order to find out which products and services to offer and, also, how and when to communicate with the consumer. This customer-centred paradigm establishes relationships with customers on an individual basis, and uses the information gathered to treat individual customers differently. This tendency towards personalized communication was introduced by direct mail and the use of the telephone for marketing purposes. Mail and telephone can also be integrated with mass media advertising, when using direct response advertising.
- This leads us to the second trend: the integration of diverse marketing communication tools to create synergy. By mixing the advantages of different tools, the marketer aims

to minimize the weaknesses of individual communication tools and maximize the strength of each tool.

- The third trend could be labelled the evolution towards permission marketing. The Internet, for example, and especially the merging of Internet and mobile communications, offers not only the opportunity to communicate to the right individual, but also at the right time and in the right place. To make this possible without irritating consumers, and without losing their trust in electronic and mobile commerce, each company has to implement a policy that offers the prospect and client some basic rights concerning the use of their personal data, and control over the possibilities and limitations to communicating with them by e-mail or by (mobile) phone. A company cannot, therefore, build one-to-one, long-term and loyal relationships by analysing only the wishes, needs and complaints of consumers concerning their products and services. Marketers also have to be alert to the wishes and remarks of consumers concerning the means used to communicate with them.

Conclusion

Advertising and marketing are central to the existence and development of all media communication industries. As this section has demonstrated, at each point in its history advertising has reflected the cultural values of each given society. It has undoubtedly affected the structure and organization of the media industries, with funding influencing the style of newspapers, magazines, film, commercial radio and television. Advertising and marketing, as we have seen, are also playing a key role in the development and 'look' of the Internet.

As we have seen, advertising and marketing are powerful tools of communication. Advertising has been particularly studied because of its use of all-pervasive images, which dominate our lives, from the billboards we see around town, to the newspapers and magazines we read, and the television programmes and films that we watch. It has been argued that people become familiar with the techniques used in advertising and marketing, and therefore view this output with a critical gaze. However, as we have seen in advertising, the reproduction of easily recognizable 'gendered' images feeds those cultural norms that we have been socialized into. We know that these taken-for-granted images exist in our culture, and therefore, we are perhaps more susceptible to them when we see them in advertising. The analysis of magazines as an example in this section has considered the rolling effect of glossy, stylized images and words from article to advert. The location and ideas presented in both articles and adverts are repeated and, due to this repetition, appear to merge: articles look like adverts and vice versa. The criticism here is that if idealized body images are represented in both, throughout a magazine, the articles and advice presented by the editor may merge with, say, an advert for a cosmetic product. We have also seen this trend in advertorials, infomercials and banner ads integrated into e-zines. The influence on the reader is believed to be greater than that for an advert alone, because of the repetition of the ideas presented. In addition, the constant reduction of the male or female persona to a gender stereotype is seen to reinforce societal attitudes about masculinity and femininity.

As we have seen, the structure and concerns of British and American advertising regulating bodies are in many respects similar. However, they do fundamentally differ in their overall philosophy. The Federal Trade Commission is primarily concerned with the rights of the consumer, while as we have seen with the controversy over the Opium advert, the British Advertising Standards Authority takes more of a moral guardian role. Generally, in both countries, advertising is not as tightly controlled as some elements of the media, such as violence and sexual content. Advertising has contributed to critical debates within society and has been a major source of controversy itself. Contemporary advertising has become more daring as media content has generally become more explicit. Today's advertising is more surreal than ever before and more self-reflective of its own content and history.

SUMMARY

- Historical transformation of society is linked to changes in advertising from simple announcement style, to a technologically sophisticated, media-driven business.

- Advertising as a cultural commodity has been analysed from many theoretical perspectives: from a critical perspective that examines the role of advertising in supporting capitalist society, to feminist theory concerned with the representation of men and women within society.

- Semiology has a central role in analysing advertising because of its focus on examining signs and meaning.

- Advertising can be seen as reductionist, in that it reduces images of men and women to basic gender distinctions. They have a role in reinforcing the stereotypical attitudes towards the sexes experienced in society.

- The British Advertising Standards Authority and Independent Television Commission, and the American Federal Trade Commission have a significant role in regulating the advertising community. The codes stated offer guidelines to advertisers on appropriate behaviour. Failure to uphold these regulations can, and sometimes does, result in legal prosecution.

- Audience members are aware of the role advertising plays in society. They are not passive recipients of the advertising message, but make an active choice as to what aspects of the information to use or discard.

- Marketers identify the needs of particular groups of consumers, and then alter products or services in order to meet those needs

- The marketing mix is the armoury of communication tools used to influence consumer attitudes, knowledge and behaviour towards a product or service. Increasingly, marketers are integrating these different mass media, direct and indirect marketing tools.

- In webmarketing, the advertising message can be delivered on a one-to-one basis – the different applications bringing together speech, sound, written words, and still and moving images, which can be adjusted to the individual targeted.

Further Reading

Fowles, J. (1996) *Advertising and Popular Culture*. London: Sage

Hart, N. (ed.) (1995) *The Practice of Advertising* (fourth edn). London: Butterworth-Heinemann

Nava, M. *et al.* (eds) (1997) *Buy This Book! Advertising and Consumption*. London: Routledge

Schudson, M. (1993) *Advertising: The Uneasy Persuasion*. London: Routledge

Palmer, A. (2000) *Principles of Marketing*. Oxford: Oxford University Press

Useful Websites

Two useful sites concerning general advertising and marketing are:
http://www.adassoc.org.uk/
http://www.zenithmedia.co.uk/adhel500.htm

For a site on product placement see:
http://www.productplacement.co.nz

A very interesting and up-to-date site for American law and advertising is:
http://www.arentfox.com/quickguide/
   businesslines/advert/advertisinglaw/

The site of the British Advertising Standards Authority is at:
http://www.asa.org.uk/

The site for the Federal Trade Commission is at:
http://www.ftc.gov/

References

Allen, C. (1998) *Internet World Guide to One-to-One Web Marketing*. New York, NY: Wiley Computer Publishing

Barthes, R. (1973) *Mythologies*. London: Paladin Granada Publishing

Branston, G. and Stafford, R. (1996) *The Media Student's Book*. London and New York, NY: Routledge

Brierley, S. (1995) *The Advertising Handbook*. London and New York, NY: Routledge

Dominick, J.R. (1987) *The Dynamics of Mass Communication* (second edn). New York, NY: Random House

Dyer, G. (1982) *Advertising as Communication*. London and New York, NY: Methuen

Eldridge, J., Kitzinger, J. and Williams, K. (1997) *Mass Media Power*. Oxford: Oxford University Press

Ewen, S. (1976) *Captains of Consciousness*. New York, NY: McGraw-Hill

FEDMA (1999) *1998 Survey on Direct Marketing Activities in the European Union*. At: http://www.fedma.org

Fill, C. (1995) *Marketing Communications. Frameworks, Theories and Applications*. London: Prentice Hall

Floor, K. and Van Raaij, F. (1998) *Marketing-communicatiestrategie: reclame, public relations, sponsoring, promoties, direct marketing-communicatie, winkelcommunicatie, persoonlijke verkoop, beurzen, tentoonstellingen, geïntegreerde communicatie*. Houten: EPN

Gelman, R. (1998) *Protecting Yourself Online*. San Francisco, CA: Harper Edge

Goffman, E. (1979) *Gender Advertisements*. New York, NY: Harper & Row

Goldman, R. (1992) *Reading Ads Socially*. London and New York, NY: Routledge

ITC Codes of Advertising Standards and Practice (1998). Autumn

Leiss, W., Kline, S. and Jhally, S. (1997) *Social Communication in Advertising: Persons, Products and Images of Well-being* (second edn). London and New York, NY: Routledge

Kotler, P. (1987) *Strategic Marketing for Nonprofit Organisations*. Englewood Cliffs, NJ: Prentice Hall

Mattelart, A. (1991) *Advertising International: The Privatisation of Public Space*. London: Routledge

Murdock, G. (1992) Embedded persuasions: the fall and rise of integrated advertising. In Strinati, D. and Wagg, S. (eds) *Come On Down? Popular Media Culture in Post-War Britain*. London and New York, NY: Routledge

Packard, V. (1981) *The Hidden Persuaders*. Harmondsworth: Penguin

Peterson, C. (1998) *I Love the Internet, but I Want My Privacy Too!* Prima Publishing

Strinati, D. and Wagg, S. (1992) *Come On Down? Popular Media Culture in Post-War Britain*. London and New York, NY: Routledge

Van Zoonen, L. (1994) *Feminist Media Studies*. London: Sage

Walrave, M. (1996) *Telemarketing: storing op de lijn?* Leuven: Acco

Walrave, M. (1999a) Telemarketing: still possible in the next millennium?. In *Journal of Database Marketing. Special Issue: Challenges for the New Millennium* 7, 138–56

Walrave, M. (1999b) *Privacy Gescand?* Leuven: University Press

Walrave, M. (2001) *e-Privacy*. Diegem: Kluwer Editorial

Interactive Electronic Media

Gillian Youngs and Oliver Boyd-Barrett

Introduction

This section assesses interactive electronic media and their diverse impacts. The main focus is on the Internet as a new social sphere, facilitating new forms of economic, political and cultural exchange. The virtual character of these processes means that physical proximity is removed from the equation. The boundary-crossing nature of the Internet marks the triumph of time over space. Communications across geographical distance can be conducted instantaneously and easily, the combined power of **information and communications technologies (ICTs)** bringing new scope for the accompanied transmission or posting of large quantities of data more efficiently than ever before.

The Internet is multi-functional and cross-sectoral. It incorporates the public face of the World Wide Web and the private platform of e-mail. It involves market, government, educational, media and civil society sectors. It is multi-media in integrating visual, audio and textual material. It is enabling advances in distance learning, which is itself, through its new patterns of flexibility, contributing to a reshaping of the knowledge environment and issues of access within it. In this section, we explore the capacities of the Internet and their meanings, its continuities and discontinuities with established media patterns. Critical attention is focused on the range of issues of inequality and power relating to ICTs and questions of connectivity and influence.

CHAPTER 37

Globalization and the Internet

Gillian Youngs

INTRODUCTION

The development and use of the Internet was one of the major social changes at the end of the twentieth century. The existence of the Internet meant that the dawning of the twenty-first century was clearly marked by a transformed mass communications environment. One of the key analytical challenges for social science scholars is to understand the implications of the main characteristics of the Internet, and the detailed ways in which it is changing forms of social interaction and their future potential. It has quickly been recognized that the Internet must be assessed not only in relation to the full spectrum of modern communications, but also in relation to the vastly differentiated social contexts within which it operates. The Internet is, first and foremost, a social space directly linked to, and interactive with, other social spaces. For all its distinctions, it needs to be understood in grounded ways that focus on existing social relations and patterns (Youngs, 2001a). For this reason this chapter concentrates on the relationship between globalization and the Internet.

It is generally taken for granted that globalization provided the overall context for the introduction and application of the Internet. It is less well understood that the nature of the Internet itself has provided an important practical and heuristic means for understanding what globalization is actually all about. Discussion about, and use of, the Internet has helped both experts and non-experts alike to come closer to processes of globalization. In their macro forms of economic and political structures and interactions, these had tended previously to appear far more distant from everyday, lived reality. Globalization was too much something that happened 'out there', involving major players such as governments, non-governmental organizations (NGOs), and transnational corporations (TNCs). It affected people's lives through the economies and polities they participated in, and the interconnected changes these moved through, but it still seemed abstract in many ways. Actual use of the Internet, and direct experience of its global reach, have helped to make these processes more concrete.

In this chapter we begin by exploring the meanings of globalization, on the basis that these provide a useful backdrop for approaching a critical and historically sensitive understanding of the Internet and its contrasting social meanings. We then move on to an introductory discussion of the nature of the Internet as a communications arena, exploring its distinctive qualities. Next we address the question of whether, and on what basis, we might consider the Internet to have launched a communications revolution. In this discussion the role of continuity in mass communications is highlighted. If the Internet can be considered revolutionary, the context is the history of mass communications and their social impact.

MEANINGS OF GLOBALIZATION

There is now a vast literature on globalization that continues to grow (see, for example, Kofman and Youngs, 1996; Mohammadi, 1997; Tomlinson, 1999). It is a phenomenon affecting all aspects of life: political, economic, cultural and social. It fundamentally concerns transformations in the ways in which distinct societies and communities and their key organizational actors interrelate. All forms of social exchange are at the heart of globalization, and thus its story cannot be told outside of the context of communications. Their role is complex. It is at one and the same time facilitative, illustrative and productive. It is facilitative in the sense that without recent developments, notably in ICTs, the very notion of a 24-hour global stock market, for example, would be impossible. This market has been symbolic of globalization. It is in fact a collection of separate national stock exchanges – for example, in London, New York and Hong Kong – operating to some extent seamlessly, thanks to the sophisticated and multi-dimensional communications systems that link them. More broadly, ICTs have been a major means by which TNCs in particular have developed their global business, production and marketing operations (see Schiller, 2000: 37–88).

Communications have been illustrative of globalization in the sense that they have been the means through which we can observe it happening, receive information about its various developments and, in some respects, actually experience it. The Internet is a specific facet of this to be explored further below. Mass communications in the form of television is the main means through which people around the world have witnessed the various political, economic, social and cultural processes of globalization and their effects. News networks like CNN, in their daily multi-regional operation and dissemination structures, have delivered news into homes around the world. This has charted many minute-by-minute happenings, such as rises and falls in stock market prices, and details of the latest corporate mergers, in addition to the grand symbolic moments of globalization such as the fall of the Berlin Wall in 1989.

Satellite, cable and digital technologies have been fundamental to the development of, and continuing changes in, global media systems (see, for example, Negrine, 1997; Thussu, 1998). They have literally shrunk the world in terms of geographical reach and speed of information-gathering and dissemination. They have done so in the context of a liberalizing global economy where cross-border investment, economic activity and trade have increasingly been facilitated by government deregulation and privatization, inter-governmental co-operation and international institutions such as the World Trade Organization (WTO).

Communications have been a productive element in globalization. Communications, and media products and services have been boom elements of the growing global economy. Hollywood's European exports are calculated to have grown by 225 per cent between 1984 and 1998, for example, and world television viewing hours to have nearly tripled between 1979 and 1991 (Herman and McChesney, 1997: 39). Communications enterprises have been prominent in the mergers and acquisitions (M&As) trends that have come to characterize globalization. This commercial conglomeration brings together diverse capabilities in production, distribution and innovation. It involves ownership, control of technology and investment, and sales. It is part of the broader M&As picture, and the heavy concentration of power in the so-called developed economies of the North as opposed to the developing and least developed economies of the South. Electronics, media and communications giants featured in the largest 100 TNCs in the world ranked by foreign assets in 1998, and included familiar names such as Sony Corporation (Japan), News Corporation (Australia) and Cable & Wireless (UK). Virtually all the top 100 were concentrated in the USA, Europe and Japan, known as the triad (UNCTAD, 2000).

It is clear that the facilitative, illustrative and productive roles of communications are interconnected. Consideration of this aids our understanding of the integral relationship of communications to globalization. Let's take another notable member of the top 100 TNC list, McDonald's, and the integrated role of communications in globalizing different aspects of its brand message. There is a high level of dependence on communications by non-communications products for their success in the global market-place. This signals the ways in which communications are highly influential or even formative in the synthesis between economic and cultural facets of globalization. George Ritzer's 'McDonaldization thesis' considers the economy–culture fusion, stressing that the brand is as much about ways of doing business as ways of eating.

> One of the things that makes McDonaldization unique is that it brings together in one
> package a threat to both European business *and* cultural practices. Previous manifesta-
> tions of the American menace have tended to represent one or other, but not both. While
> the invasion of, for example, Harvard Business School techniques and a corporation like
> DuPont represented a threat to European ways of doing business, they had relatively little
> impact on European culture in general. In contrast, the coming of MTV, Coca-Cola and
> Disney threaten to homogenize culture, but they do not greatly affect European business
> practices. McDonaldization involves *both* a revolutionary set of business practices and a
> revolution in one absolutely key element of culture – the way in which people eat (Ritzer,
> 1998: 74).

Taking Ritzer's emphasis on business and cultural practices, it is straightforward to see how communications facilitates the dissemination of them both. It goes beyond the obvious importance of advertising in developing brand associations. TNC models of business are dependent on information technology and communications systems for companies' internal as well as external operations. The attention to interactions between economic/commercial and cultural factors is particularly interesting in Ritzer's much-debated thesis. It presents perspectives on internal dynamics of globalization. Quite clearly he is also focusing on the question of American hegemony, a key theme in globalization studies relating to the economy and culture (see also Slater and Taylor, 1999; Youngs, 2000a).

Inequalities have been a major feature of global economic growth. Benefits have been heavily concentrated in the North, and analysts have highlighted in recent years the problem of growing gaps between the haves and the have-nots, both among states and within them (UNDP). Technology has been an important part of this picture; the levels of ownership of, and control and influence over it by the North have been of growing concern, particularly with the recent development of the digital economy and economic growth related to ICTs (US Department of Commerce, 2000). Existing technological gaps and the speed of technological change are relevant here. The problems of the South being left behind relate to them both.

The 'digital divide', much discussed at the turn of the century, was not only key because it related to the vast ICT gulf between North and South, but because it was built on a long history of technological inequality. Even though Internet access was growing significantly in the less developed regions of the world by the turn of the century, the level of its concentration in the North was staggering. According to figures from Nua Internet Surveys quoted in the US government's *Digital Economy, 2000* report (US Department of Commerce, 2000), worldwide Internet access grew by 78 per cent between March 1999 and March 2000, from 171 million to 304 million. All regions showed significant growth, with Africa being in second position in these terms with a 136 per cent rise from 1.1 to 2.6 million people online. But this share was still minimal compared to the domination of the USA and Canada (136.9 million), Europe (83.4 million) and Asia-Pacific (68.9 million). South America had 10.7 million and the Middle East 1.9 million.

Understanding the Internet

There are a number of issues that are basic to understanding the Internet. They relate to its distinctive qualities as a social and communicative sphere, and their relevance to actual and potential changes in the exchange processes that are so much a part of the fabric of human society. To begin with, the Internet is a product of the ICT age. It is a result of the fusing of informational and communications power. This is the main starting point for thinking about its capacities and implications. It is now well known that the development of the Internet owes its origins to military research in the USA, related to the need for a communications system that could continue to function in a nuclear era where central nodes could be destroyed. A system (ARPANET) that operated on decentralized (chaotic) principles where information could travel along multiple routes was rational in such circumstances.

> The ARPANET eventually evolved into a communications tool for public research organizations and universities in the United States, to be followed by other similar systems elsewhere. Using what was originally intended to be merely a sidebar feature of the network – electronic mail – discussion groups proliferated on a wide range of esoteric topics and issues. By the time Internet became the successor to ARPANET in the late 1980s/early 1990s, networked communications had exploded to include private individuals around the world linked through a truly *anarchic* web of computers, searching and sharing databases and entering into *unmediated* online discussions. (Deibert, 1997: 131–2; my emphasis)

Issues of anarchy and lack of mediation are central to the nature of the Internet. These point to the horizontal – rather than vertical – forms of communication that it facilitates. It helps if we use these as the basis for considering how the Internet has changed the traditional mass media environment; but it only helps us to do so effectively if we keep a strong purchase on the information *and* communications sides of the picture.

The fusing of computational and communications power in the digital era permits the transfer and posting of textual and visual material in quantities and at speeds never known before. The Internet is a multi-functional interactive environment, so these processes occur in many different forms, both private and public.

Some private and public uses of the Internet

The Internet incorporates starkly different unmediated and mediated activities such as:

- exchange of personal photographs and intimate documents on a one-to-one basis via e-mail
- participation in a moderated discussion group
- engagement in 'cybermeetings' and exchanges in live chat rooms
- posting of NGO information on a complex website including membership, policy and campaigning information
- shopping for goods and services
- researching a topic using the World Wide Web and available sources from, for example, media outlets, universities, NGOs, governmental and international institutions.

Anarchic might seem a rather extreme way of describing the Internet, but it does have some useful indicative aspects. For a start, in the familiar mass media environment, which became established during the last century, vertical informational structures dominated. Most of the information people received came via national and local governments, agencies and media systems. Satellite, cable and, more recently, digital multi-channel environments added international elements and diversity to this picture without substantially changing it.

The British Broadcasting Corporation (BBC) remains an icon of this mass media era. As a public service broadcaster it has demonstrated the high level of national political importance attached to media services in one of the leading democratic systems. Even today the mass media, in terms of television, newspapers and magazines, retain a predominantly national structure, not least because of language, interest and cultural considerations. There has been synergy between the development of modern nation-states and media systems for the obvious reasons that the former have been the principle organizing structure for human societies. Democracies, in particular, function on the basis of participation and informed citizenship, identifying the media as central to their operation (see discussion of relevant themes in Tehranian and Tehranian, 1997).

The Internet can be regarded as anarchic because it expands the informational environment in ways that directly oppose national vertical definitions of it. It is inherently cross-boundary in its reach, not only internationally but in many other ways too. Let's stay with the national issue for the moment. In international relations the term anarchy has a particular application. It captures what are traditionally considered to be the key characteristics of the international scene. This is described as anarchic, in contrast to the ordered nature of the internal realm of states where there is governmental control.

States retain their unique status by being the only legitimate users of force, both internally and externally, in this context (see extensive discussion of this area and critical debates about it in Youngs, 1999a). The nature of this legitimacy may be open to question in relation to the specific circumstances, as demonstrated in recent times, for example, by the international protests at the former apartheid regime in South Africa. In simple terms, anarchy is the condition beyond the boundaries of the nation-state, because there is no comparable overarching authority in the international realm. States are formally equal, although, in practice, matters of military, political, economic and cultural power tend to be of prime importance, as witnessed in the limited membership of the collective security body, the United Nations Security Council.

In these terms the Internet has produced a new anarchic information era. Citizens with access to it can easily and quickly, and both are very important, move well beyond their national mediated channels of information. They can gain access to a whole host of informational sources that extend outside their own national boundaries. Such sources can be diverse in nature, and both mediated and unmediated. They can include different kinds of 'official' and civil society outlets, and varied national and international news media. It should be stressed that this applies to issues that may be considered national or international.

It is possible via the Internet, in a very short space of time, to access, and in some cases download, vast amounts of information on a particular topic. Take, for example, some kind of environmental disaster. The World Wide Web could offer:

- coverage by various newspapers and news organizations at home and abroad
- statements by governments, and other national and international agencies
- reactions and relevant policy concerns of NGOs active on the issues
- background on any companies involved and their pronouncements.

Relevant websites may be hosted by the bodies involved themselves, or others commenting on their activities or concerns. Interactive possibilities might include joining e-petitions or e-mailing inquiries or protests. Such circumstances are in sharp contrast with the pre-Internet age when national (and international) media would have been the prime *accessible* sources of information.

The question of accessibility is not only a technical one, although that is important. When we are thinking in terms of a horizontal communications environment, as opposed to a vertical one, we are addressing issues of who has access to information. In a vertical, mainly mediated system there are information gatherers (traditionally journalists and other such individuals privileged by their professional status and roles) who have access to information and disseminate it, as it were, on behalf of the larger public. Thus access is narrowed to the few who provide information to the many. The Internet does not, of course, wipe out this system. It transforms it by moving more towards a many-to-many and multi-level, multi-source model of communication. This is the essence of its horizontal characteristics. Let us look in more depth at those now.

The Internet is a horizontal communications sphere in a number of ways. Some of these relate to the status of information. In a vertical system, different levels of status are generally clearly allocated as part of the hierarchy of legitimacy in the system. Hence the high status accorded to the BBC, for example, with its public service mission. In a vertical system there tends to be an overt ranking of information sources according to recognized levels of authority. In a horizontal system things are potentially far more complex. The issue of authority is one that can be intrinsically open to question. While the recognized weight of established media retains its influence, it is in the context of a more diverse and multi-source informational environment. In principle, it is possible for an individual to make extensive searches for material and viewpoints on a specific topic, well beyond the usual mediated sources. Such a search might not take much more time than watching a television news item or reading a newspaper article, although of course it could extend well beyond that.

COMMUNICATIONS REVOLUTION?

The grounds for suggesting that the Internet marks a communications revolution have been introduced in part above. There are four main reasons for arguing that this is the case.

1 The combination of computer and communications systems permits the posting and transfer of large amounts of data on a many-to-many as well as a one-to-many basis.
2 The speed and cross-boundary nature of communication in the digital era permits intensified and diverse forms of information-sharing and networking never known before.
3 There is new emphasis on the connectivity and skills required to be an active participant (rather than passive consumer) in this communications environment.
4 The Internet brings together text, audio and visual material, including music, radio and film, in a multi-media interactive environment, the potential of which will increasingly be realized with growing bandwidth availability. *entertainment*

Let us now expand further on these interconnected areas and the background to consideration of the Internet era as a revolutionary one. Together they help us to understand the quantitative and qualitative changes the Internet has introduced in relation to the nature, patterns and volume of communication. In the twentieth century, the mass communications of radio, television and film were key. These media and the study of them have informed how we think about communications processes in societies. They have also informed how we think about what it means to be involved in different parts of these processes.

These media fit largely into the vertical, hierarchical (one-to-many) model of communication. Public and commercial providers supply a menu of items to mass audiences, which can be active in their choices from that menu but remain fundamentally passive consumers. Much research has stressed that this notion of passivity should not be pushed too far. Audiences can engage with the material they consume, bring to it their own views, needs, desires, perspectives and cultural resources, and may well use it to inform their own future actions, thoughts and challenges (see various contributions on these and other areas in Boyd-Barrett and Newbold, 1995). Mass media consumption should therefore be regarded as an integrated part of other forms of social and communicative action.

This is a point that signals the continuity of relevance of many findings in mass media research to new work on the Internet. The sense of the Internet as an integrated part of

social and communicative frameworks aids awareness of historical continuities in communications associated with it, as well as the distinctive developments it represents.

In a horizontal, many-to-many communications environment like the Internet, the emphasis
shifts from passive consumer to active participant. Many more choices are there to be
made. As distinct from the traditional mass media environment where there is a set menu
of choice from a set, albeit growing, list of providers, the Internet offers ever-expanding
sources of information from an ever-expanding range of providers. These include governments, businesses, schools and universities, local, national and international organizations
and groups, and individuals. Importantly, as well as providing different kinds of information,
there are multiple sources on the same topics and subjects, facilitating a wider critical spectrum from which to view something or make judgements.

Because the Internet is a multi-sphere as well as a multi-media environment, the diversity
of the subjects referred to here is noteworthy. They can be anything from the pop star
Madonna and her latest performance or album, to the deliberations and decisions of the
WTO, or the publication of the latest research report for the Central Intelligence Agency of
the US government. As much of the material can be downloaded, it can be considered at
length and utilized for enjoyment, debate, teaching, research, political and other activities.

The multi-sphere nature of the Internet is one of its distinctive elements. Search engines
help those navigating the Internet to track different forms of information on specific topics
from contrasting sources. The hypertext links within and across sites facilitate the continuing search for supporting details and associated material, as well as knowledge about
organizations active or interested in the subject. The informational tracks that can be pursued on the Internet are as much about identifying actors concerned with or involved in the
subject matter as about the information itself. We are back here to the sense of the Internet
as an integrated part of social and communicative frameworks.

The boundaries that can be crossed on the Internet in this way are also part of its revolutionary capacity in information and communications terms. National boundaries can be
transcended in seconds on the Internet, and so also can the boundaries between different
social spheres and information sources such as the media, government, civil society, educational institutions and individuals. There are many new possibilities for those connected to
the Internet to gain access to direct sources of information and views in this context. But
these are only possibilities until they are taken up. They require a rather different approach
to the 'pick from a menu' one of the established mass media setting.

New kinds of media literacy and competence are relevant to the Internet era. Internet
users have opportunities to take far more active roles. New kinds of curiosity can help them
get the full benefit of this new media environment. The Internet offers a vast range of individual user profiles in terms of its different functions. Its many-to-many communications
structure offers a whole new, more individually as well as collectively oriented, media framework. Individual Internet strategies are appropriate for thinking through action plans, to get
the most out of what's on offer and to link it effectively to life goals and problem-solving. The
Internet is used in various work, school and social settings for specific collectively designated tasks, and by the vertical structures of business (including for marketing and selling),
government and mass media. It is also an informational exchange and linking sphere that

individuals can use to their own political, cultural, economic, social and personal ends, and in which NGOs, for example, can enhance their public presence and interactive contact.

The Internet's global potential is also part of its revolutionary character, but at this point this is no more than just a dream. Solving the digital divide between North and South is one of the major challenges of the twenty-first century, and in some ways it seems an overwhelming one. Built on the technological inequalities of the past, it is a divide that encourages critical thought about the central importance of advances in communications to political, social and cultural developments. It is highly contradictory that the global reach and promise of the Internet is hindered by so much exclusion. Because it is a setting shaped, as all communications settings are, by those who have most influence on and control of it, it can be regarded currently as a far from global sphere. We should expect and hope for more change in it as it moves closer to its potential global character in the coming years, and as the diversity of its shapers and users grows.

The Internet, then, takes us into a new communications era, which should be understood in the context of processes of globalization. These intensify the speed and density of all kinds of exchange between communities across the world. The benefits of globalization have been heavily concentrated in the North. This has applied to the Internet, which has begun, not surprisingly, by being dominated by business, institutions and other users in the rich regions of the world. Its nature as a boundary-crossing arena, however, has opened new horizontal forms of communication, including those between North and South. These represent an expansion beyond the vertical structures of the traditional mass media environment, a richer informational setting beyond the limits of the one-to-many mass media traditions.

As well-known media giants like the BBC, and other broadcast organizations and daily newspapers around the world, move firmly into the Internet era too, it can be seen as a new stage in the transformation of these familiar mass media players. They are influenced by the new interactivity of the Internet, which is contributing to changes in the ways they relate to their audiences. These players are developing their roles, including in relation to the new many-to-many communications settings, where mediated information no longer holds the same kind of supreme position it did some years ago. References to websites for direct sources of relevant information at the foot of newspaper articles indicate not only that we live in a multi-media digital era, but also that newspapers recognize themselves as part of a wider informational sphere than was previously the case.

Such developments will continue as will the levels of cross-media interactivity the digital era permits. These enable, for example, listeners on BBC Radio 4's main morning news programme, *Today*, to e-mail in suggested questions for an upcoming interview, or to go to their screen to see, say, an ancient coin being held up to the webcam in the studio by an interviewee. If we keep a strong focus on the Internet as part of the overall social and communicative framework, we will not miss the implications of such developments. They demonstrate the significance of the new multi-media environment, including to the most well-established and prominent members of the traditional media. The full dynamic influence of the Internet can only be recognized in such ways.

One of the biggest steps for the future is the move to a culture of the active Internet user as opposed to the significantly passive viewer/listener/reader of earlier mass media times.

This is a dramatic change and an exciting one. Many are already embracing it in their use of the Internet, whether for learning, political mobilization, community-building or whatever. It allows new individual and collective strategies for communication and action in the distinctive international setting of the Internet. The capacity the Internet offers for posting and transferring large amounts of information at high speed, and for conducting transactions across the globe instantaneously, all relatively cheaply and easily, provides a richer and more accessible communications environment than has ever been available. As the online community grows to include more of the world, currently excluded due to economic, technological and social inequalities, that richness will be all the more diverse and valuable.

CHAPTER 38

Information and Communication Technologies
Gillian Youngs

INTRODUCTION

This chapter explores in more detail some of the main social meanings embedded in ICTs. The discussion links the examination of technological capacities and phenomena to the ways in which they both affect, and potentially change, understanding of the social world around us, and actions and imaginings connected to it. The basis for what follows is the recognition that technologies are endogenous to societies and their transformations (see fuller discussion of this and associated themes in Talalay, Tooze and Farrands, 1997). This is a holistic and integrated perspective on technology and its functions, recognizing that the origins of technological innovations are part of the histories, aims and functions of societies; further, that the introduction of technologies is a dynamic process shaped by human inputs and ideas in incremental and socially located ways. The approach also recognizes that the use of technologies contributes to future ideas and social goals, including the specific manner in which these may be conceived of and arrived at.

Technologies, and ICTs more specifically, are not treated as merely pieces of hardware and software, but as socially contextualized in their origins and operations. This includes awareness of the different kinds of perspective (actual and possible) on such technologies among their vastly different users, for example. It counters homogenous views of technologies that assume too unified a sense of their social applications. Its focus is rather on the differences that are manifest in terms of their impact, and the strategies associated with them. Straightforwardly, it is on the human dimension of technological developments.

> The recognition of technology as an expression of human creativity . . . reminds us that technology is fundamentally a form of human interaction with the environment, an expres-

sion of the relationship of humans to the world. It puts the human element back into our consideration of technology. It is less abstract in this way than the reduction of technology to technical rationality – to an ideology of progress. It is more concrete in that it discourages us from assuming technology as a given . . . and encourages us to view it in a social context, to relate it to meaning and power and the forms of organization, production and consumption, through which they are formed and transformed. (Youngs, 1997: 35)

In probing further what is distinct about the Internet it is inevitable that we need to talk more about its technologies, their functional capacities and the meanings behind them; but this should be done in ways that prompt thinking about much more than the technologies themselves. For the key to understanding them is to do so in full recognition of their social implications and possibilities, the latter being equally as important as the former. This makes it clear that the story of any technology is an unfolding one that can be embellished by new ideas, innovations and applications at any point.

We begin by thinking further about the nature of electronic information and its qualities as the central fabric of the digital era. We then move on to discuss the World Wide Web and infrastructural issues related to the Internet, including the role of search engines. Next we consider e-mail and its range of functions and flexibilities as a form of one-to-one, one-to-many and many-to-many communication.

ELECTRONIC INFORMATION

The dawning of the age of electronic information has facilitated a number of developments with far-reaching implications. They relate to communications within and across different societies, including market transactions of all kinds, and business-to-business linkages. Their main features are:

- the creation of a virtual realm of social interaction, which combines unique facilities of speed and access across distance in information-rich circumstances
- a range of interactive possibilities, which facilitate new linkages between individuals, organizations and groups in interpersonal, political, cultural and commercial contexts
- a new multi-media platform, which encourages innovation in the association of visual, audio and textual forms.

This new era is one of virtual presence, communication and exchange. ICTs link material places, people and organizations, allowing them to interact, engage in political and social activities, and select and purchase goods and services, without actually being physically present.

In practice this virtual world signals the triumph of time over space. It definitely shrinks the world in terms of its accessibility: instead of physically travelling to reach a specialist shop or supplier, for instance, it is possible, direct from your home or desk, without moving an inch, to order the goods you want, which may be delivered the next day. The shop or supplier could be just round the corner or thousands of miles away – the transaction time is the same (delivery times, of course, may vary, but not necessarily). Furthermore, the World Wide Web offers an equal platform for those near or far. Presence in virtual space and access to it overcomes challenges of physical space, or the restrictions that impractical lengths of time covering vast distances would involve. The scope for selecting and comparing what is on offer is defined in virtual rather than physical terms.

The digital era brings the world to you in whole new ways. These do, however, have deep associations with the ways in which traditional mass media have changed the social environment. The television remains the central motif of these changes. Through its central place in the home, and as a multi-faceted and major deliverer of national and international information and entertainment, the television has been pivotal in aspects of both the functioning of modern societies, and citizens' associations and identifications within them. It has been an integral part of social processes – political, economic and cultural. Through one medium it brings together, literally side by side, the spheres of advertising, news and entertainment.

Like television, the Internet is also a multi-faceted platform crossing different spheres including advertising, news and entertainment, but it does so more powerfully than has traditionally been done by television for a number of reasons. As a horizontal rather than a vertical communications environment, the diversity of the Internet's offerings is incomparable in its scope to the relatively limited output of television, even in its continually expanding multi-channel forms of cable and satellite and, more recently, digital terrestrial broadcasting. The Internet brings much more of the world into the home than television ever has, and in completely new ways that could be argued to democratize the informational environment more deeply than television has.

The horizontal nature of the Internet brings together direct and indirect (mediated) forms of information. This allows people, in effect, for the first time, to act as their own news processors. They can research and cross-check information from an often wide range of sources, including those of an official (e.g. governmental) nature. Information providers no longer have to rely totally on traditional media to reach their publics. The World Wide Web enables them to make direct (unmediated) contact with them, and to build relationships with them that have a far more secure informational basis than in the previously mediated conditions. Let us now explore this a little further. The traditional media, whether radio, television, newspapers or magazines, have always had a premium on available time or space. In the production of news, for example, this has made selection a key factor in what specific information and how much of it has been transferred from information providers via the media to the public.

The digital era's new informational capacities create quite different circumstances, where organizations can, through their web pages, ensure that all the information they wish to communicate is available to the public, whether people have come to the site directly or have been referred to it by an article in the media. This may include, perhaps, background policy documents and historical details associated with a current issue, and links to the websites of other relevant organizations. The news media themselves are, of course, taking full advantage of these new possibilities, enabling them not only to make their news material available via the web, but to make their archives accessible, and to offer background pages on major topics and include in them links to other websites.

The interactivity of the Internet complements and reinforces its qualities as a **horizontal communications sphere**. Interactivity is far from totally new in relation to mass media. Radio phone-ins, telephone voting on television shows etc., have all been elements of growing interactivity; but the Internet takes interactivity to a whole new level of intensity and significance. It also enables and encourages, and the latter is as important as the former, a permanent presence through websites. This is notably the case for media programmes that used to have clearly defined time slots, such as BBC Radio 4's *Today* and *World at One* news programmes. The BBC maintains one of the most prominent sites on the web as a media organization, but within it, specific programmes such as these extend their presence and activities beyond the usual time slot confines. For instance, after the programme one of the guests can be available on the site for question-and-answer sessions.

Such developments demonstrate how the Internet facilitates an interactive ongoing news environment. The news production process is not only extended but it is extended in a way that the audience is actively involved in. This is a quantitative *and* qualitative change. It gives us a deeper understanding of the kinds of meaning associated with the horizontality of the Internet as a communications arena. It signals that we are not just talking about more information but different kinds of informational processes. Such issues are at the heart of critical thinking about not only what is already happening on the Internet but future possibilities, many as yet not thought of.

There are multiple forms of interactivity on the Internet. This may be one of the bases for arguing that we are entering a whole new culture of interactivity thanks to digital capabilities. We will be talking in more detail in the next chapter about the social meanings behind some of these forms of interactivity. These include private e-mail exchanges, ongoing group e-mail (listserve) discussions, chat room engagements, various forms of feedback, such as reactions to website content and design, e-mail questions and comments to radio and television shows while on air, and so on. The different types of interactivity include instant/live interactions, but they also include, as in private e-mails, the convenience for both sender and receiver of choosing their own timings. In the latter case interactivity is not dependent on synchronization. As the Internet is a 24-hour system, forms, for instance, can be completed online in the middle of the night for instant dispatch to be dealt with during office hours the next working day.

These kinds of interactivity give concrete meaning to the notions of flexibility frequently discussed in association with the concepts of the information age or knowledge society (for assessments of some of the issues see, for example, Harvey, 1989; Drucker, 1993). They demonstrate new ways of manipulating time and space to individual and organizational ends. As such, their implications are worthy of critical and imaginative thought. Some commentators remind us that this should not be too utopian.

> Now we are facing a new revolution that will combine a multitude of the paradoxical and contradictory trends of our civilization as it has developed so far. It will liberate in some ways, and enslave in others; it will enlarge consciousness in some ways, and destroy self-respect in others; it will enable greater human compassion in some ways, and unleash the ugly Other within ourselves; and through its subversive enhancement of control for

particular tasks, it will create an engine of innovation that defies societal control. (Sardar and Ravetz, 1996: 12–13)

This is a fairly dark perspective on the cyber age. However it does firmly remind us that the implications of innovations are what societies make of them. One of the reasons it may be helpful to think in terms of a new culture of interactivity is the recognition that we are probably a long way from understanding yet what this will mean for the way societies operate and interrelate.

The multi-media capacities of the Internet are directly relevant to its interactive range. All forms of media – visual, audio and textual – come together in the Internet. It is a truly integrated media sphere that enables virtual activities of the most diverse kind. Take, for example, computer games, which can now be played over the Internet with participants from around the world rather than the neighbourhood. The multi-media Internet age is only in its infancy due to the high bandwidth (network transmission capacity) requirements of audio-visual material such as film. The recent high-profile merger of AOL and Time Warner – bringing Internet, broadband cable and content services together, and forming the biggest media conglomerate in the world – demonstrated clearly that the integrated media path is the future.

Such a merger highlights the continuing importance of vertical power in the media industry. It was yet another stage in the media merger trends that defined, in large part, both the global industry in the latter stages of the twentieth century, and the influential role of communications and media in the growth of the global economy (see, for example, Herman and McChesney, 1997). Like other major areas of the economy, the ICT scene is dominated by key players and their influence, Microsoft being among the notable examples.

There are important contradictory tensions between the horizontal qualities of the Internet as a communications sphere, and the vertical world of corporate concentration that substantially shapes its operation and future potential. Part of this picture is the integration of the Internet with television and mobile phones. Among other things, this means a growth in the commercially structured range of forms of access to the Internet. Use of the Internet is increasingly commodified via such developments, at the same time as it is undoubtedly made more available – in conventional terms, becoming more of a mass medium.

THE WORLD WIDE WEB

The World Wide Web is the shop window (literally in many cases) of the virtual world of the Internet. It is the dynamic, ever-present and continually expanding arena of websites and their diverse interactive facilities. It is the public face of the Internet. It captures the full complexity of what is possible on the Internet and holds the seeds of future potential for its further development. It is frequently stressed that while the origins of the Internet were in the USA, the World Wide Web was conceived in Europe, at the end of the 1980s at the Conseil Européen pour la Recherche Nucléaire (CERN). The World Wide Web was the major step towards a linked informational world. Through its hypertext environment, coding enabled the linking of documents to one another, one of the key means of multi-dimensional, rather than linear, movement. The inventor of the World Wide Web, Tim Berners-Lee, indicates powerfully issues of social meaning in his thinking towards this seminal development:

> In an extreme view, the world can be seen as only connections, nothing else. We think of a dictionary as the repository of meaning, but it defines words only in terms of other words. I liked the idea that a piece of information is really defined only by what it's related to, and how it's related. There really is little else to meaning. The structure is everything. There are billions of neurons in our brains, but what are neurons? Just cells. The brain has no knowledge until connections are made between neurons. All that we know, all that we are, comes from the way our neurons are connected. (Berners-Lee and Fischetti, 1999: 14)

Such reflections indicate the degree to which the innovation that the World Wide Web represented was deeply embedded in ideas about how the world works, and how meanings are generated within it, both individually and collectively. These comments also take us deeper into the story of ICTs: the thinking about what it means to *integrate* the capacities of computers to store and process vast quantities of information with the capacities of communications systems to disseminate it effectively *and* creatively. My emphasis on integration, and effectiveness and creativity points to a series of issues relating to the qualitative differences produced by fusing the power of computer and communications technologies.

In combining the technologies, the capacities of both are transformed. Their integration produces quite different technological forms. In the case of ICTs, the social dimension is essential for understanding the meanings of these transformations, as is so often the case with technological developments. The idea of single computers or computer systems holding pockets of information is quite distinct from the idea of a networked system where these pockets can be shared and associated with one another. This unpacks some of the meaning behind the use of the term dynamic in relation to the Internet. This sharing and association can enable new meanings (ideas/decisions/plans for action, etc.) to be generated, which in turn may be shared and associated, and so on and so on. This is part of the explanation of the World Wide Web as a social sphere. It may be virtual, but it is embedded in other more familiar social spheres, and is part of their processes of communication, decision-making and action. We will look further at this in the next chapter in relation to virtual communities.

For now let's stay with the concept of integration and ICTs. It is interesting to note the extent to which Marshall McLuhan's work on communications warrants fresh readings in the context of the Internet. This is particularly the case when considering the kinds of continuity and discontinuity between the mass media era of television and the new ICT world discussed above. We are moving from a largely electric media era to an electronic one, and in order to understand the changes this implies, both sides of the coin are influential. This is not just because of integration of the Internet with television, for example, but because of the degree to which the televisual (electric media) framework has formed the social basis on which we are moving into the multi-media (electronic) environment. McLuhan's famous 'the medium is the message' stand remains highly relevant to critical thinking about living in and through electronic media. As two commentators have put it:

McLuhan . . . forces us to see how our sensory lives change in response to the media we use. Our transformed perception can lead to powerful discoveries. . . . McLuhan stressed environments and the inter-connectedness of things, the ecology of thought, and the pervasive, inescapable power of electric process to change socio-political existence . . . his vision has been borne out by events. (McLuhan and Zingrone, 1997: 5–6)

A number of questions are prompted by such thoughts. How well do we understand the full impact of the electric media age on social existence, structure and meaning? How much and in what ways will the electronic multi-media age transform these developments? Fundamentally, such questions maintain a firm hold on media history and its relevance to thinking about the present and the future. They have informed some of the assessment in the chapters of this section. The merging of technologies in some ways represents the merging of historical and contemporary influences too. Thinking about new media, far from leaving thinking about established media behind, requires us to look at it afresh, and to consider, among other things, how far or correct was our understanding of its social effects.

The electronic era includes a heavy emphasis on textual as well as visual, audio and audio-visual forms. It would be absurd to think that this textual emphasis has no links to traditions in print and other text-based forms in its social implications – not least as print media, for example, are actively involved in merging their operations with the web realm. But the discussions here have also stressed that this realm has a scope and instantaneous forms of interconnection as well as access to quantities of diverse information never possible before. The ICT textual world has unique qualities, including its chaotic horizontal nature, linking contrasting sources of mediated and unmediated material.

The terms navigating and surfing the Internet signal the degree to which it is a sea of information. Browser software that enables this process and search engines that facilitate identification of websites connected to specific topics are both essential tools in this respect. Major search engines have become key advertising nodes on the Internet due to their integral function for its users, resulting in high numbers and frequency of hits on the sites. For these reasons they are prominent in the vertical structures of the Internet. Search engines and Internet Service Providers (ISPs) also feature among portal sites, as do various commercial and civil society web presences.

Portals have developed as part of the navigational infrastructure on the net. Sometimes they offer services such as e-mail, home pages and news, securing regular and extended use, and thus attractiveness to advertisers in the case of commercial sites. Part of the hidden interactivity on the net that has caused some controversy is the use of so-called cookies. These are information files that allow the gathering of data about an individual's web use by interested commercial parties (for further discussion of these areas see, for example, Miller, 2000).

E-MAIL

E-mail is the private face of the Internet compared to the World Wide Web, but it is no less powerful in its own fashion. Its nearest relatives in earlier communication formats would be the letter and fax, but it has incomparable capabilities in relation to speed and volume. E-mail is flexible in its operation as a one-to-one, one-to-many and many-to-many form of communication. Thanks to the Internet's decentralized operating structure its messages can travel virtually as quickly to the other side of the world as to the next road, in fact in certain circumstances they might even arrive more quickly to the former than the latter. Via attachments e-mail also facilitates the instant dispatch of long documents over a great distance – a process that previously would have been impractical via fax.

E-mail has been transforming communications at all levels – personal, professional and social. It has been as important within organizations as across them, so much so that managers and employees rely increasingly on the use of e-mail for communications inside their home bases as well as with other branches or outside entities. E-mail's effects on the interactional structure of daily life have been pervasive in many cases. It has affected patterns of face-to-face and telephone conversation. It is commonplace that, rather than leave their desks to speak to colleagues about a matter, or ringing them up, individuals will choose to e-mail them. Once again, it is the flexible qualities of e-mail that influence these developments. Its asynchronicity means that there is no dependence on the receiver's simultaneous presence as required in face-to-face and telephone communications. The message can be flagged as urgent, but otherwise it can just wait there for a response as fits in with the receiver's schedule. If it is a complicated issue, including perhaps one that would be useful to retain in textual form for further reference for one reason or another, it is far more effective than a long answerphone message. Software also permits a live discussion via e-mail, which can be useful when the exchange of views, say, is more important than just passing on information.

The ability through e-mail to copy a message to as many receivers as required, including attachments, is much quicker and more efficient than previous methods of duplicating communication. Listserve discussion groups, which enable messages to be simultaneously copied to an e-mail list of receivers, facilitate group exchanges across geographic distance and time zones.

The different forms of flexibility that e-mail features are powerful when considered in combination. The ease and instant qualities of e-mail can be argued to encourage communication, producing its own different effects in specific settings such as work, political activism and interpersonal relations. Much has been made of the problems of overload, which such circumstances can produce, particularly in work contexts. As many have discovered, the instant demands of e-mail can severely interrupt the cycle of ongoing activities. An information-rich environment means more pressure on individuals to assess and manage the information that confronts them. To come back to 'the medium is the message', the nature of e-mail can also be considered to be impacting on the actual nature of our communication. Writing in the virtual realm of the Internet is rather different from its more material printed and posted counterpart.

In general, e-mail is less formal and more anonymous than regular mail. People say things in e-mail they would not say in ordinary mail, perhaps because it is so easy to send mail to large numbers of people. They seem to press the send button without thinking about it and

without the cooling-off period that would follow if they carried a letter around with them until
they reached a mailbox. (Stefik, 1997: 119)

This chapter, then, has explored the Internet and its main elements as integral parts of
the social framework. It has promoted an approach to ICTs that is sensitive to history and
context. It has had a number of intentions in this respect. The first has been to note how
ICTs highlight the relationship between technology and social change. The wide, and relatively easily identifiable, effects of ICTs on societies provide us with an important opportunity to think more critically and deeply about technology as a social force. They direct us to
fresh challenges in integrated understandings of technology.

The chapter has considered continuities and discontinuities across the electric (television) era and the new electronic (multi-media digital) one. To a significant degree the two
eras are contiguous in global terms, particularly with the current level of exclusion from the
digital revolution. The integration of the television and the Internet may lead to this contiguity
being the overarching setting for the new mass media era. In any event, this discussion has
signalled that the critical work on the mass media of the twentieth century, including that by
figures such as Marshall McLuhan, remains pertinent to the consideration of media developments in the new millennium.

The Internet is in its infancy and the ways in which it grows will depend on the decisions
that societies, organizations and individuals make about how it should be used and for what
purposes. None of these are self-evident or necessarily predetermined, although of course
they are heavily influenced by historically created circumstances. These include the increasingly concentrated commercial power in the media and ICT sectors. Giants like Microsoft
and the recently merged AOL and Time Warner have significant influence over the Internet
environment, its capacities and contents. Market power will continue to substantially shape
the Internet as it has the traditional mass media sphere.

The horizontal communication capacities of the Internet are, to significant degrees, in
tension with the vertical forms of power affecting it. This is bound to continue to be the case.
Therefore analysis of the Internet will need to take account of both the horizontal and
vertical processes. This should be done on an open basis so that the possibility of the full
horizontal potential, is not lost sight of due to the existence and impact of the vertical
structures.

As a social arena the Internet, like any other, is one of conflicting interests. It is a site of
struggle, and presumably will be even more so in the future, as societies become increasingly dependent on it. It is technologically complex and involves a whole host of expert
knowledge systems concerning its operation. The implication of much of the assessment
conducted here is that education about the Internet will become an increasingly political
issue, the more societies integrate it into their ways of life.

CHAPTER 39

Virtual Communities

Gillian Youngs

INTRODUCTION

This chapter explores how relating electronically is impacting on society, particularly in the political and economic realms. The notion of virtual communities is indicative of ICTs as increasingly integral to different forms of social organization and action. We will consider the qualities of virtual communities that may distinguish them from the types of social groupings and interactions with which we are most familiar. These have been far more place-dependent than virtual communities may be, the latter being less constrained by the accessibility of participants to each other in physical terms.

A **virtual community** may just as easily operate across a number of continents as across several villages in one small region. They can be, although of course are not necessarily, more open to the involvement of people who are geographically and culturally distant from one another. In their reach, ICTs enable new kinds of imaginings about the nature of communities across national, cultural and social boundaries. They potentially go beyond, or perhaps it would be more accurate to say they add to, established patterns of thinking about communities in predominantly national and local terms.

We return here to the need to understand fully the informational and communications functions of ICTs. Identification with specific communities involves a host of influences including associative factors. ICTs make it possible to develop associative links across vast geographical distances at a level of intensity never previously possible. Because they permit virtually constant interaction, if that is desired, they facilitate new levels of human proximity in such circumstances (see Tomlinson, 1999). The capacity for substantial amounts of information to be exchanged and accessed via the Internet is influential for the potential development of new associative bonds. Information is a fundamental part of the learning processes that can lead to identification with other individuals and collective entities.

Prime associations with national and local environments are based, among other things, on the integral role of knowledge about and experience of them in the formulation of individual and collective identities (see Anderson, 1991; Youngs, 1996). ICTs and the possibilities they offer for virtual experience and association – that is, experience and association across distance rather than being reliant on physical proximity – can transform the overall associative environments within which those who have easy access to them live. It is important not to overstate these possibilities, but to be aware of the changes they may be contributing to as part of the processes of globalization.

A NEW AGE OF TRANSNATIONAL COMMUNICATION?

Have we entered a new age of transnational communication and what does this mean? Let's begin to address this rather large question in the spirit of the wider discussion in this section. The arguments presented would tend to indicate positive responses based on ICTs' boundary-crossing and horizontal qualities, as well as their promotion of easy, intense and continuous communication over time and distance. ICTs, in particular the Internet and its diverse functions, move us beyond primarily nationally mediated and vertical informational environments, to circumstances where many more horizontal and cross-boundary (including international) interactions, access to and exchange of information, are possible. Global media have impacted on national informational arenas but they have not transformed them in the way that ICTs potentially do. This is due to the active rather than passive, horizontal rather than vertical, forms of communications ICTs enable.

While media and communications conglomerates are working hard through their vertical power to shape the Internet, it is at the same time being used by NGOs, groups and individuals to forge new horizontal links, campaigns and communities of interest and action, reflecting and championing different political and economic agendas. The protests in Seattle, USA, at the WTO's meeting in 1999 were among the first high-profile instances of cyber-activism's contribution to new kinds of political demonstration.

The Internet had played a major role in the international networking and preparation leading up to the event. These are the kinds of activity that may be considered to be contributing to the development of new communities of interest and/or association. It is often noted that the demonstrations themselves should not necessarily be read as particularly significant; it is harder to argue this for all the virtual communication and strategizing that precedes and follows them. Communities are formed over time and, to some extent, time will tell to what degree virtual processes are actually producing new communities as such, what shape they may take, which ones will be fluid and changing in form, and which may endure in more consistent make-up.

The global women's movement(s) has been a notable example of community-building through ICTs. The arrival of ICTs accompanied a growing international focus on women's issues and women's movements, with the UN conferences on women and its decade for women (1976 to 1985) playing key roles. International networking and the use of traditional media and communications systems such as newsletters, fax and telephone were well established in women's activism. The ICT dimension came to the fore in major ways at the fourth world conference in Beijing in 1995 as well as earlier, in the preparations for it (Gittler, 1999). ICTs extended the established practices and networking possibilities that had already been contributing to building different strands of international women's movements (Gittler, 1999: 92). The Beijing and post-Beijing processes were examples of the potential of the Internet to deepen women's global connectivity and to transform their collective sense of political action.

It is helpful to explore the idea of connectivity in this context in order to understand further the interrelationships between political and ICT processes. They have, in many ways, proved inseparable in recent developments in international women's activism. As the political motivations for connectivity have expanded, in part stimulated by the growing numbers of organizations involved and contrasting interests represented, the awareness of ICT problems and issues has grown. It has done so in specific relation to the differentiated and particular circumstances and concerns of women in separate settings. Connectivity has been important in the multi-level nature of the work, with lobbying operating at national and regional, as well as global, levels. This demonstrates the extent to which global activism is integral to, and interactive with, other sites of activism.

> Increasingly in the years following the Beijing process women have taken up their concerns directly with national governments and global telecommunications bodies. Participation in regional and global preparations for the 1995 meetings built a network of women concerned with gender and information technology policy. Women's achievements and difficulties in taking hold of new technologies served to inform and spur on efforts to influence policy makers. Continuing disparities in access and infrastructure, issues relating to knowledge and control of electronic spaces, and the lack of women's input and involvement in information technology development, design and policy making are among these concerns. (Gittler, 1999: 98)

ICTs are highly political in themselves when considering questions of control and inequality related to North/South and gender divides. This is evident in the work of organizations like the Association for Progressive Communications (APC), which integrates ICT and democracy issues. APC's women's programme, which played a leading role in the Beijing processes, addresses women's access issues internationally (see http://www. apc.org).

Debates focusing on questions of inequality related to ICTs open up consideration of a number of things. These include the distinctive differences that ICTs can make for different sectors, groups and communities. It is possible to argue that ICTs can make *most* difference for those who have been least advantaged in the communications realm, including the poorest parts of the world. ICTs offer possibilities for kinds of international connectivity that could only be dreamed of in previous times. ICTs also bring distinct advantages for groups such as women, who have been especially restricted in both their international activities and linkages with one another in historical terms.

> Women can seek women in cyberspace in new and extended circumstances which disrupt national/international boundaries that have been so powerful in separating them behind layers of socially-constructed domestic politics and life. Feminist visions of cyberpossibilities assert the priority of such women-to-women linkages and women's full social potential to work together to reimagine as well as recreate the world. . . . Critical perspectives on cyberspace have an obvious potential to disrupt the degree to which women have historically been contained predominantly within masculinist (especially state and home) boundaries and thus withheld from each other. The seeking of collective spaces has been intrinsic to women's transformative practices and cyberspace provides real opportunities for extending the scope of these explorations. (Youngs, 2000b: 14; see also Youngs, 1999b)

A new age of transnational communications may have dawned, but it is not a homogeneous one. Too many people around the world are not even part of the Internet revolution yet. Among those who are, the levels and kinds of involvement and influence vary enormously. Literacy and technological capabilities are part of this picture. The key role of English language has also been much debated as a major problem affecting the Internet's potential for inclusion. It is far from being a universal communications sphere in any deep sense of that term at present. This means that analysis of its heterogeneous qualities remains a priority for critical awareness of both what is currently possible and the sorts of changes that need to be made for its future development.

Often, approaches that highlight the positive aspects and potential of the Internet are viewed as overly utopian. They can be perceived differently. There are too many social barriers currently affecting the Internet, as this section has indicated in some detail. These should be recognized and tackled analytically and in practice. But the heterogeneity of the Internet means that, for example, an increasing number of organizations and individuals in the North and South are coming online all the time. New linkages, particularly those promoted by NGOs, are being forged across North/South and other divides. It is important to assess these developments while taking into account the overall inequalities characterizing the Internet. There are major structural changes that are yet to happen in this context, but the incremental work towards change that is going on and expanding day by day on the Internet should not be overlooked as part of these longer-term processes.

Furthermore, utopian thinking may not be out of place in relation to the Internet for many reasons. As a revolutionary technology in communications and information terms, its potential is unfolding. Creative thinking about it and experimentation with it is part of this unfolding. How people use the Internet, for what social purposes, and the impact that it has in these orientations, feature largely in determining its future. Issues of inequality are not just related to straightforward economic and practical areas, as important as these are. They also concern the significance of diversity in creative input into the future of the Internet. Feminist assessments of the Internet, for example, address the unequal part that women have traditionally played in the invention and application of technologies in general (see, for example, Haraway, 1997; Youngs, 2001b).

Serious focus on the Internet's potential as a new inclusive transnational communications arena produces a host of critical questions about the ways in which exclusions affecting it operate, how they can be countered and new patterns of creative thinking about its potential that could result from such efforts.

> Cyberculture is only as diverse and interesting, or as violent and boring, as the people who contribute to it. It's about numbers and critical mass . . . It can promote communication across cultures, and between people of very different social groupings, because they meet as minds first, and only later, if ever, begin to reveal aspects of their identity (age, sex, country, culture, religion, race, sexuality, ability, etc.). Connectivity provides us with the means for communicating, acting together in the real world, and for sharing information and resources. Critical engagement enables us to develop discernment, to rise above the hype and seductiveness of this new and powerful medium. And creativity should not be

underplayed in the electronic culture, as it could be an important source and sustenance for social change in the future. (Hawthorne and Klein, 1999: 14)

THE INTERNET AND POLITICAL ECONOMY

The Internet as part of contemporary processes of globalization is integral to the changing character of the global political economy. A virtual mode is speeding up and intensifying exchange across distance. This mode is most appropriately regarded as an enhancement rather than a replacement of the established materiality of political economy. Goods and services remain fundamental to its operation as do logistics ensuring their adequate delivery. In fact the emphasis on speed of access in the new digital economy increasingly places more demands on logistics. Some of the greatest challenges in the coming years lie in this area.

In this launch period of the digital economy we are only seeing the early stages of its effective integration into, and to a certain extent transformation of, existing economic structures. There are two main areas in this regard – business to customer (B2C) and business to business (B2B). Both take time to develop fully. There are obvious profit imperatives in businesses linking to their customers via the Internet to generate instant orders in this new sales environment. It is revolutionary in two main respects: it delivers an instant and growing international market, and is accessible to customers in the comfort of their home, office, etc. The Internet literally brings the mall into the living room in ways that would be hard to compare with its earlier forerunners such as television shopping channels and catalogues. Its multi-site nature makes comparisons – so essential to bargain hunting and choice – far easier and quicker. As an environment it offers comparable dimensions to a shopping trip, apart from the physical aspects of browsing, touching and trying that remain important. How much virtual experience will in the future be able to adequately replace such physical experience remains open to question at this stage.

The B2B market has deep implications for economic and commercial infrastructures. It concerns the integrative ways in which businesses use the Internet in their operations. B2B activities involve complex supply and demand chains that are internal elements of organizational patterns and commercial strategies. The move to a more Internet-driven B2B environment implies at least some rethinking in these areas. This not only concerns the use of ICTs but what this actually means for business structures and policies. There are new mind-sets involved as much as new practices, planning, investment and training. The US government's *Digital Economy, 2000* report stated that:

> There is growing evidence that firms are moving their supply networks and sales channels online, and participating in new online marketplaces. Firms are also expanding their use of networked systems to improve internal business processes – to coordinate product design, manage inventory, improve customer service, and reduce administrative and managerial costs. Nonetheless, the evolution of digital business is still in an early stage. A recent survey by the National Association of Manufacturers, for example, found that more

than two-thirds of American manufacturers still do not conduct business electronically. (US Department of Commerce, 2000: v; see also Schiller, 2000: 1–36)

Major business trends in the digital economy include existing businesses adapting to it and modifying their operations to take full account of its benefits. The trends also include the phenomenon of new forms of Internet business – companies oriented towards the Internet directly and the sales environment it offers, the bookseller Amazon.com being one of the notable examples.

The electronic business world – e-business as it is often termed – is a diverse environment with small and large players. It has been stressed that there are levelling elements of the current electronic market for smaller commercial entities.

The new economy is being shaped not only by the development and diffusion of computer hardware and software, but also by much cheaper and rapidly increasing electronic connectivity. The Internet in particular is helping to level the playing field among large and small firms in business-to-business e-commerce. In the past, larger companies had increasingly used private networks to carry out electronic commerce, but high costs kept the resulting efficiencies out of reach for most small businesses. The Internet has altered this equation by making it easier and cheaper for all businesses to transact business and exchange information. (US Department of Commerce, 2000: v)

The driving principles of the Internet revolution in business remain those consistent with the history of political economic development and the globalization of commercial activity and marketing. Ownership, control, growth and profit are key in Internet capitalism. Despite its comparative cheapness, virtual space costs, through domain name registration fees, for example. Access to it, and effective presence and operation on it, come at a price, and the relative nature of this varies depending on different market circumstances. The structural concentrations of control and wealth shaping the Internet reflect those of the global political economy at large and its US-centred neoliberal orientations (see the detailed discussion of relevant issues in Schiller, 2000).

The debate about digital divides and digital democracy is taking place at a time when basic problems of survival persist in the world. A total of 1.2 billion people live on less than US$1 a day, more than 1 billion people in developing countries lack access to safe water, and more than 2.4 billion people are without adequate sanitation (UNDP, 2000: 4). AIDS has ravaged Africa, expected to have 40 million orphans by 2010 (UNDP, 2000: 31). Growing gaps have been charted between the richest and poorest within and between countries. The income gap between the fifth of the world's people living in the richest countries and the fifth in the poorest rose from 30 to 1 in 1960, to 60 to 1 in 1990, and 74 to 1 in 1997 (UNDP, 1999: 3).

The global inequalities in communications infrastructures have mirrored other forms of inequality. By the turn of the century the fifth of the world's people living in the highest-income countries had 86 per cent of world gross domestic product (GDP), 82 per cent of world export markets, 68 per cent of foreign direct investment (FDI) and 74 per cent of telephone lines. The bottom fifth had just 1 per cent in the first three areas and 1.5 per cent in the fourth. Communications conglomerates have featured in the recent M&As trends that have helped to keep FDI flows concentrated within the triad of the European Union, USA and Japan (UNCTAD, 2000). Technological innovation and convergence are among the influences at work here.

CYBERCULTURE(S) AND GLOBALIZATION

Cyberculture should be viewed in the context of the political, economic and social realities of dominant patterns of globalization. The latter tell an often depressing story of the ongoing concentration of wealth and influence in the North that seems, in some senses, starkly at odds with the boundary-crossing possibilities of cyberspace. Perhaps this approach is too much rooted in dualisms that plague perspectives on globalization. Is it a good thing or is it bad? The picture rather tends to be that it is a complex set of processes that bring both good and bad, and not surprisingly tend to favour those with the existing lion's share of structural power. But can we leave it there? A comment on ICTs by Fatma Alloo, founder of Tanzania Media Women's Association (TAMWA), gives a clear answer to that question: 'We must recognize that this information technology is here to stay. . . . What we have to decide is we either play the game . . . and turn it to our advantage or lose out completely' (Society for International Development, 1998: 14).

The Internet is not an ideal sphere. It is infused with influences of power and inequality like all social spheres. It has distinctive qualities facilitating connectivity that have been discussed at length in this section. Vertical structures of government, commerce and media are taking leading roles in shaping and utilizing that connectivity to generate new kinds of linkages with citizens, customers and audiences; but new kinds of horizontal civil society connections are also being forged, with a growing number of NGOs around the world playing roles, including in relation to the democratization of ICTs, and their effective use for a wide range of community-building and campaigning efforts. NGOs in the South and North have been at the forefront of developing the Internet as a political and social tool, including with overtly transnational aims. Fatma Alloo relates TAMWA's path following assistance from the APC women's programme, as follows.

> TAMWA had one of the first e-mail nodes in Tanzania at a time when technology was treated with great mistrust as a type of monster. In using this new information technology TAMWA challenged the prevailing view that technology is only something for the haves, and therefore to be shunned. Even more challenging, TAMWA was an NGO working in media and in addition one that focused on women.
>
> Within TAMWA, however, there was still a struggle to encourage members to use information technology. Taking TAMWA as an example, it seems that women are particularly shy, even scared of technology and it takes quite some time before they will dare to try to use it. And here I include myself.
>
> We did persevere however, and the experiment in TAMWA bore fruit. The information technology enabled us [to] link with the broader women's movement. The local and the international could be connected and could work together on various issues such as

violence against women, reproductive health, in general women and empowerment issues. (Society for International Development, 1998: 17)

There are numerous examples of ICT application of this kind, often involving the input of different local and international NGOs and/or other agencies and grant-givers. They demonstrate the dynamic contribution that ICTs can make to local/global change. They signal practically ways in which, through ICTs, local and global processes can more effectively be integrated. They also demonstrate the direct relevance of ICTs to different forms of collective political work (see Harcourt, 1999).

Intrinsic to thinking about cyberculture and globalization is an awareness of the vast range of social contexts that exist, the contrasts in access to, experience of, and perspectives on ICTs. We are back to questions of heterogeneity rather than homogeneity. Focus on heterogeneity suggests that cyberculture is partly about awareness of differences, and learning about them and their implications. It may be much more appropriate to talk in terms of cybercultures to capture the diversity of ICT communities and orientations. The Internet as a network of networks can be viewed as a giant collection of meeting/working/socializing/transactional/campaigning/community-building places.

One of the problems with the scale and nature of the Internet, particularly in its relative infancy, is that a lot of what actually happens on it is not necessarily known by many beyond those involved in or affected by specific communications tracks or communities of interest within it. There are random and invisible qualities about the Internet, particularly when we compare them to the vertical communications settings that are most familiar. The headline structure of managed vertical news environments (including those on the Internet) produces a sense of boundaries to knowledge. There is a kind of (false) security in being able to think the headlines tell us what we need to know or what is most important. Critical awareness that this is not actually necessarily true in many circumstances does not wipe out the dominant tendency to allow our informational needs to be taken care of, as it were.

Cyberculture in its multiplicity of sources and perspectives offers incitements to leave that false sense of security behind, to move away from complacency to a more curious and critical proactive stance. Market and institutional forces will continue to exert their managing influence on use and experience of the Internet. The expanded bandwidth multi-media (mobile) Internet of the future is probably key in this respect. Will the Internet become little more than a consumer sphere, a means of buying and viewing, including on the move via the mobile phone? Some commentators see the Internet as the next stage in the triumph of corporate logic: a symbol of the desire for unbounded activity in terms of both geographic reach and social function (Schiller, 2000: 203–9). In this sense the limited and fragmented nature of cyberactivism and community-building on the Internet may seem substantially overshadowed by the centralized and coherent forces of global conglomerate capitalism. It is early days to make judgements about the Internet; e-government is in its initial phases. We should work on the basis that the political potential of the Internet may well be as powerful as its economic potential.

This chapter, then, has discussed different aspects of the Internet and political economy.

It has returned to the theme of globalization including in relating inequalities and ICTs to the wider context of inequality in the global political economy. A number of points raised indicate the importance of assessing the Internet in connection with the material structures of political economy. The Internet is at least in part a complex expression of those structures and the power relations that have shaped them. It is a dynamic aspect of the ongoing importance of ICTs to globalization, and the transnational operation of the powerful corporations that have significantly defined it.

The Internet represents a powerful virtual market, which is being used to bring about transformations in B2C as well as B2B transactions. It transcends boundaries, offers 24-hour non-stop trading, and helps to cut costs for businesses large and small. The Internet has generated completely new business models in online companies as well as facilitating changes in the operation of existing enterprises.

The vertical structures of the global political economy have produced and steered the Internet, but at the same time it has been an important sphere for growing transnational linkages between civil society actors such as NGOs, for campaigning, community-building and empowerment strategies. Horizontal political and social forces have harnessed the Internet's full capacities to lobby and work for change. Because of the nature of the Internet, much of this activity may remain hidden, only known about by those directly involved or affected. The ease with which networks can link to other networks via the Internet helps to address this problem, but does not eradicate it.

Different kinds of creativity are being undertaken on the Internet. Corporate wealth and technological concentration steer economic investment in its future patterns and applications. There are fears that this will turn it increasingly into little more than a grand sphere of intensified consumption. Convergence – the combination of the Internet with other technologies such as the television and mobile phone – can be regarded as supportive of such a trend. This is not to overlook the fact that a lessening of digital divides in the future should play different parts in widening involvement in, and benefit from, the global economy, including among those in the South.

The signs are that the problem of concentration of wealth and corporate power in the North is likely to be embedded by the Internet and the continuing trends in conglomeration. Will the market take all on the Internet in the years to come? This is one of the main outstanding questions. It will depend on the degree to which other influences, particularly those in government and civil society, work to create and maintain a more diverse virtual environment. If the Internet becomes the major transnational communications sphere in the future, there will be plenty of grounds for arguing its political and social importance.

Current NGO activities on the Internet, and their impact in local and global contexts, as well as their effectiveness in connecting those contexts, help provide bases for those arguments. As a technology, or more accurately a combination of technologies, the Internet is open to an infinite number of social meanings that can only be given to it through its different uses. Digital democracy may be partly about ensuring that the scope of this potential remains as wide as possible, and that the kinds of creativity and diversity involved are encouraged, facilitated and supported.

CHAPTER 40

Media Technology for Distance Learning

Oliver Boyd-Barrett

MEDIA STUDIES, TECHNOLOGY AND EDUCATION

Discussions about technology in media studies, like discussions about media in general, focus on mainstream, large-audience media. This reflects the history of a discipline that set itself in opposition against presumptions of the superiority of 'great literature' and the worthlessness of popular culture. Concentration on big media in turn suggests a presumption that large audience equals great influence or significance, for individuals or for society. This is unlikely always to be true. The drive for audience size more likely limits attainable depth of significance, by contrast with media products that address specialist needs and interests. Conventional presumptions marginalize the study of specialist media, or of mainstream media in specialist contexts. I include here the educational media, and the ways in which formal education and media texts interrelate. Studies of these generally adopt an insufficiently critical, prescriptive, 'administrative' framework of enquiry that focuses on media effectiveness for learning.

My topic here is media technology for distance teaching in higher education. Just as technology applications in mainstream media often transform audience experience of narrative traditions that are as old as humanity, so they transform experience of the learning process and of what counts as learning. In mainstream media as in the world of education, the choice of technology is determined by a range of social factors, many of them institutional and ideological.

Ways of Making and Taking Meaning from Texts

My starting point is the cultural specificity of approaches to teaching and learning, and the extent to which issues of technology in education are also ideological contests about how teaching and learning should take place, and about what constitutes teaching and learning, and even knowledge. I take my cue from the focus of socio-linguistics on the cultural determination of the ways in which people interact with, talk about and take meaning from texts.

Heath (1983) looked at three communities in South Carolina – middle-class white, working-class white and working-class black – and examined their different literacy practices, including the hallowed place of the bedtime story among white middle-class families. This literacy event involved interaction of text, pictures and talk within the context of an intimate child–parent relationship. Heath interpreted the typical question-and-answer routines of this ritual as a form of early preparation of the child for the prevailing literacy of formal education. Eve Gregory (1993) looked at processes of teaching children to read in the classroom. She argued that such processes cannot be passed off simply as the transmission of textual decoding skills. Rather, they need to be understood as a form of socialization, both into the range of talk and meanings that formal education considers appropriate in relation to texts, and into the appropriate relationship between teacher and learner. The Russian psychologist Vygotsky (1962) found much the same thing in his study of language acquisition, namely that learning to talk is also a process of learning how to learn. This process is embedded within and contributes to the relationship between a learner and someone who has more language competence – often a parent. Barry Street (1993) demonstrated how the conventions of literacy – which determine the use of speech as it relates to texts, and the appropriate uses of written texts – are very different from one society to another, or from one literacy form to another within a given society.

Conventions for the use of language in academe vary between different subject areas and between cultures. These pertain to conventions for the presentation and formulation of knowledge, and for what counts as argument. Researchers (e.g. Scribner and Cole, 1973) examining the relationship between literacy and scientific rationality contest the claim that literacy is essential for rationality. They argue that there are many forms of literacy. Some play no part in rationality and the development of rationality is more related to the institution of formal schooling than to literacy *per se*.

These sources demonstrate how, in the terms of Heath (1983), the taking and making of meaning from texts is as culturally specific as the texts themselves. The one-to-one parent–child, print-related bedtime story for middle-class whites in one community is set against the communal, oral, print-free, story-telling skills of working-class blacks in another. There are different ideas about what constitutes a text, about how to talk about texts, present and appreciate them.

Distance Learning and the Sociology of Knowledge

Such considerations address issues about what constitutes knowledge, and how knowledge is constructed and framed to count as such. They help dissect the culturally specific and ritualistic aspects of any educational 'tradition' – i.e. the determination as absolute that which is, empirically, relative. Educational traditions are built on such decisions as the duration of courses, divisions between subjects, and ideas about what counts as appropriate presentation via lecture or research article etc., how academics and students should interact, how learning is assessed, and the determination of suitability for study (admission) and progression.

The traditions of western higher education have always been open to challenge. Changes in technology, while they may not constitute challenges in themselves, do expose the cultural relativity of much of what passes for education by exposing just how diverse and how available is the range of alternative ways of doing things.

A set of conventions about learning has developed in the West (I will refer to these as the 'dominant mode') that are overdue for critical overhaul. These provide the framework and ground rules for students from other societies who study with western institutions. Their global adoption reveals processes and patterns not unlike those revealed in the dissemination of media forms and practices.

The radical alternatives of **distance education** have to do with the reduction of constraints of time and space, greater dependence on non-oral and non-print media, greater attention to adult learners, flexibility of starting points and progression, and enhanced student choice. Not one of these is especially dramatic nor even foreign to conventional university education. This is partly because conventional and distance education are not truly dichotomous. Each supposed feature of distance education is also to be found within specific varieties of the dominant mode. What distance learning often does is bring most of these alternatives together in one radical package that I shall call the 'presumptive mode'.

The two modes, dominant and presumptive, are not diametrical opposites but are sometimes institutionalized as such. They are identifiably separate ideological formations about the nature of learning. The dominant mode variously sees the presumptive mode as a threat or as a resource of ideas and experiment from which it can pick and choose without challenge to conventional institutional features. Neither mode is actually homogenous. Talking about them as though they were impedes progress towards our understanding the complexity of practices in higher education.

Putting technology in context: defining criteria of distance education

Criteria that determine the nature of distance education provision in higher education:

- the provider is state-supported or private
- the provider is 'dedicated' – distance education is its sole or most-important activity – or is a conventional campus-university that has incorporated some distance learning
- distance learning is strategically governed from a 'whole-institution' perspective, or is non-strategic – an incremental add-on by particular departments
- there exists an institutional philosophy for distance education, and the extent to which that philosophy penetrates everyday culture, or not
- there is strategic planning with implications for the availability of whole degree programmes, and for balance between credit and non-credit courses, or not
- the provider originates the courses that it delivers or outsources them
- faculty are mainly full-time and responsible for day-to-day course development and presentation or teaching, or part-time with limited responsibility
- the look and feel of distance education is determined by any of a mix of technologies, including face-to-face encounters
- distance education is treated separately from campus education, possibly as a self-sustaining profit centre, or is completely integrated
- providers have substantial upfront investment in distance education, or consider that it requires little or no additional financing (funding levels depend in part on

> whether the origination of materials centres on a single academic expert or on a multi-professional team)
> - the student 'market' is on or off-campus

I shall explore some different shapes that the presumptive mode has adopted in higher education. Institutional, historical and social contexts are also important, and underline the danger of focusing exclusively on technology. I shall say most about the British Open University because, despite having a relatively low-technology approach up to the 1990s, it is possibly more influential worldwide than other providers. (Much of what follows was originally published in the journal *Information, Communication and Society* (Boyd-Barrett, 2000).)

MODEL 1: 'PUBLIC, DEDICATED, STRATEGIC' – THE BRITISH OPEN UNIVERSITY

This first model inspired and legitimated distance education in many countries. I describe it as a public, dedicated, strategic distance learning institution, with a commitment to making higher education available to everyone, on demand. It is the principal originator of its own courses. Full-time faculty are responsible for course development, in collaboration with broadcasters and consultants. Tutorials and marking are undertaken by part-time faculty, usually hired from other institutions of higher education. Its mission is strategically governed on an institution-wide basis. Its technologies are combinations of print, audio-visual programming and face-to-face tutorials, extending increasingly to Internet and compact disc. This mix allows students to achieve degrees entirely 'at a distance'. Finance comes from government and tuition, supplemented with sponsorship from foundations and industry. Courses have substantial development time (at least two years) and investment (estimated at almost US$2 million per credit course in the early 1990s). Courses are developed by multi-disciplinary groups of academic experts working alongside pedagogical advisers, designers and graphic artists, audio-visual production personnel and developmental testers. The market is defined inclusively. Anyone in the EC over 18 can apply for undergraduate admittance, regardless of previous qualifications (numbers admitted in any one year are, however, limited by funding availability). The Open University recruits students from many other countries and, in 1999, it opened the United States Open University. It has undergraduate, postgraduate, advanced diploma, masters and doctoral degrees, as well as diploma and certificate courses.

The Open University prefers the term 'open learning' to 'distance learning'. Its first students enrolled in 1971; by 1996 there were 257,000 students (120,000 undergraduate and 137,000 postgraduate). Daniel (1998) calls it a 'mega-university', arguing that size yields significant economies of scale, and facilitates high quality for modest fees.

Brainchild of a Labour government, the Open University took root in a conservative society divided by social class, whose academy revered elitist 'Oxbridge' traditions. Correspondence teaching was widely deprecated as an activity of grubby, huckster institutions exploiting the educational pretensions of unworthy lower-class losers. In 25 years the Open University had so overcome this ideological challenge that it ranked as fourth-largest higher education institution in receipt of government funding (and first for teaching), and tenth within UK league tables of teaching excellence. It boasted tens of thousands of graduates in every profession and was expanding internationally. What could account for this transformation?

The Open University model was a calculated response to prevailing problems of the time. It enabled government to expand higher education for less money. It responded to anticipated growth in demand for education throughout life. It enabled adults to maintain jobs and support families as they acquired a university education. It harnessed media to education, a reassurance of countervailing influence to the government-sanctioned commercialization of television.

Many responses to these trends were possible, and some would have failed. To understand the success of the Open University, I have drawn liberally on my own experience, but equally on accounts by its first vice-chancellor, Sir Walter Perry (1977), and its current vice chancellor, Sir John Daniel (1998; 1999a; 1999b).

Still remarkable 30 years later, the Open University offered open access, on a 'first come, first served' basis, regardless of previous qualifications – demonstration of its commitment to those with little other opportunity to achieve higher education, notably adults of modest income and with family commitments. By the 1990s, approximately one-third of its graduates had entered without conventional university entrance requirements. Challenging the rigid 'ladder' principle of educational advancement, this gave weight to world experience and motivation. Students paid relatively modest fees for admittance. By the judgements of government league tables, many professional associations, students and professors, the 'standards' of teaching and learning at the Open University compare well with those of conventional universities. Some original planners had wanted the university managed by a consortium of existing adult education departments; this would likely have relegated distance education courses to a bureaucratic consortium of non-prestigious faculties.

A factor almost as important as open entry in explaining the growth and survival of the Open University was its link to the highly regarded and nationwide British Broadcasting Corporation (BBC), subcontracted to produce radio and television programmes for both students and larger 'listening-in' audiences. This invaluable publicity (through the programmes themselves, programme announcements, and programme listings in newspapers and guides) was reinforced by production quality of general broadcast standard.

Strong and consistent government sponsorship was crucial. Initial Conservative Party scepticism on the party's return to power in 1971 gave way to respect. Government later exerted pressure towards self-sustainability for all universities, and this has fostered entrepreneurship. Although the Open University exudes a public-service ethos, specifically entrepreneurial programmes date from the late 1970s with the introduction of a self-sustaining MBA programme. Government funding has fallen from 80 per cent to around 60 per cent or under, but the Higher Education Funding Council grant is still considerable. The Open University must balance its books, yet develops many courses that are uneconomic, while maintaining breadth of choice.

Its 'Rolls-Royce' model of course development may have overcompensated in order to prove that distance education was not third-class education for the poor. Large course teams did not displace department or faculty structures, but constituted strong work groups with lives of two to three years (then diminishing in size during course presentation). Supported by a total budget of £215 million in 1999, including government subsidy, and delivering to large numbers, Open University course fees are inexpensive; UK fees in 1997 were US$540 for a full-credit course (6 credits are needed for a pass degree). Programme development contracts from government agencies in fields such as health, social welfare and education (including, from 1995, the first UK government-recognized teacher training qualification by distance learning) enhanced prestige.

Dedicated to distance learning, with faculties of arts, social sciences, education, science, mathematics and technology (later including business, social services, languages and law), the Open University occupied a greenfield site in central England (close to the new town of Milton Keynes) with 13 regional centres throughout the UK. Each region maintains networks of study centres for local tutorials: 311 UK study centres and a further 330 in continental Europe. Locally organized face-to-face teaching by 7000 part-time 'associate lecturers', addresses the needs of students for day-to-day contact and tutorials. Tutorial participation is mostly voluntary after year one.

Quality BBC broadcasts were secondary to the principal learning components – namely printed course units – easily deliverable through the reliable nationwide postal service. These comprised voluminous original works, vetted every step of the way by course teams, in specially prepared course readers, set books, broadcast notebooks and cassettes. A total of 32 original course units, each of them approximately 10,000–12,000 words long, constituted the typical 'whole credit' course in social sciences, humanities and education. Courses often amounted to daring new conceptualizations of whole disciplines of study, drawing on faculty expertise and experts worldwide. The Open University's 'popular studies' course in the 1980s, for example, was virtually the first higher-education course of its kind. Course readers and set books fostered ties with publishers and book stores; course materials were adopted widely throughout higher education. Printed texts did not challenge conventional ideas about teaching quality in the same way as television-led learning. Print conformed to the self-imposed restraint of universal access, which cautioned against precipitate enthusiasm for newer technologies. VCR was incorporated only when most people had easy access to video players. A similar attitude prevailed towards computers; most courses now have online tutoring, but online communications for mainstream learning were still (in 1999) confined mainly to courses about computers or distance education. Easy visibility of high-standard course materials provided reassurance to the general public as to 'standards', but exposed controversial materials to wider scrutiny, even ministerial intervention.

Part-time tutors for tutorials and marking mainly worked as full-time lecturers for other higher-education institutions. Their co-option contributed to the university's image, establishing collaborative rather than competitive relations with other higher educational institutions. Each region had full-time directors and academic-related staff, who recruited tutors and students. The regional model endorsed the university's commitment to all peoples of the UK. Part-time tutors' marking practices were monitored by central academic staff. The regions provided multiple sites for the taking of examinations, set and marked by the national centre. The university spent US$2 million annually in the late 1990s training its associate faculty.

Until the 1980s the Open University did not compete for conventional higher education's main market: the under-21s. Many early students were teachers upgrading their teaching certificates to degree level, in a profession converting to graduate-level entry. Demanding clients, they were largely content with their experience, supplying word-of-mouth endorsement. (Teachers today constitute only a small proportion of total student numbers.)

In addition to print, broadcasts, cassettes, CDs and online tutoring, local face-to-face tutorials are provided fortnightly or monthly. Foundation courses had additional week-long summer schools. A course portfolio encompassing four levels, introduced modular, 'a la carte' education to England and Wales. Students had to take foundation courses in two disciplinary areas (later reduced to one and no longer an absolute requirement). The system was responsive to student needs and interests. Its credit structure (adopted from the Scottish university tradition) was different from the American one. Individual courses were long – eight credits were needed for an 'honours' degree. An American model would have provoked criticism in a country that considered its own system more specialized and demanding. A 'non-rigid uniformity' of operations, standards and practices governed the length of courses, layout and design, pre-course evaluation and quality control, constructed a distinctive 'brand image' and reduced the temptation to constantly re-invent the wheel.

Faculty were required to research, and the university has achieved commendable results in national research productivity rankings. This emphasized its commitment to scholarship and its equal status with existing universities. The university has greatly expanded its post-graduate programmes, including a taught educational doctorate, attracting substantial numbers of students, including its own graduates.

Cautious international expansion involved collaboration with other large-scale quality providers, including the Institute of Management in Singapore and the Open Learning Institute in Hong Kong. Providing consultant support to distance ventures globally, the Open University enjoyed the accolade of its own government. Its 25,000 non-UK students include 17,000 from the former Soviet bloc (Daniel, 1998). The Open University of the United States was incorporated in Delaware in 1999. This built on collaborations with the state university systems of Florida and California. In California, the Open University worked with California State University (CSU) teams to re-develop a teacher training programme for emergency permit teachers, and comprised print, video technologies and online materials. The Open University also partnered with the Western Governors University (Blumenstyk, 1999).

MODEL 2: 'PUBLIC, INCORPORATED, STRATEGIC' – LEICESTER UNIVERSITY (UK)

Leicester University is a chartered British university approximately 100 miles north of London. It is mostly a conventional campus, with over 14,000 students. But the establishment of an

MBA by distance education in 1989, recruiting several hundred students in Southeast Asia and elsewhere, led senior administration to encourage other departments to develop distance MAs or MScs. The range includes a general MBA, and specialist MBAs in human resource, sports and educational management, and MAs in international law, mass communications, museum studies, psychology and public order. The university funded these courses from accumulated revenues. Students register knowing they can study for their entire degree entirely by distance. Building on the credibility of distance education that the Open University has established, Leicester is more entrepreneurial.

Distance-learning programmes here exist to make surplus revenue; most of them do. Departments were largely autonomous in determination of formats, content, pedagogy, marketing and advertising. Ten years later central administration exerted pressure for common formatting and publicity to establish 'brand image' and because standardization spares course teams the trouble of re-inventing the wheel with respect to book design, logo design, copyright issues, structures of assessment and so on.

To reduce faculty resistance to distance education (perceived to be demanding, time-consuming and 'different'), many (short-term) appointments were made specifically for distance education, including clerical and other office staff for each programme. New faculty worked under considerable pressure while exposed to market risk, yet subject to similar or less attractive terms and conditions of employment. But, in some departments, faculty developed programmes on release time.

By targeting the postgraduate market, the university appealed to students who were accomplished learners, capable of independent study. Additionally, the focus for recruitment was mainly on niche markets and professional groups. This 'cream' rather than public-service model, appeals to conventional institutions needing to offset near-permanent threats to grant income, and which find it difficult to compel faculty to commercialize. Students were both domestic and international. Where there were significant concentrations of students in overseas countries these were serviced in collaboration with educational agents or overseas universities. Commercial agents required careful monitoring to avoid abuses, but at their best were more flexible and responsive than universities.

The prevailing model was of commissioned materials (printed and bound through university printers or through external subcontract), set books, with some relatively cheap audio/video components and some online interaction. Most arranged face-to-face tuition. The MA in Mass Communications organized periodic weekend course conferences in Britain, Greece, Hong Kong, Singapore, Taiwan, Thailand and the United Arab Emirates.

In summary, I describe Leicester as a 'public, incorporated, strategic' model of distance learning. This was a conventional institution that largely assimilated distance learning within existing academic and management structures. Yet it simultaneously ring-fenced it within an environment of entrepreneurial practice, subject to oversight by a specialist advisory committee (in addition to the academic board) chaired by the academic registrar. Distance learning staff appointments were arguably more dependent on programme viability than conventional academic appointments. Critics argued that this overlooked the pressures on all university staff to act 'entrepreneurially'. While the university may not have rewarded distance learning faculty for exposure to market risk, it tended to privilege distance learning

units managerially, allowing programmes to operate relatively autonomous budgets. Originating as incremental innovations at departmental level, programmes were increasingly subject to central strategic planning since, together, they represented a multi-million-dollar
operation and accounted for a substantial proportion of all students. The fundamental purpose here, in contrast to that of the Open University, was to generate surplus revenue. Yet
Leicester could justly claim to be making postgraduate education practical and affordable
for working adults who could study in their own time without obligatory classroom attendance, achieving their qualifications entirely at a distance.

The university originated most of its course materials, although some early courses were
constituted principally from 'readings' of existing texts. Course developers were full-time
faculty, supported by some external consultants. Teaching, unlike in the Open University
model, has principally been in-house, with some support from part-time staff. Funded from
accumulated reserves, sustained because they generated revenue, these programmes
helped finance projects the university might otherwise not have funded. Surplus revenue was
shared between university and faculty or programme.

Programmes required substantial upfront investment, but not at Open University
levels. The MA in Mass Communications that I developed from 1994 had a float of
approximately US$400,000. The course was in presentation to students less than a year
after start of development. The course was still in development as the first students
enrolled, and development continued to the end of the first year of presentation.
Audio/video productions were either re-recordings for which educational re-use was
protected under copyright, or inexpensive in-house productions, and considerably less
than the cost of comparable productions from the Open University. Parsimony took
advantage of postgraduate familiarity with study discipline. Yet many students did not
have English as a first language, and were studying in cultures quite different to that of
the UK. Course teams were smaller than at the Open University, working for shorter
periods and meeting less frequently. Many degrees had parallel on-campus equivalents
(unlike at the Open University) that were both a resource and a point of reference for the
maintenance of 'standards'. Students were both international and domestic. Courses
were almost exclusively English. Student numbers were typically several hundred for
each programme.

MODEL 3: 'PUBLIC, INCORPORATED, NON-STRATEGIC' – CALIFORNIA STATE POLYTECHNIC UNIVERSITY, POMONA

California State Polytechnic University, Pomona, is one of the 23 campuses of California
State University. Up to 2000, the system had a relatively *laissez-faire* approach to distance
education. Policy was left much to the discretion of campuses. In 1997–98, the system
recorded 18,081 enrolments on courses that used satellite, video-cassette, ITFS, cable and
other means of delivery. The non-credit portion of television instruction served an estimated
1 million students annually. Three degree programmes and five certificates were available

exclusively through the use of the Internet. A total of 3300 registrations were recorded in all forms of Internet programming (CSU, 1999).

There was significant inter-campus variation. Anticipated increases in conventional enrolments to 2010, following the baby-boom impact of 'tidal wave 2', were technically an incentive to use distance learning to reduce demand on physical resources, but were perceived by many faculty as confirmation that traditional teaching practices were safe. Online courses were boosted during the 1990s by digital summer schools. Additionally, in 2000 the university's cabinet provided development money for as many as 30 technology-mediated courses. There was no single source of information as to how many of the university's courses were online, in whole or in part. A very small proportion of all courses was delivered entirely online, principally for the benefit of on-campus students. No degrees could be achieved entirely online, although there was one four-course distance learning 'LEP-UPLINK' programme leading to CLAD/BCLAD certification for teachers in bilingual classrooms. This used videos, workbooks and Internet interaction between students and instructors. Online certificate extension programmes were in preparation.

Development of online courses was mainly secured by faculty release time, and courses were taught by single instructors, with technical support and advice from the instructional technology advisory centre and professional development centre. The multi-media LEP-UPLINK programme recruited up to 100 students for each of its four courses. A few online courses for on-campus students regularly recruited up to 100 students. Students mostly lived within or near the university's service area. With the exception of courses or programmes from institutions with strong regional or national brand identity, US online education may be a surprisingly local phenomenon. Online courses at Pomona principally included web-delivered text, online interaction between instructor and students, and among students, with supporting workbooks and textbooks, and occasional face-to-face orientation or examination sessions.

In brief, Pomona is a conventional state university that has incorporated some distance learning, but without a substantial strategic policy or philosophy. Distance learning traditionally favoured satellite television and video, but is increasingly moving online. Online courses are developed by interested faculty, largely on the basis of courses they already run, and who can secure some (modest) funding or release time, or both. External funding, as in the case of support from the Department of Education for the LEP-UPLINK programme, can yield more substantial funding, preparation time and corresponding quality of resource, but these are generally one-off occurrences. (Some larger distance learning developments elsewhere had substantial external funding, as in the case of the University of California online extension courses, which had funding from the Sloan Foundation.) There are no credit programmes other than LEP-UPLINK, that may be achieved entirely 'at a distance'. In the past, the University Senate's attitude towards expansion of distance learning has been cautious. Further development may depend in part on the attitude and requirements of the university's accreditation agencies, but for the short to medium term a principal barrier is the shortage of motivated faculty. This limitation potentially opens the door to external 'content providers', but no such deal has been seriously considered. The beneficiaries of distance learning initiatives are principally on-campus students, and select groups of non-matriculated students of certificate programmes. Overall numbers are modest and unlikely soon to reach a critical mass at which significant economies of scale could be achieved.

CSU Pomona represents a context of provision that is common across the United States. For some institutions distance learning is a matter of incremental growth, as at Pomona, in others its growth has been more strategic and driven by scale, as at Leicester. Such examples could be described as 'public, incorporated, strategic' but unlike Leicester, they are increasingly tending to be online. Established examples would include the University of California online programme, which by 1998 had recruited 1400 students to 59 courses (Almeda, 1998). Examples emerging from pre-online technologies include the Old Dominion University of West Virginia, whose Teletechnet programme used satellite technology for distance learning programmes in more than 40 locations across several states, accounting for more than 15,000 student registrations. The 1998 Campus Computing Project survey records more than one-third of all higher-education institutions using or having formal plans to use the Internet in distance education. Many such courses have been designed for on-campus students. A large but unknown proportion of online courses available for off-campus students are non-credit. Online players include prestigious institutions such as Stanford, which began an Internet masters in electrical engineering in 1998, and Harvard Business School, which is developing online business courses. Many state college systems offer web-based learning, including New York, which offered 1000 online courses in 1999, and the University of Maryland, which has some 10,000 students taking online courses. Growing online education attracts a significant service industry, representing a process of institutional 'unbundling' of functions. Organizations like Blackboard.com, Convene International, Generation 21, Parliament Software, Real Education, and the University of Delaware's SERF, provide packages that include access to course architecture, administration and tracking software, online faculty training courses and technical support. A new generation of companies such as Skillsoft are providing content that can be used within wholly online or conventional courses.

MODEL 4: 'PRIVATE, INCORPORATED, STRATEGIC' – UNIVERSITY OF PHOENIX

A second group of models includes institutions that are neither conventional campus universities nor, using the British Open University as a standard, conventional dedicated distance learning institutions. The University of Phoenix is of interest because, like the Open University, it had achieved considerable success and economies of scale, even before the availability of online teaching. Unlike the Open University, whose predominantly 'correspondence' character would still classify it as 'technology mediated', the University of Phoenix had adopted principles of flexible learning and customer-focused provision that was still based on traditional classroom methods. Phoenix locates classes as near as possible to the students, wherever there are students to be found. This is similar to the use of extension satellite centres for the delivery of programmes taught by university faculty travelling out to teach (a model common to Australian universities, which ship faculty out to teach classroom courses in Southeast Asia).

The University of Phoenix has extended this practice distinctively in scale and in the use of part-time faculty, many of whom are not otherwise employed in higher education. There is a strong specialist interest in job-centred management programmes. Phoenix appears to have responded to adult demand for flexible and convenient higher education in ways that other universities have not matched.

Phoenix is a privately owned unit of Apollo Group, Inc. The group made a profit of US$46 million on US$391 revenues in 1998 (*Business Week*, 8 September 1999: 91). Its stock rose by more than 1500 per cent in the period 1994–99 (Guernsey, 1999). The original Phoenix model offered conventional classroom teaching, flexibly taught in many different learning centres (119 sites in 34 states, Puerto Rico and London, with sites located in leased buildings near major highways), by part-time faculty (of whom many are suitably qualified non-academic professionals) to suit the timetables and domestic constraints of working adults. The university claimed 50,000 students by autumn 1997, rising to 74,500 by late 1998. From 1989 it had also offered online courses (accounting for approximately 10 per cent of its students). The Phoenix model caters to working adults, mostly between the ages of 35 and 39, who want to earn their degrees quickly (reportedly, it is possible to complete an undergraduate degree in two years, depending on the amount of prior credit earned). Students take courses one at a time and these are accelerated, lasting five weeks for undergraduates and six weeks for graduate students, scheduled mainly in the evenings and at weekends. (Leatherman, 1998; Padilla, 1999). The company employs 5200 instructors, all but 150 of whom are part-time, and who receive between US$1000 and US$2500 per five-week course. Undergraduates spend less than half of the time (17.5 hours over five weeks, not counting time for breaks) that traditional university students spend (40–45 hours) face to face in a classroom setting with a professor during a three semester course. The deficit is made up by mandatory, though largely unsupervised, weekly small-group study sessions of class length, in which students are supposed to meet independently with other class members.

In brief, the University of Phoenix is a non-conventional institution that has incorporated online distance learning as an increasingly significant supplement and alternative to its dispersed provision of degree level programmes. Its mission is profit-driven, but succeeds because of its response to demand from adult learners in search of career-relevant degree qualifications that they can achieve with maximum flexibility and speed under accredited conditions. Its part-time faculty deliver courses subject to the standards and criteria established by the institution. Part-time faculty, while qualified, may pursue industry or professional as opposed to academic careers. Phoenix has explored the potential of developing courses around online materials provided by external online training sources such as Skillsoft. The technology mix is classroom and online learning. Course development is not seen to require the high levels of investment characteristic of the UK models discussed earlier, and is largely the product of individual faculty working in collaboration with technicians. The market is a broad one, principally made up of working people who are looking for professional degree-level qualifications.

MODEL 5: 'PUBLIC/PRIVATE, DEDICATED, STRATEGIC' – THE CLEARING HOUSE/CONSORTIUM MODEL

Farrell (1999: 8) noted that the USA has generated many different models of distance education, including broker-type organizations designed to acquire or broker programmes from
a variety of institutional providers, and to add value through flexible entry and credit transfer
policies. The 'clearing house' seeks to overcome fragmentation of the educational market
by pooling distance courses, course support, marketing, even technical infrastructure and
training from a variety of different institutions. Consortia can thus improve the overall
strength and quality of their collective portfolios (Mendels, 1999).

Clearing houses are conduits for distance learning programmes from member institutions. These include the Western Governors University (WGU) and California Virtual
University (CVU). The WGU, one of whose principal backers was AT+T, had still attracted only
100–120 students by summer 1999, and was reported to need 3000 students enrolled in
order to break even (EDUCAUSE Edupage listserve, 23 August 1999). Many potential
students who visited the WGU website may have registered directly with the member universities. CVU was launched in 1998, listing 2000 courses, but in 1999 control shifted back
to participating universities who balked at a proposed marketing bill of US$3 million over
three years. During the first year of operation, CVU had attracted 25,000 enrolments; about
120,000 people visited the website monthly (Mendels, 1999). Downs (1999) has argued
that money was not the problem (there was US$6.1 million backing from UC, CSU and com-
munity college systems). All it had to do was catalogue university courses, not create them.
But each participant wanted something different. Corporate sponsors wanted profits;
member institutions wanted autonomy, the government wanted a good press. Downs also
queries why a student would want to sign up with the CVU when s/he would get their degree
from another institution?

The Kentucky Commonwealth Virtual University (KCVU) started with 160 students
enrolled in 21 classes in summer 1999, with an annual operating budget of US$8 million
(Associated Press, 23 August 1999). The state planned to invest nearly US$18 million over
two years. The university has no professors, does not deliver its own courses nor grant
degrees, but offers a directory of online courses statewide, a central online library, and
support services for distance learning students. A total of 22 of the state's 59 colleges and
universities participated. KCVU pays for technology used on individual campuses and sometimes pays for release time for professors to develop courses. It operates a toll-free 'call
centre' where students can seek technical or academic help. Courses use standard software
for the same 'look and feel'.

Another 1999 initiative, R1.edu, brought together 14 large US research universities to
market their distance education efforts through a central web directory, co-ordinated by the
University of Washington (Young, 1999a). Unext.com, another example, invites universities
to contribute course materials that can be sold to major corporations for employee training.
Participants include Columbia University's business school, the University of Chicago,
Stanford University, Carnegie Mellon University and the London School of Economics and

Political Science. Its first customer was IBM, whose Lotus Development unit, called LearningSpace, is used for delivery and sales. Participating universities benefit from sales revenue, royalties and equity (Guernsey, 1999). One objective is to achieve accreditation as an online business school for MBA degrees. A 1998 initiative, Caliber Learning Network, Inc., involves a Baltimore company and three universities – the Wharton School of the University of Pennsylvania, Johns Hopkins University and the University of Southern California (Guernsey, 1999; McGeehan, 1999) – in offering business courses via satellite television and the Internet.

Other examples of the clearing house model include the National Technological University, an accredited, degree-granting university that offers for-credit and non-credit courses delivered via what it calls 'leading-edge telecommunications technologies' produced by a working alliance of universities and training organizations. Knowledge TV, a television channel designed to meet diverse needs for education, information and instruction, focuses primarily on for-credit, college-level 'telecourses', available both for registered students and a much larger 'eavesdropping' audience. Programming comes from 30 affiliate universities, colleges and other providers around the United States. Degrees are conferred by affiliate institutions, not by Knowledge TV. The channel is delivered by satellite, broadcast, cable and the Internet, to individuals or to institutions. Instructor contact is maintained via telephone, mail, e-mail and periodic teleconferences (Jones, 1997).

Palomar College, California, offers 4200 hours of original educational programming in San Diego County and is involved in the construction of a satellite uplink facility that will provide all 106 California Community Colleges with the ability to transmit their courses to students anywhere in the state. The PBS (Public Broadcasting Service) Adult Learning Services (ALS) 'Going the Distance' project assists colleges in developing distance degree programmes. ALS was established in 1981 to co-ordinate with 190 public television stations and some 2000 colleges to deliver telecourses for college credit. Colleges pay for a licence to use the materials for local delivery within their own credit and non-credit programmes.

In summary the clearing house model is driven by allure of relatively modest start-up costs, economies of scale and strong brand name. Participating institutions may or may not have a management or ownership stake in the clearing house; they may include both public and private institutions, profit and non-profit. The clearing houses will typically have no full-time faculty of their own. The model allows for a mix of technologies and delivery systems, including online, terrestrial, satellite or cable television and radio, and correspondence. By bringing together courses from different sources, the clearing house may be well positioned to construct entire degrees online. But, equally, course portfolios may merely reflect the idiosyncrasies of individual member portfolios. Course credit is generally awarded by the source institutions that have originated the courses. The courses themselves usually result from the efforts of individual staff working in relative isolation. Not always well resourced, clearing houses are by definition strategic, designed to maximize dissemination, but not all are effective. They target both existing on-campus students, who can better juggle their timetables if they have distance learning options, and external students who benefit from programmes that do not require physical class attendance.

MODEL 6: 'PRIVATE, DEDICATED AND STRATEGIC' – JONES INTERNATIONAL UNIVERSITY (*ET AL.*)

This model is represented by commercially driven private institutions dedicated to distance delivery. Some are offshoots of older publishing and media interests, some have links with conventional universities. Internet-only institutions include private operators such as Jones International University (accredited), and non-accredited institutions such as Concord University School of Law in Los Angeles, and OnlineLearning.net, owned partly by Houghton Mifflin, which has exclusive rights to market non-credit versions of courses given at the University of California at Los Angeles.

Jones International, an offshoot of Knowledge TV (described above) was the first Internet-only school accredited to grant college degrees. It counted 950 registrations for its various courses in March 1999; of these 10 were enrolled in the bachelor's degree programme and 64 in the master's degrees (Blumenstyk, 1999). At fees of US$4000 a year, Jones competes hotly with the US$3200 average of a state college, but it has been estimated that Jones would need 3000 students in two years to become profitable (*Business Week*, 8 September 1999: 90). The decision of the North Central Association of Colleges and Schools to accredit Jones International in March 1999 was formally protested by the American Association of University Professors (AAUP), alleging that Jones instructors taught courses prepared by others and had little say over how material was presented, that nearly all instructors were part-time and that there was little emphasis on research.

In July 1999, publisher Harcourt General, Inc. announced its intention to introduce a programme called Lifelong Learning, an Internet university and an Internet high school. It wanted to become the first major publishing house to offer accredited college degrees, through the New England Association of Schools and Colleges, the same organization that certifies Harvard University and other major colleges in the region (Hechinger, 1999).

In summary, the institutions of this model are largely profit-driven, and some have strong commercial roots in the publishing and entertainment industries. They tend to employ only as many full-time faculty as are needed for accreditation purposes, if that. Like the University of Phoenix they depend heavily on part-time faculty for both course development and presentation. They are dedicated to distance learning, and their approach is strategic. Their technology is online, involving both content delivery, synchronous and asynchronous interaction between instructors and students, and among students. Not enough is currently known about the upfront investment available for the preparation of individual courses, nor whether there is any significant shift away from the traditional instructor-centred approach in favour of course team operation. Courses tend to concentrate on areas of high potential revenue, inevitably strong on management and computing.

These different models of the incorporation of technology for the provision of higher education by distance learning demonstrate, first, how technology greatly expands the range of options available to institutions. The options that particular institutions choose, however, are not technologically determined, but reflect institutional, cultural and market imperatives. Surprisingly, none of them suggests a radical diminution in the importance of institutions and their faculty as primary definers of what counts as worthwhile knowledge. But technology has had implications for the range of providers that are motivated to enter the field of higher education, and this in itself, more than the technology, may be the major threat to the dominant mode of education provision.

Conclusion

This section has adopted a multi-faceted approach to interactive electronic media. It has explored the qualities of the Internet, and the ways in which they both intersect with mass media traditions and transform them. It has stressed that continuities and discontinuities are equally important to the new digital informational environment. In this context, it has suggested that work on the Internet should retain strong purchase on the traditions of mass media research and its critical aspects. The dangers of utopian views of the Internet have been noted, but so has the importance of creativity and diversity to its further development. The Internet is a heterogeneous environment and digital divides mark it as a highly unequal one. It features contradictions and tensions between vertical power structures and horizontal forces. Concerns about increasing market colonization of virtual space are clearly justified, but political and other influences may guarantee a more balanced and holistic environment.

Focus on distance learning requires consideration of media technology within higher education. It has been argued that media research generally concentrates on mainstream media. This is bad for media research, because specialized media or media uses are under-researched. It is bad for research into educational media, which tends to be overly prescriptive and insufficiently critical. Media technologies in education are not uncontroversial forces for good, rather they are the sites for contestation about the nature and purposes of education and educational knowledge. The idea that technologies are neutral often leads to presumptions about technological determinism. These under-rate the significance of institutional and ideological factors, among other components of the full social and cultural contexts of education. The discussion has demonstrated the extent to which distance learning alternatives in education may in fact be independent of technological sophistication and are always reflective of important institutional, strategic and ideological choices.

SUMMARY

- **The Internet has launched a new integrated multi-media digital era in which the combined power of ICTs facilitates growing levels and forms of interactivity.**

- Vertical structures (media, market, government) are shaping and being shaped by the new horizontal, many-to-many communications character of the Internet, through which unprecedented levels of easily accessible direct (unmediated) information sources are now available.
- Traditional media can extend their presence via the Internet. Its interactive functions are also influencing their practices. E-mail input from audiences, for example, can be immediately included in interview questions in broadcasts.
- The Internet has global potential but, because of digital divides, notably between North and South, this remains just a dream at present.
- ICTs have opened up new patterns of communication across North and South, promoted especially by the work of growing numbers of NGOs.
- NGOs have been at the forefront of efforts to use ICTs for community-building, campaigning, and the effective linkage of local and global concerns.
- Convergence – integration of the Internet with television and mobile phones – will be key to future developments, with the growth of bandwidth expanding multi-media applications.
- There are fears that cyberspace will turn out to be little more than a new intensified realm of consumption. However, continuing civil society cyber-activity and the development of e-government could help bring increasing political balance to the market thrusts of the virtual world.
- The Internet has contributed to recent advances in distance learning, which incorporates a range of different private and public models using synchronous and asynchronous interaction between tutors and students.
- Distance education is concerned with the reduction of constraints of time and space, greater dependence on non-oral and non-print media, greater attention to adult learners, flexibility of starting points and progression, and enhanced student choice

Further Reading

Daniel, J. (1998), *Mega-Universities and Knowledge Media: Technology Strategies for Higher Education*

Harcourt, W. (ed.) (1999) *Women@Internet: Creating New Cultures in Cyberspace.* London: Zed

Stefik, M. (1997) *Internet Dreams: Archetypes, Myths and Metaphors.* Cambridge, MA: MIT Press

Useful Websites

Association for Progressive Communications (international Internet community for environment, human rights, development and peace): http://www.apc.org

UK Department for Education and Skills (e-business strategy): http://www.dfee.gov.uk/e-business

US Department of Commerce, Economics and Statistics Administration, Secretariat on Electronic Commerce (US government electronic commerce policy): http://www.ecommerce.gov

World Bank global development gateway portal on development: http://www.developmentgateways.org

References

Almeda, B. (1998) University of California extension online: from concept to reality. In *Journal of Asynchronous Learning Networks* 2(2), 1–20

Anderson, B. (1991) *Imagined Communities: Reflections on the Origin and Spread of Nationalism*. London: Verso

Berners-Lee, T. and Fischetti, M. (1999) *Weaving the Web: The Past, Present and Future of the World Wide Web by its Inventor*. London: Orion Business

Blumenstyk, G. (1999a) In a first, the North Central Association accredits an on-line university. In *The Chronicle of Higher Education*, 19 March, A27

Blumenstyk, G. (1999b) California virtual university will end most of its operations. In *The Chronicle of Higher Education*, 2 April, A30

Blumenstyk, G. (1999c) The marketing intensifies in distance learning. In *The Chronicle of Higher Education*, 9 April, A27

Blumenstyk, G. (1999d) Distance learning at the Open University. In *The Chronicle of Higher Education*, 23 July, A35–7

Boyd-Barrett, O. (2000) Distance education provision by Universities: how institutional contexts affect choices. In *Information, Communication and Society* 3(4)

Boyd-Barrett, O. and Newbold, C. (eds) (1995) *Approaches to Media: A Reader*. London: Arnold

California State University (1999) *Access in Action: Extended University Annual Report, 1997–1998*. Los Angeles, CA: California State University

Daniel, J. (1998) *Mega-Universities and Knowledge Media: Technology Strategies for Higher Education*

Daniel, J. (1999a) *Distance Learning: The Vision and Distance Learning: The Reality. What Works, What Travels?* Conference presentation: Leadership in the Knowledge Economy. Boca Raton, FL, 10–12 January

Daniel, J. (1999b) *Building in Quality: the Transforming Power of Distance Learning*, Council for Higher Education Accreditation, second annual conference. San Diego, California, 2 February

Deibert, R.J. (1997) *Parchment, Printing and Hypermedia: Communication in World Order Transformation*. New York, NY: Columbia University Press

Downes, S. (1999) What happened at California Virtual University. In *Threads*

Drucker, P. (1993) *Post-Capitalist Society*. New York, NY: HarperCollins

Farrell, G.M. (ed.) (1999) Introduction. In *The Development of Learning: A Global Perspective*. London: Commonwealth of Learning

Gittler, A.M. (1999) Mapping women's global communications and networking. In Harcourt, W. (ed.) *Women@Internet: Creating New Cultures in Cyberspace*. London: Zed

Gregory, E. (1993) Negotiation as a criterial factor in learning to read in a second language. In Graddol, D. *et al.* (eds) *Researching Language and Literacy in Social Context*, Clevedon: Multilingual Matters

Guernsey, L. (1999) Click here for the ivory tower. In *New York Times on the Web*, 2 September

Haraway, D.J. (1997) *Modest_Witness@Second_Millennium. FemaleMan© Meets_OncoMouse™Feminism and Technoscience*. London: Routledge

Harcourt, W. (ed.) (1999) *Women@Internet: Creating New Cultures in Cyberspace*. London: Zed

Harvey, D. (1989) *The Condition of Postmodernity: An Enquiry into the Origins of Cultural Change*. Oxford: Blackwell

Hawthorne, S. and Klein, R. (eds) (1999) Introduction. In *Cyberfeminism: Connectivity, Critique and Creativity*. Melbourne: Spinifex Press, 1–16

Heath, S. (1983) *Ways with Words*. Cambridge: Cambridge University Press

Herman, E.S. and McChesney, R.W. (1997) *The Global Media: The New Missionaries of Corporate Capitalism*. London: Routledge

Jones, G.R. (1997) Cyberschools: an Education Renaissance. Englewood, CO: Jones Digital Century, Inc.

Kofman, E. and Youngs, G. (eds) (1996) Globalization: Theory and Practice. London: Pinter

Leatherman, C. (1998) University of Phoenix's faculty members insist they offer high-quality education. In The Chronicle of Higher Education, 16 October

McGeehan, P. (1999) Unext.com, 4 more schools agree to deals. In Wall Street Journal, 23 June

McLuhan, E. and Zingrone, F. (eds) (1997) Essential McLuhan. London: Routledge

Mendells, P. (1999) Hurdles for online education efforts. In New York Times on the Web, 29 March

Mendells, P. (1999) Online classes let small colleges expand offerings. In New York Times on the Web, 18 August

Miller, V. (2000) Search engines, portals and global capitalism. In Gauntlett, D. (ed.) Web-Studies: Rewiring Media Studies for the Digital Age. London: Arnold, 113–21

Mohammadi, A. (ed.) (1997) International Communication and Globalization, London: Sage

Negrine, R. (1997) Communications tech-nologies: an overview. In Mohammadi, A. (ed.) International Communication and Globalization. London: Sage, 50–66

Padilla, A. (1999) The University of Phoenix, Inc. In On the Horizon, 30 July

Perry, W. (1977) The Open University: history and evaluation of a dynamic innovation. In Higher Education, Jossey-Bass

Ritzer, G. (1998) The McDonaldization Thesis: Explorations and Extensions. London: Sage

Sardar, Z. and Ravetz, J.R. (1996) Introduction: reaping the technological whirlwind. In Sardar, Z. and Ravetz, J.R. (eds) Cyberfutures: Culture and Politics on the Information Superhighway. London: Pluto, 1–13

Schiller, D. (2000) Digital Capitalism: Networking the Global Market System. Cambridge, MA: MIT Press

Scribner, S. and Cole, M. (1973) Cognitive con-sequences of formal and informal education. In Science 182, 553–9

Slater, D. and Taylor: J. (eds) (1999) The American Century: Consensus and Coercion in the Projection of American Power. Oxford: Blackwell

Society for International Development (1998) Women in the Digital Age: Using Communication Technology for Empowerment, Rome: SID

Stefik, M. (1997) Internet Dreams: Archetypes, Myths and Metaphors, Cambridge, MA: MIT Press

Street, B. (1993) Cross-Cultural Approaches to Literacy. Cambridge: Cambridge University Press

Talalay, M., Farrands, C. and Tooze, R. (eds) (1997) Technology, Culture and Competitiveness: Change and the World Political Economy. London: Routledge

Talalay, M., Tooze, R. and Farrands, C. (1997) Technology, culture and competitiveness: change in the world political economy. In Talalay, M., Farrands, C. and Tooze, R. (eds) Technology, Culture and Competitiveness: Change and the World Political Economy. London: Routledge, 1–9

Tehranian, M. and Tehranian, K.K. (1997) Taming modernity: towards a new paradigm. In Mohammadi, A. (ed.) International Communication and Globalization, London: Sage, 119–67

Thussu, D.K. (1998) Electronic Empires: Global Media and Local Resistance. London: Arnold

Tomlinson, J. (1999) Globalization and Culture. Cambridge: Polity

United Nations Conference on Trade and Development (UNCTAD) (2000) World Investment Report (published annually). New York, NY: United Nations

United Nations Development Programme (UNDP) (1999; 2000) Human Development Report (published annually). New York, NY: Oxford University Press

US Department of Commerce (2000): Digital Economy, 2000. Economics and Statistics Administration, Secretariat on Electronic Commerce (June). At: http://www.ecom merce.gov

Vygotsky, L.S. (1962) Thought and Language, Cambridge, MA: MIT Press

Young, J.R. (1999a) Universities create on-line education 'portal'. In The Chronicle of Higher Education, 25 June

References

Young, J.R. (1999b) Kentucky's virtual university will serve as an on-line course catalogue. In *The Chronicle of Higher Education*, 3 September, A52

Youngs, G. (1996) Beyond the 'inside/outside' divide. In Krause, J. and Renwick, N. (eds) *Identities in International Relations*. London: Macmillan, 22–37

Youngs, G. (1997) Culture and the technological imperative: missing dimensions. In Talalay, M., Farrands, C. and Tooze, R. (eds) *Technology, Culture and Competitiveness: Change and the World Political Economy*. London: Routledge, 27–40

Youngs, G. (1999a) *International Relations in a Global Age: A Conceptual Challenge*. Cambridge: Polity

Youngs, G. (1999b) Virtual voices: real lives. In Harcourt, W. (ed.) *Women@Internet: Creating New Cultures in Cyberspace*. London: Zed, 55–68

Youngs, G. (2000a) Globalization, technology and consumption. In Youngs, G. (ed.) *Political Economy, Power and the Body: Global Perspectives*. London: Macmillan, 75–93

Youngs, G. (2000b) Women breaking boundaries in cyberspace. In *Asian Women* 10, 1–18

Youngs, G. (2001a) Theoretical reflections on networking in practice: the case of women on the net. In Green, E. and Adam, A. (eds) *Virtual Gender*. London: Routledge 84–99

Youngs, G. (2001b) The political economy of time in the Internet era: feminist perspectives and challenges. In *Information, Communication and Society* 4(1), 14–33

Selective Glossary of Key Terms

Glossary entries are marked **bold** on their first main appearance in the text.

administrative research This tradition of media research has as its principal purpose service of the needs of media organizations and their regulators. It is typically media-focused, and takes little account of media in relation to their total social and historical context.

aesthetics This relates to perceptions of beauty, taste and what is considered to be artistic. It is idealist, in that its connotations relate to rather subjective opinions as to art and beauty.

branded The manufacturer places its name on the product to make it easily identifiable for audiences. The brand name is part of the overall image, encouraging the consumer to believe in the quality of the product and aspire to the lifestyle associated with the brand through advertising.

collective identity Identification with a community and/or the institutions by which it is represented, expressed or symbolized. Collective identity has different aspects based on class, gender, lifestyle and nation.

consumer sovereignty This term refers to the consumer having the power in a free market to make an active choice as to the products s/he buys. It can also be said that consumer desires influence what is produced and the amount that is produced.

critical research Critical media research examines media within their total historical, social, political, economic and cultural contexts. Its principal purpose is to.serve the general public or social good.

cultural studies This tradition of research holds that culture, defined as the totality of human expression, is of fundamental importance for the understanding of human and social behaviour. Study of the media is inevitably part of the study of culture.

cumulative Developing and increasing steadily, building on past knowledge to move forward.

depth of field Where everything is in focus, this is important in guiding the viewer's eye to particular areas or characters on the screen. Close-up focus or distant focus is largely determined by the kind of lens being used and its aperture. A deep-focus shot, however, in allowing for a great depth of field, where everything within the frame is in focus, theoretically leaves the audience to focus where they wish on the screen. Great claims are made for Orson Welles' use of deep focus in *Citizen Kane* (1941).

distance education Any form of teaching and learning in which the teacher(s) and learner(s) occupy non-contiguous physical or temporal spaces, and which depends substantially on the mediation of media technology.

effects research   This tradition of research focuses on the impact or effects that media texts have for audience or consumer cognition, attitude or opinion, and behaviour.

epistemology   The theory behind knowledge, i.e. what a particular discourse can bring to a topic, what can we learn, and what are the strengths and weaknesses of a given approach; so we can talk of a post-modern epistemology, or an empirical one.

ethnographic research   This tradition of research applies the approaches of social anthropology to the study of how audiences interact with and take meaning from media texts, and to the study of how the producers of media texts inscribe them with meaning. This tradition foregrounds the importance of in-depth experience of and familiarity with groups, institutions and cultures in the study of media.

formalist   Formalism is the study of the formal structures and properties of a text. It is not concerned with the relationship of the text to reality, audience or social context. Formalists examine texts for their own intrinsic value, being concerned mainly with meaning and its creation within the text.

functionalism   This sociological tradition posits the analysis of social behaviour on the idea that there are meaningful entities called 'societies', whose component parts are usefully analysed in terms of their functional significance for social cohesion and survival.

gender   Can be defined as the cultural differentiation of male from female. While the term 'sex' refers to the fact that women and men are born different in physiological and biological terms, 'gender' refers to the cultural meaningfulness attributed to these natural differences. Especially since the 1960s much academic – and at times public – attention has been paid to the idea that the social definitions of 'femininity' and 'masculinity' are culturally constructed, and have to do with ideology and power rather than being 'natural'. Indeed, as some emphasize, the definition of the terms gender, masculine and feminine is based on cultural expectations of behaviour. This idea has been discussed from many perspectives, drawing attention to the macro level of the social powers at play to the micro level of the psychological construction of identity.

German expressionism   From 1919 until about 1931 German film is said to have reflected the disturbed social state of the country, its political disarray and trauma following its defeat and humiliation in the First World War. The term originates from painting, describing an anti-realist and anti-naturalist approach. In the films of this period – *The Cabinet of Dr Caligari* (Robert Wiene, 1919), *Nosferatu – A Symphony of Horror* (F.W. Murnau, 1922) and *M* (Fritz Lang, 1931) – the visual style was characterized by low-key lighting, oblique camera angles, a sharp juxtaposition of light and dark, and the painting of geometric shapes on sets. Combined with Gothic narratives, this made German expressionism a unique and theatrical film style.

hegemony   Applied to culture, the term signifies the maintenance of power by elite groups by means of ideological constructions (or representations of the world) that work in such a way as to secure the voluntary compliance of the oppressed to the conditions of their own oppression.

holistic   Can be described as the premise that the 'total' is more than the sum of its parts.

horizontal communications sphere   Description of the nature of the Internet where the vertical structures of government, media, business etc. operate within a many-to-many environment, allowing, for instance, non-governmental organizations (NGOs) comparable presence on the World Wide Web and direct (unmediated) contact with the public.

identity   This complex concept lies at the heart of current debates in cultural studies and social theory. From current literature it becomes evident that identity can best be under-stood as a fluid process, always in formation, negotiated and re-negotiated. Moreover, 'iden-tities in the contemporary world derive from a multiplicity of sources – from nationality, ethnicity, social class, community, gender, sexuality – sources which may conflict in the con-struction of identity positions and lead to contradictory fragmented identities' (Woodward, 1997). This view recognizes the idea that the modern self is composed of a multiplicity of identities. The various products of the media are viewed as providing materials out of which we forge our identities as individuals and as members of social groups.

information and communications technologies (ICTs)   Reference to the combination of the capacities of information and communication technologies as the central character-istic of the digital era.

Internet   Information and communication network of networks that incorporates both e-mail and the World Wide Web.

mass society   This sociological tradition holds that individual members of society are directly controlled by the major centres of power in society, without the protective media-tion of intervening organizations such as churches, professional or civic associations, etc.

media tycoon   A person who has managed to build a media empire 'single-handedly'. Historically it was often concentrated on one medium, such as Hearst's press empire, now tycoons own multi-media conglomerates. Prime examples are Murdoch, Berlusconi and Kirch.

merger   A fusion of two (or more) companies to form one corporate-industrial body. Merg-ers can take different forms, from a purely formal or financial coming together on the one hand, over total integration to a takeover of one company by another (whereby the first 'dis-appears') on the other hand.

myth   The Barthesian semiological device in which a culture speaks to itself, and repro-duces its ideological structures; this uses signs to create naturalizations of socially con-structed and culturally necessary ideologies. Myths in the West may include, for instance, the sexual prowess of the black, the stupidity of the Irish, the inability of women to drive, and many others; these hide and naturalize politically expedient ideologies.

pluralist   This sociological tradition holds that power in society is distributed across many different sectors or centres, and that the balance of power between each of these different sectors or centres is maintained through continuous processes of negotiation whose ultimate goal is social integration and survival.

political economy   This sociological tradition analyses society and social phenomena, including media, in terms of the interplay between politics, economics and ideology.

post-feminism   The third wave of feminism, which accepts 'sexpositive' attitudes, the celebration of previously taboo areas such as sexual attractiveness, fashion and pro-capitalist ideologies; perhaps partly inspired by 1980s role models such as Madonna. It can be seen as a backlash against writers such as Andrea Dworkin – post-feminism sees woman as equal but different, and that they can 'have it all'.

prospects   Potential buyers of a product. In other words, a prospect is someone who has particular characteristics that could make him/her want or need a product. For example, a man has booked a holiday, therefore he is a prospect for travel insurance and may need a hire car at his destination.

public sphere   This concept refers to any meeting place, be it physical or virtual, in which people come together as equals for rational discussion of issues for the public good, without the intervention of the forces of the state or of capital.

race   The term 'race' is problematic and, far from being an innocent term, it carries much ideological weight. In much of the existing media studies literature, the term race is actually assumed to refer to black people of African-Caribbean origin, although current writing addresses further groups outside the ethnic and cultural mainstream of Anglo-Saxon society (in fact, some writers draw attention to 'white' as a racial category).

reinforcement effect   The reinforcement school of media effects research holds that the most important effect of the media is their power to reinforce the existing cognitions, attitudes or opinions, and behaviours of audience members or consumers, through processes of selective exposure, attention and retention.

representations   This term refers to the signs and symbols that claim to stand for, or re-present, some aspect of 'reality', such as objects, people, groups, places, events, social norms, cultural identities and so on. These representations may be constructed in any medium and are an essential feature of social life; they allow us to communicate and make sense of our surroundings. Within media studies the assumption is that how members of society see themselves, how they are viewed and even treated by others, is determined to a great extent by their media representation. The focus for media research in this context is the ideological role of representing and representation, the ways in which representations are made to seem 'natural'.

scopophilia   The Freudian concept of the desire to see the unseeable; this is one of the leading arguments behind the nature of the pleasure of the media text. Many texts have explored this, such as the 1960 film *Peeping Tom*, and it has influenced later work on voyeurism, pleasure and the ideological implications of viewing.

spot advertising   This term refers to adverts used in the breaks during and between television programmes.

subgenres   A subgenre is best understood as the development of a new strand or dynamic of a genre, which, while retaining some similarities, especially in terms of origins, develops specific themes of the original genre.

synergies   Situations in which the result or effect of two or more co-operating or combined corporations or functions, is bigger than the sum of the effects each of the corporations or functions could obtain separately.

target audience   A term widely used in market research to refer to a section or group of people that advertisers are trying to attract to a product. Through market research the advertisers discover all they can about the target audience (through discussion, groups, interviews, etc.) – for example, lifestyles, tastes, class, age, gender etc. This information is then used when determining the best method of advertising a particular product.

text   In the context of media research, a 'text' is any media product, whether in whole or in part, whether linguistic, numerical, visual, aural, or tactile, in which meaning is purposefully inscribed and from which meaning may be taken.

theory   A theory is any reasoned proposition, or set of propositions, that purports to explain the nature or behaviour of any phenomenon or set of phenomena.

transgressivity   Etymologically derived from 'to sin', this is particularly relevant in the light of many post-modern texts and relates to the breaking down of barriers of bourgeois taste, arguably with precedents in the US underground cinema of the 1970s and 1980s. This goes a long way towards explaining the popularity of pornography, S&M styles and transgressive sexuality in all its forms from non-PC jokes on television to the boom in drag/cross-dressing.

verisimilitude   This simply means believability, and relates to the imperative that all moving image products should be grounded in reality, even if that reality is a generic one. Thus, even a science fiction film should have a relationship to reality within the bounds of its generic discourse.

virtual community   The idea that communities of interest/action can now be built using the Internet, their distinction being a lack of dependence on physical proximity and the possibility of operating across multiple international boundaries.

Subject Index

Name and Title Index